Ca...an
criminology

John A. Winterdyk
Mount Royal College, Department of Criminology

Prentice Hall Canada Career & Technology
Scarborough, Ontario

In memory of Thomas Dick, a dear friend and true inspiration. A man who epitomized the zeal for life and caring. Your influence will continue to glow brightly.

Canadian Cataloguing in Publication Data

Winterdyk, John
  Canadian criminology

1st ed.
Includes index.
ISBN 0-13-014096-1

1. Criminology. 2. Criminology—Canada. 3. Crime. 4. Crime—Canada.
I. Title.

HV6025.W56 2000   364   C99-930440-2

Prentice-Hall, Inc., Upper Saddle River, New Jersey
Prentice-Hall International (UK) Limited, London
Prentice-Hall of Australia, Pty. Limited, Sydney
Prentice-Hall Hispanoamericana, S.A., Mexico City
Prentice-Hall of India Private Limited, New Delhi
Prentice-Hall of Japan, Inc., Tokyo
Simon & Schuster Southeast Asia Private Limited, Singapore
Editora Prentice-Hall do Brasil, Ltda., Rio de Janeiro

ISBN 0-13-014096-1

Vice President, Editorial Director: Laura Pearson
Acquisitions Editor: David Stover
Marketing Manager: Sophia Fortier
Developmental Editor: Susan Ratkaj
Production Editor: Cathy Zerbst
Copy Editor: Gillian Scobie
Production Coordinator: Peggy Brown
Art Director: Mary Opper
Cover Design: Sarah Battersby
Cover Image: Robert Karpa/Masterfile
Page Layout: Jansom (Janette Thompson)

1 2 3 4 5 04 03 02 01 00

Printed and bound in Canada

Visit the Prentice Hall Canada Web site! Send us your comments, browse our catalogues, and more at **www.phcanada.com**. Or reach us through e-mail at **phabinfo_pubcanada@prenhall.com**.

Table of Contents

Introduction

Criminology is a "hot" topic these days. One cannot read the paper, listen to or watch the news without being bombarded with some local crime story (let alone national or international crime). Many criminology and criminal justice programs have to turn students away as there are not enough seats available in their programs to accommodate them all. Our program for instance, has had an annual ratio of about three applicants for every seat and the demand has been increasing! The general interest in criminology, and more particularly Canadian criminology, is also being reflected in the growing number of crime fiction books and academic textbooks. So, why yet another one?

Almost as quickly as the interest in criminology has grown so has our understanding of crime and criminality. Criminology is a dynamic area of study that is continually evolving in its aim to better understand and control crime and criminal behaviour and ultimately remove social inequalities.

This book, while intended as an introductory textbook, reflects the emerging *integrative* and *interdisciplinary* approach to the study of crime and criminality. And while the underlying theme and orientation is relatively new, the subject areas covered are consistent with the way many programs teach their introductory level criminology courses.

Before undertaking this project, I compiled an extensive list of chapter headings along with brief descriptions from a variety of textbooks. I then asked my students and fellow faculty members to rate the relative importance of the prospective chapters. I also asked them to offer comments on chapter content where they felt it might be appropriate. In addition, I invited feedback regarding any topics that they felt should be addressed which were not covered in the list. With a few minor exceptions, such as reviewers' feedback and my own decision-making process, the framework of the book was generated by my students and colleagues. However, the orientation and pedagogy is solely my responsibility.

Aside from the impressions I have garnered from attending criminology conferences and international meetings, throughout my education I have been influenced by a number of people whose ideas and writing have helped to forge my current orientation. Most notably, I have been influenced by the works of criminologists such as C.R. Jeffery, Paul and Patricia Brantingham, the psychologist and research methodologist Vernon Schafer, and my grandfather, whose approach to education and the pursuit of knowledge were both pioneering and inspirational. When he retired from teaching, he was awarded a special medal by the Queen of The Netherlands for his years of service and his contribution to education. Hence, the purpose of writing this book is to not only to fill a void in the Canadian market but also to bridge the gap that has existed in criminology virtually since its inception in our country. That is, too many disciplines have been competing to claim criminology as their domain. However, social science recognizes that human behaviour involves social, individual, environmental, political, biological, and other social and scientific attributes. Criminology is a complex concept and criminality cannot be explained in simple terms, or from a singular perspective. As Barak (1998:xi) recently noted, criminology needs to not only be interdisciplinary but also integrative—"getting down to the business of filling in the space between the different disciplinary perspectives on crime and justice."

This textbook represents another step towards creating such awareness. Although most of the traditional areas of more conventional criminology textbooks are still covered, I have attempted to provide a balanced review. For example, **Chapter 1** introduces the reader to the meaning of crime, deviance, and criminology. It also traces the evolving history of criminology and provides the basis for understanding why an interdisciplinary and integrated approach is necessary for criminology.

Chapter 2 examines the role of the public and the media. Both play an integral role in forging the identity, the issues, and even directing criminal justice policy. The chapter offers an overview of why criminology needs to understand the importance of the role of the public and the media when studying crime.

Criminological theory and criminal justice policy is influenced by cultural values and politics. These elements can be tempered by objective criminological data. In **Chapter 3**, we will review the various methods of collecting and analyzing information about crime and criminals. Such data can be used to support policies and educate the public. This chapter concludes with some cautionary observations on criminological data. **Chapter 4** is unique. While many textbooks include some coverage on the history and evolving nature of the discipline, in this chapter we explore the major schools of criminological thought as well as present profiles of some of the pioneers and their ideas. An appreciation of our heritage is an essential ingredient in preparing for the future. In addition, the Appendices provide concise, yet detailed, reviews of six important Canadian pioneers who have played a significant role in forging Canadian criminology. It is hoped that providing such coverage will prompt others to expand on the coverage as well as help students to better appreciate the need for Canadian criminology.

In **Section II** attention shifts towards criminological theories. Criminological theories represent the various epistemological perspectives used to engage in criminological inquiry. Textbooks vary in their orientation and method of coverage when it comes to criminological theory. However, they generally reflect competing disciplinary approaches rather than offer an interdisciplinary approach. In keeping with the interdisciplinary approach, the major criminological theories are divided into their primary multidisciplinary areas such as biology (**Chapter 5**), psychology (**Chapter 6**), and sociology (**Chapter 7**). **Chapter 8** includes some of the emerging integrated and interdisciplinary approaches used to explain crime. Coverage ranges from the *routine activity theory* to *social conflict theory, left realism,* to some of the new *bio-social theories.*

Section III is divided into six chapters. **Chapter 9** includes an overview of the violent crimes that are most recorded by the police and which tend to draw the most attention from the media and the public. In addition, there is a brief overview on some of the "new" forms of violence (e.g., hate crime, stalking, and terrorism). **Chapter 10** includes an overview of crimes against property. In particular, the chapter focuses on conventional property crimes such as fraud, theft, arson, and motor-vehicle crimes. In **Chapter 11** the focus shifts to organized and economic crimes, sometimes referred to as non-conventional crime because standardized data is seldom available. In addition to providing coverage on such areas as organized crime, political crime, and economic crime, the chapter addresses some of the explanations of the various crimes. **Chapter 12**, meanwhile, addresses what are often referred to as public order offences such as gambling, prostitution, and drug/substance abuse. Although these crimes often involve organized crime groups, they have been placed in a separate chapter because of their general nature. They are sometimes also referred to as "victimless" crimes since those involved are often willing participants. They are also crimes concerned with issues of morality, which some argue do not belong in the domain of state control. However, whether moral issues or not, these behaviours involve acts that have a direct impact on public safety and well-being.

Women and crime is dealt with in **Chapter 13**. There was considerable outside support for this chapter, yet divergent opinion about its format. It reflects one of the major shifts within criminology. Several years ago, very little attention was paid to female crime. Although criminologists have been paying increasing attention to female crimes, it is an area that can be characterized as being still in its infancy. In the chapter, I provide an overview of the history and current status of criminological understanding of female crime.

Finally, in **Chapter 14**, the focus shifts to future criminological issues. Issues such as the future of crime, the need for comparative research, dealing with the knowledge explosion, and crime prevention are examined. The chapter concludes with an overview of restorative justice—one of the "new" trends in criminology that reflects an integrated and interdisciplinary approach to social order.

Where appropriate, most chapters include an overview of some of the major historical antecedents, key concepts, and important findings that contribute to our understanding of the topic's relevance to the study of crime and criminality. In this way, the reader can acquire an appreciation of how the discipline has evolved as well as how current theories have come into the fold.

The textbook does not include any detailed discussion of the police, the judicial system, corrections, or the role of law in the study of crime. Except for the latter topic, these are aspects of the criminal justice system that, although covered in many American-based criminology textbooks, would make the book somewhat overwhelming. As noted below, we have prepared a special chapter on the role of law in criminology and placed it on the Prentice-Hall Web site at **www.prenticehall.ca/winterdyk**. Since not all programs cover this topic in their introductory courses, for practical and economic reasons it was decided to place the chapter on the Web. You are all welcome to visit it.

Sometimes reading pages and pages of new material can make assimilating it difficult. Therefore, each chapter begins with a set of important *learning outcomes.* The outcomes are intended to help the reader focus on necessary conceptual aspects. Also, at the end of each chapter is a set of *discussion questions* that are intended to help integrate the material, as well as a list of *key concepts* and *key names*—where appropriate. Finally, where possible, the end of each chapter also includes some helpful *Weblinks*.

At the end of the textbook is a *glossary* of the concepts highlighted in bold text throughout the book. Although it may appear redundant, standardization is becoming increasingly important as criminology continues to evolve and become increasingly international in scope. Readers are likely to find some discrepancies because of different theoretical perspectives, but overall the glossary should help to develop a better understanding of criminology.

As you progress through the book, you will notice that some chapters have more footnotes than others. I have endeavoured, however, to keep them to a minimum because, while they are intended to offer additional information, they are infrequently accessed by undergraduate students—at least that was the case when I was a student. But you are encouraged to peruse them as they provide additional information that might prove helpful for those seeking more insight into a topic or issue.

Finally, although I have tried to do justice to the evolving nature of criminology by adopting an interdisciplinary and integrated approach, I suspect I must call on students and instructors to fill some voids from time to time. However, the effort has been made and I see this book (like criminology itself) as a work in progress. In the meantime, to facilitate the journey, we have prepared, with the assistance of Sandie McBrien and Rosemary Burk, a glossary of key terms at the end of the book, as well as an Instructor's Guide with a testbank.

Should you find this textbook interesting and intellectually stimulating then my efforts have not been in vain. Nevertheless, rest assured the journey is not complete and any constructive feedback is welcome. Finally, please feel free to visit our department homepage where we have compiled a list of Internet links to helpful criminology Web sites: **www.mtroyal.ab.ca/programs/commhealth/ criminology**.

John Winterdyk
Department of Criminology
Mount Royal College
Calgary, AB.
e-mail: **jwinterdyk@mtroyal.ab.ca**
fax: (403) 240-6201

Note: Since some criminology and criminal justice programs have criminal law courses, not all introductory courses may cover this chapter in detail. However, it is an essential component of the criminological enterprise and therefore is included.

The meaning of crime and our response to it are often defined and understood through the laws society has created in order to maintain a balance between social order and individual freedoms. An overview of criminal law also reflects those areas and issues that society seems to think most warrant formal attention. An examination of the laws serves as a barometer of social attitudes and trends. The Web site chapter examines such issues as historical concepts of justice, the function and purpose of criminal law and a description of the *Criminal Code* and the court system. In addition to surveying various criminal defences, the chapter concludes with a discussion of the role of law in criminology.

Acknowledgments

Although I am solely responsible for the content of this textbook, it reflects the input and support of numerous people. While some of these persons are aware of their impact and/or contributions, many are not. I am indebted to all of them. And while not everyone's name may appear below, my heartfelt thanks goes out to them all.

Whenever I undertake an effort such as this book, I realize not only how important friendships and loved ones are but how important it is for us to recognize and appreciate that we are all one.

As mentioned in the Introduction, my grandfather, Dirk Winterdyk, has been the most influential academic force in my life. In addition to embodying all the quintessential traits of a wonderful grandfather, he was an educator extraordinaire and his ideas and enthusiasm have remained a powerful influence on me. Throughout my school years I have been touched in various ways by the ideas and works of Vern Schafer, Bruce Hunsberger, Ronald Roesch, Deanna Buckley, Ray Corrado, Vince Sacco, Paul Maxim, Paul and Patricia Brantingham, Elizabeth Loftus, Hans Eysenck, and C.R. Jeffery. I would also like to acknowledge several of my fellow graduate students who in their own way helped me to survive the demands of graduate school so I can enjoy what I do today. They were truly memorable times. Thanks in particular to Jane Debbo, Klaus Kohlmyer, Linda Fischer, Darryl Plecas, Dan Beavon, and David Horne.

Of my colleagues at Mount Royal College, I would like to recognize a dear friend Sandie McBrien who provided invaluable feedback on most of the chapters and was invaluable with the Instructor's Guide. With assistance from Rosemary Buck, she prepared the lion's share of the Instructor's Guide for *Introduction to Criminology: An Integrated and Interdisciplinary Approach.* To Gary Brayton, Don Fetherston, and Doug King who read various chapter drafts. To Janne Holmgren who checked all the chapter references and to Rosemary Buck who is the most recent sessional instructor in our department. In addition to helping with the Instructor's Guide, Rosemary provided invaluable assistance tracking down permissions and following up on other "incidents" that allowed me to meet the submission deadline. A special thanks goes out to our department secretary Brenda Laing who has always been there to do, to provide the little extras that make my life at the college and the demands of writing a little easier. To the Kootnet Internet providers in Libby, Montana for enabling me, while spending my summer in Montana, to stay in touch with the "outside" world.

To Karen, who provided me with the support that only a caring friend is capable of. My demands on her time had, on numerous occasions, necessitated tolerance and empathy, all of which, and more, she gave. However, I am also thankful for those moments when she reminded me of "the bigger picture." There is more to life than working! To Ted, Luke and Matt, whose presence taught me the value of having an open heart.

Last but not least, I would like to thank Prentice-Hall and my senior editor David Stover. After some early difficulties with the concept of the book, David eagerly embraced it and encouraged me to see this project to completion. I would also like to thank developing editor, Susan Ratkaj, and Cathy Zerbst, production editor, who both, on short notice, helped to nurse this book into a much better project than what even I had envisioned. And Gillian Scobie, my copy editor, who has an incredibly fine eye for details (some of which I would rather not disclose) and also demonstrated a sound knowledge of the subject matter. Finally, I would like to thank all the anonymous reviewers who spent many hours offering constructive criticisms and insightful suggestions. While many have contributed to the success of this book—and without their feedback this textbook would be a mere shadow of what it now represents—the final product is my responsibility.

CHAPTER 1

Criminology: Its Nature and Structure

"When there is crime in society there is no justice."

Plato

"Crime, for its part, must no longer be conceived as an evil that can not be too much suppressed ... crime is not pathological at all ... and its true function must be sought elsewhere."

Emile Durkheim (1858–1917)

Learning Outcomes

After you have completed this chapter, you should be able to:

- Recognize the importance of having a Canadian criminology textbook.

- Understand the complexity of both criminology and crime.

- Identify misconceptions about criminology.

- Understand the role of criminologists, their various methods of inquiry and the elements that make up the discipline of criminology.

- Differentiate between crime and deviance, fully understanding the evolving and relative nature of both.

- Recognize the many ways we gain knowledge regarding crime.

- Appreciate the impact of the social sciences on the development of criminology and recognize the necessity for an integrated and interdisciplinary approach.

Introduction

Although the chapter's opening two quotes are about crime, they reflect diametrically opposing views. Welcome to the controversial subject of crime and, more generally, the discipline of criminology.

Before we begin, take a few minutes to answer a few questions that I like to ask my students at the start of my introductory criminology class(es). You might want to do this exercise in a group setting and jot down your responses.

- **Criminology**: What does it mean to you?
- What does the word **crime** mean?
- Is there a difference between a **crime** and **deviance**?
- What is a **criminal**?
- What do **criminologists** do?

While these are specific questions, you will likely get a wide range of responses. Explore possible reasons for this with your classmates.

The next set of questions is a little more abstract but are questions we have probably all thought about at some point. Follow the same procedure as you did with the previous questions.

- Has crime increased?
- What are the most serious crimes and why?
- Who is committing the most crimes and why?
- How many feel capital punishment/the death penalty should be reinstated and why?
- Why does the crime rate vary within Canada and internationally?
- Why are certain types of crimes committed by certain individuals and not others?
- Why do we respond differently to alleged criminality?
- What can we do to control crime?[1]

These questions are intended to get you thinking about the sources of information and the perceptions of crime and criminality. They will also raise a number of questions that may encourage you to explore these basic issues, in detail. If so, welcome to the exciting subject of criminology. In addition, the questions serve to establish a foundation on which we can begin to examine some misconceptions about crime and criminality, as well as develop a framework in which to study criminology.

Finally, I end the introductory portion of the first class by asking students why they are taking the course and/or enrolled in criminology. Again, take a few minutes to share your impressions. Do some of you want to work with young offenders, to be police officers, to practise (criminal) law, to study forensics, or are you just taking this as one of your electives? If the responses are varied, what impression might you be able to draw about criminology as a discipline and what it has to offer interested students (see Appendix 3)?

The answers to the above questions represent the cornerstones and building blocks of this course. In addition, since this textbook is intended to serve as an introduction to criminology, in this chapter we will begin by examining the fundamental principles of crime, criminality, and deviance. We will then review the historical roots of criminology. This will provide the backdrop by which we understand and appreciate how and why criminology has evolved into an enterprise that has become increasingly integrated and interdisciplinary in nature. The chapter will conclude with some practical issues that criminologists must consider. Before we begin, however, let's examine why this book has adopted a Canadian slant.

A Canadian Flavour eh!

As reflected in the title, this book is not only an introduction to criminology, but also an introduction to Canadian criminology. Is there a difference, you ask? Is there any constructive purpose in trying to separate Canadian criminology from criminology in general? Some Canadian criminologists have noted that we are modest players on the international scene. For example, a review of articles in such journals as the *Canadian Journal of Criminology* will reveal how we regularly give credit to the same scholars, most of whom are American. And we are not the only ones who regularly turn to American sources for our theoretical perspectives and notions of what is important in criminology. In his book on comparative juvenile justice, Winterdyk (1997b) presents twelve different countries (including Canada), most of which trace the inception of their respective juvenile justice systems to the influence of the American model used at the turn of the 1900s. However, the contributions show that although youth crime has remained a universal issue, a number of different juvenile justice models (six in all) have emerged over the years. The different models emerged because of different cultural, geographical, political, and social attributes unique to each country. The same is true for Canada and the United States (see Box 1.1).

REALITY CHECK BOX 1.1

CANADA AND THE UNITED STATES: DIFFERENCES THAT COUNT

Even though Canada and the United States share a common heritage. there are a number of unique social, cultural, and political differences that make our differences "count".

	CANADA	UNITED STATES
Population ('93)	28.7 million (2.9 per km2)	257 m. (27.5 per km2)
Languages	English/French	English

Visible Minorities	East Indians/other Asians/Caribbean	African-American/Hispanic
Indigenous Peoples	First Nations People/Métis/Inuit	Native Americans/Alaska Native/Asian/Pacific Islanders
Government	Parliamentary/Constitutional Monarch	Federalism Executive/Bicameral
Basis of Government	Constitutional Act/Charter of Rights and Freedom	U.S. Constitution/Bill of Rights
Criminal Law (1) Federal Statutes	National Criminal Code	State Criminal Statutes/
:	Young Offenders Act (Federal)	State Juvenile Acts
:	• age limits 12–17	• age variable
:	• modified justice model	• crime control model
:	No capital punishment	Capital punishment
:	Indictable/summary offences	Felonies/misdemeanours
Justice Officials	Appointed by government	County sheriffs/City and County prosecutors/State judges—all elected
Policing (2)	Municipal/provincial/federal	Municipal/county/state/Federal
Sentencing	Indefinite	Indeterminate/determinate Varies from state to state
Corrections (3)	Federal/Provincial	Federal/state
	• Jurisdiction determined by length of sentence	• Jurisdiction determined by code violation
Crime Rates '95	5,278 per 100,000	8,954 per 100,000
Violent Crime	685	995
Property Crime	4,593	5,237

(1) see Kerans, 1993, (2) see Seagrave, 1997, (3) see Ekstedt and Griffiths, 1988; Lines, 1996.

These differences do not mean that one country's system, or criminological approach, is better than the other's. They are simply different and, if for no other reason, deserve to be treated as such. Canadian criminology has begun to forge its own identity,[2] as evidenced by the growing number of criminology programs, criminology books with a Canadian focus, and Canadian-based criminologists who have made significant theoretical and practical contributions to criminology (Chapter 4). This textbook provides students with an introduction to criminology that, where appropriate, places the content within a Canadian context.

With this foreknowledge, it only seems justified that this textbook is also biased toward the work of Canadian criminologists. The premise for this orientation and emphasis is also based on feedback from my students over the years. They want Canadian content. However, they also want Canadian material put into a realistic perspective. Therefore, where appropriate, international material has been used in an effort to provide a *balanced* overview and one that will enable practical and, I hope, insightful conclusions and comparisons.

Criminology, Crime and Deviance

"The objective of criminology is the development of a body of general and verified principles and of other types of knowledge regarding this process of law, crime, and treatment." Edwin Sutherland and Donald Cressey, *Principles of Criminology* (6th ed.) (1960:3).

What is Criminology?

Many introductory textbooks define **criminology** as "the scientific study of crime, criminals and criminal behaviour." This general sociological definition was first introduced by Edwin Sutherland in one of the first criminology textbooks in North America, during the 1920s (see Chapter 7). While the definition tells us that criminology is a scientific discipline, it tells us nothing about the meaning of the terms crime, criminals, and criminal behaviour. A more precise description of what criminology means is dependent on the disciplinary orientation used to define the nature of crime and criminals (see Box 1.2). Thus, criminology can be defined as *the scientific study of human behaviour, crime causation, prevention and the punishment and rehabilitation of offenders.*

The study of crime emphasizes the scientific study of human behaviour. Criminology attempts to explain how and why crime occurs. Therefore, *a criminologist is a behavioural scientist who is interested in the identification, classification, and description of types of criminal behaviour.* Since a **criminologist** is concerned with the study of human behaviour, he or she draws on the behavioural sciences rather than elements of the criminal justice system (e.g., law enforcement, courts, and corrections) to explain criminal behaviour. The behavioural sciences can include a wide range of subject areas, including biology, anthropology, economics, political science, psychology, and sociology, as well as policy sciences (criminal law, policy, administration, and ethics). Therefore, criminology is an **interdisciplinary** and **integrated** science. But, until recently, most criminologists tended to be trained in a particular discipline (e.g., biology, political science, sociology, psychology, and law). These criminologists, then, tend to be multidisciplinary specialists who, while acknowledging other disciplinary perspectives, study crime and justice in accordance with their particular disciplinary training. However, as the discipline has evolved, an increasing number of scholars are being educated in an integrated and interdisciplinary environment.

Criminologists who subscribe to the latter approach to the study of crime believe that the various disciplinary perspectives are interrelated and provide a richer approach to methodological, practical issues and theoretical debates, than that of a single discipline or body of knowledge.

The plea for an interdisciplinary approach can be traced back to at least 1933 when Jerome Michael and Mortimer J. Adler, in their book entitled *Crime, Law and Social Science* called for the establishment of a separate criminology program in which criminal law and the behavioural sciences would be taught in an integrated and interdisciplinary manner. However, during its gestation period in North America, sociologists (in particular the Chicago School—see Chapter 7) quickly came to dominate criminological thought and research. It wasn't until the 1960s, with the flourishing of criminology, that the schools provided criminology with an opportunity to evolve an interdisciplinary approach and to bridge paradigmatic differences. Noted scholars such as Jeffery (1978, 1990) in North America and Radzinowicz (1965) in Europe have championed the cause. In Canada today, the integrated and interdisciplinary approach to the study of crime is attracting a growing number of followers.

FYI BOX 1.2

Two Misconceptions About Criminology

While criminology is the disciplined study of crime and crime control, it has had to contend with a number of misconceptions that arise from its efforts to apply its findings to practical policy. For example:

1. Criminologists have been crusaders for fair laws, fair punishment, more reliable treatments, removal of the death penalty, and a better sense of social justice. For this reason criminology has often been viewed as a humanitarian movement (see Chapter 4). However, it is also a scientific discipline that relies on empirical evidence to support humanitarian reforms.

2. The norms, beliefs, and values of society often dictate the formalization of laws. Consequently, some mistakenly think that criminology is a *normative* discipline concerned only with understanding the values and norms of society. While crimi-

nologists do study the relationships between norms and their entrenchment into the values and practices of society, the method adopted is non-normative. Rather, criminology is scientific and interdisciplinary in its approach to the study of criminological issues.

How might humanitarian and normative issues either assist, or hinder, our understanding of crime and its control ?

What is Crime?

"Everyone knows what crime is, or so it seems." Silverman, Teevan Jr., and Sacco, 1991:1.

Crime (from the Latin word *crimen* meaning "accusation") is a generic term that people use to refer to a wide range of acts that have been socially, culturally, and/or legally defined as being "wrong" or "anti-social" (Siegel, 1995). Crime is a social phenomenon that commands considerable attention from the (Canadian) public. Canadian criminologist John Hagan (1987), while commenting on crime, simply described it as a "hot" topic.

The meaning of crime has changed over time. Originally, crimes were private wrongs. Individuals who were wronged would seek "self-help" retribution, or revenge, against the wrongdoer or the wrongdoer's family. In time, this practice of personal justice broke down as the family structure changed and private vengeance became difficult to enforce. This gave way to the emergence of the legal concept of crime that today is commonly used within the criminal justice system. A legal definition of crime simply states that *a crime is what the law proclaims it to be and a crime is an act punishable by law.*[3]

Crime vs. Offence

In the media, the terms **crime** and **offence** are sometimes used interchangeably. Is there a difference? British criminologist Nigel Walker (1987) has observed that the concept of crime used to mean a serious breach of criminal law. The Scots and French still distinguish between "crimes" (breach of the law) and "offences" (violation of morality), while in the United States, crimes are distinguished based on a perceived serious breach of law. Less serious crimes or breaches are called "misdemeanours" (e.g., public drunkenness), while the more serious offences are called "felonies" (e.g., murder and rape). Until 1967, England made the same distinction. However, that country now simply classifies crimes as "arrestable" and "non-arrestable" offences. Arrestable offences are crimes for which a person can be arrested without a warrant and non-arrestable offences require a warrant.

Be Careful What You Do!

According to the Law Reform Commission of Canada, there are more than 40,000 crimes and offences that appear in federal and provincial laws and regulations as well as in local government statutes and by-laws.

In Canada, we use the term **indictable** to refer to more serious crimes (e.g., homicide, assault, and robbery). The penalty for indictable convictions varies depending on the seriousness of the crime. The other term used is **summary offences**. Summary offences denote less serious crimes (e.g., certain types of property offences, and theft or fraud under $5,000). Summary convictions carry a general punishment "of a fine of not more than $2,000 or imprisonment for six months or both." *Therefore, crime refers to the general infraction, while offence refers to the specific crime, such as homicide, theft, and robbery.*[4]

While the term crime is central to criminology, there is not a universal definition! We can note, however, that all definitions are based on legal constructs that define crime as the violation of a criminal law. In other words, *without law there is no crime.* Furthermore, we can note that the meaning of crime can vary with time and place since those who make the law also change over time. What is fundamentally important to recognize is that how we define a crime will influence how we view and study it. In Section II, we will examine the theories criminologists use to study crime and criminals.

Although there is no universal definition of crime, we can note that as a term, crime is a normative concept (i.e., based on norms and values) that carries a pejorative (i.e., negative) connotation. Any definition is influenced by our *frame of reference*, that is, the product of our economic, ideological, political, social, and disciplinary training. For the purpose of this book crime is defined as "a socially constructed concept used to categorize certain behaviours as requiring formal control and warranting some form of social intervention."

The list of what constitutes a crime is long and varied. One method that has been used to organize the various types of crimes is to divide them into **conventional** and **non-conventional** categories (although other classifications exist). Conventional crimes have been characterized as those crimes committed by individuals or small groups in which some degree of direct (e.g., personal) on indirect (e.g., property) contact occurs. These crimes can include street crimes such as robbery, assault, motor-vehicle theft, and break-and-enter. They are also the kinds of offences that most frequently come to the attention of the criminal justice system, as well as the media (Chapter 2). As Canadian sociologist, Daniel Koenig (1992), observed, conventional crime represents a subset of crime and may, or may not, include offences which cause great financial loss, physical harm, or death. In Chapters 9 and 10 we will focus on the most common of the conventional crimes as well as take a look at some of the emerging variations of these crimes (e.g., stalking, home invasion, and hate crime).

Non-conventional crime refers to those offences not usually pursued by the criminal justice system. Yet their social, financial, and personal impact may be far more serious than their conventional variation. For example, computer crimes (Chapter 11) have been described as a type of theft, but the impact of these crimes can have a devastating and more far reaching impact than "'simple'" theft. Other examples of non-conventional crime include: organized crime, various public order crimes, various forms of terrorism, transnational crime and white-collar crime. In addition, as with conventional crimes, there are new and emerging forms of non-conventional crimes that the criminal justice system is only now realizing or which have emerged in response to some social, economic, or political situation (e.g., Russian Mafia, trade in human organs, child pornography on the Internet, etc.). We will examine some of these crimes in Chapters 11–12.

Regardless of whether we are dealing with conventional or non-conventional crimes, all crimes are defined by laws.

REALITY CHECK BOX 1.4

CYBER CRIME—NOT QUITE CONVENTIONAL ... YET!

- On July 18, 1996, 16 individuals were charged with trafficking in child pornography. The accused, part of an international Internet pedophilia ring, came from ten different U.S. states, Australia, Finland, and Canada. They belonged to an online chat group that swapped stories about child sex and conspired to produce and exchange sexual images of females as young as five years old. (*Calgary Herald* – Online).
- Robert Glass from North Carolina and Sharon Lopatka from Maryland found each other on the Internet and had a romantic liaison via e-mail until they finally decided to meet face-to-face. Glass was subsequently charged with Sharon's death when she did not return home. Glass claimed she died while the two were having sex (Death on the Internet, 1996).

Both cases, and there have been many that are similar, raise a number of issues surrounding the nature of human behaviour, censorship, and (crime) prevention (see Chapter 11).

Deviance

Deviance is another term that is sometimes misunderstood and deserves clarification. While occasionally used interchangeably with the word crime, there are subtle differences in meaning.

Deviant behaviour is a term used to encompass a wide spectrum of conduct that, to varying degrees, may be considered offensive. *Deviant behaviour involves actions that depart from social norms. These actions may, or may not, be against the law*. For example, is the use of a "soft drug", such as marijuana, illegal? Is its use considered deviant? Boyd (1993) cites studies that found the use of marijuana to be quite common. Using Canadian data, Boyd also observed that "(m)ore than 90 per cent of those jailed for cannabis possession receive sentences of less than six months in prison" (p. 79). Since so many people experiment with marijuana and the court imposes relatively light sentences, should we continue to view the use of marijuana as deviant? Is marijuana any more socially harmful than alcohol or cigarette-smoking?

For obvious reasons, society cannot, and would not, sanction all undesirable behaviour, but where do we draw the line? The line between crimes and non-crimes or deviance or even normal behaviour is often a fine one. How do the examples serve to illustrate the point that the concept of crime is relative (to time and place) and evolutive (changing—a term coined by Maurice Parmalee in 1918)?

The relativity of crime is an important concept because it reflects the attention that should be placed on how we respond to criminal acts as well as the extent to which we want to control social behaviour. The concept of crime as a **relative** construct is also important because by definition it is fundamentally incompatible with the notion that criminals are born to crime or predisposed to crime through heredity. This has major theoretical implications, some of which we will explore in Section II.

The notion of crime being **evolutive** refers to the historical pattern: there are ample indicators that acts deemed criminal at a given time, in a given community, often turn out to have a different or more positive value for human beings. Examples in Canadian history include prohibition, abortion, and the use of morphine and cocaine. At one time or another all these behaviours were legal before being legislated illegal.[5]

But what, if any, boundaries of criminalization should be set? Is criminal behaviour qualitatively different from non-criminal behaviour? Answers to such questions can also have social policy implications and represent major challenges to criminologists.

The Crime and Deviance Hierarchy

University of Toronto criminology professor John Hagan (1985) developed a schematic diagram to illustrate the difference between crime and deviance. As illustrated in Figure 1–1, the difference between what is a crime and what is simply deviant is sometimes subtle. At the bottom of the pyramid there are *social diversions* that are considered relatively harmless, and there is no consistent

FIGURE 1—1

HAGAN'S PYRAMID CONSENSUS VS. CONFLICT

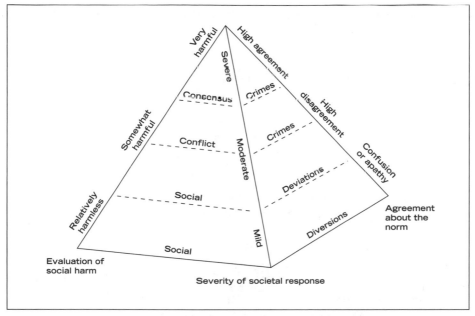

Source: J. Hagan "The Disreputable Pleasures" 1991 Toronto: McGraw-Hill Ryerson Ltd. Reprinted with permission.

agreement as to whether such actions should be regulated. Examples of social deviations could include an individual's preference in dress, language, and lifestyle. In certain social settings, however, a social deviation may be regulated, such as a school dress code or the use of offensive language directed towards a police officer or the court.

At the top of the pyramid are those behaviours for which there is both very high agreement as to the social harm of certain actions and a strong support to sanction and control such behaviour. These are referred to as consensus crimes. Examples of **consensus** crimes in Canada might include homicide, sexual assault, and treason. However, not everyone necessarily agrees that these crimes are wrong. They are subject to dispute, as not everyone agrees these behaviours should be considered crimes at all.

The **conflict** and social deviation crimes represent actions for which there is mixed support: whether such actions, although legally defined as crimes, should be considered as such. In Canada, in the 1990s this could include smoking mari-juana, procuring the services of a prostitute, appearing topless in public in some provinces, driving without your seat belt fastened, or smoking in a public place (see Chapter 12).

In essence, we can say that our perceptions of behaviours are not constant. Our attitudes about them can vary over time and from one place to another. This shifting of our definitions of deviant behaviour closely parallels our concepts of crime.

Sacco (1988:7) perhaps best encapsulated the meaning of deviance when he wrote, "the essence of deviance is to be found not in the behaviour defined as deviance, but in the social processes that define deviance." That is, deviance is defined by the norms and values within society, and while they are usually defined by the majority, they can also be defined by a minority group that defines certain societal practices as deviant.[6]

What is key is not just why an act becomes deviant but the reasons why people behave in ways unacceptable to most of us. Furthermore, as criminologists, we are interested in the concept of deviance and its relationship to criminality.

So far we have defined the major concepts and terms that make up the terminology of criminology. We have seen that their meanings are specific and perhaps somewhat complex. Next, we will look at how criminology and how its terms originated.

The Origins of Criminology

As early as 2000 BC, the subject of crime was a point of debate amongst philosophers, legal scholars, medical doctors, and even theologians. Socrates, for example, was known to have commented on the plight of young people. He argued that they were disrespectful and in need of certain disciplining. Even today, within institutions of higher learning, you might enter any one of those disciplines to study crime as part of the curriculum. Naturally, as noted earlier, your approach and understanding would be greatly influenced by the particular disciplinary orientation— i.e., its *frame of reference*. For example, how might a lawyer, as opposed to a theologian, approach the causes of crime? What line of reasoning would each be likely to adopt when considering an appropriate response to a criminal offender?

For centuries, these bodies of inquiry (i.e., philosophy, law, medicine and theology) constituted the core means by which to study crime—by studying human behaviour. However, it was not until the works of several social philosophers in the eighteenth and nineteenth centuries that the natural and social sciences became recognized as disciplines. This era is often referred to as the Enlightenment because of the marked proliferation of non-secular intellectual thought (see Chapter 4).

The Emergence of Criminology

In 1885, Raffaelo Garofalo, an Italian law professor and former student of Lombroso (see Chapter 4) coined the term "criminologia" and the French anthropologist Phillip Topinard used it for the first time in 1879, as "criminologie." Both Garofalo and Topinard used their terms in reference to the study of punishment and treatment of criminals rather than the scientific analysis of observation of crime and criminals. Not only did this reflect their respective disciplinary training but it also had a significant impact on the meaning of criminology for nearly a century thereafter. Writers and thinkers of the time were more interested in reforming criminal law than in attempting to understand the etiology (i.e., origin) of criminal behaviour. The orientation is referred to as the classical school of criminological thought (see Chapter 4).

At the turn of the twentieth century, one of the leading European criminologists, Bernaldo De Quiros, while discussing theory, noted that the science of criminology was a secondary evolutional consequence of the study of penology (i.c., the study of punishment) (Quiros, 1911). In fact, two of the major reformers of the time, Cesare Beccaria (1738–1794) from Italy and Jeremy Bentham (1748–1832) from England, wrote about penal reforms based on humanitarian grounds and classical principles rather than scientific ones (see Chapter 4).

Gaining Stature

The late 1800s were a period of considerable change for criminology. As it gained acceptance around the world, universities began to offer courses in programs that specialized in criminology. Today, in Canada, we have three different, although not necessarily independent, criminology-oriented programs (also see Appendix 2). They include:

1. Criminology—focusing on etiology of crime,
2. Criminal justice—focusing on the agencies of social control, and
3. A "human justice" program at the University of Regina focusing on preparing undergraduate students for employment in the criminal justice field, as well as conducting research within the province.

The growing acceptance of criminology as a subject of study was marked by a shift from legal reforms to a more scientifically-oriented approach. In North America, the first real breakthrough for criminology as a discipline occurred in 1918 when Maurice Parmalee, a sociologist, wrote the first textbook on criminology, albeit with a sociological orientation. It was simply titled: *Criminology*. Even though Parmalee drifted into criminological obscurity, Edwin H. Sutherland's *Principles of Criminology* (see Chapter 4 for further discussion), which appeared six years later in 1924, became a major force in furthering the influence of sociological positivism (Gibbons, 1979). His textbook, with updates and later revisions with his former student Donald R. Cressey, had been reprinted more than a dozen times by the early 1980s, a testament to its content, ideas, and enduring impact on criminological thought. While Sutherland is generally regarded as the most influential North American criminologist, John Henry Wigmore (see Chapter 4), former dean of the law faculty of Northwestern

University in Chicago, is recognized as the first to give criminology a credible platform in North America. Wigmore arranged for the first conference on the subject in 1909. Out of the conference proceedings emerged the prestigious publication for scholars to publish their related works, the *Journal of Criminal Law and Criminology*.[7]

Sutherland's work not only spawned a plethora of sociologically-based textbooks dealing with the subject of criminology, but between 1930 and 1950 in North America, that orientation helped forge an alliance between criminology and sociology departments (see Reckless, 1970). Many of the more prominent sociological theories of crime emerged during this era (see Chapter 7).

In **summary**, we can see that the discipline of criminology has not only evolved in its meaning and scope but continues to be a fluid and evolving area of study. Criminologists are no longer concerned with penology or the sociology of law. Rather, criminology can be, and has been referred to as a criminological enterprise. Let's explore what is meant by this phrase.

The Criminological Enterprise: What Criminologists Do

Today, criminology is increasingly recognized and accepted as an interdisciplinary and multifaceted enterprise. The notion of criminology as an enterprise can be attributed to the writings of Marvin Wolfgang and Franco Ferracuti (1967), who recognized that the study of criminology involves several sub-areas (e.g., biology, law, psychology, psychiatry, and sociology). We can say it is multifaceted because it encompasses the study of several major areas, where they pertain to the subject of crime and criminality. In such an enterprising discipline, a criminologist is likely to specialize in one or more of these sub-areas. This is not unlike a sociologist who might specialize in urban sociology, gender issues, social ecology, or demography, among a variety of other sub-areas.

Students studying criminology are usually required to take at least one course in each of these primary sub-areas. So let us take a brief look at the core sub-areas (Figure 1–2) that make up the criminological enterprise.

1. **Criminal statistics:** In an effort to understand, describe, predict, and access the impact of crime prevention or intervention programs, researchers often rely on crime data. For example, how serious is the incidence of youth crime in Canada? When and where does it usually occur? Will such measures as "toughening" the *Young Offenders Act* help to control the problem? How do our violent crime rates compare to other nations? (see Box 1.5) Answering these types of questions involves gathering scientific data from a variety of sources and using appropriate research methods and statistical tools.

FIGURE 1-2

THE CRIMINOLOGICAL ENTERPRISE

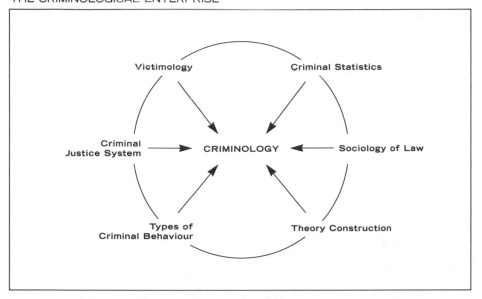

BY THE NUMBERS BOX 1.5

VICTIMIZATION RATES FOR SELECTED VIOLENT CRIMES BY COUNTRY—PER 100,000

COUNTRY*	HOMICIDE	SEXUAL ASSAULT	ROBBERY
Northern Ireland	9.4	15	12
Italy	5.2	4	5
Canada	3.0	10	13
France	2.4	18	11
Switzerland	2.4	18	4
Netherlands	1.6	0	5
Sweden	1.5	9	9
England/Wales	1.4	8	3
W. Germany	1.3	3	7
Scotland	1.0	8	5
Norway	1.0	6	5

Source: *CCJS:* Violent Crime in Canada, 1996, 16(6):17

---

*Annual data varies between countries. They cover the years 1989 to 1993.

By "scientific" we mean data that can be observed and (repeatedly) measured to test theories and ideas for their validity and reliability: Does the evidence fit the explanation? Otherwise, if we obtain information based on erroneous sources we might make a (policy) decision which could be counter-productive. For example, should we reinstate capital punishment? Would that behaviour act as an effective deterrent? Will requiring Canadians to register their firearms reduce the incidence of offences resulting from the use of firearms?

Obtaining dependable answers to these and many other criminological questions is critical if the criminal justice system is going to maintain social control and command the support of the populace (see Chapter 14). Hence, criminal statistics is one of the most crucial aspects of the criminological enterprise. In Chapter 3 we will review some of the data-gathering techniques commonly used in the study of criminologically-related issues. In Chapters 9–13 we examine how data can be used to describe the patterns and characteristics of crime.

A CLOSER LOOK BOX 1.6

The Cost of Crime

A crime statistic: The conservative Vancouver-based think tank, the Fraser Institute, published a report titled *The Crime Bill*, in which it conservatively estimated that crime costs Canadians approximately $16.7 billion, or 2.3 per cent, of the nation's gross domestic product (*Fraser Forum*, 1995 – Internet Online).

---

2. **Sociology of law:** In Canada, as elsewhere around the world, the provinces and federal government are constantly concerned about maintaining social order. Criminal law, as prescribed in the Canadian *Criminal Code*, is the backbone of the formal description of non-acceptable behaviour. The Criminal Code also describes the range of punishment, rules of law, and the limits of law. For example, in Canada, there can be no crime without a law and you are considered mentally incapable of committing a crime if you are under the age of 12.

These formal definitions are all very well, but they leave many questions unanswered. For example, how do laws come into effect? Do they help ensure a better quality of life and safer communities? Do they give rise to a feeling that justice has been exacted for those who have violated the law? Was Paul Bernardo punished fairly for the killing of two girls in Ontario? Was it fair, or right, that in December 1997 he was granted the right to have a public defender plea his appeal? Was it fair that his wife and partner-in-crime, Karla Homolka, had further charges dropped because of her plea bargain arrangement prior to the full disclosure of her involvement?[8]

The sociology of law is concerned with determining the origin of law and legal thought. By better understanding that history, criminologists try to gain a better understanding of how various economic, political, and social forces work to influence the formalization of social control and social order. Noted American criminologist Richard Quinney (1977) argued that the definition of law is simply created by authorized agents who have vested interests (also see Chapter 8). Is this true? Who decides whether soliciting should be legal? To what extent is law an effective instrument for curbing tax evasion or cigarette-smuggling? Should the law be used to regulate issues of morality (e.g., how old do you have to be to buy alcohol, purchase pornographic literature, etc.)? The sociology of law is also concerned with the study of how and why changes in the law occur. Crime being a *relative* and *evolving* concept (e.g., computer crime and high technology crimes, international drug cartels, etc.), the law must be sensitive to changing conditions within society. It is interesting to note that Edwin Sutherland (1947) observed that the sociology of law received little attention during the early years when sociology dominated criminological thought. It was accepted as "a given." However, as the discipline of criminology evolved, so did its focus. Some of the elements relating to law and the sociology of law can be found on the Prentice-Hall Web site (www.prenticehall.ca/winterdyk).

3. **Theory Construction—Etiology:** This area of study has grown considerably throughout the twentieth century. It is concerned with understanding the causes of crime and its rates and trends, as well as predicting individual or group behaviour. For example, why and how could Clifford Olson kill 11 children? How could two English ten-year-olds, Robert Thompson and Jon Venables, bludgeon to death five-year-old James Bulger in 1993? How could otherwise well-trained and disciplined Canadian soldiers, while serving in Somalia in the mid-1990s, kill innocent local residents? What about the incidents involving the peace-keeping troops in Bosnia who were charged with gross misconduct at a local mental hospital? Is this type of behaviour triggered by "primitive" physiological characteristics? Is society somehow to blame? Were the offenders suffering from some biological or neuropsychological problem (see Chapter 5)? Was their behaviour somehow learned? Were there other social, economic, or mitigating causal factors?

In order to answer these kinds of questions in an objective and "value-free" manner, criminologists rely on criminological theories to help describe, explain, and predict criminal behaviour. This approach is also known as a scientific approach—using facts to "speak for themselves."

All theories, however, reflect the ideological or political sentiments of the day. In the 1960s, Cloward and Ohlin's theory of differential opportunity (see Chapter 7) arose in part because of the political belief that lack of opportunity was the root of most crime. In fact, in the United States, the Kennedy and

Johnson Administrations launched an all-out campaign against what was believed to be the root of crime—the slums. The $12 million initiative referred to as the War on Poverty involved a program called Mobilization for Youth, based in the slum areas of New York City. Unfortunately, as a result of poor management and practical and conceptual limitations, the program was unable to bring about structural social changes to the slums. The initiative was, however, instrumental in establishing such well-known programs as Job Corps, VISTA, Neighbourhood Legal Services, Community Action Programs, and one of the most successful programs—Head Start (see Krisburg and Austin, 1978). In Chapter 14 we will explore the issue of whether the "new" restorative initiative is socially, economically, and/or politically motivated.

Because the study of criminology is interdisciplinary in nature, there are a variety of criminological theories and theoretical orientations. Researchers have developed several methods for classifying these variations. And because of its multidisciplinary roots, almost every criminology textbook offers a somewhat different twist to classifying theories (also see Appendix 2). Unfortunately, this practice has not only done little to facilitate students' understanding of theories, it also reflects the ideological biases and conflicts that permeate the study of crime and criminality. So, for the purposes of this book, we will group theories according to their disciplinary orientations (Chapters 5–8) in an effort to demonstrate the need for an integrated and interdisciplinary or "bridging theories" orientation.

4. **Types of Criminal Behaviour**: The use of criminal typologies is a way of trying to understand and organize behaviour. Official police data (known as the *Uniform Crime Reports*) record crimes according to specific types as defined by law. These data include several types of violent crimes and property crimes, as well as a number of other *Criminal Code* offences (e.g., prostitution, arson, drugs, etc.). Many criminologists believe that different crimes have different explanations and causal factors (see Section II). For example, Fredrick Desroches' *Forces and Fear: Robbery in Canada* (1995) represents a fine analysis of robbery as well as a discussion about how we might consider preventing robberies. Silverman and Kennedy (1993) offer a similar study of murder in Canada.

In addition to the study of crime types, criminologists interested in this subarea often attempt to link crime types with criminal behaviours, that is, different types of criminals commit different types of crimes. This is known as crime typology. This area of inquiry is concerned with understanding the causes and motivation underlying such areas as violent crime, corporate crime, serial murder, property offences, soccer hooliganism, and more. In Section IV we will address some of these areas.

5. **Law Enforcement, Judiciary and Corrections**: The criminal justice system (CJS) consists of three formal elements: detecting crime, processing crimi-

nals, and protecting society. How these elements, individually, and collectively as a system, fulfill these tasks is subject to much debate and research (see, for example, Ekstedt and Jackson, 1997 and/or Goff, 1997). For this reason, many criminology programs offer several courses that allow the student to examine each element in detail. Therefore, we will not be examining these elements in any specific chapter. Only those issues pertinent to the study and etiology of crime and criminals will be covered.

A CLOSER LOOK BOX 1.7

The Cost of Operating the Criminal Justice System

After adjusting for inflation, the per capita cost of crime has risen dramatically from $4.38 per Canadian in 1961 to $16.85 per Canadian in 1980 (Griffiths and Verdun-Jones, 1989) to $340 for every person in 1994/95 (*CCJS*, 1997, 17(3)). Total government spending on police, courts, Legal Aid, and Corrections increased 13 per cent (after inflation) between 1988/89 and 1992/93 to $9.57 billion (A graphic ..., 1996) and nearly $10 billion for 1994/95.[9]

---

6. **Victimology**: In recent years the growing interest in and awareness of criminal–victim relationships has prompted both public and academic interest. As a subject of interest, however, some of the early positivists (Lombroso, Garofalo, Ferri, and Tarde, among others) had already recognized the importance of the victim's relationship to the crime he or she suffered and to the offending individual. However, as Ellis (1986) has noted, the relationship is not always clear. One of the first pioneers of victimology, Hans von Hentig (1948:383), posited that many victims precipitate their own victimization through their lifestyle, mannerisms, or other forms of behaviour and expression—"the relationships ... are much more intricate than the rough distinction of criminal law." A classic analogy, taken from von Hentig's early work, might be that someone who goes to "seedy" bars alone and is not dressed to fit in may be inviting "trouble." Based on Fattah's (1991:101) typologies, such a potential victim could be described as a *deserving victim* because his or her "reckless behaviour (is) seen as deserving their victimization."

Victimology can also include the scientific study of the relationship between the victim and the criminal justice system (see Box 1.8). Ellis has pointed out how victims can be further victimized by the system. This can involve insensitive questioning by police, harsh cross-examination in the courts, or withholding of evidence until a case is resolved. For example, I once had a student whose driver's side bucket-seat was removed and kept as evidence while the case was being tried. She was not provided with another car seat. Since no effort was made to provide her with a temporary seat, she was being further victimized—

but this time by the criminal justice system. The student had to use an orange crate (and hoped she would not be caught) with a pillow for the few weeks it took before her seat was returned!

Alternatively, the state can be viewed as an "offender." It could neither provide sufficient protection for the victim nor could it restrain or deter the criminal, because of some fault in the social control network. As well, there could be connections between victims and other societal groups and institutions, such as businesses, the media, and social movements (e.g., Gay Rights, Greenpeace, etc.).

REALITY CHECK BOX 1.8

FROM VICTIM TO VINDICATED

One of the controversial issues that has plagued the criminal justice system has been its inability to ensure due process and reach a just decision as to the guilt or innocence of an accused based on legal protocols. John Monahan (1981) wrote about the issue of *false positives* (incorrect predictions of behaviour) among psychiatric predictions of the future dangerousness of offenders. If psychiatrists can be wrong 56 to 80 per cent of the time, how often are innocent people falsely convicted when lawyers and judges regularly make decisions on interpretation of the law? What price is society willing to pay for a sense of security? What are the moral and ethical limits to justice being exacted? Does society have the right to make examples of innocent people? How can criminology help to reduce these problems?

Science can, and has, played a critical role in protecting the rights of the innocent and ensuring the conviction of the guilty (see Hans Gross and Issac Ray in Chapter 4). One of the more powerful scientific tools, in recent years, has been the development of the DNA test in 1988. DNA testing was introduced into Canada in 1989 and the first case in which such testing was successfully used to free a wrongfully-convicted individual occurred in January of 1995. This was the case of Guy Paul Morin, who had been charged with the brutal sex slaying of a young girl in 1984. After years of appeals, and denying any involvement in the murder, he was finally proven innocent as a result of DNA testing. Another case of note is that of David Milgaard. He spent 23 years behind bars for the murder of a 20-year-old Saskatoon nurse's aide that he didn't commit. At age 40, he was finally freed when the Supreme Court of Canada admitted that, based on the evidence, there had been a miscarriage of justice. However, it was not until the summer of 1997 that he was fully exonerated by DNA tests. Finally, on December 24, 1997, Milgaard was granted a full pardon. He is now free to enter the United States and travel abroad. The final act had been delayed as a result of an escape in 1981 when he failed to return from a day pass. Conversely, in

October of 1995, Jason Scott Good of British Columbia was finally convicted of slaying Denny MacDonald, using DNA testing results.

Given the growing interest in victimology, relevant material has been incorporated throughout the textbook. Mendelsohn (1963), another pioneer in victimology, has argued that victimology deserves to be a separate and autonomous science. This view has not been widely embraced, as evidenced by the paucity of criminology programs offering courses on victimology. As for the CJS, there is also a dearth of victim assistance/support agencies. Most of the agencies that do exist are privately run and often rely on volunteer support to support themselves.

FYI BOX 1.9

The "Dark Figure" of Crime

The 1993 victimization survey, the General Social Survey (GSS) of Canadians revealed that 90 per cent of sexual assaults went unreported to police, along with 53 per cent of robberies. The same survey reported that more than 70 per cent of perceived violent criminal incidents were not reported to the police (Johnson, 1996).

In **summary**, as an enterprising and interdisciplinary area of study, criminology has evolved to become a multifaceted discipline. As an enterprise, the sub-areas often pursue the same issues (i.e., the possible means of controlling criminality), but generally come out with different solutions or interpretations. For (social) policy analysis this often presents major hurdles when trying to make sound policy (see Chapter 14). As the great Greek philosopher Plato observed over 2,000 years ago, "existing conditions are imperfect reflections of operating principles" (cited in Wright and Fox, 1978:317). Furthermore, this lack of consensus can lead to confusion. So how does criminology attempt to make sense of crime, and how can it put that knowledge into effect?

In the next two sections, we will review the primary disciplinary perspectives that make up the study of crime and criminality. Then we will look at the importance of linking criminological findings with (social) policy.

Viewing Crime Through the Eyes of a Criminologist

"Crime is present not only in the majority of societies of one particular species but in all societies of all types" Emile Durkheim (1858–1919).

We have just identified the main sub-areas of study within criminology. What we did not clarify is how criminologists view crime. Because of the complexity of crime and its pervasive influence on all levels of society (individually, societally, economically, politically, environmentally, and even spiritually), virtually every major discipline has contributed something to the study of crime. Criminologists, regardless of their disciplinary bias or theoretical orientation, however, are all primarily interested in the study of human behaviour, or, more specifically, crime and criminality (i.e., Why are crimes committed by certain individuals and not others?).

If you are in a criminology program, as you read this section see if you can identify which disciplinary perspective(s) the faculty members within your department might align themselves with, then ask them, to see if you were right. How many different perspectives are there in your program?

We will summarize six of the more important criminological specialties that you are likely to be exposed to as students of criminology:

1. **Sociology:** Sociology is the science of interaction among people, the effects of the interaction on human behaviour, and the study of the forces (e.g., values, norms, mores, laws, etc.) that underlie regularities in human behaviour. In essence, sociologists are interested in the study of culture and social structure.[10] The French sociologist, Emile Durkheim (1895) defined crime in this way: "An act is criminal when it offends the vigorous and well-defined states of the collective conscience."

Sociology, like all other major disciplines, views crime and criminal behaviour from a variety of perspectives. These range from *social structure* to *social process* to *social organization* orientations. The sociological perspective is the most dominant criminological perspective in North America.[11] A number of these orientations will be discussed in Chapters 7 and 8.

2. **Psychology:** Psychology is the science of individual behaviour. More than 2,000 years ago, Plato, in *The Republic*, spoke not only about assigning citizens to different roles based on their aptitudes, but that some such measurement be developed. Psychologist Olaf Kinberg (1960) defined crime as "a form of social maladjustment which can be designated as a more or less pronounced difficulty that the individual has in reacting to the stimuli of his environment in such a way as to remain in harmony with that environment."

As with most other social sciences, the manner in which individual behaviour can be tested and quantified varies depending on one's orientation. For example, as will be elaborated upon in Chapters 5 and 6, one can focus on mental abilities such as IQ (see Box 1.10) as a gauge of normality, or on differences in physical characteristics (see Chapter 5). In addition, psychologists focus on differences in personality and mental characteristics of criminals. Even as early as the fourth century BC, the father of modern medicine, Hippocrates, associated physical characteristics with behaviour.

ARE CRIMINALS INTELLIGENT AND/OR CREATIVE?

Noted Harvard University psychologist, Howard Gardner, published his controversial book *Frames of Mind: The Theory of Multiple Intelligence* in 1983, refining his theory that intelligence cannot be measured through intelligence quotient tests. Gardner believes we have multiple intelligences: linguistic, logical/mathematical, musical, spatial, bodily kinesthetic (e.g., skills possessed by athletes, actors, and dancers), interpersonal, intrapersonal, and even naturalistic, i.e., a good understanding of flora and fauna. For example, have you ever felt you were better suited to, or felt more comfortable with, one of these areas than others? My spatial skills are much more acute than my wife's, but she has exceptional interpersonal skills—a skill I envy as a teacher. To support his general premise, Gardner cites an example of the frontal lobes of an individual being removed so that he is never able to move again, yet can still score 130 on an IQ test. Rather than believing that IQ alone is indicative of what we are capable of, Gardner suggests we need to broaden our understanding of intelligence (Jahrig, 1996). Platt (1969) suggests that *creativity* may be a better indicator of intelligence. In order for a crime to be successful, a criminal must not only be intelligent enough to form the intent but also display a degree of creativity that enables him or her to evade apprehension. Guilford (1954) has defined creativity as behaviour characterized by fluency, flexibility, and originality.

What kind of implications might this have in our attempts to understand criminal behaviour and our response to it? Do you think that social forces in life are more important than individual factors in determining criminal behaviour?

Although psychology represents a popular area of study, it is less well-established in criminological literature than the sociological perspective. One of the more notable Canadian contributions include Donald A. Andrew and James Bonta (both at Carleton University) who collaborated to produce *The Psychology of Criminal Conduct*. In their 1994 Preface, Andrew and Bonta offer a strong argument on the need for a psychological examination of criminal conduct, commenting that sociologists have tended to discredit and often ignore individual elements in explaining criminal behaviour. We will examine some of the different psychological interpretations of crime in Chapter 6.

3. **Biology:** Bears know when to hibernate, salmon always return to the river they were spawned in, and vultures seem to know when death is close at hand. These are instinctual and biologically-triggered mechanisms. Why could it not be possible that certain human traits are biological, or "hard-wired"? Or that certain crimes are a function of chemical, genetic, and/or neurological influences? In

Chapters 5 and 8 we will examine some of the traditional and more recent biological interpretations of criminal behaviour.

Until recently, the biological perspective was met with a fair degree of skepticism. However, the book that had perhaps the greatest impact on the re-emergence of biological explanations of crime is the acclaimed 1985 work of J.Q. Wilson and R. Herrnstein: *Crime and Human Nature*. As we will see in Chapter 8, the biological perspective has evolved into an interdisciplinary perspective and appears to be gathering a strong following.

4. **Economics:** To paraphrase a famous dictum from the works of Karl Marx (1818–1883): "Money is the root of all evil." Over the years many studies have been done, demonstrating a link between unemployment, economic recession, and capitalism that forms the basis of all crime. Is it possible that crime is a function of competition for limited resources and/or social status/power? Do people who have "everything" commit as many crimes as those who do not?

As we will see in Chapter 8, Karl Marx is most often associated with this notion of economic determinism and its relationship to crime. However, other than using economics as an explanatory variable (or as part of a grander theoretical model), few researchers since the classic work *Criminality and Economic Conditions* in 1905, by the Dutch criminologist Willem Adriaan Bonger (1876–1940), have produced a book using economics as the primary predictor (dependent variable) of crime.[12]

Although the economic perspective of crime has never been as widely embraced as some of the other perspectives by Canadian criminologists, there have been a number of interesting works that can (however loosely) be aligned with that view.[13] We will explore some of the economic perspectives in Chapter 8.

5. **Geography/Environment:** Crime cannot occur in a vacuum. Take a minute to reflect on some of your favourite crime or horror movies. Are there "typical" scenes that tend to show up often? How about a foggy night down by the waterfront, or an unlit alleyway in a rundown area of town, or even a clear night with a bright full moon? While these and other classic images may make for suspenseful movie scenes, a number of criminologists have developed sophisticated models and theories based on a wide range of environmental factors that include such factors as phases of the moon, barometric pressure, even the physical appearance and layout of a business, residence, social area or community. Is it possible that crime rates are a by-product of physical and environmental forces?

What is unique about this theoretical orientation is that, in addition to its potential for practical applications, the results from this line of inquiry can often be used in a proactive and preventive manner. For example, adding an alarm system to your new home or making sure that your lawn is cut and mail picked up while you are away are simple crime prevention designs using elementary environmental modifications. This approach is examined in Chapter 8.

6. **Political Science:** How is it that a small but empowered group of officials can produce laws or ignore the will of the public they serve? How criminal justice officials make decisions has a direct impact on the community at large. In addition, since criminal justice is not perfect, like most social service systems it presents many interesting issues for study among certain criminologists.

All societies require some coordination among people. The more complex and heterogeneous societies are, the greater the need for a formal infrastructure that tries to coordinate all the activities that might affect its citizens. This can range from identifying privileges, rights, and obligations, to defining the administration of justice. The organizing principles of a country, province, or municipality "indicate how conditions and concepts such as life, liberty, property, civil rights, prestige, status, jobs, and information should be distributed among members of society" (Wright and Fox, 1978:314).

As a student studying criminology you might be interested in trying to understand why it took more than 20 years of debate before the *Young Offenders Act* was passed in 1984 (see Hak, 1996). You might also ask what the politicians were trying to accomplish, and whose interests were being served—especially given the Act's current public reception. Alternatively, you might ask why political decisions do not always appear to reflect the interests of society. For example, why is it that capital punishment has not been reinstated when, in a 1994 Gallup survey, 59 per cent of Canadians supported its reintroduction?

Throughout this textbook, and in particular in Chapter 14, we will provide examples of how political science as well as the other disciplines have contributed to the study of criminality and social policy.

Finally, it is interesting to observe that while North American criminologists tend to align themselves with one of the above social science perspectives (as multidisciplinary specialists) when studying crime, Europeans have approached crime from a legalistic standpoint. For example, most European criminologists are predominantly lawyers by training who have taken an interest in social science.[14] Yet neither approach seems to be very successful at solving the crime problem (see Box 1.5).

Criminology—An Integrated and Interdisciplinary Approach:

Until recently, few Canadian criminologists had been trained within a criminology program. This is primarily because criminology programs in Canada did not exist until 1960 and graduate-related programs until a number of years after. Furthermore, as reflected above, in the past criminologists have usually come from diverse fields, with sociology and psychology representing their primary orientation. However, since Denis Szabo's pioneering efforts, a growing number of criminology, criminal justice and human justice programs have sprung up across the country (see Appendix 1). Chunn and Menzies (1997:18) estimate that over the years, "nearly 1,000 students have graduated from Montreal, Toronto, Ottawa, and Simon Fraser Universities with M.A., M.Sc., M.C.A., or Ph.D. degrees in criminology. Today five schools offer graduate-level programs in criminology"[15] and have become increasingly interdisciplinary in their approach to the study of crime and criminality (see Figure 1–3 and Box 1.11). The new undergraduates and graduate students will further help to shape the interdisciplinary and integrated identity of the discipline.[16]

FIGURE 1–3

INTERDISCIPLINARY CRIMINOLOGY

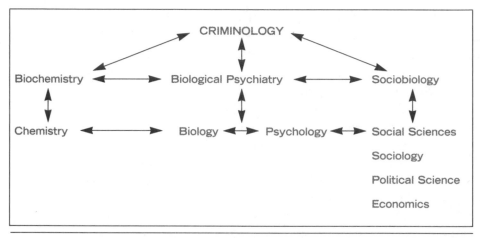

Source: Adapted from C.R. Jeffery (1990). "Criminology: An interdisciplinary approach."
Englewood Cliffs, NJ: Prentice-Hall.

WHAT DO YOU THINK? BOX 1.11

SO MANY QUESTIONS AND SO FEW ANSWERS!

A critical review of the literature will reveal that there are both disciplinary and ideological arguments for trying to address only certain questions and issues as they pertain to criminology (see, for example, Shearing, 1989; Miller, 1973). However, it is the intent of this book to argue that an interdisciplinary, holistic, and flexible approach may be more realistic and practical. The following questions represent a cross-section of questions you can explore individually or as a class exercise. There are no right or wrong answers. Rather, the exercise serves as an introduction to the complexity of crime as well as how difficult it is to solve criminological issues.

How might one best begin to answer each of the questions?

1. Is crime (really) increasing in Canada? Why is it increasing? What factors play a major role in understanding crime patterns (e.g., age, gender, region, climatic conditions, etc.)?
2. Are certain groups in Canadian society more over-represented than others in the Canadian justice system? If so, why? Is the CJS racist? If so, is anything being done to correct the situation?
3. Should pornography be censored? Should lap dancing be banned? Should prostitution be legalized? Why were/are books, like Canadian author Margaret Laurence's *The Stone Angel* banned from public schools?
4. Should soft drugs such as marijuana be legalized? Why do we allow people to drink alcoholic spirits and smoke cigarettes when we know these substances can lead to premature death? Would legalizing drugs help the CJS?
5. Should the insanity defence be abolished?
6. Should terminally ill patients be allowed to have assisted suicide?
7. Do we need more prisons? Is punishment the best way of dealing with criminal offenders? Should men and women in prison be allowed conjugal visits?
8. Are victims' rights and assistance programs succeeding?
9. Should we focus on general theories of crime as opposed to specific ones?
10. Should criminology be recognized as a separate discipline?

An integrated and interdisciplinary approach attempts to treat all disciplinary perspectives equally, as well as integrating the competing notion that crime is a product of choice or free will as opposed to being a product of fixed external and internal factors.

For example, why did former hockey czar, Alan Eagleson, commit fraud against the players who had entrusted him with the management of their pension funds? Those who support the free will model might say he knowingly calculated the risk based on his influential position, limited knowledge and/or concern of his agents. He responded to an "opportunity" that seemed too good to ignore. By contrast, it may also have been true that pressure from his legal firm to generate revenue, family stress and/or having a troubled childhood predisposed him to commit the offence.

An integrated and interdisciplinary approach would say that Eagleson committed the crime based on a combination of rational and irrational factors. Once tempted, he may have become consumed by greed and lost sight of his ability to maintain any perspective.[17]

Hence, an integrated and interdisciplinary approach may be general (e.g., all crimes) or specific (e.g., a particular crime) and may rely on some perspectives more than others to understand a situation.

What Are Your Chances?

In 1997 there were 2.5 million *Criminal Code* incidents (excluding traffic incidents)—there were nearly 30 million Canadians of which approx. 21 million were of legal age. Therefore nearly 1 in 10 Canadians could have committed a crime (*CCJS*, 1998, 18(11) and Canadian Census (Online)).

Can different theoretical perspectives offer politicians informed responses to the criminological issues confronting society?

Can These Ideas Work?
Bridging Theory and Policy

"Every man is guilty of all the good he didn't do" Voltaire (1694–1778).

The subject of crime, as John Hagan, then president of the American Society of Criminology, said in 1987 is "hot." It receives considerable media coverage (see Chapter 2) and levels of public fear are higher than ever before. Annual surveys conducted across Canada for *MacLean's* magazine all report that Canadians rank crime as an important issue.

Politicians often run their campaigns around crime issues—especially the Reform Party (see Appendix 5). Many political pundits believe that George Bush won the 1988 presidential election because he succeeded in labelling his opponent being "soft on crime." Interestingly, Clinton also took a hard stand on crime (Siegel, 1992). Allan Rock (Minister of Justice in 1996) was applauded for taking a hard stand against crime when he toughened the *Young Offenders Act* and repealed Bill 745 (the "faint hope" clause, as it was referred to in the press). The Bill had opened a loophole for serious offenders to get out on early release. In 1998, following Ontario's example, Alberta began to seek public input on revamping the justice system. Alberta's Minister of Justice, John Havelock, explained that Albertans were disgusted with the government's apparently lax attitude towards justice. Is this an astute observation or simply a means by which the government can absolve itself from responsibility if the public's ideas do not work?

As has been noted already, criminology is an "applied" social science. Criminologists use their theoretical perspectives to study crime and formulate workable solutions to the problem. The perspective in this book deals with the challenge of bridging theory and policy in criminology. It is a challenge because numerous studies have been done along with numerous policy recommendations and the "successes" have been few. Furthermore, there are often competing approaches to addressing the same issue. For example, what is the best method by which to address sex offenders? As we will see in Chapter 10, different explanations and different solutions have been put forth, yet according to official statistics the rate of incidence of sexual assaults has not declined significantly over the years.

While criminologists may not boast a perfect track record, making policy decisions without theoretical guidance would be like playing Russian roulette. There would be no basis on which to decide how to respond to sex offenders or how to address any other issue confronting criminologists and the criminal justice system. Hackler (1994:62–63) offers an interesting explanation for the dilemma:

> If criminologists would be *inconsistent* in their ideology and more *consistent* in their use of science, we would probably create a more reliable knowledge base. In the end, this could contribute to a better society... Criminologists in Canada would probably be more productive if they understood and utilized scientific procedures more than they do at present.

Despite the difficulties confronting criminologists in conducting sound research and being able to make sound policy recommendations, criminology has much to offer in the study of crime. For example, without scientific proof, capital punishment would likely be reinstated, we would likely still be torturing wrongdoers, and we might never have introduced such programs as Victim Offender Reconciliation, Community Service Order, or used DNA technology in investigative work.

Throughout this textbook there are examples of how theory, coupled with research, have been used to lead to social policy (see Chapters 9–13).

A final point about integrating theory and policy that deserves mention is the ethical issues criminologists must face when espousing a theoretical perspective or offering policy recommendation. There are potential social and political consequences to doing applied research. As Barak (1997:10) cautions, however, "criminological knowledge is also a product of ethics and notions of justice." In other words, policy recommendations are driven by the dominant and prevailing values and disciplinary structures of the time.

When Do They Go Public? Ethical Issues

To study any social issue with the intent of proposing solutions raises a number of ethical dilemmas. Ekstedt and Jackson (1997:242) define ethics as "the application of moral values or principles to decisions in public or private life."

Researching a social issue such as child abuse or prostitution, or deciding whether to subject inmates to "experimental" treatment programs can have many profound associated ethical issues. For example, many people's lives may be affected by these findings—be it considering chemical castration (see

"Chemical castration ...", 1996); legalizing prostitution (see Lowman, 1995); random drug testing of police officers in England ("Random drug ...", 1996); or managing sex offenders (Bernier, Mailloux, David, and Cote, 1996). In October of 1970 the federal government enacted the *War Measures Act* in response to the controversial activities of the FLQ (*le Front de Liberation du Québec*). Before that, the FLQ had plotted to kidnap the United States' and Israel's consul-generals in Montreal. They had planted a bomb in the Montreal Stock Exchange, which injured 27 persons, and had been involved in the murder of a member of the Québec cabinet, Pierre Laporte (Berger, 1982).

When might any of the above examples represent an infringement of our basic civil liberties and a violation of our moral standards? How should criminologists interpret such issues? How do we separate prevailing competing disciplinary biases and values to address criminological concerns?

Given the dynamic nature of crime, some criminologists try to understand the extent to which society attempts to maintain social order and how far the public is prepared to acquiesce in that attempt. In addition to dealing with these practical and ethically related issues, we need to consider how the findings can, or should, be used: towards social control or, one of the central themes of this book, crime prevention? There is also the question of which criminological perspective to study. Answers to these questions can, in part, be found within whatever disciplinary perspective is being exercised.

In **summary**, criminologists need to exercise caution when interpreting their findings. They should ground their research in sound theories and sound methodologies. However, they also need to move beyond conventional ideas and strive to create new images and new meanings for concepts that do not work. This postmodernist conceptualization embraces an integrated and interdisciplinary approach. Then these findings should be replicated over time and in different settings before they are applied. This is why many criminologists are reluctant to state anything conclusively. As you read the conclusions to research reports or journal articles, you will inevitably notice this.

Summary

In 1995, at their international crime conference, the United Nations declared that crime was a global issue. However, we began the chapter by suggesting that criminology could justifiably be examined from a *Canadian perspective*. Although the first Canadian criminology program did not emerge until 1960, we now have nearly 40 diploma and degree related programs across the country (Appendix 1). In addition, while we may not be a major player on the international scene some significant studies and scholars have already made their mark (see Chapter 4).

After defining the essential terms in criminology, we explored the roots of the discipline. While the subjects of *crime* and *deviance* have been of interest since ancient times, criminology is a comparatively young area of inquiry. We saw how criminology has evolved, and continues to evolve, into an *integrated* and *interdisciplinary* science.

We have seen that criminology is the systematic and objective approach to the *study of human behaviour* involving crime, criminality, victims, and the criminal justice system, as well as the laws that define crime and its administration. Criminology has evolved into a dynamic integrated and interdisciplinary field which, in North America, has its roots steeped in the behavioural sciences. Although sociological thought has played a major role in criminological inquiry in Canada, no single theory can provide all the explanations regarding the crime problem. Yet, as the noted American sociologist Thomas Kuhn (1970), among others, noted, the paradigm criminologists use will naturally influence the type of information they seek, the strategies they employ, and the interpretations they make.

It was also observed that criminology is an applied science, a *criminological enterprise* that uses *theory* and *research methods* in an effort to explain the causes of criminal behaviour. In addition, *criminologists* use their findings to provide informed opinions to help *guide policy-making* throughout the criminal justice system. Finally, it was noted that as an applied discipline, criminologists must deal with a number of *ethical issues* when conducting their research.

Criminology is like a living organism. It is dynamic. It is constantly evolving and presenting new challenges. It is an exciting discipline and one that will allow students to make a positive contribution, especially if they are prepared to embrace an integrated and interdisciplinary approach to the study of criminal behaviour. The number of professions and related areas in which students can seek employment is large (see Appendix 3). Because of the practical implications of working in these areas, the jobs can be personally very rewarding.

Having laid the foundation of the discipline, let us now turn our focus to how the public forms its images of crime and criminal behaviour. For, where once criminological knowledge was largely confined to the arena of academia, the organs of mass communication and mass media are now also producing criminological "knowledge." Their perceptions can, and do in many cases, become the driving forces behind formal responses to maintaining social order.

Discussion Questions

1. Other than simply wanting to refer to Canadian crime data, why should we want a Canadian criminology textbook?

2. What is the difference between a crime and an offence?

3. What is the importance of understanding the historical roots of criminology?

4. What are the major elements that make up the criminological enterprise?

5. Why should we want to embrace an integrated and interdisciplinary approach to the study of crime? What are the strengths and weaknesses of such an approach?

6. In 1999, the Mayor of Grand Forks in British Columbia proposed applying for federal licensing to become Canada's chief supplier of medical marijuana. Explain how this proposal reflects the relative and evolutive nature of criminal/deviant behaviour.

7. Towards the end of the chapter, it was noted that there are a number of ethical issues that criminologists must contend with. How can they resolve these challenges?

Key Concepts

Criminology	criminologist	criminological enterprise	summary offences
Criminal	interdisciplinary	offence	non-conventional crimes
Integrated	consensus	conventional crimes	
Conflict	etiology	relative	
Crime	deviance	indictable	

Key Names

C. Lombroso	R. Garofalo	P. Toppinard
C. Beccaria	J. Bentham	M. Parmalee

Weblinks

www.mala.bc.ca/crim/htm is the homepage for the Department of Criminology at Malaspina College in Nanaimo, BC. It is perhaps the best general Canadian source for accessing a wide range of topics, data, international crime and criminological material.

➔ **www.fsu.edu/~crimdo/imges.html** University of South Florida criminologist Cecil Greek, has created one of the most comprehensive criminology Web sites anywhere. Although American-based, he provides numerous links to Canadian and other international Internet links on virtually any subject area.

Footnotes

1. Gibbs (1987) identifies the last four questions in the list as representing the "four major questions" that criminologists traditionally strive to answer.

2. For example, American born Edwin Sutherland is often recognized as the "Dean of American criminology" (Reid, 1982:153) while Denis Szabo, the "Dean of Canadian criminology," born in Hungary and educated in Europe, established the first criminology program in Canada in 1960 (see Chapter 5). Their different heritages have had a significant impact on their approaches to the study of criminology.

3. Students interested in learning more about the role of law in criminology can visit **www.prenhall.ca** and **www.prenticehall.ca/winterdyk**.

4. It should be noted that many offences are what are referred to as hybrid offences. Depending on the seriousness of the offence, the crime can be proceeded with as an indictable charge or as a summary charge. For example, if someone commits a break-and-enter and steals goods whose value is in excess of $5,000, then the offence is treated as an indictable offence. If the value of the goods does not exceed $5,000 then the offence is punishable as a summary conviction.

5. Boyd (1988) and Linden (1996) offer a general review of some of these concepts.

6. Environmental groups such as Greenpeace, for example, may consider the commercial development of wildlife habitat areas as both deviant and criminal. In Section II, we will examine the labelling and symbolic interactionist perspectives.

7. Other major contributions of historical note include John L. Gillin's 1926 textbook, *Criminology and Penology* and Philip A. Parsons' textbook, *Crime and the Criminal*, also published in 1926 (see Gibbons, 1979:34). Gillin's textbook included 36 chapters which were divided into two main sections—theoretical explanations of crime and punishment and control of crime. His etiological approach paralleled that of Parmalee as they are both relatively supportive of the Lombrosian perspective. Parsons' book, while having drawn fewer accolades than Gillin's or Sutherland's, was intended for the general public and college students (Gibbons, 1979).

8. An informal survey was conducted in July 1996 through one of the crime Web sites on the Internet. The survey results showed that nearly 50 per cent of the respondents felt the court should have been able to charge her since she had not been completely truthful about her involvement at the time of the plea bargain.

9. *Juristat* reports note that these figures do not reflect all government spending! They neglect to explain which elements of government spending are not included in the estimates.

10. In many universities and colleges, sociology and anthropology programs can be found grouped together. Both tend to address human behaviour from a macro (or larger) social perspective. While sociology is more typically the "study of systems of social action and their interrelations" (Inkeles, 1964:16), anthropology is the science of human beings. Social anthropologists deal with the description and analysis of the forms and styles of social life of past and present. Meanwhile, Canadian criminologist Clifford Shearing (1989) contends that criminology is, and has always been, concerned about ordering and the struggle over social order. Therefore, cultural anthropological studies can help us to understand diverse systems of social control as well as how they came to be, and how they expanded or disappeared.

11. Other Canadian books on crime and criminal behaviour have also been dominated by the sociological approach. Today, virtually every major sociology program across the country has at least one instructor/professor who specializes in criminological issues.

12. Bonger attributed criminal acts, in particular those against property, directly to the poverty of the lower/labouring class in a competitive capitalistic system. And while there is now

sufficient evidence to indicate that poverty alone does not cause crime, nor do the poor commit most crimes, his observation that wasteful consumption tends indirectly to set goals that are impossible to legitimately be achieved by people in the lower strata of society, still holds true.

13. Included in the list are Brian MacLean (Kwantlen College); John Lowman (Simon Fraser U.); Ronald Hinch (U. of Windsor); Walter DeKeseredy (Carlton U.); and Dorothy Chunn (Simon Fraser U.).

14. Among some names you are likely to come across are: David Farrington and Barbara Wooten from England, Nils Christie from Norway, Josine Junger-Tas and Gert-Jan Terlouw from the Netherlands, David Garland from Scotland, and Hans-Jörg Albrecht, Hans Juergen, and Hans-Jörg Kerner from Germany.

15. The University of Montreal was the first to grant a doctoral degree in criminology in 1968 while Simon Fraser did not begin its doctoral program until 1985 and the University of Toronto until 1990–91 (Chunn and Menzies, 1997).

16. Also of interest is the fact that in the 1990s, "women have come to surpass men numerically" at the graduate level and are bringing with them gender and feminist perspectives that have not been traditionally embraced in (Canadian) criminology (Chunn and Menzies, 1997:19). Collectively, the respondents to Chunn and Menzies' survey felt that effective social change could be more readily obtained through the promotion of social justice than through the prevention of crime and that a multi-disciplinary field of study and practice be adopted. The identity of criminology is ever evolving.

17. Eagleson received an 18-month sentence at a medium-security provincial prison near Toronto. On July 7, 1998, after serving six months (one-third) of his sentence he was granted parole. Even though he had defrauded many of his clients over a long period of time, the parole board decided to release Eagleson "because the former lawyer did not pose a threat to the public and was not likely to reoffend"(Graham, 1998).

CHAPTER 2

Images of Crime and its Control

*"Accounts of life in the urban centres of the late 1800s
and early 1900s are hair-raising. Crime was a real
threat, but then as now the picture of the crime problem
painted by official statistics was seriously distorted ..."*

H. Pepinsky and P. Jesilow (1984:22)

Learning Outcomes

After you have completed this chapter, you should be able to:

- Recognize the various methods of forming images of our reality.

- Know what influences our frame of reference choice.

- Identify the five basic ways in which we acquire knowledge and understanding.

- Understand the difference between rationalism and empiricism and how they affect our conception of crime and criminality.

- Discuss and appreciate the importance of ethics in disclosure and have an appreciation of the "social responsibility" inherent in social science discovery and disclosure.

Assuming you have read Chapter 1, you now know that the subject of crime and criminality is a complex area that has been influenced by different ideologies and disciplinary perspectives. In fact, even among those who consider themselves criminologists, there is some disagreement over what criminologists should be studying, how they should study it, and what to call their program. In Section II, we will examine some of these diverging views. However, before we do, let us look at some of the images the public has of crime and the role of mass media in shaping our images of crime.

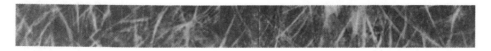

Up until the early 1970s, researchers tended to examine only people's perceptions of crime. They felt that the public was greatly concerned about crime and that the mass media played a significant role in the creation and dissemination of perceptions of crime. Comparatively few researchers, however, have examined where people gain their ideas about crime (DeKeseredy and Schwartz, 1996). Yet, as Ballard (1998) recently noted, media coverage of crimes can play a major role in the legislative processes, that may not always be warranted.

As will be seen in this chapter, the average person has a general knowledge about a variety of details around crime. However, as some researchers have observed, their awareness of crime tends to be based on an information-rich and knowledge-poor foundation.[1] How do we form opinions about the world (of crime) around us? To what extent is our fear of crime justified? Do the media distort crime news? Are official sources of crime data reliable?

The objective of this chapter is to examine how the public comes to know about and form perceptions of crime and criminality. First, the chapter will focus on the four main methods of how people come to perceive their reality. Thereafter, the focus will shift to a brief discussion on the ethics of information disclosure.

Public Perceptions of Crime

"Ignorance is preferable to error; and he is less remote from the truth who believes nothing, than he who believes what is wrong" Thomas Jefferson (3rd President of the U.S.A.—1801–09).

Knowledge vs. Belief

Before delving into methods of knowing, it is helpful to clarify a few terms of reference about the concept of image formation. How we form images of our reality has been the subject of numerous philosophical debates and social science studies. Kerlinger (1979), for example, notes that *knowledge* can be viewed as either being *dynamic* or *static*. "The static view holds that science is an activity that contributes systematized information to the world" (Ibid:7). It views knowledge as cumulative to the extent that we keep inquiring.

The dynamic view, by contrast, regards knowledge as a process of self-discovery. Knowledge is seen to be important in and of itself but it only serves as "a base for further scientific theory and research" (Ibid:7). The view, or *frame of reference*, we choose is influenced by our socialization process, psychological character, and various biological factors. Nettler (1984), among others, has observed that how we view something is not necessarily the same as our knowledge about something. You might believe that capital punishment is an effective deterrent but over the years, research (i.e., knowledge) has continually been unable to support your view. Furthermore, the type and amount of reading or viewing you engage in will determine how much knowledge you have to make an informed decision about a particular issue. For example, because the media have a code of conduct that requires them to report the news accurately, the public may feel that the media are reliable sources of crime information. However, also knowing that the media "focus upon what is out of place: deviant, equivocal, and unpredictable" (Ericson, Baranek, and Chan, 1991:4), represents additional insight into the role of the media that may help the public to view such news more warily. Yet the public may not always be aware of this. A number of studies have shown that as many as three-quarters of people polled overestimate the amount of crime involving violence (see Ekstedt and Jackson, 1997). Therefore, there are many avenues by which to gain knowledge and they do not always result in the same outcome! How then does the public acquire its knowledge about crime?

General Methods of Knowing

Facts vs. Fiction

What is the difference between knowledge, belief, and truth? Based on information (e.g., crime statistics) available to you, you might *know* that the crime rate declined in the 1990s. However, based on personal experience and/or other methods of knowing, you might not *believe* everything you read (see Box 2.1). So what is the *true* (real) scenario?

The great French philosopher, René Descartes (1596–1650) introduced us to the *method of doubt*. Unless every belief can be demonstrated with absolute certainty, then we must doubt its existence. He introduced us to the concept of **rationalism,** which means knowledge is based on reasoning. It is from Descartes' work we have the famous saying "I think therefore I am." Another way of understanding knowledge comes from the **empiricist** perspective. Such great scholars as John Locke (1632–1704) and David Hume (1711–1776), argued that knowledge comes though experience. Locke used the analogy of *tabula rasa*: our minds begin as a blank slate on which life experiences form our reality (Wolff, 1971).[2]

If one considers the work of Immanuel Kant (1724–1804), perhaps one of the greatest thinkers since Aristotle and Plato, then the line between fact and fiction becomes even more nebulous. In his work titled *Critique of Pure Reason*, published in 1781, Kant argues that we never have knowledge of reality. Instead, our mind forms our appearances of reality. Hence, *our ways of acquiring knowledge simply represent the mental window through which we view and construct our reality.* Therefore, it is possible for two researchers (or other people) to describe the same thing from two different paradigms and produce considerably different accounts. It is not unlike the Crown and defence bringing in their own experts to counter each others' sworn impressions. Each believes their experts' knowledge to be superior to and therefore more believable than the other's expert. Yet all the experts are speaking on the same subject. Who is telling the "truth"? We must assume they all are since their testimony is provided under oath!

While it is beyond the scope of this chapter to debate the strengths and weaknesses of the above views, they are intended to serve as reminders that what we believe to be facts (e.g., the news) may only be illusions compared to a greater reality that we have not yet seen. Change in our knowledge can occur through what Thomas Kuhn (1970) coined a **paradigm shift**. This concept encapsulates the premise that there can be no one objective truth but rather multiple theories, that arise from the different beliefs and values that researchers and scientists have. Hence, reality can be described as consisting of multiple paradigms (beliefs) or theories. However, research paradigms come under scrutiny and when new findings overwhelm previous knowledge, researchers experience a paradigm shift. For example, criminology was once dominated by law and the sociological perspective. However, as we have gained more empirical knowledge about crime and criminality we have seen a shift towards embracing other perspectives such as psychology, political science, and an interdisciplinary approach.

So again we come back to the importance of knowing. It can perhaps be generally said that, whether we choose to view crime as either "bad" or "good," functional or dysfunctional, it is a phenomenon that draws considerable attention. What does crime mean? What does it really represent? What can or should we do about crime? Why do some people tend to commit more of certain crimes than others? And why do they commit one crime instead of another?

Criminology, like any area of study, is a collection of information that forms a knowledge base. This becomes the foundation for theory, policy, and social and political responses.

In more concrete terms, criminologists have synthesized the above issues into two principles of crime. The concept of crime is both *relative* and *evolutive*.[3]

On Sundays, in Indonesia it is illegal to express affection in public. To do so can result in a prison sentence. If you were to visit the beautiful open squares in Rome on a warm Sunday you would likely find the steps covered with lovers espousing their affection towards their partners. Similarly, in Canada such expressions are not sanctionable unless they violate public conduct orders. The above examples serve to illustrate two points. First, our knowledge of crime is limited by our knowledge of social and cultural values around the world. Second, these examples illustrate that the concept of crime is relative to time, place, culture, and values. Therefore, we can further note that there are no absolutes about our knowledge of what constitutes a crime.

Today we view alcoholism as a disease, a view endorsed by Alcoholics Anonymous, whereas at the turn of the century it was seen as a moral failing (Schlaadt, 1992). Yet the Old Testament tells of how Noah cultivated grapes to make wine. In Canada our attitudes toward the use of alcohol have also varied. In 1878, the *Dominion Temperance Act* gave local jurisdictions the right to vote "dry" (Hatch, 1995) while in the 1960s through the 1980s ads associating alcohol consumption with good times were readily displayed on television and in print.

Both the *Dominion Temperance Act* of 1878 and World War I brought about the prohibition era in Canada. However, in the late 1800s and early 1900s it was legal to consume kola nuts and marijuana. In fact, as many of you might have heard, Coca Cola used to have a kola nut base—hence the derivative Cola! Today, kola nuts are on the Olympic list of banned substances because they have a stimulant effect on the body. Since the banning of kola nuts Coca-Cola has substituted sugar and caffeine. Both sugar and caffeine in excessive amounts also have addictive properties, but they are legal (Fishbein and Pease, 1996). This example further illustrates the points about crime being relative and evolutive.

What constitutes a crime can change over time. The definition and meaning of crime is influenced by changing values and beliefs. For example, homosexuality is no longer a crime; smoking in public places is a violation, in many places; and not wearing your seat belt, or bicycle helmet in some parts of Canada, is not a crime.

What is the purpose of making laws that have no permanence? Why do we create laws that in a few years may be considered either too liberal or conservative? Do such laws have a place in our complex society? How do we **know** when to legislate laws or to repeal them? What constitutes a majority of opinion?

In **summary**, our images of crime involve a complex interplay of the knowledge (i.e., information) we have available and the choice we make as to how strongly to believe such information (i.e., based on experience, values, and norms). We have also seen that what may appear factually accurate at one point in time and place, may later take on a different meaning. Collectively, the ethical implications of these elements play an important role in how, when, and why we control crime.

Acquiring Knowledge on Crime

In the previous section, it was observed that the line between "fact and fiction" is often obscure and subject to change. Today, the problem is further complicated by the fact that our world has become so highly specialized. It is no longer possible for the average person to be a "jack of all trades." Instead, we tend to acquire varying degrees of expertise in one or two areas.

We tend to develop and master skills that enable us to obtain employment that often requires we have these specialized skills. For example, police officers must go through rigorous physical and personality screening procedures before they are accepted into the police training academy. Then they must successfully complete the training, in many cases at their own expense, before they become police officers. The days of going straight from high school into a police force are becoming increasingly rare.[4]

In 1984, Canadian sociologist Gordon West, identified four major influences that shape our images of juvenile delinquency that can also be generalized to crime. They include: (1) personal knowledge, (2) the mass media, (3) official state knowledge, and (4) sociological knowledge. We will examine the first three influences and, based on the assertions made about criminology being interdisciplinary and integrated, we will expand on point four to include theoretical knowledge.

Because crime is so pervasive today, the public relies on a variety of sources to obtain some understanding of a subject that, according to various polls over the years, ranks consistently at or near the top of social concerns (Livingston, 1992). Based on the work of Kidder and Judd (1986), we will review five basic means by which we acquire information and understanding about crime and criminological issues. They include:

1. **Speculation and logical analysis**. We often form conclusions based on what appear to be logical speculation of ideas and observations. For example, being idle provides free time and boredom, which in turn can lead to committing deviant acts to alleviate that boredom. However, our deductive process may be influenced by our limited knowledge and our wishes and desires, as well as our capacity to ignore contradictions in our thinking.

2. **Authority**. An authority (e.g., Bible, parent, teacher, or an "expert") says that something is so, and we accept it as fact. Using an expert to affirm our belief lends credibility to it. In fact, research shows we are likely to seek out experts who we can identify with just as we tend to seek out friends and partners with whom we feel a "connection."

3. **Consensus**. Rather than appeal to wisdom, we appeal to the wisdom of our peers. Our peers, however, are likely to share the same views as those inquiring, and Kidder and Judd (1986:15) note that "groups of people can be notoriously poor as independent judges."

4. **Observation**. You might have heard that a certain instructor is very demanding of his/her students. To decide whether you should avoid taking a class from the teacher you decide to sit in on a class and observe for yourself. Since you are limiting your impressions to one or two classes and the opinions of others, you might not be objective in your assessment.

5. **Past experience**. Kidder and Judd suggest that this is the most common means of generating support for our hypotheses. We draw on prior instances or

events that confirm our assumptions and then attempt to modify incongruent elements.

Studies have shown that information that is consistent with our expectations is more easily remembered than information that is not. Therefore, it is generally "unlikely that hypotheses will be disconfirmed by recollected observations" (p. 17).

Although the above methods of knowing are readily available to most people, they lack a number of critical elements. Most important, they are not systematic or objective in their approach. These methods lack a representative sample, and typically they are small samples based on a limited number of questions. These approaches are "naive" in nature (see Box 2.1). By contrast, scientific inquiry relies on the collection of observable and measurable data in which ideas are tested following prescribed methodological techniques (see Chapter 3). These techniques are the subject of research methods courses which most criminology programs require their students to take.

BY THE NUMBERS BOX 2.1

PUBLIC PERCEPTIONS: FACT VS. FICTION

A Special Report feature in the *Calgary Herald* (May 24, 1996) noted that concern for personal safety climbed from 56 per cent in 1991 to 62 per cent in 1996. The fact is however that the number of criminal incidents (and their rates) has been declining in recent years nationally and regionally (Chapter 10). Calgary, because of its continual growth, can serve as an illustration.

YEAR	CRIMES AGAINST PERSON	CRIMES AGAINST PROPERTY	POPULATION
1990	9,614	62,993	692,885
1991	12,660	76,466	708,583
1992	9,871	72,755	717,133
1993	6,991	65,648	727,719
1994	7,014	56,136	738,184
1995	6,734	55,690	749,073
1996	7,046	56,663	767,059
1997	7,856	56,231	790,498

Source: City of Calgary Community and Social Development Department, Social Research Unit. *Crime and Safety in Calgary, Alberta.* (1999). www.gov.calgary.ab.ca/81/81dcrime.htm.

One does not need to be familiar with statistical techniques to see that the number of crimes has dropped while the population has risen. Why do people seem to have the wrong impression? There are a number of possible explanations. With fiscal cutbacks, police are prioritizing responses, the public may be reporting less as their faith in the system wanes, and the increase in youth crime may be distorting the overall perception and trend. Nevertheless, your odds of being a victim of a violent crime are 1 in 119, of a property crime, 1 in 14, death from a heart attack, 1 in 538, dying from smoking, 1 in 606, of dying in a fatal car accident, 1 in 10,526. Therefore, perhaps our fears are not illogical. What do you think? (See Chapter 3 for further discussion.)

What is needed to help separate facts from public misconceptions is the use of the scientific method of inquiry. The primary building blocks involve four steps. The process is illustrated in Figure 2–1. The fact that the model is circular indicates that knowledge is a process of retesting and refining our understanding of a phenomenon, program, or event. Theories, for example, are constantly being tested under different conditions to see whether they can stand up to the rigours of objective evaluation and the test of time. Theories that do so tend to become the dominant perspectives embraced by researchers. We will examine some of these perspectives in Chapters 5–8.

FIGURE 2–1

THE WHEEL OF RESEARCH

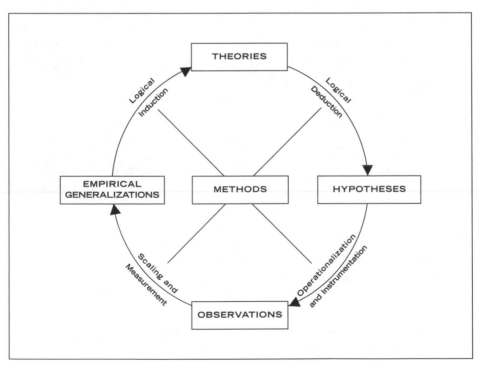

Reprinted with permission from: Wallace, Walter L. *Sociological Theory: An Introduction*. (New York: Aldine de Gruyter) Copyright 1969, Walter L. Wallace. In Miller & Whitehead (1996:15).

These naive methods of gathering information can sometimes result in misconceptions of crime because our perceptions are often coloured by one or more of the above factors.

Personal Knowledge and Crime

The viewpoints formed by the public can have a dramatic impact on the criminal justice system and criminology in general. Public pressure has been successful in bringing about judicial reform. The public has been described as the *hidden element* of the criminal justice system (Griffths and Verdun-Jones, 1994). In many cases, it is the public that dictates how money is spent in addressing crime and criminality, as well as on criminal justice administration.

One of the more dramatic examples, in recent years, has been the growing dissatisfaction the public has had with young offenders, because of stories such as the Ryan Garrioch case in 1992, and the 1995 incident in Montreal which involved the senseless killing of Reverend Frank Toope and his wife for a paltry $100 cash and some jewellery. The crimes were committed by young persons. They have all helped to fuel public criticism of the Young Offender system, and in particular the *Young Offenders Act*. Public outcry at these incidents eventually led to an increase in the penalty for murder, from seven to ten years and in 1999 a bill was tabled to replace the *Young Offenders Act* with the *Youth Criminal Justice Act*.

Similarly, a growing decline in public confidence in the criminal justice system, in particular because of certain sentencing and correctional practices, prompted the *Daubney Report (Taking Responsibility)* to verify the impressions expressed by the public in the media. Subsequent studies by Doob and Roberts (1982) and, more recently, Roberts (1988) indicated, however, that most Canadians appear to have limited knowledge about the actual crime rate and tended to overestimate the amount of violent crime, along with being ill-informed about other key aspects of criminal justice functions. Similar observations have also been reported in the United States (see Barkan and Cohn, 1994) and in Germany (see Boers and Sessar, 1991).

Public images of crime and criminality can also have a direct impact on how people conduct themselves. According to Sacco and Kennedy (1998), women tend to feel less safe alone at night, and the elderly are more fearful of being victimized than are other age groups. Because of their fear some people go to great lengths to secure their property, from sophisticated car and house alarms to protective devices such as pepper spray and personal alarms. Based on 1996 figures, Canadians spend approximately 195 million dollars, between 2.3 and 5.3 per cent of the nation's gross domestic product (GDP),[5] on personalized security systems (Easton and Brantingham, 1998). This compares to an estimated $425 million (US) each year in the United States (*Business Week*, 1993). Do these devices work? Are they necessary? Has their presence created other problems? Consider the following media captions:

- "Lorrie McClinton has a big dog, bolts her doors and keeps a knife and a baseball bat nearby." The photo caption to an article on peoples' increasing fear levels of being victimized (*Maclean's*, Jan. 7, 1991:30).

- Sales of "The Club," a steering-wheel lock to discourage auto theft, increased from $22 million in 1990 to $107.3 million (US) in 1992 (*Business Week*, Dec. 13, 1993). Yet, according to Statistics Canada, the rate of auto theft increased from 184 per 100,000 in 1983 to 355 by 1993. And based on his review of Canadian motor vehicle theft, Morrison (1996) observed that contrary to advertisement claims for automobile security devices "little is known on the deterrent effect of anti-theft devices ..." (see Chapter 9 for further discussion).

Public perception of the risk of being victimized by crime versus the actual risk varies according to factors related to lifestyle, age, gender, occupation, and a variety of personal attributes (see Karman, 1990).

Beginning in the 1980s, Canadian researchers have conducted a number of major victimization studies. Brillon (1987) and, more recently, Fattah and Sacco (1989) examined victimization among the elderly. They observed that actual victimization of the elderly was low but that fear levels increased due to feelings of fragilility and defencelessness. Vulnerability factors included:

1. **State of health**: 28 per cent of the elderly versus 19 per cent of those younger required hospitalization after being victimized.

2. **Financial situation**: 65 per cent of those surveyed experienced a drop in income. Two-thirds of those people experienced a 25 per cent drop in income levels.

3. **Social milieu**: Due to their lifestyle, the elderly are generally less informed about their risks than younger generations.

Brillon's research was pioneering as very little until then had been conducted on the victimization of the elderly. Yet, by the year 2000, those 65 years of age and over will represent at least 30 per cent of the Canadian population (Foot, 1996). More recently, research on elder abuse and other forms of elder victimization has been growing. However, researchers must guard against creating a social problem that, according to current victimization data, indicates the elderly are not at as much risk as they believe themselves to be. For example, an American study reported that while, in 1992, seniors represented 14 per cent of the population, only 2 per cent were victimized. Furthermore, between 1973 and 1993, both the rates of theft and violent crime against the elderly dropped.

In addition, as witnessed in Canada, the elderly are more likely to be victimized at or near their homes than are the young. The American study also reported that the elderly are more susceptible to crimes motivated by economic gain than mere crimes of opportunity (*Elderly Crime Victims*, 1994).

While we should not view the problem lightly, Canadian criminologist Brian Maclean (1986) argues that the growing awareness of victimization may well represent an excuse for widening the net of social control. He notes, for example, that the rate of criminal justice spending increases faster than the rate of growth for overall state expenditures. Yet crime rates remain comparatively stable. In fact, during the mid-1990s there was a decrease in crime rates. Maclean also points out conviction rates have remained relatively stable over the years.

As noted in the biographical sketch of Denis Szabo (Chapter 4), there are two sides to social reality. There is social reality as perceived by the public, and that perceived by researchers and criminology/criminal justice officials. The challenge for criminologists is to try to discern which reality is more plausible and how to balance the two perspectives. This is why most criminologists ground their research in theoretical principles and empirical data. However, it is clear how the public can become confused or misled trying to learn about the realities of crime.

Mass Media Knowledge and Crime

"It is likely that in one week of prime-time television drama one will see more homicides than will occur in Canada in the course of a year" (Silverman, 1988: 209).

Much of what people know about the issues in the world come not from direct experiences but from media portrayals. And there is plenty to choose from. Most radio stations, including CBC radio, provide news on an hourly basis. On television, there are several all-news stations such as CNN and CBC Newsworld, not including the number of crime-based sitcoms, movies, and documentaries that are aired regularly. These media, in many respects, represent our conventional methods of knowing. They represent authority (the trusted news anchor),[6] consensus (all the channels tend to cover the same stories), observation (we see pictures of the crime around us), and the news is often just "more-of-the-same" (i.e., past experience). In addition, television, radio and newspapers are entertainment media that must sell themselves to the public.

Using Canadian data, Smith (1983) found that the public and policymakers are generally concerned about the effects of television and movies on violent behaviour. Ericson, Baranek, and Chan (1987, 1991), and others, have found that the presentation of news content varies between media and newsprint because of the distinct format differences; however, the research has been unable to find consistent patterns. For example, Gollins (1988), the vice president of a national advertising agency, argues that the impact of the mass media is far less than critics fear and that the media simply reinforce prevailing attitudes and beliefs. At the other end of the spectrum, LaHaye (1988), a conservative Christian spokesperson, argues that the media, by displaying violence, sex, and crime, undermine morality in society.

The lack of congruence in the literature not only reflects the different intellectual heritage of the authors but also methodological limitations. Such limitations include being able to control for the characteristics of the source or controlling less tangible elements such as public interest and the characteristics of viewers/readers.

Representative crime coverage falls into a "catch-22" because people are inclined to pay to see only what fits their frame of reference. Therefore, the media have a stake in reinforcing certain images. Moreover, since the public has limited access to or experience with crime, their misconceptions are perpetuated in the media (Silverman, 1988). The formations of such misconceptions have been well documented in the literature. Among the first to do so was the noted social psychologist Albert Bandura.

The Mitigating Role of the Media

Bandura (1979), in a series of experiments, found that one way in which behaviour is learned is through *symbolic modelling*. Drawing on the principles of the *social learning theory* (see Chapter 6), Bandura observed that children readily imitated behaviour they observed on television and controlled video presentations. This process is referred to as *vicarious reinforcement*. The theory asserts that our social environment contributes to the learning process. Given this line of reasoning, it is possible to learn not only from those around us, but also from what we see, hear, read, and who we associate with.

How, or why, people imitate what they see, read, or hear is not clear, but there is sufficient scientific evidence to indicate that imitative and vicarious learning does occur at some level. For example, if violence and punishment are used in the home to settle disputes, children are likely to model that behaviour when they find themselves in a similar situation. The mode of vicarious modelling has been extensively documented in child abuse literature (see CSOA-CY, 1984).

Using several figures from the National Centre of Health Statistics, sociologist David Phillips found that suicides increased significantly just after the appearance of a non-fictional suicide story that appeared on television. In conjunction with related studies, Phillips concluded, "all these findings support the hypothesis that publicized suicides trigger imitative behaviour," sometimes in overt ways (i.e., an explicit suicide) or covertly (i.e., in the form of automobile or aircraft accidents) (cited in LaHaye, 1988:114). In addition, while an association between what we are exposed to and what we do does not imply a causal relationship, the media do appear to play a role in influencing human behaviour. However, since we do not have a clear picture as to the strength of the relationship, nor fully understand why some people are more susceptible to media images than others, the role of the media and crime will continue to intrigue behavioural scientists

In Chapter 6, we will explore other elements of the social learning and cognitive theory which, according to Stitt and Giacopassi's (1992) research on theories, are among the most frequently tested theories in criminology.[7] However, as an instructor once told us, "the more people write and talk about a subject, the more they realize how little they know about it."

A Growing Concern

Since the 1960s, there has been a dramatic growth in news media coverage of crime (Wilson, 1994) (see Box 2.2). Is this due to the increase in crime or is it a response to the media's realization that sensational news sells? What type of crime stories do you typically hear, see, or read about? Is the coverage representative of the "true" crime picture offered by official sources? Does the coverage provide a fair balance of local, national, and international crime experiences? If you answer "no" to any of these questions, what concerns or issues might that raise regarding our understanding of crime?

A report from the conservative think tank, the *Fraser Forum* (1996, Sept.), points out that while the murder rate declined each year between 1991 and 1995, media coverage (i.e., CBC and CTV) increased significantly. It was also noted that even though in 1995 just 16 per cent of the murders were committed by someone unknown to the victim, these types of cases were over-represented in the media (54 per cent of CBC and 66 per cent of CTV coverage). In fact, only "18 per cent of CBC and 11 per cent of CTV news stories on Canadian murder focussed on those committed by someone known to the victim" (p. 2).

FYI BOX 2.2

Media Violence

- A Laval University survey revealed that the violence index for Canadian television was 23.4 per cent lower than that for American television.
- Children's programs were 68 per cent more violent than programs for adults.
- "The tendency of adolescents to challenge conventional authority makes them particularly susceptible to imitating some kind of television violence, crime, and portrayals of suicide."

- Domestic violence comprised approximately 25 per cent of CTV and less than 10 per cent of CBC coverage of violence against women.
- Though the murder rate has dropped since 1994, murder reports were 33 per cent more frequent than the previous year (Quick facts—Media Violence, 1998).
- A three-part American study found that the number of prime-time shows containing violent scenes rose slightly from about 50 per cent in 1994 to approximately 66 per cent in June 1997.
- 92 per cent of programs aired by pay networks in the United States contain violent crime.
- Overall, the national average of violent programming is around 61 per cent (*CNN Interactive*, 1998).

In an earlier study by West (1984), a survey revealed that stories about delinquency and crime tended to feed on **moral panic** rather than upon actual behaviour. For example, in 1992, stories surrounding the Ryan Garrioch case tended to focus on the growing problem of violent youth crime, and the need for amendments to the YOA (Mofina, 1996). (Ryan, a 13-year-old, had been stabbed to death by a 15-year-old on May 11th, 1992, in a Calgary school yard.)

The type of coverage by the various media was similar to the infamous and sensationalized killing of a 12-year-old Toronto youth in July 1977. The youth was "homosexually assaulted and raped, forced to take illicit drugs, then murdered" (West, 1984:5). The story received considerable coverage, but no mention was made of the rarity of such crimes, the risk of victimization, or the fact that physical coercion for this type of crime was also very uncommon (see Chapter 9). Instead, the media focussed on stories such as campaigns to clean up Yonge Street and to combat homosexuality.

As Ericson et al. (1991) found in their extensive study on the role of the media in Canada, the media are powerful and persuasive. However, as Chermak (1995), among others, argues, the public's fascination with crime often has little to do with the reality of crime. For example, he suggests that our reading of crime news is a "ritual move exercise" that is not dissimilar to other routines we engage in such as exercising, having our morning coffee, or late night snacks (p. 72). Nevertheless, he also acknowledges that it may be possible for certain individuals, in particular youth, to imitate or be influenced by what they read or see. Hence, from a criminological standpoint it may be interesting to explore the relationship between the frequency with which people attend to the news media and their perceptions of crime. What kind of impact does TV have on people's perception of the seriousness of crime?

Several years ago, an Ontario-based study reported that there was a significant relationship "between media use and perceptions of crime seriousness"

(Geboyts, Roberts, and DasGupta, 1988:3). The more people watched television news the higher their ratings of crime seriousness became. The researchers also found that women and those respondents who **had not** been victimized within the past year expressed greater fear than did males and recent victims. Geboyts et al.'s work reaffirmed the findings of earlier Canadian studies by Akman and Normandeau (1967), Sacco (1982), and, more generally, the views expressed by the Canadian Coalition Against Violent Entertainment and the Coalition for Responsible Television. What was not taken into account were any possible social, economic, and/or demographic variables.

In 1991, Martinez (cited in Barbara, 1995) presented a report to the CRTC in which the report provided a detailed analysis involving hundreds of studies that link radio and television violence to individual aggression and violent crime. In particular, the report notes that children are particularly affected by media violence (e.g., GI Joe, Teenage Mutant Ninja Turtles, Power Rangers). However, the report points out that adults can also be affected by media violence because it tends to erode their ability to socialize and moral development. Members of the coalition report that violent content on television increased over 30 per cent during the late 1970s and early 1980s. Statistics Canada data indicate that in 1994 Canadians viewed nearly 23 hours of television per week. Children (2–11 years) viewed nearly 18 hours and adolescents viewed just over 17 hours[8] (Average hours per…, 1994). An American study by Burns (1989:35) reports that the "average 18-year-old has watched close to 100,000 beer commercials … spends in the classroom by graduation (about 12,000 hours) … spends approximately 22,000 hours watching television … in direct contact with parents (an average of 3,600 hours), it is clear that electronic input into the minds and brains of our young is an overwhelming fact in our society."

DeNew argued for stricter legislation on violent television content. However, the general manager of a television station from Ontario pointed out that viewers dictate programming by making television stations aware of their interests and concerns. In the same article, the television manager is quoted as saying, "The fastest way I can go bankrupt is to program shows that you will not watch" (Marron, 1983).

"Heads or Tails?"

It cannot be denied that many television programs contain violence in one form or another, be it physical, verbal, or occasionally, symbolic. Moreover, even though there have been "more than 1,000 studies published worldwide on violent entertainment" (Brady, 1992 cited in Murphy, 1995:109) the evidence has not always been conclusive. As early as the late 1950s researchers began to examine the relationship between television viewing and maladaptive behaviour. Most studies failed, at that time, to find any significant relationship between the viewing of violence on television by children and subsequent maladaptive behaviour. Most other studies since, especially those done by Bandura and his colleagues in the 1960s, have consistently shown an increase in anti-social and aggressive behaviour because of exposure to aggressive models. In addition, as former CRTC chairman Keith Spicer noted, "common sense tells us that this must be true ... why else do advertisers spend millions on television commercials if there is no impact on our behaviour?" (Murphy, 1995: 109).

The evidence points to a relationship between the viewing of violence and subsequent maladaptive behaviour. Moreover, while there might not be a direct link, some experts suggest that the cumulative effect of such exposure can be harmful to future behaviour. In 1976, Canadians viewed an average of 3.2 hours of television per day. By 1987, their viewing time had increased to 3.4 hours a day. Perhaps contrary to popular belief, children watch less television than adults. For example, in 1987, children aged 2–11, averaged 3.1 hours of viewing per day, while youth between ages 12–17 averaged 2.7 hours, adult females averaged 3.8 hours and adult men watched approximately 3.2 hours per day. Young (1990) reports that the type of viewing varies by gender and age. Children tend to watch more drama and comedies while men watch twice as much sport as women.

Unfortunately, since most studies on the effect of media violence have been conducted under laboratory conditions, the evidence cannot be readily extrapolated to real-life viewing. However, Surette (1992) reports that the media can shape criminal behaviour (e.g., "copycat" crimes such as the one that occurred in northern Saskatchewan when a 15-year-old male youth, who got his ideas from watching the movie *Warlock*, brutally killed a 7-year-old boy in 1995 (*Globe and Mail*, August 2, 1996). The death of child model sensation Jon Benet Ramsey, on December 26, 1996 was thought to have been influenced by Mel Gibson's movie *Ransom*. Surette also points out that print media are not as powerful as visual media. Film and video technology are able to capitalize on both visual and audio capabilities which "greatly enhance its connotative capacity and allows it to bind its message to the context in which they were produced" (Ericson et al., 1991:23).

Understanding the roots of public perceptions is important because it affects how the public view elements of justice and how justice might view (use) the public—a sort of double-edged sword! A few years ago, the Calgary Police Association placed an ad in one of the local papers with the caption "We have just one police officer for every 674 Calgarians." It seems clear the police were using the media venue to gain public support in their fight with the city to allocate more funding for law enforcement. The ad began by citing police ratios of between 439 and 571 to one in most other major Canadian cities. And while the ad acknowledges the level of satisfaction Calgarians express towards the police, the ad states that unless things change "sooner or later, something's got to give." Interestingly, the ad neglected to mention that there is no research supporting the premise that more police officers will reduce crime, improve response time, or improve overall service. Conversely, the police have also used the media bridge for public relations through cooperative initiatives to combat crime with such programs as *Crime Stoppers*. However, while most *Crime Stoppers* programs can point to the success of their programs (see Box 2.3), it is not clear to what extent programs like *America's Most Wanted*, and *American Justice*, among others, create an unreal perception of crime seriousness, increase public fear levels, and generate the sale of unnecessary security devices. For criminologists, these types of questions have both theoretical and ethical implications and raise further questions as to the role of the media as a social and political instrument in the fight against crime.

REALITY CHECK BOX 2.3

CRIME STOPPERS—A COMMUNITY EFFORT

In July 1976, in Albuquerque, New Mexico, a university student was killed during a gas station robbery. After nearly two months of investigation, police were unable to come up with any leads. Then police detective Greg MacAleese obtained permission to reenact the crime on a local station. A reward was offered to anyone who could provide information leading to an arrest. Within 72 hours of the reenactment being aired, the police had enough leads to arrest the two men responsible for the killing. This was the beginning of *Crime Stoppers*.

Today, there are more than 950 *Crime Stoppers* programs worldwide. Most major cities across Canada have a *Crime Stoppers* tip line and use television and/or radio to seek public support for difficult-to-solve cases and/or wanted persons. Rewards of up to $2,000 are offered to anyone providing information leading to an arrest. All information can remain anonymous if the caller so wishes. Funds for the project are supported by donations of money, goods or services from the community.

As of November 23rd, 1996, *Crime Stoppers International* statistics indicated:

• 577,688 cases cleared.

• $40,004,333.00 (U.S.) in rewards paid out.

• $1,017,169,438.00 in property recovered.

• $3,604,762,486.00 in total dollars recovered.

• 112,595 total convictions made.

• 4,760 homicides cleared (CSI Statistics, 1997).

Since Victoria, British Columbia, first introduced their *Crime Stoppers* program:

• 1,406 cases cleared, up until April 1995.

• $2,483,800 in property recovered, up until April 1995.

• $7,561,717 in total dollars (CDN) recovered, up until April 1995.

• $212,123 in rewards given out, up until April 1995. This involved 973 persons (Greater Victoria..., 1996).

Theoretical Explanations

Basing his argument on the principles of the *conflict theory* (see Chapter 7), Richard Quinney (1970) argued that various media are some of the vehicles within a capitalistic society that are used to interpret social reality in terms of interpersonal violence and property crimes. He further argued that the media tend to convey an image of rapidly increasing crime rates. These views have been more recently supported by the *left realist* perspective (see Chapter 8) in the writings of Jock Young (1986) and others. It can be said that collectively, the media play a significant role in society "because they have the power to decide what issues are worthy of public consumption and crime is an important topic in society" (Chermak, 1995:167). Is this interpretation of the role of the media "real" or simply the product of *social constructionism*—i.e., if we pay it enough attention, it suddenly becomes a social issue? Lippert (1990), in his study of Satanism in Canada, suggests that the perceived problem of Satanism may be nothing more than a perceptual image fed by the media. LaHaye (1988) reports a similar phenomenon with President Richard Nixon. After he wrongfully accused Alger Hiss of being a Communist, the media and the public never forgave him, and the Watergate fiasco simply gave the American populace the opportunity to publicly humiliate and disgrace him. However, if the media are so influential why, then, do not even more viewers, both young and old, commit crime? If the media are such powerful communicators, when should censorship be enforced? Should the networks adopt a voluntary rating system as opposed to government interference? Where do we draw the boundaries of freedom of speech and expression?

One recent example, from the United States, involved a debate over whether executions should be permitted on television. Only 29 per cent of those surveyed believed showing an execution would serve as a deterrent (Sherman, 1994). Ironically, the notion of public executions serving as a deterrent is not new! Executions were carried out during the Roman Empire and again with great regularity during the Inquisition and the French Revolution, and did little to deter people from committing more crimes (Johnson, 1988). Meanwhile, in Canada, there has been controversy about the use of the "V-chip" in lieu of the media monitoring themselves. Invented by Vancouver engineer Tim Collins, the chip is designed to help parents screen out sex and violence on television. Collins notes that in spite of growing public concern, the public is "not winning the battle in the United States." President Clinton recently signed a new law requiring all new television sets to have a V-chip by 1998. Canada is considering similar legislation (Marotte, 1997).

In **summary**, while social scientists may not fully understand how media coverage of crime affects public perceptions of crime, we do know that the media provide information, and some more than others. But, in defence of the media, no or few studies have ever proven that reading, viewing, or hearing about violence leads to violent behaviour.

One of the difficulties in studying the impact of the media is understanding how people respond to different channels of information (radio vs. newsprint vs. television), which ones they prefer to rely on, their personal experiences preceding participation in the survey, their state of emotional and physiological arousal at the time, etc. The problem is analogous to selecting jury members for a case that has received considerable media attention. Almost everyone will have heard something about it, so it is impossible to determine anyone's objectivity.

Official Knowledge and Crime

Within the criminal justice system there are three primary sources of (official) knowledge: the police, the judicial system, and the corrections system. As we will see in Chapter 3, these sources are required by law to produce information, primarily in the form of statistics, that are intended to reflect their performance. The collection and dissemination of these data can be viewed as a form of public accountability. Many of the statistics and general information used by the media and criminologists come from these primary sources. For example, the justice department regularly provides press releases to the media covering a wide range of issues and information requests. In addition, the Canadian Centre for Justice Statistics annually publishes a variety of information service bulletins titled *Juristat*. These publications summarize criminal justice information on a variety of topics, ranging from criminal justice expenditures to violent offences among young offenders to issues about sentencing, and correctional and law enforcement practices.

While an undergraduate student I was required to read Darrell Huff's (1984) entertaining little book, *How to Lie with Statistics*. Lying with statistics has become something of a cliché. However, clichés often miss the central issue, that is, the real concerns, the meaning, and the interpretation of statistical data. Brantingham and Brantingham (1984) point out that, while official sources may have their inherent limitations, the data they produce is consistent, regularly collected and published, and readily available. The inherent limitations refer mostly to the fact that the information collected is dependent on being reported or processed by the criminal justice system. Therefore, the interpretation of data is somewhat dependent on the knowledge and skill level of the user. Courses in research methods usually devote a part of the course to teaching students how to analyze data, and how to manage data, as well as the ethics of data management.

Let us take a brief look at some of the limitations of official data before offering a rationale for its use.

Limitations of Official Data

In Canada, the system for collecting and disseminating criminological data has evolved with the growing demands for that knowledge, both in the professional and public sectors. It is important to identify a number of common errors that plague those who use criminological data. The use of criminological data is based on sampling, an important factor for virtually any survey project. Counting anything is always subject to limitations. These limitations affect the **reliability** (i.e., does the instrument measure the event consistently each time?) and **validity** (i.e., does the instrument measure what and only what it is supposed to measure?).

- **Random error** refers to the unintentional mistakes made during the data collection process. For example, all municipalities are required to report counts of the same criminal offences to Statistics Canada. However, due to variances in administrative differences, enforcement practices, or even public attitudes, there may be unknown errors in their counting procedures. One way to minimize the amount of random error is to have a large enough sample size. Then we can assume that data from the different municipalities and provinces are still comparable.

- **Systematic errors** refer to a predictable error during the data collection process. When recording crime data, municipalities need to be sensitive to such details as the difference in the reporting rates between certain property-related offences and most serious violent crimes. For example, it is a well-established fact that property crimes are more likely to go unreported than are most serious violent crimes. Therefore, researchers know that the margin of error for officially recorded property crimes is greater than that for serious violent offences. Knowing the differences regarding the dependant variables (i.e., types of crime) is important to properly controlling for systematic error.

- **Measuring crime data at different stages** can lead to potential interpretative errors. For example, during the seventeenth and eighteenth centuries, the French Royal Warehouses promised to buy all the hemp (i.e., cannabis) that Canadian farmers could grow. Then in the 1920s, with the assistance of *Maclean's* magazine, a number of articles by Emily Murphy were published that talked about the "evils" of smoking narcotics. The articles provided the RCMP and the government with the leverage needed to make cannabis hemp illegal, under the name of "marijuana," in the *Opium and Narcotic Drug Act* of 1923. In 1971 and again in 1993 "smoke-ins" were held in Vancouver, BC, which in turn spawned a number of grassroot organizations demanding the law be changed. However, in 1996, Bill C-7, introduced by the Liberals, if passed, would make the penalties even harsher. Therefore, depending on when the use and enforcement of marijuana use was measured, the picture would be incomplete without knowing the history (i.e., different stages) of the cannabis laws (The complete history ..., 1997).

Similar Canadian examples can be found for prostitution (Lowman, 1995; Sansfacon, 1985), murder (Boyd, 1991), crimes against women in Canada (Boritch, 1997), and, more generally, official crime data. Before 1962, when the Uniform Crime Reporting process was introduced, Canada did not have a standardized crime recording procedure for the provinces (see Chapter 4 for further discussion).

These and other studies illustrate that even if agencies are not making recording errors, they may be indicators of what agencies do. From this, we can conclude that variations between and within systems are inevitable.

- **Interpreting data at different stages of the system** represents another potential pitfall when using official data sources. When you collect Canadian crime statistics (or crime data from any other country) that spans a significant period of time, you will most likely observe that data are not always reported and recorded in the same manner from year to year. That variation may be the result of administrative changes, changes in the law, or some other intervening variable that is not always readily observable.

Another factor that can affect the interpretation of crime data is what is referred to as the **crime funnel** (Chapter 1) analogy. This concept is based on the knowledge that the numbers of cases at each level get smaller as a result of "information processing." For most offenders, the police are the point of contact with the criminal justice system. Whether the police lay a charge or not determines whether the offence proceeds to the next stage of the system. Then, depending on the decision of the courts, the case may, or may not, proceed beyond the court level. If you were to compare law enforcement statistics with correctional data, you would get two different pictures as to the nature and extent of crime.

Similarly, depending on what type of crime data municipalities are collecting, its relevance can be affected by the social, cultural, and/or political climate at the time. For example, if municipalities were interested in studying youth crime, they might want to be aware of how much attention was being paid to the youth problem at the time the data were being collected. Hence, certain assumptions about the reliability of the source may warrant scrutiny.

We can see, then, that these "information contaminates" represent potential risks when interpreting data at different stages of the system. Fortunately, by being aware of the potential pitfalls, steps can be taken to identify potential information contaminates. Understanding these types of systematic and/or random errors can then enable researchers to make sound comparisons and analysis. While official data are usually readily available, researchers need to be familiar with the characteristics of their crime statistics in order to be able to draw valid conclusions.

Suffice it to note, at this stage, that in a course such as "The administration of criminal justice," these issues and their implications are explored in detail. Even though there are methodological strategies that can be employed to guard against the various pitfalls when using official data sources, it is important to be aware that no matter how diligently data are collected, or at what level they are accessed, all crime statistics are, at best, only suggestive in what they reveal about the true nature of crime.

Why Use Official Data?

Criminologists have long debated the merits and the intent behind official data sources. Those with a more *critical* or *radical theoretical* orientation suggest that official sources are controlled by the ruling classes. They use the information to reflect the interests of the state in such a way that it allows them to continue to exert control or engage in **net widening** activities. For example, are there more laws today than there were 50 years ago? Are there more police officers per capita than there were 50 to 100 years ago? Who is primarily responsible for legislating new criminal laws? Why are there so few statistics on "white collar" crime, political crime, and environmental crime? Some of these issues will be explored in subsequent chapters. At this point, however, it can be noted that official data, according to a conflict perspective (see Chapter 7) only serve the interests and needs of those recording from an administrative standpoint. They are simply doing what they need to do in order to meet their goals and objectives.

On the other side of the proverbial fence we have the *consensus model* (see Chapter 1), or *moderate/conservative view.* Synnott (1996:11) suggests "indeed the 'small c' conservative perspective paradigm is the dominant paradigm in Canada." This view asserts that official sources provide the information that the public appears to want. As the prime consensus theorist, Emile Durkheim (1858–1917), once noted, all events serve a purpose. The media are simply part of a unity of interdependent institutions that serve to maintain the social structure. So are we more interested in general information than in understanding the causes of the act(s)? Again, there is no clear answer to such a question. Rather it depends on one's frame of reference and (theoretical) knowledge base.

Theoretical Knowledge and Crime

As was noted in Chapter 1, whether it is viewed as *dynamic* or *static,* theory represents the building block to systematic and objective knowledge. It was also observed that, until recently, (at least in North America), criminological thought was dominated by the sociological perspective. Crime and criminality were largely seen in a macro-social context, in which the causes of crime were seen to be related to such factors as poverty, unemployment, heterogeneous settings, peer pressure, family, and education, among other social indicators.

And while theoretical concepts are supposedly based on scientifically verifiable and reliable observations, the **operationalization** of variables is often subject to criticism. For example, are official crime data reliable indicators of youth crime? Numerous self-report studies have shown official data to be limited for most property-related offences, while theoretical knowledge often has a direct impact on public opinion and social policy (DeKeseredy and Schwartz, 1996). By way of example, beginning in 1965 a growing volume of literature in the area of developmental psychology provided some of the critical information for the eventual replacement of the 1908 *Juvenile Delinquency Act* with the *Young Offenders Act,* in 1984 (Hak, 1996). Similarly, after Robert Martinson published his controversial, yet widely read, work on "nothing works" in 1974, there was a dramatic shift away from the rehabilitative models to a more conservative approach to justice administration. The rehabilitation programs' growth had corresponded to the emergence of positivism (Chapter 4) and psychology in the 1960s and early 1970s (Williams and McShane, 1994).

Virtually every social science program has a course on the theory of knowledge. In order to understand crime and criminality it is important to realize that how we form our sense of reality is fundamental to how we think about problem solving. In recognizing the complexity of human behaviour, criminological knowledge needs to be interdisciplinary in nature and embrace theories that bridge the social and physical sciences. Without this integration of theory, the knowledge sources and framework we have traditionally relied on will continue to frustrate our ability to move forward as a science.

Ethics in Disclosure

This chapter has addressed a number of different aspects of how we come to form perceptions of reality and acquire knowledge. By now you have probably deduced that the understanding of how we acquire knowledge, what it means, and what it represents is filled with controversy. Yet, notwithstanding some of the issues advanced, it can be noted that whether knowledge comes through personal experience, via the media, through official accounts, or grounded in theoretical knowledge, it should pass the same "test of meaningfulness, verifiability, and reasonableness before it can be accepted" (Wolff, 1971:257).

Since knowledge can be said to be *relative* and *evolutive*, how then do we rationalize the disclosure of what we believe to be meaningful, verifiable and reasonable? Students of criminology and policy makers often deal with critical issues that can have sweeping political and social consequences. For example, public opinion surveys show that most Canadians are in favour of:

• Reinstating capital punishment.
• Increasing penalties for young offenders.
• Lowering the age of responsibility.
• Using fixed sentences for serious crimes.

Criminologists who study these, and other controversial topics, have found themselves divided on even the most basic criminological issues, such as:

- What should criminologists study?
- What is crime?
- Is criminal behaviour pre-determined?
- Should we have gun control?
- Is punishment good crime control?
- Are prisons a good idea?

It is important to recognize the power of an applied discipline. As we have seen, crime affects us all, either directly or indirectly. Therefore, criminologists must not only be aware of the ethics of their profession, but they must also be prepared to defend their work in the light of public scrutiny. They also need to feel self-conscious about what they say. Scientists have a social responsibility to re-examine their goals and the implications of their findings.[9]

Finally, perhaps all researchers could adopt the physician's oath, given by the father of medicine, Hippocrates (460–377 BC): "*Above all do no harm.*"

Summary

This chapter has detailed how the public constructs its images and its control of crime. It was noted that public perceptions are important in that they can have a direct influence on criminal justice policy. For example, Sprott (1996) notes how many of the amendments to the *Young Offenders Act* were influenced by public perception and public pressure.[10] It was also noted how the public forms its knowledge of crime, which, although varied, is often naive and limited. Four primary sources of knowledge of crime were discussed. They included victimization, mass media, official crime data, and theoretical evidence. With each strategy a number of strengths and weaknesses were identified. This was followed by a brief discussion about whether it is possible to truly know anything about crime. It was noted how our concepts of crime have historically been subjected to paradigm shifts—that the concept of crime is a *relative* and *evolutive* construct.

The mass media are powerful environmental stimuli that affect not only our knowledge about crime, but also our physiological reactions to it. Increasingly, criminologists recognize the complexity of human behaviour and how that influences our images of crime. However, conventional perspectives (e.g., sociology and psychology) have never adequately explained how the media influence behaviour. For example, while we know that there is a relationship between media violence and violent behaviour, we do not fully understand why some people are more affected than others. Researchers need to adopt an interdisciplinary approach, one that acknowledges such areas as neurological learning theories and the role of the brain in learning behaviour. Until these basic issues are addressed, it will be difficult to formulate policies that will balance individual freedoms with the protection of society.

The chapter concluded by identifying a number of essential ethical dilemmas about when and how information about crime should be shared and used. This area represents a growing area of concern and interest among criminologists. Every major educational institution now has an ethics review committee that is responsible for ensuring that research conducted through the institution meets strict standards. However, as we saw, ethical issues are subjective, and it is never possible to predict with certainty that criminological findings will be accepted or interpreted in the same manner the author(s) intended when presenting them to the public.

Although it is not a fail-safe strategy, formal laws have been used in an attempt to ensure a sense of continuity and fairness in our interpretation and handling of crime. In the next chapter the role the law plays in the study of criminology is examined.

Discussion Questions

1. Where do you get your knowledge of crime? Having read this chapter, how accurate have your perceptions been?

2. Which of the four basic kinds of data do you consider superior? Explain your answer.

3. How could the media better present knowledge of crime?

4. What kinds of challenges do public perceptions of crime pose for criminologists and social policy makers?

5. Examine your perceptions about your fear of crime. Why do you feel the way you do about your risk of victimization? How does it influence your behaviour?

6. Survey a local or national newspaper for approximately two weeks and collect all crime-related stories. What kinds of stories are covered? Using the points raised in this chapter, what are the strengths and weaknesses of the crime articles?

7. Do you have a *Crime Stoppers* program in your area? If you had information that could assist police in arresting someone, would you want the reward money? Do you agree with the concept of *Crime Stoppers*?

8. How can the public and media benefit from an integrated approach to the study of the media and crime?

Key Concepts

Rationalism	empiricist	paradigm shift
Methods of knowing	mass media	moral panic
Juristat	validity	systematic error
Reliability	random error	crime funnel
Net widening	operationalization	

Weblinks

There are no specific links offered for this chapter. However, most major Canadian (and international) newpapers and magazines have their own Web sites. Southam Corporation, for example, operates a chain of newspapers across the country. By accessing one of their papers, you can usually access sister papers across the country. You might want to "bookmark" a few of these to follow major crime stories. An interesting exercise too is seeing how different parts of the country (or world) cover similar stories (e.g., Bre-X, the Latimer case, the Somalia affair, the war and killings in Kosovo, or any other current story).

Footnotes

1. Using a major drug story as an example, Potter and Kappeler (1998) report how the *San Jose Mercury News*, in 1996, despite distorting the facts, ended up garnering national and political attention. Their case study illustrated how the media and the state can sometimes work together to preserve ideologies (e.g., the war on crime) that may not have any substantive foundation.

2. Although the empirical perspective has dominated criminological thought in recent years, the debate between rationalism and empiricism has not been resolved among philosophers.

3. As noted in Chapter 1, the term *evolutive* was coined by Maurice Parmalee in 1920. He used the term to describe the evolving nature of the meaning of crime.

4. Normandeau and Leighton (1990) offer a comprehensive review on the future of policing in Canada.

5. The GDP calculation varies depending on the method used to perform the calculation.

6. Every year, *Maclean's* surveys 1500 Canadians across the country about different aspects of their behaviour, attitudes, and values. While some of the questions vary from year to year (they tend to reflect current social issues and concerns) the subject of crime remains consistent. In 1994, the greatest consensus (85 per cent) believed that violent crime has increased in the last ten years. Only 4 per cent believed crime had decreased!

7. Richard Wright (1998) reports that Travis Hirschi's *social control theory* was the most cited criminological theory. Edwin Sutherland's *differential association theory* was a distant second. In fact, the top five theories were from the discipline of sociology, reflecting the powerful influence sociology has had on criminological thought and research (see Chapter 7).

8. Children and adolescents in Newfoundland spend the most time in front of the television (23.8 hours vs. 18.9) while children and adolescents in British Columbia spend the least amount of time watching television (15.2 hours vs. 13.9) (Average hours per..., 1994).

9. Canada's own David Suzuki's CBC show, *The Nature of Things*, along with several of his books, carry a similar theme. As a scientist with a public platform, he often calls on other scientists and his viewers to treat our environment ethically and responsibly.

10. See Winterdyk, 2000 for an update on the proposed *Youth Criminal Justice Act* which calls for new actions on three complementary levels: prevention, meaningful consequences, and harsher punishment for violent repeat offenders.

CHAPTER ③

Gathering and Interpreting Crime Data

"It ain't so much the things we don't know that get us in trouble. It's the things we know that ain't so."

Artemus Ward cited in Huff, 1954

Learning Outcomes

After you have completed this chapter, you should be able to:

- Understand and appreciate the purposes of crime data.

- Identify the main methods of counting crime.

- Understand the aims of research.

- Recognize and have knowledge of the official and unofficial crime collection methods and their limitations.

- Realize the importance of an interdisciplinary, multi-methods approach when collecting crime and criminal justice information.

Crime ... "It is Everywhere"

In Chapter 2, it was observed that the public tends to believe that crime is everywhere. As early as 1975, Daniel Koenig, from the University of Victoria, reported that crime was seen to represent a serious concern among Canadians (Linden, 1996). In 1991, a poll conducted by *Maclean's* magazine found that 62 per cent of respondents said they are taking more precautions to ensure their personal safety

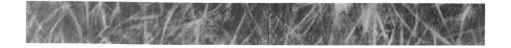

than they used to (Underwood, 1991). The poll also "revealed signs of an increasing interest in handgun ownership" (p. 30). Much of their social reality of crime, however, is based on statistics which, when covered by the media, are distorted, biased, and otherwise incomplete, or include exaggerated information about ordinary events (Winterdyk, 1996). Furthermore, if the growth of Canadian criminology programs since the mid 1970s is any kind of indicator, then academics also seem to think that crime and criminality deserve closer attention. A review of international news indicates that crime appears to be omnipresent (see Brady, 1996, and United Nations, 1995).

An additional indicator that might be used as a benchmark of the crime picture is the increase in financial expenditures to support the various elements within the criminal justice system. Griffiths and Verdun-Jones (1989:34) note that "during the twenty-year period 1961–1980, expenditures for criminal justice services in Canada rose dramatically. Total federal spending on police, courts, and corrections in 1961 was $4.38 per Canadian; in 1980, it was $16.85 per Canadian (adjusted to Implicit Price Index)" (see Box 3.1). In 1980, annual expenditures were nearly $4 billion; in 1989–90 expenditures had risen to $7.7 billion (Griffiths and Verdun-Jones, 1994). By 1995–96 the total criminal justice budget was nearly 17 billion dollars for a per capita cost of $586[1] (Easton and Brantingham, 1998).

BY THE NUMBERS BOX 3.1

WHERE DOES THE MONEY GO?
JUSTICE SPENDING IN CANADA: 1994–95

AREA:	PERCENTAGE OF TOTAL CRIMINAL JUSTICE BUDGET:
Policing	58
Adult corrections	19
Courts	8
Legal Aid	7
Youth corrections	5
Prosecution	3

Source: *CCJS:* Justice Spending in Canada, 1997, Vol. 17(3):1

While Chapter 2 focused on the *qualitative, subjective* or *ideological* interpretation of reconstructing criminological phenomena, this chapter will focus more on the *quantitative, objective,*[2] and *empirical* statistical reconstruction of crime. Four main methods of counting crime (i.e., official agencies of social control—police, courts and corrections, victimization surveys and self-report studies and observational methods) will be examined in terms of their strengths and weaknesses. We will conclude with a discussion about the importance of applying the scientific method of research when counting and using crime data. First, however, we will discuss the purpose of gathering crime data.

Before we proceed, it should be pointed out that this chapter only focuses on the primary sources of collecting crime data. It is only meant to introduce you to the primary data sources in the field. However, depending on the issue being studied, other valuable sources range from hospitals, insurance companies, banks, high school and university surveys, to archival data and academic literature. Most criminology programs offer qualitative and quantitative research methods courses in which students learn to use a variety of information sources to answer criminological issues from a rich interdisciplinary perspective.

Purpose of Crime Data

Another important sub-area of the criminological enterprise is crime statistics. Criminologists who use crime data try to generate *reliable* (i.e., consistent) and *valid* (i.e., accurate) measures of criminal behaviour, criminal trends and patterns. Crime data can also be used to conduct research on crime. Without such data, it would be difficult to construct criminological theories and answer such pressing questions as "Do the expenditures necessarily reflect an increase in crime?" and "What is the social and financial impact of crime on society and its citizens?"

Since criminologists are interested in crime control, it is important that the measurement strategies used to gather crime data are accurate reflections of what is happening in society. In fact, British criminologist Jason Ditton (1979) suggests the term criminology should be replaced with *controlology* to more accurately reflect what criminologists are concerned with. As Nettler (1987:36) notes, criminological data serve five key purposes:

1. **Description**: Being able to describe the nature and extent of crime is necessary in order to form good crime control policies. A description of crime also serves as a barometer of community well-being. As discussed in Chapter 2, the public plays a major role in reporting crime incidents to the authorities. What they choose to report provides a descriptive profile of what they consider worthy of attention. The first step toward being able to understand, explain, and ultimately predict/control crime and criminality is the ability to accurately provide descriptive information about criminal phenomena.

2. **Explanation**: Most criminologists rely on criminological theories to explain crime patterns and trends. Theories enable researchers to extract testable **hypotheses** that have empirical references (see below). Most research observations rely on quantifiable (measureable) data in order to verify their theoretical (causal) statements. Then, based on the empirical findings the researcher is able to either support, or not support, the theoretical assertions tested. In Chapters 5 through 8 we will see how various theories use strategies data to explain crime rate patterns and their situations.

3. **Program evaluation**: As noted above, it is expensive to operate the criminal justice system. Accountability has become a major issue among policy-makers and their constituents. What are we getting for our money?

An effort to control and/or prevent crime, as well as to determine which strategy should be used (i.e., deterrence, incapacitation, rehabilitation, retribution, just deserts, or restorative) requires the ability to enumerate criminal incidents. In the late 1970s, a pilot program for serious young offenders was established in Ontario. Based on the therapeutic wilderness models popularized by the Outward Bound movement and introduced to North America in the 1960s, the program was carefully monitored financially, and its success was measured against the cost of running the more traditional programs such as probation and community service programs. After two years, the wilderness program was found to be more expensive to operate than the conventional-based programs. As a result the project was shut down. What the politicians choose to overlook, however, was the cost benefit of the program. With a less than 20 per cent recidivism rate, the program was considerably more effective than the programs against which it was compared (Winterdyk and Roesch, 1982).[3] However, even data obtained objectively can be subject to different interpretations (see Chapter 2) depending on whom, and for what, the information is being used.

Program evaluation is easy to conduct but difficult to do well (Franklin and Thrasher, 1976). Today, most criminology programs have a number of courses that teach students how to engage in sound program evaluations. Nevertheless, designing an evaluation and interpretating the data obtained is often challenging. This is one reason why many criminologists suggest that research should be grounded in scientific rigour.

4. **Risk assessment**: While crime may appear to be everywhere, on closer reflection we know that this is not true. By measuring criminal activity in accordance with time, settings, location, and other social and environmental characteristics, criminologists are able to calculate the *relative risk* of being victimized or of becoming an offender. For example, relying on data from a 1973 cohort group, Wolfgang (1996) reported that Chinese youth who have a history of dropping out of school, have a father who is employed as a "worker," a family history of disharmony, and goals that are focused on the pursuit of power and money, were more likely to be delinquent. In Canada, if you are male, you are more likely to be the victim of homicide, serious assault, and robbery while women are more likely to be victims of sexual assault (Sacco and Kennedy, 1998). Risk assessment for the elderly has become an important area of study in recent years as their numbers continue to increase (Foot, 1996).

WHAT DO YOU THINK? BOX 3.2

DOES LOCKING UP OFFENDERS HELP?

Based on a survey of 37,000 provincial inmates across seven provinces in the late 1990s, a federal study revealed that about 49 per cent of prisoners would likely reoffend. The conclusion was based on a history of prior convictions, behaviour while on supervision, employment history and substance abuse (Reoffence risk high—study, 1998).

5. **Prediction**: From a humanitarian and utilitarian perspective, it would be better to prevent crimes than to react too strongly and punish individuals for their transgressions. Historically, social scientists have been intrigued with the possibility of predicting human behaviour. How will we respond to it? Many criminologists specialize in trying to predict who (i.e., serial killers, sex offenders, bank robbers, cheque forgers, computer hackers and so on) is likely to commit particular types of crimes. Others are interested in trying to articulate what the criminal justice system will be like in the twenty-first century. For example, what will the law of the future look like? Will we move toward community-policing? What will our criminal courts look like? What theories will dominate the future?

To be prediction-oriented is to be future-oriented, *proactive*, and prevention-oriented while the punishment model and a crime control model are past-oriented and *reactive* to crime. Most of the research conducted by the Brantinghams on environmental criminology is prevention-oriented. They have found, for example, that altering certain environmental factors (e.g., street lighting, storefront visibility, street location of businesses, etc.) has a direct impact on crime. Criminals are not interested in being seen since it increases their risk of being caught. Just as medical and alternative practitioners use the tools of their trade to diagnose potential future risk of heart disease, tooth decay, premature bone deterioration or aging, so criminologists can apply an interdisciplinary approach to predicting potential dangerous offenders. A former graduate student of the Brantinghams, Kim Rossmo (now a Detective Inspector with the Vancouver City Police) has developed a new computer mapping technique referred to as "geographic profiling" in which he is able to predict the homes or workplaces of various types of offenders based on crime site information. This computer technique relies on innovative research on the spatial behaviour of criminals, for which there is a growing body of literature (Grescoe, 1996). Unlike the more conventional approaches to studying the "why" of crime, Rossmo and the Brantinghams are interested in the "where" (see Box 3.3).

Geographic Profiling: Pinpointing Crime

In a relatively short period of time, geographic profiling has become a "hot" new tool in the fight against crime. In 1998, there were at least three major police forces across Canada using this new computer technology to effectively target criminals who commit a series of crimes. They include the Vancouver City Police, RCMP, and the Ontario Provincial Police (OPP).

In early 1998, the OPP announced that they would be using the Canadian-made *Rigel* computer program that can be used to track down serial killers, repeat rapists, bombers, bank robbers, and arsonists, among other repeat offenders. As a test, the *Rigel* system was able to locate a four-block area where serial killer Clifford Olson had lived. Their system was also able to identify the St. Catherines area where Paul Bernardo and his wife Karla Homolka lived when they killed two teens in the 1990s. It also worked in the case of the Abbotsford killer in the mid 1990s. *Rigel* was developed by Kim Rossmo and police forces from around the world have been lining up wanting to buy the system.

You can visit the OPP Internet site at **www.gov.on.ca/opp/**. For a more formal, yet comprehensive overview of geographic profiling visit **www.ecriccanada.com/geoprof.htm**. It is a rich source of current information on geographic profiling in Canada.

The *Rigel* model is based on the premise that we are creatures of habit. Just as we go through our daily rituals when we rise in the morning, geographic profiling involves collecting as much data as possible about the crime and comparing it to behaviour patterns of persons caught committing such criminal acts. The more data available on a particular type of crime the greater the likelihood of being able to predict the type of person who commits the crime and where he might live. For example, do you usually take the same route to and from school every day? Do you usually shop at the same store for your groceries? If you have not already noticed, watch how your fellow classmates come and go to class. Also note their mannerisms. See if you can differentiate your classmates' movements based on specific characteristics.

Although it sounds promising, criminology is still a young discipline and in many cases limited in its approach. Developing reliable and valid prediction models is as much an art as a science. Monahan (1981) was among the first to point out the risks in making predictions, especially in the social sciences. One of the most serious risks in trying to predict human behaviour is the per cent of *false positives* (i.e., "misses" or inaccurate predictions). Based on his review of psychiatric predictions, Monahan concluded that their predictions of dangerous behaviour were wrong two out of three times. Canadian researchers Hucker, Webster, and Ben-Aron (1981) compiled a collection of ten articles on recent legislative approaches to mental illness issues surrounding the prediction, management, and treatment of dangerous and mentally ill patients. The article illustrates that we need to re-examine our theories, practices, and assumptions about prediction issues.

A number of years ago, while attending a regional criminology conference, a researcher from Saskatchewan claimed he could predict, with nearly 90 per cent accuracy, the likelihood that a young person would become a young offender. Aside from some methodological concerns, questions were raised as to the ethical and moral implications of testing young people for their propensity to act badly. Furthermore, how many non-delinquent youth would be erroneously predicted to have the "bad seed"? Even if one could predict with reasonable accuracy which interventions would work best, how long would a person need to remain under such a treatment modality? The list of concerns regarding infringements on young people's lives seemed to far outnumber any possible benefits. The line between interference as treatment versus punishment for the greater good of society is a highly subjective issue for which there are no clear answers, but it is one that a criminologist must struggle with.

To further illustrate the importance of the concept of false positives, imagine if you had been asked to lock a person up for life for a crime he or she had legally been found guilty of (based primarily on the testimony of eyewitnesses) but for which the accused maintained his or her innocence. What would your decision be? What would you base it on? Research on eyewitnesses has found eyewitness testimony to be far less reliable than we have intuitively believed (Loftus, 1979). For example, in Canada there have been several notorious cases in which innocent people have been wrongfully found guilty, largely on the evidence of an eyewitness. Perhaps the most famous of such cases involved Donald Marshall, in Nova Scotia, who spent eleven years in prison before new evidence finally cleared him, eventually awarding him $898,000 for his wrongful conviction.

You say you need hard scientific data such as DNA evidence? With the recent use of DNA evidence, a number of Canadians have been found innocent of crimes for which they had been convicted. One highly publicized case involved Guy Paul Morin, who was exonerated in 1995 when DNA evidence showed he was not the killer of a nine-year-old girl. At the time, he received $1,000,000 for his suffering. How many other innocent people have been falsely punished? As our means of crime detection and prediction improve, we will, perhaps, be better able to prevent these mistakes.

Finally, the American sociologist Edwin Schur (1973) spoke about the option of not punishing young offenders, because over 90 per cent of them grow out of their delinquent behaviours. A variety of studies have since found that only about

6 per cent of young offenders become chronic offenders. Are we creating a criminal justice system to combat crime or to perpetuate a system that is designed to support and justify its existence? Prediction appears to be little more than "chance" or as Ennis and Litwick (1974) wrote, prediction in the criminal justice system is about as accurate as "flipping a coin."

In this section, we have seen that although the purposes of gathering crime data are diverse, they are essential to the reliability and validity of the study of criminal phenomena. However, we have also seen that some of the purposes have their ethical, practical, and theoretical limitations, so any crime data, and observations drawn from such data, should be viewed with caution as there will always be some unpredictable influences.

Let us now look at the sources of crime data. We will begin with the official crime data sources and then examine a number of key unofficial sources.

The Looking Glasses of Crime

Before we begin, it might be helpful to identify three important terms of reference that will be used throughout this section. *Actual crime* refers to all crimes that occur but are not necessarily detected, reported, or processed by official criminal justice agencies. *Official crime* refers to those criminal events that have been detected, reported, and recorded in some official fashion (e.g., police data and self-report data). Finally, the *dark figure* of crime refers to those criminal events that go undetected and/or unreported by official criminal justice agencies.

Official Sources of Crime Data

"There are three kinds of lies: lies, damned lies, and statistics" Benjamin Disraeli (1804–1881).

The above quote reflects the attitude many people have about official crime statistics. As Darrell Huff (1954:8) cautions "the secret language of statistics, so appealing in a fact-minded culture, is employed to sensationalize, inflate, confuse, and oversimplify." But "love or hate" them, statistics are an essential source of information for social scientists and policy makers.

While official data are the most readily available and most widely used, they have also been subjected to the greatest criticism. Rather than condemn this source we will review the three most commonly used official sources of crime.

By far the most common measures of crime are official statistics. These types of data are primarily collected by the various elements of the criminal justice system—the police, courts, and corrections. Other public control agencies such as mental health and social service agencies that deal with alcohol and drug abuse, crisis centres, as well as academics have come to rely on official data to conduct research and make informed policy decisions.

Police Data

Historically, it was not police data that was the first type of official data to be collected, but correctional-based data. However, today police reports are the most frequently used form of official crime data (see Box 3.4). This makes sense if we realize that the police are usually the first point of official contact for reported and detected crime.

In Canada, police crime data are based on criminal events that are known to the police. Therefore, unless a crime is reported or detected, it will go unreported or in some cases unrecorded, even if reported (see "Factors affecting crime data" below). For criminologists, this unknown, but assumed, quantity of criminal activity is called the **dark figure** of crime. The term was first coined by the British criminologists Richard Hood and Richard Sparks in 1970. The concept of a dark figure of crime has, for some criminologists, become a major area of study in itself. Why do crimes go unreported and undetected? What can be done to improve the detection and reporting of crime? In 1978, University of Ottawa criminologists Waller and Okitiro reported that the dark figure of crime in Canada might have been much greater than was believed. Since then, through public education, changes in demographic characteristics, and increased media attention, reporting rates have gone up.

The collection of police data began in 1920 when the Dominion Bureau of Statistics voluntarily tabulated the crimes known to police forces servicing communities with populations of 4,000 or more. As crime rates increased, there was a desire to standardize police data and include more detailed information. In 1962 the **Uniform Crime Reports (UCR)** system was introduced (see Box 3.5). The collection model was borrowed from one already being used in the United States. The results were collated and published by Statistics Canada in the annual **Crime and Traffic Enforcement Statistics** and can be found today in Statistics Canada *Juristat* publications. Today police-reported crime statistics are published in a variety of issues under catalogue number 85–002.

The UCR is a standardized survey used by all police departments across the country that collects and collates crime data and makes them available to interested users, government departments, scholars, media sources, special interest groups, and (criminology) students.

CRIME RATE DROPS—WE'RE JUST TOO OLD!

- Looking through crime data to filter demonstrable, plausible, and irrefutable facts requires some creativity. And sometimes the line between coincidence and fact is little more than a difference in opinion. While some experts were scratching their heads over a decrease in official crime rates between 1991 and 1994, sociologist Rick Linden, from the University of Manitoba, suggested that "we're getting too old to be criminals." Drawing on official crime data as well as demographic data, he noted that most crimes are committed by people between the ages of 15 and 29. The baby boomers are now between the ages of 30 and 50. Linden further observed that similar trends (i.e., replication) have been observed in many American cities ("Crime rate..." Oct. 23, 1995).
- David Foot (1996:141) also notes that "demographics explains the different growth rates in types of crime over the past three decades." He cautions that the lull in crimes rates will be short-lived, and that they will rise "in the last half of the 1990s" (Ibid, 143).

For a number of years the UCR data seemed to satisfy our fascination with the question of who was committing crimes, what was happening to offenders, and just how much crime there was. Scholars, criminology students, politicians, government departments, the media, and even the curious public relied on these sources as a barometer of efficiency, effectiveness, and enumeration of criminal justice and crime related matters.

Since 1982, the Canadian Centre for Justice Statistics (see below), a division of Statistics Canada, has been responsible for gathering information from 140 police agencies in six provinces.[4] Together, it accounts for approximately 46 per cent of the national volume of *Criminal Code* violations and makes up the data for the Uniform Crime Reports (Hendrick, 1996).

UNIFORM CRIME REPORTS (UCR)

The UCR surveys involve two sets of data. The original survey included the "aggregate" (i.e., total) counts of crime provided by police departments on a monthly basis. Since these counts were prone to a number of interpretative problems (see below), in 1988 a "revised" UCR survey was introduced as a measure to correct many of the data deficiencies in the original survey. For example, aggregate counts did not distinguish between crimes completed versus crimes attempted. In addition, the original surveys required that only the most serious act be counted if a crime included several offences. This process resulted in a natural attrition of actual offences known to the police.

The new UCR has shifted from relying on aggregate counts to an "incident-based" reporting system. Now, rather than providing summaries of criminal events, data are collected on the criminal event, the offender, and the victim on an incident-by-incident basis. Consequently, the UCR data contain more and richer information than in the past. Look up some crime statistics from the 1960s and/or 1970s. Select a crime, such as homicide, robbery, or motor-vehicle theft. Compare the nature of the statistics with a current *Juristat* report on the same crime.

Police crime statistics are divided into two categories, based on the classification of crimes in the *Criminal Code*: **summary** offences that involve a maximum penalty of six months in jail and/or a fine not exceeding $2,000, and **indictable** offences that involve a maximum penalty of life imprisonment but no maximum fine. However, the *Juristat* publications reproduce the data into a variety of publications (see Box 3.6 on page 81). Table 3–1 shows the breakdown of adult and youth court offences for the year 1995–96.[5]

Table 3–1 reveals that, proportionately, youth commit far more property offences than adults and that conviction rates are fairly high.

TABLE 3–1

MOST SERIOUS OFFENCES, ADULT AND YOUTH COURT: 1995–1996

TYPE OF CRIME	PERCENTAGE OF TOTAL OFFENCES	CONVICTION RATE	
	ADULT/YOUTH	ADULT/YOUTH[*]	
Violent	20/21	49	N/A
Property	26/48	65	
Other *Criminal Code*	25/17	56	
Traffic	17/10	78	
Drug related	6/4	71	
Other Federal Status	6/0.2	78	

Total number of adult cases: 435,569

Total number of youth cases: 111,027

Source: *CCJS:* The Justice Data Factfinder, 1997, (Vol. 17(13).

---

* Although there are no data on conviction rates for young offenders, data exist showing that about one-half of violent crimes involved minor assaults (49 per cent), and that aggravated assaults with a weapon accounted for 17 per cent of all violent crimes in 1995–96 (Youth court statistics 1995–96 highlights, 1997).

Judicial Statistics

Historically, court records were the first type of official crime statistics to be collected. The French began collecting such data, known as *Compte General* in 1825. Information was gathered on the number of charges and convictions that appeared before the courts (Brantingham, Mu, and Verma, 1995). In addition, the French collected information about the offender's gender, income, education and occupation. Durkheim (1897) used this data source in his classic work on suicide.

Not long after the introduction of judicial statistics, researchers began to use the data to describe crime trends and patterns. Brantingham and Brantingham (1984) note that Guerry and Quetelet, from Belgium and France respectively, were among the first to use such data to examine the spatial and temporal distribution of crime, i.e., where and when crime happens. Having information available on age, education, gender, income, and occupation enabled them to conduct studies on suicides and to determine the distribution of the seventeen most common crimes by age and gender, as well as by geographic distribution (see Elmer, 1982).

The English started collecting court information around 1805, but it wasn't until 1857 that they developed the system in use today. Canada started to collect judicial statistics in 1876. Until the late 1960s, judicial statistics represented the primary source of national crime statistics. This process continued until 1973 when, due to federal and provincial disputes over jurisdiction and cost, it was stopped (Winterdyk, 1996).

National judicial data were not collected again until the *CCJS* attempted to resurrect the process. In 1991, two publications, with limited data, were published. By 1997, there were approximately a dozen publications. On the other hand, the Centre regularly publishes data on youth court statistics through the *Juristat Bulletin*.[6] Statistics Canada cautions against comparing the cost of court services, suggesting it is a risky practice (see Locke, 1993). Notwithstanding the general caution, court costs increased from $0.6 billion in 1988–89 to $0.98 billion by 1995–96. Expenditures on Legal Aid were the fastest-growing component of the justice system: up from $0.3 billion in 1988–89 to $0.64 billion in 1995–96—the largest growth for any segment of the criminal justice system (Easton and Brantingham, 1998). Even if the numbers are somewhat suspect, the trend does not bode well for criminal justice administrators. It would also be helpful to know to what extent any variations in the data can be explained by knowing other factors, e.g., political (who is in power), racial/class-based (what is the proportion of Native and/or marginal groups), or demographic (the proportion of youth). For example, Hackler (1994) offers a comparable argument using the number of Native peoples as a possible means of explaining the higher court costs in the western provinces.

Table 3–2 shows that in 1995–96 the majority (50 per cent) of all adult provincial offenders received prison sentences of less than one month. (It is worth noting that the data only represent about 30 per cent of nationwide coverage). Are we too "soft" on adult offenders?

TABLE 3–2

SENTENCE LENGTHS FOR ADULT OFFENDERS: 1995–96

SENTENCE LENGTH	PER CENT OF ADULTS SENTENCED
1–6 months	50
6–12 months	38
1–2 years	3
2+ years	3

Source: *CCJS:* The Justice Data Factfinder, 1997, (Vol. 17(13):6). See Vol. 18(7) for additional details.

Correctional Statistics

Although English prison statistics date back to 1836, the data appeared only in appendices to special reports. It was not until 1856 that correction statistics became part of a regular composite of criminal statistics. The types of information included in these records included age, gender, education, number of prior convictions, occupation and birthplace. These procedures remained in place until 1963 when the data were published separately as *Prison Statistics* (Brantingham and Brantingham, 1984). With the establishment of the *CCJS* in the 1980s (see below), statistics on adult correction services have been published annually in the *Juristat Bulletin.* The bulletins provide information on the number of persons being held in federal and provincial custody facilities, as well as data on the number of those charged awaiting trial and the number placed under supervision (e.g., community facilities, parole, and probation). Limited data are provided on demographic information of offenders (e.g., age, gender, and ethnic background). Data on federal and provincial expenditures are also published.

In 1993–94, adult corrections cost each Canadian $65 per year while provincial per capita costs were slightly higher than those for federal institutions ($34 vs. $31 per capita per year) (Trends ..., 1994). Total federal expenditures in 1996–97 reached $970 million—up 13 per cent over 1992–93 (7 per cent after adjusting for inflation).

For 1995–96, the Canadian incarceration rate was 151 per 100,000, which is significantly lower than that of the United States (600) and Russia (694) but significantly higher than the rate in most European countries (Corrections in Canada, 1997).[7] On any given day in 1996–97, there were 152,000 adults in Canadian prisons. The cost of incarcerating offenders is not cheap. In 1995–96 it cost an average of $50,375, per year, to incarcerate an offender in a federal institution, as compared to $9,000 to supervise an inmate on parole (Ibid). Even so, we continue to rely heavily on incarceration as a means of protecting society.

While public protection is the most important mandate of Corrections it is not the most effective means. As the Solicitor General of Canada has noted "building more prison cells to lock up more people for longer periods is not an effective response or a greater guarantee for safer communities" (Solicitor General of Canada, 1998). In an effort to address this dilemma, an international symposium entitled "Beyond prison," was held in Kingston in March of 1998. Examining statistics on incarceration enables criminologists and criminal justice agencies to better respond to related issues.

In addition to Statistics Canada reports, every year Correctional Service of Canada publishes a handy little booklet that is filled with lots of interesting facts on federal inmate populations (see Table 3–3). A review of the annual publication will show that our incarceration rates are increasing and that we are moving toward a more punitive and more expensive correctional system. Other statistical information on the adult correctional system can also be found under government catalogue number 85–211. Both official data sources reveal a great deal about the correctional system and raise serious questions about what can be done to address the increasing costs of the current retributive approach to corrections.

TABLE 3–3

INMATE PROFILE: MARCH 1994 AND MARCH 1997

PROFILE:	MALE OFFENDERS PER CENT	FEMALE OFFENDERS PER CENT
Age 20–34 yrs	53.6/46.7	51.7/51.5
Single	56.6/57.2	57.3/56.3
Common law	29.0/29.7	18.0/19.3
Married	12.3/11.8	13.3/10.6
Serving 1st penitentiary term	49.6/53.7	74.3/74.2
Serving less than six years	53.4/49.4	61.9/58.0
Serving sentences for:		
• Murder	13.7/15.5	15.5/19.9
• Schedule I offence	62.0/62.4	47.4/45.7
• Schedule II offence	7.1/8.8	21.1/23.5
• Non-schedule offence	17.1/13.2	16.1/10.9

Source: *Corrections in Canada* 1994 edition and 1997 edition. The Communications Branch, CSC.

What Do Official Data Measure?

The esteemed British criminologist, Leslie Wilkins, once noted that official crime data are not, strictly speaking, statistics of criminal events per se. Rather, they reflect police, court, and correctional responses to social behaviour with respect to a particular set of offence categories as defined by the *Criminal Code*. Along this line of reasoning, *symbolic interactionism* (a term coined by Herbert Blumer in 1937) can be used to clarify Wilkins' observation. Blumer (1969:2) identified three premises of the perspective:

1. "Human beings act toward things on the basis of the meanings that the things have for them.
2. "The meaning of such things is derived from, or arises out of, the social interaction that one has with one's fellows.
3. "These meanings are handled in, and modified through, an interpretative process used by the person in dealing with the things he encounters."

Given Blumer's points, it can be said that official statistics are collected and used to meet the source's particular needs since they are inclined to collect only data that has meaning to them and which they can use for their own needs.[8] In fact, all organizations have roles and interests that serve to create particular "mind-sets" as to what is important. At the other extreme of the spectrum, *radical criminologists* see official sources of crime data as nothing more than a measure of political success in that the data "mystify and cloud the fact that the major 'crimes' against society are committed by the state" (American Friends Service Committee, 1971:10–11).

The impetus for such views, stems, in part, from the fact that the volume of recorded criminality is smaller than that of actual criminality. In an earlier edition of his book *The Disreputable Pleasures*, Canadian sociologist/criminologist John Hagan (1977) discussed the concept of a *crime funnel* (see Table 3–4). As discussed in Chapter 2, the extent to which the funnelling effect takes place is subject to considerable debate. At one end of the debate, researchers such as Chambliss (1988), adopting a *conflict/radical* perspective, argue that official statistics are highly unreliable because of competing social factors and political interests. Evans and Himelfarb (1992), on the other hand, are less pessimistic. They conclude their review of URC data by stating, "we can probably learn something about crime from these data, but we are not sure how much" (p. 78). Several years earlier, Nettler (1987:49) had already made a similar observation when he concluded that when the various modes of counting yield similar results, confidence in public records increases. However, "judgement is required" when using or interpreting such data.

TABLE 3-4

THE CRIME FUNNEL—CRIME NET

- Total incidents reported to police in 1996   =   2,832,800 (100 per cent)
- Offences recorded as actual (determined to have occurred)   =   96 per cent
- Offences cleared   =   34 per cent
- Offences cleared by charge   =   22 per cent
- Convictions   =   15 per cent
- Sentence of custody   =   4 per cent

Source: *CCJS:* The Justice Data Factfinder, 1997, (Vol. 17(13):1).

"The government are very keen on amassing statistics. They collect them, raise them to the nth power, take the cube root and prepare wonderful diagrams. But you must never forget that every one of these figures comes in the first instance from the village watchman, who just puts down what he damn pleases." Sir Josiah Stamp ((1880–1941) cited in Nettler, 1987:39).

Based on the data presented in Table 3–5 we might deduce that Prince Edward Island has a serious crime problem. We might further be left with the impression that Manitoba is the most lenient of the provinces—perhaps more community-oriented than the rest of Canada. If we believe that a society that strives to maintain harmony and abhors social disorder will have a lower crime rate, the west should have a lower crime rate than the east, right? Well, such is not the case (see, for example, Hackler (1994) and/or Easton and Brantingham, 1998). Referring to Table 3.5, the report indicates that jurisdiction variation may be offence-dependent. In Prince Edward Island, drinking accounts for 75 per cent of all admissions as compared with the national average of 16 per cent! (Sentence admission ..., 1998).

TABLE 3-5

SENTENCE ADMISSIONS FOR 1996–97 IN ADULT AND PROVINCIAL/TERRITORIAL CUSTODY

PROVINCE	RATE PER 10,000
Newfoundland	1,946
Prince Edward Island	4,446
Nova Scotia	1,273
New Brunswick	2,384
Quebec	2,517
Ontario	2,060
Manitoba	819

Saskatchewan	1,569
Alberta	2,832
British Columbia	1,513
Yukon	2,670
North West Territories	N/A
PROVINCIAL	2,057
FEDERAL	87

Source: *CCJS:* Adult Correctional Services in Canada, 1998. (Vol 18(3):p.6).

Finally, depending on its purpose, official data can serve as useful indicators. It is all a matter of how and for what purpose the data are being used. Furthermore, since crime data do not explain themselves, it is helpful to use an interdisciplinary and theoretical approach to using and interpreting official counts of crime. And while theories are also not immune to shortcomings, by employing a structured approach that has observable and measurable concepts and constructs that can be tested, they represent reasonably objective means to study crime and its control. We should guard against the careless use of statistics when they are influenced by factors that are not well-understood.

One thing is certain: Currently there is no sure way of assessing the gap between official and unofficial crime data. As Sellin (1951) noted nearly 40 years ago, what is the "real" value in knowing the exact numbers of crime? More recently, Jeffery (1990) offered a scathing, yet insightful, assessment of how we measure crime. He suggests that "if we had a radar system or an emergency medical system that operated at the level found in the criminal justice system, we would not be alive for very long" (p. 125). Part of the dilemma lies in the relative, and changing, meaning of crime and the fact that our criminal justice system is reactive in its handling of crime. Therefore, while measuring crime may be of some value in developing theories of crime and criminal law, they serve us less well in developing theories of human behaviour. However, since laws are constantly changing, along with social points of view, such theories will always be limited in their ability to explain and predict. After reviewing the points raised in the next section, you will better appreciate the difficulty of relying only on official data to formulate theories of human behaviour.

Factors Affecting Crime Data

Official crime counts are subject to artificial fluctuations. The fluctuation, or distortion, of actual crime can be attributed to a variety of factors that influence the collecting and processing of crime data. Fattah (1997) offers several important factors. They include most of the following:

1. According to research by Conklin (1975), among others, media coverage of crime can influence crime counts. Focusing on certain crimes or crises draws

public attention and affects the reporting rates. As noted in Chapter 2, the media can serve as a barometer of public interest.

2. The dark figure of crime may be subject to fluctuation over time and even within settings. Fattah (1997), among others, notes that fluctuations in the dark figure can be attributed to variables pertaining to police enforcement practices, victims' willingness to report their victimization, and the public's attitude towards the criminal justice system.

3. Changes in recording procedures affect crime data collected by the various law enforcement forces throughout Canada (e.g., RCMP, OPP, QPP, municipal forces, Canadian National Railways, Canadian Pacific, and National Harbours Board Police) which are reported to Statistics Canada. Judicial statistics are the responsibility of the provincial and federal courts across the country. From time to time certain police forces or courts may not be able to provide complete information to Statistics Canada. For example, a review of annual statistics at different times shows that certain jurisdictions did not provide crime data for Statistics Canada. While Statistics Canada notes these differences in their reports they are seldom discussed by the media, or, in some cases, in academic accounts of crime. Some of the reasons for non- or over-reporting may be due to:

a) Changes in the number of police forces/officers.

b) Changes in police/court administration. Mandates for policies at the municipal, provincial, or federal level may change (e.g., shift from a crime control model to a community-based prevention model).

c) Changes in the legal definition of crime. On the recommendations of the Wolfenden Report in the 1970s, attempted suicide and consensual homosexuality were no longer subject to criminal prosecution. These changes reflected the government's disinclination to interfere with moral issues. In 1985, several major crimes were redefined or amended: rape (C.C. sections 270–273) (renamed sexual assault and redefined), hate crime (C.C. sections 318–320), and prostitution (C.C. section 213). And since its inception in 1984, various sections of the YOA have been amended. These changes reflect the evolving attitudes in public opinion towards accountability and clearer defininitions of certain crimes.

d) Changes in the population base. Both the media and the police are notorious for using absolute numbers of crime when trying to create an impact. However, these crime figures are meaningless unless they are linked to population size, political and social changes, or some combination of the those factors. Ideally, only crime rates should be used when drawing comparisons. In the mid-1990s, when our local police were trying to earn public sympathy so they could obtain more resources, they used absolute numbers of crime counts to create an image that crime had increased considerably in recent years. In fact, however, the crime rates showed no such increase; they simply coincided with the city's population growth.[8]

Using base rates to convert crime counts to rates that are expressed as the number of crime cases, charges, or complaints per unit volume of the population has become the norm. In Canada, as in many other western countries, crime reports use units of 100,000 for all crime statistics. For certain crime categories, for which the population base is smaller, crime reporting units of 1,000 and 10,000 may be used. To calculate the crime rate, the following formula is used:

$$\text{Rate per } 100{,}000 = \frac{\text{\# of reported crimes}}{\text{Total population}} \times 100{,}000$$

Yet in spite of using a common denominator to equalize the counting process, the base rates are prone to several technical problems. First, in Canada a major census is undertaken only once every ten years, with a smaller census at the midpoint between each major census. Over that ten year span, fertility, emigration, and immigration rates can fluctuate significantly (see McKie, 1994), enough to distort the actual crime rates. Even using the midpoint to adjust the base rate is not fail-safe, because the counts are not as comprehensive as those at the ten-year mark.

Other strategies have been suggested as a means of calculating base rates: using counts of the population at risk rather than of the total population (Boggs, 1966); calculating break-and-enter rates in terms of the number of dwellings; basing motor-vehicle thefts on the number of vehicles; and basing sexual assaults on the population of females. However, since circumstances surrounding victims of crime are not consistent, these strategies also have their limitations.

The final technical problem Brantingham and Brantingham (1984:55) identify "involves a change in the *format* used to collect police data." As noted above, redefining certain crimes can cause significant problems for researchers wishing to compare crime data from year to year. The most obvious of these changes occurred in 1962 when Canadian police statistics were completely reorganized. Again in 1980, with the establishment of the Canadian Centre for Justice Statistics, a number of changes were made, and collection and recording practices continue to evolve (Ross, 1993).

e) Changes in public attitudes toward crime and the police. The **Canadian Urban Victimization Survey** (CUVS) found that only 42 per cent of all recorded crimes are reported by the victim or another member of the public. Depending on the type of offence, only around thirty per cent of recorded crimes are the result of police observation or intervention. Therefore, public reporting patterns can have a dramatic impact on crime counts.

As crime rates rose throughout this century, it became increasingly important to establish a comprehensive system that would coordinate criminal justice data and address community justice needs. The Canadian Centre for Justice Statistics was the national response.

Canadian Centre for Justice Statistics[9]

"... no formal system has the ability to count crime with one hundred per cent accuracy" Winterdyk (1996:16).

When the Uniform Crime Report (UCR) was introduced in 1962, official crime counts were considered to be more uniform and reliable than previous methods used for recording crime data. However, as crime rates increased (from 2,771.2 in 1962 to 9,233 incidents in 1988), and then dropped (to 8,758 per 100,000 in 1996) and public awareness grew via newsprint, radio, and television, the public appetite for the *facts* of crime also grew. Along with the introduction of self-report and victimization survey results (see below), during the late 1960s and early 1970s, it became evident that official data were limited in a more serious way. The concept of the dark figure of crime began to draw increasing attention.

Between 1974 and 1981, several task forces and advisory boards attempted to reorganize the national data collection methods in an effort to meet both federal and provincial needs. This seven-year process culminated with the opening of the Canadian Centre for Justice Statistics (*CCJS*) as a satellite of Statistics Canada, in 1981. For the next six years, the Centre continued to be plagued by operational and directional difficulties. A 1984 evaluation gave it a modest passing grade. Nevertheless, it was decided to extend its funding for another three years.

In spite of its difficulties, the Centre has grown. In 1981, it produced only two reports; in 1992, twenty-five. The Centre released 17 publications in 1994, 13 in 1997 and 14 in 1998. Today, the benchmarks of the Centre for crime and criminal justice data gathering and publication are the ***Juristat Bulletins***. These special topical publications not only inform administrators within the criminal justice system about issues they are interested in, but also fulfill one of their mandates, which is to satisfy the "public's right to know." In addition, the Centre also undertakes specific studies in such areas as corrections, impaired driving, and legal aid (see Box 3.6). However, as several researchers have noted, the Centre continues to experience difficulties trying to meet the needs of different sources. Some key limitations include:

- no national information on court decisions.
- inconsistencies in the way provinces report, as well as count, their crime incidents.
- data on crime incidents, arrests, charges, convictions and dispositions lacking depth.
- reports providing little insight into crime and criminal behaviour.
- no reports on white collar crime, organized crime, victimless crime, or other types of non-conventional crimes.

In fairness, however, the Centre tries to provide information that is of value for policy makers, criminal justice administrators and planners, academic researchers, the media, as well as the public. And since its inception, the Centre has had a major impact on the study of crime and criminal justice in Canada.

Criminology students in completing course projects will most likely use these publications. Academics have already begun to make use of these services and the *CCJS* has assisted scholars by providing relevant data.[10]

FYI BOX 3.6

Your Best "Official" Source of Canadian Justice Information

Today, the Centre responds to information needs on:

- Adult Corrections Service
- Impaired driving
- Violent and property crime

- Drug violations
- Justice spending
- Victimization
- Justice Data factfinder

- Family violence
- Legal Aid
- Young Offenders
- Justice spending

- Firearms
- Police administration
- Homicide

Publications can be found in most college and university libraries obtained via fax (613) 951-6615 or by calling the toll free number 1-800-267-6677.

In **summary**, the official data gathering techniques in Canada have evolved over the years. Today primary sources for criminological-type data can be obtained through the *CCJS*. The quality and variety of data have improved considerably since the formation of the service in 1981. In the future it will remain the primary source for such data, and with rapid technological changes, such as sophisticated Internet search engines, the services provided by the *CCJS* will likely improve. However, it is important to remember that criminological data are only as good as their applications to scientific theory that is interdisciplinary in nature. The *CCJS* does not (yet) provide such rich information. Therefore, students and scholars are encouraged to familiarize themselves with other theoretically significant sources. Among the more conventional unofficial sources that criminologists have come to rely upon are **victimization surveys**, **self-report data** and **observation data**.

Unofficial Sources of Crime Data

As was described in Chapter 1, crime involves both an offender and a recipient of the offence. Given this observation, we could deduce that other natural sources of crime data can be obtained from the offender. One such source is formally referred to as self-report data, from the recipient of the offence, while the other is formally referred to as victimization data. As Chambliss (1988) and Elias (1993), among others, point out, without such data the crime picture would be incomplete.

Victimization Data[11]

The study of victimology is an immensely interesting area of investigation within criminology. In Canada, unlike many European countries, the study of victimology is still in its infancy (see Chapter 4). Until the pioneering efforts of Ezzat Fattah in Canada and Hans von Hentig and Stephen Schafer in the United States, the area of crime victims was not considered an important topic for criminological study. This may be because victimology has historically not been viewed as an area of study that belongs to criminology. Up until the 1980s most North American textbooks overlooked the impact of the victim on crime causation. Even as recently as 1997, courses on victimology were only available in the larger criminology programs/schools in Canada. No Canadian university offers any extensive concentration on the study of victimology. This, in spite of the fact that even as early as 1947 Edwin Sutherland pointed out the public is always the victim of a crime. More recently, Sacco and Kennedy (1998) identified three elements that are essential to describing a criminal event. Their elements complement Sutherland's observation. The first element is the *precursor* of the event that refers to the "situational factors that bring people together in time and space." The second element pertains to how "*interactions among participants* define the outcomes of their actions" (e.g., victim-offender relationship), and the third element is the *aftermath* of the event. This approach not only offers a convenient mode for studying crime but also illustrates that there is a relationship between the victim and the offender.

Objectives of Victimization Surveys

While the early victimization surveys (VS) were designed to provide more complete measures of the rate of occurrence for selected crimes, today the purpose and objectives have expanded. Writing in the *Canadian Journal of Criminology*, John Evans and Paul Legar (1979) identified four major objectives:

1. Measure the extent and distribution of selected crimes. The intent is to produce more complete information on the extent and distribution of selected crimes than is available from official data.

2. Measure the impact of selected crimes by assessing injury and cost to victims (i.e., emotional, financial, and physical). This can be highly useful data otherwise not available through official sources.

3. Assess risk of criminal victimization. By using VS data it is possible to compare victims with non-victims as well as to provide information on the perceived risk and the social and physical context of such experiences.

4. Provide indicators of criminal justice functioning. Such feedback can provide useful information about the functioning of different aspects of the criminal justice system from both the victim's and perpetrator's perspective.

Victimization Surveys in Canada and Elsewhere

In spite of its limited role in Canadian criminology, the use of victimization surveys is more solidly established in Canada than elsewhere. The roots of victimization surveys in North America can be traced back to the efforts of the now defunct LEAA (Law Enforcement Assistance Administration) which, in addition to playing a major role in the forging of American criminology, funded the first national victimization survey conducted by Biderman, Johnson, McIntyre, and Weir in 1967 (DeKeseredy and Schwartz, 1996).

As with official data-collecting methods, the LEAA underwent several bureaucratic reorganizations until 1980, when the National Criminal Justice Information and Statistic Service, formed in response to the national crime problem, became known as the Bureau of Justice Statistics. In 1980 the United States hosted the First World Congress of Victimology in Washington, D.C.

Beginning in 1973 and every year since, The National Crime Survey (NCS) in the United States has conducted annual victimization surveys that involve more than 100,000 people who, as part of the methodology, are interviewed several times a year. In their twentieth annual report, the NCS included over 120 numerical tables describing criminal victimization (see Greenfeld, 1994). General areas of coverage included: costs of crime to victims, the nature and extent of criminal behaviour, establishing probabilities of victimization risks, and studying victim precipitation of crime and culpability.

To undertake such surveys is both time-consuming and very costly. Furthermore, acquiring stable estimates of less common crimes would require even larger samples that would add to the high cost and methodologically-intensive process. Other methodological concerns relate to more specific issues such as differently-worded questions, the sensitivity of wording used, different techniques used to collect data, and people's ability to remember past events accurately. Fortunately, in recent years there have been many articles written on this subject, including how to improve the reliability and validity of the surveys.

Even though some critics question the cost benefit of these surveys, their popularity is growing and we are seeing a number of international surveys in the literature. For example, the International Crime Survey, in which Canada was a participant, involved seventeen countries and employed computer-assisted telephone interviews (Van Dijk, Mayhew, and Killias, 1990).

Overall, victimization rates were higher in the United States, Canada, and Australia than in Europe. However, over a five-year period the Netherlands had the highest victimization rate (60.4 per cent) followed by the United States (57.6 per cent), while Canada ranked fourth (53 per cent). It is possible that the Dutch statistic could be mostly accounted for by the number of bicycle thefts that occur in that country. Focusing on common conventional crimes, Canada ranked highest in only one category, "risk of damage to car." Nearly 9.8 per cent of those surveyed had experienced some deliberate damage done to their cars in the past year. And while Canada and the United States had higher overall victimization rates than their European counterparts, fear of street crime was highest in Germany and Great Britain. Other interesting findings included: the international average for gun ownership: 6 per cent (3.7 per cent in Canada and 29 per cent in the United States); 28 per cent of those surveyed favoured imprisonment, while 41 per cent supported community service order as a viable sentencing disposition.

In Canada, the **General Social Survey** (see Box 3.7) has a criminal-victimization component. These national surveys have been conducted every five years since 1988. Smaller in format and depth than its American counterpart, the survey asks people about only eight types of crime: assault, break-and-enter, motor-vehicle theft, sexual assault, theft, theft of household property, theft of personal property, and vandalism (Sacco and Johnson, 1990). Perhaps the most frequently-cited Canadian victimization survey was the Canadian Urban Victimization Survey conducted in 1981. The survey involved seven large metropolitan areas (Vancouver, Edmonton, Winnipeg, Toronto, Montreal, St. John, and Halifax-Dartmouth). More than 700,000 persons over the age of 16 were interviewed. The huge volume of data has been reported in ten separate publications over a period of five years, from 1983 through 1988 (see Box 3.7 and 3.8a).

REALITY CHECK BOX 3.7

HIGHLIGHTS OF THE GENERAL SOCIAL SURVEY (GSS)

Published for the second time in 1993 the General Social Survey involved a sample of approximately 10,000 participants. Some of the key findings include:
1. Since 1988 there has been a small but measurable increase of fear of victimization.
2. Compared with 12 other western countries, Canada ranks in the lower third for risk of being victimized.

3. There has been an increase in the public's perception that levels of crime have increased.
4. Actual victimization rates declined with increasing age of respondents.
5. Approximately 28 per cent of violent victimizations are reported to the police.
6. Of those crimes reported, 64 per cent expressed "satisfaction" with how the police responded to their incident. Females were less (54 per cent) satisfied than males (75 per cent).
7. Compared with official counts of crime, Canadians tend to overestimate both the frequency and seriousness of violent crime.

Source: *CCJS*, 1994:14(3)1–19.

REALITY CHECK BOX 3.8A

HIGHLIGHTS OF THE CANADIAN URBAN VICTIMIZATION SURVEY (CUVS)

1. Fewer than 42 per cent of crimes are reported to the police.
2. The majority (66 per cent) said they did not report because the offence was "too minor" while 61 per cent did not report the crime because they felt the "police couldn't do anything."
3. The more evenings spent out of doors the greater the risk of being victimized.
4. Only 5 per cent felt unsafe in their own neighbourhood during the day, while 40 per cent felt unsafe in their neighbourhood during the evenings.
5. The major determinants of fear are: being older; living in an urban setting; being female; having a lower income; and living in heterogeneous housing.
6. Social determinants of fear include being previously victimized and/or knowing someone who had been victimized. These concepts are referred to as the *ripple effect,* that is, based on mutual reinforcement.
7. Personal-type offences occur most frequently in the summer (30 per cent) and least frequently in winter (18 per cent).
8. The time of occurrence for personal-type crimes is Monday through Friday between the hours of 8 am and 6 pm (33 per cent).
9. Weapons are used in 35 per cent of personal violent crimes (only 13 per cent involved guns).

Source: Canadian Urbanization Victimization Survey—assorted volumes 1984–1985.
Solicitor General Canada: Program Branch, Research and Statistics Group.

HIGHLIGHTS OF THE VIOLENCE AGAINST WOMEN SURVEY (VAWS) (ONLINE: WWW.LIB.UWATERLOO.CA/ UWEBS/VAW/VAWABT.TXT)

1. Nearly 25 per cent of all Canadian women have experienced at least one incident of violence since the age of 16.
2. Approximately 25 per cent of the assailants were men known to the women victims while another 25 per cent were strangers.
3. Slightly more than 15 per cent of currently married women reported violence by their spouse and half of those respondents with previous marriages reported being victimized by their ex-spouse.
4. Sixty per cent of Canadian women expressed feeling at least "somewhat" worried about being out after dark.

Given their different formats and questioning structure, the CUVS is not compatible with the GSS. However, the CUVS marked Canada's entry into the victimization survey market. And just as official crime data have evolved to become more reliable and richer in content, so too will victim data. For example, in 1993, the first **Violence Against Women Survey** (VAWS) was undertaken. The survey involved over 12,000 respondents and 472 variables (see Box 3.8b above). While informative, there are no plans to repeat it (Johnson, 1996b, also see Weblink for related Internet site).

Since criminal victimization in Canada is a relatively rare occurrence (especially for violent offences), it is difficult to conduct such surveys with special groups and/or on special topics (e.g., elderly abuse). But because of the wealth of information to be obtained from such research, academics will likely continue to conduct their own research in these areas.

As researchers increasingly recognize the need for a multi-method approach to collecting data on crime (see "Triangulation" below) many of the existing concerns are likely to be addressed and perpetual limitations will be addressed through other means. Also, as we move away from what Andrew Karmen (1996) terms "offenderology" to being more victim-conscious and integrating victimization into theoretical perspectives, the refinement of victimization surveys is likely to continue. For example, sociologist Jack Katz (1988) expresses the view that criminologists need to broaden their objective and deterministic perspectives of deviance. He suggests that criminologists need to embrace a spiritual approach. In so doing, criminologists will use victimization data to better understand the role of the victim and offender. Meanwhile, the critical theoretical perspective *Left-Realism* (Chapter 8) makes extensive use of victimization data when testing its principles (see, for example, Lowman and MacLean, 1992). Similarly, feminist researchers have not only used victimization data but have developed means of looking into behaviours (e.g., child abuse, motor-vehicle theft, etc.) not covered in traditional victimization surveys. And finally, The Netherlands is currently co-ordinating an international survey of victimization suffered by businesses, which will have both theoretical and policy implications. As for Canada, the variety of victim assistance-based programs that exist will ensure that victimization surveys and the study of victimology in general, will become a major force in criminological study. This may be further fuelled by the 10th International Symposium on Victimology that will be hosted by Montreal in August, 2000.

Self-Report Data

In North America, Thorsten Sellin (1931) was one of the first criminologists to argue that in order to understand crime, it is important to start by asking about the offender's behaviour and motivation. Since Sellin's article, self-report surveys have been conducted with young offenders, judges, lawyers, law enforcement officers, inmates, senior citizens, business persons, and virtually any sub-population that might be thought to engage in criminal acts.

Self-report studies take a pragmatic approach to the enumeration of criminal behaviour—was a crime committed or not? Based on the responses the scores are cross-analyzed against the fundamental demographic and socio-economic characteristics of the respondents, such as age, gender, known criminal record, and social class. These data are then used to assess both the validity of criminal justice statistics as a pattern index of crime, and the validity of criminological theories based on inferences drawn from the patterns found in criminal justice statistics.

Findings of Self-report Surveys

The flavour of self-report studies has changed over the years. One of the earlier self-report studies was conducted by Austin Porterfield (1943), Texas, Christian University. He asked students to respond to a survey on deviant behaviour. While most of his findings might appear trivial by today's standards, he observed that there was a strong gender bias in favour of males—they commited more delinquent acts than females. Among his more amusing findings were such observations as: 79 per cent of males admit to using abusive language and 77 per cent admit to throwing spitballs. Only 8 per cent admitted to committing break-and-enter.

The early self-report studies offered criminologists some fruitful insights into their understanding of crime. The studies revealed that the gap between official and self-report data varied by age, gender, offender type, and race. Offenders who are not part of the official data base (i.e., haven't been caught) tend to commit a wide variety of offences, rather than specializing in one type of offending behaviour. Only about one-quarter of all serious, chronic young offenders are officially apprehended.

In Canada, self-report surveys have been limited. What studies have been conducted tend to focus on youths and adolescents. For example, during the 1970s and 1980s two University of Montreal researchers conducted repeated self-report surveys on a large group of high-risk and known delinquent French-speaking boys. The survey included 39 questions asked of the youths about their delinquent behaviour over the past 12 months. The questions covered a broad range of offences, ranging from property-related offences, to violence, sexual habits, and crimes against their families. LeBlanc and Frechette (1989) attempted to describe delinquent patterns for all high-risk Canadian boys and men. While their study included a number of strong elements, they neglected female delinquency and ignored cultural and social differences between English- and French-speaking Canadians. Also, given that they only surveyed urban males in one major city, their generalization to all Canadian youth is highly suspect in terms of reliability and validity.

In another major study, Gomme, Morton, and West (1984) conducted a self-report study in a small rural-urban southern Ontario community involving senior elementary and junior high school students. Consistent with other self-report studies (see, for example, Siegel, 1995), West found that males commit significantly more delinquencies than do females. The exception was running away from home. Males were more likely to be involved in damaging property and fighting. Minor theft was reported with similar frequency by both genders, while, proportionately, males committed more medium-serious thefts.

Limitations of Self-report Surveys

Despite a comparatively long history, self-report studies have been fraught with methodological problems. Even though they guarantee confidentiality and anonymity, there have been problems with comparability. Similarly, until recently, few studies were standardized, as they were often done at different times by those with different interests. One exception was the study by West and Farrington (1977), in England, that investigated the development of young offenders in a sample of delinquent and non-delinquent boys over a ten-year period. They found that differences did exist between delinquents and non-delinquents on factors relating to family background and several personal characteristics. Similar results have been reported recently in a study of Chinese delinquents by Wolfgang (1996).

Another limitation of self-report studies has been that they seldom use comparable questions, or use comparable areas or time frames. These drawbacks render the studies almost useless for any assessment of the efficiency of criminal justice statistics. Walker (1987) has identified several other factors that bring into question the reliability of self-report surveys. They include:

1. The respondent may mistrust the interviewer.
2. Respondents may not answer truthfully because of embarrassment.
3. Respondents may feel a deep sense of guilt and not disclose their behaviour.
4. Respondents may exaggerate the truth, especially if they are young.
5. Respondents may simply forget.

As a result of their numerous methodological limitations, self-report studies are plagued by reliability problems, are of doubtful validity, and have led researchers to draw unfair and incorrect inferences. However, with creative efforts, and being sensitive to possible limitations, it is possible to minimize the problems. For example, Dentler and Monroe (1961) in a two-week follow-up, found a 92 per cent concurrence rate, while Clark and Tifft (1966), who used the threat of a polygraph test on a sample of youths, found the variation between different testing periods to be statistically negligible.

More recently, Junger-Tas, Terlouw, and Klein (1996) have compiled a collection of sixteen articles of mostly European origin, along with one from New Zealand and another from the United States, involving an international self-report survey of juvenile delinquents. The study was conducted between 1991 and 1993 and the countries used a variety of sampling techniques, making direct comparisons between the participating countries difficult. Nevertheless, the general findings are consistent with other self-report literature: that the ages from 16 to 17 years are the peak ages for offending; that violence is strongly related to lower educational levels; and that school failure is related to violent offences.

Viewing it as a preliminary study, the editors note the importance of engaging in comparative research. However, they also note such efforts have not been quick in unfolding; in fact the "path to this book started back in Wuppertal, Germany in 1981" (p. 385).

In **summary**, self-report studies have undergone steady improvement over the years but as DeKeseredy and Schwartz (1996:138) write, "we still have a ways to go to make them completely useful." In the meantime, we should treat these types of studies as reasonably reliable but subject to qualification, i.e., less reliable for trivial questions (e.g., theft under $20), for personally embarrassing questions, and for very serious crimes. In addition, researchers need to expand their topic base. For example, our knowledge base about self-report adult crime is very small. Furthermore, the majority of such surveys have been conducted with (male) young offenders. This is probably due to the ease of access to young male offenders and the relatively low cost of administering such surveys. However, in spite of the number of self-report studies conducted on young people, the findings have not shed a great deal of light on our understanding of youth crime. For example, Vold's (1979:226) observation that "the basic motivations for crime are common in all social classes, not just to the lower class" is not very enlightening.

The limited advances in understanding crime through self-report studies is due in part to the limited methodological limitations discussed above, as well as the lack of an interdisciplinary approach to surveying those who have already committed offences. For example, rather than simply enumerate trends and patterns of offences committed by various groups, self-report surveys could embrace an integrated interdisciplinary approach that includes questions regarding biological and environmental factors that are more in keeping with our understanding of crime and criminality today. However, an American study conducted by Michael Hindelang, Travis Hirschi, and Joseph Weis (1981), suggests that official and unofficial data collection techniques have improved over the years and that the problems of accuracy and reliability in self-reports fall well within the range of acceptability. They argue that in spite of the skepticism among some criminologists, self-report studies serve an informative function as long as researchers conduct their research within the methodological parameters identified.

Observational Procedures

The final source of data that is regularly used to obtain accurate data on crime is observational data or *field research*. As Jackson (1995–1999), among others, has commented, you cannot gain insight into people's motives for committing crimes if you are sitting at your desk analyzing data or reading crime surveys. Would it not be more informative to actually be able to follow and watch a prison riot rather than hand out surveys after the fact? Would it not be more informative to sit in a court and watch a trial unfold or to go on police ride-alongs than to administer a survey?

The German sociologist, Max Weber (1864–1920), was instrumental in developing methodological approaches that emphasized the importance of how individuals interpret their actions as well as how they interpret the actions and reactions of others. Weber used the term **Verstehen** to refer to this *qualitative* approach to understanding. The concept is defined as the process of trying to understand an event by placing oneself in the situation and trying to see it through "their" eyes—aligning oneself with another's social viewpoint. Since then a number of major theoretical perspectives have emerged: the *symbolic interactionism* perspective (see Ritzer, 1992); the *ground theory* (see Galser and Strauss, 1973); and the *ethnomethodological* perspective (see Garfinkel, 1967). From this general *social-constructionist* perspective, crime statistics tell us more about the agencies and individuals (e.g., police, courts, and corrections) who are responsible for constructing them than about the crimes and criminals they are reporting.

Over the years, a number of classic studies have employed one of the above perspectives to study crime and criminals. Among the list are Sutherland's *The Professional Thief* (1937); Chambliss's *The Box Man* (1975); Snodgrass's *The*

Jackroller at Seventy (1982); and in Canada, Letkemann's *Crime as Work* (1973). For his book, Letkemann interviewed 45 bank robbers and burglars in an effort to describe and explain the lifestyle of a safe-cracker.

Advantages and Disadvantages of Observational Procedures

All field observation techniques are comprehensive data collection methods. They are excellent techniques for gathering information, when going directly to the event is essential or helpful. When events are better observed in their natural setting, observational procedures can be information rich. As Mark Hamm (1998) notes, criminological field research enables the researcher to transcend abstract theoretical analysis by immersing him- or herself in the situated meanings and emotions of the criminal event.[12] These techniques are also useful for gathering data on social processes over time (e.g., youth gang activities, police investigation procedures and the interaction between prostitutes and their johns). Collectively, these procedures have a strong appeal value to the reader because they have good **face validity**. You only report what you see!

When collecting data in social settings (e.g., inmate vs. guard interactions), these methods enable data collection on at least three levels:

1. The act itself, the activities surrounding the act, and the meaning of the activities;
2. The dynamics of the participants and their inter-relationships; and
3. The setting in general (Lofland, 1984).

Observational techniques entail varying degrees of involvement in and observation of the events. This raises a number of methodological and ethical considerations. For example, the now oft-cited "tearoom trade" study of homosexual activities by Laud Humphrey (1970) has become a classic study in field research ethics. His doctoral dissertation involved observing (male) homosexuals meeting in public washrooms, without getting their consent. Was this a violation of their privacy and personal liberty? Could Humphrey be considered no better than a "peeping-tom" or voyeur? Humphrey admitted to being less than candid with his respondents (p. 171). Is this practice of deception acceptable? In a report on some of the criticisms, Horowitz and Rainwater (1970) argued that the study was conducted within ethical boundaries. Either way, the point is that collecting data through observational methods can be subject to controversy. As an interesting footnote to this study, Canadian sociologist Fredrick Desroches (1990) attempted to replicate the results of Humphrey's study by means other than personal observations. While his methodology was much different (he used observations made by police), he found the behaviour of male homosexuals to be remarkably consistent over time, from community to community, and across national boundaries.

Another drawback of observational procedures is that they tend to be much more labour-intensive than victimization or self-report surveys. The data are also more subjective and sample sizes tend to be considerably smaller than the unofficial and official means of data collecting mentioned above. In addition, depending on the method of data collection employed, the type of information gathered is dependent on the recorder's biases and mental and physical limitations. As a result, there is no allowance for causal assertions or generalizations beyond the study group. Nevertheless, as noted above, there have been a number of major studies conducted using one or more of the observational methodologies, and in some areas they appear to be gathering a strong following.

Types of Observational Techniques

Most criminology research methodology textbooks include a section of observational methods. Two of the more common observational procedures will be introduced briefly. They both share the theme of being more directly involved in observing and recording their subject matter.

1. **Field (Covert) Observation:** The intent of covert, or *non-participant,* observations is to observe and collect data in its natural setting without altering the setting in any way. And while the methodology can be somewhat haphazard, the information obtained can be most enlightening (Jackson, 1995–1999).

Field observation techniques are the least obtrusive method of the observational techniques. It is a procedure that we have probably all engaged in at some time or other. Going to a hockey or baseball game, sitting at your favorite coffee bar and watching "life pass by," or simply hanging around a crime scene and observing the sequence of events all constitute field observation.

As an undergraduate student, I assisted one of my instructors in a study which required working in one of the first sex shops in Toronto posing as a sales person, with the consent of the store manager. My task was to observe daily transactions without questioning or prying into people's lives. I was simply to observe and later record everything as it pertained to a set of pre-established criteria. I found the experience both entertaining and extremely informative as it helped to dispel a number of misconceptions I had about the types of people who might visit such a store.

Field research can provide rich and detailed information. Observing verbal and non-verbal interactions (i.e., micro-analysis), as well as elements of some theoretical paradigm that you might be testing, can prove very insightful. Other groups have identified, in accordance with Hagan's (1997) definition of deviance, a variety of *social diversions* and *social deviation,* and conducted field studies around behaviours ranging from seat belt use at different times of the day and within major urban vs. rural settings, to stopping for stop signs, and a variety of other behaviours that reflect norm violations. Each study produced an understanding of human behaviour that a general theory would be hard-pressed to describe.

2. **Participant Observation:** This is a methodology more commonly used by anthropologists although the Chicago School (Chapter 7) produced a number of classic sociological studies (see Theodorson, 1982). The methodology involves "going natural" or engaging in *field research*. Humphrey (1970), for example, was a *participant observer* or a "watchqueen," as he termed it. In return for being able to watch he acted as his study group's watch guard to warn of any unwanted visitors.

The researcher can vary his or her degree of involvement as a participant observer and become totally involved in what he or she is observing. In a classic illustration of this approach, John Howard Griffin had his skin impregnated with a black dye so that he could blend in with the blacks he wanted to observe and live with, so he could provide a more realistic description of what life was like for blacks in America. His story is told in his book *Black like Me* (1961). Although a compelling story, this type of research is considered to be primarily qualitative. Griffin had become a *complete observer-participant* whereas the *complete observer* does not participate in anything, but only observes, as if sitting behind a "one-way mirror."

Engaging in this type of research often places great demands on observers' time. In addition, observers must be able to operate on two levels. First, they must immerse themselves in what they are observing. Second, they must remain detached from what they are observing. Imagine going to your favorite sporting event and being asked to observe but not get personally involved—like a broad-caster or sports reporter. Police officers are also often required to play a passive observational role when conducting an investigation. Ethical dilemmas can arise if they find themselves in a position where an event of which they strongly dis-approve might occur. Longmire (1983) found that such dilemmas are common among those who engage in research questions in criminology and criminal jus-tice. Surveying a sample of members of the American Society of Criminology, Longmire found that 63 per cent indicated experiencing some ethical dilemmas when conducting research. The most common (9 per cent) ethical dilemma per-tained to issues surrounding confidentiality. What do they do? They can follow some of the basic guidelines such as: don't harm participants, ensure voluntary participation, maintain the anonymity and confidentiality of participants, and be honest at all stages of the study (Jackson, 1995, 1999). When students take a research methods course they will become familiar with these and other related issues. And if you are interested in substantive issues regarding ethics in crimi-nology and criminal justice policy, aside from seeking out related textbooks, con-sult the journal *Criminal Justice Ethics* for a broad selection of articles.

As noted above, most criminology research methods courses include a section on field research. Aside from learning the essential tools for conducting such research, students acquire an understanding about the strengths and weaknesses of relying on participant observation as a means of acquiring knowledge. As criminology moves closer to being more interdisciplinary it has increasingly begun to combine qualitative and quantitative methods of data-gathering. The process of combining multiple sources to better understand criminological phenomena is referred to as triangulation.

Triangulation

To this point, we have observed that no one data source is able to demonstrate the validity and reliability of one measurement of crime and criminal justice concerns completely. Official data sources and unofficial data sources each have their strengths and weaknesses. Paul Lazerfeld (1959) and Donald Campbell and Donald Fiske (1959) were among the first to suggest that multiple measurements or *data triangulation* can be used to better illuminate a particular issue. For example, criminologists can recreate a great deal of a past incident by using indirect observations (e.g., examining physical evidence) and combining them with current statistical trends and patterns to better explain and predict the phenomena.

Using triangulation increases *convergent-discriminant* validity. According to Campbell and Fiske (1959:81), by using different data sources "of measuring a construct, the results should be similar, whereas the same method measuring different things should yield dissimilar results." Police data provide an official indicator of crime as do victimization data (*convergence*) but the results are seldom identical (*discrimination*) since they measure the same phenomena from different perspectives. Triangulation has enabled criminologists to illuminate the dark figure of crime. Letkemann's study (1973) of cheque forgers included three different sources of information in order to develop his cheque forger typology. A similar method was used by Clarke (1982) to develop his typology of assassins, while Boyd (1988) used at least three sources of information to develop his typology of murderers in Canada.

Research methodology textbooks, almost unanimously, take time to point out that, while the validity of information sources is critical, no single method or multi-method strategy can demonstrate or prove any phenomena with one hundred per cent accuracy. Rather, the "invalidity is lessened, or researchers are able to express greater degrees of confidence in their data" (Hagan, 1989:247). This is why, when reading academic research articles, statistical techniques and their probabilities are used to objectively state the degree of confidence found in the data. However, that is a completely different subject, best left for a behavioural statistics course, because it is not practical to discuss it in this textbook.

Now that we have examined the purpose of crime data and how data are collected, let us look at how criminologists use the various sources of crime data to study criminological issues and criminality. The procedure by which crime data are used to study criminological issues is known more generally as **research methodology**.

Research methodology is the scientific process whereby criminologists strive to understand and explain criminological issues through a variety of social science methods. Methodology is a sub-area of *epistemology* (the science of knowing) and has also been called "the science of finding out" (Maxfield and Babbie, 1995:5).

The Purpose of
Studying Criminological Relations

Correlation and Crime

One of the oldest formal techniques for trying to understand crime is to examine those factors that are associated with the phenomenon being studied. Nothing happens in a vacuum. For a ball to move, there has to be some type of energy directed at the ball. For a crime to occur there has to be a target, and the offender must be motivated and must have the skills in order to commit the crime.

Hartnagel (1995:95) notes that discovering correlates or relationships is "an important first step for any scientific discipline such as criminology." And while correlations do not imply *cause* they are often seen as somehow being related to each other in contributing to a crime. While a correlation does not imply cause, it usually prompts researchers to examine why and how two (or more) variables correlate. A correlation thus refers to a relationship between two or more phenomena that, based on specified criteria, are related, or vary together—as one changes so does the other. For example, some criminologists have claimed that crime is related to phases of the moon, to economic conditions in society, to the amount of violence on television, and even to different body types. (We will explore some of these correlates, among others, in Section II). Once correlates have been established, criminologists attempt to discern whether the association somehow contributes or causes a change to the phenomenon in question.

Cause vs. Probability

What do we mean by "cause"? Cause implies that the occurrence of one event is directly affected by the presence of one or more variables or factors. For example, most people believe that human responses have certain reliable causes. If you stab someone he or she will probably bleed. If you tell a good joke people are likely to laugh. However, if you are a trained Yogi or Sufi master you might not bleed if stabbed. In the second example, people might not understand your joke. So believing in a cause does not necessarily imply that an event is **deterministic**. Nothing is ever perfectly predictable. As the social anarchist Paul Feyerabend (1986:55) writes, "no theory ever agrees with all the *facts* in its domain, yet it is not always the theory that is to blame." Many researchers, therefore, prefer to use the term **probability** to express the likelihood that two or more events are related. The process of measuring the probability that certain effects will occur when certain causes are present involves the use of statistical techniques (e.g., chi-square, t-test, analysis of variance, regression, etc.). Because of the importance of behavioural statistics, virtually every social science program offers such courses.

The stronger the degree of association between the variables measured the greater the likelihood that it will be accepted as being true or valid. When we test the likelihood of two or more variables, researchers formulate a **hypothesis** that is usually a declarative statement about the relationship. For example, if you had been abused as a young person (cause) then your chances of becoming an abuser yourself are greater (effect) than if you had not been abused. Theory contains the constructs that are of theoretical interest and that attempt to explicate, or account for, a set of propositions or statements.

Although criminologists are concerned with humanitarian issues regarding the fair treatment of criminal offenders, they attempt to base their decision on scientific evidence. Among the advantages of the scientific procedure is the ability to provide clearer guidelines to let you know when you are wrong. This is why research methodology is a major component of any criminology program. Through the varied techniques available, researchers strive to accomplish four basic aims:

1. **Discovery:** Research can never prove a hypothesis. It can only provide supporting evidence. To the uninitiated, research findings sometimes seem to state the obvious. As a young criminology student, one of the first "common sense" observations I remember reading was a study that reported that if you associated with a "negative" element, it would increase your chances of becoming delinquent. I thought, how original, go figure! However, in addition to verifying the "obvious," researchers also attempt to understand or clarify facts that may be less obvious. For example, why doesn't everyone who associates with a "negative element" turn to crime? Similarly, while the practice of punishment and corporal punishment has been around since the dawn of time, it was not until the 1990s that a growing volume of literature, suggesting a proactive and restorative stance towards justice, started gaining momentum (see Fattah, 1995, Zehr, 1995). By examining data through different "lenses," researchers are discovering alternatives to punishment (see Chapter 14).

2. **Demonstration:** It has often been said that there are very few original ideas, only variations on a few themes. One way to illuminate such assertions is to put the assertion or observation to the test—to prove a point, so to speak. This process can offer insight and clarity into the relationship between crime and ideas, such as whether the restorative justice concept works as well in small communities as in major urban settings.

Not all variations are better than the original version. For example, are new drugs of today better than the herbs used thousands of years ago by our "primitive" ancestors? Until recently, the Amazon was thought to be little more than a wild jungle where primitive people dwelled. Then the rainforest began to be appreciated for its essential contribution to the world's ecosystem, and, more recently, for its medicinal plants. One such plant that only caught North American attention in the 1990s is gurana. Its natural properties help sustain energy and combat a variety of ailments (see Straten, 1994). Only after scientists have been able to document (i.e., empirically demonstrate) the evidence of the benefits of numerous primitive cures has there been a renewed interest in these old remedies.

Closer to home, social control agents have tried to use (demonstrate) punishment as a deterrent. In spite of evidence to the contrary, the social control agents have tried to improve (a variation in the demonstration) on their methods of punishment. Yet the results are still the same. Most criminals are seldom deterred by the threat or nature of the punishment (e.g., capital punishment in the United States).

It is important to realize that research can only be consistent with or demonstrate a hypothesis. No demonstration can ever prove the hypothesis. Just because we might be able to demonstrate that fear of crime is related to safety precautions a person takes does not mean that there are not alternative explanations that are equally consistent with the research results.

3. **Refutation:** Since the late 1970s, capital punishment has been illegal in Canada. Pioneering research by Fattah and others suggested that capital punishment was not an effective deterrent. Fattah's work was instrumental in abolishing capital punishment in Canada. His work challenged a long-standing belief and practice. Similarly, in the 1990s a number of studies on boot camps were found to refute the notion that hard work, harsh discipline, and a regimented lifestyle deter young offenders from re-offending (Cowles and Castellano, 1995). The highly publicized "Scared Straight" program from the 1970s was also later refuted (Lundman, 1994). Yet shortly after its introduction, some Canadians who had only a limited amount of information to base their observations on, noted, "shock treatment, if run properly could be most effective as is proven by ... 'Scared Straight'" (Leard, 1980).

Science provides an opportunity for "checks and balances" of all ideas. And sometimes even good intentions are later refuted as being not very sound. After all, we once believed that the world was flat until Christopher Columbus proved otherwise, just as we once believed the sun circled the earth, before Galileo proved that the earth was not the centre of the universe. So, while the power of science can provide the objective tools to test (i.e., discover) ideas and gradually move closer to the truth, it can also be used to refute existing beliefs. Canadian scholars Fattah and Grygier (see Appendix 4.A) have been strong crusaders against the use of punishment as a means of social control. For example, in a talk given in honour of professor Koichi Miyazawa of Japan, Fattah (1995) listed nine reasons why punishment does not have justifiable merit as a means of social control (see Box 3.9). Unfortunately, while they have lauded criminologists for their research and ideas, Canadian criminal justice policy makers have done little to embrace their ideas (see Chapter 14).

WHAT DO YOU THINK? | BOX 3.9

PUNISHMENT: REFUTING ITS "MERITS"

Consider:

1. Punishment is ineffective: United States and China, with their high incarceration and execution rates, are prime examples.
2. Punishment achieves nothing: Punishment does little more than breed anger, hostility, resentment, and antagonism... violence breeds violence.
3. Punishment is costly: The financial costs have been escalating year after year (see "Trends...", 1994).
4. Punishment is degrading, humiliating and stigmatizing: Any form of deprivation of liberty is degrading and humiliating.
5. Punishment is never personal or individual: Although we might be imprisoning the offender we are also having an impact on his/her family, friends and social network. Punishment extends beyond one's immediate circle.
6. Punishment treats human beings as a means to an end: While punishment may have some cathartic effects on the public, it does little for the person being punished. The person is sacrificed to achieve some other goal.
7. Punishment looks at the past: Punishment is retributive in nature. It is retrograde in its approach and does little for the offender's future well-being.
8. Punishment perpetuates rather than settles conflicts: Fattah argues that punishment does not settle anything. Rather, it only serves to generate further animosity and antagonism among the parties involved.
9. Punitive penal sanctions amount to punishment of the victim: By its very practice, punishment only serves to victimize the victim further. Society also loses since it refuses to accept failure.

Fattah uses these points to argue in favour of a restorative model of justice, a model which started to receive considerable interest from government and non-government agencies concerned with the growing problems of our current criminal justice system in the mid 1990s.

Do these arguments make sense? Do you think they could work in our society? What roadblocks might exist?

4. **Replication:** The more times you can confirm an observation the greater its predictability and consistency. A review of the academic journals reveals numerous studies that represent replications of previous studies but perhaps using different participants, different settings, and/or the introduction of additional measures. For example, Sutherland's differential association theory (Chapter 7) has been the subject of hundreds of articles and earned the respect of most critics (see, generally, Williams and McShane, 1994, 1999). However, we must be careful not to accept observations at face value. After all, we once believed the world was flat, and that criminals represented some kind of throwback to a more primitive type of human being.

Because social scientists are trained to be inquisitive, critical thinkers and because nothing is absolute, they strive to contribute to the existing state of knowledge. Therefore, theories are constantly evolving and changing. At the turn of the century, ecological theories (Chapter 7) received widespread support until the 1940s, when a variety of sociological perspectives gained prominence. Starting in the 1970s, with growing social and political unrest, we moved towards more conservative interpretations of crime and used conservative strategies to control crime (i.e., incarceration). When crime increased dramatically and steps had to be taken to understand it, a shift took place from theoretical issues to practical concerns, and a new discipline emerged, criminal justice (Williams and McShane, 1994, 1999). Similar observations could be made by a number of major theories covered in Section II. Therefore, while replication can serve a vital function, as already stated, it must be viewed with caution.

As a final note, it should be pointed out that, as sophisticated and structured as research methods may appear to be, they have also been described as an "art" form (Palys, 1998), that is, even though there are certain fundamental guidelines that researchers attempt to follow when conducting research, the flexibility and quality of their research design is limited by such factors as cost, time, and practicality. And while scientific inquiry may not provide the definitive answers we seek to complex criminological questions, scientific theories offer at least an "objective" approximation of reality, as scientific theories are premised on observable, measurable, and usually empirically testable hypotheses or assertions.

One of the reasons for the lack of "success" is that most criminologists have viewed, and continue to view crime and its causes, as well as its control, from classic one-way cause-and-effect relationships (Normandeau and Hasenpush, 1980). Instead, successful research must recognize the interdisciplinary nature of crime. Crime is influenced by a complex interaction of biological, environmental, political, psychological, sociological, and other factors that are generally beyond the scope of legal mechanisms and decision-makers.

Until the political decision-makers and criminologists embrace an interdisciplinary approach we must learn to work within the parameters available. In the next section, we will examine what kinds of official data are available and how they are collected and disseminated. Just as we must learn to recognize the complexity of human behaviour, we must look at crime statistics from many angles over short- and long-term periods in order to move towards a better understanding of crime and its control.

Summary

The main objective of this chapter was to describe and evaluate four of the primary methods of gathering and interpreting crime data. Crime data are essential to explaining and describing crime trends and patterns, and for developing criminological theory and formulating social policy. Criminal statistics are part of the criminological enterprise.

In reviewing the various crime data sources it was noted that they each have their strengths and weaknesses. Even though some criminologists have used such observations to refute the use of any crime data, it was observed that as long as they understand their subject matter, the results can be interpreted accordingly. The choice of crime data is usually dependent on the resources available to the researcher, the researcher's scholarly training and theoretical bias combined with the parameters of the phenomena being studied.

Criminologists have typically fallen into "schools of thought" and "camps of research methodology." For example, it was noted that North American criminology has been dominated by American ideas and research techniques. However, crime is not limited to North America. Therefore, it is recommended that an interdisciplinary and multi-method approach be used when collecting crime and criminal justice information. In addition, given the various strengths and weaknesses of the sources covered, the chapter concluded by suggesting that criminological research relies on data from a variety of sources. Triangulation, for example, is a practical and effective method by which to increase the validity of the subject being studied. As Simon (cited in DeKeseredy and Schwartz, 1996:148) observed, "a research method for a given problem is not like the solution to a problem in Algebra. It is more like a recipe for beef stroganoff; there is no one best recipe."

Discussion Questions

1. Why is crime data essential to the study of crime?
2. How should we deal with offenders who display high-risk re-offending characteristics? How might we determine the best intervention strategy?
3. What are some of the major problems of the different sources of crime data?
4. In Box 3.3 it is suggested that crime can be predicted using demographic trends. What policy implications might this have?

5. What are the advantages and disadvantages of being interdisciplinary and integrated in our efforts to collect crime data?

6. How can the various sources of information on criminal events be used to either support or distort actual crime rates?

7. Using a current *Juristat Service Bulletin*, pick two or three common crimes and examine their official rates compared to other crimes. Then collect approximately a dozen media stories on these crimes. Compare and contrast the media stories with the official data. Is the media coverage consistent with the official data? What might account for any differences? What implications might this have for criminal policy?

8. To what extent is it safe to generalize self-report data from convicted and/or known high-risk offenders to the criminal population? Why, or why not, is self-report information superior to UCR data?

Key Concepts

Crime data	false positive	police data
Uniform Crime Report (UCR)	indictable offence	summary offence
Judicial statistics	correctional statistics	correlation
Canadian Urban Victimization Survey (CUVS)	General Social Survey (GSS) *Juristat*	probability hypotheses
Violence Against Women Survey (VAWS)	cause vs. prediction victimization data	deterministic unofficial data
Dark figure	field observation	ethnomethodology
Self-report data	participant observation	
Triangulation	Verstehen	
Canadian Centre for Justice Statistics		

Weblinks

www.ecriccanada.com/geoprof.htm An excellent source for those interested in geographic profiling of crime.

www.statcan.ca/english/pgdb/state/justice.htm The homepage for Statistics Canada. Numerous related government crime links. Unless your institution has a site licence, you may not be able to access this link.

http://library.usask.ca/data/social/violence.html The site for the survey on female victims of violence.

Footnotes

1. New Brunswick had the lowest per capita cost at around $230 while Ontario had the highest per capita cost at $308. The Yukon and the North West Territories had consider-

ably higher per capita costs (i.e., $1084 and $1250 respectively) but their rates are artificially inflated due to their small population.

2. The term objective refers to the process of using crime data (i.e., numerical data) to describe, explain, and predict criminological issues.

3. For a more current update on the status of boot/therapeutic camps see Bourque, Cronin, Felker, Pearson, Han, and Hill (1996).

4. The Yukon and Northwest Territories were not separately identified until 1967.

5. For students interested in seeking a career in policing, *Juristat Service Bulletin* also publishes reports on police personnel and expenditures across the country.

6. Prior to the introduction of the YOA in 1984, separate statistical data on juvenile delinquents were kept, since 1920. Even though data were available on the number of outcomes of cases brought against juveniles in each province and territory, one must exercise caution when using the data. Under the JDA, the maximum age of responsibility varied between the provinces and there was variability in the handling of charges between jurisdictions.

7. Other rates for 1994–95 include: New Zealand, 127 per 100,000; United Kingdom, 99; Australia, 89; German, 81; Sweden, 66; and Norway, 56 (Corrections Population Growth, 1997).

8. For an entertaining account of how statistics can be misused and abused, see Darrell Huff's little book, *How to Lie with Statistics*, 1954.

9. Most of the information for this section is adapted from "The Looking Glass: Canadian Centre for Justice Statistics," Winterdyk (1996).

10. See, for example, Silverman and Kennedy (1993) who used *Juristat* data for their work on homicide; Desroches (1995) used *CCJS* data in producing his account of robbery, while Kennedy and Sacco (1996) collected seventeen articles on crime and criminal justice issues based largely on material compiled by the *CCJS*.

11. Not included in this section is data from the recent 1998 International Victimization Survey. *Juristat*, vol. 18(6) has highlights from the survey.

12. In 1997, as part of a field research project on Timothy McVeigh, Hamm spent three days living in the hotel room in which McVeigh stayed before bombing a government building in Oklahoma City.

CHAPTER 4

The History and Pioneers of Criminology

"While we read history we make history."

George William Curtis (1824–1892)

Learning Outcomes

After you have completed this chapter, you should be able to:

- Discuss the three major schools of criminological thought.

- Recognize the impact these schools have had on our current view of crime, criminals, and justice.

- Evaluate the major schools in terms of their impact and their implications.

- Be cognizant of the pioneers who have contributed to criminological reform in Canada.

- Appreciate the necessity of an interdisciplinary approach to the study of crime, criminals, and the justice system.

- Recognize the need to include "prevention" as a critical element in an integrated and interdisciplinary model.

What is the Point of History?

How often have you heard the phrases "history just repeats itself," "we've heard it all before," "we never seem to learn from our past," or "you are just reinventing the proverbial wheel"?

In Chapter 1, it was observed that our interest in crime has existed as long as recorded history. Throughout the centuries, many scholars have offered various

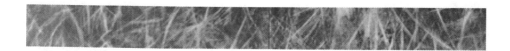

opinions as to the causes and "cures" for the problem. Some of them have had an enduring influence on how we view crime and study criminality. However, the scientific study of crime and criminality is a relatively recent development. In this chapter we will go into greater depth and examine both the history of criminological thought and some of its major contributors. For example, you will find biographical profiles on some of the prominent pioneers spread throughout.

The selection process for determining who should be highlighted is, as Mannheim noted in his preface to *Pioneers in Criminology*, "open to criticisms from many quarters" (1973:xiii). However, I have attempted to focus on those important pioneers who receive attention in many other books covering similar topics. And some discretion was exercised, given the limited space. For students who would like to read more about the pioneers in criminology, there are several textbooks that provide excellent biographical accounts of them (see Mannheim, 1973; Martin, Mutchnick, and Austin, 1990). In fact, much of the biographical detail presented here has been drawn from these two sources.

In addition to tracing the past and present origins of criminological thought, this chapter also includes biographical sketches of some of the key legal, penal, and law enforcement reformers. By familiarizing yourself with some of the fundamental ideas and principles of each school and its major contributors, you will gain a better appreciation of how criminology and its sub-areas have evolved into an interdisciplinary area of study.

Finally, including such a chapter provides an opportunity to highlight some of the prominent Canadian researchers and scholars who have made significant contributions to the discipline, both nationally, and, in a growing number of cases, internationally. However, given the theme of this book and not wanting to detract from the fundamental contributions to criminology and criminological thought, the six Canadian profiles are presented in Appendix 4. The fact that these profiles have been placed in an appendix is not meant to undermine their contribution. You are strongly encouraged to read them and/or refer back to them as they are referenced throughout the textbook.

As you will learn in subsequent chapters, individuals have long debated the causes of and cures for crime, as well as the means by which to address them. The major schools of thought represent an end product of the evolutionary process. We will address three major schools of thought: the classical, neoclassical, and the positivist. In addition, a fourth perspective that represents a blending of the classical and positivist principles will be discussed. The "school" of crime prevention, while not generally considered a school of criminological thought, is a perspective that is being embraced by a growing number of scholars and by the criminal justice system. Let us begin with the first criminologically-oriented school—the Classical School.

Classical Criminology[1]

The Roots of Social Reform

The roots of the classical school of criminology emerged in response to the harsh, retributive punishments that existed throughout the Dark Ages (450–1100 AD), Middle Ages (1100–1300 AD) and the Renaissance (1300–1600 AD).

After the fall of the Roman Empire (476 AD), most of the progressive legal reforms disappeared and were replaced with superstitions, fear of magic and satanically-based thinking. People who violated social norms were thought to be witches or possessed by evil spirits. The Dark Ages was marked by ritualistic killings such as burning at the stake, branding, pillory, and the stocks, and other variations of humbling corporal punishment survived up to the seventeenth century. During the sixteenth and seventeenth centuries in Europe, justice was extreme in its measures and in many cases the distinction between criminal cases and private actions to seek compensation for wrongdoing was indistinguishable (Johnson, 1988).

Attempts to "reform" and regulate the meaning and punishment of crime emerged during the early feudal period. One of the first such attempts occurred in 1670, in France. The *Criminal Ordinance* represented an attempt to codify legal sanctions. However, for a number of cases it was not specific enough and still allowed judges discretion to diminish or increase punishment (Siegel, 1995). These were times marked by a number of ritualistic practices of exacting justice, often in the form of vengeance. Some of the more "civil" practices of resolving disputes involved monetary payments as punishment for crimes. Three examples included:

(1) Wergild, practised by some German and Anglo-Saxon societies, was a form of financial compensation for certain crimes. Victim compensation was an important element of the punishment model. Then in 601–604, Aethelbut of Kent introduced a wide range of fines for the crime of theft, called "dooms." For example, stealing from the church was punishable by "compensations ranging from three times the value of the property to the maximum of twelve times the value of the assets taken" (Johnson, 1988:46). (2) Once "blood-feuds" were replaced with trials, it was sometimes thought necessary to determine the truth of testimony by means other than the court. Ordeals were occasionally used to determine guilt. In such instances, disputed questions were referred to the judgment of God. Ordeals typically involved the use of fire, water, and the wage of battle. For example, a suspect might be held under water for long periods to see if God would intervene, thus showing the individual to be innocent. The practice fell out of favour during the middle of the thirteenth century. (3) Those charged with a crime could challenge the accusation with the help of oath-helpers. This involved a practice in which the accused called on 12 to 25 people who could testify as to his or her innocence. Today we simply call them "witnesses for the defence."

In addition to the harshness and brutality of justice, punishment was often inconsistent and chaotic. In fact, Martin Luther called for rulers to pursue, beat, strangle and torture offenders, since rulers were the representatives of divine retribution (Johnson, 1988). Crime was viewed as a rebellious act committed by the poor against the rich and the political structure. Punishment was justified as a means to establish order. In Chapter 7, we will see how the conflict theory has entrenched some of these principles into its theoretical framework. Martin et al. (1990) note that a special disadvantage fell on peasants, wanderers, and vagabonds. Many were punished for theft that was often done as a means of survival. Combined with the famines, wars, excessive taxes, and plagues that characterized this period, social reform was slow in coming.

Towards Enlightenment

It wasn't until the seventeenth century that Europe entered into what is referred to as the Enlightenment (1500–1700). This period marked the beginning of the scientific revolution and the Protestant Reformation (1517). The Polish astronomer, Nicholas Copernicus (1473–1543), who proved the earth revolves around the sun, is often credited as the first major scientist of the Enlightenment era. Jan Weir (1516–1588) wrote the first refutation of the existence of demons and incantations. He also argued that those thought to be possessed were merely mentally ill —*sans deleria*.

Humanism also became a significant force that challenged the existing concept of punishment. The prevailing ideology of the time was called **utilitarianism**. One of its fundamental principles was the notion that punishment should be fair, not cruel, excessive, or capricious. The turning point came on March 2, 1757 after a mentally-challenged man, Robert-François Damien stabbed, but did not kill, King Louis XV of France.

Damien's torture is described in graphic detail in Foucault (1977). His public execution involved a progression of brutal attacks on his body culminating in all parts of his body being hurled into a nearby fire. Throughout the ordeal, he was asked several times if he had anything to say. He said he did not other than "Pardon, Lord."

These forms of unfair punishment, abuse of power, and corrupt economic systems that taxed the poor to support the rich and powerful, would contribute to social revolutions in the American colonies, in 1774; in France, in 1789; and much later, in Russia in 1904.

The ideas of humanism and utilitarianism were put forth by a number of major scholars of the time. Among the most notable was the English philosopher John Locke (1632–1704), who founded the **school of empiricism** and had a profound impact on political ideology.[2] In France, the philosopher and social and political theorist Jean Jacques Rousseau's (1712–1778) ideas also contributed greatly to the emancipation of people from the absolutism of church and state oppression. These ideas appear in his famous political treatise *The Social Contract*, published in 1762. Other writings spoke to the need for more humane and psychologically oriented methods of child rearing (see DeMause, 1988). And René Descartes (1596–1650) helped bring mathematics, philosophy, and social science together into a unified scientific method.

As the Enlightenment produced many nonsecular ideas, the traditional religious doctrine of divine rule and absolute devotion to the church began to wane and the old aristocracy was called into question. As mentioned earlier, the concept of justice was one of the areas to be challenged. The person generally considered most responsible for this evolutive process was Cesare Bonesara, Marquis of Beccaria, more commonly referred to as **Cesare Beccaria** (see Box 4.1).

PROFILE BOX 4.1

CESARE BECCARIA

Beccaria was born on March 15, 1738 into an aristocratic family in Milan, Italy. In 1758, he graduated from the University of Pavia, where he obtained a law degree (Monachesi, 1973).

Upon graduating, he returned to Milan were he joined the "Accademia dei Transformati," a group interested in literary and social issues. It was through this society that he read some of the great philosophical writings of the day (e.g., Francis Bacon, David Hume, and Jean Jacques Rousseau). He also met and formed a new and stronger political group with Pietro Verri, a noted economist. The new society called itself the "Accademia dei Pugni" (Academy of Fists).

With much encouragement from Verri, Beccaria wrote about legal and prison reform. Pietro's brother Alessandro took Beccaria into the prisons to see for himself the need to write about penal issues. Beccaria anonymously published his essay *Dei delitti e delle pene* (*On Crimes and Punishment*) in 1764. He was only 26 years of age. This small monograph of approximately 100 pages has been heralded as a masterpiece and the foundation of the classical school of criminological thought.

History is somewhat vague as to whether Beccaria actually wrote the essay himself. In fact, Graeme Newman and Pietro Marongiu (1990) suggest that he may have plagiarised the work. Based on known facts, various scholars feel that Pietro and/or his colleagues may have somehow contributed to the final manuscript (Monachesi, 1973). Either way, beginning with the second edition, Beccaria was listed as the author.

Initially his treatise was not widely embraced. In 1765, the Pope placed Beccaria's work on a list of banned books for its "extreme rationalism" (Bierne, 1991). In time, however, his plea for the ending of torture drew increasing international acclaim. The great French philosopher Voltaire (1694–1778) invited him to Paris to meet with his group. He also received requests from a number of foreign governments to assist with the revision of their criminal codes. Among them was the Russian Empress Catherine II. However, Beccaria did not follow through with many of the invitations.

Beccaria never produced anything else of note. He eventually took a position as a professor of political economy in the Palatine School, but after two years left to become a magistrate and returned to a relatively quiet life. He died on November 11, 1794 at age 56.

Beccaria's Key Ideas

In their summary of Beccaria's work, Martin et al. (1990:8) point out that Beccaria "did not specifically set out to develop a theory pertaining to crime and justice, but rather simply wanted to delineate the parameters of a just system with criminals. Whether he intended to or not, Beccaria developed an outline for a theory of justice."

In his 1764 essay, Beccaria argued for a minimal punishment as being necessary for social defence and the protection of society. He emphasized fair and proportionate punishment for the harm done to society, and he embraced the concept of free will, arguing that if three basic conditions could be met, most potential offenders would be deterred. The conditions are **certainty** of punishment, **swiftness** of justice, and measured **severity** of punishment. To this day, many legal systems struggle to maintain these essential elements as part of their criminal justice systems.

From Beccaria's essay (1963) it is possible to identify four general and grand principles that epitomize the classical doctrine.

1. **Equality:** By strictly and objectively interpreting the law, all will be treated equally. In the classical sense, there can be no consideration of personal character, no entertainment of motive, or any justification for individualized punishment when trying a criminal case. As Beccaria notes, "the measure of punishment is not the sensibility of the crime, but the public injury" (p.70).

2. **Liberty:** We have the inalienable right to be protected from the potential abuses of power by the state. Beccaria states, "only the law can decree punishment for crime" (p.13). He also argued that the law cannot be applied retroactively and that there can be no punishment without law—"nor can society deprive him of public protection before it has been decided that he has in fact violated the conditions ..." (p.30).

3. **Utilitarianism:** Beccaria believed the major goal of the sovereign is the greatest happiness for the greatest number. Hence, justice should entail utility rather than retaliation and retribution—punishment is to be useful—"to instil fear in other men" (p.30). Therefore, as noted above, punishment should be

viewed as a deterrent. Only by ensuring the conditions of certainty, swiftness, and severity is it possible to achieve the maximum deterrent efficiency. "The severity of the punishment of itself emboldens men to commit the very wrong it is supposed to prevent" (p.43); therefore, "it is better to prevent crimes than to punish them. This is the ultimate end of every good legislation" (p. 93).

4. **Humanitarianism:** Punishment should not only be fair but humane. Beccaria was opposed to torture and cruel punishment (see pp. 30–36) and he was against the death penalty (see pp. 45–52): "This useless prodigality of torments" (p. 45) for "(i)t is not the intensity of punishment that has the greatest effect … but its duration" (pp. 46–47).

An Enduring Influence

It has been over 200 years since Beccaria's classic work was first published and yet it continues to command several pages in virtually every introductory criminology textbook. His fundamental principles still represent the foundation on which social policy in Canada, and in many other countries, is based.

His work, however, has not gone unchallenged (see, for example, Newman and Marongiu, 1990). Criticism should take into account, though, that Beccaria wrote his essay in a time of considerable turmoil, when the scientific technique of gathering objective data to support one's views was not yet in vogue. Furthermore, it was not, apparently, his intention to produce a theory on penal justice (Maconochie, 1973).

In **summary**, his enduring influence on justice policy and the foundation his work gave to social control theories, social learning theories, and rational choice theories should not be overlooked. His enduring influence on criminology arguably places him in a league by himself and renders him worthy of respect and careful reading to this day.

Many others have carried forward Beccaria's ideas, among them, **Jeremy Bentham** (1748–1832) (see Box 4.2). In his book *A Fragment on Government and an Introduction to the Principles of Morals and Legislation*, published in 1789, Bentham developed the foundation of **utilitarianism**—"the greatest happiness of the greatest number." Like Beccaria, he subscribed to the concept of free will. He argued that people weigh the probabilities of pleasure against the risk of present and future pain. In recognizing the complexity of the process involved in decision-making, Bentham developed a quasi-mathematical formula for calculating how much pain was needed to deter someone from committing an offence. He referred to his formula as *felicitous calculus* (moral calculus) (Geis, 1973). But, as DeKeseredy and Schwartz (1996:164) observed, it might more appropriately be termed "interesting guesswork."

JEREMY BENTHAM

Jeremy Bentham could read by the age of three, play the violin by age five and study French and Latin by age six. He entered the University of Oxford at age 12! And as Geis (1973:66) points out, while his ideas of moral calculus may not have been the most sound, "the practical results ..., stand as major monuments." His ideas of justice were instrumental in mitigating the severity of punishment, removing the exclusionary laws of evidence, and introducing principles of crime prevention into the judicial process. In 1799, Bentham was asked to design a prison that would embody his fundamental ideas. He subsequently made plans for what he called "Panopticon" or "inspection home." The intent of the design was to enable all cells to be viewed from a central control area, which he believed would allow for constructive supervision and reform. Although never built, some of the early American prisons were modelled after the design, and today, certain young offender institutions in Canada have incorporated a modified version of the architectural concepts. As Geis notes in his concluding quote, "I do not know of a single law reform effected since Bentham's time which cannot be traced to his influence" (p.67).

In the classical tradition, Bentham focused on legal reforms that would support the utilitarian doctrine. He suggested that since punishment is in itself harmful, it can be justified only if it prevents greater social harm than it produces. Therefore, the certainty of apprehension and punishment could serve as a better deterrent than the severity of punishment itself. Hence, while punishment brings pain, if it can prevent crime, then it will give society at large greater pleasure.

Bentham, along with other noted British philosophers such as James Mill and John Stuart Mill, believed that since we are rational and **hedonistic** (pleasure-seeking), the risk of punishment (i.e., harm or pain) could **reform** criminals and prevent them from wanting to offend. From this notion we derived the term "penitentiaries" (to do penance), which could serve both as punishment and an opportunity to reform oneself (i.e., corrections). Punishment in the form of incapacitation not only removed the risk from society but also deprived offenders of their "greater good." Furthermore, the certainty of punishment could function as a **deterrent** to would-be criminals (see Box 4.3). In other words, people learn to become afraid to commit crime because they fear punishment and loss of freedom.

Deterrence Concepts and Theory

Deterrence theory, a fundamental dictum of the classical school, is based on the premise that individuals have free will and that they are rational in their thinking. Proponents of the deterrence theory also base their ideas on learning theory principles (Chapters 6 and 7). Zimring and Hawkins (1975) identified two levels of deterrence: The first is **specific**—it focuses on the individual offender by punishing the offender. Offenders learn from their exposure, referred to as associational learning: one learns to associate a specific painful stimulus with a specific behaviour pattern. The second level of deterrence is **general,** which refers to the deterrence of non-criminals from any possible future criminal activity. This is imitative learning. Through the principles of certainty, swiftness, and severity of punishment, society in general will be deterred from wanting to commit crime. There may, however, be "conditional" circumstances in which legal threats only affect those who are interested in conforming to the norms of society (see Sherman et al., 1992).

Evaluation of the Classical School

It all sounds good, you say, but does the fear of punishment really prevent crime? Can criminals be rehabilitated?

Attempts to answer these questions have produced many publications, textbooks, and "new and better" programs. This is not the place to try to do justice to such a loaded issue. These questions are the subject of other courses. However, a brief observation at this point is warranted.

Overall, the research on **deterrence** is inconclusive (Paternoster, Saltzman, Waldo, and Chiricos, 1983; Winterdyk, 2000b). Some of the earlier studies reported that under certain circumstances it does appear to work (see Gibbs, 1975). Williams and Hawkins (1986) found that the fear of arrest could act as a deterrent especially when linked to the indirect social penalties of arrest. They identified three types of social costs:

1. *Commitment costs*: Arrests may have an adverse effect on future opportunities such as employment.
2. *Attachment costs*: Arrests can result in harm to, or loss of, personal circumstances.
3. *Stigma*: Arrests can negatively affect one's personal and/or public image.

Overall, however, based on his review of the deterrence literature, Akers (1994:55) concludes that the correlations found "between the perceptions of risk and subsequent offenses are too weak to validate deterrence theory." Even when a modified version of the deterrence theory (e.g., Ronald Clarke's *Rational Choice Theory* (see Chapter 8)) came into vogue, the empirical evidence was limited by the inability of the theory's supporters to clearly define the concepts of "reasoning criminal" or the "rational component" in crime (Ibid). Furthermore, Clarke argued that the rational choice theory is little more than a revision of the social learning theory.

Although the Canadian public feels that the law reflects its values, we are less optimistic about whether the laws are enforced equally (Brillon, 1987). In fact, when there is a high risk of apprehension, the administration of punishment deterrence is likely to have some impact. However when the risk of sanction is low, deterrence has a limited impact (see, for example, Ekstedt and Griffiths, 1988). In addition to various methodological problems, (being able to interpret data in the absence of controlled studies, and the inherent complexity of the concept), the elements of punishment will continue to be debated and researched for some time yet (see Chapter 14).

As for reforming and rehabilitating criminals, the classical doctrine has met with yet another nemesis. "Success" of punishment or correctional practices is often measured by **recidivism** or relapse into crime. Aside from methodological and definitional issues, recidivism rates among both adults and young offenders across Canada are not promising (see Chapter 3).

Where does this leave the classical school of thought? Mannheim perhaps best summarized it when he said the classical school is "too static and sterile to guide further progress" (1973:35).

Classical School Influence on Canadian Criminal Justice Policies

Attempts to control crime through the classical doctrines fell short of their good intentions and sound rationales. Nevertheless, some of the major concepts derived from the school are entrenched in the *Canadian Constitution*, the *Criminal Code*, and the *Young Offenders Act*. These include:

- The idea that humans have free will;
- The concept of utilitarianism;
- The existence of civil rights and due process of law;
- Rules of evidence and testimony;
- Being held accountable for one's misdeeds;
- Determinant sentences;
- The swiftness and certainty of punishment;
- The threat of punishment serving as a deterrent; and
- No justification for capital punishment.

Perhaps the most influential modern-day revisionist of the role of punishment has been Michel Foucault (1926–1984). Many of his ideas about the role of punishment can be found in his 1977 book, *Discipline and Punish*. And although it is beyond the scope of this chapter to discuss his points in detail, the essence of his argument is that punishment should not be seen simply as "the independent development of legal or economic institutions" (Barak, 1998:87). Punishment, he argues, is, rather, an interrelationship between power, knowledge, and the body, that is affected by such factors as economics, social development, political ideologies, and changing mass communication (Ibid).

In spite of its attributes, the classical perspective failed to acknowledge individual differences, motivation, and situational circumstances (Geis, 1973). For example, if you are caught speeding because you are rushing a dying or injured person to the hospital, should you incur the same penalty as when you are speeding simply for pleasure? Similarly, should a woman who, after years of being physically abused kills her partner, receive the same punishment as someone who kills for greed? Some might argue that "the law is the law" (e.g., Beccaria's principle of equality), while others might beg for some compassion and discretion when examining the particular incident. These types of questions gave rise to the neoclassical perspective.

Neoclassical Criminology

The concepts of the neoclassical school of thought were first incorporated in the French code of 1791. Although its assumptions have remained the cornerstone of criminal justice policy, from a criminological perspective the neoclassical school did not receive much attention until the 1980s and 1990s. This revival was in response to the failure of rehabilitation and a public outcry for a return to harsher punishments (deKeseredy and Schwartz, 1996). The public began to demand lengthier prison terms, a return to corporal punishment and even a reinstatement of capital punishment (see Box 4.4)—a **just deserts** model. The public asked that punishment should fit the crime—a concept in keeping with the classical school.

REALITY CHECK BOX 4.4

THE SINGAPORE EXPERIMENT—A CANADIAN INTEREST

Singapore has one of the most punitive penal codes in the world. In 1994, Singapore drew considerable media attention when Michael Fay, a native of Ohio (then 18 years of age), was detained for defacing automobiles with spray paint. Fay received four lashes after a four-month prison sentence. While the media debated the severity and rationale of corporal punishment, the decline in the crime rates suggests that—it works! The overall crime rates of the United States run between 200 per cent and 380 per cent higher than those in Singapore (Weichman, 1994). However, while the overall crime rate decreased from 1988 through 1993, the number of youth crimes increased by almost 30 per cent. More than a third were caught shoplifting and about 1 in 10 youths were arrested for stealing bicycles.

Alberta Reform MP Art Hanger, a strong advocate of corporal punishment, drew considerable media attention when, in March of 1996 he announced plans to go to Singapore to study the country's system of corporal punishment. However, due to party politics he backed out at the last minute. Afterwards, he defended his views by stating that, through public meetings, he had received support for his planned trip (Albert, 1996) (also see Appendix 5).

WHAT DO YOU THINK? BOX 4.5

BRING BACK CORPORAL PUNISHMENT?

During Canada's pioneering days, corporal punishment represented the most common method of punishing offenders and it was typically imposed in public (Carrigan, 1991). Should we bring back corporal punishment? If so, what kinds of limits would you impose on its use?

Spawned by the limitations and criticisms levied at the classical school, the ideas of the neoclassical school were pioneered by Rossi in Italy and Garraud and Henri Joly in France (Fattah, 1997). While endorsing the major principles of the classical school, this new perspective entailed two fundamental exceptions:

(1) Rejection of the rigidity of the classical system of punishment; and

(2) A degree of subjectivity when assessing criminal responsibility—**discretion**. The French Penal Code of 1804–1811 was the first legal code to incorporate these ideas and the Canadian *Criminal Code* has been written in a neoclassical fashion.

The neoclassical perspective assumes that individuals choose to commit crime after calculating whether crime's potential rewards outweigh its potential risks (Cornish and Clarke, 1986). Today the perspective is generally grouped under the rubric of *rational choice theory* (Chapter 7). For example, the *routine activities theory* (Chapter 8), can be seen as a rational choice theory. It assumes that criminals base their decisions on the perceived attractiveness of a target, the absence of guardianship, and level of motivation (Clarke and Felson, 1993).

DeKeseredy and Schwartz (1996) suggest that James Q. Wilson has been instrumental in the revival of neoclassical thinking. Many of his ideas and the arguments for the revival can be found in his frequently-cited book *Thinking about Crime* (1975). Wilson argues that since we cannot seem to identify the root causes of crime, policymakers should direct their attention to better deterring people from committing crimes. This is very much in line with the writings of Beccaria and Bentham. For example, Wilson agrees that punishment should be both swift and certain and that the punishment should be proportionate to the severity of the crime. However, none of the classical or neoclassical scholars have defined how one measures the degree of seriousness of a crime. Is this a moral issue that implies that crimes are not constant but relative to time and place, or, as a Calgarian lawyer was once quoted as saying, "How much justice can we afford"? Could the seriousness of a crime change with circumstances? For example, during times of war, killing is considered "acceptable."[3]

Wilson is less concerned with severity than with certainty and swiftness, because the more "Draconian" (see Box 4.6) the sentence, the greater the chances for a **plea bargain** (Wilson, 1995). A plea bargain is characteristic of a neoclassical approach because it provides an opportunity for the defence and Crown to reach an arrangement in which the accused agrees to plead guilty for certain considerations (Cousineau and Verdun-Jones, 1979).

WHAT DO YOU THINK? BOX 4.6

DRACONIAN LAW AND CAPITAL PUNISHMENT

In 621 BC, Athenian law was codified by the Greek statesman Draco—hence its name. The codification brought greater equality to all Greeks as the lower class was given the right to vote. Considering this, one may wonder why the name carries such pejorative connotations. This is easily explained: Draco's codification prescribed death for most criminal offences (Bedau, 1996).

Reference to capital punishment can be found in the Code of Hammurabi, Mosaic Law, and even the Bible, which prescribes death for more than 30 different crimes ranging from murder (see Exodus 21:12) to fornication (see Deuteronomy 22:13) (Bedau, 1996). Canada practised capital punishment until 1976 (see Boyd, 1988). The last execution took place in 1962 at the Don Jail in Toronto (see Chapter 9). And although the murder rate increased by nearly 70 per cent between 1962 and 1975, the rate had decreased some 30 per cent by the late 1990s (see Table 9.3 – Chapter 9).

The death penalty is still in effect in 40 U.S. states—in October 1998 there were 3,517 inmates on death row. Since January 1, 1973, when the Legal Defence and Educational Fund was established and started to keep death row statistics, there have been 481 executions, 76 commuted cases, 1,642 cases where convictions/sentences were reversed, and 98 inmates who died of natural causes while under the death sentence.

Whether capital punishment is Draconian or a "cruel and unusual" form of punishment or whether it is a "punishment fitting of the crime" has been subject to numerous philosophical, moralistic, and secular-based arguments. In 1994, 59 per cent of Canadians indicated they were in favour of reinstating capital punishment (*Fraser Forum*, 1995). How do you feel about the use of capital punishment? Can, or should it be, justified under certain circumstances?

Please see Box 9.2 for additional details.

WHAT DO YOU THINK? BOX 4.7

CAPITAL PUNISHMENT ACROSS CANADA

A 1998 POLLARA survey found that while 48% of Canadians favour the return of capital punishment there is considerable regional variation. Residents of BC expressed the strongest support (61%) while the Atlantic Region expressed the lowest level of support (48%) (Naumetz, 1999). As recommended by some Reform Party members, should the choice of reinstating capital punishment be left to the provinces' discretion?

Today, those interested in the neoclassical perspective are mainly economists (deKeseredy and Schwartz, 1996). Assuming people are rational and calculating, all that differentiates a criminal from a non-criminal is the degree to which any individual feels the benefits of a criminal act outweigh its cost. An economist might suggest, for example, that the reason property crime is more prevalent than violent crime is because the chances of being caught are considerably less. In addition, the neoclassical perspective is closely aligned with *deterrence theory*, which assumes that "good" laws (i.e., punishment) can deter criminals. Therefore, the current orientation of the neoclassical perspective is to stress the **deterrent** effect of punishment. Is the pain of being caught and the severity of the punishment enough to make any rational person think twice? (See Chapter 14—restorative justice.) Similarly, imprisonment can be justified on the grounds that removal of liberty and social comforts can and should be severe enough to deter not only the specific offender but anyone who might even remotely think about committing a crime.

As mentioned earlier, the literature on the effectiveness of deterrence, both specific and general, has not been promising. Numerous studies have shown that a majority of prisoners return to their former life of crime on release (for a general review, see Esktedt and Griffiths, 1988). Similarly, in many North African countries, theft used to be punishable by severing the offending hand. However, pickpocketing and theft are still practised. In the United States, 40 states still exercise capital punishment for certain serious offences, yet these offences are still being committed. In 1995–1996, Ontario and British Columbia introduced zero tolerance for speeding—people still speed. Cigarette packages clearly advertise the negative consequences of smoking—statistics show smoking has increased among young people (McKie, 1989). Is there an alternative?

The Roots of Positivism: The Statistical School

Before the emergence of the (Italian) positivist school, positivistically-oriented research on crime had already been conducted by Adolphe Quetelet (1796–1874) of Belgium and André Guerry (1802–1866) of France. Both statisticians, they examined the **social statistics** on information that was available. Their line of inquiry and examination represented the forerunner of the *ecological school* (see Chapter 7). Among other findings, they observed "variations in crime rates by climate and season and observed the same age and sex differences we find among criminals today" (Williams and McShane, 1994:3).

Other pre-Italian positivistic research included scientifically-oriented studies such as those of Jean Baptiste della Porte (1535–1615) who studied the relationship between body characteristics and crime. He is generally considered to be the founder of human physiognomy (the art of judging character from features of face and form of body). Francis Gall (1758–1828) studied the relationship between the external conformation of the brain and behaviour. This "science" is referred to as **phrenology**. Gall and Johann Spurzheim (1776–1853) collaborated to map the relationship of bumps on the head to behaviour, especially abnormal behaviour. Spurzheim would later acknowledge that the bumps were predisposing factors and that free will could be a mediating factor.[4]

Towards the latter half of the nineteenth century a unique form of **positivism** began to emerge in Italy.

The Italian Positivist School of Criminology

The French sociologist and philosopher **Auguste Comte** (1798–1857) is generally credited with coining the term "positivism" and is recognized as the **father of sociology**. He used the term "positivist" to describe what he considered the final social developmental stage. This occurs when people embrace a rational, scientific view of the world, as opposed to relying on metaphysical (i.e., philosophical, abstract general reasoning) explanations (Williams and McShane, 1994, 1999).

In criminology, the positivist perspective was first embraced by the **holy three of criminology**—Cesare Lombroso (1835–1909), Raffaelo Garofalo (1852–1934), and Enrico Ferri (1856–1929). It is Lombroso (see Box 4.8), however, who is most often recognized as the father of modern criminology. As noted above, in the neoclassical school, there were a number of other researchers before him who had applied the scientific method to identify criminals but it was Lombroso who focused exclusively on criminals.

PROFILE BOX 4.8

CESARE LOMBROSO—"THE FATHER OF MODERN CRIMINOLOGY"

In his account of Lombroso, Marvin Wolfgang (1973:232) begins by noting that "in the history of criminology probably no name has been eulogized or attacked so much... More has been written by and about Lombroso than any other criminologist." Encouraged by his mother, Lombroso pursued, and excelled at, education. In 1859, at the age of 24, he obtained a medical degree with a specialty in surgery from the University of Genoa. Upon graduating, he volunteered as an army physician. With time on his hands, he decided to take anatomical measurements of soldiers as a possible way of determining from which region of Italy they came. During the course of observing over 3,000 soldiers he found a positive correlation between soldiers who had tattoos and those who were involved in some type of military or civilian rule infractions. He later obtained permission to study mental patients and began to solidify his theory of criminality. Many of his ideas and observations were first published in *l'Uomo delinquente* (*The Criminal Man*) in 1876. By its fifth and final edition in 1896 the book had been expanded from 256 to 1,903 pages and had received international acclaim (Schafer, 1976).

It was at the University of Turin, with the assistance of two students, Garofalo and Ferri, that Lombroso refined his general theory that criminals are distinguishable from non-criminals by different physical anomalies, which he considered to be **atavistic** or degenerative in origin. He would also later collaborate with William Ferrero, his daughter Gina's husband, to write the first book on female offenders. It was simply called *The Female Offender* (Wolfgang, 1973).

By all accounts, Lombroso was a celebrated man and much sought after. In fact, in 1908 Professor John Henry Wigmore* (1863–1943), Dean of Law at Northwestern University in Chicago, offered him the position of Harris Lecturer. However, due to ill health, Lombroso was not able to accept the position. On October 19, 1909, Lombroso passed away and, as requested, his brain was placed in the Institute of Anatomy at the University of Turin.

*In 1909, Wigmore was the primary architect of the National Conference on Criminal Law and Criminology in Chicago. It was the first conference of its kind in North America and represented the dawn of a new era in the history of American criminal jurisprudence. He was the founder of the prestigious *Journal of Criminal Law and Criminology* in 1907 (see Millar (1973) for an extensive review).

Lombroso's Key Ideas

Lombroso's ideas of criminality were influenced by the works of such notables as Charles Darwin and his evolutionary theory, Ruldof Virchow's ideas on organic regression, and Paul Broca's methods of describing and classifying anatomical features. To make sense of these ideas he grounded his thinking in Comptian positivism (the need for observable and measurable facts). The process led Lombroso to develop his biological deterministic theory of criminality, based on the concept of **atavism**. Lombroso used the term to characterize those individuals who, based on some morphological (i.e., the study of body forms) characteristics, were considered not fully evolved. They were "throwbacks" to a more primitive time. He believed the cause was hereditary. Among the physical malformations (he called them "criminal stigmata"), he catalogued the asymmetric face, excessive jaw, eye defects, large nose, large ears, receding forehead, long arms, swollen lips and many others. These physical anomalies could be inherited or indirectly manifested because of insanity, syphilis, epilepsy, or alcoholism (Martin et al., 1990), the latter point reflecting the fact that Lombroso recognized that environment can play a role in an individual's development.

Types of criminals: Lombroso's criminal typology involved four main classifications:

1. The **born criminal**. This term, which was coined by Ferri, was used to describe criminals who were born moral imbeciles and epileptics. Born criminals supposedly accounted for one-third of all criminals.

2. The **criminal by passion**. This criminal type was mainly used to describe female offenders. Criminals by passion commit crimes based on their "pure spirit of altruism," for example, the brother who kills the man who raped his sister, or the wife who kills her unfaithful husband. He also noted that because of their nature, this type suffers more from remorse than from the penalty of the law. Criminals by passion are more likely to commit suicide after the crime.

3. The **insane criminal**. These individuals commit crimes because they lack the mental capacity to understand or appreciate their acts. Kleptomaniacs, nymphomaniacs, imbeciles, and habitual drunkards are among the insane types. They tend to commit cruel, impulsive, and obscene acts.

4. The **occasional criminal** has four sub-types. *Pseudocriminals* break the law by accident; *criminaloids* have weak dispositions; *habitual criminals'* constitution predisposes them to crime: poor education, poor family upbringing, and other native environmental factors can bring on criminal tendencies; and *epileptoids*, born with epilepsy, could "form the basis for the development of their criminal tendencies" (Wolfgang, 1973:253).

WHAT DO YOU THINK? BOX 4.9

THE INFLUENCE OF THE POSITIVIST SCHOOL

Modern scientific criminology emerged out of the work of the Italian Positivist School of Criminology. It attempted to eliminate the notion of free will and focus on individual biological and mental traits that predispose people to crime. To what extent do you think individual and biological traits are predictors of crime? Discuss how positivist principles are portrayed in the movies.

It is interesting to note that while Lombroso's findings have been largely discredited, the impact of the scientific method and possible deterministic or "soft" deterministic links to criminality have spawned numerous theories. Most notable among these theories are those based on biological and psychological principles (see Chapters 5 and 6).

Ferri and Garfalo (see Box 4.10), both lawyers by training, not only contributed to Lombroso's ideas but introduced some significant elements into the conception of criminal causality. Aside from coining the term *born criminal*, which Lombroso was happy to embrace, Ferri argued that crime was caused by "physical" (race, geography, temperature, and climate), "anthropological" (age, gender, organic, and psychological), and "social" (customs, economic, population density, and religion) factors (Williams and McShane, 1994:33).

PROFILES BOX 4.10

ENRICO FERRI

Ferri's work and novel ideas did not go unnoticed. When fascist leader Benito Mussolini came to power in the early 1920s he asked Ferri to prepare a new criminal code. Ferri did so but it was never accepted by the Italian parliament. Sellin (1973) described Ferri as the most brilliant of the "holy three" and his distinguished career is a testament to his significance to the positivist movement. One of his most famous works was *Criminal Sociology* (1884). It contains many of his theoretical ideas, which place him deservedly among the holy three.

RAFFAELO GAROFALO

Garofalo's contribution came through his insightful challenges against *"naturalistic" criminals*. He argued that the concepts of crime and delinquency need to be defined before attributing deterministic causal factors. While he did acknowledge that certain people are morally less developed than others, he believed behaviour is eventually influenced by an interaction of environmental, circumstantial, and organic variables. From this premise he developed his *natural crime theory*, which was meant to address the shortcomings he saw in Lombroso's theory and the "lack of accuracy and exactness" in Ferri's model (Schafer, 1976).

An Enduring Influence

Collectively, "the holy three" of criminology helped to forge a school of thought and a line of inquiry that has given rise to much investigation and theoretical development. Several of the more recent lines of inquiry that are positivist in character include: sociobiology (Mednick and Christiansen, 1977); biopsychology (Jeffery, 1990), and evolutive theory (Ellis, 1982, 1988) (see Chapter 8 for further discussion).

Evaluation of the Positivist School

Which came first, the chicken or the egg? Or, in the case of traditional criminology, what is more important when trying to prevent crime: (1) changing social conditions such as lack of opportunity, peer pressure and early childhood socialization, through the classical model that relies on social reform via the law; or (2) changing individual factors, such as diet, drugs, alcohol, or genetic or constitutional conditions, through treatment strategies? Is there such a thing as a "criminal type" or a "constitutional crime marker"?

Both the classical and positivist themes have supporters and both continue to have an impact on the operations of the criminal justice system and research venues of criminologists today. And although Hackler (1994:109) suggests that "Neither of these schools serve us well in terms of reducing crime ...," positivist ideas continue to have an impact on the trial process. Judges tend to be more willing to consider genetic conditions, dietary influences and biochemical imbalances (see Chapter 8). Correction programs continue to experiment with "better" treatment programs such as those for particular types of offenders (e.g., sex offenders, compulsive gamblers, etc.). In addition, young offenders continue to receive "special" treatment under the ***parens patriae*** doctrine—from the Latin meaning "pseudo parent," a concept derived directly from the positivist school of thought. Under English common law, the doctrine held the king responsible for those individuals who were deemed unable to abide by the law. This doctrine was later entrenched in the *Juvenile Delinquents Act* of 1908, which granted juvenile courts procedural rights to deal informally with young offenders in the same way as their parents would have. In addition, crime-fighting strategies such as social engineering (e.g., increased street lighting and the provision of health services and subsidized housing for the poor) are based on deterministic principles. Finally, with the emergence and growing acceptance of an interdisciplinary perspective, recent positivist-based research in the biosocial, bioenvironmental, and biopsychological areas, as well as in urban planning, have resulted in some promising findings (see Chapters 5 and 8).

Nevertheless, biological, psychological, and sociological determinism continue to be challenged on four key issues:

- Weakness of methodology;
- Limited application to the understanding of white collar crime, organized crime, and political crime;
- A general fear that positivist-based policies will be intrusive and possibly lead to totalitarianism; and
- The failure to distinguish clearly between the role of environment and heredity (Schafer, 1976).

In **summary**, the battle between law and science (free will and determinism) may not have lived up to all the expectations of either side, but the struggle has nonetheless had a major impact on criminology, criminological thought, and criminal justice.

Law vs. Science

By the turn of the twentieth century the two primary schools of criminological thought had forged their identities and made their mark on how we view criminology and criminal justice today. Figure 4–1 illustrates how their principles have become integral characteristics of the criminal justice system.

Classicism is based on reforming criminal law and maintaining social order through criminal responsibility. It assumes individuals are capable of intent (free will) and that punishment is therefore justified on the grounds of moral guilt and a criminal mind. **Retribution** and **revenge** are the traditional objectives of criminal law under the classical school of thought.

Positivism is an outgrowth of the scientific revolution. It embraces determinism. Rather than punish someone who may not be fully capable of controlling his/her criminal actions, special consideration and conditioning might be required. Positivists subscribe to the doctrines of **reform** and **rehabilitation**. Scientific criminology (i.e., positivists) has given us juvenile court, parole and probation, indeterminate sentences, and special "correctional" programs for different types of offenders (e.g., sex offenders, compulsive gamblers, shoplifters).

LAW AND SCIENCE IN CONFLICT

ELEMENTS OF THE CRIMINAL JUSTICE SYSTEM

Law Enforcement   Judicial Process   Corrections   Trial   Sentencing

CLASSICAL IDEOLOGY   POSITIVIST IDEOLOGY

- enforce the law   - guilt or innocence   - rehabilitation—mitigating
- maintain order   - due process   circumstances
- minimal discretion   - legal rights   - best interest
- "follow the book"   - individual/public
- apprehension

Although Figure 4–1 may suggest that there are two schools of thought present, operationally the criminal justice system is based on the classical legal doctrine. For example, even today, police and lawyers make decisions based on the law first and seldom acknowledge human nature or information from other behavioural sciences (Brantingham and Brantingham, 1984). While mandated to offer special rehabilitation and reform programs, corrections are usually underfunded, have insufficiently-trained staff, and are too over-crowded to adequately execute individualized/group treatment programs (Ekstedt and Jackson, 1996). Criminological ideas and research, on the other hand, are based on the scientific and positivist models and are interested in the etiology of crime and criminals.

This dualism has created conflict between the criminal justice system (i.e., law) and criminology (i.e., science). As Jeffery (1973), along with others, has noted, historically there has been a lack of theoretical integration between law and science. In Figure 4–1 it can also be seen that there is no common integrated model of criminal justice by which the primary agencies operate towards a common goal through common strategies. It is essential for students studying criminology to recognize these inherent conflicts, as they play a significant role in how we study crime and criminal behaviour.

A Move Toward an Integrated School of Thought

Criminology must find a way to integrate these theoretical differences. Even though crime has been one of our major concerns for the past two decades, we have few positive outcomes to show for the time and vast sums of money we have put into programs dealing with crime and criminals. Crime rates, for the most part (Chapters 9 and 10), have been steadily escalating since the early 1960s and the cost of maintaining our criminal justice system gets more expensive each year (see Chapters 1 and 2).

As was suggested in Chapter 1, what is needed is an interdisciplinary approach that can study crime and criminality scientifically. Sociologists and psychologists need to know, or work with, the law or lawyers, while lawyers need to know the behavioural sciences. Most criminology programs across the country are composed of staff from a variety of disciplinary backgrounds. They have the foundation to offer interdisciplinary training to the student. The common interdisciplinary approach that should be adopted by all programs is one that addresses the problem of crime and criminals through prevention.

Before we delve into this new, emerging criminological perspective, let us take a brief look at some of the pioneers who have helped shape the discipline, and influenced our thinking about crime, criminality, and criminal justice.

Following the reasoning of Jeffery (1973) we will present these pioneers in chronological order, rather than try to locate them in a particular school of thought. It is their contributions to criminological reform that are of primary interest. However, as Martin et al. (1990) note in their compilation of pioneers, by placing them in chronological order they often fall within the parameters of the existing ideology.

The list, for practical reasons, has been abbreviated. However, every attempt has been made to acknowledge most of the major sub-areas within criminology. In order to do so, this section will again follow the lead of Jeffery (1973).

Criminology at Work: Pioneers in Criminal Justice

Prison Reform

Earlier it was noted that corrections and incarceration have not always been as we know them today. One pioneer who has had a very measurable impact on penal reform is Scottish-born Captain Alexander Maconochie (1787–1860). In Australia he is probably best remembered for his services at the prison colony at Van Dieman's Land on Tasmania and Norfolk Island in the South West Pacific. It was while serving as the private secretary to Van Dieman's Land Lieutenant-Governor, Sir John Franklin in Tasmania, that Maconochie formulated many of his penal reform policies, many of which were adopted and put into practice.

His firsthand witnessing of the treatment and transportation of English convicts to Van Dieman (discovered by Dutch navigator Abel Tasman in 1643) prompted Maconochie to point out "that cruel and harsh punishment debase not only the victim, but also the society which employs them ... rather the objective be to reform the offender so that he should leave prison capable of useful citizenship, and a better man than when he entered the prison gates" (Barry, 1973:86–87). From his various writings he devised five ideas of prison reform, which were considered novel at the time. They were:

1. Sentences should not be measured by time but by the ability of a prisoner to complete a specified quantity of labour—a task-oriented sentence and a concept of indeterminate sentences;

2. The quantity of labour is determined by the gravity of the offence and the degree to which the prisoner improves himself;

3. While in prison, a prisoner should earn everything he receives;

4. When working in groups, all are answerable to each other's conduct; and

5. As the prisoner nears his release date, attention should be given to preparing him for release into society.

During Maconochie's service he introduced other novel practices, such as allowing prisoners to use proper utensils, providing educational and spiritual services, and granting a variety of other privileges formerly considered unworthy of prisoners. In essence, Maconochie recognized that prison was *not a place to punish but was a place where one served one's punishment*. Barry (1973) summarizes Maconochie's major contribution in four points: (1) reward: prisoners must earn their release through industrious labour and good conduct; (2) individual influence: for prisons to offer constructive support, prisons should not exceed more than 300 persons, or 100 for more serious offenders; (3) prisons should provide opportunities for gradual approximation of release (e.g., half-way houses); and (4) there should be strict supervision after discharge.

FYI BOX 4.11

Confinement in Canada

The building of Kingston Penitentiary, in 1835, marked the beginning of the prison industry in Canada. Before it was built, there was considerable debate over whether confinement should be viewed as punishment or an opportunity for reformation. The *Brown Commission,* of 1848–1849, was the first major report calling for more humane treatment of prisoners.

Many of Maconochie's ideas of penal reform have found their way into Canada's penal history at one time or another and he could be considered the most important of these early pioneers. However, other reformers have also made their mark in the history of penal reform. For example, John Haviland (1792–1852) gave us the radical model, which was used in building a number of the earlier prisons in Canada, and John Howard (see Box 4.12) was instrumental in the establishment of prisoner advocacy groups. The writings of the French lawyer Charles Lucas (1803–1889) set the foundation for a system of maximum and minimum sentences and a system for the classification of prisoners. He also emphasized the need to separate adults from young offenders (Normandeau, 1973). Many of Lucas's ideas can be seen across Canada in today's correctional system (see Jackson and Ekstedt, 1996).

Modern Law Enforcement

There are other courses within criminology programs that focus on policing and its related subject areas. Therefore, rather than try to do such a broad topic justice, the purpose here is to provide a brief biographical sketch of one of the major pioneers of modern policing.

Western policing can be traced back to around 1035 when the Danish King Canute set up a system in which all males over the age of 12 were bound by law to keep the peace. This was referred to as the **frankpledge** and participants were members of a **tithing,** a small administrative division. Until the eighteenth century, law enforcement came under the rule of the sovereign and was somewhat informal in structure (see Box 4.13). With the advent of the Industrial Revolution, the problems society faced under an agricultural setting began to change. They could no longer be dealt with on an informal basis. The solution that emerged was the creation of a bureaucracy—the foundation of modern policing (see Stansfield, 1996).

From a criminological viewpoint, it is interesting to examine the roots of modern policing from a number of perspectives, including administrative, social, psychological, and legalistic ones.

FYI BOX 4.13

The Roots of Policing

Some of the terms and phrases we use today had very practical origins. For example, remember those old western movies where the sheriff rounded up his **posse comaitatus**? This phrase, derived from Latin, means "power of the county," and **sheriff** is derived from the old English practice of the king appointing a representative, called a "reeve" from each shire (county) to enforce the laws. He became known as the shire-reeve or sheriff. As for **constables**, they came into being in 1285 through the Statute of Winchester. A constable (derived from Latin and meaning "officer of the stable") assisted the king in suppressing riots and other violence.

Sir Robert Peel (1788–1850) is most often recognized for his ideas on policing, at least in the arenas of criminology and law enforcement. However, Peel had a very distinguished and full career in other areas. Like so many great English thinkers, he was educated at Oxford University. After graduating, he entered politics and became a very successful politician. In fact, Peel was Prime Minister (for only four months) in 1834–1835. He is credited as the founder of the modern Conservative party in England and his political efforts in 1829 succeeded in granting Roman Catholics political equality (Stansfield, 1996).

From a criminological standpoint, Peel's most significant contribution came in 1829 when he reorganized the London metropolitan police force after a somewhat frustrating and less than successful attempt by Henry Fielding, the author of *Tom Jones* (1707–1758), to establish uniformed and armed officers. However, due to poor funding, his "experiment" failed.

FYI BOX 4.14

Policing in Canada

The first Canadian police force was established in Toronto in 1835. In addition to the responsibilities they have today, early Canadian police officers were also required to collect taxes, serve as bailiffs, be firefighters, and be jailers (Dantzker and Mitchell, 1998).

In re-establishing the London constabulary, Peel instituted uniforms, strict discipline, banned the bearing of firearms, and set up the fundamental principles still used in policing today. Some of the most important principles include:

- The power of the police is dependent on public approval of their existence, actions and behaviour.
- Maintaining the respect of the public means securing their willing co-operation in the task of securing observance of laws.
- The police must demonstrate absolute impartial service of law, readily offer individual service and friendship by exercising courtesy and friendly good humour.
- The police must use minimal force when trying to restore the law.
- The test of police efficiency is the absence of crime and disorder, and not the visible evidence of police action in dealing with them (Normandeau and Leighton, 1990:140).

Peel's efforts met with considerable success. His officers became known as little **Roberts** or **bobbies** and his system was adopted throughout England. Whether the expansion of police forces was necessary or was simply an attempt by government and other power brokers to control and suppress the poor has, and continues to be, a subject of debate.

By the twentieth century, policing was well-established. Many of the principles from Anglo-Saxon times as well as Peel's criteria are entrenched in Canadian professional policing today.

Legal Aspects of Crime

Since the Hammurabi Code, law has been the cornerstone of the criminal justice system. Law represents the formal means of maintaining social control, for without law there is no crime—*nulle crim sin lege*—and without law there cannot be any punishment—*nulle poen sin lege*, two legal principles that can be traced back to the influential writings of Beccaria.

There have been many great legal reformers. Bentham introduced us to the principles of utilitarianism (see above) while the American legal scholar Charles

Doe's (1830–1896) writings helped to clarify the meaning of criminal responsibility. Doe also called for medicine and law to work more closely together. Meanwhile, the writings of the Spanish legal scholar Pedro Montereo (1861–1919) had a significant impact on North American law. He argued that the judiciary should be preventive in nature and that judges and lawyers should be trained in the social sciences—especially sociology and psychology—in order to better prevent and cure criminals, ideas that have received considerable attention over the years.

Perhaps one of the more enduring pioneers was the American **Isaac Ray** (1807–1881), who has been described as "the most influential American writer on forensic psychiatry during the whole nineteenth century" (Overholser, 1973:177). Before the work of Dr. Ray, law was strictly interpreted. Issues pertaining to mitigating circumstances were limited. In one of his early articles, Ray charged the legal profession with failing to recognize the importance of medical evidence. He wrote that the legal definition of insanity was too limited in its scope and that lawyers were ill-equipped to assess such a mental disorder. Expert testimony in cases involving insanity pleas was needed.

Being a staunch supporter of phrenology, Ray developed a line of reasoning that came to have a major impact on jurisprudence. In an 1835 article, he argued that criminals could experience periods during which their ability to reason was temporarily interrupted. He referred to this state of being as **moral insanity**. These states of being could, he thought, be related to the study of phrenology and Ray posited that perhaps the brain was compartmentalized. Therefore, while a person might act rationally in one situation, the same person might behave quite differently in others.

FYI BOX 4.15

Redefining Insanity in Canada

Since 1992, claiming insanity is no longer a true defence in Canada. Under section 672 of the *Criminal Code* an accused can be found "not criminally responsible on account of mental disorder."

Although not without his critics (see Overholser, 1973), Ray drew the attention of many legal scholars. One such scholar, Judge Charles Doe[5] later wrote the decision that is now referred to as the New Hampshire Rule (see Box 4.16). In addition to being one of the founders of the American Psychiatric Association (APA) in 1844, Ray went a long way towards bridging the gap between law and medicine. In recognition of his contribution, the APA annually gives out an award to a lawyer or psychiatrist who promotes a closer working relationship between law and medicine—a truly integrated and interdisciplinary approach.

And while the New Hampshire Rule has been replaced in the United States with the **Durham Rule**, much modern thought and influence can be traced back to Isaac Ray and his enduring efforts to improve jurisprudence, not only through medicine, but also through science in general.

A CLOSER LOOK BOX 4.16

New Hampshire Rule—1871[6]

This legal decision was seen as an improvement on the **M'Naughten Rule** of 1843. The M'Naughten Rule provided for a plea of insanity, but failed to provide any clear legal definition or universally applicable test of irrational reasoning. Daniel M'Naughten, a British citizen during Sir Robert Peel's premiership (see above), was distraught over the Prime Minister's efforts to curtail human liberty. On January 20, 1843, M'Naughten attempted to kill the Prime Minister. The person he shot was not Peel, but Peel's private secretary. The case drew wide attention and M'Naughten was eventually acquitted by reason of insanity. The decision was based on the grounds that he had lost all self-control—and had submitted to an "irresistible impulse."

The New Hampshire Rule refined the cognitive test for insanity and an irresistible impulse test as initially defined under the M'Naughten Rule. The New Hampshire Rule was applied in the case of *United States v. Durham*, (subsequently referred to as the Durham Rule).

The Canadian legal system uses the M'Naughten Rule when considering an insanity plea.

Criminalistics

Criminologists in North America have until recently paid little attention to what happens between the time of an offence and the sentencing or corrective processes. A review of several prominent Canadian introductory criminology textbooks shows that they make no specific mention of this "relatively static phase ... where only the administrators of social control ... are in action" (Schafer, 1976:4). It is generally seen to be peripheral to criminology and a subfield of criminal justice. Only when the process overlaps with criminal etiology and correctional theory do criminologists become involved. Otherwise, criminalistics or police sciences, police learning foundations, or police foundation programs (descriptions vary across the country—see Appendix 1) fall under the domain of applied two-year law enforcement and correctional programs.

However, for criminology to maintain an interdisciplinary perspective, it must also embrace all aspects of social control. As implied earlier, in North America criminalistics has not fallen within the dominant domain of criminological thought. In the past sociology and psychology were deemed the only acceptable ways of studying crime and criminality. However, today the integrated and interdisciplinary approach to the study of crime and criminal justice has begun to change this mindset.

Criminalistics refers to the use of scientific techniques in the detection and evaluation of criminal investigation (e.g., police crime scene analysts, laboratory personnel, etc.). **Alphonse Bertillon** (1853–1914) is generally acknowledged as the first modern-day criminalist to develop the practice of *anthropometry*— criminal identification. While working for the Paris Police Department, Bertillon refined and standardized the process of photo identification. The procedure involved positioning measuring guides beside suspects so that their physical characteristics (e.g., skeletal size and shape, ear form, etc.) could be determined. Photographs were taken, using both front views and profiles. Meanwhile, Sir Francis Galton (1822–1911), a cousin of Charles Darwin, popularized the use of fingerprints, which was officially adopted by Scotland Yard in 1901 (Saferstein, 1998).[7] Although both techniques of identification have become modernized, both methods of identification are still used today.

European criminology, on the other hand, has been dominated by the legal profession. Lawyer **Hans Gross** (1847–1915), born in Graz, Austria, pursued a career as an "examining justice," i.e., criminal investigation. He observed that while the police were good at maintaining order, they were often less adept at solving crimes, often relying on evidence from informers who were also often engaged in criminal activity.

As a lawyer, Gross was witness to how poorly prepared many cases were. There was a serious lack of evidence. How could a case be fairly tried under such circumstances? To this end, Gross made the best of his position to gather information and formulate ideas so he could improve crime investigation techniques. In 1883, after 13 years of careful research, he published his ideas in a book titled *Manual for the Examining Justice*, which eventually went to seven editions. Roland Grassberger (1973) described it as the "pièce de resistance" of its time. In the book Gross says that every criminal case should be treated as a scientific problem and every effort should be made to use and apply scientific investigation techniques in solving and resolving criminal cases.

The manual provides detailed, articulate descriptions and illustrations for such investigative strategies as medicine, ballistics, chemistry, microscopy, physics, anthropometry, fingerprinting, serology, and several other relevant areas. He also argued that experts in these fields testify in court. In addition, Gross developed several new methods of material evidence which technology has since refined (Grassberger, 1973).

The work of Franz von Litz and Hans Gross, among several other Austrian scholars, has been referred to as the **Austrian School** (Fattah, 1989). Today, crime investigation techniques such as DNA, fingerprinting, photo identification, voice-print identification, hair and fibre analysis, and crime scene analysis illustrate that Gross's pioneering work and ideas have become the heart of virtually all crime investigation practices. Today Canada operates seven forensic police labs.

Virtually every crime investigation today follows Gross's and Seelig's seven golden rules of crime solving: who, what, where, when, why, how and with what. These elements are more commonly referred to as the **modus operandi**. As Grassberger (1973:316) concludes in his biographical account of Gross, scientific evidence "is the hope of any wrongfully-suspected person and it is feared by any offender conscious of guilt."

Beyond Social Defence

In 1973, Mannheim speculated that a third school of criminological thought might be emerging. Referring to the work of French Judge **Marc Ancel,** it was called the school of social defence (see Box 4.17). The era of social defence emerged as a reaction against the prevailing retributive systems throughout Europe in the 1700s, through the writings of Jean Jacques Rousseau, Voltaire, Beccaria, Bentham, and others (Schafer, 1976). Its principles were later adapted by the United Nations Organization in 1948 for "the prevention of crime and the treatment of offenders" when it was formed. In spite of its European roots, in the concluding chapter to Mannheim's book, Jeffery suggests that the concepts and principles of social defence might more accurately be termed a **neopositivist** position. Jeffery subsequently called for a perspective that would transcend the classical and positivist schools of criminology.

The new perspective would focus on prevention and would be interdisciplinary in nature. The distinction is quite clear in his final remarks "The Classical School said 'reform the law.' The Positive School said 'reform the man.' The environmental school would say 'reform the environment'" (p. 498).

A CLOSER LOOK BOX 4.17

Principles of Social Defence

1. Social defence is not deterministic.
2. It disapproves of a rigid classification of offenders into types, and stresses the uniqueness of human personality.
3. It believes in the importance of moral values.
4. It appreciates the duty of society towards the criminal and tries to establish an equilibrium, and
5. While fully using the resources of modern science, it refuses to be dominated by science. (Mannheim, 1973:35).

6. The aim of social defence is not to punish a fault but to protect society from criminal acts.
7. Penal policy should promote individual resocialization rather than the collective approach to the prevention of crime currently used.
8. The process of resocialization requires a *humanization* of new criminal law so that individual self-confidence and sense of personal responsibility can grow and human values can be respected.
9. The humanization process should be based on scientific understanding of the phenomenon of crime and the offender's personality. (Ancel, 1994).

The ideas of social defence speak to the need to protect the rights of citizens against the arbitrariness of the courts, but the theory also recognizes that the state has a right to protect itself and society should an individual choose to break the law.

Today, the social defence model is more widely supported in Europe than in North America. It is characterized by its focus on crime prevention, a theme expressed by many criminologists and criminal justice practitioners.

Prevention as a School of Thought

Most North American criminology textbooks have been written by sociologists and, understandably, reflect their disciplinary bias towards the concept of crime prevention. This domination has hampered the development of an integrated and interdisciplinary approach in Canada. Any notion of prevention has tended to focus attention on modifying elements within a social context.

Wolfgang and Ferracuti (1967:40) perhaps summed it up best when they wrote, "It is possible to trace the development of criminology along traditional lines of biology, psychology, and sociology without much overlapping or integration of these approaches." However, with the emergence of a new school/perspective of thought, the need to embrace an interdisciplinary approach is even more necessary.

Crime Prevention

The traditional etiologies of crime have not been able to fully explain, understand, predict, or suppress crime. It is a dismal fact that the varied methods of law enforcement practices, correctional protocols, and legal reform have failed. Combined with the general level of public distrust toward all elements of the criminal justice system (see Chapter 2), criminology needs to move away from the reactive and antiquated notion that punishment (see Chapter 14) will prevent crime and protect society. Crime prevention can only be achieved through understanding what law is, why laws make some human behaviour a crime (see Prentice-Hall weblink at end of chapter), and human behaviour (see Chapter 8).

The notion of crime prevention is nothing new! Anyone who has visited European, African, or Asian countries will have seen buildings, centuries-old, that incorporate elementary, yet highly effective, crime prevention strategies, for example, moats around a castle or houses facing onto a street with no, or very small, windows. Many older quarters, especially in southern Europe and parts of Africa, share a common open inside courtyard for natural surveillance. Curfews also were, then and now, not uncommon in early times for youth and adults alike. However, even with the emergence of modern architecture and crime prevention technology, crime was, and is still, a major social problem.

Crime prevention is more than sophisticated door locks and expensive house and car alarm systems. It is more than relying on "visibility" gimmicks like leaving your radio/television on, using a light timer, or having someone cut your lawn and pick up your mail while you are away. And it is more than using police escorts to the parking lots on college and university campuses for night classes.

Although these strategies work reasonably well for most property-related crimes, they are less effective for crimes against a person (e.g., murder, rape, and assault) (Jeffery, 1990). At this point you might want to take a few minutes to write down or discuss how many things you do directly and indirectly on a daily basis to minimize your risk of becoming a victim of a crime. How does it make you feel to take such precautionary steps? How does your concern about your safety make you feel about people in general, about our country, about the state of humanity? Would you rather not have to think about your risk of being victimized?

Sociology, which colonized the study of crime in North America, has not helped crime prevention efforts. Sociologists, along with most other social sciences and the policy sciences, have made little or no effort to acknowledge what, or how, other disciplines might contribute to the study of crime and criminals (Lejins, 1983). This lack of integration and sharing also can be seen when comparing criminology and criminal justice programs. Criminal justice students (e.g., law enforcement and corrections) tend to take practical courses and express minimal interest in behavioural science courses. Criminology students, meanwhile, tend to take theoretical and more behavioural science-based courses.

Key Ideas

In order to embrace the crime prevention model for crime control, we must alter the goals of criminology and the criminal justice system. One of the pioneers of this model is **Clarence Ray Jeffery** (see Box 4.18). The following points are an integration of Jeffery's (1990), Schafer's (1976), and Wilson's (1975) ideas.

Crime prevention:
1. Must involve proactive measures (see Chapter 14).
2. Must accept short-term gains over immediate change.

3. Must replace punishment (i.e., revenge and retribution) as the basis for crime control (see Chapter 14).
4. Must embrace an integrative and interdisciplinary approach (Chapters 5 and 8) in which:
   a) We strive for a better understanding of the limits of law and crime (see Weblink).
   b) "We do not believe that the criminal justice system should have the 'sole' responsibility for dealing with crime" (deKeseredy and Schwartz, 1996:464).

In order for a crime to occur, three elements must be present: **skill + motivation + opportunity**. Attempts to address skill and/or motivation, to date, have been minimally successful. Therefore, crime prevention should focus on opportunities that entail an interaction between the environment and the brain (see Chapter 8).

PROFILE BOX 4.18

C. RAY JEFFERY

Jeffery was one of Edwin Sutherland's (*differential association theory*) last students. His academic career has been marked with controversy as he has challenged a number of the conventional viewpoints on crime and criminality in North America. While at the Department of Psychology at Arizona State University, Jeffery developed a version of *social learning theory* based on Skinnerian principles as opposed to the social control theory of Hirschi that focused on social variables. In the 1960s he proposed replacing all of Sutherland's theory with a single statement of operant conditioning— essentially rejecting the theory! Although his efforts were not successful his ideas evolved into an interdisciplinary explanatory model of crime. In various writings starting around 1977, Jeffery proposed that criminal behaviour was the result of interactions between biology, behaviour and the environment. In his 1977 book *Crime Prevention through Environmental Design*, Jeffery argued that all behaviour lies in the brain. This became the basis for his sociobiological theory of crime.

In 1963, he started the newsletter *Criminologica* and in 1970 became the founding editor of the journal *Criminology* that is now the official journal of the American Society of Criminology (ASC). In 1978, he was elected President of the ASC.

Today he continues his pioneering efforts at the School of Criminology at Florida State University in Tallahassee, Florida. Many of his ideas on crime prevention and the sociobiological perspective can be found in his textbook *Criminology: An Interdisciplinary Approach* (1990). It may have been a book before its time because most criminologists still continue to cling to more conventional modes of criminological inquiry.

The "new" crime prevention model is not yet widely embraced. However, this will change (see Box 4.19). The criminology students of today and tomorrow will pioneer these ideas and help bring about change. As the British philosopher Bertrand Russell once wrote, "We need the creation of a school of men and women with scientific training and philosophical interests, unhampered by the traditions of the past" (cited in Jeffery, 1990:464).

A CLOSER LOOK BOX 4.19

Restoring Order: "Fixing Broken Windows"

In 1982, George Kelling and James Q. Wilson wrote a groundbreaking article for the *Atlantic Monthly*. In the article they discuss how broken windows breed disorder. They suggested that if citizens and community-oriented policing (COP)[8] were to more aggressively protect public spaces it would help to control the spread of crime. Since their article was published a number of others have written on this method of restorative order. In 1996, Kelling teamed up with Catherine Coles to write a book on the concept. They argue that the "three-strikes-and-you're out" rule is fine, but it is a reactive measure. Instead, employing COP to help keep neighbourhoods safe is both proactive and more effective (as well as more cost-efficient). Even more recently, Peter Knobler and William Bratton (the former commissioner of the New York Police Department) co-authored *Turnaround: How America's Top Cop Reversed the Crime Epidemic* (1998). When Bratton assumed his position as commissioner in 1994, he promised to combat crime in every borough of the city ... and win. Over a 27-month period he reduced crime by 33 per cent. The book is an autobiography of his success story. How did he do it? He took an apathetic police force and turned it into a progressive community-oriented crime-fighting entity. The concept involves such elements as: *involvement of the citizen* in crime-fighting ventures; *officer participation* in the process of sharing problem-solving with the community police are serving, and *reduction of fear and crime deterrence* by encouraging citizens to provide helpful information, and using their input to fight crime and reduce fear. In his own charismatic way, Bratton helped to instill a sense of pride among his officers and got them to work with the boroughs to "take a bite out of crime" at all levels.

Summary

We have covered a lot of criminological history in a few pages. By tracing the roots and development of criminological thought, it is hoped that you have acquired a better sense, not only for the complexity of criminology, but also of the need for an integrated and interdisciplinary approach.

In reviewing the three major schools of criminological thought, it should be clear that criminology is *evolving*. Yet, the *classical* and *positivist* principles still dominate criminal justice practices and policy and many of the criminological theories we will examine (Chapters 5–8) can trace their influence to the various schools' principles. Furthermore, as criminology has evolved as a science, and in its theoretical repertoire, criminology has moved towards an integrated and *interdisciplinary* science. The study of criminology is no longer only concerned about penal reform, or law reform. Increasingly criminologists are focusing on human behaviour as being the product of social, economic, individual, environmental, and biological factors. In addition, there has been a shift, from being reactive to proactive in its approach to addressing the crime problem.

The pioneers of criminology illustrated how criminological ideas are influenced by our experiences at the time. They are *relative* and subject to change. Yet this is what makes criminology exciting and dynamic. But it also should serve as a caution. What we think may be "right" today may not hold true tomorrow and the consequences of our ideas can have profound implications. This is why it is important to understand not only what the past has given us but to learn from it.

Finally, in Appendix 4 you will find a review of six resident Canadian pioneers (one has since returned to the United States). Their profiles reflect many of the points made above. Although the official study of criminology in Canada is relatively young, they have each made significant contributions to the study of criminology, both nationally and internationally. Students are strongly encouraged to read these profiles and reflect on their contribution to Canadian criminology and criminological thought.

Having laid the foundation of criminology and placed it in a historical framework, we can now move on to examine and review some of the conventional and non-conventional methods for explaining, describing, and predicting criminal behaviour. We will begin with biological theories.

Discussion Questions

1. How important is having a sense of criminological history when attempting to predict future criminological issues and future policy?

2. How does the classical and positivist approach to the study of crime complicate our ideas about crime prevention and criminal justice policy?

3. Which of the pioneers covered in the main the text do you feel has made the most significant contribution to current criminology? Why?

4. Which of the Canadian pioneers (Appendix 4) do you feel has made the most significant contribution to current (Canadian) criminology? Why?

5. In this chapter, we examined four major schools of thought (i.e., classical, neoclassical, positivist, and the "school" of crime prevention). Which of these schools appears to offer the best approach for the study of crime and crime control?

6. In the summary, it was suggested that criminological ideas are influenced by our experiences. What kind, or type, of experiences do you feel will affect how we view crime in the future?

Key Concepts

Classical school	neoclassical school	positivist school
Neo-positivist school	Austrian school	Social Defence
Self-help justice	utilitarianism	just deserts
Retribution	discretion	phrenology
"holy three of criminology"	atavism	frankpledge
moral insanity	criminalistics	M'Naughten Rule
Durham Rule	"fixing broken windows"	moral calculus
Deterrence (general vs. specific)		

Key Names

C. Beccaria	J. Bentham	A. Comte
C. Lombroso	E. Ferri	R. Garofalo
A. Maconochie	J. Howard	R. Peel
A. Bertillon	H. Gross	M. Ancel
C.R. Jeffery		

From Appendix 4—Canadian Pioneers:

D. Sabo	E. Fattah	J. Hackler
T. Grygier	A. Normandeau	Paul and Pat Brantingham

Weblinks

www.gov.on.ca/opp/cpdc OPP community police development centre.

www.community.policing.org/ The community policing consortium.

www.prenticehall.ca/winterdyk Specially prepared chapter on law and crime designed to complement this textbook.

www.ieway.com/~csukbr/calcrime.html A novel site with an extensive listing of historical criminal events and an impressive list of various historical document of crimes, criminals, and legal cases.

Footnotes

1. In the strictest sense, the term classical is used to characterize the art and literature originating from the ancient Greeks and Romans. In a much broader sense, however, it can refer to a specific historical period (circa 1750–1820) that marked historically significant systems of thought (*Encarta*, 1996).

2. Locke challenged the divine right of kings and argued that sovereignty should rest with the people and not the state. Many of his ideas regarding natural rights, property rights, the duty of the government to protect our rights, and the democratic principle of majority rule have been embodied in the Canadian Constitution.

3. Points taken from DeKeseredy and Schwarzt, 1996; Mannheim, 1973; Williams and McShane, 1994; 1999.

4. For a modern day discussion on this controversial subject see Peters (1995) whose article focuses on methodological issues and Montagu (1997) whose critique is based on anthropological factors. Both suggest that in spite of the work of Canadian researchers Rushton and Ankey (1995), this line of inquiry holds little scientific merit today.

5. See Kenison (1973) for a detailed account on the life and times of Judge Doe.

6. For further discussion on the implication of criminal defences and the insanity plea visit the Prentice-Hall link on Crime and Criminal Law at: **www.prenticehall.ca/winterdyk**

7. Evidence suggests that as early as the Tang Dynasty (618–906 AD), the Chinese were using inked fingerprints as personal seals on important documents (Soderman and O'Connell, 1945).

8. The acronym COPPS is also used in the literature. It stands for Community-Oriented Policing and Problem Solving.

CHAPTER 5

Biological
Explanations

*"I have called this principle, by which each
slight variation, if useful, is preserved, by
the term Natural Selection."*

Charles R. Darwin
(On the Origin of Species, Chapter 3)

Learning Outcomes

After you have completed this chapter, you should be able to:

• Appreciate the importance of a biological orientation.

• Recognize and realize the mitigating impact of the environment on biology.

• Have an awareness of, and appreciation for, the research dedicated to the study of biological variables and their possible correlations to crime.

• Have an awareness of, and appreciation for, the research dedicated to biological/environmental correlates of crime.

• Recognize the myths versus the facts regarding biological explanations of crime causation.

• Appreciate and strive for an integrated and interdisciplinary theory that includes biological, social and psychological dimensions.

Among North American criminologists biological explanations of crime have received limited attention. When they have been addressed they are usually grouped with psychological explanations. The rationale commonly used is that they can both be characterized as subscribing to a "positivistic–deterministic"

framework (Chapter 4). What is ironic, however, is that criminology emerged out of the disciplines of anthropology, biology and medicine. Evidence of this can be found in the works of Charles Darwin (1809–1882), Cesare Lombroso and his colleagues (Chapter 4), as well as Sigmund Freud (Chapter 7) and a number of early geneticists such as **Gregor Mendel** (1822–1884) and Francis Joseph Galton (1822–1911). Mendel, in his now famous studies involving the ordinary garden pea, discovered and proved the concept of inheritance and what would later become know as the gene. Genetic research has become a major area of study today, one that we will also look at.[1]

When criminology was first introduced as an area of study in North America in the 1920s, most academics were sociologists by training (see Gibbons, 1979 for an overview). Not surprisingly, the sociological frame of reference and inquiry quickly became the dominant theoretical paradigm. However, psychology and biology were not completely overlooked. In 1943, Barnes and Teeters wrote, "not until we recognize the fundamental truth that the individual is made a delinquent by forces beyond his control operating on his structure, can we make much progress in understanding such behaviour and correcting it" (cited in Einstadter and Henry, 1995: 73).

The early *positivists* recognized that behaviour could be influenced by internal (i.e., nature–biology) and external, or environmental (i.e., nurture–psychological) factors. Similar views were more recently expressed in the frequently cited work, *Crime and Human Nature*, by James Q. Wilson and Richard J. Herrnstein (1985). In their book, they carefully review the biological and psychological literature and forcefully suggest that criminology needs to be interdisciplinary and not overlook findings from these areas. They argue that most crimes, but not all, are carried out by persons who are mesomorphic, exhibit relatively low IQs, are extraverted, impulsive and usually deficient in other personality attributes (see below). Similar views had been expressed earlier by Shah and Roth (1974) who also argued that not to adopt an interdisciplinary perspective would leave the dominant sociological explanations incomplete, and inadequate as explanatory models.

Finally, while sociological theories see the criminal as someone who has been somehow estranged from society, who is undersocialized, and who is in need of social structure (e.g., family, religion, education, and work), they also define delinquency and criminals in terms of social labels. These labels do not necessarily relate to human behaviour, but merely aid society in identifying law-breakers. However, as was discussed in Chapter 3, there are many more people involved in delinquency and criminal behaviour than are convicted. Therefore, the answer to the crime problem is found not only in studying known offenders, or in looking at social factors, or at who is undersocialized. Rather, supporters of the biological perspective argue that we must identify the role of heredity, the importance of biophysical as well as bio-social factors in the environment. As Hippchen (1978:12) observed, "we must strive to understand what is optimum —optimum chemistry, optimum physiology, optimum psychology, and the optimum socio-culturally." Only by embracing such an interdisciplinary perspective can we begin to fully understand human behaviour.

In this chapter, we will examine a number of different biologically-based factors that have been linked to criminal behaviour. These factors fall into one of two camps. They either assume a direct inheritable link or they are associated with some internal or external mediating factor. After presenting an overview of some of the biologically-based explanations of crime, the chapter will conclude with a summary of some of the myths and facts about the biological perspective.

Before we begin, consider the following observations, which illustrate the importance of environmental (external) and natural (internal) factors in understanding aggression, violence, and suicide in society. Throughout the chapter we will elaborate on many of the findings.

- Children of families on welfare demonstrate twice the rate of psychiatric disorders as children from better-off families ... (and) ... have serious difficulties such as alcoholism and criminality in adulthood (Justice Association, 1989).

- A study on the prevalence of mental health problems among male federal inmates revealed that a significant number of the offenders (homicide, robbery, sex and drug offenders) surveyed met the criteria for anti-social personality disorders (Motiuk and Porporino, 1992).

- Comparing 41 murderers to 41 matched control participants, Raine and associates (1997) found that murderers had significantly lower levels of glucose uptake in the prefrontal cortex of the brain.

- In a study of 43 young offenders, Unis and associates (1997) found that those youths who expressed impulsive aggression, suicidal behaviour and a variety of other abnormalities, had abnormally high levels of the neuro-chemical serotonin. While an association was observed among males, no similar correlation was seen among female participants, lending support to a biological/environmental interaction.

- In summarizing the observations of several keynote speakers at the June 1995 conference called "Violence as a Public Health Issue," in Midland, Ontario, Carter noted that "young people are more violent than ever before" (p. 28) and that there appeared to be some organic (biological) linkages (Carter, 1995: 28–29).

The "Golden Age of Criminal Biology": The Foundations of Biological Determinism

WHAT DO YOU THINK? BOX 5.1

CAN YOU JUDGE SOMEONE BY THEIR APPEARANCE?

William Shakespeare in his play *Julius Caesar*, describes Cassius as having "a lean and hungry look... such men are dangerous." Have you ever judged someone based only on physical appearance? Do Charles Ng, Paul Bernardo, Karla Homolka, or David Walsh look like criminal types? Why might we put so much stock in judging people based on their appearance?

According to Schafer (1976:50), the "golden age of criminal biology" occurred in the late 1800s and early 1900s. Some of the pioneering, biologically-based research on criminals involved the study of physical features and attributes. In scientific circles this is known as **somatotyping** (i.e., body-typing). And while scientists were busy trying to empirically verify that there is an association between body appearance and criminal behaviour, storytellers have long reflected these notions in classic "good-guy/bad-guy" stories. For example, in Robert Louis Stevenson's novel, *Dr. Jekyll and Mr. Hyde,* the character of Hyde is portrayed as an evil and grotesque-looking character. In her novel, *Frankenstein,* Mary Shelley (1799–1851) describes Frankenstein's transformation as resembling a monster who also acts destructively. And in the 1994 remake of the original movie *Frankenstein*, the monster appears to become destructive because Dr. Frankenstein's assistant stole an "abnormal" brain rather than a "normal" one for the monster's body. As reflected in Box 5.1 above, the list could go on. The next time you watch a crime or horror movie, take note as to whether the characters are stereotyped in this fashion. Darwin described these traits as *atavism,* a word that comes from the Latin *atavas*, meaning ancestors. In other words, such criminals look like a throwback to a lower level of human development. It would appear that the concept of "character" has and continues to conjure stereotypical images of physical features, stature and accompanying psychological dispositions. Let us now look at some of the early biologically-based theories that tried to prove that criminal behaviour is inherited.

Early Theories of Physical Appearance

Many of our stereotypes about the good-guy/bad-guy image can be traced back over two thousand years to the time of Socrates, who noted that unsavoury characters were recognizable by their physical features (Ellis, cited in Vold and Bernard, 1981:52). One of the earliest "scientific" attempts to validate such assertions was the study of *physiognomy* (i.e., the judging of facial features). One of the more prolific researchers in this area was the Swiss theologian Johan Casper Lavater (1741–1801), who produced four volumes of work on physiognomy. He identified such classic relationships such as "shifty" eye, a "weak" chin, and an "arrogant" nose. While many of his ideas are no longer considered to have any scientific basis, they continue to intrigue us.[2]

Franz Joseph Gall (1758–1825) was among the first to develop a systematic method of the doctrine of *phrenology*— the study of the exterior of the skull. However, the rationale for the skull's measurements being an indicator of human behaviour can be traced back to Aristotle's notion of the brain representing the organ of the mind.

While Gall identified 26 faculties of the mind on the skull, his fellow collaborator John Gasper Spurzheim (1776–1832) not only expanded the list but also brought the idea to North America (Vold and Bernard, 1981). Although Spurzheim's ideas reflected a biological determinist perspective, he recognized that criminal tendencies could be held in check through intellectual and moral development. A novel and interdisciplinary approach for the times!

In the late 1800s and early 1900s phrenology was widely used in penitentiaries in the eastern United States. As scientists developed better research skills, the concept was quickly discredited and abandoned. Because of a lack of scientific evidence, phrenology and physiognomy have all but disappeared—or have they? (see Box 5.3)

FYI BOX 5.2

Criminality—Is It All On Your Head?

Although crude, phrenology represented an early quasi-scientific method of attempting to understand the relationship between physical characteristics of the brain and criminal behaviour.

Today, while the practice of relying on phrenology may have fallen out of favour, other practices still rely on observable physical features or markings, such as iridology and palm reading. It appears that, as much as we do not want to believe in fate, many people still have a fascination (or at least a curiosity) with deterministic theories (e.g., astrology, biorhythms, the I Ching, Angel and Medicine cards, Runes, etc.) and how they affect elements of human behaviour.

PHYSIOGNOMY AND FETAL ALCOHOL SYNDROME (FAS)

It is commonly believed that there is a strong relationship between (illegal) drug use and crime. We are constantly bombarded with such accounts from public officials and news media. In 1986, Prime Minister Brian Mulroney claimed there was a drug epidemic in the country. The problem group is Canadian youth (between the ages 15–24) (Eliany, 1994). They consume more illicit drugs and tobacco than any other age group. Young men are more likely to use and abuse illicit and legal drugs than young women.

Every year the federal and provincial governments spend millions of dollars on various health expenditures. From 1975 to 1994 health expenditures increased from $12.2 million to $72.4 million (*Canada Year Book 1997*, p. 110). Yet the "drug problem," remains a poorly-understood phenomenon, both culturally, politically, and from a public health perspective. Like so many aspects of crime, it is a relative and evolutive concept. In the seventeenth century, for example, when coffee was first introduced to Europe, the Catholic Church forbade its consumption and advocated wine as a more appropriate substitute.

Even though the debate as to the relative harm of illegal versus legal drugs has been the subject of numerous publications and debates, there is little dispute over whether drugs in general take a toll on society. In recent years the effects of fetal alcohol syndrome (FAS) and its relationship to crime and learning disabilities has received increasing attention. In addition, just when some might have thought that physiological measurements are not reliable indicators of cognitive development, a growing body of research evidence has shown that FAS can be characterized by observable measures. These include intelligence scores (mean IQ score of 68), cardiac defects, central nervous system impairment, growth abnormalities, and physical and facial patterns (Dobbie and Bill, 1978). For example, *dysmorphic* features that appear due to prenatal alcohol abuse include:

- eyes widely-spaced
- nose is often short and upturned
- the area between the bottom of the nose and upper lip (the philtrum) is elongated and flat
- upper lip is thin
- small chin
- ears low-set and rotated to the back of the head
- teeth often misplaced and misshapen (Schroeder, 1994).

The syndrome was first discovered in the late 1960s at the Seattle, Washington County Hospital by Dr. Christy Ulleland. Confounded by six of the infants entrusted to her care who were not responding to medical treatment, she found that the mothers of all six were chronic alcoholics. On further investigation, she found that in over 80 per cent of the cases the babies were undersized at birth and were either retarded or borderline. Then in 1972 two colleagues from Seattle, Washington, Kenneth L. Jones and David W.

Smith, published an article in *Lancet*, where they first coined the term *fetal alcohol syndrome* (Dobbie and Bill, 1978).

In spite of the volume of research linking FAS to criminal behaviour and other social and physical abnormalities, the well-known author-anthropologist Ashley Montagu once wrote "it can be stated categorically, after hundreds of studies ... that no matter how great the amount of alcohol taken by the mother – or by the father ... neither the germ cells nor the development of the child will be affected" (cited in Dobbie and Bill, 1978: 4). However, in the 1990s, science has carried the day. In fact, today FAS has been identified as the third ranking (behind Down's Syndrome and spinal bifida) cause of being mentally-challenged.

Streissguth and colleagues (1997) found that of 415 individuals diagnosed with FAS or FAE (fetal alcohol effect), 60 per cent had committed a crime, nearly 50 per cent exhibited inappropriate sexual behaviour, 60 per cent experienced school problems (failure and/or dropping out) and 94 per cent exhibited mental problems. In 1998, Streissguth and his associates at the University of Washington School of Medicine began to develop a Fetal Alcohol Behavior Scale that is capable of describing the behavioural essence of FAS and FAE. The scale is able to control for variable effects such as age, race, gender and IQ and has a test-retest reliability of nearly 70 per cent.

Later in this chapter we will discuss the general biological effects of alcohol and illicit drug usage on criminal behaviour.

Anthropological Measurements and Criminal Behaviour

Although Lombroso is the most famous of those who have propounded the idea that criminals can be differentiated based on their physical attributes, there have been other notable contributors to this line of inquiry. For example, although they did not focus on criminals per se, the German scientist Hans Kurella and his American counterpart, August Drahms, were also strong supporters of the *somatic* approach. However, **Charles Buckman Goring** (1870–1919) in his most noteworthy work, *The English Convict* (1913) presents data on 3,000 recidivist criminals whom he compared with a control group consisting of British soldiers, hospital patients, and university students (Vold and Bernard, 1981).

Goring examined 37 physical (e.g., nasal contours, colour of eyes and hair, head circumference, etc.) and mental traits that "led him to believe that a defective state of mind combined with poor physical condition *unavoidably* makes a person a criminal personality" (Schafer, 1976:51—emphasis added). He named this constitutional predisposition *criminal diathesis*. This orientation has been referred to as Goring's *feeblemindedness* theory. Drawing on his observations from parental (father–son) and fraternal (brother) resemblance comparisons, Goring concluded that criminality has a hereditary link.

Goring's contribution to criminology may not lie with the specifics of his findings but with the indirect findings. Unlike those before him, Goring did not restrict his explanation of crime to either the environment or to heredity. Instead he was among the first to suggest that criminal behaviour may be the result of interaction between the two:

crime = heredity x environment.

While Goring was not able to figure out how to explain and describe that interaction his assertion has since become the focus of and basis for numerous studies and theories. In fact, this is a view that can be found among many of the criminological theories today (see, for example, Williams and McShane, 1999). Few criticized his findings until **Earnest A. Hooton** (1887–1954), a Harvard anthropologist, questioned his work. Hooton's criticism focused primarily on the methodological issues and the resulting conclusions. His study (1931) had an impressive sample size of 17,000 people from ten states, of which 14,000 were prisoners, the balance representing a non-criminal control group.

Hooton did not try to imply that physical differences *caused* crime. He believed rather that the information could be used for predictive purposes, along with other social and environmental factors. Among his findings, Hooton reported that:

- In 19 out of 33 measurements there was a significant difference between criminals and civilians.
- Criminals were inferior to civilians in nearly all their bodily measurements.
- Low foreheads, high-pinched nasal roots, nasal bridges and tips varying to both extremes of breadth and narrowness, excess of nasal deflections, compressed faces and narrow jaws, fit well into the picture of general constitutional inferiority.
- The basic cause of the inferiority (probably) is due to heredity and not to situation or circumstances.
- Tattooing is more common among criminals than among civilian controls.
- Thin lips and compressed jaw angles occur more frequently and marked overbite less frequently among criminals than among civilians.
- Low and sloping foreheads, long, thin necks, and sloping shoulders, are similarly in excess among criminals compared with civilians (Vold and Bernard, 1981:62).

In spite of his impressive sample size (especially given that he did not have the use of a computer to calculate all the data!) and the fact that many of Hooton's[3] findings have been and continue to be found in gangster-type movies, his findings were subjected to severe methodological criticisms. Among those who took issue with Hooton's work included Edwin Sutherland, Robert Merton, and Ashley Montagu. They all pointed out that even if heredity did play a role, what is inherited is never made clear. Nevertheless, the supporters of the positivist-deterministic model did not disappear. Instead, they developed other classification strategies.

Body Types and Criminal Behaviour

"The widely held supposition that physique is irrelevant to behaviour and personality is downright nonsense. Your carcass is the clue to your character" E.A. Hooton (1887–1954).

While Lombroso tried to establish a relationship between a person's temperament and physical characteristics (Chapter 4), it was the pioneering efforts of the German scientist **Ernst Kretschmer**, in the 1920s, and **William Sheldon**, in the 1940s, that have been most often associated with this line of inquiry. Kretschmer believed that there were two fundamental types of mental states: *cycloids* and *schizoids*. In addition there were two subdivisions known as the *eliptoids* and *hysterics*. Cycloids were characterized as suffering from manic-depressive temperaments while schizoids were generally hysterics. However, as Martin et al. (1990:129) point out, these subdivisions "did not fit any particular physical type." Depressive temperaments were allegedly predisposed to commit more intelligent and less serious crimes. Schizothymes were characterized as being either insensitive or hypersensitive and tended to commit more serious and violent crimes. In addition to labelling personality types, Kretschmer identified three body types: (1) *Leptosome* or *asthenic*: the tall, lean and thin individual, which typically displays a schizothyme temperament, (2) *Pyknic*: the short, rotund, and soft figure, which represents the cyclothyme temperament, and (3) *Athletic*: the broad, muscular, strong type.

Kretschmer and his supporters found that most criminals (50–90 per cent) were of the schizothyme type while the cyclothyme type made up 10–20 per cent of the criminal population. Again, as with the positivists before him, Kretschmer's findings were challenged on their lack of empirical rigour. For example, his body types were not always mutually exclusive: a significant number of offenders could be characterized as having the athletic body type.

In the face of such criticisms, the American physician William H. Sheldon (see Box 5.4) set out to refine and improve on Kretschmer's work. Sheldon based his *constitutional* theory on the belief that human embryos are made up of three tissue layers. The inner layer is the **endomorph**, the middle layer is the **mesomorph**, and the outer layer is the **ectomorph**. Combining knowledge from his psychological training, Sheldon constructed corresponding temperaments.

WILLIAM HERBERT SHELDON (1898–1977)[4]

In their account of Sheldon, Martin, Mutchnick, and Austin (1990:119) write that he "represents the last of the trend setters who carried on the work of early twentieth century biological determinism... (his) concepts became almost household words and continue to do so..."

Sheldon was born and raised in Warwick, Rhode Island. After his father died, the prominent American psychologist William James became a second father to the young Sheldon. Under James's influence, he entered college and pursued a degree in psychology. He eventually completed his Ph.D. in psychology at the University of Chicago. Thereafter, he spent a few years teaching before returning to school to obtain his medical degree at the University of Chicago.

After finishing medical school, Sheldon visited Europe from 1933 to 1934. There he met Ernst Kretschmer. After returning to the States, he began to do research on somatotypes at Harvard. There he met another pioneer of constitutionalism, Earnest Hooton (see above). In time, he came to believe that biology not only formed the basis for psychology and psychiatry, but also religion. In sum, Sheldon believed that the body, mind, and spiritual world were all based on biological determinism.

Sheldon's first major work on somatotypes, *The Variety of Human Physique* was published in 1942. This volume was "devoted entirely to determining physique and arriving at somatotypes while his second major publication, *The Varieties of Human Temperament*, also published in 1942, provided guidelines for assessing personality temperaments based on physiques (Martin et al., 1990:133). His final book on somatotypes, titled *Atlas of Men: A Guide for Somatotyping the Adult Male at All Ages*, in 1954, comprised "mostly photographs" with little theoretical explanations or justification (Ibid, 133). Sheldon wanted to include women but was unable to secure enough volunteers to complete his detailed requirements.

While Sheldon spent his early years at Harvard University, he spent the longest part of his professional life (1951–1970) at the University of Oregon in Portland. After a long and distinguished career, Sheldon died of heart failure at age 78.

The relationship between (a) the body types and (b) temperament were as follows:

1. (a) *Endomorphic*: have a well-developed digestive system and a tendency to put on weight and become heavy-set and soft in appearance. Their skin is usually smooth and soft, their bones small.
   (b) *Viscerotonic*: tend to be extroverted, easy-going, and enjoy the "good" and easy life.
2. (a) *Mesomorphic*: are predominantly muscular, strong boned, and lean.

(b) *Somotonic*: are assertive in their mannerisms and quite active in their behaviour.

3. (a) *Ectomorphic*: appear thin, pale, with delicate bodies, small and delicate bones, fine hair, and sharp noses.

(b) *Cerebrotonic*: are introverted complainers, troubled by insomnia and chronic fatigue (adapted from Vold and Bernard, 1981: 67).

WHAT DO YOU THINK? BOX 5.5

PHYSICAL TYPES AND HEALTH

The ancient Hindu science of healing known as *Ayurvedic* medicine has long associated physical body types (similar to those of Sheldon) with "psychological and physiopathological functions of the body, mind and consciousness" (Lad, 1985:25). Since our physical appearance is often influenced by social expectations, how might we begin to determine a person's "true" somatotype and compare the findings to different criminal behaviours?

Recognizing Kretschmer's theoretical limitations, Sheldon did not view the types as being mutually exclusive but rather interrelated, to varying degrees. To quantify this assertion he developed a seven-point rating scale, with each type receiving a score based on appearance and measurements. One meant a virtual absence of the mental or physical trait while seven represented a preponderance of the trait. Hence, a person with a score 6–1–4 would be a strong endomorph with some ectomorphic attributes. Many of Sheldon's ideas and evidence were based on a study over a ten-year span involving 200 young males who lived, at some time, at the Hayden Goodwill Inn for Troubled Youth in Boston. Sheldon found that most delinquent youths were predominantly mesomorphic. However, unlike traditional sociology and the law, Sheldon did not use the term delinquent in the same way. Instead, his notion of delinquency was more akin to psychiatric ideas and he used the term "biological delinquency" to describe those youths with mesomorphic attributes.

Subsequent strong support for Sheldon's findings came from Sheldon Glueck and Eleanor Glueck during their 1956 study involving 500 chronic delinquents and 500 proven non-delinquents. They added a fourth constitutional type— *balanced* and also used a multi-factor approach.

Their initial findings received considerable attention. However, their data also fell prey to methodological criticisms, in particular, their prediction scale, until the late 1980s when John Laub and Robert Sampson revisited the Gluecks' self-report data after discovering sixty boxes of their data in the basement of the Harvard Law School Library. With the aid of modern computers and more sophisticated analytical techniques, Laub and Sampson re-analyzed the Gluecks' data (see Sampson and Laub, 1988, 1990, and Laub and Sampson, 1993). Their efforts paid off. In their important work, *Crime in the Making* (1993), Laub and Sampson used the *life course* perspective to demonstrate that delinquent behaviour can be affected by events that occur at different stages of life. They refer to these events as "turning points." For example, two critical turning points that enable an adult offender to desist from crime are marriage and a career.

Life events help people accumulate social capital, positive experiences with individuals and institutions that become life-sustaining. Similarly, negative experiences throughout adolescence and early adulthood can also influence the direction of delinquent and criminal careers. While representing a new integrated approach to explaining crime and delinquency, Siegel (1995) raises a number of questions which the **life course theory** has not been able to address. For example, "Why do some kids change while others resist? Why do some people enjoy strong marriages while others fail? Why are some troubled youths able to conform to the requirements of a job or career while others cannot?" (p. 286).

The body-build type theories eventually lost their credibility as an explanatory model when they were not able to provide convincing evidence regarding the influence of the biological influence. The lack of a sound methodology continued to plague those who championed the biological perspective. However, more recently, Ayurvedic medicine, which is premised on physical constitution and temperament and principles which emphasize understanding the body as a whole—as body, mind, and spirit—has received widespread support and interest (Chopra, 1990). Based on an ancient Hindu healing tradition, ayurvedic doctors focus on identifying the patient's metabolic body type. Each metabolic body type corresponds to different temperaments, and treatments vary according to one's constitution. Interest in this area of medicine has grown considerably in recent years.

In **summary**, if criminology is going to continue to move forward, it cannot simply think in terms of biology versus environment. Such approaches are not only simplistic, but counterproductive to understanding the complexity of human behaviour. Therefore, future studies should attempt to see body build as a potential risk factor, along with social risk factors to violent and/or antisocial behaviour. It might be useful to ask here, typically, who were the bullies in public school? Who usually started trouble?

Chromosomes and Criminal Behaviour

In spite of the criticisms levelled at the positivists, the belief that physiological and behavioural tendencies have a constitutional foundation continued to evolve. The positivists' interests were spurred on with the development and discovery of new methods of measurement and improved methodologies. One area of inquiry that was dependent on the discovery of an appropriate scientific measurement instrument involved the study of a possible link between an abnormal number of sex chromosomes and criminal behaviour.

Sex chromosomal abnormality is a biological defect that may either be inherited (nature) or be the result of some genetic mutation (nurture) during conception or during the development of the fetus in the uterus.[5] And from high school biology, you may remember that every cell of a normal human being contains 23 pairs of chromosomes. One of these pairs is the gender chromosomes that determine gender and gender characteristics. In the genetically-normal female, the chromosomes are both similar in size and shape. Under a microscope they resemble two "X's", hence their name. By contrast, the normal male has an XY pairing, with the Y chromosome being smaller in shape and size than the X chromosome.

For reasons not yet fully understood, when there is improper separation of the chromosomes during meiotic cell division (see Box 5.6) sex chromosomal abnormalities occur. According to Herrnstein's (1989) accounting, this occurs in less than 1/10th of 1 per cent of the male population. There are several known combinations of abnormal numbering of sex chromosomes, two of which have been reported to be associated with criminal behaviour. The possible combinations wherein a new embryo has more or less than the usual gender chromosomal constellation include:

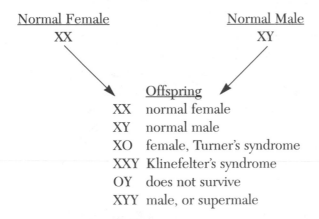

Normal Female
XX

Normal Male
XY

Offspring
XX normal female
XY normal male
XO female, Turner's syndrome
XXY Klinefelter's syndrome
OY does not survive
XYY male, or supermale

FYI BOX 5.6
- -
The Ultimate "Jigsaw" Puzzle

Genes, hundreds and thousands of them, are situated along amino acid chains known as chromosomes. After the egg (female) and sperm (male) unite during intercourse they form a new organism. Once they have formed a union the meiotic process of cell division begins in which the number of chromosomes are reduced to half. The meiotic process is different in females and males. For females a part of the meiotic division is complete at birth, while in males the entire process occurs at birth. Geneticists

The first of the criminal sex chromosomal abnormalities to be discovered was the **XXY** karyotype or **Klinefelter's syndrome**. While Klinefelter first described the condition in 1942 it wasn't until the 1950s that researchers began to identify males with the extra sex (X) chromosome. The syndrome is reported to be associated with degeneration of the testes, sterility, breast enlargement, and social and/or school learning problems. In addition, alcoholism, homosexuality, frustration-based outbursts, and overrepresentation among the mentally-challenged have also been reported among those with the XXY karyotype (Vold and Bernard, 1981). It is probably the most common chromosomal variation in humans—approximately 1 in every 500 live-born males.

Research by Patricia Jacobs and her associates in 1965 also drew considerable criminological interest. Studying patients in a maximum security mental hospital, Jacobs demonstrated the existence of males with an extra Y chromosome, the XYY, and also found that the disproportionate number of males with this constellation was statistically significant. These males were characterized as being exceptionally tall (mean height 6' 1" vs. 5' 7" for other patients), more introverted, and having a strong propensity towards violent and criminal behaviour. Later Borgaonkar and Shah (1974) identified other traits that were commonly observed among males found to have the XYY makeup. These included a predisposition to facial acne, abnormal EEG patterns, extra-long extremities, and additional testosterone. Their findings were based on a limited sample size and should therefore be viewed with caution.

A number of subsequent studies supported both the existence of the XYY make-up and its accompanying traits. However, none of the studies demonstrated an increased link between those who have an XYY constellation with an increased risk of developing violent or anti-social tendencies. This is in part due to the fact that the exact function of the extra Y chromosome is still poorly understood. Research conducted in Denmark by Mednick and Christiansen (1977) found that of nearly 4200 males, while only a dozen were XYY cases, almost 42 per cent of those had criminal records, compared with 9 per cent of the XY cases.

Perhaps the most notorious case to draw attention to the possible link between the extra Y chromosome and violent behaviour was that of Richard Speck. In 1968 he was convicted of killing eight Chicago nurses. Because of his size and emotional instability he was suspected of having an XYY predisposition

—but he did not (Fox, 1969). However, there were a number of other international trials throughout the 1960s that put forward the XYY condition as the basis of a plea of insanity. These cases included: Daniel Hugon in Paris in 1968, Ernst-Dieter Beck in Germany in 1962, Sean Farley in New York in 1969 and Raymond Tunner in Los Angeles in 1968 (Shah and Roth, 1974). Although experts testified that these men were predisposed to be criminally dangerous, the XYY syndrome was not considered a valid excuse by the courts. In fact, there is conflicting evidence that suggests that many XYY individuals are normal but until some effort is made to determine exactly what percentage of the male population is XYY, most of these questions will not be answered. And given the expense, time, and socio-political environment surrounding this controversial relationship, it is unlikely they will be.

The controversy surrounding the XYY syndrome and whether it represents a biological link to criminality does not seem to have received wide social or legal support. Yet indirectly it has prompted a call for an interdisciplinary approach to the study of criminal behaviour. One of the first non-biologists to do so was Nicholas Kittrie, a law professor at the Washington School of Law, American University. Kittrie observed (1971:28) that we must employ an eclectic framework to explain the cause of crime and that the XYY constitution "is merely one more piece of evidence that man is not his own master."

The likelihood that the legal system, let alone criminologists, will readily embrace XYY studies (let alone any biological explanations) has perhaps best been encapsulated by one of the leading North American proponents of this general line of inquiry, **Sarnoff Mednick,** and colleagues Terri Moffit and Susan Stack (1987). In their book, Mednick recounts that his XYY studies have been referred to as "demonism revisited" and how a Washington columnist's story about Mednick's ideas of using physiological data on serious violent offenders being "voodoo" stuff ended by Mednick's research proposal funding being withdrawn! Subsequently, Mednick has done, and continues to do, most of his research along these lines in Denmark.

As we will see in Chapter 8, inquiries into such lines of investigation are not readily supported. As Jeffery (1990:184), another supporter of the positivist frame of reference writes, "we can put criminals in a hell-hole called prison, and we can execute them, but we cannot do research as to the causes of criminal behaviour." And even though the XYY pattern is rare enough not to represent a major factor in law-breaking (see Stoff and Cairns, 1996:6) it should not prevent criminologists from recognizing the role biological factors play in criminal behaviour.

Twin and Adoption Studies and Criminal Behaviour

With each of the preceding biological lines of investigation researchers have not:

- Been able to clearly delineate the biological influence;
- Been able to account for possible intervening variables such as IQ, emotional instability, EEG patterns, etc.;
- Known at what stage of development biological factors begin to exert their influence on behaviour; and
- Been able to determine why the influence is not the same for all people who possess the biological characteristic(s).

Aside from the methodological criticisms, we are left with the question, "just how important (if at all) is the environment in explaining human behaviour"?

Twin Studies

Another biological line of inquiry that has tried to clarify the relationship between the biological basis of criminality and the environmental basis involves identical and fraternal twin studies.

Identical twins share identical genes and are the product of a single fertilized egg called a *monozygote*, while fraternal twins are the products of two eggs fertilized by two separate spermatozoa called *dizygotes*. The physical (i.e., height, weight, blood type, and general appearance) and personality traits of identical twins are more similar than those of fraternal twins. While identical twins may share common traits, careful attention reveals differences. When I remarried, I "inherited" a set of identical twins. For a time I had to be extremely vigilant in order to discern who was who. Physically, they were almost identical but they had different personalities and mannerisms that they sometimes seemed to (intentionally) mask—just to confuse me I think. Even my wife was occasionally stumped about who was on the other end of the telephone, especially when the twins were still in their mid-teens.

In spite of what the term "identical twins" (monozygotic twins) might imply, as we will see even among identical twins the concordance rates (i.e., rate of agreement) are not perfect either. This suggests that in addition to a heritable component the environment must also play a role. The question remains as to what extent the environment plays a role and whether it is possible that some of the gender trait genes are not reproduced.

One of the first twin studies to focus on criminality was conducted by the German scientist Johannes Lange in the late 1920s (cited in Schafer, 1976). Using 30 pairs of twins, of which one of each pair had been incarcerated, Lange found that the concordance rate was significantly higher among identical twins than among fraternal twins. Based on these findings, he suggested there was evidence for inherited criminal behaviour. Although Lange's work received much acclaim initially, his methodology quickly became the subject of much criticism. But the seed had been planted and researchers around the world set out to try and verify his work. Over the years there has been a wide array of studies conducted around the world in monozygotic (MZ) and dizygotic (DZ) twins. While the concordance rates for MZ were always higher than in DZ, none of the studies reported a concordance rate of 100 per cent (see Walters, 1992, or Wilson and Herrnstein, 1985 for a comprehensive review). Given the consistent differences between MZ and DZ twins, it seems fair to conclude that they indicate some degree of genetic predisposition for criminal behaviour. And as Raine (1993) points out, the evidence speaks for itself and, with better biometric modelling, twin studies are likely to make increasingly important contributions to genetic research on crime.

WHAT DO YOU THINK? BOX 5.7

CAN YOU BLAME YOUR PARENTS?

"Heredity is one of the reasons that parents with problems often have children with problems" J. Harris, 1998:294). Do you agree with this statement? If so, what theoretical implications does it raise?

Adoption Studies

A further methodological modification for determining the effects of heredity on criminality was the study of the records of adoptees. One of the first such studies was undertaken by Fini Schulsinger in the early 1970s. The study involved 57 psychopathic adoptees who were matched with 57 non-psychopathic adoptees on the basis of age, gender, social class of adoptive parent, and age of transfer to adoptive home. The concordance rate among the psychopathic patients was 14.4 per cent, compared with only 6.7 per cent of the biological relative of the non-psychopathic adoptees. Again, while the concordance rates were not 100 per cent, the results were statistically significant. However, the results do raise the question, "How do we account for the difference?" Below is a summary of some of the major adoptee studies. As with Schulsinger's findings, they all demonstrate that heredity does play a role in determining human behaviour, whether criminal or otherwise (cited in Vold and Bernard, 1981).

Approximately 15 studies on adoption have been conducted in Europe and the United States. The following summaries represent a cross-section of some of the major ones.

- Crowe (1974) studied 41 female criminal offenders and their 52 adoptee babies. Thirty-five per cent became involved in criminal behaviour as compared to four per cent control adoptee babies.

- Hutchings and Mednick, in a study cited in Mednick and Volavka (1980), studied male adoptees and their biological and adoptive fathers. They found that 36.4 per cent of the delinquent adoptee boys had biological fathers with criminal records. The risk did not depend on whether the child and/or the adopting parents knew about the biological parent's criminal record. In addition, criminal adoptees had a higher per cent of criminal adoptive fathers (23 vs. 9.8 per cent). Overall the results showed the interaction of genetics and environment (36 per cent). The effect of the environment in the absence of genetics was only 11 per cent.

- A Swedish study conducted by Bohman and his colleagues (1982) included 258 male adoptees. Just over 13 per cent of the biological fathers or mothers had been charged with a crime, compared with 10 per cent of male adoptees whose biological parents had no convictions. Although not statistically significant, when alcohol abuse among the biological parents was added to the analysis, the risk of the adoptees committing a crime increased. This evidence lends support to the fact there is some genetic correlation between violence and alcohol abuse.

Finally, although their study is not a twin or adoptee study, Rowe and Farrington (1997:177) report that "criminal convictions were highly familial because convictions in a parent increased the risk of convictions in a child." Their findings are based on a longitudinal study of 344 families with two or more children.

Correlations between siblings were stronger in same-gender siblings (.45 to .50) than in opposite gender ones (.27). Even though Rowe and Farrington used sophisticated statistical models, they were unable to provide strong support for the importance of the family environment (e.g., family size, parental supervision, and parent child-rearing style). They suggest the lack of support of environmental effect "could be taken as indirect support for the genetic inheritance element of the heritability toward criminality" (p. 190). In summarizing their findings they further observe that "unless criminologists routinely adopt behavioural genetic research designs that estimate genetic components in environmental effects (e.g., twins or adoptive studies), no unambiguous evidence can be obtained for family environmental effects on children's criminality" (p. 197).

In **summary**, the volume of research evidence demonstrating a heredity link between MZ twins and criminality is quite impressive, though not conclusive. International studies indicate that while heredity (i.e., genetics) does play a role, the environment is also a factor whose influence has not yet been clearly understood. Yet Stoff and Cairns (1996:7) note that children are more vulnerable than adults and suggest "that common environment may play a more important role than it does for adults." It probably comes as no surprise by now that other lines of biological inquiry also emerged. In his summary of the research on twin studies, **Richard Herrnstein** (1989:4) concludes "the evidence suggests a more complex chain of connections: genes affect psychological traits that in turn affect the likelihood of breaking the law. Intelligence and personality are the two traits most strongly implicated in this chain." If so, let us begin with intelligence.

Intelligence and Criminal Behaviour

"How a person behaves is determined largely by how he thinks. Criminals think differently." S.E. Samenow, 1984.

There is a plethora of evidence to show that a majority of the criminal population has an average IQ of about 91–93, compared to an IQ of 100 for the general population. For a recent review of this literature, see Herrnstein (1989) and Quay (1987). The premise of criminal behaviour being related to mental abnormality had been proposed a few years earlier by the prominent German psychiatrist Gustav Aschaffenburg. One of the pioneering studies asserted that inherited "feeblemindedness" was the now classic study of Henry Goddard (see below). The study was conducted at the New Jersey Training School for the Feeble Minded at Vineland (cited in Vold and Bernard, 1981:81). Goddard used the then newly-developed intelligence test that had been developed by the French team Alfred Binet and Theodore Simon (today known as the Stanford-Binet IQ Test).

In a commonly-cited study, Goddard found that intelligence, like criminal behaviour, is inherited. In fact, in his study of the Kallikak family in 1913, Goddard went so far as to conclude "that crime is the result of low-grade mentality; primarily feeblemindedness, which is an inherited quality" (cited in Schafer, 1976:60–61). Goddard choose the Kallikak family because one of them, Martin Kallikak, had had an affair with a feebleminded girl who gave birth to an illegitimate son. Martin then later married a girl of good reputation. Goddard traced 480 relatives of the son and 490 relatives of his wife. He found that a significant number of the son's relatives had a wide variety of abnormal problems ranging from prostitution to criminal behaviour and psychiatric problems. As for the relatives on Martin's wife's side, Goddard found very few such incidents. During the 1870s Richard Dugale made similar claims in his study of the Juke family (Vold and Bernard, 1981). So powerful were the claims that they led to the sterilization of feebleminded women as a measure to prevent future generations of feeblemindedness. Science was used to "justify" this practice of eugenics. Even the Supreme Court of the United States got into the act by condoning sterilization of the feebleminded. For example, Justice O.W. Holmes said, when referring to a case involving a feebleminded woman, that "three generations of imbeciles are enough" (Rennie, 1978, cited in Jeffery, 1990:181).

Contrary to the findings of Goddard and Dugale, intelligence **does not** predict delinquency or crime very well. Unfortunately, neither study examined the role of the environment and the role it might play. For example, lower standards of living and being raised in a family with limited education are strong environmental cues that can predispose youth to deviant behaviour. More recent research cited by Kotulak (1997), and others, suggests there has been sufficient evidence to indicate that we should not completely discard the relationship between intelligence and criminal behaviour. McCord and McCord (1959) were among the first to suggest that parental discipline, family cohesion, religious upbringing, and exposure to peer and social opportunities are better indicators than IQ at predicting criminal behaviour. Several years later however, Gordon (1987) demonstrated that the higher the verbal IQ score, the lower the probability of delinquent behaviour. Gordon also attributes differences in the delinquency rates between whites and blacks to IQ scores (see Sowell's work on p. 179). Similarly, Rutter and Giller (1984) found that lower IQ scores correlated to an increased risk of delinquent behaviour which also affected youths' self-esteem. Herbert Quay's (1987) evidence indicates that, on the average, delinquents have IQs of about 92, which is about one-half of a standard deviation lower than the general population. In addition, Quay believes that a lower IQ places youths at social risk and Herrnstein (1989) adds that this often leads to poor parenting and eventually becomes a negative spiral of disadvantages for youth—an integrated approach.

Finally, recent research at the John Radcliffe Hospital in Oxford, England, has found evidence that appears to link intelligence to pH levels (see below) in the cortex of the brain. Although preliminary, the study found that teens with higher IQ scores tended to have higher alkaline pH readings than those with lower IQs. Graci (1997) notes that this is the first time intelligence has been linked to a biochemical marker in the brain. It would be interesting to see whether the findings hold true for offenders with low IQ test scores.

In an attempt to synthesize the vast volume of literature that has accumulated over the years, Akers (1994:78) concludes: "it is difficult to dismiss entirely the evidence of correlation between IQ and delinquency." The prominent sociologist, Don Gibbons (1992:148), arrived at a similar conclusion. However, he cautions "the extent to which measured intelligence is itself a social product of sub-cultural variations in learning environments and similar factors, rather than an index of innate intelligence."

Intelligence tests, on the other hand, attempt to measure two primary functions and at least one secondary function. The first primary function is to obtain an estimate of a person's current level of cognitive functioning (verbal as opposed to spatial/performance IQ), called intelligence quotient (IQ). The second primary function is to assess intellectual deterioration in organic or functional psychological disorders. The secondary function is that therapists use the information for clinical purposes. Overall however, Wilson and Herrnstein (1985:159) conclude their review of psychological intelligence tests by describing them as a "blunt instrument of measurement."

Notwithstanding the previous observation, Herrnstein (1989b) suggests that with the growing redistribution of childbearing toward lower social strata, there will be a drop in the average intelligence of the population. This will happen because the parents of the children are also likely to have a lower verbal IQ, as opposed to lowered spatial/performance IQ. They are unable to provide the stimuli needed to nurture the intellectual growth of their children. According to Herrnstein, this is likely to continue through successive generations at a declining increment of one point per generation. Unfortunately, he argues, schooling alone does not guarantee success of improved IQ. As he notes "schools are being criticized for their lack of rigour, for failing to instill a love of learning; society as a whole is criticized for underpaying and underappreciating teachers" (p.78).

So while schools and homes (i.e., parents) can be improved to ensure that intelligence does not decline any further, it must be recognized that while environmental factors play a role, genetic factors in intelligence also contribute significantly to IQ. In addition, future researchers need to examine the mechanisms by which low IQ predisposes individuals to crime and to determine the extent to which low IQ is a product of the social and cultural environment, as opposed to early brain dysfunction.[6]

Personality and Criminal Behaviour

Again, we are confronted with the "horse and cart" scenario. How do we acquire personality? The popular answer is that personality is the product of psychological factors since personality refers to characteristic patterns of acting, feeling, and thinking as defined by age, gender, race, ethnicity or geographic region. However, as with language, personality may also have a biological foundation (see, for example, Lenneberg, 1967).

In recent years, there has been an abundance of evidence showing that most offenders' personalities are distinctive, though not necessarily abnormal. However, earlier research found little or no relationship between the personalities of offenders and non-offenders. One of the earlier studies, Schuessler and Cressey (1950), examined 113 studies and found that only 42 per cent of the studies reported a difference in personalities of offenders and non-offenders. Schuessler and Cressey relied on a sociological perspective. However, many of the earlier studies were either methodologically flawed and/or the measurement instruments lacked the sophistication to adequately measure personality traits. In his update on the personality literature (44 studies between 1965 and 1975), Tannenbaum (1977) found that 80 per cent of the studies reported a personality-crime association. All the studies reviewed, however, relied on psychological indicators rather than biological measurements.[7] The biological component of personality is not well understood because measurements of personality have not been well-standardized. As Herrnstein (1989) notes, personality tests only measure an approximation of personality. Even though most tests have reliability and validity scores, they are all subject to an error measurement as well.

The variety of psychometric (i.e., personality assessment) tests that have been developed over the years to measure personality take up entire books. For example, in their first volume, Corocoran and Fischer (1987) divide their measurement textbook into three major parts: instruments (approximately 90) for adults, instruments (N=19) for children, and instruments for couples and families (N=15). In addition, personality is probably more multi-faceted than intelligence. There are, for example, two different types of personality tests. With projective personality tests, the test taker is presented with an ambiguous stimulus (e.g., ink blot or incomplete sentence test) and asked to respond to them. And while projective texts may yield important information, Weiss (1988), among others, has observed that the analysis and interpretation of these tests is subject to wide variations. The other types of personality tests are the objective inventories. In these tests the test taker responds to a list of "questions" from which an answer is selected. The *Minnesota Multiphasic Personality Inventory* (MMPI) is perhaps the most widely-used personality inventory. The test consists of 567 statements that are divided into sub-scales.

The assumption underlying personality and intelligence tests is that they rely on standardized psychological assessment procedures, which are seen to be primarily the product of one's experience. Herrnstein (1989) suggests, however, that the different aspects of personality may have different heritabilities. Just as there are genes for the colour of our eyes and hair and for the growth and development of our limbs, it might well be possible that inherited personality traits predispose individuals to criminal behaviour. Combined with environmental cues (i.e., experience and context) these factors provide the opportunities for which crime(s) an individual is likely to commit. Therefore, personality and intelligence may have a biological link. More precisely, personality and intelligence are not simply the result of environmentalism but are an interaction between the environment and the brain (organism)—a bio-environmental model (see Chapter 8). This notion is not new. In fact, one of the early pioneers in experimental abnormal psychology, **Emil Kraepelin** (1856–1926) proposed that personality disorders could be directly linked to organic brain disorders (Schafer, 1976). As noted above, he developed a diagnostic classification system for disorders. Due to the poor methodological and measurement techniques of the time his findings had a limited lifespan, but his system became the basis for diagnostic categories in the *Diagnostic and Statistical Manual of Mental Disorders* (DSM–IV).

In **summary**, we have explored a variety of inheritable factors that have been, and in some cases continue to be, linked to criminal behaviour. And while some of the earlier notions such as phrenology, somatotyping, and physiognomy have met with considerable skepticism, there still remain elements of these perspectives that cannot, or should not, be completely discarded.[8]

As noted earlier, the premise of biological determinism has not been in vogue for some time. But, just as allopathic medicine is beginning to re-evaluate some of the complementary practices (e.g., acupuncture, colour therapy, homeopathy, and naturopathy) criminologists should not be so anxious to reject scientific evidence for which there is a substantial following. Until a theory, or perspective, comes along that can solve and/or prevent all crime, criminologists should continue to entertain all new ideas and subject them to scientific scrutiny.

We will now shift our review to biologically-based explanations whose origins may either be heritable or the result of lifestyle factors. We will examine such factors as alcohol and drugs, endocrine imbalances, diet, and environmental conditions.

WHAT DO YOU THINK? BOX 5.8

TRANSCENDING CONVENTIONAL THOUGHT

"Significant problems we face cannot be solved with the same level of thinking we were at when we created them" (Albert Einstein (1879–1955). How might we begin to overcome socio-political resistance and look more closely at the possible relationship between biological influences and criminality?

Alcohol and Illicit Drugs and Criminal Behaviour

Extreme drunkenness has been used as a legal defence.[9] Such a defence is premised on the assertion that the offender did not have the mental capacity to appreciate his/her actions. Although the drunkenness defence is based on legal principles, a biochemical malfunctioning must occur in order for the brain not to function properly.

Burns (1989) notes that, in the United States in 1962, fewer than one per cent of adolescents had experimented with drugs, but by the early 1980s, 57 per cent of adolescents had tried some type of illicit drug—usually marijuana. Similarly, in their review, Smart and Jansen (1991) found that most Canadian and American surveys report that use of alcohol among adolescents varies between

60 and 90 per cent (see Box 5.9). Perry (1996:147) notes that, "the late 1960s and early 1970s saw adolescent substance use become more widely publicized," perhaps accounting for some of the increased usage among adolescents. But, Doweiko (1993 cited in Perry, 1996) comments on how the 1960s and '70s marked a period of rapid evolution in North American society. Substance abuse became a legitimatized way of expressing frustration and rebellion. And although it was not the only factor identified, Carter (1997) notes that Canada's most notorious serial killer, Clifford Olson, was an alcoholic when not in prison. He also comments on how many other serial killers also had histories of alcohol abuse.

WHAT DO YOU THINK? BOX 5.9

- -

ALCOHOL AND ILLICIT DRUG USE AND CRIME

The following examples are but a small sample of the growing body of literature showing a link between substance use/abuse and criminal behaviour.

From Boyd (1991):

- Approximately 20 per cent of all visits to Canada's emergency rooms are alcohol-related.
- Alcohol-driven violence creates about 300,000 annual visits to emergency wards.
- Men are twice as likely to be treated for alcohol-related violence then women.

From Synnott (1996):

- More than half of the 5,500 criminals sent to jail since 1990 had consumed either alcohol or used drugs on the day they committed the crime. More than two-thirds had related problems requiring treatment while in prison.

From O'Neil, Wish, and Visher (1990):

- Approximately 70 percent of all offenders are substance abusers. How might we best address the problem of alcohol and drugs? Should it be treated as a crime or as a disease? To what extent does the risk of punishment serve as a deterrent?

In addition to the increased experimentation with illicit drugs, Burns (1989) also reports that the average age of onset has dropped over the years. These views can also been found in the Canadian literature (see Eliany, 1994). Given the dominant sociological perspective in North America, these trends have been explained from a social constructionist perspective, viewing society as a constructed representation of reality in which the world has no underlying objective character (see Pfuhl and Henry, 1993). However, as the evidence suggests, an interdisciplinary perspective may provide greater predictive and explanatory potential.

Both alcohol and drugs (legal and illegal) affect metabolic processes and the central nervous system. And while relatively little attention has been paid to the biogenic effects on criminal behaviour, the effects have been extensively studied in the medical arena. For example, Caboret and Wesner's (1990) findings of a genetic factor that operates from the biological parent to the adoptee and the chance of alcohol abuse occurring in the adoptee was statistically very strong. They also found, however, that the environment played a role. Having an alcoholic in the adoptive home increased the risk of alcohol problems in the adoptee, but not to the same extent as having a biological parent who was an alcoholic. And, since the 1970s, as the genetic-link evidence has accumulated, and as new and more sophisticated techniques have been developed, researchers have been attempting to localize the gene(s) responsible as well as to find out how the gene(s) operates (Wijsman, 1990).

While some researchers are trying to localize the genetic component for alcoholism, other investigators have been looking for risk factors or markers for alcoholism. Tabakoff, Whelan, and Hoffman (1990) have found neurotransmitters in the brain that are related to alcoholism. In one of the first such studies, Julius Axelrod (who won a Nobel Prize for his work on brain chemistry) demonstrated that when cocaine was placed on the brain of dead rats, it was absorbed into the brain and displaced the existing neurotransmitters. Axelrod found that over time, "drugs actually drive out the brain's own chemicals" (cited in Burns, 1989:49). A corollary to the biochemical changes that take place through drug use is the fact that certain individuals have different sensitivity levels or responsiveness levels to alcohol. If you have ever attended a drinking party, you have probably noticed how some people can "hold" their drink/drugs better than others.

In **summary**, Barros and Miczek (cited in Cairns and Stoff, 1996) perhaps best summarized the status of the drug (including alcohol)–aggression link. For example, they observed, "ethanol clearly stands out as the drug most frequently associated with violent and aggressive behaviour in humans" (p. 342). However, while drugs and alcohol correlate highly with aggression and risk in suicide, homicide, motor-vehicle accidents, and domestic violence, the research has not established a clear causal relationship. While we know that drugs act on the neurotransmitter system of the brain, research is less clear about the influence of environmental, cultural, gender, and individual differences. Future research should study the effects of alcohol and drugs from a multiple-level and interdisciplinary perspective.

The notion that race may represent an explanatory factor in crime is, as Ashley Montagu (1997) clearly points out, one of social science's most dangerous myths. Yet there are some who continue to report the existence of such a relationship.[10] Even the late, and highly-respected psychologist Richard J. Herrnstein and the political scientist Charles Murray received considerable attention for their racist book *The Bell Curve: Intelligence and Class Structure in American Life*.

Fortunately, few scholars pursue such lines of inquiry, but those who do only retard the progress of biologically-based research in criminology.

Endocrine Imbalances and Criminal Behaviour[11]

Hippocrates and Galen, two of the most influential physicians of ancient Greece, believed that the human organism is a single hierarchical complex in which mind (e.g., imagination and humour), body (e.g., nerves, blood, and muscle), and soul (e.g., vital spirit) are closely linked. In fact, Hippocrates, the father of modern medicine, asked his students to divide their patients into classifications according to blood, phlegm, and colour of the bile. The idea of classifying the human body has since evolved into the relatively new science of endocrinology (from two Greek words, *within* and *separate*) (Beiler, 1965).

Today, there is a growing body of literature that relates various physical and behavioural conditions to endocrine imbalances. However, it was not until the pioneering work of the German chemist, Fredrich Wohler, in 1828, that it became possible to study endocrine systems (Vold and Bernard, 1981). After synthesizing the organic compound urea, Wohler speculated that humans are chemical entities. Excited by this new line of thinking, researchers began to identify some of the physiological and psychological effects of the endocrine glands (i.e., the hormones, from the Greek "to arouse"). Louis Berman (1938, cited in Vold and Bernard, 1981:109) was among the first to develop a chemical-glandular theory of personality differences. One of the areas that received considerable attention in this regard was the brain.

Hormones Gone "Bad"

Our brain is responsible for managing all the hormones released from our *pituitary gland,* located near the middle of the brain (see Figure 5–1). The *hypothalamus* is the nerve centre for the autonomic nervous system and is also the control centre for sex hormones—our libido. It is also the seat of our emotional reactions: fear, aggression, hunger, and thirst. Jeffery (1990:200) refers to the functions of the hypothalamus as the "food, sex, fight or flight" syndrome. Below it is the *substantial nigra,* whose main function is to send signals throughout the body. The brain communicates with itself by neural transmission. The thalamus is the sensory relay location that transmits neural information from the sensory organs to other parts of the brain. The chemical transporters that carry the message along the *axons* are the **neurotransmitters**. How information gets around the brain depends on the amounts of each neurotransmitter present at the synapses where the neurons join. Neurons are transmitted via an electrical and biochemical impulse (Burns, 1989, Colgan, 1996). There are four main types of neurotransmitter.

Neurons can either increase (excite) or decrease (inhibit) the level of activity of receptor neurons. The primary *excitatory* neurotransmitters are *dopamine* (DA) and *acetylcholine* (ACh) while the two main inhibitory neurotransmitters are *serotonin* (5-HT) and *noradrenalin* (NE) (norepinephrine). And while considerable monies and research efforts have been invested to understand how hormonal imbalances lead to health problems (e.g., low sex drive, lack of mental alertness, prostrate problems, and female reproductive problems) criminologists have not been very interested in examining the role endocrine/hormone imbalances might play in understanding criminal behaviour. For example, consider the well documented medical finding that shows that depression among women increases dramatically after normal births (Colgan, 1996). While there are sociological (e.g., strain) and psychological (e.g., frustration) explanations for such behaviour, could the depression be related to hormonal and biological factors?

There is no strong evidence that links female depression to crime—not because it may not exist but because it does not fall within the conventional lines of criminological inquiry. Recent research, for example, has shown that in order for a mother to protect and nurture her baby during *in utero* development and early infancy, a stronger immune system is required to protect the baby. Mothers need more estrogen in order to have strong immune systems. However, increased levels of estrogen in the body stimulate both the acetylcholine and dopamine systems which, in many cases, lead to the classic symptoms of anxiety, irritability, and hypersensitivity—premenstrual syndrome (*PMS*) (Colgan, 1996).

One of the first studies to examine the influence of hormonal changes on female behaviour found that 46 per cent of the samples (N=156) committed their crimes either four days before or following menstruation (Dalton, 1961). However, in spite of more recent supporting evidence (e.g., Fishbein, 1992), it is still not clear whether the psychological and physical stress of aggression might trigger menstruation and not vice versa. Nevertheless, in the 1980s there were a number of successful defences of women who had killed men while experiencing PMS (Katz and Chambliss, 1995).

As for hormones and their effect on men, a recent study by James Dabbs, of Georgia State University, (cited in Gibbs, 1995) found that those male prison inmates with higher **testosterone** concentrations are more likely to have committed violent crimes. If the hypothalamus and striatal cortex are sensitive hormonal imbalances which can affect our health, is it not also possible that hormonal imbalances might also predispose us to criminal behaviour?

Canadian researchers Philippe Rushton and Julie Harris (1994) tested salivary testosterone levels of prosocial and aggressive behaviour in both male and female twins (228 pairs). They found that testosterone was higher in males and in those males who expressed more aggressive behaviour. They suggested that male violence is largely genetic in origin, whereas female violence is often triggered by environmental factors. They propose that the differences between gender violence are related to testosterone levels. What remains unclear, however, is the effect of the interaction between biology, gender roles, and socialization processes.

Finally, there is a growing body of research into the possible link of low **serotonin** (5-HT) levels to violent behaviour and impulsive and suicidal behaviour among criminals and psychiatric patients. While most of these studies have been conducted with animals, Stoff and Vitiello (1996) present a summary table that includes 24 of the more recent studies reporting links between adolescent and adult aggressive and antisocial behaviour with serotonin levels. However, due to the limited number of studies and some questionable methodologies, the use of serotonergic drugs in childhood aggression has not been clearly delineated. In fact, the studies "do not reveal the consistent pattern of reduced 5-HT function" (Ibid, 116) but that the growing body of literature does offer supportive results that should prompt continued research along these lines of inquiry.

Therefore, since brain levels of serotonin may be partially determined by genes, a percentage of individuals may be genetically predisposed to violent behaviour. Increasingly, criminologists are revisiting the possible links of the brain and are incorporating areas ranging from psychology, biochemistry, neurology, and sociology into an interdisciplinary approach to a theory of human behaviour.

FIGURE 5-1

THE BRAIN

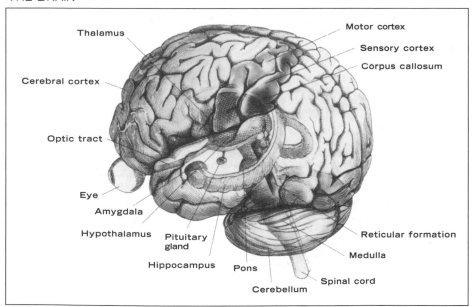

Source: C.R. Jeffery (1990:200). *Criminology: An Interdisciplinary Approach.* Englewood Cliffs; NI-P-H.

EEG Abnormalities

Although their ideas were not grounded in scientific evidence, in 1928 Max Schlapp and Edward Smith wrote the first criminological textbook, to try and explain criminal behaviour as a product of hormonal imbalances (Vold and Bernard, 1981). The idea of being able to explain certain criminal behaviours based on endocrine imbalances was popular in the 1930s. However, by the end of that decade, a study conducted by Matthew Molitch seemed to put to rest any assertions that endocrine imbalances were related to crime (see Vold and Bernard, 1981:111). Then a study conducted by Dennis Hill and D. A. Pond, in 1952, on 100 serious offenders found that approximately one-half had abnormal electroencephalograms (EEGs). While interesting, they failed to use a control group and therefore no conclusions could be drawn from their findings (Vold and Bernard, 1981). Even though the studies since Hill and Pond's work have not provided a strong theoretical case for a link between EEG abnormalities and crime, there is sufficient evidence to indicate that EEG abnormalities are more commonly found among serious and/or violent offenders than among other offender populations (see Shah and Roth, 1974, and Wilson and Herrnstein, 1985). Referring to some longitudinal research conducted in Scandinavia, Wilson and Herrnstein (1985) observed that the results confirmed that there was a relationship between low-level arousal and certain crimes. Low levels of brain arousal have also been linked to psychopathic behaviour and criminality (see Box 5.10).

A CLOSER LOOK BOX 5.10

Psychopath: A Personality Disorder or Chemical Imbalance?

Although estimates vary, somewhere between 20 and 60 per cent of provincial and federal inmates suffer from some type of mental disorder. Throughout the 1800s and early 1900s it has been referred to as *mania sans délire* ("madness without confusion"), "moral insanity," and even as "irresistible atavistic impulses." Today, mental disorders have been referred to as **psychopathy**, sociopathy, or antisocial personality.

The late Hans Eysenck (1977) and the Canadian researcher, Robert Hare (1996), described psychopaths as extraverts who have low internal arousal levels. They argued that psychopaths must constantly seek stimulation and do not respond well to learning by direct experience, such as punishment. To Eysenck and others, psychopathy is viewed as a behaviour disorder that has been blamed on familial and sociological factors. Eysenck believed that many chronic young offenders suffer from psychopathy and if we could understand and treat it, we could significantly reduce the problem of delinquency.

By contrast, there is a growing body of literature suggesting that psychopathic behaviour does **not** stem from bad parenting but rather from fundamental differences in the psychopathic brain. For example, recent research has found that psychopaths have smaller heart rate changes and skin conductance changes in response to fear-provoking stimuli; their prefrontal cortexes do not function normally; they do not respond normally to startle potentiation; and the visual cues of their left/right brain responses differ from non-psychopathic individuals. There is also a growing body of evidence indicating that young offenders diagnosed with psychopathic traits tend to have lower resting heart rates when committing their deviant acts. Raine (1993) reviews fourteen studies between 1971 and 1993. He observes that while there was statistical variation between studies, all found the same effect. Explanations range from fearlessness, autonomic underarousal and an autonomic nervous system that favours parasympathetic rather than sympathetic autonomic processes. However, among adult psychopaths, there is no evidence to suggest that they also experience lower resting heart rates. Therefore, while there may be a stronger biological association among psychopathic adolescents the effects are less compelling among psychopathic adults. Again, we find a possible link between biological and social factors.

WHAT DO YOU THINK? BOX 5.11

PSYCHOPATHY: IS IT BIOLOGICAL OR PSYCHOLOGICAL?

Among conventional psychologists, there are different interpretations of the psychopathic personality, while among biologically-oriented psychologists, psychopathy is believed to be related to measurable physical conditions. If that is true, should psychopathic offenders be treated or punished?

As noted above, criminologists to date have only dabbled in this area. However, if the medical literature is any indication, then perhaps we need to pay closer attention to the possible relationship between endocrine imbalances and criminal behaviour. In the next section we will examine the relationship between nutrition, environmental toxins and crime.

Nutrition and Environmental Toxins
and Criminal Behaviour

Dr. Marnie Rice, director of research at Oak Ridge Psychiatric Hospital in
Penetanguishene in Ontario, when asked what she would do about violence in
Canada if she were given a blank cheque, said she would "spend it feeding good
food to young mothers-to-be" (P. Carter, 1995:34).

In the previous section it was noted that endocrinology means "as within so
without." The same could be said about nutrition—you are what you eat. If that
is true, then perhaps there is a connection between nutrition and crime. And
while we may exercise free will in what we eat, we have less control over how
certain foods affect our bodies and mind or, more specifically, our brain. In addition to what we eat, we are also affected by what we drink and by the air we
breathe. Any time I spend time in a large city like London or Paris, as much as I
enjoy the experience, my throat usually gets sore within a few days. And everyone is probably familiar with "Montezuma's revenge"—the poor quality of drinking water that can be found in less well-developed countries.

Perhaps the most frequently-documented example of nutrition as a source
of crime is *hypoglycemia*, or low blood sugar. And perhaps the most famous
case involving the use of diet as a defence involved Dan White who, in 1979,
was convicted of the voluntary manslaughter of San Francisco's mayor, George
Moscone and his fellow supervisor, Harvey Milk in a case dubbed the "Twinkie
defence."[12] White's successful defence was based on the premise that he suffered from "diminished capacities" as a result of eating too many junk foods
high in sugar (e.g., Coca Cola, chocolate, and Twinkie bars) which aggravated a
chemical imbalance.

One of the functions of the pancreas is to secret insulin into the blood system
to remove sugar in order to convert it to fat for energy use. The fat is stored in
the liver until the body needs it. The brain regulates and controls blood sugar
levels in the body. Philpott (1978:128) found that after studying blood sugar levels "before and after exposure to addictants in known narcotic, alcohol, and food
addicts I arrived at convincing evidence that hypoglycemia can consistently be
observed as relating to the stress of the addictive withdrawal state" (also see
Virkkunen and Linnoila, 1996 for an update).

In 1980, **Alexander Schauss** was among the first to popularize the notion that
violent delinquent behaviour might be related to bio-environmental factors—
more specifically, dietary factors that produce biochemical imbalances. Along with
several associates at the University of Puget Sound, he found that on average juveniles ingested 32 per cent more sugar than a control group who were behaviourally-
disordered but had no criminal record. Several supportive studies linking dietary
habits with violent behaviour appeared soon after in such journals as the

International Journal of Biosocial Research and, more recently, in the *Townsend Letter for Doctors.* For example, Werteim (1995) reports that in 1902 the average American consumed about 10 pounds of sugar per year. By 1982 it had risen to 123 pounds and by 1988 to 133 or 1/3 pound per person per day! And while the concept of diet being related to violent crime may have appeared outlandish to conventionally-trained criminologists, students of nutrition have amassed considerable data showing a link between dietary habits and anti-social behaviour.

The following summaries represent a sampling of the growing body of literature linking the effects of certain dietary practices to criminal behaviour and general behavioural disorders:

- Adams (1998a) reports on a study by Jacqueline Stordy, among others, who have found a link between attention deficit disorder (**ADD**) and a diet high in saturated fats (i.e., processed foods). ADD is characterized by restlessness, hyperactivity, and forgetfulness. It has been related to conduct disorders, sensation-seeking and early adult offending among delinquents (Farrington, 1994). And in a follow-up article, Adams (1988b) reports that two-thirds of ADD cases likely go unreported and undetected. It is estimated that ADD affects between 5 and 12 per cent of Canadians—including 1.2 million children.

- A British psychiatrist, Kathy Smith, reports that women whose diets were low in the amino acid *tryptophan* were at greater risk of depression than those who had normal diets. Trytophan-deficient diets are more commonly found among women with eating disorders (Nutrition cited ..., 1997).

- Lonsdale and Shamberger (1980) found a positive correlation between those youths displaying a high rate of irritability and aggressiveness and the amount of junk food and fast food they ate.

- Schoenthaler and Doraz (1983) tested 276 incarcerated young offenders to determine whether a change in their sugar intake corresponded to a change in their institutional behaviour. Simply altering their sugar intake produced significant disciplinary actions for the experimental group. Meanwhile, Schoenthaler, Amos, Eysenck, Hudes, and Korda (1995) point out that the improvement in behaviour may be not so much due to decreased sugar consumption as to the increased intake of the vitamins and minerals contained in the fresh fruits, vegetables, and whole grain foods. They studied 402 male prisoners over a 15-week experimental period. Two groups received different strengths of vitamin–mineral supplements (100 per cent vs. 300 per cent of the USRDA) and one group, the placebo. They found that the groups receiving the supplements had a mean rule violation reduction (16 per cent for the 300 per cent group and 38 per cent for the 100 per cent) while the placebo group had a mean rule violation increase (i.e., 20 per cent). The authors concluded that while environment should still be considered when studying violent behaviour, more research needs to be done to understand the relationship between nutritional intervention and controlling anti-social behaviour.

As with any line of inquiry, however, not everyone was impressed. Morris, in 1987, (cited in Vito and Holmes, 1994:111) "reviewed several studies and concluded that no reliable evidence exists to suggest that a high-sugar diet causes hypoglycemia, that the condition is common among offenders, or that it causes violent, criminal, or antisocial behaviour. She further recommends that correctional administrators not take any drastic steps to modify the sugar intake of prisoners."

Support for Morris's ideas appears to be limited. The study and science of the treatment and prevention of disease adjustment of the natural chemical constituents of our body is called *orthomolecular* medicine. First coined by the late Dr. Linus Pauling (the guru of vitamin C) in 1968, it is an enigma among conventional practitioners. But its supporters, and the evidence, are increasing voluminously. In 1959, Dr. Frank Boudreau, of the Milbank Fund of New York, said: "If all we know about nutrition were applied to modern society, the result would be an enormous improvement in public health, at least equal to that which resulted when the germ theory of infectious disease was made the basis of public health and medical work" (Williams and Kalita, 1977:ix). A major study cited in Williams and Kalita reported that in 1975 one-half of the population was suffering from some degenerative disease and the number of children classified as hyperactive, retarded and schizophrenic was steadily increasing. Why? The authors point a finger directly at the changing dietary habits of North Americans and environmental pollutants. Along similar lines, Beasley and Swift (1988) reported that the average Scholastic Aptitude Test (SAT) scores among young people has been steadily declining over the past 25 years! Why? Again, they also point to diet and environmental deterioration as possible markers.

More recently, the University Medical Research Publishers, based in Tempe, Arizona, cite a study by Dr. Emanual Cheraskin, professor emeritus at the University of Alabama Medical School. Cheraskin surveyed over 1,400 healthy individuals over a twenty-year period and found that not only do healthy people eat better than less healthy people but that their diets consistently exceeded the government recommended daily allowance (RDA) anywhere from five to nine times! His work has been replicated with young people and the results were very similar. The researchers of the later study report that only 5 per cent of the American population is "clinically well" (University Medical Research Pub., 1993). The overall implication, aside from the obvious one—that most North Americans have a sub-standard diet—is that it subjects them to physical and emotional problems and that dietary deficiencies may result in genetic mutations. For example, in a 1992 article that appeared in the prestigious medical journal *Lancet*, Dr. Lucas reported that pre-term babies who had not been fed mother's milk, but cow's milk and/or soya-based infant formula, had an 8.3 IQ deficit by the age of 8.5 years.

Other diet links to crime include studies on an excess or undersupply of vitamins such as C, B3, and B6, as well as the relationship between food allergies and anti-social behaviour (see Raine, 1993 for an excellent review). In addition to suffering from learning disabilities and cognitive deficits, excessive exposure to, or high intake of, certain common minerals such as cadmium, copper, lead, magnesium, manganese, and zinc have also been linked to aggression (for reviews of this literature see Denno, 1988; Marlowe, Bliss, and Schneider, 1994). Of these minerals, manganese has received considerable interest in recent years. The following is a brief list of some observations and findings relating to a possible link between manganese and crime.

- The notion that manganese might be a dangerous substance can be traced back to 200 BC when the Greeks referred to it as the **voodoo metal** because of its apparent harmful effects on humans (VRF, 1994).

- In 1820, Captain Flinder of the sailing ship the "Beagle," on arriving at Groote Eylandt off Australia, observed that it was the only island visited in the South Pacific where the women were sent into the bush and the men came prepared to do battle. He also observed that the water had a blue hue suggesting a high manganese concentration. Many years later the island boosted the world's largest manganese mine (VRF, 1994).

- Over one hundred years later, in 1987, Cawte and Florence reported that, based on 50 years of data, the incidence of violence and murder was 299 per cent higher on Groote Eylandt than in any other area in Australia.

- James Huberty, who in 1984 killed 21 innocent people after firing into a McDonald's restaurant in San Ysidro, California, and Patrick Purdy, who in 1989 went on a killing spree in a Stockton, California school, were both found to have excessively high levels of cadmium and manganese in their hair (Walker, 1994).

FYI BOX 5.12

Environmental Toxins Inherited

An in-depth study of Canada's 1991 Gulf War veterans "raises serious questions about the incidence of birth defects in the children of soldiers." The study revealed that children born to veterans of the war were 20 per cent more likely to have physical defects. The veterans meanwhile expressed feelings of depression, insomnia, and irritability. The study speculates the causes of the symptoms to include exposure to chemical and biological weapons, use of anti-nerve gas pills, toxic fumes from oil fires, and war-related stress (Bronskill, 1998, June 28).

In one of the first comprehensive studies to explore a possible link between high levels of manganese and crime, Gottschalk et al. (1991) conducted a three-phase study over a six-year period on over 200 violent offenders and a control group of 200 non-violent offenders. In addition to finding significantly higher levels of manganese among the violent offenders (regardless of race) they suggested that factors such as alcohol, diet, or psycho-social events might affect the elevated manganese levels. Subsequent support came from Barnes et al. (1993) and Marlowe (1993), and from Canadian researchers Donaldson and James Owen from Montreal, who showed that manganese ions can: "wreak considerable havoc among the catecholaminergic nerve cells localized (in the brain) ... looks exactly like the signs and symptoms of Parkinson's disease ... Symptoms of manganese toxicity span a continuum from mild features such as extreme fatigue, somnolence, and irritability, to ... involvement in 'stupid crimes' and (irrational) violent behaviour (manganese madness)" (cited in Walker, 1994:1332).

Finally, the issue of whether "potential" environmental harm will ever be taken seriously received a major blow in 1998 when the Canadian government lifted its ban on the controversial gas additive MMT—a manganese-based fuel additive designed to increase octane levels in gas. Rather than heed pleas from environmental and health groups the Liberals, by lifting the ban, avoided a $250 million American lawsuit. Politicians simply argued the scientific evidence was lacking (Eggertson, 1998).

A CLOSER LOOK BOX 5.13

Crime and pH Saliva

Several years ago, Dr. G. Bonham, then Medical Officer of Health for the City of Calgary, publicly warned of the epidemic of small babies being born in the city. He attributed this shift to improper nutrition and a variety of lifestyle factors of the mothers. He further stated that "If you think prevention is expensive try treatment for size" (Reich, 1994). Reich was referring to the higher cost of treating the increased incidence of psychiatric and physical diseases that occur in these children as they grow up. A few years later, Dr. Brent Friesen, the new Medical Officer of Health reiterated the same observations (Lowey, 1997). Friesen pointed out that between 1986 and 1995 the percentage of total newborns born underweight went up one per cent (to 6.8 per cent) and that the incidence of allergies had also increased. He further suggested that many of the social ills in Canadian society (e.g., alcohol and drug abuse, depression, suicide, and crime) may be based on specific nutritional deficiencies combined with increased indoor work and recreation lifestyles. Together these deficiencies can compromise our states of mental and physical wellbeing.

Based on documented cases of patients over a long period of time, Reich believes that specific nutritional deficiencies are the result of a diet high in acid-producing foods and deficient in alkaline-producing foods. Combined with a deficiency of sun on the skin this results in an excess of acidic ionic hydrogen in the body. That physiological effect can be manifested in hyper-physical activity which in turn can lead to criminality and to drug addiction.

Is there any easy or cost-efficient way to test for this complex biochemical imbalance? Reich suggests there is such a (2 cents per test) technique. It involves using simple pH paper to test saliva. Doing the salivary test before or several hours after eating, and not preceding it with strenuous exercise, will provide a reliable pH reading, indicating whether the individual is calcium and vitamin D deficient. Although a seemingly viable and inexpensive method for testing violent and/or anti-social offenders, Dr. Reich, despite offering many times to conduct the research virtually for free, has not been able to find support for his ideas.

You might want to test this simple concept. Using pH paper test yourself under different conditions (e.g., first thing in the morning, just before an important exam, after a strenuous workout, eating different kinds of foods, etc). Then also note how you are feeling. If your body is rested, the pH should read alkaline and if you are "stressed" it should read acidic.

In **summary**, there is a growing body of evidence that links nutrition to crime. However, the factors are quite divergent, with no consistent food type, mineral, or vitamin being fingered as the ultimate marker. Similarly, most of the evidence also suggests that there may be environmental and/or psycho-social factors playing mitigating roles. Overall, the findings point to the complexity of human behaviour and how it may be altered through what we eat, drink, or breathe. Perhaps Beasley and Swift (1989:447) provided a cogent summary when they noted that "chronically poor nutrition, environment, variously affecting the embryo, fetus, and infant at their most vulnerable moments of development, wreak much of this burden."

Summary

Biological explanations of criminal behaviour emerged in an era when concerns for social control had been addressed in an environment of retribution and "just deserts." Issues of eugenics and "politically correct" concerns about implications of racial and class bias had not yet become social concerns. Subsequently, in this positivistic environment, the biological perspectives received considerable and wide-spread academic and social respectability.

As the strategies for conducting research methods improved and the technologies for collecting observations and improving measurements were refined, the scope of biological perspectives grew. They have ranged from phrenology to somatotyping to genetics to personality to nutritional factors. However, with each new perspective we saw that their ability to explain "all" criminal behaviour remained incomplete. The question of environmental (nurture = experience and context) seemed to be inseparable from the biological (nature) theories. In other words, biology may affect experience or context, but environment also influences biology. Alternatively, as the eminent anthropologist Ashley Montagu (1997) points out, crime and aggression, while having biological potential, need to await the appropriate environmental trigger before expressing themselves. Therefore, both perspectives need to be studied and we need to recognize that criminal behaviour (and behaviour in general) is a *multidetermined* phenomenon spanning the sciences and social sciences.

Criminology needs to separate the myths of biological ideas from the facts. For example, the biological perspective does not assume that all crimes are committed by "born criminals." Rather, their research focuses on exploring possible links between biological and intervening social, personal, and environmental-outcome variables. In addition, the biological perspective does not assume that social control can only be altered through law and order. Their research focuses on an *integrated* and *interdisciplinary* approach that emphasizes individualized treatment through biological and/or genetic intervention strategies. Finally, proponents of the biological perspective do not assume their theories have all the answers. They feel that while the "root causes" of crime might lie in the genetic and/or biochemical makeup of individuals, they are also dependent on environmental (i.e., social and personal) cues and stimuli. As Stoff and Cairns (1996:xiii) state, "biological variables influence social behaviour, vis à vis, social behaviour influences biological variables."

Although biological explanations have suffered in the past from a lack of methodological soundness and adequate empirical testing, today, with technological advances, the use of larger samples and more rigorous methodologies, the picture is changing. For example, Terri Moffitt and her partner, Avshalom Caspi, have been conducting a longitudinal study on young offenders in New Zealand since the 1970s. Their research focuses on the biological and psychological causes of delinquency and crime.

The above points can perhaps be best illustrated in Figure 5–2.

It was suggested several times throughout this chapter that biological research and biological explanations remain controversial socio-political issues. Beirne and Messerschmidt (1991:487) observe that the "recognition of biological factors is gaining importance among criminologists."

I would like to conclude this chapter with a quote from the 1996 Annual Presidential Address at the American Society of Criminology as it appeared in the journal *Criminology*, which reflects the general theme of this chapter:

FIGURE 5-2

THE MAJOR CLASSES OF VARIABLES INVOLVED IN CAUSING BEHAVIOUR

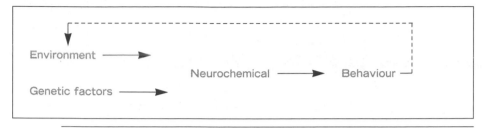

Source: L. Ellis, 1982:44.

"I strongly believe that the future development of causal theory is dependent upon our movement toward integrated theories that involve biological, social, and cultural dimensions" (Wellford, 1997:4). In Chapter 9, we will discuss the bio-social theory, which represents one of the new promising integrated and interdisciplinary perspectives linking biological factors with sociological elements.

Discussion Questions

1. In spite of the growing body of research suggesting that criminal behaviour may have a biological basis to it, which myths pose the greatest hurdle for criminology? How might we overcome these myths?

2. Referring to the apparent increase in youth violence across the country, how might we explain this trend from a biological perspective? Applying at least two different theoretical models, explain the phenomenon.

3. Describe the major biological theories discussed in this chapter. What are the relative strengths and weaknesses of each theory? What are the primary differences between early vs. more recent biological approaches to criminal behaviour? Which theory do you think has the most explanatory power? Why?

4. What challenges might exist in accepting one type of biological theory over another?

5. Canadian criminologists Richard Tremblay and a colleague (1993) have suggested conducting psychological tests that assess children's ability to adjust to social settings as early as their pre-school years. Should we consider screening or testing for the possible existence of a genetic marker? Why or why not?

6. To what extent might other aberrant behaviours have an organic (biological) basis to them? To what extent might psychopathic behaviour be the result of an interaction between brain differences and social/familial factors?

7. How have social structures affected biological theory, crime research, and crime policy?

8. After reading this chapter, to what degree do you think that biological explanations of crime have been, and are, currently grounded in scientific principles?

9. How might biological components be incorporated into an integrated and interdisciplinary criminological perspective? Which components do you think would be the most important?

Key Concepts

Somatotype	physiognomy	fetal alcohol syndrome
Endocrine system	neurons	neurotransmitters
"voodoo metal"	life course theory	chromosomes
Klinefelter's syndrome	XXY	psychopath
Serotonin	testosterone	ADD

Key Names

F. Gall	C. Goring	E. Hooton
W. Sheldon	E. Kretschmer	E. Kraepelin
A. Schauss	G. Mendel	R. Herrnstein
S. Mednick		

Weblinks

www.crim-times.org/ Although a small publication by most journal standards, *Crime Times* is the most up-to-date and comprehensive source for research in the area of biology and crime.

Footnotes

1. In February 1997, researchers at the Roslin Institute near Edinburgh, Scotland, received worldwide attention when they released the news that they had successfully cloned a sheep whom they named "Dolly"—a Finn Dorset lamb. The news drew immediate worldwide attention. In a follow-up public opinion poll, people were asked whether they would be interested in cloning themselves in some form. Ninety-one per cent said **no** to cloning themselves, 74 per cent said that cloning was against God's will, and 65 per cent said that the government should regulate animal cloning practices (Nash, 1997).

2. Ashley Montagu (1997) offers one of the most comprehensive and compelling discourses on the relationship between physical traits and the ability to predict human behaviour.

3. For an excerpt of Hooton's *The American Criminal*, see J.E. Jacoby (1994).

4. For a detailed history of Sheldon's life and ideas see Martin, Mutchnick, and Austin (1990).

5. In Chapter 9 we will see that this line of explanation and inquiry has evolved to include such factors as injury, diet, and chemical and other environmental factors. While this line

of investigation can trace its influence to the work of Goring, it also represents a refinement of the Mind + Environment model. It is one of the interdisciplinary perspectives that is gaining acceptance among criminological investigators.

6. For an extended examination of the intelligence debate see H. Eysenck's (1998) *Intelligence*. NY: Transaction.

7. In Chapter 6, we will review some of the psychologically-based perspectives that attribute the "antisocial" personality to some personal experience or individual conditioning process.

8. In April, 1997, University of Calgary researcher Julio Arboleda Flores began conducting research into a new method of determining genetic predisposition to schizophrenia. Along with several of his colleagues, he is comparing the number of fingerprint ridges of people's hands to test for genetic predisposition to schizophrenia (Toneguzzi, 1997). Flores has since moved to Toronto.

9. Visit the Prentice-Hall Web site, **www.prenticehall.ca/winterdyk** where you will find a chapter on crime and law.

10. For a controversial look at the relationship between race and crime see Philippe Rushton's (1995) controversial book on race evolution and human behaviour). Rushton, a Canadian, drew international attention at the 39th Annual Meeting of the American Society of Criminology in Montreal, in 1987, when he presented a paper describing how racial differences correlated to crime variations among different ethnic groups. He asserted there was a genetic influence. Focusing on methodological problems with Rushton's research, Roberts and Gabor (1990) point out that: (1) Rushton's independent variable, race, assumes people are racially pure, yet the literature has provided ample evidence that shows "close to 50 per cent of those classified as black are over half-white by lineage" (Ibid, 295); (2) correlation between two variables does not constitute evidence of a causal relationship; (3) over representation may have less to do with a genetic predisposition as opposed to a "consequence of their social situations and in response to prevailing criminal opportunities" (Ibid, 298–299), and (4) Rushton appears unaware of differential victimization patterns. The fact that blacks may be over-represented may be a simple consequence of environmental factors. It was not until 1978 that Thomas Sowell demonstrated that the difference in IQ score could be accounted for by social and cultural differences! Once these were controlled the differences disappeared (Stark, 1992). This line of reasoning has been abandoned for some time by those familiar with biological perspectives (see Beardsley, 1999).

11. Since the Twinkie defence, few subsequent junk-food defences have been successful. It is not clear whether the legal system fully understands the effects of diet on the biochemical structure or whether diet is simply seen as a mitigating factor. See, for example, the section on automatism and insanity in the "crime and law" chapter specially prepared for this textbook. It can be found at the Prentice-Hall Web site, **www.prenticehall.ca/winterdyk**.

CHAPTER 6

Psychological Explanations

"Fifth, there is now much evidence to discredit the type of sociological theory so prominent and widely accepted ...; criminals require socialization by properly planned conditioning treatments."

H.J. Eysenck, 1977:12–13

Learning Outcomes

After you have completed reading this chapter, you should be able to:

- Recognize and appreciate the impact psychology has had on the understanding of criminal behaviour.

- Appreciate the complexity of human behaviour.

- Recognize and become familiar with some of the important methods of treatment advocated by therapists.

- Appreciate the fact that knowledge is a relative concept, unable to be accounted for with only one perspective.

- See the importance of the learning theory in understanding criminal behaviour.

Phrases like "just what makes that person tick," "they must be really warped to be able to commit that kind of crime," or "that person really needs some serious help" can sometimes be heard when people talk about the behaviour of a criminal. As we learned in Chapter 4, this type of orientation belongs to the positivist school of thought. This perspective assumes that behaviour is **deterministic** and is related to individual and/or environmental factors. Scientific psychology divides the causes of human behaviour along the continuum between *nature* and *nurture*.

Focusing on individual factors to explain behaviour is probably the oldest explanatory mode known to us. In addition, like sociological explanations (Chapter 7), the field of psychology is both broad and diverse in its study of human behaviour.

In this chapter, we will focus on the psychologically-based factors as opposed to the individual biological factors (Chapter 5) that fall predominantly under the realm of "nature." Until recently, however, psychological approaches to under standing criminality were not always distinct from the somatic-biological orientation. In fact, Schafer (1976) suggested seeing them as being on a continuum. As recently as a few years ago, introductory criminology textbooks typically grouped the biological and psychological explanatory approaches together. However, today, with the growing volume of research in both the biological and psychological arenas, it is prudent to divide the two perspectives. As criminology becomes more integrated and interdisciplinary in focus and recognizes the need to separate theories of law and criminal justice from theories of human behaviour, biological, and psychological theories and research have slowly begun to receive individualized attention.

We will first begin by reviewing the oldest known explanatory model of deviant behaviour—**demonology**.[1] Then we will review several of the main psychological explanations of criminal behaviour. It should also be noted that this chapter, as with all the theory chapters, is not intended to provide an exhaustive review of psychological theories of crime and criminality. The objective is to provide a cross-sectional introduction as to how psychology attempts to explain and predict human behaviour. Hence, while psychological theories focus on identifying individual factors as the primary cause of criminality, most theories also acknowledge the influence of social and/or environmental factors.

In this chapter, we will focus on five major psychological theories and/or orientations. They will include *psychodynamic*, *behavioural*, *personality*, *cognition*, and *moral development*. Yet, as diverse as these psychological perspectives are, they all tend to "focus their examinations on basic components of human nature, such as appetites and aversions, motives and emotions that are viewed as characteristic of the human species" (Barak, 1998:127).

The Legacy of Demonology and "Evil"

"The devil made me do it" Flip Wilson (comedian).

Flip Wilson was a popular comedian during the 1970s and early 1980s who would use the above phrase to excuse his actions whenever he got into trouble in his show. The insinuation was that he became possessed by a "bad seed" or evil thought beyond his control. Although it was usually good for a laugh, as the old saying goes "there is usually a grain of truth in every joke." In his thought-provoking and widely-acclaimed book, *The Soul's Codes* James Hillman (1996) uses the term "bad seed" to describe a psychopathic criminal. Using case studies ranging from Adolf Hitler to Jeffery Dahmer, Hillman argues that there are those who are born without a *soul* and in whose character one can see evil—in psychological terms, *psychopathic* traits. Many of his ideas are a refinement of Lombroso's earlier notions of the *born criminal* (Chapters 4 and 5). Moreover, in keeping with the positivist model, Hillman describes how it is possible to exorcize—"redressing the balance between the psyche's weakness and the daimon's (soul's) potential" (p. 242).

Before the 1700s, also referred to as the "dark ages" in criminology, most authorities thought that criminal behaviour was caused by supernatural forces or "some other-world power or spirit" (Vold and Bernard, 1989:5). The ancient Greeks had a word for this evil—*hubris*, as did early Christian tradition—*superthia* (Hillman, 1996).

Anthropological and historical records describe how primitive and preliterate societies believed that all living and non-living objects held some symbol of power. Depending on the source, the powers could represent either good or evil. Out of these beliefs emerged the practice of black magic, witchcraft, and satanic worship. Today, we can still find evidence of these *metaphysical* belief systems. Some people believe that gemstones, pyramids, and various bioenergetic devices possess certain healing properties. Different religious groups still practise ceremonial sacrifices or homage that must be given in order to appease one's wrong-doings. Even certain rock music has been used as a medium. Performers such as Marilyn Manson, through his musical lyrics and stage attire and presence, encouraged his listeners to rebel against Christianity and to love Satan (Brundt, 1997). In 1996, the popular music magazine *Rolling Stone* crowned him Best New Artist!

There is no shortage of alternative practices that share the common theme of placing faith and trust in constructs whose influence has never been proven. Woodward (1997) observed, even in the historically Christian-based institutions of higher learning, Canadian universities are offering more and more non-Christian-based courses in religious studies than ever before. Although the characteristics may vary, they are all a means of balancing the good and evil in us and subscribe at some level to a belief in a "mystical" or "supernatural" power. Over time, the line between "good magic" and "evil" has become blurred (see Box 6.1).

As European societies evolved from primitive tribes to agrarian cultures and then to the formation of communities and urbanization, weaknesses in the Catholic church led them to form an alliance with the existing ruling bodies (deKeseredy and Schwartz, 1996). Abstract faith was being substituted by formal intervention agencies created by the state. In their zeal to convert and control the populace, these agencies engaged in a reign of terror that would span the Middle Ages. The practices are today referred to as the Inquisition. Under this reign of terror, both the church and the state tortured and executed anyone they felt was a threat to the state or the church. The most common victims were the poor. Pfohl (1994) estimates that over a two-hundred-year period, approximately a million people, mostly women, were burned alive. Were these people possessed by evil thoughts or were they simply the victims of a narrow-minded social, cultural, and political mindset?

The historical overview of demonology further serves to highlight several of the points about the *relative* and *evolutionary* meaning of crime (see Chapter 1). Throughout the ages, evil's associations with criminal behaviour has been well-documented, but we also see that the meaning of possession or evil took on different connotations over time. We can also see how the *consensus* and *conflict* perspectives (see Chapter 1) of justice emerged from these times. In ancient times there appeared to be a greater level of consensus as to what constituted "evil." However, as societies evolved and became more heterogeneous, so did the meaning of evil. Chambliss (1988), for example, suggests the Inquisition was a time when those in power used their influence to attack and "scapegoat" those less able to defend themselves. The poor, and often innocent, were punished in order to mask the shortcomings of the state and the church. Pfohl (1994) reports that, while exact numbers do not exist, throughout history a million people, mostly women and members of the lower and middle classes were put to death in extreme ways. One of the more classic accounts involved the execution of a mentally-ill man by the name of Robert François Damiens, who in 1757 stabbed King Louis XV.

Another way of interpreting the behaviour of those thought to be engaging in evil acts is to view their behaviour as *"subjectively adaptable* to a response pattern that a person has found to be effective, or thinks to be effective, in certain circumstances" (Bartol, 1995:92). In other words, people simply act in accordance with what they feel, or know, enables them to cope and deal with life. In other words, evil behaviour can be seen as a form of maladaptive behaviour rather than as a psychopathology. When some people are exposed to a sudden shocking or violent scene they simply faint. Humans and animals alike regularly engage in subjectively adaptable behaviour in order to suit their needs and environment. As Shakespeare once wrote, "All the world's a stage, and all the men and women merely players."

The notion that people must possess, or be possessed, by an "evil mind" to be guilty of crime has been refined over the years (see Box 6.1). Today, our criminal law doctrine of responsibility and punishment is based on the principles of *mens rea* and *actus reus* (see Prentice-Hall—**www.prenticehall.ca/winterdyk**—

Web site). We do not punish people unless they have committed a wrong with foreknowledge of the act. While we may not talk openly about the intent being a product of a possessed mind, our criminal justice system still advocates the use of punishment to condemn the criminal act. Or the system might attempt to rehabilitate, treat, or simply prevent the offender from "infecting" others with his/her evil ways. As part of the interdisciplinary nature of criminology and the criminal justice system, in the sentencing process we cloak such notions by framing them in a legalistic context.

REALITY CHECK BOX 6. 1

MODERN-DAY DEMONOLOGY

The notion that individuals can be "possessed" by evil spirits can still be found today. During the Roman Empire these beliefs were used to justify persecuting Christians. Later, the Christian church used persecutions against witches. More recently, the Nazis used the belief against the Jews, and various religious and spiritual groups still hold to these assertions as a means of expressing their beliefs and controlling their followers. Among the extremist groups, some continue to engage in ritual abuse exercises to rid the "victim" of demonic possession. The practices have included cult-related abuse, satanic ritual abuse, ritualized abuse and sadistic abuse (Ritual Abuse, 1996).

Many of our ritual behaviours are harmless—e.g., getting up every morning and brushing our teeth before we have breakfast. Virtually every society has rituals related to important life situations such as baptism, marriage, graduation, and death. By contrast, ritual abuse has been defined as psychological, physical, and/or sexual assault on an unwilling victim. It can be committed by one or more individuals whose primary motive is to act out a sequence of events in order to satisfy the perceived needs of their deity. The Aztec used to sacrifice young virgin girls to appease their gods. Meanwhile, Christians and Mormons, among others, give financial donations and perform other rituals (e.g., regular church attendance, prayer, abstaining from certain foods and drink, etc.) as an expression of their devotion to their deity. Where do we draw the line between acceptable and non-acceptable rituals?

Six different forms of ritual abuse can be identified in the literature. They all share the common theme of religion. Although difficult to substantiate, in recent years there have been reports of an infant dying of exorcism in Ontario and a young child dying in Alberta as a result of satanic exercises. Another Canadian example was the ill-fated **Order of the Solar Temple** and its leader Luc Jouret in 1994 in Quebec. Portraying himself as the "New Christ" the Swiss-born Canadian preached of an impending catastrophe. Then, after a series of macabre events, nineteen members were found dead, dressed in their ceremonial robes and lying in a circle with their feet pointing toward a common centre.

The scenario and unfoldment of the Solar Temple was similar to the tragedy in 1993 at Waco, Texas, where more than 80 Branch Davidian members died following a shootout with authorities, and a fire. However, the most famous cult event to draw international attention occurred in 1978. Californian Reverend Jim Jones led a group of followers to Jamestown, Guyana, where 914 members committed mass suicide. And as we enter the new millennium, groups such as Heaven's Gate are likely to proliferate. Heaven's Gate gained international attention when in March 1997, a number of its members committed mass suicide at its multi-million dollar Rancho Santa Fe in California.

In **summary**, reliance on demonic approaches and other metaphysical explanations of behaviour have been used throughout the ages by some people to excuse their behaviour while the church and state used it as a means of justifying social control. And since the wrongdoing was considered something supernatural, people were not subjected to horrific punishment. Yet, according to a scientific perspective, there has never been any demonstrable proof of God's existence or the existence of evil. Nevertheless, the notion of spirits and demons as possible causes of criminal behaviour prevail. With the emergence of the *classical* and *positivist* schools of thought psychological theories emerged as one means of trying to explain and predict human behaviour through scientific methods.

The Emergence of Psychology and Criminality

Interest in the psychological and psychiatric aspects of crime emerged during the middle to late 1800s. Jeffery (1973) identifies three essential individuals.

1. **Gustav Aschaffenburg** (1866–1944), a pioneer of psychiatric criminology argued that we are less influenced by heredity than by our social environment (von Hentig, 1973). Aschaffenburg's ideas were instrumental in forging the notion that, from a psychological perspective, criminal behaviour is not a mental pathology but a form of socially maladaptive behaviour.

2. **Henry Maudsley** (1835–1918), described as a brilliant medical doctor, believed that criminals are the product of "moral degeneracy"—lacking in moral development (Scott, 1973). Many of the principles that were expanded on by the famous Swiss child psychologist Jean Piaget (1896–1980) were further developed by Lawrence Kohlberg (1969) (see p. 195). Beginning in the 1970s their ideas also formed the basis of Canadian prison education programs (see Duigud, 1979, and Ross, Fabiano, and Eweles, 1988).

3. **Issac Ray** (1807–1881), the "father" of the American Psychological Association and a very influential forensic psychiatrist, wrote a great deal on the subject of "moral insanity." He considered it a "disease ... never established by a single diagnostic symptom" (Overholser, 1973:183).

A widely-cited article by two well-known psychologists, Samual Yochelson and Stanton Samenow (1976), argued there may be a "**criminal personality**," or at least a different thinking pattern among criminals. Their research was based on extensive case studies of only criminally insane patients in a Washington, D.C. hospital. Although they overgeneralize the evidence, their work drew considerable attention from federal government circles (Williams and McShane, 1999). The view that there might be something "wrong" with the mind of a criminal gave support to the notion that sentenced individuals be required to undergo various sorts of treatment.

In this chapter we will limit coverage to some of the major theoretical psychological contributions to the study of criminal behaviour. As Bartol (1995:ix) noted, "the study of criminal behaviour must be *interdisciplinary.*" Therefore, it is necessary to acknowledge the many ways an individual's behaviour can be formed.

The psychological causes of criminal behaviour can be divided into two major theoretical categories: those that emphasize family conflict or *intrapsychic* factors, and those that attribute the origins of criminal behaviour to learning factors (Johnson and Fennell, 1983). Within the later classification, there are varieties of sub-classifications of learning. They each focus on different elements of learning. Because the learning approaches are more widely accepted, we will focus on five of the primary sub-categories that include frustration-induced criminality, learning, behaviourism, cognition, and moral development. First, however, we will review the intrapsychic or psychodynamic approach as it was one of the first approaches to consider individual personality as an observable and measurable factor in (criminal) behaviour.

Intrapsychic: Psychodynamic Explanations

Perhaps the best known psychodynamic theory is the Viennese Freudian-based psychoanalytical approach. It is a mixture of the Kantian (i.e., rationalism) and Lockean (i.e., behaviour is the result of sensations and experiences) models. According to the Freudian approach, criminal behaviour is the result of internal conflict and tension among the three aspects of one's personality that emerge in early childhood because of developmental and/or interaction problems between parents and their children.

Freud (see Box 6.2) believed that the mind has three levels of *consciousness*: the unconscious, the preconscious, and the conscious. According to Freudian theory, when combined with the **id**, **superego**, and **ego**, these elements of personality can result in criminal behaviour. The outcome of our behaviour is dependent on how we process our early childhood experiences—traumatic or otherwise.

The id and the superego are considered part of the *unconscious* mental process while the ego is considered part of the *conscious* mental processes of the personality. The id consists of basic unconscious biological urges and desires for immediate gratification and satisfaction, which include the desire for food (i.e., the will to live), sex (i.e., pleasure), and survival (i.e., aggression). The id is also referred to as the *pleasure principle* because it attempts to avoid pain or unpleasant experiences.

The power of the unconscious can be used to explain how some people are driven to steal or fight for their survival—out of necessity. The id is the amoral, immature instinctive passion within all of us. As Freud noted, the id is our life source or *eros*, our creative side, and the basis for both positive and negative aggression. However, due to the influence of the id and its self-centred focus we start life in a state of immorality (Bartol, 1995). The humanist-oriented psychologist, Rollo May (1970), later simply referred to the id as *will*.

PROFILE BOX 6.2

SIGMUND FREUD (1856–1939):
"THE FATHER OF PSYCHOANALYSIS"

Freud was born on May 6, 1856, at Freiberg, Moravia, which at that time was part of the Austro-Hungarian Empire. His family moved to Vienna in 1860. On entering the University of Vienna he became a medical student and specialized in anatomy and physiology. (Because he was a Jew, opportunities were not readily available (Hall and Lindzey, 1970)). Out of necessity, he opened a private practice where, amongst other interests, he specialized in the treatment of nervous disorders. He subsequently developed a treatment modality based on patients talking about their problems, which he later called *free association*. Freud believed sexual factors were the key to understanding hysteria.

 Freud was a prolific writer, and some of his writings today continue to be published as classics in the field of psychoanalysis. His commitment to clearly explicating his psychoanalytic theories and the importance of dreams is perhaps best reflected in the observation that at the end of the day he would set aside half an hour for self-analysis (Hall and Lindzey, 1970).

When the Nazis overran Vienna in 1938, he fled to London, where he died of cancer 16 months later, on September 23, 1939. While his work is voluminous, there has perhaps been an equal amount of literature that has tried to debunk his psychoanalytic theories. Nevertheless, they have withstood the test of time and there continue to be prominent supporters of his general ideas (e.g., Alfred Adler, August Aichorn, Eric Ericson, Erich Fromm, Karen Horney and Alice Miller). Freud's work will continue to command a place in personality theory and psychotherapy.

The ego and superego by contrast, are products of our individual learning experiences. We each experience different events throughout our childhood, adolescent, and adult years. Our ego (the "I" or *reality principle*) represents an adaptive outgrowth of our id. Based on early childhood experiences our ego learns to weigh the consequences of acting out the id within the boundaries of social convention, and serves as our control mechanism.

The other unconscious aspect of our personality, the superego, represents outer world influences. The superego arises out of the relationship between our early life experiences and the moral values of our parents and the community at large. The superego is an indicator of our socialization process. This notion is well illustrated in August Aichcorn's (1935) classic book *Wayward Youth*. In addition to defining delinquent groups according to their id and ego, he notes that those with criminal superegos belong to criminal groups or identify with a delinquent father—a very sociological orientation of criminality according to Jeffery (1990). The superego is our "psychic police officer" (Bischof, 1964) that polices our id through conscious thought. Redl and Wineman (1951) coined the concept *delinquent ego* to describe those youths who, because of inadequate ego and superego development are able to rationalize their delinquent aggression and frustration. They also report that such youth lack close personal relationships with adult figures.

Together, these three aspects of our personality (id, ego, and superego) can be in conflict. In fact, they usually are to varying degrees. Some of the more common forms of intradynamic conflict take the form of *neuroses* such as anxiety, phobias (fear of different things), amnesia, or sexual disorders.

The source of the conflicts can be either organic or functional in nature. Organic disorders are based in the brain or brain chemistry (Chapter 5) whereas functional disorders have no known physical base but rather a mental, experiential, or psychic base (Jeffery, 1990). Hence, we derive the term "mental illness" or *mana sans delieria*—a mind without reason.

When we experience internal psychic conflict it can lead to the *repression* of desires or unpleasant memories that in turn can lead to personality problems. For example, victims of sexual abuse can sometimes go for years without remembering the traumatic experiences they were subjected to as children (see Box 6.3). These repressed feelings can lead to fundamental personality problems such as difficulty feeling close to someone for whom they care or not feeling comfortable engaging in certain sexual acts that they were subjected to. If left unattended, the unconscious memories can cause anxieties around the repressed desires and memories. Victims are then likely to resort to one of four defence mechanisms[3] in order to avoid confronting the reality of their hidden desires. When the mental anguish begins to negatively affect their behaviour Freud felt they were suffering from neuroticism—emotional instability.[4]

Freud and Human (Psychosexual) Development

As the id represents the core of our personality and is the dominant force at birth, Freud argued that our early childhood experiences most directly affected our later psychological development. In particular, Freud believed that since sex was an instinctual need, how we progress through the five stages of child development significantly influences our *psychosexual* development.

The first stage is the *oral* stage (birth–age 1), which centres on the mouth and the pleasures associated with sucking and eating. Examples of its manifestation in later life include being passive or dependent, or chewing gum or smoking.

The *anal* stage (ages 1–3) focuses on the control and elimination process—the toilet training period. Examples of its manifestation in later life include being compulsive, stingy, and concerned with orderliness.

The *phallic* stage (ages 3–5) when children discover their sexual parts and derive pleasure in masturbation and their genitals. This is also the stage when boys form an attachment to their mother and when they must compete with their father for their mother. When this happens, conflict arises between son and father. Freud labelled this the *Oedipus* complex, named after the Greek tragedy in which the son kills his father. The son normally resolves the conflict by identifying and obeying his father. This is a superego development.

The *sexual latency* stage (ages 6–13) is one of repression of sexual feelings and interest in young people. This is when boys play with boys and girls with girls.

The final stage of development is the *genital* stage (age 13 and beyond) when the superego is well enough developed for youth to move into wider socially and culturally acceptable behaviours and to act in morally- and socially-prescribed ways.

Problems experienced during any of these phases could trigger problems, and thus unacceptable or criminal behaviour. The means to determine if a person is experiencing problems is through dream analysis, and through a process Freud called *free association*. Freud, along with many of his followers, believed our dreams contain many of the repressed feelings and hostilities our conscious mind (i.e., superego) would not let surface for fear of embarrassment or some other unpleasant experience.

Freudian Explanations of Criminality

In accordance with the basic assumptions underlying Freudian theory, human behaviour is inherently anti-social and delinquent, and criminal behaviour is an indication of personality conflict. Unresolved conflicts can lead criminals (the ego) to feel the need to be punished but the id may prevent them from confessing to the crime. However, when the perceived harm diminishes (e.g., know they're dying) they (superego) might confess to their wrongdoing.[5] Criminals on death row are given the opportunity to spend time with a minister before being executed. Halleck (1969), among others, has observed how many criminals readily tell all and feel a sense of relief after being caught. For example, serial killer Heriberto Sedo, known as the Zodiac killer, used to leave an encircled cross with three sevens at the scene of each crime. Even after signing his confession statement to the police, in 1996, Sedo sealed his statement with his trademark—a confession? Psychoanalytical interpretation suggests this type of behaviour allows criminals to shed their guilt—the classic battle between the driving forces, *cathexes*, and the restraining forces, *anti-cathexes*—a term coined by Freud.

Hence, as Warren and Hindelang (1986) observed:

- Criminal behaviour is the product of an uncontrolled id. It is a form of neurosis—an unconscious internal conflict that is expressed through an overt act.
- Criminals have an unconscious need to alleviate their sense of guilt and anxiety.
- Criminal activity may be an alternate means to gratify those needs that were not fulfilled by their family.
- Some criminal and delinquent behaviour is the result of traumatic (non-pleasurable) experiences whose memories have been repressed.
- Some forms of delinquent behaviour may be the result of displaced hostility and/or an unconscious desire for punishment.

    In **summary**, Freudian theory has met with varying criticism (Einstadter and Henry, 1995), as has his treatment modality of psychoanalysis (Finckenauer, 1984; Jeffery, 1990). Nevertheless, he can in many ways be considered, along with Darwin, a founding father of the psycho-biological concept of humankind (Sulloway, 1979), for Freud attempted to find both a neurological and biological link to personality. In fact, his ideas were interdisciplinary in nature as he placed a strong emphasis on biological and social factors as well as on multiple mechanisms to explain behaviour.

    Today, researchers continue to think of new ways to validate the theoretical assertions of the psychoanalytic approach. And since no one theory has yet been able to explain all aspects of criminal behaviour, perhaps any theory that has withstood so much debate deserves some serious consideration in our quest to understand criminal behaviour.

Cognitive Explanations

Plato and Kant both suggested that human behaviour is the product of mentalism, which involves processing the physical and social factors in our lives

(Mannheim, 1973). In psychology, the term *cognition* is used to refer to the ability of individuals to make sense of their sensory experiences. Jeffery (1990:213) offers the following illustration of the mentalistic/cognitive model of human behaviour (also see Figure 6–2):

ENVIRONMENT————> MIND—————> BEHAVIOUR

How the mind processes its sensory experiences is based on the premise of free will and intentionality. This general premise of explaining behaviour is related to cognitive and learning theories in psychology. Cognitive explanations claim that criminal behaviour is the result of faulty or irrational thinking.

Frustration-Aggression Model

The notion that frustration and aggression are linked is a popular conception of anti-social behaviour. Have you, for example, ever done something out of frustration? Have you ever become angry following a frustrating experience? A growing concern in many North American cities is the increase in road rage (see Box 6.4). This occurs when a driver's temper flares up at the slightest provocation (e.g., being cut off, someone not merging properly).

REALITY CHECK BOX 6.4

THE ISSUE OF ROAD RAGE

The issue of road rage has drawn so much attention in the late 1990s that various associations have attempted to understand it and implement programs to curb the growing trend of irate drivers. In one report, Vest, Cohen, and Tharp (1997) observed that road violence has gone up 51 per cent in the 1990s. In the cases studied, 37 per cent of offenders used firearms while 35 per cent used their cars! Obscene gestures are also very common. The American Department of Transport estimates that two-thirds of road fatalities are partly caused by aggressive driving. One expert suggests that we are simply reacting to having our sense of space constantly violated since cars represent an extension of our personal space (Coyle, 1998). In March of 1998, the Ontario Provincial Police introduced a traffic section nicknamed the "Highway Rangers," whose members drive around and spot people expressing road rage. They are then pulled over and given a survey. Based on their response, they are either given a warning or a ticket (Question: How do you feel about stupid quizzes?, 1998). (See Web site links at the end of the chapter for a link to road rage).

The modern frustration-aggression conception of criminality can be traced back to the work of Dollard, Doob, Miller, Mowerer, and Sears in 1939. They identified several premises that have become widely accepted under this social learning model of behaviour. These premises "linked Freudian concepts with the methods and concepts of an emerging behavioural perspective of human behaviour" (Andrews and Bonta, 1994:93). Freud believed that we are susceptible from birth to a build-up of aggressive energy and from time to time it must be drained—"to blow off steam." Andrews and Bonta (1994) identified five elements of Dollard et al.'s study.

1. Aggression is always a consequence of frustration. Strasberg (1978) observed that communication problems were more common among violent young offenders than non-violent offenders. He also noted that speech and language disorders are more common among young males than young females. Frustration results from an aversive state of arousal towards a valued goal-response. There are two types of aggression (Fesbach, 1964). *Hostile aggression* refers to expressive or acting-out (e.g., insults and physical assault) behaviour. *Instrumental aggression* occurs when the "offender" weighs his or her options in order to gain his or her intention—using just enough coercion (physical and verbal) to gain another person's compliance.

2. The risk of aggression escalates with the degree of outside interference, frequency of frustrating experiences, and intensity of the event that instigated the frustration.

3. The greater the risk and perception of punishment resulting from an aggressive act the greater the likelihood the act will not be committed. This is one of the premises of the Classical doctrine (see Chapter 4). Certainty and severity of punishment can serve as an effective deterrent.

4. If the "victim" perceives that the cost of directing aggression towards the offending agent could result in more harm then he or she will likely redirect his or her aggression. Rather than take your hostilities out on the police officer who ticketed you, you might go home and verbally vent your frustration on your partner.

5. Once a person has vented his or her aggression, there is a temporary reduction in the desire to act out. This is also referred to as "catharsis." You feel better after getting it off your chest—at least for a while.

Although the state of criminological knowledge was still in its infancy in the 1930s, this model was thought to provide a viable explanation for most criminal acts.

Subsequent research on the frustration-aggression perspective by Leonard Berkowitz (1962) both updated and refined the theory. For instance, he divided criminal personalities into two main classifications: the *socialized* and the *individual* offender. The socialized offender's behaviour is a result of learning, conditioning, and modelling. By contrast, the individual offender's behaviour is a product of persistent, intense episodes of frustration resulting from unmet needs (see Box 6.5).

Copycats and Modelling

Alfred Bandura, of Stanford University, and his fellow student Robert Walters (who taught at the University of Toronto and the University of Waterloo before his tragic death in 1968) conducted a number of studies on aggression and violence that were based on the learning model. Bandura (1965) identified three kinds of learning: (1) Observation learning is based on *modelling* in which the observer copies behaviour that he or she identifies with. For example, children may mimic television characters from their favourite programs or they might mimic the behaviour patterns of their parents. (2) Response stimulation is similar to the "monkey see, monkey do" tendency.[6] Children who grow up in an environment where their father abuses their mother might grow up to copy that behaviour. Research has shown that viewing violent movies or sexually explicit videos can stimulate a desire to copy that behaviour. (3) Raising and lowering restraints depends on how our view of a model affects our attitude. If we admire someone and see his or her conduct pay off, we are more likely to emulate him or her. We tend to identify with winners, not losers. A number of studies have been conducted showing that young offenders became more aggressive after viewing "warranted" violence in which "unwarranted" aggression is directed towards a sympathetic movie character. These stereotypes are often played out in the wrestling world where the "hero" is momentarily beaten into near defeat before rising from a choreographed devastating loss to avenge his punishment, all to the adulation of his fans.

One of the most recent dramatic examples of a copycat crime was the high school gun-and-bomb attack by two teenagers at a high school in Littleton, Colorado in May of 1999. Less than two weeks later in the small town of Taber, Alberta, a 14-year-old youth killed a schoolmate and critically injured another. Like the shooters in the Littleton incident (who were members of a gang known as the "Trenchcoat Mafia"), the Taber youth wore a black trenchcoat and conducted his shooting spree in a similar manner to the Colorado incident.

In their collaborative book, Bandura and Walters (1959) note that while violence and aggression may result from neurological mechanisms and/or brain damage, they argue that most types of aggression in young people are based on emotional arousal that is learned and based on certain environmental cues. They also note that the type of reinforcement plays an important role in whether violent acts are repeated (see classical conditioning on p. 198). These ideas are very similar to the learning theories developed by sociologists (Chapter 8).

In their review of the Berkowitzes' update and revision, Andrews and Bonta (1994) note that the model is regularly used for treatment programs that target the control of anger. It might appear quite appealing as an explanatory tool, but one of the difficulties confronting this perspective is: How does one measure concepts such as frustration, aggression or feeling better? What is an "attitude," and how does the mind assimilate and process sensory stimuli (the triggering observation)? How "intense" do the stimuli need to be, and are some environmental factors more important than others? Not only do elements of these questions lack adequate *operational* definitions, the questions also highlight the fact that the "mind" can never be directly, empirically observed (Jeffery, 1990). However, the model does assume a mind-body dualism that is congruent with the key elements of criminal law; that is, *mens rea* (the ability to form intent) and *actus reus* (the physical element).

In **summary**, the frustration-aggression model is based on social learning theory that is part of cognitive psychology. While Dollard et al. (1939) based their social learning approach on imitation, Bandura's model advocated a social learning process based on cognitive process coupled with life experiences. Other variations of the social learning model include modelling (see Box 6.3) and symbolic interaction (Blumer, 1969).

The social learning theory does not account for individual biological states due to the brain, genetics, or learning differences. We do not all respond in the same way to similar stimuli (Jeffery, 1990). In Chapter 7, we will see that sociology interprets social learning differently than does psychology. For example, sociology uses social learning theory as an all-encompassing experience of learning rather than as an aspect of the cognitive process.

Moral Development Theories

"Kids have no respect for people or property." "Such a heinous act! How could anyone do a thing like that?" Such statements might well reflect elements of another cognitive-based theory—theories of moral development.

There are a number of theories of moral development but a central theme to all of them in understanding criminality is the manner in which individuals develop a sense of *morality* and *responsibility*.

The Swiss psychologist, **Jean Piaget** (1896–1980) was the founder of the mental and moral development theory. Studying children, Piaget hypothesized that children experience four primary stages of mental development. The *sensorimotor* period (birth–age 2) involves children learning to respond to their immediate environment and developing their motor reflex skills. The *preoperational* period (ages 2–7) involves learning language, drawing, and other skills. The *concrete operation* period (ages 7–11) involves the development of logical thinking and problem solving skills. The final *formal operations* period (ages

11–15) involves learning to deal with abstract ideas. Piaget believed children learn to progress from being self-focused in their mental awareness to being able to understand and integrate their outer environment. As they mature, children learn to process moral-conflict situations in an intelligent manner.

Although Piaget did not apply his theory directly to delinquency or criminality, the American psychologist, **Lawrence Kohlberg** (1986) applied the concept of moral development to criminality. Kohlberg (1969) theorized that all individuals pass through the same stages, in which they develop their moral reasoning skills. As we progress through the stages, we learn to make decisions about right or wrong and determine the ethically/morally acceptable course of action based on the surrounding circumstances.

Kohlberg divides moral development into three levels, each with two stages of moral reasoning (see Figure 6–1). For example, adolescents typically reason at the conventional level. At this level they believe in and adopt the values and rules of society. Hence, they try to abide by the laws—not to steal, not to lie, etc. However, according to Kohlberg and his colleagues, most young offenders (and criminals, in general) reason at the preconventional level. They might be familiar with the dos and don'ts but they think in terms of: "If I commit a break-and-enter, what are the chances of getting caught and/or being punished?" By contrast, if a youth was at the postconventional level, his or her reasoning would include respect for human rights and the dignity of human life.

Moral Development and Criminality

Kohlberg theorized that not everyone makes it through all the stages of moral development or progresses at the same rate. Moral development depends on how we deal with the learning experience at earlier stages. Based on these ideas, Kohlberg reasoned that incomplete moral development was a major reason for criminal and deviant behaviour. Studies by Kohlberg and his associates (1973), among others, found that adolescent and adult offenders were significantly lower in their moral development than noncriminals of the same social background.

In **summary**, given the impression some people have of the character of many types of criminals, it is not surprising the moral development theory has been an important cognitive theory for criminology (Siegel, 1995). Steven Duiguid (1979) developed a training module to help inmates develop their moral reasoning skills. He has reported some success with his model.

In spite of its pragmatic appeal, the theory also has its critics. For example, Kohlberg's theory is not able to clarify whether an individual's lower level of moral reasoning predisposes him or her to offending or whether offending predisposes him or her to staying in the lower stages of moral development. Peer pressure, family conflict, or biochemical imbalances might have triggered this developmental behaviour for a variety of reasons.

FIGURE 6—1

KOHLBERG'S LEVELS OF MORAL REASONING

LEVEL OF MORAL DEVELOPMENT	STAGE OF REASONING	APPROX. AGES
Preconventional "do's and don'ts"	*Stage 1:* Right is obedience to power and avoidance of punishment. *Stage 2:* Right is taking responsibility and leaving others to be responsible for themselves.	< 11
Conventional	*Stage 3:* Right is being considerate: "uphold the values of other adolescents and adults' rules of society" *Stage 4:* Right is being good, with the values and norms of family and society at large.	adolescence and adulthood
Postconventional	*Stage 5:* Right is finding inner "universal rights" balance between self-rights and societal rules — a social contract. *Stage 6:* Right is based on a higher order of applying principles to all human-kind; being non-judgmental and respecting all human life.	after 20

Source: Adapted from L. Kohlberg, 1986:57–58.

At what level of moral development might the following individuals be?

- The boxer, Mike Tyson, biting the ear of his opponent Evander Hollyfield during a match in retaliation to an alleged low punch.
- Former head of the NHL Players' Association in the 1980s, Alan Eagleson, was found guilty of skimming profits intended for NHL pension funds. He was also found guilty of mail fraud. He had even been bestowed the Order of Canada—the highest civilian award in Canada.[7]
- Former Bre-X owner David Walsh who, in the mid-1990s, allegedly defrauded thousands of Canadians of their investment in a bogus gold mine.[8]
- Albert Walker, who was charged in 1998 with the cold-blooded killing of Ronald Platt, the man whose identity he assumed during the final three years of his six years on the run from Canadian authorities. He had fled Canada after bilking many of his clients in Paris, Ontario of their savings.[10]

Gilligan (1982) argued that Kohlberg's theory is biased in favour of males. She points out that there are variations in moral standards between men and women. Women, she suggests, tend to be more care-oriented while men are more justice-oriented when making moral decisions. This difference has never been clearly resolved.

A final criticism pertains to the ability to quantify moral development. Although the general evidence suggests that the level of moral reasoning is related to behaviour (the theory is not able to differentiate between types of criminal behaviour and stage of moral development), "the correlations reported in many studies is often quite low" (Cox, Roesch, and Zapf, 1996:243).

Behavioural Explanations

Most psychological theories of crime support the assertion that human behaviour emerges from the mutual interaction between a personality variable and situational variables. However, Bartol (1995:106) notes in his review of the literature that "much crime research and theory neglects situational variables in favour of dispositional factors." An exception to this limited frame of reference lies in the behavioural approach. Of all the psychological theories, behavioural psychology has been described as perhaps the most economical and elegant (Jeffery, 1990). Rather than focus on abstract concepts such as attitudes, interests, nature of past experiences, or personality patterns of the individual, behaviourists focus on specific behaviour (see Figure 6–2).

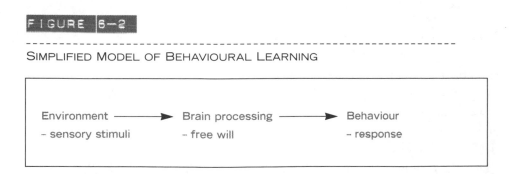

FIGURE 6–2

SIMPLIFIED MODEL OF BEHAVIOURAL LEARNING

Environment ⟶ Brain processing ⟶ Behaviour
- sensory stimuli   - free will   - response

With respect to criminal behaviour, behaviourists view crime as learned responses to life situations that do not necessarily have to represent abnormal or morally immature responses. For example, the wife who kills her abusive husband/partner or the starving survivor of a plane crash who resorts to cannibalism in order to survive, do not necessarily commit these acts because they have some personality pathology or maladaptive personality trait.

There are two basic behavioural models of associative learning, classical conditioning and operant conditioning.

Classical Conditioning

The *Stimulus-Response* (S–R) theory can trace its origins to the pioneering work of the renowned Russian physiologist **Ivan P. Pavlov** (1840–1936) who won the Nobel Prize in Physiology and Medicine in 1904 for his work in this area. Using dogs, he was able to demonstrate that through the simultaneous presentation of an *unconditional stimulus* (US) (piece of meat) combined with a *conditioned stimulus* (CS) (sound from a tuning fork, a neutral stimulus), the conditioned stimulus, through repeated presentations, would eventually elicit a conditioned response (CR) (salivation) in the absence of the *unconditioned stimulus* (UCS). This type of learning was referred to as *conditioned response* (CR), *Pavlovian conditioning*, or *Classical learning*. The model asserts that the dog (or person) has no control over the situation or over what happens to it (Bartol, 1995).

FYI BOX 6.6

Is Doing Psychology Also an "Art"?

Although considered the father of classical conditioning, Pavlov considered himself more a physiologist and had little respect for psychology. He once said "it is still open to discussion whether psychology is a natural science... at all" (cited in Adams, 1976:91).

There are four kinds of classical conditioning that are defined by the relationship between the CS and the UCS (Adams, 1976).

- Simultaneous conditioning occurs when the CS and UCS come together and go off together. In treating certain pedophilias, a picture of a child (CS) is accompanied by an electric shock, noxious smell, or aversive taste (UCS) to extinguish any sexual arousal (CR) (see Marshall, Laws, and Barbaree (1990) for Canadian examples).
- Delayed conditioning occurs when the CS precedes the onset of the UCS and may continue after the commencement of the UCS. With the pedophile a picture may be displayed to see if it elicits a reaction before the shock is administered (see Box 6.7). The picture and shock may stay on together until the patient's sexual reaction subsides.
- Trace conditioning occurs when the CS is terminated before the onset of the UCS. There is delay between the two stimuli.

- Backward conditioning occurs when the UCS precedes the CS. Adams (1976:94) notes that "little or no conditioning is found with backward conditioning ... so it is dubious as one of the main kinds of conditioning."

Paraphilias

Pedophilia is a term used to describe those who obtain sexual pleasures through sexual activity with underage youth, usually prepubescent children. The disorder is a type of paraphilia (from the Greek "para"—"to the side of", and "philos"—"loving") which refers to abnormal or bizarre sexual practices that range from children, animals or others who cannot grant consent; humiliation (sadomasochism); or nonhuman objects (e.g., leather, shoes, underwear) (see Holmes, 1991).

The widely-respected American psychologist Seymour Halleck (1967:176) observed that the line between what is legally defined as a sex crime and what society considers sexual deviation "is almost incomprehensibly muddled by value judgements, conflicting concepts of normality and an aura of secrecy." For example, in the 1960s it was illegal to have intercourse outside of marriage in ten American states. Referring to patients he has treated, Halleck also points out that many sex offenders readily confess their "sins." He wonders whether their problems should be treated solely as crimes or as deep personal problems that they feel shame and guilt over and wish to be punished for.

Applied to the treatment modality, classical conditioning is often based on a process called avoidance learning or aversion therapy. By associating the fear of punishment with the crime or diversion, the offender would learn to avoid and "extinguish" the behaviour. In addition to controlling the type of conditioning, the therapist can also control the duration and intensity of the punishment, and aversion to the individual patient (Maletzky, 1991).

Over the years behaviourists have compiled a considerable volume of literature demonstrating that an aversive stimulus has a strong effect on behaviour. Maletzky (1991:90), in reviewing aversion therapies for sexual offenders concludes that "their techniques not only were highly effective but also provided a framework upon which to develop theories about the origin of maladaptive sexual approach disorders." However, Lykken (1957 cited in Bartol, 1995:80–81) was among the first to demonstrate that psychopaths have an unresponsive autonomic nervous system that does not respond in the classical reflex manner. As discussed in Chapter 5, noted researchers like Robert Hare and Hans Eysenck have focused on social learning related factors, such as poor parenting and an impoverished learning environment. Although their models differ slightly, both argue that psychopathic and anti-social behaviour is linked to a breakdown in learning inhibition and/or lacking in the ability to process information. Other psychologists have pointed out that psychopaths suffer from a lack of *empathy*— the capacity to put oneself in another person's shoes.[11] Yet, in spite of the growing volume of research on criminal psychopaths, Bartol (1995), among others, concludes that while we know they do not seem to think like the rest of mainstream society, there is much we still do not understand about them and treatment programs have only been marginally effective.

Hans Eysenck (1977) coupled his personality theory of criminality (see Chapter 8) with classical conditioning to suggest that the problem with criminals is that they do not condition in a socially-accepted manner. The break-and-enter offender, for example, may not be deterred (UCR) by the presence of a house alarm sticker (UCS). Based on Eysenck's theory, the alarm decal is not critical enough to deter the offender because of his or her personality traits. Yet the decal might deter another potential offender.

Operant or Instrumental Learning

While **John B. Watson** (1878–1958) is often recognized as the father of experimental psychology and behaviourism (Bartol, 1995), B.F. Skinner (see Box 6.8) has been one of the most influential behaviourists in North America. Although Skinner accepts the belief that human cognition exists, he maintains that unless one can observe and measure it, cognition can not be scientifically studied. Only that which has a physical basis, and can be publicly observed, can be studied.

PROFILE BOX 6.8

BURRHUS FREDERICK SKINNER (1904–1990)

Skinner was born and raised in Susquehanna, Pennsylvania. He majored in English in university, determined to become a writer. However, after graduating, his attempts to make a living at writing dried up. He went back to school to study psychology at Harvard University. On graduating in 1931, he quickly became an acclaimed leader in experimental psychology and later received the distinguished President's Medal of Science (Hall and Lindzey, 1970).

In addition to his numerous academic works, Skinner wrote the famous utopian novel *Walden II* in 1948, in which he "described the evolution of an experimental society based on psychological principles" (Hall and Lindzey,

Section II: Etiology of Crime

1970:478). His model community is based on a planned order that eliminates punishment, along with any form of aversive control. In 1967, an actual community, Twin Oaks, based on the book, was established in Virginia. In 1971, he published his scientific position in another popular book, *Beyond Freedom and Dignity*. On its release the *New York Times* suggested that if one read only one book that year, it should be Skinner's book.

On the value of punishment, Skinner (1971:68) wrote, "the trouble is that when we punish a person for behaving badly, we leave it up to him to discover how to behave well." This view may have been influenced by his father, a lawyer, who had taken him on prison tours while young, and from his grandmother, who constantly stressed the evils of wrongdoing (Skinner, 1979). He has been described as the most influential representative of behaviourism, constructing one of the major psychological theories of the twentieth century.

For Skinner all behaviour is situational, deterministic and void of independent thinking. That is, we are at the mercy of stimuli in our environment and simply react to the stimuli around us. In addition, while our environment might appear complex and filled with stimuli, careful research can identify the causal factors. This line of reasoning is known as operant conditioning and forms the basic principles of *behaviour modification* or *behavioural therapy*. Behaviourists believe that behaviour is influenced whenever someone attempts to exert some power and control over others. Thus, behaviour is not based on free will but instead is viewed as the product of chains of stimuli and responses. One of the most powerful elements of behaviourism is *reinforcement*.

We can probably all relate to examples of how our behaviour was changed as a result of being rewarded for some responses and not others. In grade school, you might have earned stars for work well done. Conversely, if you did something wrong you might have been grounded or had a curfew levied. Psychology has extended this general knowledge to changing the anti-social behaviour of delinquent boys and changing inappropriate behaviour through treating emotionally-challenged patients. This is known as behaviour modification. The key to initiating any change is dependent on the *discriminative stimuli* which, when present, can bring about the desired change. The discriminative stimuli can either be *positive* reinforcement (results in increases or rewards behaviour) or *negative* reinforcement (either reduces, eliminates, or causes the avoidance of undesirable behaviour) (Bartol, 1995).

One common form of positive reinforcement used in many correctional settings is the use of token economy. "Tokens" such as poker chips, points, and stamps are symbolic rewards that are given whenever the desired response occurs. The tokens can be submitted in exchange for "backward reinforcement" of value to the participant (e.g., buy food, watch a favourite television program, etc.).

Negative reinforcement focuses on trying to extinguish undesirable responses by creating a negative association between the response and the discriminative stimulus. As noted above, negative reinforcement has been used in a variety of programs designed to treat sex-offenders.

Reconditioning behaviour is also dependent on different types of reinforcement schedules. Reinforcement is not always delivered in the same manner. The two basic schedules are:

- *Ratio schedules:* reinforcement occurs after a specific number of responses regardless of time frame.
- *Interval schedules:* reinforcement is delivered on a time schedule independent of the number of responses.

These two schedules can be further classified into *fixed* and *variable* schedules, "depending whether number of responses or time between reinforcements is fixed or is variable with a statistical definition" (Adams, 1976:47).

When these elements are applied to a treatment or therapeutic setting, it is referred to as behaviour modification. The principles and elements of this modality have largely been derived from research in experimental psychology—hence its often stark and sterile image.

Behaviour modification (BM) can be illustrated with the following steps:

- The purpose of BM is, first, to define the problematic behaviour (e.g., shoplifting).
- Unless one can identify the specific problem, it cannot be properly changed. For example, when the client feels stressed he or she turns to shoplifting to alleviate his or her tension.
- Usually the behaviourist designs contracts for patients that involve specific contingency elements, for example, being placed under house arrest and not being permitted to leave the property between certain hours, to report in every day at a predefined time, etc.
- The aim of the program is to shape the behaviour of the offender using either an *aversive* approach (e.g., fines, lock-down, loss of privileges) or a *positive* approach (e.g., earned remission, praise, "tokens" that can be put towards a reward of choice).

Applying Behavioural Conditioning

In their extensive review of Canadian correctional programs, Gendreau and Ross (1987) identified a number of advantages and disadvantages of behaviourally-based treatment programs. Among the advantages they include:

- Treatment does not dwell on past experiences. There is no need to assess the validity of such experiences.

- Because patients must focus on the current aspects of their behaviour they cannot use explanations of prior experiences or events to excuse their behaviour.

- BM-oriented programs do not require trained therapeutic personnel to administer them.

Among those elements that are considered limitations of the behavioural treatment approach, Vito and Holmes (1994) found:

- When reinforcement is based on negative conditioning some researchers question whether it is simply designed to gain control of "troublemakers."

- Are adequate steps always taken to protect the rights of the inmates?

- BM programs tend to create artificial situations that do not resemble the natural environment the patient must live in. As Vito and Holmes (1994:132) observe, "not all good behaviours are rewarded."

The recent interest in restorative justice may be a viable alternative to conventional approaches. These programs are based on the philosophy and criminal justice model of *restorative justice* (Fattah, 1995; Zehr, 1995) (see Chapters 4 and 14).

In summary, behavioural learning represents a stark contrast to most of the learning-based theories. The model (classical and operant) asserts that behaviours change in response to the stimuli in the individual's environment. Behaviourists do not assume that behaviour is rooted in an inherently abnormal personality.

Applications of the behavioural approach were popular models of treatment during the 1970s (see, for example, Gendreau and Ross, 1987). Treatment modalities varied in their description but they all emphasized modifying behaviour through a variable system of rewards and punishments. Targeted behaviour was based on observable and quantifiable actions. However, in partial response to a variety of ethical and practical concerns there was a waning of the behavioural approach in certain areas of the system. Nevertheless, in keeping with theoretical trends in criminology, behaviourism has evolved into a broader integrated and interdisciplinary model of learning. One such variation is the bio-social theories (see Chapter 8).

Summary

Psychology has made a number of important contributions to the study of criminal behaviour. In this chapter, we began with a look at the "roots" of psychological theories and the influence of demonology. At one time, it was thought that criminal behaviour was the result of a possessed mind/body. The only way to exercise the evil was usually by some torturous means. The key was a focus on the individual rather than his or her environment or any social forces.

Demonology set the stage for psychology and the medical model where treatment could be rationalized as an appropriate way of correcting deviant or criminal behaviour.

We then examined one of the most enduring psychological approaches to the study of (criminal) behaviour—psychoanalysis and the psychodynamic perspective. Criminality was seen as a product of unresolved conflict, a maladaptive behaviour that could be traced to early childhood experience(s). Left unresolved the emotional disturbances could lead to unhealthy habits and/or behaviours. Psychoanalysis relies on free association to treat offenders. In addition to the theory being difficult to test empirically, its effectiveness seems "limited to generally intelligent, articulate, adult neurotics" (Finckenauer, 1984:27).

The second major perspective of the psychological theories we examined was the cognitive-based learning theories. Here, we focused on three varied learning approaches—the frustration-aggression model, moral development, and behavioural conditioning theories. Although each theory applies a different set of principles to explain how people learn, they all assume individuals have free will and assert that they can learn to alter their criminal actions. The behavioural models were the most divergent of the learning models presented.

Even though there have been a number of significant variations between the perspectives and theories covered, the length of time they have withstood scientific testing, and their ability to satisfactorily account for some forms of criminal and deviant behaviour continue to receive support in the literature. Yet, as was discussed in Chapter 2, knowledge is a relative construct and therefore no one theory can account for all criminal behaviour. In fact, human behaviour is too complex to simply rely on a theoretical perspective that focuses on only one aspect of human behaviour. However, the emergence of the bio-social perspective from the behaviorial models shows that psychological theories have evolved to become more interdisciplinary in their approach. The theories illustrate that criminal behaviour is learned behaviour based on personal experiences whether on negative unresolved childhood experiences or on the type of reinforcement received while interacting in the environment. As Jeffery (1990:247) concludes, "learning theory is critical to any understanding of criminal behaviour."

All the theories are concerned with classifying and responding to individual behaviour. This medical model has been the foundation for numerous individualized treatment and prevention programs within the criminal justice system. Programs range from *probation* to specialized treatment programs for specific types of offenders.

Summary: Psychological Theories of Crime

PERSPECTIVE	THEORIST	CAUSES OF CRIMINALITY AND CORE ELEMENTS
Demonology		• Demons, evil spirits, and gods cause evil behaviour
Intrapsychic Theories		
Psychodynamic	S. Freud	• Intrapsychic processes
	C. Jung	– unconscious conflicts
	A. Aichorn	– importance of childhood experiences
		– defence mechanisms
		– anger
Learning Theories		
Cognitive	J. Piaget	• Information processing
	L. Kohlberg	– thinking and planning
	S. Yochelson and	– memory
	S. Samenow	– perspectives
		– developmental issues
		– ethical values
Social Learning	J. Dollard et al.	• Situational processing
	W. Bandura	– frustration-aggression
	B.F. Skinner	– modelling/imitation
	H. Eysenck	– stimulus-response

Discussion Questions

1. Although the percentages vary, we have seen an increase in the number of offenders who experience some degree of mental/emotional challenges. How might we explain this trend from a psychological perspective? Apply at least two different theoretical models to explain the phenomenon.

2. Describe the major psychological theories discussed in this chapter. What are the relative strengths and weaknesses of each theory? Which theory do you think has the most explanatory power? Why?

3. What challenges might exist in accepting any one type of psychological theory over another type?

4. How have social structures affected psychological theory, crime research, and crime policy?

5. After having read this chapter, to what degree do you think that sociological explanations of crime have been, and are, currently grounded in scientific principles?

6. How might psychological components be incorporated into an integrated and interdisciplinary criminological perspective? Which components do you think would be the most important?

Key Concepts

Deterministic

Order of the Solar Temple

Frustration-aggression model

Intrapsychic

Psychoanalytic

Classical conditioning

Paraphilia

Operant/instrumental learning

Schizophrenic

demonology

road rage

psychodynamic

behavioural learning

organic disorder

avoidance learning

behaviour modification

cognition

criminal personality

modelling

moral development

id, ego, superego

functional disorder

token economy

psychopath

Key Names

G. Aschaffenburg

S. Freud

I. Pavlov

A. Bandura

H. Maudsley

J. Piaget

J. Watson

I. Ray

L. Kohlberg

B.F. Skinner

Weblinks

http://heavensgate.com The Web site of the cult group Heaven's Gate. An interesting insight into their agenda and propaganda.

www.schizophrenia.ca/ Schizophrenia Society of Canada. Although it doesn't strictly deal with crime, it offers lots of interesting information about an illness that many criminals seem to suffer from.

www.stop-roadrage.com In the late 1990s, road rage seems to have become the rage. This Web site offers a number of interesting links. It includes information from Dr. Leon James who is considered an expert on the subject. There is a workbook, road rage survey, and even a link for ordering road rage bumper stickers.

www.hare.org/ Since a growing body of research suggests that many chronic offenders suffer from some form of psychopathy, this Web site might prove interesting.

Footnotes

1. While some readers might feel the subject matter of demonology should be placed elsewhere (e.g., history), its legacy has had a significant impact on how we view crime and criminality from a psychological perspective.

2. Schizophrenia is a psychological and physical disease of the brain similar to Alzheimer's Disease. While some research suggests it may be present at birth (possibly inherited), it only begins to manifest itself when the prefrontal cortex matures in late adolescence. The Canadian Schizophrenic Society estimates schizophrenia affects about one per cent of the population. Symptoms usually involve bipolar disorder (manic depression) and hallucinations (visual and auditory). Unlike psychopaths, schizophrenics can have difficulty maintaining reality.

3. The unconscious mind can result in defence mechanisms that are established by the ego. There are four main forms. *Displacement* or *sublimation* occurs when the substituted object represents a higher cultural goal than immediate gratification. *Repression* occurs when memories (e.g., sexual abuse) are forced into the unconscious mind and their existence is denied. *Reaction formation* takes the form of an irrational adjustment to anxiety. For example, you might not like somebody but you pretend to get along. *Projection* occurs when an individual rationalizes an appropriate motive for an inappropriate one (Vold and Bernard, 1981). One of the better known sociological adaptations of Freud's defence mechanisms application is the *technique-of-neutralization* developed by Graham Sykes and David Matza in the later 1950s. The theory was used to explain how youths come to commit delinquent acts.

4. By contrast, Freud referred to a complete breakdown in emotional stability that may be accompanied by episodes of hallucination, as **psychosis**.

5. Freud used the term **thanatos** to refer to our unrecognized desire to be potentially self-destructive. For example, knowing the potential harm of smoking, speeding, bad diet, "picking fights," and even leaving assignments to the last minute, and so on, why do some of us do one or more of these things?

6. In 1996, a 14-year-old boy from La Ronge, Saskatchewan was found not guilty by reason of insanity for killing a seven-year-old and then boiling his flesh in liquid fat. He was modelling a scene from the 1991 movie *Warlock*.

7. On February 1998, Eagleson became the first Canadian ever to be stripped of the honour.

8. In June 1998, Walsh died at his home in the Bahamas after suffering from a brain aneurysm. He was 52 years old.

9. For an intriguing account of the Walker case, you might be interested in reading A. Cairn's (1998) *Nothing Sacred: The Many Lives and Betrayals of Albert Walker*. Toronto: Seal Books.

10. A psychopathy test can be found on the Internet at **www.hare.org/**

CHAPTER 7

Sociological Explanations

"The sociological imagination enables us to grasp history and biography and the relations between the two within society."

Charles Wright Mills (1916–1962)

Learning Outcomes

After you have finished reading this chapter, you should be able to:

• Appreciate the contribution that sociologists have made to the study of crime.

• Appreciate the uniqueness that sociologists bring to the study of crime causation.

• Identify the factors that contributed to the emergence of the sociological school.

• Provide an historical outline of Canadian sociology.

• Identify the numerous different sociological perspectives.

• Appreciate the strengths of the major sociological perspective.

• Recognize the limitations of each perspective.

• Better understand and appreciate the need for a multi-factor, multi-disciplinary approach.

In Chapter 1 it was noted that *crime*, in an absolute sense, refers strictly to violations of criminal laws, and that the term *deviance* is used (primarily by sociologists) to mean the violations of certain norms, ranging from folkways and mores to formal laws. Together, criminal acts and acts of deviance are largely recognized as social problems and people as social beings are shaped by social forces

in their environment. As the prominent American sociologist C. Wright Mills (1959) observed, individual problems are rooted in their social structure (see Box 7.1). This general perspective, in North America, has dominated the study of crime and deviance.

Even though other disciplines (e.g., biology, economics, political science, and psychology, among others) are vying for acceptance in criminology, the sociological approach is still the dominant discipline used to describe, explain, and predict crime. No other discipline offers as many theories of crime, and no other discipline has influenced criminal justice policy as has sociology. In fact, although not the first to do so, sociologist Ronald Akers (1992) tries to make the case that criminology belongs to a subfield of sociology. He makes this argument because most criminologists are primarily trained in sociology and because much of the theorizing and research is conducted from a sociological perspective.

Given the historical dominance of sociological traditionalists, it is a somewhat daunting task to offer a representative overview of sociological theories. In fact, some might feel that certain sociological perspectives have been ignored in this chapter. However, given the integrated and interdisciplinary orientation of this textbook, the purpose is to present a cross-sectional and summative overview of some of the important sociological theories.

A CLOSER LOOK BOX 7.1

A Sociological Assessment of Crime

Sociologists suggest there are two central questions in the study of criminology. According to Barken (1997:3) they are:

1. Why do crime rates differ across locations and over time?
2. Why do crime rates differ according to the key dimensions of structured social inequality: race/ethnicity, class and gender? For example, the Routine Activity Theory (Felson, 1997) suggests that the decline in crime in the 1990s is due to a reduction in suitable targets. People are carrying less cash and consumer goods like televisions weigh more than they did in the late 1970s when property crime was much higher. The explanation changes in our social environment over time. We will examine this theory in greater detail in Chapter 8.

Let us begin by examining the meaning of social structure and its significance for sociology and sociologically-trained criminologists. We will then proceed with a brief historical overview of sociology as a discipline before discussing several of the more established and traditional sociological theories of crime. It is intended that each of the theories, although different in approach, share common sociological orientation to the study of deviance and crime. Some of the more contemporary integrated sociological perspectives will be briefly addressed in this chapter. For example, although we will introduce the routine activity theory and conflict-based theories, they will be expanded on in Chapter 8. There we will review a variety of those theories whose explanatory approaches strive to bridge disciplinary boundaries. The chapter will conclude with a brief summary and evaluation of sociological theories of crime and deviance.

Social Structure and Crime

One of the questions many sociologists typically ask is whether as social beings we are innately "good" or "bad." While biologists and psychologists look to the individual and some personal trait or attribute for an answer, sociologists look to the social structure and social forces of society for their answers. For example, individualists such as Lombroso (Chapter 5) believed certain individuals were simply born criminal. The social environment provided the setting and opportunity for a crime to occur. Freud (Chapter 6) meanwhile believed humans were essentially amoral and it was only because of the socialization process (i.e., super-ego) that people had to struggle (defence mechanisms) to function within the confined bounds set by society. Hence, social forces are seen as contributing but not causal factors.

While recognizing the diversity of sociological perspectives addressing the issues of crime and deviance, it is possible to speak of a "sociological approach." Rooted in the classical statements of Emile Durkheim, Karl Marx, and Max Weber, sociology starts with the idea that all behaviour is social—that is, it is necessarily shaped by the social structure. Instead of placing emphasis on the processes of personality or individual determinants for behaviour, sociology stresses behaviour through the internalization of social roles.

Through the notion of social structured behaviour, sociology makes a significant departure from both the classical model and positivism. This notion asserts that individuals are socialized into any given social structure through the parameters of their social roles. In this way, social structures pressure individuals towards conformist behaviour.

In relation to crime and deviance, sociology is concerned with the impact the social structure has on deviance and criminality and the pressure within the social structure on some people to engage in nonconformist behaviour.

Our social structure provides an environment for learning, or socialization. What is considered acceptable behaviour is defined through *prescriptive norms* (define what we can do) and *proscriptive norms* (what we cannot do). Some of our norms are informal in that there are no written laws defining what we can or cannot do. Rather they are simply part of our social environment that have been established over time. However, as societies moved from more informal structures to more formal ones it became necessary for some laws to be converted into formal laws (Wright and Fox, 1978). Given that not all aspects of our social environment can be controlled, or all laws enforced, sociologists argue that such situations can lead to crime and deviance.

One of the founding fathers of sociology is Emile Durkheim (see Box 7.3). He perhaps best encapsulated the above ideas when he observed that even in a society of saints there would be deviance. He also observed that some acts would be defined as criminal and even some saints would commit crimes (1938 cited in Wright and Fox, 1978:134).

Durkheim believed that human groups make rules and someone within the group always breaks some of these rules. The exact reasons, according to Durkheim, are not always clear but the individual's behaviour is perceived as being related to his or her social environment rather than intrinsic traits. For example, when you were younger and had your group of "best friends" (social environment) were you ever asked to keep a secret and never tell anyone? How many of you did tell the secret to someone else (intrinsic traits)? Is it possible, as the great English philosopher Thomas Hobbes (1588–1679), Sigmund Freud, and others have suggested that without a hegemonic (i.e., preponderant influence or authority) social structure, deviance and crime are simply expressions of disharmony? If so, then criminal laws are necessary as a means of social control and as a reflection of the social consciousness of society at large. Furthermore, this line of reasoning lends support to a sociological interpretation and analysis of what can be viewed as a social phenomenon.

The traditions of the sociological understanding of crime and deviance are repeated, explicitly or implicitly, in its many more current theoretical statements. Since the 1930s, there has been a significant volume of work developing various aspects of the sociological approach to crime and deviance. Consequently, this chapter can only give an overview of the more significant developments. Nevertheless, the link between current expressions and the traditional statements is clear. As expressed by the American sociologist Robert Merton, the aim of the sociological explanation is to discover how some social structures exert pressure on certain persons in society to engage in nonconformist rather than conformist conduct.

History of Sociological Criminology

"In the first place crime is normal because a society exempt from it is utterly impossible" (Durkheim, 1893, cited in Jacoby, 1994:65).

Sociology emerged from the social and political philosophies of nineteenth century Europe—a period characterized by considerable social unrest marked by such major events as the French Revolution (1789). **Auguste Comte** (1798–1857), in addition to being recognized as the "founder of sociology" was also the founder of the positivist school of philosophy. The positivist school advocated that the study of social phenomena be conducted through the use of a "systematic observation and the accumulation of evidence and objective facts within a deductive framework (moving from the general to the specific)" (Williams and McShane, 1994:32). Hence, it is not the perspective that is important but the process or methodology of the study. In his six-volume *Cours de Philosophie Positive* (Course in Positive Philosophy) Comte argued that human behaviour is dictated by forces beyond the individual's control (Barkan, 1997). Comte believed that the social development of humankind could be classified into what he referred to as the *law of the three stages*:

1. **Theological**: Events are largely attributable to supernatural forces which cannot be directly observed or measured. For example, the phrase "it is God's will" may be used to explain an experience but it is a statement that cannot be proved or disproved.

2. **Metaphysical**: Natural events are seen to be the result of fundamental energies or ideas. For example, a murder could be explained as the result of an offender's soul being occupied by an evil spirit.

3. **Positive**: Phenomena are explained through observation, hypothesis, and experimentation. This is the basis of scientific inquiry.

According to Comte, the explanation of crime and criminality passed through these three stages until the nineteenth century when the positivist school of thought emerged.

The final stage has two main elements. The first is the notion that our behaviour is a function of external forces beyond our immediate control. These forces, as noted already, can range from elements like wealth and class, to political and historical famine and war. These forces have been grouped into *macro*-based sociological theories (Williams and McShane, 1994). Macrotheories are broader in scope and attempt to explain social events in terms of their social structure and its effect on behaviour. As Williams and McShane (1994:8) note "they paint a picture of the way the world works."[1]

Comte's second element focused on individual traits and characteristics including brain structure and an individual's biological makeup. Although he was a sociologist, Comte's elements share an interdisciplinary context. Even though Comte believed that sociology was based on biology, he maintained that sociology represented the key to understanding social change. In time, Comte adopted a hierarchical stance of the sciences and eventually placed sociology above all others. While recognizing the role of individual traits, he felt that the social environment was the best indicator and predictor of human behaviour.

While Comte may have been somewhat conciliatory in his approach to explaining social behaviour, his fellow compatriots **Gabriel Tarde** (1834–1904) and Emile Durkheim (see Box 7.3) were not. In his effort to explain criminal acts at a social level, Durkheim rejected both biology and psychology. Today, even though sociologists subscribe to Durkheim's perspective rather than Comte's they embrace Comte's scientific approach to the study of human behaviour (Jeffery, 1990).

Although Gabriel Tarde's work initially made significant contributions to the analysis of social and environmental influences on human behaviour, his work has gone largely unrecognized in recent years. His ideas about behaviour being learned largely by association have now been replaced by more contemporary theories such as Edwin Sutherland's Differential Association, Daniel Glaser's Differential Identification, and C. R. Jeffery's Differential Reinforcement Theory (see later in the chapter). Yet his book *Laws of Imitation*, published in 1890 "are eloquent expositions of the association, or learning theory of criminality" (Schafer, 1976:233). Tarde was also one of the first to refute and challenge Lombroso's theories of atavism and criminal types. Focusing on the social environment, Tarde believed that everyone behaves according to customs of the cultural environment. Tarde suggested there are two basic social processes:

1. **Invention**: May be considered a prototype, but it occurs infrequently. Most "original" acts can be traced back to earlier variations. For example, during antiquity, unwanted children were simply killed at birth. Today it is illegal to kill a newborn child. Therefore, women will have an abortion to rid themselves of an unwanted pregnancy. Some consider abortion simply a prototype of infanticide.

2. **Imitation**: According to Tarde, this is the typical element of social life. However, its psycho-biological mechanism is not yet well-defined. Similar to the social contract, we tend to behave in very similar ways and when someone chooses to commit a crime, he or she typically commits a crime that others have already committed.

In accordance with his views on the importance of imitation, Tarde identified three laws of imitation. The first is the *law of proportion*. We imitate events in proportion to the frequency, the closeness and stability that they have with those events we experience. (Therefore, criminal activities can become a "fashion" by the contagious influence of the behaviour in question.)

The second law is the *law of direction*. It asserts that a superior act (i.e., low risk of apprehension and high return for effort) is usually imitated by those who are impressed and influenced by prestige. Gangs, for example, might offer protection, easy access to drugs, and a carefree lifestyle. Tarde observed that deviant and criminal behaviour that originates in one country may be imitated in another. The skinhead movement, for example, first appeared in Europe before it was imitated in North America. Tarde cites the example of crimes that were originally committed by members of the upper classes but over time spread to lower social levels. They reflect a sense of continuance and continuity in social structures.

FORMS OF IMITATION

According to Tarde, imitation could be expressed in one of two forms—fashion and custom. *Fashion* tends to occur where contact is close and frequent. *Custom* occurs where contact is less frequent and change occurs less often. Using these distinctions, how might we explain differences in crime in urban as opposed to rural settings?

The final law is the *law of insertion*. This occurs when two mutually exclusive fashions are in opposition (e.g., abortion vs. infanticide) and one tends to be substituted for the other. Substitution is influenced by what is fashionable or superior. Such changes in social behaviour may reflect social, economic, or political shifts occurring at the time within a community. In his book *High Society*, Boyd (1991) discusses how certain drugs considered illegal today used to be legal at one time or another in Canada. Boyd suggests that legalization was in some instances politically motivated (e.g., as in the case of morphine) while in other instances (e.g., alcohol) socially motivated.

Unlike Durkheim, Tarde treated crime as a social phenomenon and likened it to the destructive nature of cancer. Hence, he argued society should spare no effort to combat it.

DAVID EMILE DURKHEIM (1858–1917)

Durkheim was born on April 15, 1858 in Epinal, France. His life has been described as "stoical, devoid of humor, and with near total devotion to study and scholarly pursuits" (Martin, Mutchnick, and Austin, 1990:47). His schooling marked by strict discipline did, however, have a lasting influence as Durkheim seemed to spend his adult life engrossed in pursuing answers to complex social issues. By the age of sixteen he had already earned a baccalaureate degree. Durkheim then went on to become absorbed with the moral philosophers of his time and in particular with the work of Auguste Comte—the "father of sociology" (Lunden, 1972).

Durkheim's interest in moral philosophy and social structure were further fuelled by the impact of the French Revolution and the defeat of Napoleon. It was a period also marked by a dramatic move from a feudal-agricultural system to an industrial economy. As Martin et al. point out, because of his educational foundation and academic interest, Durkheim became interested in trying to understand and explain "societal influences upon morality, religion, deviance, and the general breakdown of traditional social institutions" (p. 48).

As for his academic work, he first introduced the concept of anomie in his Ph.D. dissertation, *The Division of Labor in Society*, published in 1893. The concept of anomie was used to describe how a society could change so rapidly. Then, while at the University of Bordeaux, in 1895, he wrote another classic, *The Rules of Sociological Method*, in which he further delineated his theory of anomie and the function of crime in society. This was followed two years later by another seminal work, *Suicide*. In the latter book, Durkheim displays his astute knowledge of the scientific method to explain the social meaning of suicide. Drawing on his theoretical principles and available data, Durkheim argued that Catholics committed fewer suicides than Protestants because their doctrine is stricter, they have clearer norms, and unlike Protestants, they condemn the practice of suicide. Hence, he asserts, Catholics have a strong *collective conscience* that is necessary for a stable society.

While teaching at Bordeaux, Durkheim also found the time to develop and edit the first sociological journal, *L'Année Sociologique*. Through the journal, Durkheim helped to forge early criminological theory and to bring sociology to full acceptance as a social science (Martin et al., 1990).

After his death in 1917, Durkheim's work received limited attention, due primarily to the fact that it was not translated into English. However, in the 1930s his work was re-discovered and translated into English. It quickly drew the attention of sociologists and, indirectly, criminologists. And although Durkheim is recognized as a sociologist, Lunden (1972) offers a profound quote from Durkheim's work that reflects a deep awareness of human behaviour that transcends a strict sociological perspective. Durkheim wrote "Man's characteristic privilege is that the bond he accepts is not physical but moral: that is social. He is governed not by a material environment brutally imposed on him, but a conscience superior to his own" (Ibid, 398).

Sociology in North America

Sociology emerged in 1892 as a disciplinary area of inquiry when the first sociology department was established at the University of Chicago (Williams and McShane, 1994). Being located in an urban centre it is not surprising that the early sociologists focused on urban life and the influences of urban life and the urban setting. For example, the pioneering work and ideas of **Ernest W. Burgess** and **Robert E. Park** can still be found in Cohen and Felson's (1979) very popular Routine Activity Theory today (Chapter 8).

> In 1921, Burgess and Park collaborated to write the *Introduction to the Science of Sociology* which was more commonly referred to as the "Green Bible" at the University of Chicago. Even today, it is considered "among the most important treatises ever written in sociology" (Martin et al., 1990:101).

While at the University of Chicago, Burgess developed his concentric-circle theory of crime. The theory involved the study of ecology—the distribution of phenomena and their relationship to the environment. In particular, Park and Burgess "produced a conception of the city as a series of distinctive concentric circles radiating from the central business district" (Williams and McShane, 1994:53). Burgess and his colleagues attempted to explain crime as a function of social changes that were accompanied by environmental change. This mode of sociological inquiry has been referred to as the **Chicago (Ecological) School** (see p. 228) since many of the studies during the 1920s and 1930s adopted a similar approach. The school also got its name from the fact that all the studies were conducted at the University of Chicago.

Borrowing from animal and plant ecology studies, Burgess applied the ecological concepts of dominance, invasion, and succession to explain how human beings could be physically mapped into zones. Burgess's theory divided the city into five major zones with each zone being characterized by different social and organizational elements. For example, Zone 1, the central business district, is defined by light manufacturing, retail trade, and commercialized recreation while Zone 5, the outermost area, is seen as the commuters' zone where wealthier residents live (see Figure 7–1). This zone includes suburbs and satellite towns like Oakville, Port Hope, Mississauga, and Brampton around Toronto. By contrast, the inner zones tend to attract the poorer and more crowded housing. For example, if you live in, or near, a large city, where do most of the wealthy people live? Where do you find the homeless and street people? Where are the shelters for the homeless, and which areas do you feel less safe in?

In addition, between the zones are areas in transition where the physical and social environment are less defined. These are the areas where newly arrived immigrants initially settle, where divorce rates are higher, and housing less well maintained. They are areas of *social disorganization* and characteristically have higher crime rates.

For a period, the concentric-circle theory enjoyed considerable success. However as the social structure changed the social ecological approach shifted from a focus on individual crime to the crime site and from physical characteristics of the environment to social traits (Brantingham and Brantingham, 1984). For example, during the pre-automobile era our mobility patterns tended to be more confined than they are today. With the advent and popularity of automobiles our social structure changed and our awareness of space became more fluid and the traditional social ecological approach could no longer adequately explain criminal behaviour. This set the stage for the emergence of numerous sociological theories that can trace their origins to the influence of human ecology and its evolution into social ecology. In Chapter 8, we will examine the integrated social ecological model known as Crime Prevention Through Environmental Design (**CPTED**).

FIGURE 7-1

ZONE RATES OF MALE JUVENILE DELINQUENTS, 1927–33 SERIES

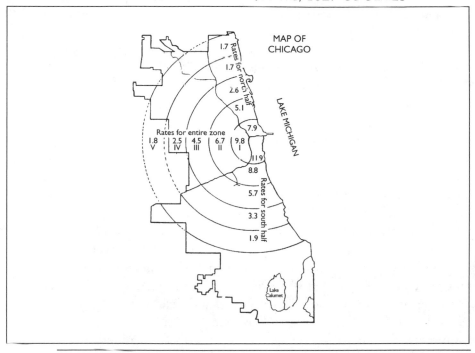

Juvenile Delinquency and Urban Areas *Clifford R. Shaw—Henry D. McKay*; 1972;
The University of Chicago Press, p. 69.

In spite of several methodological critiques, the intellectual heritage of the Chicago School runs deep and has had a lasting influence on North American sociological criminology. Its adherents range from Fredrick Thrasher's work on youth gangs in the 1920s to Edwin Sutherland's formation of the *differential association theory* in the 1930–40s, to Howard Becker's *labelling theory* in the 1960s (see Williams and McShane, 1999).

Canadian Sociology

Sociology in Canada was slower to emerge and evolve.[2] Because of colonial ties, Canadian academics have historically looked to Europe for leadership. Therefore, in the beginning of the Canadian sociological movement, anglophone schools followed the British in "hesitating to give recognition to sociology which was viewed as a present-oriented and shallow American discipline" (Hiller, 1983, cited in Teevan, 1986:12).

McGill University was the first Canadian school to establish a sociology department under **Carl A. Dawson** in the 1920s, who was influenced by functionalist approaches of the University of Chicago and at Columbia.[3] Throughout the 1930s and 1940s most of the research done in the area can be viewed as historical sociology with little emphasis on crime or deviance (Teevan and Blute, 1986). Francophone schools influenced by the French Catholic sociologists did not embrace Durkheim's view of God as a symbol of society rather than a real entity. The Francophone schools viewed sociology more as an adjunct to Christian social doctrines than as a science (Ibid). However, this all changed as the "baby boomers" of the 1960s entered universities in record numbers. Schools sought new solutions to a growing number of social problems (e.g., ethnic relations, poverty, and separatism) and universities established sociological programs to provide an academic venue for studying social conflict. With the rapid growth of sociology departments, the demand for trained faculty could not be met by Canadian sociologists. Teevan and Blute (1986) note that by 1970–71 only 40 per cent of sociology and anthropology faculty were Canadian citizens, the remainder mostly American. As sociology emerged as an academic discipline, Canadian programs were based on the dominant American perspective of *functionalism* or a systems approach.[4]

In their summary, Teevan and Blute (1986) comment on how difficult it has been for a Canadian sociology to emerge. This view is reflected in the fact that most of what is presented in this chapter has American roots.

In **summary**, the emergence of sociology had European roots and as a discipline it is a little more than one hundred years old. The American universities (Chicago School) were the first to embrace sociology as a mode of scientific inquiry into human behaviour. Canadian sociology did not come into existence until the 1920s. Today, however, sociology has become a major area of scientific inquiry and along with its growing popularity, different sociological perspectives emerged (see Box 7.4).

To this point, we have presented some general thoughts on crime and deviance and a number of questions have been raised. In this chapter, we will draw on some of the major sociological theories of crime and deviance to provide a general understanding. Given the parameters of this textbook and the chapter, we will include four sociological theories that have been used extensively to explain crime and criminality. They include: (1) *anomie*, (2) *ecological school*, (3) *differential association*, and (4) *labelling and situational theories*. Taken alone, each theory provides useful insight into crime and deviance. Collectively they serve as powerful explanatory models. However, as Schafer (1976:49) observed, sociology alone is not "able to offer satisfactory explanations of the causes of crime." Sociology has however made a significant contribution to the study of crime and deviance and has drawn attention to the importance of studying social process, social structure, and the social environment.

Overview of Sociological Perspectives and Some Related Theories

PERSPECTIVE	KEY POINTS	RELATED THEORIES
Social/Process Learning	– behaviour is learned in social context – law-breaking and motives are acquired through interaction with others	Differential Association Neutralization/Drift
Social Reaction	– focus upon social and institutional response to an individual – less interested in initial delinquency than in how social control agents respond – view individual as a passive being who is forced into delinquency/crime as a result of societal definition	Labelling Dramatization of Evil
Social Disorganization	– societies strive for a state of equilibrium/stability – changes in social structure and environment create instability which can lead to crime	Concentric Circle CPTD
Strain	– stress, frustration, or strain prompt deviance – norms violated to alleviate the strain – greatest pressure within the lower social echelons	Anomie
Social Conflict*	– society composed of competing interests – competing values and interests lead to conflict between groups vying for power – state represents interest of those groups with the most power	Conflict
Social Control	– crime and deviance result from inadequate social roles or association with deviant others – social policy focuses on changing responsibility of the offender	Differential Association Social Learning Social Control

* In Capter 8 we will address some of the more contemporary versions of the conflict perspective (e.g., critical criminology, radical criminology, and left-realism).

Anomie/Strain Theory

We begin with anomie theory because of the nature of its fundamental concepts. Anomie is also seen as a pivotal idea in the sociological study of deviance and crime and is an easily understandable example of sociological explanations.

Conceptual Basis

The idea of anomie was first set forth by Emile Durkheim and later modified by the eminent American sociologist Robert K. Merton (1910–). Durkheim introduced the term in his 1893 book, *Division of Labor in Society,* to describe a condition of "deregulation" or "normlessness" occurring in society. Moreover, while it was not fully an empirical theory, it had good face validity—it made good sense (see Chapter 3).

Two themes are central to Durkheim's thesis: (1) social organization is necessary to keep our natural (i.e., innate) tendencies in check, and (2) under conditions where social order breaks down and social norms lose their influence, then a condition of anomie develops and crime significantly increases (Durkheim, 1951, cited in Wright and Fox (1978:136)). Based on his central thesis, Durkheim employed a deductive process to develop a dichotomy based on the principles of mechanical and organic solidarity. He argued that all societies start in a "mechanical form that is socially characterized by *homogeneity* (uniformity). Mechanical societies are self-sufficient and autonomous and there is little division of labour or non-specialization of labour. However, Durkheim notes that all societies evolve (at different rates) from simple towards more complex highly specialized forms. He referred to this process as *organic* solidarity. As societies become more specialized in labour they need more laws to maintain social order.

Durkheim further felt that societies are in a constant state of change. This state of change creates a natural environment of strain (i.e., helplessness or normlessness) among different social groups. It is when the force of the "collective conscience" weakens that rates of crime, suicide and other deviant behaviours increase. In addition to the theory's good face validity, Durkheim advocated that crime and punishment be empirically measured and tested.

Believing that every social structure is in a state of flux, Durkheim regarded crime as a natural and inevitable element of society. To this end, he recognized two types of criminals: altruistic and common. The *altruistic criminal* is one who becomes offended by the rules of society and is intent on trying to change them for the better. Animal rights groups and certain environmental groups (e.g., Greenpeace and the Sierra Club) would fall under this category. The *common criminal* is the more typical offender. These individuals reject the laws and norms of society and intentionally violate laws with little regard for the rights of others (Vold and Bernard, 1986). Together the crimes of altruistic and common criminals produce the social ills of society. Durkheim argues that due to structural and societal differences crime is not only inevitable and necessary but also functional. People who feel a sense of helplessness or normlessness adopt unconventional means by which to obtain their needs.

Although a compelling interpretation of social structure and the appearance of crime in society, Durkheim's theory lacked empirical references and his concept of anomie was never clearly operationalized. For example, when does mechanical solidarity become organic solidarity? Why and how do some criminals choose to commit altruistic crimes while others choose common crimes? Why doesn't everyone commit crime? How do criminals come to choose the type of crime they commit? Where do the criminals acquire their unconventional means? Why do some disenfranchised people choose suicide over crime? Wright and Fox (1978:137) summarize their description of Durkheim's theory as being simply "quite general."

In spite of its conceptual limitations and generality, Durkheim's thesis found wide support at a time when sociology was the dominant perspective for studying human behaviour in Europe. However, because his work was written in French it almost went unnoticed in North America. It was not until sixty years later that the American sociologist, Robert King Merton, became aware of Durkheim's work and modified and applied theory to other forms of deviance.

Robert Merton (1910–) and Anomie/Strain

It was in his seminal article published in 1938 ("Social Structure and Anomie"), which Barkan (1997) suggests is perhaps the most cited work in criminological literature, that Merton began to define his explanation of crime. In the opening paragraph to his article Merton notes that the earlier "tendency in sociological theory to attribute the malfunctioning of social structure primarily to those of man's imperious biological drives" should be discounted (Merton, 1938 cited in Jacoby, 1994:130). Instead he argued that "certain phases of social structure generate the circumstances in which infringement of social codes constitutes a 'normal' response" (Ibid, 130).

While Durkheim saw anomie arising out of some upheaval in society, Merton believed that societies did not necessarily have to be undergoing rapid social change in order for crimes to occur. In order to support this orientation, Merton's version of anomie is premised on four major assumptions about modern societies that appear in another of his classic works *Social Theory and Social Structure* (1968). The assumptions include:

- All modern societies have a core of common values.
- The majority of the members of modern societies have internalized values (that is, have accepted them).
- The significant values are those which channel energy towards the achievement of certain success goals; and

- All members of society do not have equal opportunity to socially-approved means of reaching socially-approved goals.

Based on these assumptions, Merton developed a typology involving five modes of "structural" as opposed to individualistic, adaptations to anomie to explain crime. Williams and McShane (1994) observe that Merton's theoretical assumptions have also been related to the popular strain theory. Merton argued that crime occurs when individuals are unable to achieve their goals through legitimate means. When this occurs the individual becomes frustrated (i.e., strained) and may either attempt to resolve his or her frustration through legitimate means or turn to unconventional methods of attaining his or her goals.[5] For example, in Canada, at a very early age we are encouraged to not only do well in school, but to strive to be the very best we can. For example, have you ever heard the phrases: "winning's not everything, it's the only thing," or "no pain, no gain," or "push it to the limit"? Such phrases reflect the perception that we need to succeed and be task-driven. Coming home with a collection of 'C' grades was usually cause for a heart-to-heart discussion while coming home with a few 'A's was usually met with "good work and keep it up because remember you'll need those grades to get into university." In sports, young people are not only encouraged to give it "one hundred and ten percent" but are regularly measured against their more successful peers and sometimes compared to adult idols in their particular sport. The pressure to succeed can be found in all areas of our lives. Agnew and White (1992) observed that the general strain of being treated poorly and feeling unhappy and frustrated was associated with delinquency and drug use.

As impressionable young people wanting to please and fit in, most of us strive to internalize and achieve socially-prescribed goals. In addition to working towards these goals we are also taught socially-prescribed (legal) means by which to attain them, which usually involve hard work, honesty, and patience. However, not everyone can become a Rhodes scholar, an outstanding athlete, or valedictorian. According to Merton, we adopt different modes of aspiring to the goals—some legitimately and others illegitimately.

The modes of adaptation involve:

1. **Conformist**: Without conformity there would be no social order. Most people, in spite of their social and personal circumstances, are conformists. They remain law-abiding and do their best to finish school, get a job, and raise a family. These people subscribe to the cultural goals of society and have internalized the means by which to achieve them.

2. **Innovator**: This type of person accepts the goals of society (e.g., getting an education) but rejects the socially-accepted means by which to achieve good grades (e.g., cheating). However innovators do not necessarily select deviant or unlawful means in their efforts to attain socially-approved goals. It is quite pos-

sible to be innovative without violating any significant norms. A student, for example, might participate in a field study tour rather than attend regular class as a means of learning.

According to Merton this adaptation strategy is more prevalent among the lower class where there are more obstacles to attaining legitimate goals. Crime can then be further exacerbated when the criminals (drug dealers, pimps, and gangs) flaunt their wealth and their fancy clothes in a way that says "crime pays" (Cohen and Machalek, 1988).

3. **Ritualist**: Individuals who adapt a ritualistic approach to the goals of society might be described as phony. They accept the means to goals but reject the goals themselves. An example could be the student who attends school because the law requires it, does well enough to pass, and then drops out.

Ritualists may not be goal-motivated but they are usually normative persons. They go along with the program but make no real effort to aspire beyond their immediate situation. They might be described as the "Archie Bunkers" of society (Vito and Holmes, 1994). And since they are not deviant per se, Merton spent little time discussing ritualistic behaviour (Barkan, 1997).

4. **Retreatist**: These individuals reject both the goals and means of society. A youth who does not want to go to school or does not want to work for his or her keep could be described as a retreatist.

This model of adaptation is likely to occur when the socially-approved means (working to afford a downpayment on a house) are perceived as being unlikely to result in success, perhaps even unattainable. Retreatism becomes an escape mechanism for some people in this predicament. They pour what little savings they are able to accumulate into alcohol and/or drug abuse—giving up the means and the goal. They may even contemplate suicide.

Not all forms of retreatism are necessarily harmful or wrong. For instance, the growing number of street people in Canada may be a burden to the social system but they are often harmless and the products of a system that could not meet their needs.

On the other hand, those who abuse drugs and alcohol and then proceed to drive their cars are responsible for a large number of automobile deaths every year in Canada. Such individuals are not only retreatists, but also criminals.

While some forms of retreatism are of some concern to society, it is only those instances which are defined by law as being wrong that are of concern to the criminal justice system.

5. **Rebel**: As the term implies, rebels not only reject legitimate goals and means but also attempt to bring about a new society whose goals are more egalitarian. They are the radicals and revolutionaries. The youth movements of the 1960s and 1970s represent rebellion. For example, hippies wanted a quieter, more peaceful world and rebelled by wearing wild clothing, doing drugs and

practising communal living, among other socially deviant behaviours. The Vietnam War draft dodgers not only refused to participate in the war; many of them fled to Canada to evade prosecution. More contemporary forms of rebellion include terrorist acts in which extremist groups (e.g., the "Unabomber" in 1996, and Timothy McVeigh and Terry Nichols who bombed the government building in Oklahoma, in 1995) use violence and propaganda to convey their objections to society.

Assessment of Merton's Theory

In accordance with Merton's theoretical principles, the lower classes should be disproportionately represented among the criminal population, because they have less opportunity to reach their goals legitimately. Based on a review of more than 100 studies, Braithwaite (1981) found general support for the assertion that lower-class people do commit more crimes than other social classes. However, the results were not 100 per cent. Why is it that not all lower-class people commit crimes? There are obviously some other factors that need to be accounted for.

According to a number of researchers, the relationship is more complex. Thornberry and Farnsworth (1982) suggest the model also needs to take into account other social factors such as race, seriousness of the offence, and education of the family, among other factors. However, when one begins to incorporate a wide variety of other factors, the model becomes too complex and overwhelming to be of much practical use. The ensuing result has been the emergence of reformulations of Merton's theory.

One of the more prominent revisions of Merton's theory has been by sociologist Robert Agnew. His general strain theory implies that strain is caused by a failure to achieve certain material goals. Agnew (1992) identifies three general forms of strain. They include strain caused by failure to achieve positively valued goals, strain caused by the removal of positively valued stimuli from the individual, and strain caused by the presentation of negative stimuli.

Although it is a sociological theory, Agnew acknowledges that individuals have differing abilities to cope with stress ranging from past experience, peer influence, temperament, pressing financial resources, etc.

While the theory is able to address some of Merton's limitations, Agnew fails to clearly show how or why valued goals differ between individuals or which of the other mediating elements are most important for helping individuals to cope.

In **summary**, the theoretical viewpoints discussed in this section (Durkheim's and Merton's) have had a major impact on sociological criminology. In general, the anomie theory, described as being a *positivist theory* (Williams and McShane, 1999), has been widely used to explain crime and deviance as a condition arising out of some partial anomie/strain in society.

The theory is primarily utilitarian in nature. For, as Merton noted, crime represents a response to the inability to attain culturally-prescribed goals through socially-accepted means. In other words, anomie is a form of strain—a function of personal motivation, frustration, and rational choice. Stated differently, anomie and strain theorists view crime as a normal response to abnormal contradictions around which society has organized itself. Although perhaps having some intuitive appeal, the theory does not clearly define the relationship between strain and deviance (Bernard, 1987). Being a *structural* theory, it tries to explain the relationship between social conditions and deviance but fails to explain why and how people from identical social situations can differ in their reaction to states of anomie (Williams and McShane, 1994).

The theory has also been criticized for not addressing middle-class and white collar crime (Hirschi and Gottfredson, 1987). Merton's theory focuses almost exclusively on the poor and assumes that most crimes are committed by this segment of the population. Furthermore, the adaptation modes of the anomie theory do not effectively explain violent crimes of assault, homicide, and rape (Barkan, 1997). Finally, MacLean and Milovanovic (1991) note the theory is not able to recognize the social process by which criminal statistics are constructed and used to explain why the working class is over-represented in criminal statistics.

Merton never intended to explain the process by which individuals become deviant. Instead, he was interested in explaining "variations in rates of deviance among societal groups" and "explain a social phenomenon in terms of its effects on ... the social structure in which it exists" (Williams and McShane, 1994:94). The theory has provided the framework for different strain theories and several researchers have taken Merton's theory and have adapted it to explain recent crime trends in the United States (see Messner and Rosenfeld, 1994; and Derber, 1996).

With recent revisions and extensions of the theory, such as Robert Agnew's *General Strain Theory;* Albert Cohen's *Delinquency and Frustration Theory* (see below), and the popular *Differential Opportunity Theory* of Richard Cloward and Lloyd Ohlin, the anomie/strain perspective will likely continue to draw a strong following (see Box 7.5). However, future research will need to:

- Discern to what extent social factors either precipitate and/or predispose some people to committing crimes;
- More clearly operationalize the level of strain that differentiates criminal from non-criminal behaviour;
- Focus on how strain works at the aggregate and individual levels; and
- Be able to explain the process by which neighbourhoods progress from a stable state to a "disorganized state" and then potentially return to a stable/organized state.

Strain Theory and Hate Crime

Hate crime (Chapter 9) is a growing global concern. While the *Criminal Code* prohibits dissemination of hate literature within Canada, computerized material transmitted across phone lines is considered to be part of sovereign borders. Hence, the Internet has been used to fuel hate crime activity. Hamm (1994) used principles of the strain theory to explain the increased activity of neo-Nazi skinheads in the United States. Based on an assessment of 36 neo-Nazi skinhead gang members responsible for more than 120 acts of violence against racial minorities he found that they did not represent underclass youth who experience frustration when their means to attain social goals are being blocked. Rather, Hamm found that the members were mostly working-class conformists "with a hyperactive commitment to the dominant goals of American society." On the same panel, Randy Blazak examined a group of neo-Nazis using Cohen's strain theory. Like Hamm, Blazak argues that the skinheads represent a "problem-solving" group who are reacting to a loss of opportunity and adopt illegitimate means to reclaim their status.

Similarly, Canadian researcher Jeffery Ross (1995:166) suggests the major factors "fueling hate crime in Canada are hard economic times and consequential loss of jobs and inflation." These factors represent blocked opportunity and create strain and frustration. However, in another publication, Ross (1995) notes that all the different subtypes of violence by and against Canadians have their own causes.

Cohen's Subcultural Theory of Male Delinquency

Albert K. Cohen (1918–), a former student of Robert Merton and Edwin Sutherland (see below) developed a theory to explain male delinquent cultures in working-class neighbourhoods. In his classic book, *Delinquent Boys: The Culture of the Gang* in 1955, his ideas about gangs and their activities triggered a rash of interest in both his theory and his attention to delinquent gang behaviour. In the book, he introduces the notion that "status frustration" can be the result of an entire subculture's life experiences and life opportunities. For example, Cohen suggested that delinquency among lower-class males is the product of the "status frustration" that lower-class boys experience when confronted with the dominant middle-class values within the public school system.

As was the case with many theories from this era, the focus was on young offenders and used a sociological positivist perspective. Williams and McShane (1994) suggest that Cohen's subcultural theory combined elements of the Chicago School (see below), Merton's anomie theory, and Sutherland's differential association theory (see Figure 7–2).

Based on his observation of delinquent males in the United States, Cohen found:

- Like Merton, Cohen believed that as members of a society we all share similar goals. Most of these goals are dictated by the middle-class members to the lower social classes.
- Among males of the lower social echelons gang delinquency was common.
- Gang behaviour becomes an accepted way of attaining status within the subculture because conventional avenues of attaining social status are less readily available to them than for the middle class.
- "Over time the 'delinquent solution' is passed on through the transmission of values from youth to youth and generation to generation" (Williams and McShane, 1994:111).

FIGURE 7-2

COHEN'S MODEL OF SUBCULTURAL THEORY[6]

```
          Middle Class
          Institutions
               ↓
Lower  → Middle → Status →    Reaction → Association → Delinquent → Support,
Social   Class    frustration formation with others   subculture    status
class    Measuring                     frustrated
         Rod[7]
               ↑
       Working Class
       Socialization
```

In **summary**, the subcultural approach emphasizes the importance of the social values of informal lower social class groups especially among delinquent boys. Although a very popular theoretical orientation in the 1950s and 1960s, subcultural explanations were all-inclusive and were not able to explain all delinquency, particularly female criminality. Nevertheless, the general concept of a campaign for the underprivileged spawned a number of multi-million dollar projects during this era. The "War on Poverty" saw the birth of the Peace Corps, the Job Corps, and Project Head Start, among others, all designed to provide the lower classes with employment opportunities and easier access to some middle-class values and status.

The programs met with varying degrees of success. But perhaps the biggest blow to the subcultural orientation was the emergence of self-report studies (see Chapter 3). These studies revealed that delinquency and subcultural activities are not the exclusive domain of the lower classes, nor is gang behaviour the exclusive domain of males.

Today subcultural theories have found a new ally in sociological theories that have attempted to integrate elements of subcultural theory with other informal groups to spawn such theories as Cloward and Ohlin's *Differential Opportunity Theory* (Williams and McShane, 1994). For example, instead of only focusing on social class subcultures, sociologists have expanded their definition of subculture. Today, subculture groups might include such groups as anarchists (groups who want to challenge the status quo), hackers (individuals who use their powerful knowledge of computers to commit deviant and/or criminal acts—see chapter 12), drug cultures, extreme religious groups, and organized crime groups (See Chapter 11).

Ecological School[8]

In the introduction to this chapter, reference was made to the pioneering work of Robert Parks and Ernest Burgess in the 1920s. Drawing on the relationship between animals in natural settings they reasoned that humans must also display behavioural patterns in their natural setting—urban environments. Using Chicago as their study area, Parks and Burgess developed the *concentric-circle theory* (see p. 216) which is based on the relationship between particular environmental characteristics and human relationships. Crime is but one aspect of urban ecology. The ecological school asserts that crime can be understood through the study of the physical and social structure of an environment. The theory focuses on the *socio-spatial* environment in which people live (Brantingham and Brantingham, 1984).

Although Parks and Burgess's work received considerable attention, it was the work of two fellow scholars from the University of Chicago, Clifford Shaw and Henry McKay, that is perhaps more widely known. However, others have also used ecological principles to explain crime. The earliest of these involved the studies of André Michel Guerry and Adolphe Quételet, in the 1830s, who examined the physical and seasonal spatial patterning of crime. Their work is referred to as the *cartography school*. This work eventually led to the school of *social and human ecology* which focused on the interrelationship between people and their environment and how different social conditions might result in social disorganization. Significant works range from Park and Burgess's work in the 1920s to the recent efforts of Rossmo (see Box 7.6).

Shaw and McKay's Work

Focusing most of their research on young offenders, Clifford R. Shaw and Henry D. McKay (1969) applied the principles of the concentric-circle theory to rates of delinquency, tuberculosis, and infant mortality. They found that the rates follow the same "decreasing pattern as one moves away from the central business district" (Williams and McShane, 1994:54). Based on ecological data they developed their theory of social disorganization which was buttressed "on a conception of primary relationships similar to those found in a village" (Ibid, 54). In essence, the more stable or homogeneous the family and neighborhood the greater the likelihood of a stable community. As primary relationships break down so does social control. Subsequently crime increases. Williams and McShane cite research by Robert Sampson and Byron Groves who list four elements that constitute social disorganization:

- "Low economic status;
- A mixture of different ethnic groups;
- Highly mobile residents moving in and out of the area; and
- Disrupted families and broken homes" (Ibid, 54–55).

Fernandez and Neiman (1997) presented data to suggest that the perception of increased crime risk (fear of crime) is related to general variations in assessments of the quality of life and satisfaction with social and public institutions. They further argued that overall satisfaction with life varies along with "a geographic gradient to quality of life." In other words, fear of crime was found to be related to how people perceive their physical conditions. For example, it does not appear in those living in the slums of Calcutta or other homogeneous ecological settings.

What is not clear is the cultural relativity of such perceptions. Shaw and McKay report that the zones of transition are more socially disorganized than other areas due to the "high degree of mobility, the decaying neighborhoods, and the encroachment of the business and factory districts" (Ibid, 55). These zones pose serious problems for crime because of the number of immigrants often found here.

This ecological explanation also represented an alternative explanation; instead of seeing crime as a product of heredity, viewing it as one of social disorganization and of conflict with existing American culture. Another variation of the ecological perspective that emerged out of the Chicago School to explain crime was Shaw and McKay's cultural transmission theory or cultural deviance theory. It tries to explain the *process* by which social disorganization youth's conformity to cultural values and norms and leads to delinquency. As the institutional control mechanisms break down within an area or neighbourhood, some youths choose delinquency. Over time, they develop norms and values that reinforce delinquency and criminal behaviour and eventually create a subculture of delinquency. It is when delinquency is transmitted to future members of the neighbourhood, from one generation to the next, that it becomes known as a process of cultural transmission.

Shaw and McKay (1969) found, however, that not all ethnic groups were equally vulnerable to social disorganization. They report that the strong cultural traditions of some ethnic groups, such as the Chinese and European Jews, showed an "ability to resist disorganization and adapt to their environmental conditions" (Einstadter and Henry, 1995:134). These findings can be accounted for under the control theory.

In the years since, researchers have modified the ideas of Shaw and McKay to more accurately account for discrepancies in their explanatory model. Georges Abeyie (1981) posited that in order to more fully understand the social/ecological elements of crime, research needs to include the site of the crime, the offender's residence, and where the offender was arrested (see pp. 100–101). Others, such as the Canadian team of Paul and Patricia Brantingham (1984:18) have observed that even more recently there has been a "shift from the sociological to the geographical imagination" (see Box 7.6). The geographic imagination refers to understanding how an individual perceives his/her physical environment. In the early 1970s, American architect Oscar Newman was among the first to note how our physical environment can influence our sense of territoriality and personal space. More recently, Newman (1996) has updated his acclaimed textbook *Defensible Space* (1972). In his more recent work, Newman presents the latest information on how to physically build or refurbish urban communities to reduce crime. The intent is to promote a sense of community through the physical design and layout of homes, office buildings, and the other structures that make up our community. Newman (1996) felt that the update was much needed as the original concepts were often misused and misunderstood.

A CLOSER LOOK BOX 7.6

"Zeroing in on Crime Spots"...Part III[9]

Former Simon Fraser University criminology graduate student and Vancouver City police officer, Kim Rossmo, has applied the principles of geographic mapping to the study of violent serial and sexual crimes. This approach is the latest variation of the ecological perspective.

Building on the work of the Brantinghams, Rossmo invented a sophisticated computer software system called Rigel. The program relies on the latest technology in digital mapping and powerful visual three-dimensional presentation (referred to as "jeopardies") to study violent serial crimes. With his ongoing geographic profiling research, along with investigative police work, the procedure has been used to indicate whether: "A series of crimes may have been committed by the same offender and victims are being hunted in a particular manner" ("Orion," 1996:2).

A unique attribute of the procedure is its ability to analyze data on an ongoing basis. As new information is obtained, the program recalibrates to construct a new geoprofile, thereby eliminating information not considered essential to the modelling procedure. Recognizing that it is not possible to determine which crimes are linked, the software system is capable of constructing different scenarios. Then, as the profile database evolves, the number of scenarios can be narrowed to pinpoint likely crime/ victim sites.

Rossmo's research has already been used by a number of Canadian police departments across the country to help them solve violent serial crimes. In fact, his research and expertise is being made available to international police organizations (Thompson, 1996). His work shows the importance of combining academic research with concrete criminal justice issues. In addition, as with the developments of DNA evidence in helping to solve crimes, geographic profiling represents a new and vital strategy for combatting crime.

Modern Applications of Ecological Principles

Perhaps one of the more powerful theories to emerge from the ecological school of thought has been the routine activities theory. In recent years, it has been extensively used to explain social/ecological elements to criminal activity (see Chapter 8). For example, Hakim and Buck (1989) found that after casinos were legalized in Atlantic City the greatest crime increase was in violent crime and auto theft and the lowest was for burglary. They also observed that there was a pattern and spatial crime "spill-over" effect moving away from the city. That is, as people move away from the city to outlying communities their crime rates also go up—a spill-over effect. These findings are consistent with what Reppetto (1974) had observed several years earlier. Reppetto wrote that when a criminal's awareness of space expanded or efforts were made to deter the criminal a shift in location referred to as *crime displacement* took place. This could take the form of a temporal displacement (a different time) and/or a physical displacement (i.e., they move to another area). However, not all types of crime respond to intervention strategies in the same manner. For instance, Rengert (1989), while studying recidivist burglaries in Philadelphia, found that recidivist break-and-enter offenders are more likely to stay within their neighbourhood than to travel long distances to commit crimes in unfamiliar areas. Break and enter offences are seen as crimes that require the offender to be familiar with the target in terms of surveillance absence of a capable guardian, type of material to be gained, suitability of a target and the motivation to commit the offence. Without knowledge of the target the potential offender is less inclined to risk committing the break-and-enter.

The ecological school and its various theoretical derivatives have played a major role in crime prevention strategies. Oscar Newman (1972, 1996), Paul and Patricia Brantingham (1984, 1991), John Baldwin and Anthony Bottoms (1976), Henry Cisneros (1995), and Ralph Taylor and Adele Harrell (1996) among others, have all produced practical works in which they have employed CPTED principles in deterring crime and building community.

In their review of the Chicago Ecological School, Williams and McShane (1994) point out how social disorganization and cultural transmission theory are similar to social control, differential association theory, situational choice theory, routine activity theory, and human ecology theory, among others (see Einstadter and Henry, 1995:121 for a complete list). Hence, it can be argued that the ecological school, and in particular the work of Shaw and McKay, played a significant role in the sociological criminological theories that came after them. For example, the Brantinghams (see Chapter 4) have taken the ecological concepts to new levels in their work on *environmental criminology* (1991). Today, their research and theory, along with the research of Rossmo (see Box 7.5), has drawn international respect and attention.

In **summary**, the ecological approach assumes that particular characteristics of the physical and social environment can precipitate crime. i.e., human behaviour is a product of the social environment and the environment defines the boundaries of our cultural values and behaviour. Furthermore, the general ecological framework has been influenced by human geography (e.g., CPTED), biology (i.e., applied the principles of plant and animal ecology), and by viewing the environment as a product mediated by cultural values and norms.

Throughout this section, we have seen that the ecological school has evolved to provide more powerful explanatory models for crime. However, as with any theory, the Chicago School has its critics. For example, what does *social disorganization* mean and how does one measure it? As used in their work, the concept of social disorganization carries a pejorative connotation and implies inadequacy and inferiority. However, not all forms of social disorganization are necessarily dysfunctional. Durkheim had recognized earlier that crimes could be functional if they draw attention to sanctions that may no longer be considered socially wrong. For instance practising homosexuality or drinking alcohol are no longer considered criminal offences. This came about in part because of changing social values and beliefs.

While the Chicago School stresses spatial relations and social ecology and makes use of official statistics to test its theoretical assumptions, the theory does not "consider the impact of law enforcement practices on spatial distribution" which can artificially skew the spatial relations of crime patterns (MacLean and Milovanovic, 1991:3). For example, by focusing on certain segments of the population (e.g., the poor, Aboriginal groups, and minority groups) crime statistics can create a picture of who is *really* committing the crimes. Such lines of reasoning form the basis of the conflict and radical perspectives on the causes of crime. On the other hand the ecological school, and in particular Shaw and McKay's studies, have had a major influence in the development of sociological criminology because their work addressed crime from both a sociological and social psychology perspective. They recognized the interaction between the influence of the community and the stability of socialization mechanisms on who and what we become.

One theoretical perspective that can trace its origins to the ecological school is the theory of differential association.

Differential Association

Sociological theorists such as the French sociologist Gabriel Tarde and the American sociologists Edwin Sutherland, and Howard Becker, among others, view the "relationship between the individual and society as integral to the formation of not only the deviant but also the adjusted personality" (Vito and Holmes, 1994:177). Although each theorist developed his own theory, they each examined crime as a social process involving the interplay between the individual (e.g., peer influence, family relationship, and self-image) and society (e.g., socialization process). In other words, the orientation can be described as a social-psychological process that is derived from operant conditioning in psychology (Chapter 6) (Einstadter and Henry, 1995). The social situations that people encounter play a major role in determining their behaviour.

Several other social process related theories have also adopted a similar orientation. Among the more notable is Gabriel Tarde's work in the 1890s on the *law of imitation*, Graham Sykes and David Matza's *neutralization theory* in the 1950s, and Albert Reiss's pioneering work on the *social control theory* in the early 1950s (see Einstadter and Henry, 1995 for a comprehensive review).

Although we will only focus on the theory of differential association, most of the social process theories are premised on the assertion that people commit crimes as a result of learning and socialization experiences with significant others. In Chapter 6 we observed that operant conditioning (e.g., Skinner) assumes all behaviour is simply the result of the response of an individual to the avoidance of a negative stimulus. From a sociological and criminological perspective, this idea is reflected in Jeffery's (1965) theory of *differential reinforcement* (DR). Einstadter and Henry (1995:176) observe that Jeffery's theory "recognized the differences in people's reinforcement history and the different meaning stimuli have to them." Jeffery's theory borrowed heavily from Skinner's theory of operant conditioning. Crime is a learned behaviour based on the variability and intensity of the exposure to experience. However, in spite of its logical soundness, Jeffery's theory has not received much attention.

Following on the heels of Jeffery's work are other socially-oriented approaches such as Ronald Akers and Robert Burgess's (1966) *differential association-reinforcement* (DAR) theory (see Box 7.7). They combined Albert Bandura's psychologically-based behaviour modelling (i.e., observation learning—see Chapter 6) with Sutherland's sociologically-based *differential association* theory.

What neither theory is able to account for is:

- How personality and/or bio-chemical makeup might predispose some to learn criminal behaviour and not others.

- Why some people who learn behaviour patterns never engage in criminal acts. For instance, I know how to break into a house but I have never done it.

- How the techniques and crimes originate.
- How the definition of the crime came into existence.
- Why children are more apt to model behaviour than adults.

Despite these and other criticisms, social process theories continue to attract a strong following. Supporters are likely to continue to revise the theory in an effort to counter its critics.

Differential Association-Reinforcement Theory

Akers and Burgess tried to provide a more comprehensive and scientific revision of Sutherland's learning process. They integrated some of B.F. Skinner's and Albert Bandura's behavioural principles into Sutherland's theory. Akers and Burgess assumed this would make the revised theory more testable while at the same time clarifying the learning processes involved. According to Akers (1977) people learn social skills by operant conditioning that is controlled by stimuli that follow the behaviour. As described in Chapter 6, behaviour is reinforced when positive rewards are associated with an act and weakened when a negative reinforcement accompanies a behaviour.

Akers argues that people learn to evaluate their own behaviour according to their inter-actions with significant others. The evaluative process involves making use of such social concepts as attitudes, norms, and orientations (Siegel, 1995). The interpreta-tion of such concepts is important in reinforcing and serves as cues for behaviour. Once a criminal is initiated, he or she can be reinforced by exposure to deviant models. The likelihood that a criminal act will be initiated depends on the frequency, intensity, and duration of the exposure.

Siegel (1995:213) observes that the theory "is an important view of the cause of criminal activity" and it "considers both the *effectiveness* and *content* of socializa-tioncondition crime." However, as with the DA theory, Akers and Burgess's theory has not escaped criticism. Reed Adams (1973), for example, argues that the theory has misused the principles of operant conditioning and thereby misled criminologists and sociologists in understanding criminal and delinquent behaviour. Vito and Holmes (1994:184) further note that while the theory has been generally well received it has not been able to define the "role of patriarchy in crime and delinquency."

Sutherland's Theory of Differential Association

Edwin H. Sutherland (see Box 7.8) first outlined his theory of differential asso-ciation in his 1939 *Principles of Criminology*. Conceptually it is a refinement of Tarde's nineteenth-century concept of imitation. However, although Sutherland made only three references to Tarde, none of the references were to Tarde's laws of imitation (Martin et al., 1990). And, unlike Shaw and McKay's (1969) notion that crime is a product of social disorganization, or that the lower socioeconomic positions are by nature dysfunctional, Sutherland explained crime as a function of a learning process that could affect any individual in any culture.

PROFILE BOX 7.8

EDWIN HARDIN SUTHERLAND: 1883–1950

Martin et al. (1990:139) begin their biographical sketch of Sutherland by noting that his reputation spanned the full spectrum from ardent critic to messiah "but most would certainly agree that he was the leading criminologist of his generation" in North America. In fact, some have described him as the "Dean of American criminology" (Reid, 1982:153).

Sutherland was born on August 13, 1883 in Gibbon, Nebraska. He was one of nine children and from an early age was exposed to an academic and religious setting. Because of his father's influence four of the five boys became involved in higher education. He displayed great attention to discipline, a strong sense of ethics, and a strong personality.

After receiving his BA degree, Sutherland taught for a short while at a Baptist College (from 1904–1906). While at the College he enrolled in a home study course in sociology through the University of Chicago. The following year he moved to Chicago where he took three courses in the Divinity School. One of the courses was his first criminology course called "Social Treatment of Crime." The course appeared to have a major impact on him and he began to take more sociology courses. He stayed at Chicago until 1909 and although he had not yet completed his degree, Sutherland returned for two years to teach sociology and psychology back at Grand Island College. In 1911 when he returned to Chicago to complete his degree he quickly became disenchanted with sociology (or at least the department) which he felt "led to nothing more than empty moralizing" (Ibid, 141). He switched to political economy and in 1913 was granted his Ph.D. with a double major in sociology and political economy. It was not until 1919, while teaching in the sociology department at the University of Illinois and through the encouragement of the Chair, Edward Carey Hayes, that he wrote his now classic introductory criminology textbook entitled *Criminology* and published for the first time in 1924. Sutherland completed three revisions in 1934, 1939, and 1947. After his death, Donald Cressey, one of his last doctoral students, published six more editions before his own death in 1987. Among Sutherland's other noteworthy publications were his books, *Twenty Thousand Homeless Men* (1936), *The Professional Thief* (1937), and *White Collar Crime* (1949). The latter book has been described as "a pioneer work and one that has remained controversial and provocative" (Ibid, 160). Regardless of how one views his work, there is little doubt about the enduring influence Sutherland has had on criminology. He died of a stroke on October 11, 1950.

In his works, Sutherland expressed the belief that people learn how to commit crimes primarily through social interactions. The more intimate the contact the more likely behaviours will be imitated. Through interactions with others, people learn not only the technique of committing crime, but also the attitudes, motives and rationalizations that support crime. Sutherland further believed that while criminal behaviour is a politically defined construct, learning criminal behaviour is a social, not a political or legal process (Martin et al., 1990).

The Nine Fundamental Principles of Differential Association

1. "Criminal behaviour is learned." Unlike previous theoretical assertions, Sutherland's theory asserts that criminal behaviour is largely a process of cultural transmission and not an inherited characteristic. Just as people learn law-abiding behaviour (e.g., driving a car and writing), criminals learn to break the law.

2. "Criminal behaviour is learned in interaction with other persons in a process of communication." However, just because we may be living in a criminogenic environment does not mean we will become criminals. If we are exposed to a family of criminals we have a better chance of becoming criminal or delinquent, but unless we actively participate in the process we will not develop criminal tendencies. Criminality cannot occur without direct interactions with others.

3. "The principal part of the learning of criminal behaviour occurs within intimate personal groups." While mere exposure to crime-related TV shows or movies may play a minor role, the primary learning process occurs from face-to-face interaction and contact with others. Vicarious exposure may provide the "script" but intimate personal relationships provide the motivation (Vito and Holmes, 1994).

4. "Learning criminal behaviour includes: (1) learning the techniques of committing the crime, which are sometimes very complicated, and (2) learning the specific direction of motives, drives, rationalizations, and attitudes." Through the strength of the association with other criminal types, the individual will learn how to commit crime. For example, prisons are sometimes referred to as breeding grounds for better criminals. People not only learn from those with whom they associate but learn also how to rationalize their deviant behaviour.

5. "The specific direction of motives and drives is learned from definitions of the legal codes as favorable or unfavorable." Within most complex societies, there are mixtures of subcultures, each with their own values and norms. A person will receive different messages as to how to respond to the prevailing laws of society depending on which one he or she belongs to.

6. "A person becomes delinquent because of an excess of definitions favorable to violations of law over definitions favorable of the law." Every day we make value-neutral decisions that have nothing to do with crime. For example, we make deci-

sions ranging from what to wear to what to eat. However, when a group of youths talk about engaging in some deviant act their attitudes begin to shift about the legitimacy of the act. These views then become part of their collective consciousness. In operant conditioning terms, the delinquent attitudes get reinforced.

7. "Differential association may vary in frequency, duration, priority, and intensity." The extent to which criminal behaviour is learned is dependent on the frequency with which the message is reinforced as well as how long the individual is exposed to the criminal messages. Youths growing up in a household where criminal activity takes place are more likely to learn (i.e., imitate) the behaviour. The behaviour is further reinforced when it is condoned and presented as an accepted method of conduct. For example, it is well-documented that many spousal abusers witnessed their fathers abusing their mothers regularly, over extended periods of time. It was accepted that the father responded violently when he didn't get his way. The fact that the mother did not leave the situation to file a complaint intensifies the act's acceptability.

8. "The process of learning criminal behaviour by association with criminal and anticriminal patterns involves all the mechanisms that are involved in any other learning." Vito and Holmes (1994:182) observe that the processes for learning criminal behaviour are no different from those processes involved in learning non-criminal behaviour and that it "is more than simple imitation by associating with others."

9. "While criminal behaviour is an expression of general needs and values, it is not explained by those general needs and values, since non-criminal behaviour is an expression of the same needs and values." Sutherland felt that material goods, money, and status do not explain criminality. Instead, since the motives for criminal behaviour are not the same as those for conventional behaviour, they can only be explained by understanding the nature and extent of association with criminality and deviant norms.

In **summary**, Differential Association theory is an attempt to bridge psychological and sociological principles under one criminological theory. According to the theory's principles, criminal behaviour represents an interaction between operant conditioning principles (i.e., association) and social and group relations, and environmental factors.

While Sutherland's textbook is considered a classic in its field, his theory of DA has met with varying degrees of support. One of the earliest challenges of Sutherland's theory came from James F. Short (1957 cited in Reid, 1982). While describing the theory, Short notes differential association is "the most truly sociological of all theories which have been advanced to explain criminal and delinquent behaviour" (Ibid: 154). However, he also pointed out that the theory is not testable in general terms. More recently, Lauritsen (1993) found that gang membership among public school youth is associated with the extent of peer delinquency and the amount of drug use. Meanwhile, Warr (1993) demonstrated that recent friendships are more influential in forging behaviour than earlier friend-ships. Can you relate to the latter finding? On the other hand, how long does it take someone else's influence to wear off?

Nevertheless, the theory seems to have appeal. It continues to prompt researchers to seek better methods by which to operationalize and measures the principles entailed in the differential association theory. For example, why do police officers and correctional officers, who regularly interact with the criminal element, not learn to become legal transgressors themselves? Have you ever had a close friend who got into trouble? Did you copy his/her behaviour or did they copy yours? Why?

As we saw throughout this section, differential association is fraught with a number of fundamental conceptual limitations:

- It lacks a clear definition of its concepts.
- The theory is limited in the types of crimes it is capable of explaining (e.g., it does not explain crimes of passion).
- People learn differently.

Furthermore, as Jeffery (1990:263) observes, "it never attempts to integrate biological and psychological theories of learning into criminology." Nevertheless, numerous studies have applied Sutherland's DA theory to explain delinquency and criminal behaviour with varying degrees of success (see, Tunnell, 1993). Perhaps the most dramatic illustration of its enduring influence has been the application of the theory's principles to intervention programs. For example, the innovative program Head Start takes disadvantaged children and/or troubled youth and teaches them to deal with their environment. Former President Lyndon Johnson approved the program in the 1960s, and in 1993, President Bill Clinton acknowledged the program's success (Kantrowitz and Wingert, 1993). More recently, North America has been witness to the rapid expansion of con-flict resolution-based programs (e.g., see restorative justice—Chapter 14). These programs are designed to teach youths and adults to resolve their frustration in a nonviolent manner. Exercises can include role-playing situations.

The LaMarsh Centre for Research on Violence and Conflict Resolution at York University in Toronto engages in research projects aimed at understanding anti-social and deviant behaviour and in developing constructive response tech-niques to resolve such conflicts (see Weblinks at the end of the chapter). In recent years, several of their studies have focused on identifying vengeful atti-tudes, hockey violence, and abuse.

Labelling Theory

Although the three previous theories are able to explain serious crime in gener-al terms, none of them is able to answer two fundamental questions: How and why do some behaviours come to be defined as normative while others are defined as deviant?

What are the individual/psychological and social consequences of being called a criminal or delinquent, on being apprehended, and/or convicted? Labelling theory addresses itself primarily to these two questions. Labelling theory integrates social process and structural explanations.[10]

It was noted at the outset of this chapter that no act is inherently criminal. Rather, the law defines which acts are criminal. Therefore, unlike traditional sociological theories, identified above, which embrace an "absolutist" definition of crime (crime is learned or inherited), the labelling theory adapts a "relativist" definition. That is, deviance is not a property of a behaviour but rather the result of how others regard that behaviour (Barkan, 1997).

Origins of Labelling Theory

Williams and McShane (1994:130) point out that the general orientation of labelling theory became known as the "societal reaction school." In fact, the labelling theory emerged in the 1950s when a number of social scientists observed that the ideals North Americans fought to preserve abroad (liberty and equality for all) had not changed much on the home front. Blacks and Aboriginal peoples were still treated as second-class citizens and unemployment and social stigmatization were still evident. Labelling theorists began to ask some probing questions of society. They focused on such major issues as:

- How and why do certain behaviours become defined as deviant or criminal?
- Why do society and the criminal justice system seem to discriminate and apply official labelling and sanctions? and
- What are the effects of labelling on continued criminality?

Contrary to some of the prevailing sociological theories, labelling theory did not view criminals as inherently evil as individuals who had a criminal label conferred upon them because of some legal and/or social process (see Box 7.9). Hence, it is not the offender who interests the labelling theorist but society's reaction to the offender.

Although considered a spin-off of earlier theories (Williams and McShane, 1994), the labelling theory became popular in the 1960s. The era was marked by social unrest (e.g., Southern civil rights movements), the Vietnam antiwar movement, the beginning of the contemporary women's movement, the "Quiet Revolution" in Quebec and the FLQ, such socially significant events as the introduction of our new red and white maple leaf flag on February 15, 1965 and the emergence of the New Democratic Party. This conflict-based perspective[11] became very popular among sociologists and criminologists in large part due to the work of **Howard S. Becker** (1928–) who, like so many other prominent sociologists of his time, came from the Chicago School. In his classic book *The Outsider*, in 1963, Becker presented the theory's definition of deviance. However, an earlier compatriot, Frank Tannenbaum also from the Chicago School, in 1938 coined the phrase "dramatization of evil" to describe the process of how youths adjust to a delinquent group. Tannenbaum further argued that a "tag" becomes attached when one is caught in criminal or delinquent activity. Given how similar Tannenbaum's terms were to the labelling theory in the 1960s, many criminologists view his work as representing the roots of the labelling theory. Over the years, however, there have been a number of variations of the labelling perspective. They include the *interactionist*, *social contructionism*, and *labelling and social reaction* perspectives (see Einstadter and Henry, 1995).

Once an individual is "tagged" or labelled (e.g., liar, thief, junkie, stripper), Becker (1963) felt that it is often difficult to live down or live up to the tag. The degree to which a person can shed his or her stigmatization is dependent on the sanction that is levied against them. For example, receiving a warning from the police as opposed to being processed through the judicial and perhaps even the correctional system can have a dramatic impact on an offender. Labelling an individual has been used as a rationale for recommending that the young offender system employ alternative sanctions when dealing with youth in conflict with the law. Similarly, penalties should vary according to the characteristics of the offender, not the severity of the crime. It is well documented that Canada's Aboriginal people are over-represented in the criminal justice system and that they get more severe sentences than non-Aboriginal people for similar offences (see generally Bonta, LaPrairie, and Wallace-Capretta, 1997). Such examples enforce the notion that the law is selectively enforced since different groups are labelled as being more crime-prone than others.

Primary and Secondary Deviance

While labels can be viewed as discriminatory, they can also be used to describe people's emotional, physical, or criminal predispositions. In turn they can be used to facilitate treatment, intervention, or prevention programs (Vito and Holmes, 1994). On the other hand, labels can stigmatize an individual in a negative way. Until Canadian Rick Hansen rolled his wheelchair around in the mid 1980s, people confined to wheelchairs were thought to be incapable of achieving much. Similarly, in schools children labelled "intelligent" as opposed to "average" or "slow" often get treated differently by their peers and teachers (see Matsueda, 1992). Finally, an "ex-con" will usually have a more difficult time finding employment because of a past criminal record (Bracken and Leowen, 1992). Labelling theorists suggest that labels create a "self-fulfilling" prophecy. This raises another issue that has been identified by labelling theorists —secondary deviance.

Edwin Lemert modified Becker's labelling theory to include secondary deviance, to further explain how the legal system can amplify the offender's criminal behaviour through intervention. Primary deviants are those who engage in deviant acts but are not considered deviant or "bad people." Others do not label them as "bad" nor do they apply self-labels. For example, the carpenter who takes home a few nails after work, without being detected, is not recognized as deviant and may not recognize that he or she has committed theft. Later he or she might recognize the implications of that act and chastise him or herself but if it remains undetected it does not affect self-concept.

Given that the social consequences of primary deviance are minimal, Lemert was less concerned about primary than secondary deviance. He points out that self-labelling combined with the social stigmatization of being labelled can result in "deviance amplification." The transition from primary to secondary deviance is summarized in Box 7.9.

A CLOSER LOOK BOX 7.9

The Deviance Process

1. A person commits a deviant/criminal act. (If undetected, the act remains primary deviance).
2. Society reacts in a retributive or punitive way.
3. The individual responds by committing more infractions (secondary deviation) which in turn draws additional attention to the criminal. The deviant cycle begins to escalate (e.g., frequency and/or intensity), a self-fulfilling process.
4. The labelled individual develops more hostility and resentment towards criminal justice agents.
5. Society and the legal system respond by further labelling and stigmatizing the offender.
6. As the individual's options become increasingly restricted, the criminal justice system sees the offender as a problem and the offender sees him- or herself as deviant.
7. The probability for future acts of deviance increases—deviance amplification. Therefore, once labelled and stigmatized, the offender's identity and self-concept evolve around deviance.

GENERAL MODEL OF LABELLING PROCESS

Primary Deviance – – → informal reaction – – → continuance of deviance – – → escalation of response (e.g., stereotyping, rejection, alienation of tagged actor) – – → more delinquency (secondary deviance) – – → formal intervention – – → individual begins to see self as delinquent – – → self-fulfilling process

As Lemert noted, secondary deviance sets in after the community, or society, has become aware of a primary deviance—real or socially created. Once tagged, the stigma can bring about dramatic behavioural changes. When I was a youth, having long hair was often associated with being rebellious. Today, having your head shaved carries those associations. Today, youths wearing certain types of clothing are sometimes suspected of being gang members. The recent craze over the pop music group the *Spice Girls* has prompted many teenagers to dress and talk like the members of the band, not unlike the *Beatles* frenzy of the 1960s.

Applying the Labelling Theory

How likely would you be to date or marry someone if you knew they had done hard time? Would you like your children to associate with a junkie, stripper, or known gang member? For most of us, the answer would probably be "no." The stigma we associate with certain labels can colour our perceptions.

From a theoretical perspective, the labelling has found many supporters. However, labelling theory, like *phenomenological* approaches in general, has also had its critics:[12]

- Why do people become involved even though they know they may get labelled?
- Labelling theory seems to imply that people are passive, but are they?
- Why do some people return to a life of deviance and/or crime after they have been subjected to treatment/intervention?

The labelling theory stresses the importance of societal reactions whose focus lies on the criminal not the act. Therefore, what is important for criminologists who are interested in the labelling perspective, is the importance of the label. As Becker (1963) noted, rule-making is an enterprising act in which certain groups profit more than others—hence, its critical perspective. Those responsible for making or enforcing the rules are referred to as *moral entrepreneurs*. The rule-makers are interested in criminalizing certain behaviours while the rule enforcers are concerned with enforcing the law. Based on his analysis Becker feels that laws are not made unintentionally. Consequently, he urges criminologists to shift their focus from the offender to those who make and enforce the rules.

In **summary**, the labelling theory enjoyed considerable popularity throughout the 1960s and 1970s. However, various researchers have shown that the stigma of crime does not necessarily result in an escalation of crime (see Murray, 1990). In addition, Schur (1972) points out that the theory does not explain the onset of primary deviation while Manning (1973) drew attention to the fact that not all labels are bestowed with discrimination. In his classic Canadian textbook, *Explaining Crime*, Nettler (1984) suggests that labelling does not always affect everyone in the same way. The labelling theory, for example, tends to favour the underdog but it is not very adept at accounting for the ability of the tagged individual to defuse the deviant label. If this assertion is true then the theory cannot be used to explain the causes of crime and delinquency. Therefore, the uses of labels are questionable. Nettler notes that the police do not cause crime and mental hospitals do not cause mental illness. Finally, sociologist Charles Wellford (1975:337) presents a convincing argument when he points out that it is naive to think "no act is inherently evil or criminal." For example, crimes such as rape and murder are almost universally sanctioned and are therefore intrinsically criminal.

Together these criticisms led to a decline in the labelling theory. However, as with Hirschi's social control theory, new versions of labelling theory have emerged in recent years. The research of Heimer and Matsueda's (1994) *Differential Social Control Theory* found that while structural and differential association factors play a role in explaining delinquency, self-evaluation is an even stronger indicator. Once labelled, youths take on roles that reflect how they appraise the label. Siegel (1995) considers their work important because "it is an alternative to 'traditional' labelling theory that incorporates concepts of social control and symbolic interaction."

Summary

In this chapter we reviewed four of the important sociological theories extensively used (usually at different times) to explain crime and criminality. First we noted how sociological inquiry emerged as a social science in Europe and then at the turn of the century was established at the University of Chicago. Sociology did not really find a home in Canada until the early 1960s.

Even though all the sociological theories focus on some aspect of social structure and social process they focus on different key concepts ranging from the effects of social (dis)organization to people's abilities to adapt to their societal goals through legitimate means. We then focused on the ecological school and examined the role our socio-spatial environment plays in crime trends and criminal behaviour. We then discussed an overview of the differential association theory that emphasizes the importance of social learning and subcultures, and how who we interact with can influence our behaviour. Finally, we looked at the labelling theory. Here the emphasis shifted towards societal reactions to what people do, or don't do.

In an attempt to illustrate the depth of the sociological perspectives, under each of the four classical theories, summary tables presented a sampling of related theories. Many of these related theories may be covered in other criminology courses or may be addressed in class depending on the instructor's orientation.

Sociological explanations act as powerful lines of inquiry into criminological issues, social organizations, and social processes. As Jeffery (1990:273) points out, they are all based on "social determinism and social environmentalism." Yet, in spite of their popularity, all sociological theories "ignore the role of the brain in criminal behaviour" (Ibid, 268). Our social environment provides us with the experiences and conceptual framework, but all this information must be processed by the brain before we can act on the external stimuli. To this extent, sociological theories neglect (or at least minimize) individual differences. For instance, why do not all poor Aboriginal males who are between the ages of 16 and 24 commit crimes? The sociological theories in criminology are still fraught with concepts that are too broad (e.g., goals, norms, social disorganization, association, zones, etc.) and clear operationalization of how the respective theories explain behaviour is not well defined (Andrews and Bonta, 1994; Jeffery, 1990). The French scholar Jules Henri Poincareé (1854–1912) was quoted as having said "sociology is the science with the greatest number of methods and the least results." More recently, sociologist Jack Gibbs (1972:4) appears to concur when he states "sociologists probably agree that testable theories are desirable, but … the proliferation of untestable theories surely signifies that testability is not taken seriously."

Since it is clear that the social environment (or one individual environment) is unable to explain all, or even certain behaviours, then perhaps it is time to move beyond mind-matter or mental-physical dualism. It is time to examine crime from an integrated, holistic, or interdisciplinary perspective—one in which criminologists explore the interaction of social, physical, biological, nutritional and other elements and how they affect the brain. In the final chapter in this section there will be a discussion of a few of these theories.

Discussion Questions

1. The region of the Commonwealth of Independent States, part of the former USSR, is widely seen as the most corrupt area in the world (Boyle, 1998). Much of this trend has occurred since the collapse of Russia in 1991. How might we explain this phenomenon from a sociological perspective? Apply at least two different theoretical models to explain the phenomenon.

2. To what extent do you think crime rates differ according to the important dimensions of structured social inequality such as urban social life, race/ethnicity, social class, and gender? Which of these factors do you feel are the more important for understanding crime? Why?

3. Describe the major sociological theories discussed in this chapter. What are the relative strengths and weaknesses of each theory? Which theory do you think has the most explanatory power? Why?

4. What challenges might exist in accepting any one type of sociological theory over another type?

5. How have social structures affected criminological theory, crime research, and crime policy?

6. After having read this chapter, to what degree do you think that sociological explanations of crime have been, and are, currently grounded in scientific principles?

7. How might sociological components be incorporated into an integrated and interdisciplinary criminological perspective? Which components do you think would be the most important?

Key Concepts

Differential Association

Laws of imitation

Primary vs. secondary deviance

Anomie

CPTED

General Strain Theory

Cultural transmission

Conflict perspective

Differential Identification

Ecological School

Labelling Theory

Concentric-Circle Theory

Strain Theory

Control Theory

social structure

Differential Reinforcement

"dramatization of evil"

Sub-cultural Theory

Chicago School

modes of adaptation

social disorganization

Key Names

E. Durkheim

E. Burgess

R. Merton

E. Sutherland

A. Comte

R. Park

A. Cohen

H. Becker

G. Tarde

C. Dawson

C. Shaw and H. McKay

Weblinks

No specific links are offered for this chapter. However, if you access and type in search words such as "crime and sociology," "sociology and crime," "deviance," etc. you will get hits for numerous links ranging from course outlines to general information sites. As an exercise, pick one of the theories covered in this chapter and see what you can find on the Net. For example, **www.yorku.ca/research/Lamarsh/** is the Web site for the study of family violence and conflict resolution at York University.

Footnotes

1. Willams and McShane (1994) identify two other levels of theoretical abstraction. Microtheories are more concrete. They tend to focus on explaining "how people become criminals," while bridging theories are those theories that attempt to tell us "both how social structure comes about and how people become criminal" (Ibid, 8).

2. Hiller (1982) provides one of the first and most comprehensive reviews on the history of Canadian sociology as well as a review of Clark, one of the pioneers of Canadian sociology.

3. Dawson even applied Burgess's concentric-circle theory to Montreal. Rather than forming circles, he came up with "'kidneys,' with many natural areas within them and a clear divide between French- and English-speaking areas" (Deutschmann, 1998:244).

4. The functional perspective in sociology views social arrangements as being beneficial to the maintenance of society. Therefore, each part of society contributes to the whole. Hence, crime can be viewed as functional as it promotes change and draws attention to

what needs attention. For example, prostitution could be viewed as functional because it meets the needs of some men. However, functionalists also recognize that concepts and values can change. While prostitution was tolerated during Canada's pioneering days, today solicitation (s. 213 C.C.) has become less socially acceptable.

5. After reading this section you might be interested in going back to Chapter 6 and reading the psychological variation of this theory—the frustration-aggression theory of Dollard, Doob, Miller, Mowrer, and Sear's work started in the late 1930s and Megargee's more recent revision.

6. One of the first sociologists to offer a theory of subcultures was Thorsten Sellin. In his theory culture conflict (1938 cited in Vold and Bernard, 1986) he argues that in heterogeneous societies there are many subcultures with divergent norms of conduct. Hence, human behaviour is seen as a social process that develops and evolves over time as people interact with others.

7. During the 1950s, Walter Miller developed a variation of Cohen's theory and coined the term "middle-class measuring rod." The term referred to the set of standards the lower classes tried to attain. They include such social behaviours as sharing, delaying gratification, setting long-term goals, and respecting others' property (Williams and McShane, 1994). When these goals are unattainable it can lead to frustration and a subcultural reaction, such as deviance. The subcultural behaviour becomes a learned collective solution to the problem of not being able to attain certain goals.

8. The term ecology is derived from the Greek *"oikos,"* meaning "household" or "living space." For criminological purposes, it refers to the interrelationship between individuals and their natural physical environment. This school of thought has also been referred to as the Chicago School and the School of Human Ecology.

9. Also see Chapter 4 and Geographic Profiling.

10. Although the labelling theory is often classified as a conflict perspective it can also be considered to share characteristics of Terence P. Thornberry's interactional theory. Used primarily to explain delinquent behaviour, the labelling theory asserts that delinquency is the result of a breakdown and an acceptance of conventional values. Influencing factors are age or cognitive development, social class position and growing up in a socially disorganized area. When these variables are present the risk of involvement increases and delinquent labels are likely to be attached to the youth. The theory interprets delinquency as part of a dynamic social process and not just an outcome of that process.

11. In his book *The Disreputable Pleasures*, in 1987, Hagan used the polarities of "consensus" and "conflict" to classify theories of crime. The consensus view asserts that crime and deviance is simply a deviation from generally accepted rules and values while the conflict perspective sees criminalization and criminal law as a reflection of competing interests of the more socially, economically, and/or politically powerful groups.

12. A phenomenological approach refers to a perspective that holds that criminal behaviour is only knowable to those who participate in it. For example, a criminal event means one thing to the offender, another thing to the victim, and something different again to the various practitioners within the criminal justice system.

CHAPTER 8

Emerging Criminological Theories: Closer to Being Integrated and Interdisciplinary

"If a little knowledge is dangerous, where is the man who has so much as to be out of danger?"

Thomas H. Huxley (1825–1895)

Learning Outcomes

After you have completed this chapter, you should be able to:

- Identify the existing integrated and/or interdisciplinary theories within criminology.

- Realize that today's criminologists are concerned less with trying to differentiate between criminals and non-criminals than with broader issues.

- Recognize the requirements of a good theory.

- Recognize and appreciate the strengths and limitations of the four selected "integrated" theories.

- Appreciate and recognize that knowledge is relative, thus we should be continually striving to gain a better understanding of how to apply criminological theory to crime control and crime prevention.

It was noted in previous chapters that criminology is a young discipline that has been dominated by sociological thought. However, we also observed that biological and psychological methods of inquiry have contributed to the study of crime and criminality. Collectively the theories may appear somewhat overwhelming and counterproductive in our efforts to understand and control crime. In addition to their different disciplinary orientations, criminological theories can also differ in other ways: determinism vs. free will, classical vs. positivist, consensus vs. conflict or they can be divided into micro, macro, or bridging theories (see Williams and McShane (1994: Chapter 1) for an excellent discussion). For the purposes of this introductory textbook, we want to keep the overview comprehensive but not overwhelming. The intent was also to provide the foundation on which to further advance the acceptance of an integrated and interdisciplinary conceptualization of criminology.

In spite of their different theoretical orientations and ideologies, many theories are actually interrelated to other theories within their discipline, in some cases even between disciplines. In recent years, a growing number of criminologists has begun to work on the integration of theories both within and between disciplines. These new approaches open a promising new line of theoretical inquiry that reflects the complexity of human behaviour, and tries to give more powerful and robust explanations of crime and deviance. The shift has been influenced by evolving moral, political, and religious values as well as the accumulation of criminological data—both nationally and internationally. Technological changes have not only produced new crimes, they have also redefined what crime means (e.g., genetic mapping, criminal profiling, and geographic mapping).

The refinement of methodologies combined with the development of sophisticated and powerful quantitative and qualitative data management strategies have made theory integration more practical,[1] because, as Williams and McShane (1994:253) observe, "as long as people see each theory as separate and distinct, there will be little real progress in criminology." Or, to paraphrase the sociologist C. Wright Mills, criminology needs to "imagine" new ways of connecting social issues with individual concerns.

In this chapter, we will review a cross-sectional sampling of some of the integrated and/or interdisciplinary theories within criminology. In addition to representing a new theoretical approach to the study of crime they also represent a new epistemological orientation within criminology. Siegel (1995) observes that criminologists today are less concerned with trying to differentiate between criminals and non-criminals than trying to understand such issues as:

- How and why people become involved in criminal activity.
- How and why some people terminate their criminal involvement.
- Why some individuals "age out" from crime.

- Why some individuals escalate their criminal activities.
- How and why some develop criminal specializations.

Siegel refers to this general orientation as *developmental criminology* while Barak (1997) uses the term *integrating criminologies*.

Before we examine some of these integrative and interdisciplinary theories let us take a brief look at their origins.

The Evolution of Theories

Human thought and knowledge is never static; it is always unfolding. For example, in Chapter 1, it was noted that crime (e.g., attempted suicide) and theory (see Box 8.1) are both *relative* and *evolutive* concepts. Just as we can never completely predict new crime trends, we cannot predict which theories will thrive and/or how they might evolve conceptually. For instance, Durkheim's anomie theory might have remained an obscure conceptualization of human behaviour were it not for the efforts of Robert Merton some sixty odd years later, when he revised and redefined Durkheim's theory (see Chapter 7). Similarly, in Chapter 5, we saw how the positive-based theories have experienced a resurgence, thanks, in large part, to advances in methodologies and in measurement instruments.

PROFILE BOX 8.1

EARL RICHARD QUINNEY (1934–): THE AVANT-GARDE CRIMINOLOGIST[2]

"I don't think we need a criminal law with punishment to make people good" Quinney (1971:52).

Born on a farm in Wisconsin on May 16th, 1934, Quinney's life has been well-chronicled (see Trevino, 1984 cited in Martin et al., 1990:404).

In 1952, Quinney entered Carroll College in Waukesa, Wisconsin. Although interested in biology because of his family roots, Quinney gravitated to sociology and psychology. However, based on the advice of his biology advisor he entered the master's program in hospital administration at Northwestern University.

As a master's student Quinney took a criminology class from William Byron and developed a strong interest in the academic study of crime. This opportunity had a lasting impact on Quinney's academic career.

On completing his master's degree Quinney entered the University of Wisconsin at Madison to pursue his doctoral studies in the area of rural sociology. Under the tutelage of such academic powerhouses as Howard Becker (labelling theory), Quinney's focus shifted from rural sociology to general social theory. Things were progressing well when suddenly Becker died of a brain hemorrhage. Quinney temporarily gave up his studies to teach at St. Lawrence University in Canton, New York. There he met the noted sociologist Marshall Clinard and decided to complete his dissertation in criminology. In 1962, he was awarded the Ph.D. for his dissertation, *Retail Pharmacy as a Marginal Occupation: A Study of Prescription Violation.* His dissertation was based on a functionalist perspective. That is, social phenomena (e.g., prescription violations) are explained in terms of their effect on social structure (e.g., retail pharmacy).

In the ensuing years, Quinney held teaching positions at a variety of universities and began to develop his critical theoretical perspectives, writing and publishing very productively. Throughout his work he developed his dynamic perspective that "there are four assumptions about people and society: (1) process, (2) conflict, (3) power, and (4) social action" (p. 387). The key theme of his ideas is not about why people commit a crime, but how they become labelled as criminals.

In the 1980s, after returning to the midwest to teach in the history department at Northern Illinois University in DeKalb, his views once again evolved into a more integrated and novel theoretical direction. Beginning with his book *Providence*, in 1980 and then more fully in his 1988 publication *Crime, Suffering, Service: Toward a Criminology of Peacemaking*, Quinney developed his ideas on the criminology of peacemaking (see below).

In many respects Quinney is a maverick in the area of theoretical criminology. Many of his ideas have prompted a growing number of criminologists to transcend the conventional parameters by which they have studied crime and criminality. Quinney epitomizes a thinker and scholar whose work has gone from a traditional and conservative approach to theories that represent a bold new direction.

Our understanding and theoretical conceptualization of our "reality" is influenced by our economic, physical, psychological, and social environment. This is illustrated in Chapter 4, where an overview of some of the pioneers in criminology is presented, and in the box inserts on the various individual profiles presented elsewhere throughout this book. We can see from the profiles how the ideas were influenced by their authors' life experiences. Williams and McShane (1994) describe how a number of these events have influenced criminological ideas and direction. The 1980s and early 1990s in Canada, for example, were marked by fiscal restraint and a plea for more pragmatic and conservative approaches to the administration of criminal justice. The influence of conservative and liberal ideology was discussed in Chapter 3.

During the conservative era of the 1980s and early 1990s we saw major changes to the *Young Offenders Act* (see Box 8.2) as well as in other areas of Canadian criminal justice. Along with the practical shifts that occurred there have been theoretical shifts. In the first edition of *Criminological Theory*, Williams and McShane (1988:133) observe that the "same variables have been used time and time again to explain crime and delinquency and, yet, each time the claim was that a new theory was being developed." They did suggest that the crime-as-self-help theory by Donald Black and the routine activities theory of Cohen and Felson (see below) represent "original approaches under development" (Williams and McShane, 1988:133). However, in their second edition in 1994, Williams and McShane note that "both the new gender informed theories and new variations on conflict theories are now demonstrating a greater degree of vitality than was the case six years ago" (p. 254). They suggest that a number of these theories have a conservative bent and have returned to focusing on traditional values and institutions such as family, friends, school, and work. Hence, they posit that "social control theories and integrative theories that incorporate social control should remain popular" (Ibid, 254).

REALITY CHECK BOX 8.2

YOA AMENDMENTS SINCE 1984—PRINCIPLED REFORM

1986
- Some children under age 12 pose a danger to society.
- s. 7, 33, 38, and 40–46 of the YOA ranging from noncompliance to records provisions and pre-trial diversion.
- Bill C-106 passed June 1986.
- Youth who commit a criminal offence before completing a disposition for a different offence may end up with an aggregate sentence of more than three years.

1989
- Call for more flexible sentencing options for young offenders convicted of murder.
- Bill C-12 passed December 1991 in spite of the lack of significant evidence to support the notion that longer sentences deter violent young offenders.
- The bill extended the maximum disposition from three years to five years less a day.

1995
- Call for stricter sentences for first degree murder; easier to transfer young offenders to adult court.
- Bill C-37 passed January 1996
- First degree murder doubled from 5 to 10 years and second degree murder increased from 5 to 7 years.

1996
- Federal-Provincial-Territorial Task Force on Youth Justice Report. The report resulted in a number of recommendations on age limits, processing of serious offenders, the use of alternatives to the courts, and matters concerning the transfer and sentencing of serious offenders.

1997
- After a series of interprovincial meetings, all provinces and territorial premiers, with the exception of Quebec, called for major amendments to the Act. Primary areas involved better prevention and rehabilitative programs.

The early trend dealt with technical and procedural issues, then the focus shifted to court outcomes rather than procedures. More recently, the amendments have addressed public safety concerns.

FYI BOX 8.3

Keeping Informed on the Web

You can keep informed with the latest events of the *YOA* and *YCJA* through the Internet at: **http://canada.justice.gc.ca**. This is the homepage for the Department of Justice.

In their final chapter, Einstadter and Henry (1995) also discuss the future of criminological theory but are a little more reserved about embracing integrated theories or "theoretical mix" as a promising line of theoretical orientations. They point out that while some theorists are currently "engaged in integrating theories that already exist" others are trying to generate new theories around existing concepts. They cite Michael Gottfredson and Travis Hirschi's General Theory of Crime as one such example (see p. 275). And although integrated theories have become more explicit in their conceptualization rather than implied in their orientation, Einstadter and Henry suggest it is not enough. Instead, they feel "we should respect their differences, retaining their integrity as part of the array of approaches instead of meshing them together with the risk of losing what is unique about their contribution" (Ibid, 302). They offer this view in spite of recognizing that there "are no simple explanations; there are no simple solutions" (Ibid, 318). Crime, like social life itself, is a complex phenomenon.

It should be pointed out that all ideas and expression, no matter how well-supported, are subject to criticism and change. For instance, one of the golden rules of any (criminological) theory is that it be *parsimonious* and *logically sound*: simple in its concepts yet comprehensive in its explanatory power. Jack Gibbs (1972) described a "good" theory as one that: (1) can be tested, and (2) fits the evidence of research.

While the above criteria might appear straightforward and easy to apply, the issue of what constitutes "good" is not that simple. This continues to pose challenges for the newer theories as well. The first criterion asserts that a theory and its concepts are based on the ability to measure and test the relationship between two or more variables. This is referred to as *quantitative* validation. Towards the end of Chapter 5, for example, some of the more recent biological theories of crime, while representing viable explanations, could not have been formulated until researchers had developed the measurement instruments that could measure the constructs. Hence, some of the existing, and most of our newer theories, are sometimes constrained not only by our intellectual biases but also by our scientific knowledge.

In addition, theories require a degree of "logical soundness," which is called *qualitative* validation. Williams and McShane (1994:4) describe this approach as "the ability to make sense out of several conflicting positions, and even the degree to which the theory may sensitize people to things they otherwise would not see." Have you ever changed your mind about some major understanding? How long did it take you to accept the new interpretation? We are creatures of habit and do not easily change our views.

Logical soundness assumes that the theory is both internally consistent and offers a logical description of the relationships between the variables defined in the theory (Williams and McShane, 1994). The sequencing of events is one of the more common problems. For instance, if you ask older people about their perceived chances of being victimized they are likely to express a greater level of fear than would a younger person (see Fattah and Sacco, 1989; Fattah, 1991). Research evidence, however, indicates that their chances of being victimized are actually lower than that for younger people. The elderly's fear of being victimized correlates to a variety of factors that include such elements as: gender, minority status, living in urban settings, extent of crime in the neighborhood, and living in a heterogenous setting.[3]

A final qualitative criterion for a *good* theory that has plagued the evolution of criminological theory is the issue of *popularity* (Williams and McShane, 1999). Like new clothing, new hairstyles or new forms of music, the acceptance of good theories depends largely on whether they can be marketed in a way that will capture pubic interest. Do you remember in 1997 when the soft drink "Orbitz" was introduced? It had little balls of gelatin floating around in it. While it never did anything for me, I remember young people finding it entertaining. Someone had obviously done their marketing homework. Other examples might include the hula hoop, the cabbage patch doll, pet rock or maybe even the teletubbies. They all had their moments of popularity, only to be replaced with the next craze. Is this true of criminological theories? They too have been affected by the prevailing social, political and religious values of the day.

As noted in Chapter 7, the sociological orientation has dominated much of criminological inquiry since the turn of the century, while the psychological and biological explanations of crime have experienced greater acceptance in Europe. A review of any criminological journal over the past 5 to 10 years (or longer) will quickly reveal which theories have been in vogue at different times. As Williams and McShane (1994:6) note, "a theory can simply echo our gut-level feelings about the causes of crime, and we tend to give credence regardless of its logical soundness and empirical support." In other words, dominant theoretical explanations tend to reflect intuitive and/or ideological appeal. For example, the popular idea of biological determinism at the turn of the twentieth century fell out of favour partly because of its link to racist political policies and partly because it was unable to explain certain patterns of crime.

Now that we have taken a brief look at the heritage of criminological theory and examined a few of the primary epistemological issues, we can now examine some of the contemporary and interdisciplinary theories. We will examine five main theories. They will include: *Routine Activity Theory*, *Social Conflict-based theories*, *Left Realism*, *General Theory of Crime*, and *Bio-Social Theory*. In addition, where feasible, it will be noted how these main theories have given rise to other theoretical explanations that continue to offer new perspectives by which to study and understand crime and deviance.

This cross-section of theories was chosen because they are not only drawing attention in the criminological literature but most of them are currently being used in Canada. Therefore, it will be possible to refer to specific Canadian research to illustrate the theoretical soundness of the theories. The chapter will conclude with a strong plea for a move towards, not only an integrated and interdisciplinary approach to the study of crime, but also an approach that bridges international boundaries.

Routine Activity Theory

Cohen and Felson's "rational choice" perspective argues that motivation alone is insufficient to explain the cause of crime. Crime risk is largely dependent on the opportunity for criminals and victims to interact (Kennedy and Forde, 1990).

Lawrence Cohen and **Marcus Felson's** (1979) Routine Activity Theory (RAT) can trace its immediate origins to the rational theories that emerged in the late 1970s (Williams and McShane, 1994). At the time criminologists realized that no sociological theory "contained an assumption of a rational, thinking individual" (Ibid, 221). A theory should also combine elements of deterrence, utility, and rational choice.

The RAT was initially viewed as a very practical approach to the study of crime because it attempts to integrate theoretical principles into social policy—something that has been largely lacking among criminological theories. The RAT quickly gained popularity because its principles coincided with the growing interest in victimology and the re-emergence of ecological crime-prevention ideas. In fact, Barkan (1997:101) describes the RAT as "the most popular theory of victimization." The theory also recognized the importance of human beings as rational beings. It considered both individual processing and the social environment, especially as each leads to social disorganization. Furthermore, the RAT approach gives equal weight to the role of both the offender and the victim in the crime process. Even though Cohen and Felson maintain that predatory crime is a matter of rational choice, they also hold that criminal opportunity is affected by the victim's behaviour and lifestyle. Hence, the RAT can be described as an integrated type of theory among the rational theories (see Table 8.1).

TABLE 8-1

VARIATION OF RATIONAL THEORIES

- *Lifestyle theory*   M. Hindelang, M. Gottfredson, and J. Garafalo
- Lifestyle is influenced by three elements: (1) social roles played by people, (2) position in social structure—the higher one's status the lower one's risk of victimization, and (3) rational component —how one chooses to process options based on life experiences.
- *Opportunity theory*   P. Mayhew, R. Clarke, A. Sturman, and J. Hough
- Crime is related to four key factors that are necessary and interrelated. They include: (1) the abundance of goods, (2) the physical security of goods, (3) the level of surveillance, and (4) the occasion and temptation for crime.
- *Rational choice theory*   D. Cornish and R. Clarke
- Crime is both offence and offender-specific. Offenders rationally evaluate and assess the level of skill required, the personal gain to be obtained from the act, and the risk of detection/apprehension. The offence becomes the act that fits the individual's rational decision process.
- *Cognitive theory*   G. Walter and T. White
- A psychologically-based theory that stresses the importance of the role of cognition in the individual. They argue that social and environmental factors tend to limit individual options rather than determine behaviour. Hence, crime is viewed as a product of irrational thinking.
- *Life-course theory*   T. Moffitt
                                                        D. Nagin, D. Farrington, and T. Moffitt
- Initially introduced by the husband and wife team Sheldon and Eleanor Gleuck in the 1930s! Moffit and several of her colleagues have been conducting a longitudinal study since the 1970s in the province of Dunedin in New Zealand. The study involves a cohort of 1,000 youths born in

1972–1973. Moffit et al. have been collecting biological, medical, psychological, and sociological information on the cohort at two-year intervals. Their life-course style analysis has revealed that a number of elements interact to predispose youth to criminal behaviour (e.g., poor neuropsychological scores, impaired communication skills, and poor nutrition). They note that the various elements manifest themselves at different developmental stages and relate their concepts to a biosocial perspective (see below). They offer a variety of prevention programs (see Chapter 14).

• *Routine conflict theory*   L. Kennedy and D. Forde

– Based on Cohen and Felson's routine activities and Hirschi and Gottredson's *General Theory of Crime* (see below), Kennedy and Forde also focus on the lifestyle of the victim and low self-esteem as predisposing factors to crime and/or victimization. Their theoretical model is based on a survey of over 2000 respondents from Alberta and Manitoba. They view the victim's behaviour as a product of rational choice based on learned repertoires for responding to conflict. However, low self-esteem does not directly affect crime (Forde and Kennedy, 1997). And as evidenced by the Canadian Urban Victimization Survey and General Social Surveys, among other victimization surveys, our repertoires are influenced by our relative circumstances in society. These circumstances can be further defined in terms of age, gender, income, race, and social class. The theory combines sociological and psychological factors.

Instead of focusing on the factors that influence an offender's decision-making process to commit a crime, Cohen and Felson's theory focuses on the "routine" (daily activities) of people. Their theory includes three major elements:

1. A motivated offender (e.g., unemployed, substance abuser, unsupervised youth, etc.).
2. A suitable target (e.g., unguarded homes, unlocked vehicle, unprotected commercial residence, unmarked items), and
3. The absence of a capable guardian (e.g., homeowners, police, or neighbourhood watch groups).

These elements illustrate the importance of rational thought processes as well as the importance of our environment in determining our actions. The

FIGURE 8–1

ELEMENTS OF RAT

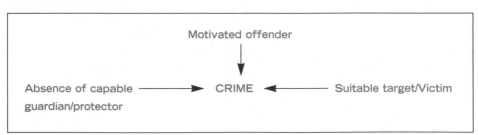

premise of the theory is that daily routine movements affect our lifestyles and activities. Or, as Cohen and Felson (1979:589) state, the rate of criminal victimization is increased when there is a "convergence in space and time of the three minimal elements of direct-contact predatory violations." Therefore, the risk of criminal victimization varies dramatically among the circumstances and locations in which people place themselves and their property. Conversely, by controlling the elements primarily through environmental situations, they suggest it is possible to reduce the risk of a crime.

Since its conceptualization the RAT has been the subject of numerous studies. It became a popular theory that seemed to complement criminal justice philosophy as well as the public's concern over victims' rights. A sampling of some of the more recent studies is presented in Box 8.4.

A CLOSER LOOK BOX 8.4

Studies on RAT

- S. Messner and K.Tardiff (1985). Examined the social characteristics of Manhattan homicide victims. The RAT effectively explained the location of victims and offender sites. General support for the theory.

- Sherman et al. (1989). Examined more than 300,000 calls to police about predatory crime and commercial crime in Minneapolis over the period of a year. The researchers found that certain predatory crimes such as robbery, rape and sex crime came from "hot spots"—small areas where all three elements converge. Hot spots can be determined empirically. In Chapter 7, we discussed how Canadian researchers are using sophisticated computer software programs to both map and predict the likely locations of serious offenders.

- "Preventing Crime: Current Issues and Debates." This was a special issue of the *Canadian Journal of Criminology* (Jan., 1990) in which a number of excellent articles discuss the specific and general application of RAT principles to the prevention of crime. For example, the article by Brantingham and Brantingham reviews several studies that have successfully focused on situational crime prevention to prevent (or at least abate) certain predatory crimes (see pages 29–34).

- L. Kennedy and R. Forde (1990:137). Using data from the Canadian Urban Victimization Survey, which contains detailed measures of routine activities, the researchers found that "personal crime is contingent on the exposure that comes from following certain lifestyles." They also found that "property crimes occur less because of conflict and more because of opportunity afforded through routine activities that remove victims from their place of residence" (Ibid, 150).

- D. Roncek and P. Maier (1991). This study included an examination of 4,400 city blocks of Cleveland in which they examined the relationship between crime sites and the location of bars and taverns. They found that the locations of these establishments turn some locations into "hot spots" for crime.

- M. Lynch and D. Cantor (1992). Using National Crime Survey and the Victim Risk Supplement data, the researchers found that victimization is dependent on ecological variables such as the environmental design of the housing unit and the social characteristics of the neighbourhood such as the level of social disorganization, perceived dangers, and the amount of time spent in the house during the day.

Summary and Evaluation

In their first edition of *Criminological Theory*, Williams and McShane (1988:133) made the observation that "none of the newer theoretical attempts have yet ... been accepted by the field as a major departure from existing criminological theories." For example, the RAT represents an attempt to integrate knowledge and research findings on ecological areas with popular opinion that emphasizes individual moral responsibility for one's actions (Williams and McShane, 1999). These two areas have been well established in the sociological and psychological literature for quite some time now.

Nevertheless, the concepts of RAT are intuitively strong and policy can be readily adopted. Many of the crime prevention programs today involve practices such as target hardening (using dead bolts in doors, security bars) and providing education programs for those who are at risk or feel they are at risk. In addition to providing a practical venue for addressing crime, the RAT has drawn attention to the important role of the victim in a criminal event. Finally, as often happens when a theory draws considerable attention to itself the RAT has undergone a number of refinements. For example, other micro and macro elements that have been variably incorporated into different variations of the RAT include:

- *Opportunities of a target*. The visibility and physical accessibility of the target. For instance, a university parking lot filled with cars during the day.
- *Risk factors*. The parking lot is located some distance from student activities —a lack of surveillance.
- *Exposure*. Can the target (car) be readily accessed?
- *Proximity*. While the parking lot may represent a suitable target it is also dependent on whether potential offenders are familiar with the area.
- *Structural/cultural proneness*. Are the targets considered suitable?
- *Defensive/avoidance behaviour*. To what extent do potential victims take steps to protect/secure their cars from being stolen?
- *High-risk activities*. To what extent is the area under natural or technologically-aided surveillance?

In spite of its practical appeal, not all criminologists support the RAT. Birckbeck and LaFree (1993) argue that the empirical tests of routine activity are generally based on false and ambiguous assumptions. For instance, the RAT asserts that those from a lower socioeconomic position are more prone to victimization than the more affluent because the latter have the means to purchase security. Yet those with the means are also more likely to go out, and because of their wealth are seen as more suitable targets. The theory does not provide an adequate explanation as to why the more affluent are not more frequently victimized.

Although the RAT acknowledges the role of choice, Canadian researchers Leslie Kennedy and Stephen Baron (1993), from the University of Alberta, found that criminal choices among young offenders, are also influenced by peer group pressures and cultural norms. These elements orient the potential offenders' choice of action. They argue that the RAT does not account for how these factors shape individual choice.

Nevertheless, numerous researchers continue to use the theory to help explain rates of victimization for specific crimes and crime "hot spots," among other criminal activity. RAT's future appears secure for the time being.

Social Conflict-Based Theories

Social conflict theories have had a long history. The modern variations of criminological conflict theories "emerged on the heels of labelling theory" in the 1960s (Williams and McShane, 1994:155). They are premised on social conditions, ranging from social and political unrest to situations involving gender, race, and social class discrimination to exploitation of the working class. The critical perspective represented an inevitable manifestation of the social unrest precipitated by the historical and political events of the time (e.g., Vietnam war, killing of President John F. Kennedy and civil rights leader Martin Luther King, domestic civil unrest, counterculture drugs, hippies, and "intense cultivation of inner subjectivity," among other dramatic social changes) (Quinney and Wildeman, 1991:71). However, being more politically oriented they have been slower in gaining acceptance among conventional mainstream criminology (MacLean and Milovanovic, 1991).

Yet it is difficult today not to read a news headline proclaiming some strife between two or more groups in Canada. Whether it is teachers threatening to strike, environmental groups protesting some logging venture, the demise of certain church leaders, or a dissatisfaction with the criminal justice system, our education and health systems, the news is filled with examples of social conflict. Social unrest seems to permeate every aspect of society today. Are we a society marked more by conflict than consensus? This is a postmodernist kind of question that has no absolute answer but represents a distinct perspective that has stimulated considerable rhetoric and a growing number of supporters.

There are several primary derivations of the social conflict perspective. In this section we will briefly summarize four of the more popular social conflict orientations. They include *conflict theory, Marxist theory, peacemaking criminology,* and *feminist theory*.

Conflict Theory

According to this perspective, crime is caused by inter-group conflict and rivalry that naturally exists in every society at every level from individuals to groups. Its origins are both instrumental (actual enforcement or control function) and symbolic (product of the social environment). The perspective has also been referred to as *critical criminology* because it challenges the social context of conditions such as poverty, racism, and sexism (Schwendinger and Schwendinger, 1970).

In defining the conflict perspective, Denisoff et al. (1974:297) "suggest that society is an arena in which struggles over scarce commodities take place. The division of labour is felt to be the source of unequal distribution in a world of scarce resources." Unlike the consensus model, which views society as a stable entity, the conflict perspective questions the system itself. Proponents of the conflict perspective argue, for example, if we all embrace the value system (i.e., consensus model), why is there so much rebellion and so much crime?

The first wave of critical theorizing in Canada emerged in the early 1980s and was followed by a second wave in the mid-1980s. Some of the key Canadian scholars included Tullio Caputo, Thomas (O'Reilly) Fleming, Brian MacLean, and Robert Ratner. However, Austin Turk was among the first to introduce a conflict perspective in his 1969 publication *Criminality and the Legal Order.* In addition, University of Toronto colleague John Hagan (1977) was the first Canadian to conceptually define the difference between a conflict and a consensus interpretation of social order.

Even though the second wave did not emerge until the mid-1980s, O'Reilly-Fleming (1996) points out that by the early 1990s the critical conflict perspective had begun to wane. It was replaced with new theoretical forms such as postmodernism, feminism, left-realism, and more recently, peacemaking (see p. 262).

While the conflict perspective has only received modest support in North America, Robert Ratner (1985) notes that the impact of the conflict perspective has had a weak following in Canada. He suggests this is in part due to the thirty-year domination of the correctionalist-rehabilitative period that lasted from the mid-1930s through to the mid 1960s. Fleming (1985) observes that the general lack of acceptance of the conflict perspective was further influenced by American sociology, which has had a major influence on early Canadian sociology (see Chapter 7). Ratner (1985) points out how the *Archambault Report* in 1938 and the *Fateaux Report* in 1956 both called for the growth of criminology in Canada, stating that universities should educate career workers in the correctional field, hence lending support to the correctional-rehabilitative philosophy. Related university programs subsequently emerged as important elements "in the infrastructure of social control" making it very difficult for the conflict perspective to find a home within academic settings. Ratner (1985:18) suggests that our criminology programs are too commercialized and that their teachers resemble "enlightened-positivists" because they support the prevailing correctional ideology.

Evaluation

For policy makers, the conflict theory may present some practical challenges. Rather than attempting to explain crime, conflict theory tries to identify the sources of social conflict and social processes through which definitions of deviance and crime are created and enforced. They point to discriminatory practices within the criminal justice system, how the lower classes are discriminated against, and how the law is used to support the status of those who make law. Yet in spite of their confrontational charges against the system, conflict theorists generally call for a peaceful evolution, rather than a revolution, to eliminate social conflict and improve the existing criminal justice system.

Austin Turk (1995) is among the few conflict theorists to identify concrete measures to reduce crime. These range from stopping the building of more prisons to decriminalizing public order offences such as consensual sexual activities and recreational gambling. Unfortunately, virtually none of his policies has received any attention from policy-makers. We will now shift our focus to the radical conflict-based theory of **Karl Marx**.

Marxist Theory

Karl Marx (1818–1883) believed that the most basic requirements of life (i.e., clothing, food, and shelter) can only be met through the manipulation of the social environment. The expression of manipulation involves labour. As human beings, we are constantly producing in order to survive. Marx saw conflict as being rooted in class differences between the *proletariat* (the working class) and the dominant *bourgeoisie* (the owners of wealth and/or power).[4] As Lynch and Groves (1989:6) note, "Above all, Marxism is a critique of capitalism," and law itself is seen as the tool of the ruling class. Marxism also shifted criminological attention away from conventional crimes to the "larger structures and forces that dominate the lives of our people," i.e., the ruling class (Quinney and Wildeman, 1991:77). And although Marx had little to say about crime and criminals per se, those who subscribed to his theoretical orientation adapted the theory to explain crime. For example, Marxist criminologists see law as primarily favouring, or protecting, the ruling class. However, Barak (1997) points out that Marxist criminologists are not a unified group.

Social conflict creates inequality and class struggle over the access to production which in turn creates social conflict and eventually crime. As Michalowski (1985:410) says, "inequality tends to increase crime by weakening the social bonds."

A leading Canadian proponent of the structural Marxism perspective is Brian MacLean who teaches criminology at Kwantlen College in Surrey, B.C. An illustration of his views can be found in an updated version of an earlier article first published in 1986. MacLean (1996) examines the implications of state expenditures on Canadian criminal justice. In the conclusion to his article he begins by acknowledging the limitations of the official data he uses. Nevertheless, he goes on to argue that the increased spending in criminal justice has simply produced "more police, more prison guards, more prisons, ... longer sentences at a time when crime rates, particularly serious crime and rates, do not increase" (Ibid, 145). MacLean says that such expenditures simply illustrate the desire of the state to widen its "net of repressive social control" (Ibid, 145). He attributes the trend to "class struggle over state expenditures ... in an attempt to transfer purchasing power and avert crises" (Ibid, 145). The nature of the expenditures gives the working class a false impression of a growing crime problem. The working class, in turn, naively supports the perpetuation of state control mechanisms. In the process the ruling class diverts attention away from itself and continues to engage in crimes that go largely unnoticed (see Chapters 9 and 10).

Evaluation

While conflict theorists have been criticized for their inability to clearly define the structural causes of conflict, Marxist theorists are also criticized for lacking realism primarily because their claims are untestable and suffer from lack of empirical evidence. Furthermore, while critical of the social structure, they offer no real solutions (Lanier and Henry, 1998).

These and other dilemmas have spawned various modifications to the conflict perspective. Among these is the peacemaking theory.

Peacemaking Theory

Former conflict theorists such as Harold E. Pepinsky and Richard Quinney (see Box 8.1) have been strong advocates of this relatively new school of thought in North America (Friedrichs, 1991:101). Quinney initially gained prominence in criminology with his powerful and influential work on the conflict theory, *The Social Reality of Crime,* published in 1970. One of his propositions included the assertion that the social reality of crime is "constructed by the formulation and applications of criminal definitions, the development of behavior patterns related to criminal definitions, and the construction of criminal conceptions" (Williams and McShane, 1994:161).

Pepinsky's ideas on conflict theory, meanwhile, were first expressed in his 1976 book, *Crime and Conflict*. Like Quinney, Pepinsky adopted a conflict perspective in his book. He argued that, rather than rely on punishment and prison, society should make better use of policies involving mediation and conflict resolution. Interestingly, while not readily embraced in the 1970s, such ideas have come into vogue in recent years (see Chapter 14).

Both Quinney and Pepinsky eventually searched from a "radical humanistic understanding of social existence and human experience" (Friedrichs, 1991:102). For example, Quinney's search led him to explore Christian socialism, liberation theology and Eastern meditative thought, among other means, to make sense of violence and to restore peace and harmony. Quinney and Pepinsky saw that even though most people recognize peace as being superior to and more powerful than violence, the use of violence seems unavoidable sometimes. But is it necessary? Or natural? Over time they came to believe such views are not necessarily absolute. Rather, they argue that the traditional way of perpetuating the "we–they" dualism and the criminal vs. non-criminal orientation has done little to alleviate the crime problem. No matter how we express crime and punishment, we cannot punish acts, only the actors. As the esteemed Norwegian criminologist Nils Christie observes, "you're more likely to see that that person's soul is not embodied in any single act, and that you can not punish an act without contaminating a complex actor" (cited in Pepinsky, 1991:107). Therefore there can be no justification in using punishment as a means of resolving disputes. Thus, peacemaking, like all conflict-based theories, posits that there must be fundamental changes to the structure of society in order to reduce crime.

Supporters of the peacemaking movement are interested in promoting a peaceful and just society through humanistic and non-violent approaches. Pepinsky (1991:109) suggests that the free exchange of information, which the American scholar Buckminster Fuller (1895–1952) called "synergetic," is the only way to peace—"punishment merely adds heat." This, he argues, is the basis of democracy. Quinney (1991) notes that peacemaking is dependent on establishing and maintaining democracy. Drawing on many religious traditions (e.g., Buddhism, Judaism, Quakerism, and Zen), the peacemaking orientation views crime as a form of suffering from both the offender's and the victim's perspective. Hence, the perspective calls for alternative strategies such as mediation and conflict resolution rather than the use of punishment as ways to address criminal acts. This perspective calls for crime control agencies to work together with the public to alleviate social ills and inequalities in order to reduce crime. Not a new concept for most religions, but a novel one for the police.

Pepinsky and Quinney, among other peacemaking advocates, point out that the criminal justice system is based on a "warlike" image in which punishment is used to avenge wrongdoing. They see punishing or controlling someone as just as violent an act as committing the crime. As Tifft (1980:6) writes, "in such instance these acts reflect an attempt to monopolize human interaction." Hence, non-retaliation, according to Graeme Newman and Michael Lynch (cited in Pepinsky, 1991:109) is the "only way to break cycles of violence." Pepinsky adds that non-retaliation alone is not enough. He adds, as noted above, that people need to indulge in democracy.

Evaluation

Based on a review of the main critically-based readers, the peacemaking model has not been embraced in any noticeable way. None of the chapters discussed the peacemaking orientation. In fact, in their table summarizing the central formulations and themes of criminological theory, Pavlich and Ratner (in O'Reilly-Fleming, 1996) neglect to include the contribution of peacemaking. And while MacLean and Milovanovic (1991) do include several brief chapter exerpts on the peacemaking perspective they are articles written by American scholars.

But perhaps peacemaking criminology is making itself felt in more practical ways. For example, starting in the mid-1990s and gaining increasing support since 1997, the concept of *restorative justice* has been drawing considerable attention. In June of 1997 the Institute for Economic and Restorative Justice and Hudson Valley Community College's Department of Criminal Justice hosted a conference on "Justice without Violence: Views from Peacemaking Criminology to Restorative Justice." In Canada similar efforts have been initiated by various provinces and by the RCMP. Chapter 22 of the Statutes of Canada (formerly - Bill C-41), which came into force on September 3, 1996, has facilitated the use of restorative justice as a new option to sentencing (Lilles, 1997). We will explore the restorative model in greater detail in Chapter 14.

Feminist Perspectives

Even though Lombroso, more than a century ago, was among the first to write a book on female criminality, the subject remained largely ignored in criminology until the late 1960s. Typically criminologists have only focused on crimes like prostitution and shoplifting when studying female crime. In fact, Leonard (1982) points out that theoretical criminology had been unable to address female crime because it has been dominated by men trying to explain male patterns of crime and delinquency. However, all this changed in the 1970s with **Freda Adler's** *Sisters in Crime* and Rita Simon's *Women and Crime*. They both point out that the women's movement provided the opportunity for female issues to be taken seriously. And while Adler and Simons reached different conclusions, they both attributed the growth in female crime to the emancipation of women. This interpretation did not sit well with other feminists (Daly and Chesney-Lind, 1988).

But their ideas, along with those of other feminists, did challenge the assumptions underlying traditional research on gender and criminal justice. Daly (1989b) has identified a number of issues that connect feminism to the discipline: (1) with the exception of rape and intimate violence criminology has not felt the impact of feminist thought, (2) some continue to believe that gender is simply another variable for the "regression equation," that asserts that the personalities women (and men) who commit crimes are somehow flawed (3) most often one hears women are simply so underrepresented they are not interesting subject matter, and (4) criminology cannot evolve unless it recognizes all components and aspects of the system—women being only one element.

Even though a variety of studies have since disproved Adler's and Simon's explanations, the two women were instrumental in bringing the feminist perspective into theoretical criminology. Since their pioneering efforts, proponents of the feminist perspective, according to Herman and Julia Schwendinger (1991) have introduced a number of significant innovations in legal discourse:

1. Universalizing rape laws. In January of 1983, the existing rape law was repealed and replaced with the general offence of assault. The new law consisted of three new categories: sexual assault (s. 246.1), sexual assault with a weapon, threats to a third party, and bodily harm (s. 246.2), and aggravated sexual assault (s. 246.3) (see Chapter 9).

2. Redefining gender crimes. By recognizing changes in women's gender roles in our evolving society, changes are also being reflected in their rates of criminal involvement.

3. Redefining gender relations in criminology. Through their writings and research feminists have helped criminological theory move beyond the male-dominated perspectives. Some of the leading Canadian female scholars include: Ellen Adelberg, Dorothy Chan, Dawn Currie, Karlene Faith, Shelley Gavigan, Rita Gunn, among several others.

4. Widening the level of awareness of how women are handled differently from men throughout the criminal justice system, from the point of arrest, to judicial processing, to incarceration. For example, LaPrairie (1990) points out that even though Aboriginal people in Canada are disproportionately represented in crime statistics, there are even more Aboriginal women held in institutions than Aboriginal males. However, she stops short of suggesting that the Canadian judicial system is discriminatory in its sentencing practices. Instead, LaPrairie expresses the opinion that the data are insufficient to draw any conclusive generalizations (see Box 8.5 and Chapter 12).

5. Calling for new methodological strategies that focus on women's experiences of oppression and discrimination.

Although the feminist approach has received considerable attention in recent years, Einstadter and Henry (1995) caution that feminist criminologists are not the only theorists who are concerned with human order, the state, law and crime. Feminists represent a perspective that takes the attributes of society and social order seriously.

REALITY CHECK BOX 8.5

ROYAL COMMISSION ON THE STATUS OF WOMEN — 1970

Although the Commission was not a feminist initiative, its investigation was probably influenced by feminist concerns over the treatment and discontent of female offenders in Canadian prisons. The Commission engaged in a comprehensive examination of female involvement in the legal and judicial system. Its report called for sweeping reforms:
- Revisions to the *Criminal Code* for such offences as prostitution and vagrancy;
- The establishment of halfway houses and hostels for women;
- Placement of female staff to deal with women when they are taken into custody;
- Better treatment, vocational and educational programs, and counselling services;
- The establishment of special programs and facilities for female offenders;
- Better arrangements for assistance at time of release and for after care (adapted from Carrigan, 1991:471).

THE KINGSTON "P4W (PRISON FOR WOMEN) EXPERIENCE"

On February 21, 1995, Correctional Investigator, Ron Stewart, released his report of the compelling 90-minute videotape in which male members of the Emergency Response Team (ERT) used excessive force and degrading tactics on female offenders in the prison for women in Kingston, Ontario.

The incident began on April 22, 1994 when female prisoners of "B" Range became involved in a physical confrontation with guards at P4W. "Six women were segregated, charged with various assault and escape charges and claims were made that the women should be placed in a Special Handling Unit" (Prison News Services, 1995). The women were awakened from their sleep by prison guards dressed in riot gear and ordered to strip and be subjected to a body search. Some were handcuffed, shackled, and forced to the floor by the attending male guards. The ordeal began at 10:37 p.m. just after lock down for the night and ended at 1:15 a.m. In all eight women were subjected to similar treatment by the ERT.

Fortuitously, the incident had been videotaped. However, even after the author of the Investigative Report, Therese LeBlanc (now Warden) reviewed the tape, she "considered the deployment and actions of the ERT as something normal" (Ibid). However, when CBC's *Fifth Estate* first aired the video in 1995, it drew nationwide outrage and shock that such things could take place in a civilized country. Solicitor General Herb Gray was forced to hold a public inquiry into the matter. The inquiry led to a number of major recommendations such as building more facilities to house women. Five new female institutions have now been approved for construction.

Depending on one's source, there are three to four primary strands or variations of feminism and feminist theory. **Sally Simpson** (1989) identifies three versions of the feminist perspective. And while they "share a concern with identifying and representing women's interests, interests judged to be insufficiently represented and accommodated within the mainstream" (Ibid, 606) they have made significant contributions to criminological theory and criminal justice practices.

1. **Liberal feminism:** Within a "liberal-bourgeoisie" tradition these feminists advocate for women's equality and freedom of choice. They see gender inequality being expressed in most spheres of influence (i.e., education, politics, the workplace, etc.). They believe it is neither necessary nor natural. They do not accept the notion that private or public division of power and labour should exist within society. Instead they call for a more "androgynous" approach (i.e., blend male and female traits and characteristics). To do so, they argue, would eliminate inequality and promote greater social harmony both within society and in the criminal justice system.

In spite of its appeal, the liberal feminist perspective has been unable to "provide an adequate assessment of the origins of gender roles" (Hinch, 1994:4). Furthermore, the notion that women are becoming more criminal as a result of their emancipation has not been empirically supported.

2. **Socialist feminism:** Proponents of this perspective see gender oppression as an "obvious feature of capitalist societies." They attempt to integrate the male domination of the class and patriarchy system since socialist-feminists believe those factors are essential to the production and reproduction of goods. For the socialist feminist the only solution is a society free of gender and class stratification. They feel that by perpetuating the existing social structure, men are more likely to commit violent street crime, while women are more likely to commit property and vice crimes (Williams and McShane, 1994).

In his summation, Hinch (1994: 9) notes that, like the radical approach, the socialist perspective is unable to "account for variations in patriarchy over time." He further states that no social structure remains constant over time though the socialist feminists imply it does.

3. **Radical feminism:** The supporters of this version of feminism believe the origins of patriarchy are rooted in male aggression and control of women. They view male aggression as existing not only within the labour force but also in men's exploitation of women for their sexuality. They feel "sex not gender is the crucial analytical category" and that male domination is the origin of female subordination. They see patriarchy as a system that defines women as subjects, with men exercising their right of control through the law. Radical feminists believe that eliminating male domination will not only reduce crime rates for women but "should even precipitate a decrease in male violence against women" (Williams and McShane, 1994:238).

The basic assertion of the radical feminists that "female subjugation is universal and originates in the biological differences between men and women" has not been supported in the literature (Hinch, 1994:6). In addition, their notion that rape somehow can exist separately from other forms of violent offences represents an overstatement and a simplification of the crime. As Hale (1990, cited in Hinch, 1994:6) points out, "the radical feminists overstate the extent of violence against women."

4. **Marxist feminism:** Williams and McShane (1994) identify a fourth theme within the feminist perspective that they call Marxist feminism. Similar to the Marxist position, Marxist feminists "see the capitalist system as exploiting subordinate groups (often based on race and gender) for capital production (profit) (Ibid, 238). Hence, they see women being relegated to lower occupational status and lower pay for equal work. That oppression and exploitation influences female crime directly since it relates to labour and gender; that is, women are more likely to commit property offences and sexually-oriented offences such as prostitution. A natural continuation of the Marxist orientation is the socialist-feminist model described above.

While we have been referring to this perspective as being part of the feminist theories it has also been classified as part of the "new" gender-based theories (see Einstadter and Henry, 1995). In fact, in his review, Barak (1997:163) notes that there has been a tendency for the different feminist perspectives to become more inclusive and shift toward "the commonalties of gender, power, and conflict." This more general classification can perhaps be best illustrated by the following two points that describe the basic function of the gender-based theories. First, the various theoretical forms all criticize traditional male *androcentric* approaches to studying crime, and second, they all attempt to develop gender-sensitive interpretations of deviance.

A variation of the strict feminist perspective that embodies the above two points is the power-control theory of John Hagan (1985, 1989) and his Canadian associates. While not a feminist theory, Williams and McShane (1994) note that the power-control theory is based on feminist/gender processes. It is also an integrated theory in that it brings together a conflict-oriented theory with social control versions of family relationships and gender-class relationships. Together these elements form the basis of the power-control theory of gender and crime. They distinguish between patriarchal and egalitarian households as key factors to understanding and explaining crime and delinquency. For example, in an egalitarian household where both parents work outside the home in positions of authority, female children are more likely to become delinquent than under a patriarchal system where mothers are more likely to be at home and provide supervision. Their research further supports the theoretical assertion that females are more likely to be controlled through informal processes than young males, who are better controlled through formal (e.g., incarceration) processes. Such findings, if supported, could lend insightful recommendations as to how the criminal justice system handles and processes female and male offenders.

Although Hagan and his colleagues have defined different effects on delinquency based on family power-control variations, critics fault the theory for ignoring such fundamental factors as school experience, and the racial context of delinquency (Chesney-Lind and Sheldon, 1992).

In **summary**, the jury is still out as to how significant the feminist perspective is, and will be, in helping to understand and explain (female) crime and delinquency. However, Barkan (1997:248) suggests that "without full consideration of gender and its intersection with race and class, the study of crime and criminal justice will remain incomplete." Nevertheless, with the changing social experiences of women and the possibilities to participate in a wider range of opportunities (including crime), these and other conditions require that criminology recognize and seriously consider women's role in society and the study of crime.

Overall, the newer social conflict-based theories cover the spectrum from conventional Marxist doctrines, to a call for more humanism in criminology. The Marxist doctrine emphasizes political economy and calls for social reform by altering the structures of corrections, courts, media, policing, and the political system. The newer Marxists are not simply concerned about rebelling against capitalist repression and exploitation but on focusing on the larger structures and forces within a social arena. Marxists view crimes as products of people alienated by capitalist social structures and institutions. By contrast, the humanistic orientation calls for the elimination of crime control through the use of punishment and retribution. In addition it calls for the elimination of the social conditions that foster inhumane conditions, moving away from conventional criminal justice practices to ones that treat victims and offenders with dignity and compassion.[5]

All social conflict-based theories share several common themes. In addition to being critical in their orientation to explaining crime, they view crime as an outcome of conflict and the domination of different groups. Second, they assume that societies are divided by conflict rather than integrated by consensus (see Chapter 1). Hence, any group that has power (e.g., the ruling class, an authority figure, men) defines the parameter of what counts as crime. And what counts as crime is seen as designed to protect the interests of those in power. A third common theme is that conflict-based theories do not accept the status quo of criminal law.

Finally, many of the newer versions of social control theories have not been adequately substantiated with sound scientific evidence. Given what evidence is available, the research findings have been inconsistent in their support. Nevertheless, they represent a level of intuitive and popular appeal that continues to draw attention. In addition, such orientations as the feminist and peacemaking ones have had practical effects on how we view crime. For example, they have challenged the age-old gender inequality issues as well as provided impetus for a (return to) humanism in criminology.

Summary and Evaluation

Collectively, the social conflict-oriented theories view crime as the product of social inequality. Accordingly, the only way to achieve real change over the crime problem is through major social reforms, in some cases bordering on revolution. Only through aggressive social reforms is it possible to correct social and/or economic inequalities that are seen as the primary causes of crime.

Can such changes be achieved? To expect a sudden and dramatic reversal of existing social and political conditions is highly unrealistic. However, we have been witness to the emergence of what Lynch and Groves (1989:128) refer to as "middle-range policy alternatives" such as the abolition of mandatory sentences, prosecution of corporate crime (Chapter 11), increased employment opportunities, and an increasing shift toward community-based alternatives to incarceration. Yet, while these theories appear to represent promise for society, like most socially-based approaches they are still unable to answer the question "why do some do it and others do not"?

Hence, while the social conflict-based approaches are important, they need to be linked with other disciplinary perspectives such as biology and psychology. In this way they will be able to integrate, as Barak (1977) and other integrationists argue, the elements of the individual, the group, and society.

It is an interesting time for criminologists. After several decades of minimal progress criminology appears to be going through a growth spurt. In the next section we will examine another of the novel theoretical approaches—Left-Realism.

Left-Realism

Historically, most conflict and radical criminologists have had a tendency to blame the ruling class and capitalism as the source of the crime problem. However, as the conventional versions of the conflict and radical perspectives evolved (see above) a number of radical theorists began to criticize the prevailing views held by conventional conflict theorists. Their proponents include Richard Quinney, Walter Dekeseredy,[6] Tony Platt, and Jock Young, among others. Relying primarily on victimization data, the new breed of theorists suggested that conflict theorists have ignored the poor and the working class to focus on crimes of the ruling (upper) class. They also charged that radical criminologists have developed weak crime control strategies. This new school of thought is known as left-realism. It argues that not only is crime a *real* problem but a problem that also exists among the lower classes.

John Lea and Jock Young (1984 as cited in Thomas and O'Maolchatha, 1989:159–160) identify six basic premises of the realist manifesto:

1. "Crime is really a problem." Considered an oversight of earlier conflict-based theories, left-realism draws attention to the "impact of crime materially, politically, and ideologically, on the maintenance of capitalism."
2. "We must look at the reality behind the appearance" since it is based on seeing through the "deception and inequality of the world."
3. "We must take crime control seriously." This departure from the positivist models involves bringing the offender into the resolution process of a crime, encouraging community involvement in crime prevention at localized levels, and using prisons only as a last resort for the most serious of criminal offenders.
4. "We must look realistically at the circumstances of both the offender and victim." This premise says that we should examine the interaction and interrelationship between the offender and the victim. In so recognizing the characteristics of the criminal event, social response can be both preventive and punitive.
5. "We must be realistic about policing." Lea and Young argue that the police can no longer be allowed to view themselves as autonomous (see Box 8.6).
6. "We must be realistic about the problem of crime in the present period." Drawing on victimization reports it seems that crime is everywhere, from the street to environmental problems to the inappropriate conduct of the police.

REALITY CHECK BOX 8.6

NOT ALWAYS ABOVE THE LAW

- Feb. 26, 1999: Judge ruled that veteran RCMP officer had no legal ground to stop, search, and seize cash on the "hunch" that the suspect was a drug courier (Slade, 1999b).
- Feb. 11, 1998: RCMP officer has charges of sexual assault withdrawn by Crown but remains suspended. (Charges against..., 1998).
- August 6, 1997: Two officers accused of falsifying evidence in the Paul Morin probe. (Officer's "lost" lighter..., 1997).
- March 21, 1997: A New Brunswick teenager received a new trial after the Supreme Court of Canada ruled that the police had obtained body evidence illegally. (RCMP violated..., 1997).

The origin of left-realism is generally connected with the writings of British scholars Lea and Young. Their ideas of left-realism are eloquently expressed in their book, *What is to be done about Law and Order?*, published in 1984. In the book they reject the Marxist perspective in lieu of a "realist" approach that states street criminals prey on the poor and disadvantaged. So the poor are doubly abused, first by the capitalist system and then by members of their own class.

While perhaps it may appear to be new, left-realism borrows heavily from conventional sociological theory, in particular the relative deprivation approach. Lea and Young (1984:88) note "the equation is simple: relative deprivation equals discontent plus lack of political solutions equals crime."

Hackler (1994) offers an interesting interpretation of the left-realism orientation. He points out that criminological theories and criminological thinking often reflect the social and political fads of the time. For example, as noted earlier, the social unrest of the 1960s seemed ripe for the emergence of the conflict perspective. Hackler goes on to suggest, however, that left-realism proponents recognize and criticize faddishness and extremism. Therefore, while we must recognize the problem of conventional crimes, we must not be too eager to get caught up in the frenzy of media and public hysteria around such incidents. For example, while child abuse is a serious problem, historical evidence suggests that it may be no worse today than in earlier times—we just pay more attention to it today.

A final example involves drinking and driving. For years, drinking and driving has existed as a "problem" in society. However, when the CheckStop program was introduced by the police to catch impaired drivers and when Mothers Against Drunk Drivers (MADD) became a tour de force in the 1980s,[7] drinking and driving became a "real" form of social deviance (the same analogy can be made about smoking)! The impression is that the problem has escalated when in fact we are simply paying more attention to it (see Friedland, Treibilock, and Roach, 1990). The latter point relates to Hackler's second theme, about how images of crime, victimization, and criminal justice issues are systematically distorted by the media.

In Chapter 2 we discussed the impact the media have on forming public perceptions about crime. For example, over the years various students in a research methods class I teach have repeatedly demonstrated the disproportionate coverage of violence between strangers over violence between acquaintances. Left-realists, among others, are keen to point out that such distorted media coverage provides ammunition for repressive, and ineffective, social-control tactics. For example, beginning in the 1980s, after a number of sexual abuse cases were reported in daycare centres, the media used them to illustrate how public concern and public policy had been misdirected. While sexual abuse incidents do occur in daycare centres[8] such incidents are comparatively rare when compared with the incident rate of sexual abuse by parents (see Rush, 1980, and *Badgley Report*, 1984).

Left-realism, according to Matthews (1987:371), can be summarized as consisting of four central elements, all of which share common themes with those Lea and Young identified above. They include:

1. A commitment to detailed empirical investigation. Left-realists rely heavily on victimization data;
2. The independence and objectivity of criminal activity;
3. The disorganizing effect of crime—all crimes are serious; and
4. The possibility and desirability of developing measures to reduce crime.

Left-realists feel that the best way to combat crime is through crime prevention that involves improving the socioeconomic conditions underlying crime, relying more on community-based policing, providing victim compensation, using imprisonment for those who pose a *real* threat to society and increasing police surveillance in those areas where crime is a problem (see Matthews and Young, 1992 for further discussion). In addition, Wellford (1997:4) argues that a first step in this process should involve "the opening up of criminal justice systems to public view and discussion." This would help to eliminate some public suspicion. These points are seen as a strength since they reflect an effort by left-realism to formulate crime policies, something that had been lacking in earlier conflict approaches.

Evaluation

Left-realism may represent a new approach to breaking out of what the Norwegian criminologist Nils Christie (1997:13) refers to as an "oversocialization in criminology." Until recently, criminological theory had not advanced much. Similar views are also expressed by Williams and McShane (1999) in their often-referred-to textbook on criminological theory. The general assertion that little has been accomplished in the area of crime control is also reflected in our crime statistics. In spite of all the financial and personal resources allocated towards crime control, the impact has been virtually non-existent (see MacLean, 1996). In fact, Christie (1997:13) sums up the impact of criminology until recently as being "dull, tedious, and intensely empty as to new insights."

In spite of its relative newness, left-realism has not gone uncriticized as a theory. Criminologist David Nelken (1994:91) argues that left-realism represented a political response in North America "for addressing the conservative forces with which it identifies." Canadian criminologist Robert Menzies (1992:140) accuses left-realism as being gender-blind and ignoring violence against women, and describes it as having "limped painfully into its crisis of middle age." Walter DeKeseredy and Schwartz (1996) argue that left-realism is too willing to inflict punishment as a tool of social control, deflecting responsibility from the capitalist system. Meanwhile University of Guelph sociologist Ronald Hinch (1994) suggests that left-realism has a poor conception of the working class and points out that members of the working class often shift roles from offender to victim and vice versa. Ruggiero (1992 cited in Hinch, 1994:19) notes that failure to clarify and operationalize these divisions make it difficult to formulate "sound theoretical or practical crime control policies." For example, in point four above, left-realism provides no clear explanation as to what constitutes "improving socioeconomic conditions" or what is meant by "victim compensation." In the abstract these ideas may make sense but, given the diversity of society and the evolutionary state of social meaning, how do we ensure utilitarian and equitable justice?

Another limitation of left-realism, according to Don Gibbons (1994), and others, is the fact that left-realism concentrates on the fear of crime and victim rates rather than studying what the working class thinks about crime control strategies. Finally, Menzies (1992:152) expresses the opinion that left-realism lacks vision and fails to "evoke a genuinely transformative politic outside of the criminological realm." So while the conflict theorists focused their attention on crimes committed by the upper class, left-realism largely "overlooks" issues of corporate crime. MacLean (1996) appears to recognize this general limitation when he calls for the elimination of conservative bias in crime surveys. In doing so, he feels it is possible to tap working class attitudes about crime control strategies.

General Summary

Whether any of these new perspectives offer promise for crime control strategies will depend on their political, social, and theoretical acceptance. It will also depend on how well they stand up to scientific testing as well as how well they can be "marketed." Otherwise, it may turn out that the new perspectives are little more than another fad. Nevertheless, some criminologists (e.g., Williams and McShane, 1999, MacLean and Milovanovic, 1991) would agree that the new perspectives have helped to break criminological theory out of its long standing mind-set; one that has produced minimal success.

On the other hand, we should also bear in mind some recent observations of the Austrian criminologist Heinz Steinert (1997) who effectively argues that "conflict" criminology is a contradiction in terms. He suggests that the process involved in studying crime and criminological issues "can only be a critique of criminology" (Ibid, 125). Criminology is the study of an interaction between individuals in society and the rules guiding such interactions. But what appears to have happened with the conflict and radical perspectives since the 1960s and 70s in the criminological movement may "have regressed into a 'critical' part of criminology" as opposed to a critique of criminology (Ibid, 111). Therefore, only time and sound theoretical research will be able to answer the question of whether the social conflict perspectives are any more enlightening than previously favoured theories. It remains to be seen whether their ideas provide any better answers to the question of crime.

The future of social conflict-based theories, left-realism, and other theories discussed above remain unclear. Nevertheless, as reflected in the breadth of their theoretical orientation, criminologists are continually striving to better describe, explain, understand, predict and ultimately control crime. They are also doing this, to varying degrees, in an integrated and interdisciplinary manner. Hence, the theories are important and will most surely be examined in greater detail in subsequent courses—especially in criminology degree-granting programs.

Next, we will look at one of the newer integrated theories in whose principles we can see how theoretical principles evolve and shift as concepts are refined, methodologies improved, and perceptions of how best to address crime change.

General Theory of Crime

The History of the Theory

How should the general theory of crime be classified? Does it represent a "new" theory or is it simply a variation of existing perspectives? As you may have gathered by now, there are no hard and fast rules for classifying theories. For example, Williams and McShane (1994) place the general theory of crime (GTC) in a chapter that includes several other "newer and emerging theories of criminology," while Barkan (1997) places the theory along with the group of theories that emphasize "social process" and Siegel (1995) groups the theory with his chapter on "integrated theories." But then in 1999, Siegel, along with Canadian co-author Chris McCormick, placed their discussion of the GCT with social structure theories. Several textbooks do not provide any, or very limited, discussion of the GTC (see Linden, 2000, or Jackson and Griffiths, 1995). Barak (1997:189) suggests that the theory is not a true integrated theory because "it emphasizes lack of self-control to the exclusion of other variables."

Regardless of how one chooses to categorize the GTC it has been placed in this chapter because of its "newness" and because it has elements that allow it to be characterized as a multi-factor and integrated theoretical approach.

Intellectually the GTC can trace its roots back to Travis Hirschi's (1969) popular (social) control theory, a theory representative of the conservative social movement of the 1970s and 1980s. The GTC was also influenced by the resurgence of the basic principles found in the Classical School (Chapter 4). These principles assert that we are rational in our decision-making processes (i.e., we have free will), that legal and socially prescribed sanctions can be used to deter potential offenders, and that the certainty and severity of punishment works. The GTC, along with rational theories and gender-class-based theories (see Williams and McShane, 1999: Chapter 10) have been called neoclassical theories as they represent the new generation of class theories.

Hirschi identified four key elements of social control based on the assertion that our behaviour reflects the degree to which we internalize the norms, values, and desire to embrace conventional behaviour. The elements include:

1. **Attachment:** To what extent does the individual feel committed to his/her social environment? The stronger our sense of attachment the greater the degree of conformity and the less the desire to commit a criminal act.

2. **Involvement:** To what extent does the individual participate in conventional activities? The greater one's involvement the less time there is to be involved in crime or deviance.

3. **Commitment:** To what extent has the individual invested time and effort to feel a part of conventional society (e.g., obtain an education, get a job, raise a family, etc.)? The more one commits to conventional values the less time there is to be involved in deviant acts.

4. **Belief:** To what extent does the individual accept and support the conventional rules and practices of his/her social environment? The greater one's acceptance of the conventional practices the less likely a person will become involved in deviant behaviour.

Together these elements affect the (social) bond between an individual and society.

Although these points have strong intuitive appeal, Hirschi was never able to clearly operationalize the extent of bonding required to minimize the likelihood of deviance or whether all elements needed to be equally strong to ensure social compliance. However, as Williams and McShane (1994:189) point out, Hirschi, in recognizing some of these criticisms, simply saw it as an empirical question that researchers should address themselves to. Researchers appear to have taken him seriously as it is "probably the most tested theory in criminology" (Ibid, 192). Kempf (1993) reports that between 1969 and the early 1990s over seventy tests of the theory were published and that the majority relied on self-report data. But, if we refer back to Gibbs' two criteria for a "good" theory and apply them to the above points of Hirschi's control theory it falls short of meeting the criteria. Nevertheless, the control theory has been successfully used to explain a wide variety of behaviour including middle-class delinquency (Linden, 1978) and white-collar crime (Hirschi and Gottredson, 1987), and many theories have since attempted to incorporate elements of the social control theory in their theories (see Williams and McShane, 1994:193). In addition, Hirschi's control theory has inspired numerous broadly-based social policy research projects that emphasized social structure and process variables such as family, school, and the religious context of delinquency. The model was less readily adaptable to treating individual offenders in correctional settings. Hence, while in vogue, there was a proliferation of social welfare policies and programs and a shift away from correctional-based programs.

While it can be argued that elements of Hirschi's theoretical model are integrated, Hirschi does not support the integrative approach adopted by some of his followers. He feels such efforts alter the basic tenets of the control theory too much. Hirschi advocates a new theory with a logically coherent set of assumptions.

General Theory of Crime

The "new" theory with a new set of logically coherent set of assumptions emerged in the late 1980s through the collaborative efforts of Travis Hirschi and Michael Gottfredson. The general theory of crime represents a modified and somewhat refined articulation of Hirschi's social control theory. In his original version of social control Hirschi emphasized the importance of our identification with conventional social control mechanisms in society, while in the new theory Hirschi and Gottfredson focus on how we use *self-control* as a mitigating force. Although social control and self-control represent two different concepts of control, Hirschi and Gottfredson (1989) assert that they are both acquired through early experiences of effective parenting.

In response to the limitations of the original theory, the new GTC has been modified. In their GTC Hirschi and Gottfredson have acknowledged some of the other new theories that have emerged since 1969. In particular the GTC has integrated concepts of control with those of bio-social (see below), psychological (Chapter 7), routine activities and rational choice theories (see above).

In formulating their new theory, Hirschi and Gottfredson (1989) were interested in being able to explain a wider range of criminality and to shed conventional social concepts like class and gender that they felt contribute to our understanding of crime. Instead, they see crime as a problem of low self-control. So essential is the principle of self-control to the GTC that Williams and McShane (1994:227) suggest the theory will soon become known as the *low self-control theory*.

It is in their defining of self-control that we see the integration of other self-control concepts found in the theories identified above. Gottfredson and Hirschi (1990) argue that we all have personality traits (ranging from impulsivity to insensitivity and basic intelligence) that affect our self-control. They argue that these traits are learnt early in life through *child-rearing practices* and tend to persist throughout life. Therefore, poor parenting, deviant parents, and/or parents who are unable (unwilling) to meet basic needs (e.g., development, security, and survival) are likely to negatively affect the child's self-control.

While the presence of poor child-rearing practices does not guarantee children will turn to crime, they will be more predisposed than those youths who experience positive child-rearing practices. Therefore, rather than subscribe to a strict determinist model, the GTC is based on soft-determinism.[9]

Assuming poor child-rearing practices exist, Gottfredson and Hirschi (1990) suggest that then social bonds weaken and criminal opportunities become attractive options. They also point out that the *criminal offender* and the *criminal act* are separate concepts. The acts simply reflect rational choice and criminal opportunity while the criminal offenders are those individuals predisposed to criminal activity because of low self-control and faulty personality traits. It is here that we see the role of a *bio-social* element being a factor in self-control. Based on an individual's trait (biological) and the quality of family upbringing over the individual's life course (social), the propensity to commit a crime may still be present but the opportunity can change.

While an individual may have low self-control it does not mean he or she will commit a crime. "In fact, low self-control results in a wide variety of behaviours, only one of which is crime" (Williams and McShane, 1994:228). Given the interplay of other theoretical concepts, Gottfredson and Hirschi (1990) believe that an individual can choose to work on low self-control, that in turn will have positive effects on all their behaviour, including a decreased likelihood to commit a crime. However, one might ask, just as people can learn to stop smoking, research shows that a majority will return to smoking several times before they are able to finally kick the habit. Can the same be said about low self-control?

Given the importance of self-control in their theory, Gottfredson and Hirschi (1990) list six elements of low self-control (see Box 8.7). They claim that the principles can be used to explain a variety of criminal behaviours, ranging from break-and-enter to fraud, murder, and rape and can even be used to explain white-collar crime such as the now famous Bre-X gold mine hoax in 1997 (see Box 8.8).

After years of only mediocre success in the mining industry it could be argued that David Walsh, the former head of Bre-X, became preoccupied with self-gratification as a result of weakened social bonds. On the verge of bankruptcy, unable to control his downward slide, he may have become directly, or indirectly, involved in "shady" business transactions. This could have been done with the intent of reclaiming some of his family's former image.

Will this debacle put an end to mining fraud? Special RCMP investigators estimate that about two per cent of mining companies set out to defraud and mislead the public. In 1998, they were investigating 15 cases of possible mining fraud. How might the GTC be applied to Walsh's case?

A CLOSER LOOK BOX 8.7

Six Characteristics of Low Self-Control

1. Human beings have innate impulsive tendencies to self-gratification.
2. Conventional socialization process is necessary to establish self-control mechanisms.
3. Improper or inadequate child-rearing practices predispose a child to trait developments that can precipitate low levels of self-control.
4. Low self-control weakens social bonds and promotes a digression to short-term, pleasure-seeking behaviours.
5. Crime and deviance become suitable self-fulfilling opportunities and behaviour.
6. Taking steps to improve self-control results in lower levels of crime as well as in other positive behaviours.

Source: Adapted from Willams and McShane, 1994:229.

DAVID WALSH (1945–1998)—FOUNDER OF BRE-X MINERALS LTD. 1988

- Grew up in the affluent Westmount area of Montreal.
- Father and grandfather were successful stockbrokers.
- Walsh had a string of mediocre successes in the investment industry first with Midland Walwyn in Montreal and then with a number of junior mining companies based in Alberta.
- Described as a dreamer with high hopes but minimal returns.
- In 1988 he founded Bre-X which was headquartered in his basement.
- In 1992, while on the verge of another bankruptcy, he hooked up with another questionable Canadian, John Felderhof, who promised him there was gold in Busang in Borneo.
- After claiming to have struck the "mother-lode of all mother-lodes" in late 1996, the shares of Bre-X went from penny stocks to nearly $280 per share almost overnight.
- After the mysterious death of one of his geologists, Michael de Guzman, suspicions arose and within a few short weeks the hoax of the century had been revealed.
- Walsh unloaded about $8.7 million in Bre-X stock before the hoax became public.
- Walsh retreated to his residence in the Bahamas and claimed no knowledge of the hoax.
- In 1997, the legal firm Deloitte and Touche became Bre-X's bankruptcy trustee and filed a class action suit against Bre-X, the Toronto Stock Exchange, securities regulators and firms that promoted the stock.
- In May 1998, at age 52, Walsh died of a massive stroke in the Bahamas. Even after his death, close friends continued to defend Walsh's innocence, claiming he was not involved in the scam. What do you think?

Sources: A. Duffy, 1997, Rubin, 1998.

Summary and Evaluation

Williams and McShane (1994:229) suggest that the "combination of propensity and event within one theory shows promise." In addition, the theory is both integrated and interdisciplinary, and bridges biological and psychological concepts along with social structural processes, that include child-relation practices and structured events.

Unlike the social conflict-based theories discussed earlier, the GTC is a *positivistic* theory that focuses on the *process* of committing a crime. An important underlying assumption of the theory is that social order is *consensus-oriented* as opposed to conflict-based. Furthermore, Williams and McShane (1994:229) note that the GTC, while tending toward a *microtheoretical* approach (e.g., different degrees of socialization process), shares characteristics of the *macrotheoretical* approach. They point out that Gottfredson and Hirschi acknowledge that social institutions such as schools can "uniformly regulate child-rearing", implying that low self-control "has origins in, or is critically influenced by, the social structure."

Again, as has repeatedly has been the case with all the theories presented in Section II, the GTC has also drawn criticisms. Williams and McShane (1994:229) argue that the theory's greatest problem is the fact that "the prediction of crime requires the identification and prediction of other outcome events as well, such as drug use, aggression, and truancy." Meanwhile, Polk (1991) feels their definition of crime is too restrictive and Bartol (1991) suggests that the theory is based on tautological reasoning since crime and other behaviours that are seen as "weaknesses" in character (e.g., drinking alcohol, smoking, doing drugs, gambling, etc.), or low-self-control, is being used to explain itself. Finally, Akers (1991 cited in Williams and McShane, 1994:230) suggests that the GTC is really no different from his own social learning theory.

Sensitive to such criticisms, researchers like Harold Grasmick and his associates (1993) devised a measure that tried more accurately to measure low self-control among male students by differentiating the short-term consequences of losing their tempers from the long-term consequences, using a factor analysis to measure low self-control. Although their study lends impressive support to the GTC, Barkan (1997) points out that because they used cross-sectional data, they could not adequately address the causal order. Grasmick et al. (1993:5) report "inconsistent with the theory are: (a) the findings that criminal opportunity has a significant main effect, beyond the interaction with low self-control … and, (b) the substantial proportion of variance in crime left unexplained by the theoretical variables." They conclude by offering a few suggestions for strengthening the theory such as "incorporation of variables that might affect motivation toward crime and to more systematically spell out what those (situational and individual) circumstances or characteristics are" (Ibid, 25).

Relying on secondary analysis of data from the Ontario Ministry of Transport, Keane, Maxim, and Teevan (1993) tested the GTC by examining the relationship between self-control and driving under the influence of alcohol. Overall, their findings revealed a positive relationship between risk taking and the effects of blood alcohol content. They conclude that while their model was incomplete with regard to a number of exogenous factors, the findings lend support to the GTC.

In spite of some of the possible theoretical limitations, Michael R. Gottfredson and Travis Hirschi have not been shy to offer the policy implications of their theory. They see no value in short-term strategies or in addressing the supposed traditional causes of truancy and delinquency since they believe they are symptoms of low self-control. They also feel any efforts to reduce poverty or other social ills will not directly affect crime because such conditions alone do not cause crime.

Instead, Gottfredson and Hirschi (1990:272–273) emphatically declare that "policies directed toward enhancement of the ability of familial institutions to socialize children are the only realistic long-term state policies with potential for substantial crime reduction." Familial institutions may involve traditional family settings composed of a natural father and mother or programs that focus on parenting skills and improving self-control in children. As for other forms of crime, the GTC is less specific but Williams and McShane (1994) suggest that perhaps the use of environmental design concepts might make crime more difficult to commit.

Overall the theory has meet with mixed levels of support. Referring back to the quote at the start of this section, the self-control/general theory of crime does not appear to adequately explain all forms of crime (see Polk, 1991). Only continued testing and practical application of the theory's concepts will provide evidence as to the theory's ultimate merit.

We will now turn to the final integrated and interdisciplinary theory in this section—the bio-social theory. Although it was briefly introduced in Chapter 5, we will examine it in greater detail here.

Bio-social Theory

"I did not even think about the Marxists. When the attacks on sociobiology came from Science for the People, the leading radical left group within American science, I was unprepared for a largely ideological argument" E. Wilson, 1978:2.

The bio-social perspective has until recently received minimal support among criminologists. It appears that the aftermath of earlier biological determinism studies (see Chapter 5) has tainted any support for the more recent variations of biological-based theories. As recently as 1992, a conference to explore the relationship between crime and genetics at the University of Maryland was cancelled because of charges of racism (Jeffery, 1996).[10] A survey of several of the theoretical textbooks also illustrates the general lack of recognition for the bio-social approach:

- R.L. Akers (1994:82–83) comments that while the modern biological explanations of crime have faired better then their predecessors (e.g., Lombroso, Hooten, Sheldon, etc.), they have not yet established adequate empirical validity. He makes no specific reference to the bio-social, but states that the assertion that there is an interaction between biology and the environment is nothing new—what is unclear is how important the role of biology is.
- F.P. Williams and M.D. McShane (1999) allocate only about two full pages (pp. 41–43) to the biological and bio-social perspectives and focus primarily on the work of Sarnoff Mednick and C. Ray Jeffery.

- W. Einstadter and S. Henry (1995:98), in an otherwise comprehensive examination of criminological theories, offer no discussion of the bio-social perspectives.
- G. Barak (1997:123) concludes his review of the biological and bio-social perspectives by stating "much of this work is provocative and promising, and, I believe, certainly worth pursuing."

Biological explanations of the causes of criminal behaviour had a less than stellar start because of poor methods of measurement, ethnocentric biases, and the fact that the classical perspective had already firmly established itself in North America. Even the more contemporary biological perspectives (some of which were reviewed in Chapter 5) have not been widely embraced. Criminologists continue to argue that "the logic of biogenic and psychogenic studies is faulty, that correlation is passed off as cause and, particularly important, alternative (and better) explanatory hypotheses are overlooked" (Brown, Esbensen, and Geis, 1996:238). However, in this section we will see that the criticisms may be unfounded.

From Chapters 5 through 7 we saw that individually the biologically-, psychologically-, and sociologically-based theories have provided only a limited understanding of crime and have only been able to provide limited policy recommendations for the prevention of crime. Collectively the theories have illustrated the complexity of human behaviour and the complexity of crime, yet they have not taken the previous points into consideration. To date, most criminological theories from mainstream lines of inquiry have focused on social or psychological variables as if they represented "main effects" or causal factors. For example, lack of self-control (GTC) may account for a certain variance of delinquent or criminal behaviour but to what extent do other social variables *interact* with self-control as predisposing or preventive factors? Raine et al. (1997:15) suggest that criminologists "who have focused exclusively on social variables have almost always ignored interaction effects between these social factors."

The bio-social perspective represents one theoretical approach that has tried to be both interdisciplinary (see, generally, Brennan and Raine, 1996) and one that is increasingly studying and questioning the interaction effects between variables. As Raine and his associates (1997b) note, this "may be due to the fact that this approach has not previously been clearly enunciated, with numerous conceptual and theoretical issues requiring clarification." For example, in addition to the concept of bio-social meaning different things to different researchers (see Box 8.9 and discussion to follow) there are also "combinations" of how the biological approach is integrated into a theoretical perspective. One such variation that received modest attention in the 1980s is the bio-environmental perspective. In his article on bio-environmental criminology, Roger Endell (1983:45) describes it as the "interaction of the biological organism with the environment." Endell suggests that such books as James Watson's *The Double Helix*, a best seller—about the discovery of the DNA code—awakened North Americans' interest to the possibilities that science, and in particular DNA, might hold in answering key questions about human behaviour and health.

As exciting as the findings were, the overriding concern, as with the Finn Dorset sheep named "Dolly" in 1996, has been one of ethics and the role science and biology can, or should, play in social policy issues. Yet is the ultimate goal of criminal policy not one of crime control—control that is effective and efficient? We will return to this issue in the final chapter.

In the bio-environmental perspective, the environmental "solution" received less criticism. This involves the concrete application of crime prevention through the physical manipulation of the environment. However, the environment alone is not responsible for determining behaviour. Therefore, borrowing heavily from Jeffery's earlier work, Endell calls for an interdisciplinary approach that involves biological factors that interact with the environment. Unfortunately, as Raine and his associates have pointed out, Endell failed to operationalize what he meant by biological factors. Nevertheless, he cites a doctoral dissertation in which the author Altemose (1978 cited in Endell, 1983:59) predicts that "computer technology, neurophysiology, behaviour modification and management by objectives will cause extensive changes in the operation of the criminal justice system." Altemose goes on to suggest that, based on his calculations, "by 2123 the criminal justice system will cease to exist" and more objective and scientific strategies will replace the current methods of justice administration (Ibid, 59). However, given our history in dealing with crime and criminals, is this something we really want? Would we ever really be able to truly eliminate, or replace, an ancient tradition?

What is clear from the writings of Endell, and other biologically-oriented theorists, is that the definition of a variable depends partly on the theoretical orientation of the construct being observed and measured. It also depends, in part, on how the variable/concept is operationally defined (i.e., method of measurement) (Raine et al., 1997). In this section we will summarize two main bio-social perspectives, that of Sarnoff Mednick, and the most recent version, of Adrian Raine and his colleagues.

A CLOSER LOOK BOX 8.9

The Birth of Sociobiology—Bio-sociology!

In 1975, Edward O. Wilson, a professor of zoology at Harvard University, wrote a comprehensive and controversial book entitled *Sociobiology: The New Synthesis*. It represented a theoretical synthesis of biology, individual behaviour, and evolutionary ecology. He defined sociobiology as "the systematic study of the biological basis of all social behavior" and as "a branch of evolutionary biology and particularly of modern population biology" (p. 4).

Relying on his entomological study of social insects, especially ants, Wilson found that, contrary to the Darwinian notion of survival of the fittest, helping behaviour (altruism) facilitates the long-term survival of the gene pool. Based on his study of social insects he hypothesized that our sense of territoriality and ability to interact co-operatively causes considerable conflict and is the basis for much of the competition witnessed between human beings for environmental resources. Wilson describes our intergroup conflicts as being a form of "tribalism," expressed through street gangs, organized crime groups, division into nations, and even extreme survivalist or retreatist groups such as the Rancho Sante Fe group in March 1997, the Solar Temple group in 1997 and 1995, David Koresh's Branch Davidians in 1993, and Heaven's Gate in 1997–98 (also see Box 6.1).[11] Wilson was careful to operationalize aggression as he identified seven principal forms ranging from "territorial aggression" to moralistic and antipredatory aggression (pp. 242–243).

Wilson believes that our genetic makeup predisposes us not only to protect our own kin but to eliminate those who appear as threats. For instance, a Canadian study found that violence against stepchildren in the homes of adoptive children was sta-tistically greater than among children living with their natural parents (see Fisher, 1991). Wilson notes, however, that "there is no universal 'rule of conduct' in com-petitive and predatory behavior" (p. 247). The theory has been used to explain why men tend to commit more acts of violence than women—they are simply acting out their "hunter instincts." Women, who are more typical of "gatherers," tend to com-mit shoplifting, simple theft and forgery.

Finally, Wilson suggests that human laws are designed to protect the genetically-based relationships we share with others, our need for material possessions, and our right to a safe space. Violations of these relationships result in crime and require legal inter-vention in a society that has not learnt how to live as well communally as social insects! Wilson also observes that if we "want to reduce our own aggressive behavior... to make us all happier, we should design our population densities and social systems in such a way as to make aggression inappropriate in most conceivable daily circumstances and, hence, less adaptive" (p. 255). Despite the criticisms directed at Wilson's work, it is interesting how the ecological school, strain theory, and a variety of other elements of other theories covered in this section of the book can be found in Wilson's ideas.

In his review of Wilson's work, Frank Schmalleger (1996) observes how traditional criminologists quickly felt threatened by this line of explanation and rushed to criti-cize the theory. Wilson (1978:1) expressed considerable surprise since he felt he "had merely been extending neo-Darwinism into the study of social behavior." The criticisms ranged from a failure to acknowledge the role of culture and social learn-ing to a lack of hard empirical support, the fact that Wilson's observations were based on other animal species and that there is no rational basis for comparing humans with other animals. Yet Schmalleger (1996:187) points out that the seeds were planted and "today many open-minded scholars are beginning to sense the growing need for a new synthesis—for a way in which to integrate the promise of biological theories… the field of criminology is now ripe for a new multicausal approach."

Before summarizing several of the bio-social perspectives let us first define what is meant by a "biological" and "social" variable. According to Raine et al. (1997) biological variables refer to biological measures of biological constructs. These can include physiological arousal, as measured by the basal level of skin conductivity, EEG arousal, and lie detectors. Such approaches have been used with sex offenders and psychopaths (see generally Stoff and Cairns, 1996).

Social variables refer to variables that reflect some measure of a social construct. This can include such variables as socio-economic status as indicated by occupational status.

In their recent book Raine et al. (1997a) identified four major interactive bio-social theories of crime and delinquency that show how an integrated and interdisciplinary approach may be a powerful theoretical alternative to conventional theories. We will only address three, as the fourth is considered too broad and empirically difficult to test. Nevertheless, contrary to Hirschi's (1979) accusation that such approaches simply represent an *end-to-end model*,"[12] these versions emphasize the need for theory to become not only integrated and interdisciplinary in nature but also to begin to evolve in the complexity of its theoretical explanatory power.

Sarnoff A. Mednick's Bio-social Theory

In many respects, Mednick is a pioneer in North American bio-social theory. As noted in Chapter 5, he has had a rough ride trying to conduct bio-social research in North America. Most of his research has been done in Europe, more specifically in Denmark. Along with his colleagues he has been involved in one of the longest longitudinal studies in the world.

In a book edited with Karl Christiansen (1977), Mednick defines his assumptions of the bio-social perspective. For Mednick all behaviour is triggered by the autonomic nervous system (ANS). He believes we are all occasionally prone to do things that violate the norms, values, and rules of society. The reason most of us do not follow through on these impulses is because we learn to control those impulses as part of our socialization process and our desire to avoid punishment. We become law abiding individuals as we learn to fear punishment. As we learn to avoid fear the behaviour gets reinforced.

Mednick feels that the ANS controls the physiological responses to fear and other unconscious bodily functions (e.g., breathing and digestion). He theorized that if one has an ANS that recovers quickly from fear he or she will easily learn socially-proscribed behaviour, whereas if one has an ANS that recovers slowly he or she will have difficulty learning to inhibit anti-social behaviour.

According to Mednick, learning noncriminal behaviour requires both individual abilities (ANS response rate) and environmental factors ("consistent and adequate punishment for aggressive acts"). An absence of both social and biological factors will greatly predispose a person to antisocial behaviour.

Hans J. Eysenck's Bio-social Theory

As early as 1964, in his controversial but frequently cited book, *Crime and Punishment*, Eysenck argued that certain biologically-based personality features that are inherited (introversion vs. extraversion) are more prone to antisocial behaviour when they interact with various socialization processes.

Eysenck further theorized that combined with our autonomic and central nervous system characteristics these biological factors affect our responsiveness to punishment and our propensity for antisocial outcomes (Raine et al., 1997b). More specifically, Eysenck found that extraverts experience cortical under-arousal and are less responsive to punishment. In other words, they do not condition well with the use of punitive discipline. This process of learning is based on classical conditioning (Chapter 6).

Raine et al. (1997) note that Eysenck's theory reflects a "paradoxical bio-social interaction for outcome." Under normal environmental circumstances, poor conditioners will become antisocial. However, given a criminogenic social environment, individuals with deficits in biological functioning (poor conditioners) would be less likely than individuals with well-functioning biological systems (good conditioners) to evidence antisocial outcomes."

Terri E. Moffit's Bio-social Theory

In Table 8–1 Moffit's work was described as a life-course theory. However, Moffit (1993 cited in Raine et al., 1997a) proposes that "the biological roots of antisocial outcomes are present before or soon after birth." Relying on longitudinal data from her New Zealand study, Moffit theorizes that congenital factors such as heredity and perinatal complications produce neuropsychological problems in the infant's nervous system (Raine et al., 1997a). These deficits then manifest themselves in childhood complications ranging from poor motor skills development to poor memory and temperamental difficulties. In one recent study they found that boys who had the poorest neuropsychological scores at age 13 were the most delinquent group by age 18—even after controlling for socioeconomic status (Moffit et al., 1994). However, the importance of an interactive effect between biology and social variables was demonstrated in their finding that showed the results did not hold true for females, or males, without taking into consideration childhood behaviour problems.

Moffit's theory asserts that while some children may be born with neuropsychological deficits, a deficient social environment might also predispose a child to perinatal complications, poor nutrition, and abuse that, in turn, would result in some biological deficiency in the child.

Overall, Raine et al. (1997a) feel that all the theories offer solid support for a bio-social approach but "none of them have violence explicitly as the outcome variable." Taking these points into consideration, Raine et al. offer a bio-social model that builds on the strengths of existing models and proclaims to provide a broader framework in which to study bio-social interactions. The model is outlined in Figure 8–2.

Figure 8–2 clearly illustrates the interdisciplinary, interactive, and integrated approach to understanding violent behaviour.

First, the model is based on biological and social risk and protective factors. Most theories have focused only on predisposing factors and have given only pass-

FIGURE 8–2

HEURISTIC BIO-SOCIAL MODEL OF VIOLENCE

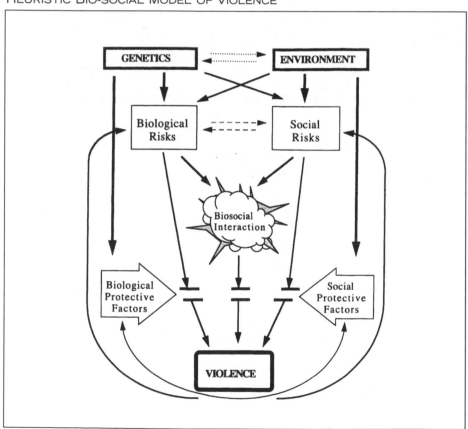

Source: Raine et al. (1997a: 15)

ing attention, at best, to protective factors. As the model suggests, "biological and social protective factors can break all three pathways ... to violence." Second, the model demonstrates that the presence of violence can produce new risk factors for violence. Raine et al. use the examples of imprisonment as presenting new social risk factors or being subjected to a head injury as a biological risk factor.

Viewed as a whole, the diagram suggests that behaviour that results in violence is the result of a complex interaction of social and biological factors, both of which need to be considered if one wants to understand violence or any form of criminal behaviour.

Again, in spite of its apparent comprehensiveness, Raine et al. acknowledge that there are a number of questions that require clarification. They are summarized below:

1. Are social risk factors more likely to interact with biological than social factors?
2. Do biological protective factors exist?
3. Do protective factors operate at their own level?
4. Does nullifying a bio-social risk pathway to violence require more protective factors than nullifying a social pathway?
5. Does violence affect risk/protective factors?
6. Are different bio-social models for different developmental stages towards violence needed?
7. Is the bio-social pathway more important for certain subgroups of violent offenders?
8. Does the model work for individual and groups?

Based on his Pulitzer Prize-winning series, Ronald Kotulak (1997) presents a compelling and comprehensive review of recent research studies that suggest that biology plays a major role in setting up the blueprint for who and what we become. However, he also notes that it is our social and physical environment that "acts like an on-the-job foreman, providing instructions for final construction" (Ibid, 4). Hence, crime is not just a legal or social problem, it is a public health and mental health issue that requires a significant shift in conventional thinking about crime.

What is perhaps most startling about the latest bio-social research findings is that violent and aggressive behaviour can be controlled by modifying the environment and/or modifying brain chemistry with such drugs as clozapine, sertaline, paroxetine, and buspirone. Kotulak (1997) says that when a number of researchers first suggested that genetic make-up and brain chemistry could be altered by manipulating the offender's environment, they gained little respect because such evidence was incongruent with conventional thinking. However, with improved methodologies and technology, researchers have begun to accumulate compelling evidence about these ideas.

Using Science to Excuse Criminal Behaviour

In January of 1999 an Alberta judge gave a man charged with robbing a liquor store a reduced sentence because "he had a neurological disorder aggravated by a mixture of beer and Valium." The store co-owner described the sentence as a joke (Slade, 1999). How important is it for the courts and/or criminologists to consider bio-social traits?

Summary and Evaluation

The bio-social theory is a controversial integrated and interdisciplinary approach to the study of crime and delinquency. In recent years it has evolved from simple correlation studies to the study of experimental bio-social effects (Chapter 5) to the study of sophisticated crossover bio-social effects.

Nevertheless, it continues to be met with guarded skepticism because of residual criticisms of racism, poor methodology, and a battery of ethical considerations. For the most part, Wilson (1975) argues that the skeptical concerns are ill-founded and usually reflect the naiveté of the critics. Similarly, Gywnn Nettler (1984:104) concluded that "to explain the 'age factor' one has to abandon sociological and sociopsychological theories of crime causation and revert to physiology, to the ways organisms differentially function with age." And Jeffery (1990:327) points out, as have others, that while social variables such as age, class, education, family, mass media, and race are used (see Chapter 8) by sociological criminologists to explain crime rates, "there is an absence of significant relationships between crime rates and all these variables."

An issue that has not been adequately addressed by those who support the bio-social perspective is, how does one resolve the conflict between law and science or, as described in Chapter 4, between the classical school and positivist school of criminology? This problem has been well described in Wilson and Herrnstein's (1985:528) critically acclaimed book *Crime and Human Nature*. In their conclusion they make the statement that "crime, like all human behaviour, has causes, and that science has made progress ... but the very process by which we learn to avoid crime requires that the courts act as if crime were wholly the result of free choice."

The bio-social theory, an interdisciplinary and integrated approach, while not the only such perspective (e.g., Jeffery (1990) prefers a psychobiolgical approach —see Chapter 5), illustrates the need to integrate criminal law and science. These views are not original. They have been expressed by the criminologist C. Ray Jeffery, psychiatrist Karl Menninger, law professor Nicolas Kittrie, and philosophy professor Michael Adler, among others.

From a policy perspective, the bio-social advocates do not subscribe to the positivist notion that biology is deterministic. Rather they argue that while genetics can make certain kinds of behaviour more likely, environmental factors may play a deciding role in whether a behaviour manifests itself. Nevertheless, some fear that proponents of the bio-social perspective might lend support to questionable controls such "as involuntary sterilization, abortion of abnormal fetuses, and genetic screening for criminological or insurance purposes" (Deutschmann, 1994:144). While they might lend support to such repugnant ideas, it is unlikely that politicians would embrace such views. More realistically, policy makers may be more inclined to entertain the idea of testing and monitoring children, involving both biological and social/environmental factors (see, for example, Jeffery, 1993).

Summary

In this chapter, we have examined a broad yet comprehensive overview of some of the new directions criminological theory is taking. We covered four primary areas (routine activity theory, social conflict theory, general theory of crime, and bio-social theory), all of which contained varying elements of an interdisciplinary and/or integrated approach.

The chapter began with a general discussion as to the merits of an interdisciplinary and/or integrated approach. While the jury is still out as to whether this line of inquiry is the "right" one, the intent of the coverage was to provide an overview of where criminological theory has been, and where it's going. Needless to say, it is this author's bias that such an approach is long overdue.[13] However, as has been expressed throughout this book, theories evolve and shift as our knowledge, values, methodologies, and political agendas change.

Whether any of the theories reviewed will become the dominant ideological perspective in the new millennium is unclear. However, it is likely that we will not see new or substantially different theories of crime. Instead, as reflected throughout this chapter, theories of the future will represent elaborations, extensions, and general "tinkering" of the classical and positivist principles that comprise the foundation on which most theories have been grounded. Furthermore, it appears likely that more integrated and interdisciplinary theories will flourish as single disciplines lose their stronghold over crime and criminological issues. As Wells (1995) observes, explanations are likely to be more *individualistic* (i.e., free will) in nature rather than collective and *voluntaristic* (i.e., deterministic). This is consistent with the current trend towards conservatism within criminology and criminal justice.

So while we recognize that criminological knowledge is a relative and evolving construct, it will remain the domain of the reader to decide which perspective best fits his or her criteria and frame of reference. As long as you apply the rigours of objectivity in your decision process then your "truth" will always prevail and be as deserving of respect as the truth of those who dare to put their ideas to pen for all to scrutinize. And, to paraphrase the noted scientist Max Planck, "an important scientific innovation rarely makes its way by gradually winning over and converting its opponents; ... What does happen is that its opponents gradually die out and that the growing generation is familiarized with the idea from the beginning" (Becker and Selden, 1985:330).

Having now covered the meaning of crime and its various elements, and characteristics (Section I), as well as reviewed various theoretical perspectives (Section II), we can now move into the third part of the book. Here we will examine conventional and non-conventional crimes as well as what we might be able to do (and what has/is being done) to address the crime problem.

Discussion Questions

1. In this chapter, we have examined several of the new and exciting emerging integrated and interdisciplinary theories. Which of these appeals to you the most? Why?

2. Although an integrated and interdisciplinary approach is being advocated in this chapter, and throughout this textbook, what challenges confront such perspectives?

3. To what extent, if any, might an integrated approach contribute to, or correct, what Canadian sociologists Richard Ericson and Kevin Carriere (1994) describe as criminology being a fragmented discipline?

4. What are the implications of each of the major perspectives in the study of crime and its control?

5. How have/might an integrated and interdisciplinary approach affect(ed) criminological research and crime policy?

Key Concepts

General Theory of Crime	Routine Activities Theory	feminist perspective
Conflict Theory	Marxist Theory	Social Conflict Theory
Gender-based Theory	Power-control Theory	Peacemaking Theory
Bio-social Theory	Life-course Theory	Left-Realism
Bioenvironmental	chaos	Social Control Theory

Key Names

R. Quinney	L. Cohen and M. Felson	K. Marx
F. Adler	S. Simpson	J. Lea and J. Young
M. Gottfredson and T. Hirschi	S. Mednick	H. Eysenck
T. Moffit		

Weblinks

Although we have no Internet links that relate directly to the integrated and interdisciplinary approach to the study of crime and criminality, you can always check the journal *Criminology: An Interdisciplinary Journal* (also see Appendix 2 for additional journals). Another source of information is the University of Montreal criminology library. Extremely comprehensive, they have an extensive listing of publications available to search through the Internet. While you cannot download any of the articles, you will be able to locate them. Their address: **http://tornado.ere.umontreal.ca/**

For more information on the Bre-X saga, sure to become a movie, you can visit the *Financial Post* newspaper on the Internet at: **www.sunmedia.ca**. Then, using their search engine type in Bre-X.

Footnotes

1. Not surprisingly, not everyone agrees that the emerging integrated and interdisciplinary theories bear much fruit. For example, Cohen and Vila (1996) and Brannigan (1998), among others, argue that while such "path-breaking" theoretical efforts are lively, none has yet resulted in a satisfactory resolution of criminological issues. However, in fairness to any new theory, many of these new theories are still in their developmental stages and have not had sufficient time to be fairly evaluated.

2. Most of the material for this profile of Quinney has been extracted from Martin, Mutchnick, and Austin's (1990) excellent discussion of Quinney.

3. See Fattah and Sacco (1989:212–225) for a more comprehensive review and analysis of how these factors affect fear of victimization among the elderly.

4. In their 1848 publication, *The Communist Manifesto,* Karl Marx and Friedrich Engels lay out many of their ideas of how class struggle is related to economic, political, and social inequality.

5. Another variation of the conflict perspective comes from the French scholar Michel Foucault (1977), as well as Michael Lynch (1988), and Stephen Pfohl and Avery Gordon (1986), who advocate a **deconstructionist/postmodernist** approach. Although the tenets are difficult to articulate, in general terms they focus on analyzing the rules and regulations in an effort to determine "whether they contain language and content that forces racism or sexism to become institutionalized" (Siegel, 1995:256). Deconstructionists believe language is value-laden and tends to extort social inequalities. They reject the apparent reality of distinction. To date, postmodernism has received marginal support, and the acceptance of one of its recent derivatives *constitutive criminology* remains uncertain. But one thing seems certain, that even if the per-

spective fails to make a significant contribution to criminological theory through its ideas it will enrich critical thought.

6. Canadian criminologist Walter DeKeseredy is often credited with popularizing left-realist notions in North America.

7. In 1994, an estimated 16,589 persons were killed in alcohol-related crashes in the United States—approximately 41 per cent of total traffic fatalities. Although there is no comparable data available in Canada, official statistics reveal that mortality rates by automobile-related accidents have been steadily declining since 1970 when they represented 25.6 per cent of all motor-vehicle accidents. In 1992 automobile-related fatalities were only 12.1 per cent (*Canada Year Book 1997*:114).

8. During the 1980s and 1990s there were a number of major cases involving the abuse of young people in daycare and youth residential centres. Among the more publicized were the incidents at St. Vincent's orphanage in the mid-1900s. In 1993, a CBC television movie was made of the incident called *Boys of St. Vincent*.

9. The term *soft-determinism* represents a middle ground stance between the traditional classical approach (free will) and positivist (determinism) schools. In his discussion of the neutralization process, Matza (1964:27) notes that we are neither "wholly free nor completely constrained but fall somewhere between."

10. The conference was rescheduled for Sept. 22–24, 1995 in eastern Maryland. This time the conference organizers were able to hold the conference. It has since set the stage for a number of other related conferences as well as opened a special area panel session at the annual meeting of the American Society of Criminology.

11. For an interesting Canadian interpretation on Heaven's Gate and other "spiritual movements," visit Jayne Gackenbach's Web site from Augustana University College in Camrose, Alberta. It includes several interesting papers related to religious movements. The address is: **sawka.com/spiritwatch/lemon.htm**.

12. A widely cited example of an "end-to-end model" is that of Delbert Elliot, Suzanne Ageton, and Rachelle Canter (1979). Their model incorporates elements of social control, strain, and social learning into a single explanatory model. The model begins by emphasizing the importance of early socialization outcomes (e.g., social control theory) and how components of the strain theory either strengthen or weaken social bonds. These elements in turn are affected by social learning components (e.g., peer association) which either result in delinquent behaviour or a high probability of delinquent behaviour depending on the sequencing of events. The theory, although not widely tested, has been applied with some success to explain drug use among juveniles (Elliot, Huizinga, and Ageton, 1985; and Winfree, Griffiths, and Sellers, 1989).

13. Support for an interdisciplinary perspective is growing. At the 1998 Academy of Criminal Justice Sciences meetings, Diana Fishbein from the University of Maryland observed that

"despite the obvious relevance of their research (interdisciplinary perspective), it remains largely unfamiliar to criminology and criminal justice scholars and practitioners." In 1999, David Farrington was elected President of the American Society of Criminology. Known for his integrated and interdisciplinary perspectives on the study of crime, it will be interesting to see what kind of impact he will have on criminological theory and research.

CHAPTER 9

Violent Crimes

"Murder! Rape! Robbery! Assault! Wounding! Theft! Burglary! Arson! Vandalism! These form the substance of the annual official criminal statistics on indictable offences… they constitute the major part of 'our' crime problem. Or at least, we are told so daily by politicians, police, judges, and journalists who speak to us through the media of newspapers and television. And most of us listen."

Steven Box (1983:1)

Learning Outcomes

After you have read this chapter, you should be able to:

- Recognize and be familiar with the major forms of violent crimes.

- Be familiar with the general trends of the major violent crime types.

- Appreciate that an "absolute" explanation of violent crime causation is currently unavailable.

- Appreciate the importance of using crime data to understand violent crime trends and patterns, explaining crime, and recommending social policy.

- Appreciate the importance of applying an integrated and interdisciplinary approach when using crime data.

- Appreciate the benefit of using comparative criminology to lend further insight into the study and control of violent crimes.

As noted in Chapter 2 and in the quote above, if the media are any barometer, crime has been on the increase. Although crime took a backseat to the unity issue in the 1997 federal election, (see Appendix 5) all parties addressed the growing public concern over crime. Between 1962 and 1991 the crime rate rose from

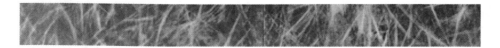

approximately 2,300 per 100,000 population to just over 10,300 per 100,000 population—nearly a four hundred and fifty per cent increase! However, as the media and official criminal justice agencies are quick to point out, since 1992 the crime rate has declined each year. In 1997, the rate stood at 5,571 per 100,000 population.[1] So does this mean Canada is becoming a safer place to live? Are our perceptions of crime, then, distorted and incorrect? What might account for the declining crime rate trend? Is the trend uniformly experienced across all criminal offences?

In the next two chapters, we will focus first on violent crimes and then property crimes. As noted in Chapter 1, these types of crimes are generally referred to as **conventional crimes**. This chapter will examine three major violent crime offences (i.e., homicide, assault, and robbery) and several "new forms" of violent crime (abduction, hate crime, stalking, and terrorism). However, it should be noted that official Canadian crime statistics also divide these crimes into a number of sub-classifications. For example, there are eleven sub-classifications for assault ranging from "aggravated sexual assault" to "unlawfully causing bodily harm."

In addition to the above mentioned crime classifications, the police also record incidents involving prostitution, gaming and betting, offensive weapons and a host of other *Criminal Code* offences. They also record offences involving federal statutes, provincial statutes, and municipal by-laws. Together these crimes make up all the police-reported incidents.[2] Some of these crimes will be covered in subsequent chapters (i.e., 11–13).

The purpose of this chapter is not to provide an exhaustive review of all reported crimes but rather to introduce you to some of the trends and patterns of various forms of these violent crimes in Canada. We will also attempt to answer several fundamental questions, such as:

1. Are rates of violent crime increasing?

2. Who is committing these crimes?

3. Are there differentiating characteristics between social groups, individuals, age groups that determine who commits more violent crime than others?

4. What are the major causal factors?

5. How does Canada compare on the international scene?

As you work your way through the sea of data in this chapter, keep in mind that the general observations and conclusions are more important than the numbers themselves. Although violent crime only represents approximately 10 per cent of the total percentage of *Criminal Code* incidents, it commands a considerable proportion of media and public attention. In 1997, there were 296,737 reported incidents of violent crime as compared with 1,458,920 property related infractions (*CCJS*, 1998). Therefore, given most people's fascination with violent crime and the fact it can potentially result in the most serious harm (emotionally and/or physically) that can be inflicted on anyone, we will examine it first.

Violent Crime[3]

"Between 1962 and 1995 instances of violent crime have quadrupled. And the youth crime rate has risen faster since the introduction of the Young Offenders Act" (*CCJS*, 1998:18(12): p.12).

In Chapter 1 we noted that the meaning of crime is dependent on one's perspective. Rather than focus on the various meanings, we will base our observations on factual data that has been collected. We will also focus on those forms of violent crime that are officially recorded by Statistics Canada. However, as will be seen by the various Box inserts, violent crime does exist in a variety of other forms as well (see, for example, Box 9.1). Given that we will be relying mostly on official data, it bears reminding that there are limitations in overrelying on statistics, believing they represent the "real" picture (see Chapter 3). All data are merely a representation of the subject being addressed.

REALITY CHECK BOX 9.2

HATE-MOTIVATED VIOLENCE

Typically, when we think of racial violence we think of the United States (e.g., the Rodney King case in March 1991), or some other foreign country. Yet Canada has a long history of hate-motivated violence towards racial and ethnic minorities. As early as 1907 in Vancouver, a mob of whites attacked the local Chinese and Japanese communities, causing extensive damage to property and, reportedly, several casualties (Data on hate..., 1995). The report goes on to cite a list of sources and references to hate-motivated violence against racial and ethnic minorities throughout the twentieth century in Canada, that, while at times thought to be related to "alleged fears of economic competition, especially at a time of recession," Patel (1980 cited in Data on hate..., 1995:1) suggests that latent racism has been behind a number of such incidents.

Citing a 1977 report by Pitman (cited in Data on hate..., 1995), it is observed that in the "majority of incidents reported and investigated, the victim did not know his assailant and had done nothing that could be reasonably construed as a provocation." Focusing his report on Toronto and the surrounding area, Pitman found that most of the victims were of Indian sub-continent origin and nearly all were males. Also of note is the fact that few of the assailants were over the age of 22 and all were male. Alcohol had been consumed just before each attack.

In recent years, there has been an increasing number of ethnic and racial hate-motivated acts of against blacks in Ontario and Nova Scotia. An indirect form of hate-motivated "violence" has also included cemetery desecration and vandalism of synagogues.

While Canada is not as progressive at addressing hate-motivated violence as Canadians might think, along with other countries such as the United States, England, and France, we have set up a reporting mechanism to enable "a more comprehensive national picture of the scale of hate-motivated behaviour" (Data on hate…, 1995). Hate-motivated crime/violence has become a serious issue in Canada, especially in light of the growing proportion of new racial and ethnic representation.

Unfortunately, to date when one examines official violent crime data, it is not possible to discern who is doing it and why. This area deserves immediate and closer attention by policy makers.

WHAT DO YOU THINK? BOX 9.3

VIOLENT CRIME RATES

In a 1979 article, University of Montreal researcher Burkhard Hasenpusch tried to predict homicide rates for 1978 through 1984. Using a variety of social and demographic variables, he predicted that the homicide rate would be 6.6 per 100,000 population by 1984. The rate was only 2.6! How could Hasenpusch have made such a miscalculation, using conventional variables? How could he have miscalculated so badly? What might the actual results tell us about homicide in Canada? What does it tell us about the methods used to understand crime (i.e., murder) rates—are we using the wrong kinds of variables to predict homicide?

From Table 9–1 it can be seen that nationally the violent crime rate has been fairly stable throughout the 1990s. Since 1991, there has been a steady decline in violent crime. Yet there is a perception that Canada is becoming more violent. Later in this section we will explore some of the reasons for this perception.

Although we have experienced a decline in violent crime since 1962, official data indicate that between 1962 and 1990, violent crime rates increased almost five-fold. This compares to a three-fold increase in property crime over the same period (see Chapter 10).

The extent of violent crime varies by type, geography, and other important characteristics. We will explore some of these elements in this section.

TABLE 9—1

VIOLENT CRIME: 1990–1997

CANADA

YEAR	RATE PER 100,000	NUMBER
1990	970	269,503
1991	1,056	296,962
1992	1,077	307,512
1993	1,072	310,201
1994	1,038	303,745
1995	995	294,603
1996	990	269,746
1997	980	296,737

Source: Assorted *CCJS* Canadian Crime Statistics. (Annual Reports)

The Cost of (Violent) Crime

Not only has crime, until recently, been increasing but so has the financial cost to Canadians over the years (see Table 9–2). According to Statistics Canada, between 1988/89 and 1994/95 total criminal justice expenditures have increased by 13 per cent on an inflation-adjusted basis (*CCJS*. Justice Spending in Canada, 1997). In the 1970s, the per capita cost was approximately $170 (Griffiths and Verdun-Jones, 1994) while in 1995/96 every person in Canada paid $586 for a total of nearly $17 billion on police, courts, corrections, legal aid, and criminal prosecution (Easton and Brantingham, 1998).[4] However, given the recent decline in crime rates, have our monies finally begun to pay off ? Or is it time to explore new and alternative strategies to address our crime problem? How can criminologists help? We will explore some of these issues in Chapter 14.

International Violent Crime Rates

When we take a moment to compare our violent crime trends with those of other countries (see Figure 9–1), the picture may seem less alarming, in some instances. For example, since a majority of the Canadian population lives within 200 km of the American border, most of us have probably spent some time reading (or hearing) about the crime problem in the United States. By all counts, violent crime is a much more serious problem for them then it is for us.

Whether one studies the UCR or the National Crime Victimization Surveys, both sources indicate that since the early 1970s violent crime rates have increased fairly consistently. Moreover, in spite of the occasional decline, the rates have remained among the highest in the world (Zawitz, 1993).

TABLE 9-2

THE COST OF ADMINISTERING JUSTICE BY SECTOR

	1989–90	1990–90	1991–92	1992–93	1995/96*
		THOUSANDS (CURRENT DOLLARS)			
All Sectors:	7.76 Billion	8.52	9.09	9.55	10.0
Police	4.68	5.24	5.42	5.71	5.8
Courts**	—	766 Million	—	867	980
Legal aid	341	412	513	602	646
Youth corrections	398	434	475	487	526
Adult corrections	1.64	1.79	1.87	1.87	1.92

Source: Statistics Canada. Cat. No. 85F0018XPE. (p. 152)
* These data represent a mix of 94/95 and 95/96. Data drawn from Easton and Brantingham, 1998.
** Figures for courts collected every second year.

As in Canada, American violent crime rates increased gradually following the Depression (circa 1930s) until the 1960s when the rate began to increase sharply.[5] Interestingly, the homicide rate had declined between the 1930s to the 1970s, when it began a period of sharp increase (Siegel, 1995). Between 1983 and 1993, the violent crime rate increased about 40 per cent.

FIGURE 9-1

INTERNATIONAL (VIOLENT) CRIME RATES—UP AND DOWN

- Western Australia: crime rates *increased* 8.1 per cent between 1994 and 1995.
- Violent crime *increased* 9.8 per cent. Robbery accounted for the greatest increase–from 1991 the rate increased from 46.8 to 78.3 per 100,000 population in 1995 (Statistics for 95, 1997)!
- England and Wales: crime *fell* by 1.3 per cent between 1995 and 1996. This represented the fourth consecutive year that the crime rate had declined after climbing from 3,848 per 100,000 population in 1986 to 5,292 in 1992.
- Most of the decline was attributed to a decline in property-related offences (e.g., 6 per cent burglary). Violent crime had increased 11 per cent between 1995 and 1996. Homicide, rape, and robbery rates went from 41 per 100,000 population in 1986 to 101 in 1996 (Home Office, 1998).
- In general, the Home Office study reports that "nearly all countries covered by Western Europe, North America, and Japan have shown a sharp *increase* in recorded crime between 1987 and 1995."

Changing demographics, economic recession and economic restructuring or increasing drug use might account for some of the similarities in international trends. However, these factors do not explain variable rates and trends. Changing police strategies and social policies and/or other more sophisticated integrated models are likely required (see Chapter 8). In the meantime, there is considerable merit in criminologists doing comparative research and applying their theories to comparative data.

The "Causes" of Violence

How do we account for all this violence? Researchers have been preoccupied with trying to explain, understand, and control one form of violent behaviour or another since criminology first became a disciplinary study in the 1800s. Yet, given our official violent crime rates, other than providing descriptive information and being bombarded with a variety of theoretical interpretations, there are no absolute explanations of what causes violent crime.

We do know, however, that the sources of violence include: (1) abusive families, (2) competing cultural values, (3) firearm availability, (4) gang motivation, (5) human instinct, (6) personality traits, (7) regional values, and (8) substance abuse. Numerous articles can be found describing how these various sources contribute to violence in society. In some criminology programs, these sources are sub-areas of study within courses.

In addition to being able to describe the sources of violence, many of the sources have been incorporated into theoretical explanations. One is the *deterministic* (e.g., human instinct and personality traits) model such as that of Sigmund Freud (Chapter 6) who argued that we possess a basic instinct for violence and Konrad Lorenz (1966) who suggested that since violence is instinctive within the animal kingdom, it is only natural that it is part of human nature too.

Other explanations have focused on *social structures* (e.g., abusive families), social forces (e.g., gangs and regional values), to measures of anomie (e.g., substance abuse). There is no lack of such explanations. However, no one theory has been able to completely explain the etiology (causes) of violence. Indeed, more recently a number of criminologists has begun to suggest that an interdisciplinary perspective may prove more promising (see, generally, Chapter 8). To date insufficient research has been conducted in this area to bear out whether this line of inquiry will prove fruitful. Nevertheless, it is incumbent on criminologists to explore new theoretical directions.

In the meantime, let us begin by examining some of the trends and patterns of violent crime in Canada. We will begin with the most serious of these—homicide.

Homicide

Both the Canadian and American Uniform Crime Reports (UCR) begin with homicide (called murder in the United States). Under s. 222 of the 1999 Canadian *Criminal Code* "a person commits homicide when, directly or indirectly, by any means he causes the death of a human being." The law goes on to define specific elements of culpable and non-culpable homicide. For the purposes of this chapter, we will only focus on murder as defined by the law.[6]

Not All Murders Are the Same

Students reading about homicide for the first time might ask "what is the difference between homicide and murder—are they synonymous?" While both terms pertain to the killing of another human being, homicide is a term used generally to refer to the killing of one human by another, while murder refers more narrowly to the unlawful, premeditated taking of another's life.

Our *Criminal Code* divides homicide into four sub-categories: (1) first-degree murder, (2) second-degree murder, (3) manslaughter, and (4) infanticide. Aside from infanticide, the placing of a murder in a sub-category is differentiated on the basis on the offender's intent and the nature of the act that causes someone to die.

Homicide Rates and Their Etiology[7]

In 1997, the homicide rate was 1.92 per 100,000 population. This represents a 9 per cent decline over 1996. Although it still is substantially above the rates for the 1960s and most of the 1970s, it is the lowest since 1969 (see Table 9–3). Statistics Canada reveals that many European countries as well as the United States have also experienced a decline in their homicide rates. Of the ten countries presented Australia had the lowest homicide rate (0.86 per 100,000) with the United States having the highest rate (6.70). Canada had the eighth-highest rate (*CCJS*, 1998:18(12)).

It is interesting to note how two "experts" offer different interpretations for the increase observed between 1966 and 1975. Boyd (1988:4) suggests the increase is due to "a rapid escalation in our *manslaughter* rate." However, Silverman and Kennedy (1992:36) point out that the manslaughter rate has remained relatively stable since 1962. Instead, they use data to show that the increase is due to the increase in males committing more murders. They state "males drive the murder rate" (Ibid, 37). If so, why do males commit more murders than females? Do the differences have a social, psychological, or biological basis?

TABLE 9—3

CANADIAN HOMICIDE RATES: 1961–1997

YEAR	RATE	TOTAL
1961	1.28	233
1962	1.43	265
1963	1.32	249
1964	1.31	253
1965	1.41	277
1966	1.25	250
1967	1.66	338
1968	1.81	375
1969	1.86	391
1970	2.19	467
1971	2.15	473
1972	2.34	521
1973	2.42	546
1974	2.62	600
1975	3.02	701
1976	2.84	668
1977	2.99	711
1978	2.75	661
1979	2.60	631
1980	2.41	592
1981	2.60	648
1982	2.65	667
1983	2.68	682
1984	2.60	667
1985	2.71	704
1986	2.17	567
1987	2.43	644
1988	2.14	576
1989	2.40	657
1990	2.37	660
1991	2.69	755
1992	2.56	732
1993	2.18	627
1994	2.04	596
1995	1.99	588
1996	2.11	633
1997	1.92	581

Source: *CCJS*. Assorted "Homicide in Canada" issues. Vol. 2(1) for 1961–1980; Vol. 18(2); Vol. 17(9); and Vol. 16(11) for remaining years.

Why Do People Kill?

What might account for the decline? This is a question that taxes even the most learned of scholars. Silverman and Kennedy (1992:5) observe that while the media want simple answers to explain homicide rates to their viewers, listeners and readers, the reality is that "these crimes need to be understood in all their complexity, especially when it comes to plan ways of preventing their occurrence."

As noted above, in spite of all the research, the question remains, does the etiology of violence (i.e., homicide) rest within the social structure of society (Chapter 7), within the biological make-up (Chapter 5) or the personality of the perpetrator (Chapter 6)? In their book on murder, Silverman and Kennedy suggest there are two classes of theory that deal with homicide. The first relates to "individual social interaction and conflict." Among the theories they review under this classification are Hirschi's *control theory* (Chapter 7) and its newer derivations (e.g., *general theory of crime* and the *power control theory*—see Chapter 8). Also included under this general classification is the *routine activities theory* (Chapter 8).

The second class of theories described by Silverman and Kennedy involve societal-level theories. The authors start their review by pointing out that human behaviour does not operate in a vacuum but is subject to the effects of the economy, inequality, and the social disorganization in the cities and towns in which they live. They cite a variety of studies that lend support to the relationship between the presence of such factors and homicide rates. What remains unanswered is a clear picture of to how extensive economic inequality must be before murder rates increase. Also, what are some of the mediating preventive elements, and to what extent can economic inequality be used to explain the different types of homicide? Similar criticisms can be made of the social disorganization condition. For example, Blau and Blau (1982 cited in Silverman and Kennedy, 1992:60) found a high correlation between divorce and crime rates. But what is not clear is the level at which crime rates "suddenly" increase. To what extent do support groups for divorcées mitigate crime rates? Do the circumstances surrounding the divorce affect the likelihood of crime? These and other factors related to social disorganization have not been clearly operationalized.

Finally, Silverman and Kennedy (1992:53–58) offer a brief overview of "alternative approaches" to explaining homicide. Here they discuss some of the micro-level approaches such as the sociobiological perspective (Chapter 5), biologically-based explanations (Chapter 5), psychological approaches that emphasize the role of moral frustration (Chapter 6), as well as psychological theories that emphasize particular psychiatric disorders. For example, in early 1999, Dr. Harold Shipman, a father of four from Manchester, England, was charged with killing 15 of his female patients. The murders date back to 1995 and involved patients between the ages of 49 and 73 (MD accused ...1999). Why did he do it? At the time this chapter was prepared, there was only speculation as to the motivation behind the killings. But it is a story you might wish to follow on the Internet.

Again, as with the two main classifications mentioned above, the latter group of theories may be able to explain some types of murder but, given their narrow theoretical perspective, they are limited in their coverage. Until criminologists begin to recognize the complexity of human behaviour and the importance of applying an interdisciplinary approach to the study of murder, or any crime, we will have to settle for interesting but limited theoretical explanations. Consequently, our ability to control and prevent such incidents will continue to fall short of our objectives.

Patterns, Trends, and Characteristics of Homicides

In 1997, 77 per cent of all reported homicide incidents were solved by the police. Between 1987–97, the proportion has fluctuated between 77 per cent and 85 per cent. However, since the process of solving homicides can take some time, some incidents are not solved until years after they were initially recorded. For example, in Nova Scotia, Donald Marshall spent nearly a dozen years imprisoned for a murder he didn't commit. In other incidents, it has taken many years to discover that innocent people had been wrongfully convicted of murder (e.g., the wrongful convictions of Norman Fox, David Milgaard, Guy Paul Morin, and Gregory Parsons). Therefore, these data underestimate final police clearance rates.

Although there are no official statistics available, it would be interesting to know what role new police investigation strategies (e.g., DNA analysis, surveillance technology, etc.) are playing in solving homicides. Data are, however, available on the manner in which homicide incidents were cleared. In 1997:

- 86 per cent were cleared by a charge being laid;
- 12 per cent were cleared by the accused having committed suicide immediately following the offence (74 per cent were of a domestic nature);
- 2 per cent were cleared by death other than suicide; and
- 11 per cent (N=56) of all homicide incidents involved youth (*CCJS*,1998: 18(12)).[8]

Other interesting facts available through Statistics Canada provide useful information by which to profile homicide victims and their accused. We will simply highlight the major findings. They include:

- Homicides (approximately 87 per cent) continue to be committed by someone known to the victim. The risk of being killed by a stranger has remained relatively stable over the past decade at around 13 per cent. The report suggests, however, that prostitutes and taxi drivers, because of their exposure and vulnerability, are at greater risk than most other groups.

- Only 6 per cent of homicides involved multiple victims—a consistent trend over the past ten years.
- Nearly half of all persons charged with homicide had consumed alcohol and/or drugs, while nearly 40 per cent of all homicide victims had consumed alcohol and/or drugs.
- Contrary to some media images, police work in Canada is still relatively safe. In 1997 only one police officer was killed in the line of duty. Since 1961, the average number of officers killed in the line of duty per year has been three. This compares to 72 police officers killed in the United States in 1995. (Source: *CCJS*, 1998:18(12)).

In recent years, domestic violence has received considerable press, and victimization surveys show that people are more fearful of stranger-related victimization. Yet, between 1987 and 1997 people were more likely to be killed by acquaintances (approx. 46 per cent) while those killed by a spouse or other family member account for just less than 30 per cent of homicide incidents, and strangers only make up around 15 per cent. The data also show that in 1997, nearly two-thirds of the victims were killed in a private residence. Only two per cent were killed in areas "unknown" to the victim. Overall, the patterns reflect the social characteristics of the incident.

Over the years the data reveal that males continue to account for two-thirds of victims and 87 per cent of all those accused of homicide. In 1997, those individuals aged 18 and 19 represented the most common single age for someone accused of homicide while those in their mid-twenties and early thirties also account for a major proportion of homicide incidents (*CCJS*, 1998:18(12)).

Homicide by Method

"The attitude here is that guns are, for the most part, just useful implements...(while) in the United States, they are an end in themselves" Donald Webster, curator of Canadiana at the Royal Ontario Museum in Toronto (Simonds, 1996:45).

If you relied on the media to deduce which method of killing was the most common, you would likely conclude it was shooting. In fact that is true, though official data reveal that stabbing and beating victims to death is also fairly common (see Table 9–4).

These trends are of interest to criminologists as they try to answer such questions as whether gun control legislation is an effective deterrent, how many deaths involve firearms as opposed to rifles, how many are stolen versus owned weapons, etc.

TABLE 9—4

HOMICIDE BY METHOD: 1992–1997

	1992	1993	1994	1995	1996	1997
All methods	732	627	596	588	633	581
Shooting	247	195	196	176	212	193
Stabbing	210	191	154	183	195	168
Beating	151	116	106	120	132	115
Strangulation	62	77	83	70	59	52
Arson	35	17	17	20	8	27
Drowning	0	0	0	0	0	7*
Shaken Baby Syndrome					7	6
Others	21	21	34	12	5	8
Not known	6	4	6	7	11	5

* poisoning.

Source: Assorted years *CCJS* publications. (Vol. 18(12); Vol. 16(11)).

In recent years, there has been considerable concern and debate about the availability of firearms and their relationship to homicide. In particular Bill C-17, passed in 1992 while allowing ownership of semi-automatic weapons (similar to those used by Marc Lepine in 1989), places a strong emphasis on their control.[9] Similarly, the controversial Bill C-68, passed on January 1, 1996, now requires firearm owners to both register and licence all their firearms by January 2001. Has all this legislation helped to reduce homicide rates (see Boxes 9.4, 9.5, 9.6)? Has it helped to reduce homicides involving the use of firearms? Since 1979, firearms have accounted for one-third of all homicides (Table 9–4). Of these incidents, handguns represent about 40 per cent of all homicides. And since 1991, handguns have only accounted for one in every 10 homicides (*CCJS*, 1998:18(12)).[10]

Based on the data it is difficult to conclusively assert that the various legislative measures have produced the impact they were designed to have. What do you think?

FYI BOX 9.4

Capital Punishment in Canada

"In 1833, Ontario reduced its catalogue of capital crimes from over 100 to 12— murder, treason, rape, child molestation, homosexuality, bestiality, robbery, robbery of the mail, burglary, arson, and accessory to murder" (Boyd, 1988:22). The common method of capital punishment was hanging. After 1867 hangings were conducted out of sight.

HOMICIDE AND CAPITAL PUNISHMENT

Capital punishment was officially abolished in 1976 and again, by a narrow margin, in 1987 (Boyd, 1988). The last Canadian hanging, a double hanging, took place at Toronto's Don Jail on December 11, 1962. Ronald Trupin was hanged for shooting and killing a Toronto police officer and Arthur Lucas of Detroit was hanged for killing an undercover narcotic agent.

While Canada no longer practices capital punishment, in the 1990s there have been a number of cases involving Canadians charged with murder in the United States who had been placed on death row. One case in 1997, involved Ronald Smith, 39, formerly of Red Deer, Alberta. He had been sentenced to death three times for the killing of two Montana cousins. As of 1998, he was awaiting yet another decision on the reinstatement of his death sentence or commutation.

Perhaps the most publicized case of the 1990s is that of Joseph Stanley Faulder. Faulder spent most of his early years growing up in Alberta. In July 1975 he was convicted of brutally killing a 75-year-old woman from Gladwater, Texas after a bungled robbery attempt. He has managed to evade several death sentences and in June of 1997 received an indefinite stay of execution after some very public appeals by friends and family members in Canada. Faulder has always claimed his innocence and says his accomplice Lynda McCann killed Ms. Phillips (*The Ultimate Price*, 1997). He was due to be executed on December 10, 1998, when a last minute appeal stayed his execution. However, he was not granted clemency after obtaining a 90–day reprieve of execution. The Texas attorney-general's office set Faulder's next date with fate for March 12, 1999, but the decision must be approved by a judge before the state can proceed with the execution...(Texas executes...). The latest decision (March 2, 1999) is that he is now scheduled to die June 17, 1999, by lethal injection—worth $86.08 U.S. As of January 1, 1999, there were 3,549 death row inmates in the United States of which 74 were juveniles. In 1988, there were 68 executions with Texas accounting for over 30 per cent of all executions in the United States (Death Row U.S.A.: Winter 1998, 1999).

The last Canadian executed in the United States was Stan Buckowski of Toronto. He was gassed in 1952 in San Quentin for the killing of a California woman.

One of the most controversial executions in recent years involved the Texas execution of Karla Faye Tucker. A former prostitute and drug addict, Tucker was convicted of hacking to death a man and woman during a 1983 break-in. Her case received worldwide publicity, including pleas for mercy from the Pope and various church groups. She had become a born-again Christian and appeared by many accounts to have transformed her life. Tucker became the first woman in the twentieth century to be executed in the United States: by lethal injection on February 4, 1998 (Texas executes Tucker..., 1998).[11]

Kids Who Kill

Young offenders have been receiving considerable attention in recent years from
the public and politicians (See Appendix 5). Homicide data show that between
1987 and 1997 youth homicide rates have remained relatively stable. The rates
fluctuated between 1.5 and 2.5 per 100,000 youths. In 1995 however, the rate
jumped to 2.7. The Statistics Canada report was at a loss to explain the increase,
suggesting that it might just be part of the annual fluctuations in the numbers.

On average, 47 youths (ages 12–17) were charged each year between 1987
and 1997, accounting for an average of 11 per cent of homicides in 1997. Over
that ten year period nearly 30 per cent of the victims were under the age of 18
years (as compared with 11 per cent of victims of homicides committed by
adults). And as might be expected, the victims of young offenders are family
members (about 45 per cent) and friends or acquaintances (31 per cent).
Interestingly, the proportion for the killing of family members is almost twice
that reported in American studies (cited in Silverman and Kennedy, 1992:165).

While able to provide detailed descriptive information on kids who kill,
researchers have been less adept at explaining why they do it. Their explanations
run the gamut from *interpersonal conflicts* (e.g., gang-related killings) to *risky
lifestyles* (drug and alcohol abuse), to being motivated by *greed*.[12]

Ecology and Homicide

Another fact that is often overlooked by the public is that homicides, like all
crimes, are characterized by environmental, ecological, and social factors. For
example, homicide rates historically tend to be higher in western provinces than
in eastern ones. Throughout the 1990s, British Columbia has consistently
recorded the highest homicide rate, followed by Manitoba and Alberta.[13] For
1997 only BC, Alberta, Saskatchewan, and Manitoba had homicide rates above
the national average. The provinces with the lowest homicide rates were Prince
Edward Island and Newfoundland.

In 1984, the Canadian environmental criminologists Brantingham and
Brantingham observed that homicide rates vary not only with geographic region but

also between nations, in regions within a country, in communities, and even within urban neighbourhoods. For example, rates vary by city and their size. Looking at long-term averages, Vancouver and Edmonton had the highest rates (approximately 3.30) while smaller cities like Saskatoon averaged 3.59 homicides per 100,000 population, Sherbrooke 2.65, and Regina 1.51. Overall, cities with populations greater than 500,000 had an average homicide rate of 1.95 in 1997 while cities with populations between 250,000 and 499,999 averaged 1.81 and cities with populations between 100,000 and 249,999 averaged a rate of 1.92. Communities with populations under 100,000 inhabitants had a homicide rate of 1.91 in 1997. The variations in homicide patterns were stable when averaged between 1987 and 1997.

While a variety of social factors including *economic deprivation* and *inequality* (see above) have been used in an effort to explain the variations, less is known about the distribution of criminal opportunities that may affect the distribution of homicide rates (see Box 9.7). Furthermore, Canadian researchers Bursick and Grasmick (1993) point out that we understand little as to how and why offenders target certain neighbourhoods over others.

A CLOSER LOOK BOX 9.7

Why is Canada Less Violent Than the United States?

Being next door neighbours, we are often drawn to making comparisons with the United States. Not only are they our closest geographical neighbour but we have many things in common. We both speak English, we can both trace our heritage to European and Aboriginal people, we are both consumer-oriented countries, and our criminal justice systems share numerous similarities. Yet we differ on a number of economic, social, and political factors (see Box 1.1). In addition, our crime rates are dramatically different. As indicated in the box below, the homicide rate in the United States is about 4.5 times higher than Canada's, its robbery rate about 2.5 times higher and its aggravated assault rate 4 times higher than Canada's.

CANADIAN AND AMERICAN VIOLENT CRIME RATES: 1993 PER 100,000

Crime	Canada	United States
Homicide	2.1	9.5
Aggravated Assault	11	440
Robbery	104	256

Source: Canada – UCR data. United States – Federal Bureau of Investigation.

A variety of reasons have been offered to account for these differences.
• Canada has less inequality than does the United States.
• Canada has stricter gun control legislation than the United States.

In **summary**, and fortunately in Canada, contrary to media portrayal and coverage, murder is still a comparatively infrequent incident and has been on the decline in the latter half of the 1990s.

While homicide rates have remained stable, we observed that young men kill more than any other segment of the population, victims are more likely to be single, separated, or divorced, they are likely to be acquainted with their assailant, and homicide rates are higher in western than eastern Canada. Explanations as to why people kill cover the spectrum from sociological and psychological to biological and sociobiological perspectives. However, given our limited ability to understand and develop social policies that can reduce homicide rates, an integrated and interdisciplinary approach that deals with ecological factors, lifestyle factors, motivations, personalities, and social settings is needed. Developing such a model, however, presents a major challenge to criminologists and its prospects remain to be determined.

Only when criminologists gain a better understanding of the characteristics of people who kill can they recommend, and subsequently implement, sound policies to apprehend, detect, punish or treat offenders and to protect citizens.

Sexual Assault

REALITY CHECK BOX 9.8

WHO CAN YOU TRUST?

- Former hockey coach Graham James was sentenced to 3 years for sexually assaulting two young hockey players more than ten years earlier. In 1997, Sheldon Kennedy of the NHL's Detroit Red Wings became the first professional hockey player to publicly disclose that he had been sexual abused by his former junior hockey coach.

- A 13-year-old boy was charged in Brampton, Ontario for sexually assaulting 8 fellow female students (ages 11–13) over a five month period in May 1997 (Boy 13, charged...).
- From 1994 to 1996, Toronto police investigated 10,000 incidents of physical, sexual, or negligent abuse of children in the Toronto area. Of this number, 2,734 cases involved sexual assaults (*Globe and Mail*, 1997, March 28).
- Based on a study of more than 1,000 cases, Edward Renner, a psychology professor at Carleton University in Ottawa, found the courts do not appear to take sexual assault cases seriously when meting out punishment[14] (Sexual assaults not..., 1997).

The above examples show that sexual assault cuts across all social classes and ages in North America. It is an issue that the courts may not be taking seriously despite what legal measures have been introduced.

In 1983, under Bill C-127, a new section was added to the Canadian *Criminal Code*. Section 266 replaced what was formerly known as "common assault." The new section now allows police to arrest a suspect when they have "reasonable and probable grounds" to believe that an assault was committed.

Today, the Code distinguishes between three levels of sexual assault. They include acts that involve:

1. No serious bodily harm or physical injury to the victim. This is also referred to as "common assault."

2. A greater degree of force or threatened force (e.g., with weapon and/or injury) and involves a degree of bodily harm such as broken bones, bruises, and cuts. A slap across the face would not constitute a Level 2 assault.

3. Aggravated assault. Under Level 3 the victim is disfigured, maimed, wounded, or has his or her life endangered.

Sexual Assault Rates

In 1997, there were over 27,063 sexual assaults. These numbers break down to a rate of 86 per 100,000 population for Level 1 offences, 2 per 100,000 for Level 2, and 1 per 100,000 for level 3 sexual assaults (*CCJS*, 1998:18(12)). And while 1997 marked the fourth consecutive year of decline, it is still 6 per cent higher than it was in 1987.

Non-sexual assault (i.e., Level 1) accounts for nearly three-quarters of all violent crimes. Therefore, these incidents have a major influence on the overall violent crime rate. Since 1983, common assaults increased steadily until 1991, when new directives to police agencies across the country to treat spousal assaults more seriously came into effect. Thereafter minor assaults have levelled off. These new directives had a significant impact on police clearance rates. Before

1983, approximately 30 per cent of all Level 1 charges laid were cleared. In 1983, the clearance rate rose to 40 per cent and in 1994 to 61 per cent. As the report notes, "it seems plausible that the charging policies police have adopted with respect to spousal violence, and the special training given to police to handle these cases, have encouraged greater numbers to come forward, which, in turn, has increased the rate of assault recorded by police" (Ibid, 8).

How Might We Explain the Trends?

Between 1983 and 1993 there was a steady increase in Level 1 sexual assault rates (Johnson, 1996). Then, as with many other forms of violent crime, Level 1, along with Level 2 and Level 3 sexual assault declined through 1997 (see Table 9–5). Can the recent decline be attributed to law reform? Referring to several studies, a Statistics Canada report suggests that the law has made it easier to report sexual attacks and has broadened the sentencing options. However, the research does not support the premise that the law alone can account for the sharp increase. The data provide no evidence to indicate that the increase in child victims, or increased reporting of spousal abuse cases, are sufficient to account for the increase. Instead, recent studies suggest a number of alternative explanations for the dramatic increase in reported sexual assaults. They include:

- The 1970s and 1980s saw significant changes in the social, economic, and political status of women;
- The media gave increasing attention to the rights of victims—in particular, women;
- The growth of the women's movement;
- Expansion of sexual assault support centres;
- The increasing number of hospitals of specialized teams trained to deal positively with victims of sexual assault;
- An increase in the disclosing of sexual assaults that occurred in the victim's distant past; and
- Intensive lobbying by women's groups, which preceded the passage of the rape reform legislation. (Source: Johnson, 1996:146–147).

Given the growing trend in sexual assaults what can/might we do about curbing this trend? Before we think about this, it should also be pointed out that according to various recent studies (e.g., Roberts and Geboyts, 1992; Roberts and Grossman, 1994) the official data are underestimates of the actual numbers. In one recent study, respondents informed Statistics Canada that they considered the assault (in the legal sense) to be "too minor" (44 per cent) while others wanted to keep the incident private (12 per cent), or were ashamed or embarrassed to report the sexual assault (9 per cent) (Criminal justice processing..., 1994). However, as noted earlier, more women are reporting sexual assaults to police.

TABLE 9-5

SEXUAL ASSAULT RATES 1990–1997

YEAR	NUMBER	RATE PER 100,000
1990	27,843	100
1991	30,351	108
1992	34,355	120
1993	34,754	120
1994	31,690	108
1995	28,183	95
1996	27,026	90
1997	27,063	89

Sources: *CCJS*, Assorted Canadian Crime Statistics. (Vol. 15(12); 6 for years 1990–1994 and Vol. 18(11):18 for remaining years).

While common sexual assaults remain high, the rates for Levels 2 and 3 have remained constant between 1 and 4 per 100,000. Between 1983 and 1994 rates for rape and indecent assault increased "only" 18 per cent (from 38 to 45 per 100,000) (*CCJS*, 1996:16(6)). This compares to an overall increase of 152 per cent for all sexual assaults from 1983 to 1993. However, when one takes into account the fact that almost 4 in 10 women have experienced at least one form of sexual assault in adulthood, it works out to over four million Canadian women! In addition, of those women who have been sexually assaulted, almost 60 per cent have been assaulted more than once. Of that number, 26 per cent were assaulted four or more times (Johnson, 1996:139). These are alarming figures and beg the question "why"?

In spite of the 1983 *Criminal Code* amendments and all the new public awareness programs and support services, when compared to Statistics Canada's Violence Against Women (VAW) survey findings official counts still reflect that "very few cases of sexual assault are reported to the police" (Johnson, 1996:143). In fact, using the 1993 General Social Survey data, Johnson (Violent Crime in Canada, 1996) observes that 90 per cent of sexual assaults were not reported to police! This compares to 68 per cent of other assaults and 53 per cent of robberies.

Characteristics of Victims of Sexual Assault

The characteristics of the sexual attacker fit the general stereotype. Over forty per cent of sexual offenders had been drinking at the time of the incident. Women under the age of 18 were the most common victims (60 per cent in 1997) and most sexual assaults occurred in a private residence. Female victims were more likely to be attacked by a stranger (23 per cent) than male victims (13 per cent). In recent years, there has been increased interest in and awareness that *date-rape* is a problem. In 1993, 12 per cent of women had been assaulted by a date or boyfriend (see Box 9.9).

A CLOSER LOOK BOX 9.9

Date rape and Date-rape Drugs

- Date rape has drawn considerable attention in recent years. In North America the issue gained front-page attention when *Katie Keostner* went public with her story in 1991. While attending college in the United States she was sexually assaulted by a fellow student.
- In 1996 a story on a new date-rape drug attracted considerable media attention. Known as "roofies" (flunitrazepam, marketed under the trade name of rohypnol), they look like aspirin but are tasteless and odourless, decrease blood pressure and have the ability to send the victim into a deeply relaxed state. But what is more alarming for the victim is that the drug also causes amnesia—the victims don't remember what happens during the time they were on the drug (Daterape—Internet, 1997).[15] In 1999, police began to respond to the growing concern of date-rape drugs. One house-raid in Vancouver resulted in the seizure of 3,500 doses of rohypnol, and similar raids in other major Canadian cities have resulted in sseizures of rohypnol and similar drugs (Williams, 1999).
- Other recent date-rape drugs that are appearing include GHB (gammahydroxybutyrate), also known as "liquid ecstasy," and "easy lay." Unlike rohypnol, GHB is a home-made drug and has been promoted as a steroid alternative for bodybuilders. Like rohypnol, GHB has a short lifespan in the blood stream—between 12 and 36 hours (Date rape: Drug..., 1998). However, unlike rohypnol, GHB has prosexual properties. This makes it difficult for police to investigate rape victims if they do not come forward quickly and defendants can claim that the sexual encounter was consensual. Prosecution is further complicated by the fact that GHB is difficult to detect in the urine.

Special K or Ketamine Hydrochloride has become something of a teen "rave" drug in the late 1990s. Originally the drug was intended as an anesthetic for pediatric patients and was used in veterinary clinics. Among its reported effects are memory impairment and deep sleep, heightened sexual elation, and "the capability of the victim to respond to verbal commands while asleep" (Brenzinger, 1998:29). Burundanga is an extract from the Datura Arobea tree in Columbia. The extract takes effect immediately and the victim usually has no recall while under its influence (Ibid).

These and probably yet-to-be discovered drugs are being used to commit sexual assaults and are being used by serial rapists.

Reducing the risk of being victimized by "sex" drugs
- Do not leave your beverage unattended.
- Do not accept any beverage from someone you do not know well or trust.
- When you are out, avoid beverages that you did not open yourself or that were not opened in front of you.
- Do not let someone talk you into trying a "new" drink.
- Adopt a buddy system when you go out.
- If you think you have been drugged dial 911 immediately and give a urine sample. Keep the beverage and give it to the police (adapted from Brenzinger, 1998:29).

Is it possible to try to control the making of such clandestine drugs? What kinds of proactive steps might law enforcement agencies initiate? Should legislators introduce new and stricter penalties for the abuse of such drugs?

Between 1983 and 1993, the rates of sexual assaults Level 2 and 3 have remained stable at about 4 per 100,000 and 2 per 100,000 inhabitants, respectively (Johnson, 1996). However, as indicated in Table 9–5 above, since 1993 the number and rate of sexual assaults has continued to decline. This compares to a rate of 40.6 forcible rapes per 100,000 females in the United States in 1993, or more accurately approximately 84 per 100,000 females in large cities, down to 49 per 100,000 in rural counties (UCR, 1994).

Meanwhile, clearance rates for sexual assaults have increased from 63 per cent in 1983 to 75 per cent in 1994 (Johnson, 1996). It appears that the 1983 legislation, along with increased social awareness and willingness of victims to report, have had a positive impact on clearance rates. However, neither social policy changes nor focusing on sex-role stereotype explanations has done much to curb Level 1 sexual assaults. Their rates have increased significantly.

Although no data are available for Canadian women, an American study found that approximately 20 per cent of females under the age of 12 had been raped by their fathers, 26 per cent attacked by other relatives, and 50 per cent assaulted by friends or acquaintances. Contrary to popular belief, only 4 per cent of rape victims under 12 had been attacked by strangers (Langan and Harlow, 1994).

Official statistics reveal that in more than one-third of all assault cases, both victim and accused had consumed alcohol or drugs before an assault (Johnson, 1996). As for the relationship between the victim and offender, it varies somewhat according to the type of assault. For example, in 1993 the majority of major assaults and common assaults involved "casual acquaintances" (about 33 per cent) with spousal or ex-spousal assault ranking near the top (Ibid).

Although laws and social attitudes have changed in recent years, the General Social Survey (GSS) (see Chapter 3) indicates that only about 30 per cent of assaults were reported to police between 1988 and 1993. As in the American study cited above, Canadian respondents choose not to report assaults because: (1) victims prefer to deal with the problem in another way (12 per cent), (2) they feel that it is a personal matter (12 per cent), or (3) they consider the incident too minor to report (44 per cent) (*CCJS*, 1994:14(7)).

When comparing official trends with the GSS results, the data reveal that, while victimization rates have not increased, there has been an increase in official reporting. In addition to demonstrating that the two surveys are measuring the same phenomenon in different ways, the differences reveal that those social attitudes and social policies are having a positive impact on victims reporting sexual assaults.

Although clearance rates have gone up from 69 per cent in 1983 to 72 per cent in 1994, the law does not seem to have had "a significant effect on the way police respond to suspects" (*CCJS*, 1996:16(6)). For example, according to the VAW survey, the perpetrator was only charged in 34 per cent of all reported sexual assault cases (54 per cent if the offender was known to the woman and 24 per cent if he was a stranger) (Johnson, 1996). The difference was accounted for by the fact that positive identification of a stranger may be more problematic.

Unfortunately data on conviction rates and sentencing of perpetrators are very limited. However, a 1994 Canadian Centre for Justice Statistics report does provide a breakdown for sentencing practices for 1991–92 (see Table 9-6). Overall, 81 per cent of those charged with sexual assault receive a prison sentence[16] while 47 per cent receive a probation order.

TABLE 9—6

COURT DISPOSITIONS FOR SEXUAL ASSAULT CASES HEARD IN PROVINCIAL COURT, PER CENT DISTRIBUTION 1991–1992

DISPOSITION	SEXUAL ASSAULT LEVEL 1	SEXUAL ASSAULT LEVEL 2	SEXUAL ASSAULT LEVEL 3
Prison	60	94	89
Probation	73	35	33
Probation	19	26	33
Community service order	2	—	—
Fine	15	2	6
Suspended sentence	20	2	—
Conditional discharge	3	—	—
Absolute discharge	1	—	—

Note: Columns do not total 100 per cent because of multiple sentences.

Source: *CCJS*, 1994:14(7).

In **summary**, sexual assault is not only classified as a serious violent crime but it is alarmingly common, especially among young women, in Canada. And while new legislation and services have been introduced to try and address the problem, the data suggest that the impact has at best been minimal.

Efforts to explain sexual violence have been varied but among the more common theoretical orientations are those that relate sexual assaults to the offenders' personal pathologies. Using a psychological approach, Groth (1979) points to sexual perpetrators being driven by pathologies: for power, by anger, or by sadism. Sociological studies meanwhile point to such social factors as the social learning process within lower-class subcultures where violence is seen as a way of life, and the mass media, which often depict the sexual exploitation of women in ways that reinforce such actions (Ellis, 1989). One of the issues Gwynn Nettler examines in his 1982 book, *Killing One Another*, is whether violence breeds violence. If we watch sporting events or watch kids in the playground during recess, the answer almost seems obvious—yes violence does breed violence! Drawing on the *social learning model* and by careful examination of the literature, Nettler came to the same conclusion.

Feminist theorists meanwhile consider sexual violence to be the product of deeprooted patriarchal traditions in which men are encouraged to dominate all aspects of life, including women (see Schwendinger and Schwendinger, 1983, and Chapter 8). In this view, women are seen as little more than property to be used and sexually exploited.

Even *biology* and *sociobiology* have offered their interpretation of sexual violence. Drawing on the notion of evolution, sociobiologists say that men have an innate drive to create offspring. The lower the degree of certainty (e.g., impotence, personal attractiveness, and social conditioning) the greater men's tendency to turn to sexually-inappropriate behaviours such as rape, child molesting, being a voyeur, and collecting pornographic material (see Holmes, 1991). Maccoby and Jenkins (1974) reported that men tend to be more visual than women are and more aggressive, curious and dominant (see Chapter 13). Hence, they may be more (biologically) predisposed to respond inappropriately to women under certain circumstances. For example, when a 29-year-old known pedophile was charged with violating a probation, of possessing pornographic material and being within a block of an area where young children were often present, the court demanded he "take any treatments provided, including chemical castration," not possess any pornographic material, not consume alcohol, and not go near children. Claiming he wanted to control his urges, the pedophile agreed to all the conditions (Slade, 1999b).

Unfortunately, these varied explanations make it difficult to identify which line *social policy* needs to, or can, take to curb the problem. Furthermore, some of the "newer" forms of assault present additional ethical and moral concerns and challenges (e.g., elderly abuse, child abuse, date rape, etc.). Therefore, criminologists should perhaps look more closely at adopting an integrated and interdisciplinary approach that might provide better prospects of insight into this and other violent crimes.

Robbery

In his book on robbery in Canada, Desroches (1995:1) describes robbery as "one of the most feared crimes common to large urban centres" because of "its sudden nature and the threat of death or serious injury." In addition, robbery also entails a double element of fear: losing one's property and the risk of suffering physical harm. The fact is however robberies account for only about 10 per cent of all violent crimes (A profile of robbery…, 1995).

Next to murder, robbery easily attracts our attention, perhaps because of its lack of predictability and element of public fascination. Movies like the "Great Train Robbery" recount the famous British mail train robbery of 1963 in which 2,631,784 English pounds was stolen by eleven robbers. One of the robbers, Ronald Biggs, who successfully escaped from Wandsworth prison after serving only 15 months of a 30-year prison sentence, has written a book about the event. The book is titled *Old Man Out* (1996). Today Biggs leads a comfortable life in Rio de Janeiro, Brazil where he is exempt from extradition (Ronald Arthur Biggs, 1996).

Biggs has a webpage on the Internet that can be accessed through: **www. bscene.com.au/biggs/welcome.html**. On November 13, 1997 Biggs successfully won an attempt against being extradited back to Britain from Brazil. The Brazilian Supreme Federal Tribunal ruled that the request exceeded their statute of limitations.

The Canadian movie *The Grey Fox* is a wonderful film on the life and times of the notorious Canadian train robber Bill Miner. Miner first made a career out of robbing stage coaches in the United States until he was caught and sent to jail for nearly thirty-four years. On his release in 1904, he drifted north to British Columbia's Nicola Valley.

Miner and two accomplices began a spree of train robberies. He became known as "the gentleman bandit" and is credited with coining the phrase "stick-em-up." Between 1904 and 1906 he became well-known to the North West Mounted Police and Canadian Pacific Railway, who offered a $5,000 reward for his capture. On his capture, he was sentenced to life in prison at New Westminster's penitentiary. On August 8, 1907 he escaped and fled to the United States.

His freedom was short-lived. In 1912 Miner was caught after robbing a train in Georgia. Again, he managed to escape but his advancing years made it more difficult to stay out of reach of the law. He was quickly recaptured, exhausted and critically-ill. He died in the prison hospital in 1913 (Anderson, 1982). The movie paints a more romantic ending, showing the locals helping him to escape to Europe with his true love and supposedly live happily ever after on his illegally-gotten gains.

Clermont (1996) observes that popular literature and the media often romanticize robbery. The most famous of such incidents might well be the story of Robin Hood who took from the rich and gave to the poor. His fictional story, set in Sherwood Forest in North Nottingham during the twelfth century, has been portrayed in television shows, cartoons, books, and movies such as Kevin Costner's 1992 version.

In this section, we will examine some of the recent trends of robbery in Canada. However, as defined in s. 343 of the *Criminal Code,* the meaning of robbery, while specific, is also broad in its characteristics and sub-types. Section 343 of the Code contains four parts that state that every one commits "robbery" who "in stealing uses violence or threats of violence against a person or property; steals from any person and, at the time of the offence wounds, beats, strikes, or assaults the victim; and, one who steals from another person while armed with an offensive weapon or imitation thereof." The definition clearly reflects the notion that robbery is an act of violence.

While the Canadian legal definition emphasizes the act of violence, Normandeau (1968) points out that in the United States robbery is more commonly associated with property-related crimes or "burglary." Robbery is defined as "the unlawful taking or attempted taking of property that is in the immediate possession of another by force or threat of force or violence and /or by putting the victim in fear." Desroches (1995:9) further notes that this is related to the fact that in some States "penal codes define robbery as a property offence while other states define it as an offence against the person."[17]

The sub-types of robbery can include highway robbery, street robbery (using force to steal a woman's purse or mugging), and armed robbery (e.g., banks). In addition to their practical differences, research shows that the various sub-types are also characterized by differences related to offender traits, motivation for the crime, and modus operandi (i.e., method of operation).

Therefore, in addition to looking at general robbery rates we will also examine some of the different robbery types and typology of robbers. They will illustrate how certain types of robberies are more prevalent than others and that not all robbers "are cut from the same cloth."

Characteristics of Robbery and Robbers

In 1997, 29,590 robberies were reported to the police, a rate of 98 per 100,000 population. Although this represents an 8 per cent decline over 1996, from Table 9–7 it can be seen that the rates have fluctuated, with the lowest rate being recorded in 1978, at 82, and the highest rate in 1991 at 118 per 100,000 inhabitants. The most popular targets for robbers are commercial establishments (e.g., banks (9 per cent), gas stations (6 per cent), and convenience stores (11 per cent)). Those accounted for 51 per cent of all robberies in 1994, while 40 per cent took place either on the street or in some other public place. What might account for the fluctuations in robbery rates?

TABLE 9–7

ROBBERY RATES 1978–1997: WEAPON VS. NON-WEAPON USE

	RATE* OF ROBBERY (USING A FIREARM)	RATE* OF ROBBERY (NO WEAPON INVOLVED)
1978	30	38
1980	35	46
1982	36	48
1984	27	41
1986	26	40
1988	23	42
1990	27	46
1991	32	53
1992	31	48
1993	28	42
1994	25	42
1995	23	45
1996	22	48
1997	18	47

Sources: Adapted from Clermont, 1996:90; CCJS. Assorted years of Canadian Crime Statistics. Vol. 15(12): 6–11 for years 1978–1993, and Vol. 18(11):18 for remaining years.
* Per 100,000.

"Causes" of Robbery

Clermont (1996) suggests that a high unemployment rate among males in the age 15–24 age group might explain the robbery trends. A 1992 Statistics Canada report on robbery indicates that about two-thirds of those accused were under the age of 25 and virtually no accused was older than 50. Tracking the robbery rates and the unemployment rates between 1978 and 1993, Clermont shows that in the early 1980s when unemployment increased for young males so did the robbery rates. Similarly, as the unemployment rates dropped in the late 1980s so did the robbery rates.

What Clermont does not take into account are the different types of robberies and whether males between the ages of 15–24 are largely accountable for the changes. For example, is there a decline in "opportunistic" robbery, those robberies committed on impulse, or a decline in "professional" robberies versus "addict" robbers? In an earlier study, Dunn (1976:9) provides data to support the notion that variations in robberies correspond to one or more "geosocial attributes"—between an "offense characteristic and an area attribute." This explanatory approach is somewhat interdisciplinary as it acknowledges both environmental factors and social attributes within an area (see Box 9.10). In his effort to explain an interrelationship, Dunn concludes by stating the "price of complexity is often an increase in the problems (both moral and operational) of control, the price of simplicity may be the total absence of control" (p. 34).

BY THE NUMBERS BOX 9.10

BANK ROBBERIES IN CANADA

- In 1982, the *Canadian Banker* published the results of a bank robbery study comparing five major Canadian cities (Montreal, Toronto, Calgary, Edmonton, and Vancouver). Between 1967 and 1972, Montreal and Toronto bank robbery rates were fairly similar when suddenly Montreal's bank robbery rate jumped. It became the bank robbery capital of the country. In 1980, Montreal's bank robbery rate was 83.9 per 1000 branches compared with Vancouver's 37.4 and Toronto's 11.4. The article notes that despite target-hardening strategies they found that "prevention is a short-term solution to criminality" (p. 41). The article concludes by refuting possible explanations such as economic differences and cultural characteristics of Quebecers.[18] Instead they suggest that the problem in Montreal can best be explained in terms of an *amplification process.* This process includes a variety of factors: low rate of solution, changes within the criminal element of the population, the number of targets, and possibly their architectural aspects, etc. No solutions were offered.

- The rate of bank robberies increased from 1160 in 1984 to 1244 incidents in 1989. Then from 1990 through 1994 the number of bank robbery incidents jumped to around 1600 incidents per year. Desroches (1995:35) suggests the increase "reflects the emergence of the so-called 'beggar-bandit'—the robber who works alone, enters the bank, and passes a note to the teller demanding ('begging for') money." In addition, the "baby boom" (a demographic hypothesis) could also account for the increase of bank robberies since young offenders who may lack self-control commit most robberies. This line or reasoning is consistent with *social control theory.*

- Official data from 1993 and 1995 shows there has been a shift in robberies according to metropolitan areas. Although there is no breakdown by type of robbery, Vancouver led the way in 1993 with a robbery rate of 458 per 100,000 followed by Montreal (379) and Winnipeg (238). For the 1993 trend Clermont (1996:92) suggests it was due to "the economic and population 'boom' experienced in British Columbia..."[19] Director of Security for the Canadian Bankers Association, Paul Sacciol (1998) provided data that showed that between 1993 and 1997, the total number of bank robberies dropped from 1782 to 1316 and similar to Clermont's observations, the data provided by Sacciol showed that between 1993 and 1997, the "bank robbery capital" of Canada has tended to shift between Montreal and Toronto.

Finally, Desroches (1995:208) offers a comprehensive overview of other possible explanations for robbery but ends by concluding "little is presently known about offender decision-making in their selection of target victims" or what motivates someone to become a robber. Using the *rational choice theory* (Chapter 7), Desroches reasons that "their rationality is limited to what seems reasonable at the time, given their financial needs and the limited alternatives and opportunities open to them" (p. 106). But why then do others in the same predicament turn to other forms of criminal activity, while others do not? How does one measure "rationality" and "seems reasonable," and what constitutes "their financial needs." I, for example, wouldn't mind having more disposable income and at times I feel constrained by my salary. Yet I have never robbed anyone including a bank. Have criminologists been missing part of the theoretical puzzle?

Robbery offenders are more likely to use weapons than are other types of offenders. Data show that nearly 25 per cent of robberies involve the use of firearms while another quarter involved the use of an offensive weapon (e.g., clubs and knives). In 1997, 18 per 100,000 robberies involved the use of a firearm. The rate has been declining every year since 1991 when the rate was 32.

Almost half of the robbers use, or threaten to use, physical violence. And while the element of violence is present, only one-quarter of robbery victims received some type of minor injury, of which only four per cent required immediate medical attention (*CCJS*, 1992:12(10)).

The perceived seriousness of robbery is reflected in the fact that more than 80 per cent of those convicted of robbery are incarcerated. Of those, over 75 per cent are placed in federal institutions (Desroches, 1995). Individuals convicted for robbery made up approximately 20 per cent of the federal inmate population between 1986 and 1991 (*CCJS*, 1992:12(10)). However, in their study of federal inmates, Motiuk and Belcourt (1995) found that the proportion of federal inmates who had been convicted of robbery was almost one-third.

A recent Canadian report indicates that "the age of onset of criminality for armed robbery offenders was, on average, 12, while occasional armed robbery offenders didn't tend to begin their criminal career until 15" (A profile of robbery ..., 1995:3). The study further points out that *association*, "both during adolescence and adulthood" seem to be more strongly correlated to the likelihood of a person becoming involved in armed robbery. Although the report does not specify, the characteristics seem comparable to the *differential association theory* (Chapter 7). However, given our discussion, this interpretation may be too simplistic, as the report fails to operationalize or clearly define what is meant by association. Furthermore, the study neglects to clarify how "association" was empirically measured.

As is the case with murder and other forms of violent crime, regular alcohol and/or drug use was common to about half of the offenders (A profile of robbery ..., 1995) (see Box 9.11). Perhaps not surprisingly, as youths they were likely to have become involved in stealing as a means to support their recreational habits. Then with age, depending on critical factors, their behaviour might escalate to robbery.

REALITY CHECK BOX 9.11

THE VANCOUVER ROBBERY PREVENTION PROGRAM FOR CONVENIENCE STORES

While the magnitude and monetary loss in convenience store robberies is not as significant a problem as other types of theft, such as shoplifting, employee theft, fraudulent cheques, or break-and-enter, it is nevertheless an important and unique type of crime (Kingsbury, 1973). In the early 1980s convenience store robbery was becoming a serious concern.[20] In 1981, a program was initiated in response to a community plea for assistance after a number of robberies involving injuries to store employees had taken place. Between 1981 and 1984 convenience store robberies were the second most prevalent type of robbery next to financial institutions.

Based on a modified *environmental crime prevention model,* the Robbery Information Program (RIP) for convenience stores was designed to proactively deter store robberies and to make it easier for employees to identify the robber(s). The RIP included a number of important elements: (1) crime prevention seminars for all businesses, (2) a package which included two height gauge charts to be placed by the door, (3) an eyewitness identification sheet, (4) stickers denoting that no large bills were kept in the till, (5) door decals identifying that the store was a participant in the RIP program, (6) emergency call number decals, and (7) two general information sheets for employees. Overall, the findings of the pilot study found that the program had a positive impact on those stores that participated. They averaged lower financial losses per incident, there was a marked decline in the number of injuries to staff, and staff were generally better informed about the procedures that should be followed in case of a robbery. One of the limitations of the RIP was obtaining store compliance, (less than 20 per cent) (Roesch and Winterdyk, 1985).

Since the introduction of the program it has become more widely accepted across Canada and it exemplifies criminological theory and research being put into practice and having a real impact. However, nothing is ever fool-proof. England has been one of the most progressive countries in using CCTV (closed circuit television cameras) to monitor problem areas. A 1998 report observed that muggers in London have simply taken to moving just out of view of the cameras to commit their crimes. In 1997, muggings went up 20 per cent. The police have taken to soliciting more community support (Hyder, 1998).

Section III: Contemporary Issues in Canadian Criminology

In **summary**, robbery tends to capture the public's interest because of the double-edged fears of loss of property, and of injury. In this section we have learnt that there is much we can say about the nature, extent, characteristics, and various motivational components of robbery. Most of what has been described is based on correlations between robbery and various aspects of different social, individual, and cultural variables. However, we have also seen that no criminological theory can clearly link a causal explanation for robbery to any specific set of variables. For example, why is it that female robbers' chief motivation is financial gain? Why do female robbers tend to act in response to external circumstances such as intoxication, financial need, or peer pressure (see Fortune, Vega, and Silverman, 1980)? None of the theories reviewed appears able to provide a clear answer. When it comes to social policy and robbery prevention, criminologists can offer little. And what they do offer should be done with considerable care for, as Desroches (1995:272) concludes, "some of the broadly based changes advocated in the social and economic structure of society are difficult and expensive to produce and may not be politically feasible."

"New" Forms of Violence

So far, we have examined the more traditional forms of violent behaviour. In recent years, however, there has been an increase in other forms of violence. In this section, we will focus on only a few of these emerging crimes of violence: abduction, hate crime (see Box 9.2), stalking, and terrorism. As with the previous sections, we will examine some of the trends and patterns of the new forms of violence and explore some of their explanations.

Abduction

- Dec. 11, 1996: A Windsor, Ontario man kidnapped his former girlfriend at gunpoint. She had separated from him sometime earlier and had obtained a restraining order against him. He had been drinking before kidnapping her (*Calgary Herald*).

- January 20, 1997: A Prince George, B.C. man armed with a knife released his hostages and surrendered peacefully to police at the local McDonald's restaurant. He had been drinking beer and wanted radio time to complain about losing custody of his children (*Calgary Herald*).

- March 26, 1997: A 75-year-old Ottawa, Ontario man was arrested after a 50-year-old man came forward recalling a kidnapping and sexual abuse incident that had happened 37 years earlier. On searching the home of the accused, numerous photographs were found of masked boys, possibly ten, in bondage and hanging by the waist from trees. The case involved serial kidnappings over a long period (*Calgary Herald*).

- There are approximately 400 abductions per year in Canada and 350,000 per year in the United States. In Canada, parental abductions are four times as likely to occur when a custody order exists (Kiedrowski and Jayewardene, 1994). By contrast Colombia averaged more than 1,000 kidnappings every year since 1993. In a feature article, Darling (1998) observed that abductions plague Latin American nations.

As can be seen from the recent examples in the Box insert, abduction can be committed for different reasons and usually carries the risk of potential harm for those being held hostage for ransom. When abduction takes the form of hostage-taking and involves risk of harm or violence, the act may then be defined as an act of terrorism (see below).

The entry, "Abduction," in the Index of the 1999 *Criminal Code,* refers the researcher to Kidnapping and Hostage Taking. They are all defined in ss. 280–283, 279, and 179.1 respectively. We will only address abductions, as the official statistics do not provide a breakdown for kidnappings or hostage takings. Abductions refer to the unlawful taking of a person under the age of sixteen, or in contravention of a custody order.

Between 1990 and 1997 the number of abductions has fluctuated from 1,046 in 1990 to a high of 1,220 in 1992. In 1997, there were 982 abductions. The rate has remained stable at 3 to 4 per 100,000 population. Therefore, while the over-all rate of abduction may be low, the majority of abduction cases involve contravening custody orders. These cases usually involve children who are often helpless pawns caught in the bitter struggle between divorced or separated parents. However, as Kiedrowski and Jayewardene (1994) report, research has not yet produced helpful psychological or sociological profiles of abducting types. General characteristics include an employed father and unemployed mother, with the majority of children being between the ages of 3 and 7 years old, no gender bias about who gets abducted, and children usually being taken during weekends or summer or winter holidays. Seldom is physical force used (Ibid).

Today, with high divorce rates, abducting children continues to present a social problem. It is an issue that requires the attention of criminologists, social workers, psychologists and sociologists to better understand abductions and the various motivations underlying the act.

Hate Crime

Given that hate crime, or bias crimes, is defined and described in Box 9.2 on p. 297, we will focus on its various roots and policy implications. In addition, while hate crime is classified as a crime of violence it can also be a property-related offence.

Jacobs and Henry (1996) suggest hate crime started from the moment European settlers arrived and made Aboriginal people a target. Since then, recent immigrants, along with other minority groups, have also been targeted. According to Jack McDevitt and Jack Levin (1993), hate crime usually involves some planning. The motives for such crimes of violence reflect three different types of motives:

- *Thrill-seeking hate crimes.* Occasionally a group of hatemongers will join forces to "raise a little hell" by terrorizing minorities and/or their property. They derive a sadistic sense of satisfaction from threatening and/or terrorizing these groups. In June 1997, the family dog of one of four Filipino sailors seeking refugee status in Canada was killed and the family threatened. Why? The Filipino crew members, on arriving in Halifax, had reported to authorities that they had witnessed six Taiwanese officers throwing three stowaways overboard from the Maersk Dubai in May 1996 (*Calgary Herald,* 1997, June 17). The attack on the family dog was an attempt to scare the family out of the community and an attempt to silence the sailors so they wouldn't testify in court against the Taiwanese officers.

- *Reactive hate crimes:* When an "outsider" is seen as a threat he or she may become the victim of a perpetrator's sense of righteousness and community. For example, in June, 1997 a Missoulian, Montana, man stabbed his roommate three times with an ice pick after failing to convince him to become a heterosexual. The two men had been drinking and the offender been trying for some time to "convert" his roommate (Moore, 1997).

- *Mission hate crimes:* The Ku Klux Klan, white supremacy groups (e.g., Identity Church, Aryan Nations, and The Order—see White, 1991), and the "skinheads" represent groups who feel it is their duty to rid the world of evil. They see it as their mission, and their right, to seek out and eliminate people who they believe threaten their religious beliefs, their racial purity, and their power. One gruesome incident that has attracted international attention was the brutal killing of James Byrd, a 49-year-old black man from Jasper, Texas. Byrd was dragged several kilometres behind a vehicle before being decapitated, by Bill King and two accomplices. King was a known member of various hate groups and had Ku Klux Klan symbols and Swastikas tattooed on his body. Even while awaiting his death sentence, King and one of his co-offenders joined the Confederate Knights of America Kings and sent a letter to a local newspaper declaring he was "still white and proud" (Whitworth, 1999). Similarly, skinheads have been associated with such acts as "gay bashing," "Jew bashing," and attacking certain East Indian groups. The heading on one of their American and United Kingdom banners simply reads "Let's kick some ass!"

And while hate crime, defined as hate propaganda in the *Criminal Code* (s. 318–320) is a comparatively new form of violence, the number of reported incidents is increasing.[21] In Canada, the number of such incidents (e.g., Ernst Zundel, Heritage Front, etc.) has increased throughout the 1990s and they tend to be more concentrated in larger metropolitan areas (Data on hate…, 1995). As for the United States, preliminary data from the FBI indicate that there are in excess of 7,000 hate crime incidents each year in the United States (Associated Press, 1994). However, because of fears of reprisal, hate crime is probably vastly underreported.

Hate crimes have probably always been with us. In Canada, they can be traced back to our dealings with Aboriginal Peoples when Samuel de Champlain established the first permanent settlement in 1608 at Quebec (Carrigan, 1991). Are its roots based in social, individual, political, or biological traits? The research provides no clear answers. Therefore, how to go about addressing it poses a major dilemma for policy makers. Amendments to the *Criminal Code* are not likely to affect individuals who are driven by some warped sense of reality. Educational programs may sensitize some of us to certain issues, but the history of prejudice and hostility based on a victim's race or religion is a long one. However, virtually every religion advocates peace, compassion, and love for our fellow man—regardless of race, creed, or gender.

Canadian author Warren Kinsella (1994) in his book *The Web of Hate* suggests that contributing factors to the rise of anti-Semitic groups in Canada may be a faltering economy and a growing segment of youths angry about the lack of opportunities available to them. In 1999, the League for Human Rights of B'Nai Brith Canada (a Jewish human rights advocacy group) reported that anti-Semitic incidents rose 29 per cent in 1998. They suggest that part of the increase may be due to cutbacks in programs against discrimination and a proliferation of anti-Semitic Web sites (Purdy, 1999). This *culture conflict* (Chapter 7) perspective has considerable appeal. However, it cannot account for differences in motivation and or target selection, nor does it explain how and why ordinary crime becomes hate crime.

Whatever the cause of hate-motivated violence, it is a sad commentary on humanity, one which deserves our concerted attention so that constructive social policy measures can be introduced.

Stalking

As Canadians, we value our freedom and independence. In fact, we have not only entrenched these rights into the Canadian *Charter of Rights and Freedoms* but in recent years have also passed specific legislation that more clearly defines these rights.

It is difficult today not to hear stories about harrassment. In 1997, a highly respected Simon Fraser University swim coach was charged with sexual harassment by a female former swim team member (see s. 264 C.C.). The story, while not an isolated incident, received considerable media coverage. Then as the story unfolded it was found that the female swimmer had been stalking the coach for some time before filing the complaint!

Intimidation under s. 423(1) of the *Criminal Code* is a new piece of legislation (passed in 1993) that defines stalking as "persistently follows that person about from place to place " In the 1980s Anne Murray, the Canadian singer, had to get a special court order to stop an ardent Saskatchewan fan, Robert Keiling, from constantly harassing (stalking) her. John Hinkley, Jr., who tried to assassinate President Ronald Reagan in 1981, also stalked the movie star Jodie Foster. Ted Bundy, the serial killer, used to stalk his victims before killing them.[22]

Although the practice of stalking has been around a long time, only recently has it been classified as an offence, and studied by criminologists. The increase in stalking may be a response to laws against domestic violence. Restraining orders provide minimal protection for the victim. However, the new legislation provides police with the power to, it is hoped, prevent more serious crimes.

Holmes and Homes (1993) list six different types of stalkers: *celebrity*, *domestic* (e.g., estranged husband following his ex-wife), *hit* (e.g., hired killers), *lust* (e.g., Stephen Stillabower and Madonna), *scorned* (e.g., the rejected lover), and *political* (The Monica Lewinsky case?). The most recent variation of stalking involves cyberstalkers. Using Internet e-mail and chat lines, there have been increasing reports of people being stalked over the Internet. One British company found that 41 per cent of their female users had been sent unsolicited pornographic material or had been harassed or stalked (Driscoll, 1999). While they all share a common behaviour, their motivation differs.

To date there is no concrete data on stalking in Canada but with social changes, such as increased sensitivity to people's rights, high divorce rates, and other social/personal hardships, stalking has become a social concern.[23] A recent American survey found that approximately 8 per cent of women experience a stalking incident in their life compared to 2 per cent of men. The majority (52 per cent) of victims are between the ages of 18–29 and the most common method is being followed (82 per cent among women and 72 per cent among men) followed by unwanted phone calls (Stalking and domestic violence ..., 1999).

In late 1997, Federal Justice Minister Anne McLellan said she would be looking into doubling the maximum sentence for stalking, from five to ten years, in response to various pleas. The concern has perhaps also been prompted by the sexual harassment policies implemented at virtually every work setting. Introducing special legislation represents a first step in addressing this new form of violence but more needs to be done to understand it before it happens.

Terrorism[24]

Canadian criminologist Gywnn Nettler (1982:227) describes terrorism as involving "the calculated instilling of fear through cruelty, killing, or the threat of both as a means to obtain or maintain power." In addition to being an act of violence terrorism is also classified as a political crime, as terrorists usually reject the goals and objectives of their society and seek to install their own goals and objectives. Stephen Schafer (1976) uses the term "convictional criminal" as a way of characterizing the political convictions underlying their illegal behaviour.

Overall, attempts to define and describe terrorism have been somewhat broad and subject to interpretation. For example, if you were an ardent environmentalist and put spikes into trees in an effort to deter logging in an area could you be considered a terrorist? Or, if a group commits a robbery in order to support their revolutionary cause (as have members of the Aryan Nations), should the act be treated as a political or terrorist crime, or as an armed robbery? The *Criminal Code* does not have a specific section that deals with terrorism. This absence has hampered both scholarly conceptualization of the term as well as the ability to provide a solid platform for intervention strategies.

Whatever form it takes, politically-motivated crimes against a sovereign state have had a long history. Some of the more recognizable people to be considered political criminals in their time include Socrates, Jesus, Joan of Arc, Martin Luther King, Jr., and Canada's own Louis Riel who led a campaign against the federal government during the late 1800s. Another major terrorist incident was the FLQ crisis of 1970.[25]

Although terrorist acts have a long history, in recent years not only has terrorism been on the increase but it has evolved into new and deadly forms. Today terrorists have access to and occasionally use such deadly weapons as chemical and biological warfare, and nuclear threats (see Boxes 9.12 and 9.13).

REALITY CHECK BOX 9.12

EXAMPLES OF TERRORISM IN THE 1990S

- February 1993: Bombing of the World Trade Centre in New York City—killed 6 people and injured more than 1,000.
- April 1993: David Koresh's followers at the Branch Davidian compound in Waco, Texas are believed to have killed themselves after U.S. federal agents attempted to investigate the community's weapons stockpile. Both the Waco and the Asahara incident (below) are examples of "doomsday cults" or "freedom fighters" who represent a new type of terrorism.
- April 1995: Bombing at the Federal Building in Oklahoma City killed 168 people.

In June 1997, Timothy McVeigh, one of the members of a right-wing militia group, was convicted of the bombing.

- March 1995:Shoko Asahara, leader of Japan's Aum Shinrokyo ("Supreme Truth") sect, placed several canisters of deadly sarin nerve gas in the Tokyo subway. The gas killed 10 and injured over 5000.

- July 1995: Letter bombs were sent to a scientist at the Alberta Genetics laboratory and the MacKenzie Institute in Toronto.

- July 1996: A homemade pipe bomb exploded at a late-night concert during the summer Olympics in Atlanta. Two people died and otherswere injured by flying shrapnel.

- March 1997: Hani Abdel Rahim Hussein al-Sayegh, a Saudi dissident, was arrested in Canada after seeking refugee status because he feared persecution in his homeland for opposing the Saudi royal family. He was believed to be a member of Saudi Hezballah, a faction of the Iranian-backed terrorist organization Hezballah. In an attempt to secure his refugee status he disclosed his involvement in the 1996 bombing of an American military building in Dhahran that killed 19 U.S. airmen. In June 1997, al-Sayegh was deported to the United States for agreeing to "tell all" in exchange for immunity and not being returned to Saudi Arabia. If his story can be verified, it could prove that Iran was behind the bombing.

- December 1997: For several decades the Provisional Irish Republican Army had been targeting British buildings in public places as part of their campaign for Irish Independence. In December 1997, Billy Wright, the infamous King Rat and a prominent Protestant terrorist, was murdered. His killing triggered retaliation killings and threatened the multi-party peace talks.

- July 1998: The group Hamas attempted to use a car bomb at a popular Jerusalem café. Police noticed the suspicious car and were able to defuse the explosives before they were timed to explode.

- August 1998: The Islamic Army for the Liberation of Holy Places claimed responsibility for the bombing of American embassies in Kenya and Tanzania which resulted in at least 210 dead and 4500 injured. One of the suspects is Osama Bin Laden, also suspected of being involved in the 1996 embassy attack in Saudi Arabia that claimed some 250 lives. He has since reportedly been hiding in such countries as Afghanistan and Iraq.

- November 1998: Alberta energy minister Steve West lashes out against so-called "eco-terrorists" who have been targeting the oil and forestry industries as well as electrical utilities across the province. Since 1996, there have been approximately 160 acts of vandalism causing $2 million in damage.

Theodore Kaczynski, nicknamed the "Unabomber" for his bombings throughout the 1980s was caught and found guilty in 1997. He was charged with killing three people and injuring 28. The former math professor has pleaded not guilty and describes himself as a delusional paranoid-schizophrenic. His defence was attempting to evade the death penalty by arguing that Kaczynski suffers from a mental defect (Kaczynski plea bargain rejected, 1997). Is Kaczynski a terrorist or simply a zealous extremist? Another story that received considerable attention was the recent case of the notorious Carlos "the Jackal." Captured in 1994 he was eventually brought to trial in 1997. Illich Ramirez Sanchez (his real name) admitted to killing 84 people and was involved in the 1972 massacre of 11 Israeli athletes at the Munich Olympics. He was found guilty in December 1997 (Prosecution calls for..., 1997). What should his punishment be?

WHAT DO YOU THINK? BOX 9.13

MAD OR BAD?

In an interview with *Time* magazine in January 1999, Osama Bin Laden, the million-aire terrorist leader called upon Muslims to attack Britons and Americans in revenge for the air attacks on Iraq in 1998 (Sapstead, 1999). Is Laden a terrorist, an (crazed) idealist? How do we counter such terrorist agendas?

Typologies of Terrorism

The difficulty in defining terrorism is reflected in the varied typologies used to describe it. Typologies range from simple dichotomous models such as Jeffery's (1991) classifications: (1) *violence against foreigners*, and (2) *violence against one's countrymen,* to Paul Smythe's (1996) three-tiered model: (1) *ethnic separatists* and *emigrant groups* (e.g., Armenians and Sikhs),[26] (2) *left-wing radical groups* (e.g., Air India bombing and the Squamish Five in British Columbia),[27] and (3) *right-wing racist* groups (e.g., Neo Nazi and Heritage Front groups). These groups are usually a combination of groups 1 and 2, are not averse to using violence and actively recruit new members. Finally, Johnathan White (1991) provides five fairly broad types—*revolutionary terrorists* who use violence to invoke fear in those in power (e.g., Palestinian Liberation Organization (PLO), Iranian-backed Hezballah), *political terrorism* is directed at specific individuals or groups who oppose their ideology (e.g., Aryan Nation and other supremacy oriented groups), *nationalistic terrorism* groups are intent on promoting their own minority ethnic or religious factions (e.g., Sikh and the Provisional Irish Republic Army (IRA), *nonpolitical terrorists* campaign for particular religious or social causes (e.g., abortion groups, Greenpeace, Animal Liberation Front), and *state-sponsored terrorism* activities tend to involve repressive political regimes who rely on force and violence to force compliance (e.g., the death squads of Nigeria, Brazil, Guatemala, Iraq, among others).

Regardless of the typology used, attempts to control terrorism through law (e.g., the *War Measures Act* in 1970 with the FLQ crisis) or the use of force (the

Oka uprising) has usually not resulted in satisfactory resolutions. In addition, Smythe (1996:19) notes that the face of terrorism is changing, since today there are other forms such as: "faction sponsored terrorism; issue-motivated terrorism; and crime-related terrorism that may provide more testing challenges in the future." This will likely represent a major area of interest to criminologists in the future.

In **summary**, the "new" forms of violence lend impetus to the need to better understand the purpose, meaning, characteristics, and theoretical causes underlying such acts. Violence seems to be evolving and spreading throughout society. We must recognize the problems that new forms of violence pose, work towards understanding their causes and develop social policy and support programs to ameliorate the problem.

Summary

We have covered a wide range of traditional forms of violent crime as well as some of the newer forms of violence. Although they may vary in nature and form, they all share the common element of violence. While official statistics suggest that violent crime has declined in recent years, its levels are still well above the rates first recorded in the 1960s. Furthermore, not all violent crime types have declined. And aside from traditional forms of violent crime, we are witnessing new forms of violence for which no official statistics are being kept. One only needs to watch, or listen to, the daily news to know that violence takes many forms and is everywhere.

It is not enough to simply be able to describe the extent and nature of violence in our society. Criminologists must also strive to gather better scientific knowledge, that is interdisciplinary, about the dynamics of the various forms violent behaviour can take. Relying on traditional legalistic approaches and conventional single disciplinary explanations can only be temporary measures. Unless criminologists are prepared to accept the facts, and unless they are prepared to see violent crime as a behaviourally-rooted problem, they are likely to witness new forms of violence not yet imagined. Society will also have to take a serious stand against violence if it wants to live a more peaceful existence.

Discussion Questions

1. What can the violent-crime statistics tell us about the crime trend and patterns in Canada? Has the picture changed in recent years? Why?

2. Who is primarily responsible for those committing violent crimes? Are there any common denominators? What are some of the major explanatory models for the different types of crimes covered?

3. Are there any common causal factors that can be used to explain violent crimes?

4. Why are the crimes covered in the chapter referred to as *conventional* crimes? How do they differ from *non-conventional* crimes?

5. Throughout the semester collect at least a dozen articles related to the "new" forms of violence. What do they tell us about the nature and extent of the problem? What kinds of solutions, if any, are offered? Do they pose a more serious threat to society?

6. Based on the highlights of the major federal parties (Appendix 5), which party do you think has the best approaches to controlling violent crimes? Why?

Key Concepts

Conventional crime	violent crime	hate crime
Crime rates	homicide	murder
Etiology	domestic violence	sexual assault
Date-rape	Bill C-127	GSS
Clearance rates	robbery	abduction
Hate propaganda	stalking	harassment
Intimidation	terrorism	bias crime
Canadian Centre for Justice Statistics		

Weblinks

www.statcan.ca/english/pgdb/state/justice.html As of January 1999, the homepage for Statistics Canada is no longer a free service. Your local library may have access to this otherwise excellent site. It is a great way to keep abreast of the latest data.

For a visual breakdown of the spatial distribution of homicide across Canada for 1996 visit **www.crimweb/stats/murdmap.htm**.

www.fbi.gov/ucr/hatecm.htm The FBI Web site on hate crime. They also include useful links to other international anti-hate sites.

www.ojp.usdoj.gov/vawgo/stalk98/chapter1.htm This site presents the findings on the first-ever national stalking survey in the United States.

www.ifs.univie.ac.at/~uncjin/uncjin/html The United Nations homepage on crime and crime statistics. Also has numerous international links.

With a little effort you can locate violent crime data/information for virtually any country around the world and/or specific reports on any type of violent crime. You can use the search engine "altavistacanada.com" and simply type in any of the violent crimes. The search will generate a wide array of related links.

Footnotes

1. The total *Criminal Code* rate, excluding traffic infractions, in 1992 was 9,981—down from 10,309 in 1991. At the time this chapter was prepared, the crime rate had continually declined from 1992 through 1996. The percentage of year-to-year decline from the previous year's crime rate was 3.2 for 1992, 5.3 in 1993, 4.3 in 1994, 1.0 in 1995, and 1.6 in 1996. Property crimes account for the greatest proportion in the rate of decline (*CCJS*, 1998:18(11)).

2. Additional crime statistics are available in *Canadian Crime Statistics*, Catalogue No. 85–205. In addition, the "Canadian Centre for Justice Statistics" published a series of Service Bulletin's known as *Juristat's* that focus specific topic areas (see Chapter 3 for a general discussion on the role of the Canadian Centre for Justice Statistics).

3. Many good statistics on crime in Canada can be found at Statistics Canada Web site: **www.StatCan.ca/english/pgdb/state/justic.htm**.

4. In terms of total government spending, the criminal justice system only accounts for about 3 cents of every dollar spent. This is comparable to the spending allotted for the environment, recreation, and culture. By contrast education receives 12 cents, health 13 cents, and social services 24 cents. Since the 1970s spending on health and justice have remained relatively constant (*CCJS*, 1997:17(3)).

5. Glenn (1988) suggests the exact year was 1964. It was marked by a number of important social changes including larger classroom sizes, rapid growth in the use of processed foods, increased consumption of alcohol and illegal drugs. For a Canadian interpretation see David Foot's book *Boom, Bust, and Echo* (1996).

6. Silverman and Kennedy (1992) point out that even though the research they discuss refers to "homicide," the precise definition will vary with the jurisdiction being covered and the context in which death occurs. For example, the law does not provide accountability for manufacturers who through negligence cause the death of those who work for them or of those who purchase their products (Box, 1983). During the Westray mine disaster in May 1992 at Plymouth, N.S., where 26 men died in a methane fire and coal-dust explosion, the deaths were dealt with in civil, not criminal court.

7. In his extensive research on the subject, Hickey (1991) was only able to identify three Canadian mass and serial killers between 1930 and 1988. They include: Clifford Olson, who killed eleven or more victims between 1974 and 1981; Marc Lepine who on December 13, 1989 entered the University of Montreal's École Polytechnique and killed fourteen women before taking his own life; and the case of Paul Bernardo and his wife Karla Homolka (see Chapter 8). Given their relative rarity in Canada, we will not address this type of crime here. The following readings represent good sources: Hickey, 1991; Holmes and Homes, 1993; Leyton, 1986; and O'Reilly-Flemming, 1996b. In addition, if you have access to the Internet you can readily find sites that provide virtually any kind of information you might want to learn about mass murderers and serial killers.

8. Between 1985 and 1995, the rate of youths accused of homicide has fluctuated between a low of 1.5 per 100,000 youth population in 1993 and 2.7 in 1995. Since 1993 the homicide rate among youth has steadily increased. Most of the victims of youth homicides involved other youths. Statistics Canada does not provide a breakdown as to how many youth homicides involve gangs, or organized crime, related incidents, accidental incidents, or domestic violence-related incidents.

9. Bill C-51, passed in 1978, prohibited the ownership of firearms that did not have a legitimate sporting or recreational purpose (e.g., sawed-off shotguns, fully automatic firearms) as well as restricted the ownership of handguns. This bill introduced the Firearm Acquisition Certification (FAC).

10. A June 1997 news release from Statistics Canada revealed that most homicides occur in urban areas and only 2 per cent involve handguns. This raises serious questions about the relevance of the gun control legislation.

11. For an excellent depiction of the emotive and social issues surrounding capital punishment you might want to rent the video "Dead Man Walking" starring Sean Penn.

12. For example, Silverman and Kennedy (1992) cite the 1990 case of Victoria youth Darren Huenemann who killed his mother and grandmother in an attempt to get a very large inheritance.

13. When the homicide rates are averaged between 1985 and 1994, Manitoba has the highest national rate (3.27) followed by B.C. (3.17) and then Alberta at 2.74 (CCJS, 1996:16(10)).

14. Renner found that sexual offenders of children get lighter sentences than do those sexually assaulting another adult. Only 13 per cent of those charged with sexually assaulting children received a sentence of two years or more, compared with 30 per cent for those charged sexually assaulting another adult.

15. Rohypnol cannot be prescribed or sold legally in Canada. It can, however, be brought into the country in limited amounts if prescribed by a foreign physician. In 1995, the drug became the first benzodiazepine to be moved to Schedule III by the World Health Organization—requiring better record keeping on its distribution (The Metro Toronto ..., 1996).

16. "The median prison sentence was five years for Level 3 offences, two years for Level 2 offences, and six months for Level 1 offences" (Johnson, 1996:147).

17. For an interesting account of the personal stories of bank robbers, see Desroches (1996).

18. More recent studies have offered conflicting explanations. Gabor et al. (1987, cited in Clermont, 1996:91) attribute the "high incidence of robberies in Quebec to the rapid social and political changes that occurred in the province"—an unstable economy with high unemployment. Clader (1992 cited in Clermont) suggests that the Quebec cultural climate may be partly accountable, as their commercial establishments such as bars, restaurants, and convenience stores operate for longer hours than other parts of Canada. This supposedly creates more opportunities for robbery.

19. According to a 1997 report, in 1986 there were approximately 7,000 bank robberies in the United States. The total loss was just under $19 million. By 1992 the number of robberies had risen to 11,000, accounting for nearly $37 million dollars in total loss (Bank robbery, 1997).

20. Based on American UCR data for 1981 a robbery occurred every 78 seconds. Even though no comparable data was available for Canada, the British Columbia Police Commission produced annual data showing that for 1981 a robbery occurred 2 hours or 114.4 per 100,000 inhabitants—up from 83.8 per 100,000 in 1977 (Roesch and Winterdyk, 1985:8). Hence, compared our neighbours to the south, robberies are rare.

21. The 1999-02-27 *Criminal Code* defines "hate propaganda" as "any writing, sign or visible representation that advocates or promotes genocide or the communication of which by any person would constitute an offence under section 319."

22. In 1993 there were only 31 American states that had made stalking a crime (Lewin, 1993). By 1996 all 50 states and the District of Columbia had passage of antistalking laws (Stalking and domestic…, 1999).

23. An American study found that 8 per cent of women (8.2 million) and 2 per cent of men (2 million) claimed to have been stalked at some time in their life. Tjaden (1997) found that stalking stopped within 1 or 2 years.

24. For additional information on the Internet see the Web site for the International Policy Institute for Counter Terrorism at **www.ict.org.il/** or the counter-terrorism site at **www.emergency.com/cntrterr.htm.**

25. There have also been terrorist incidents which took place in Canada but which originated elsewhere. In 1982 Armenian terrorists shot the Turkish embassy military attaché as part of an ongoing protest against the slaughter of Armenians by the Turks back in 1895 and 1896. Similarly, the Air India jetliner bombing in 1985 originated in Canada. The fatal bomb was placed on board the plane at Toronto's Pearson International Airport (Carrigan, 1991). These examples illustrate the extremes to which terrorists will go to have their message heard.

26. They tend to focus on parochial issues, are often ethnic-centred, and tend to be quite violent.

27. These groups tend to have a broader following and purport ideological spectrum-based issues.

CHAPTER 10

Property Crimes

"... Canadians are losing at least $5.7 billion each year to [all forms of] property crimes. This figure must be considered conservative because there is a substantial amount of loss occurring that has not been reported to the police."

Kean and Assoc., cited in Vancouver Board
of Trade Information, 1997:13.

Learning Outcomes

After you have read this chapter, you should be able to:

- Recognize and be familiar with the major forms of property crimes.

- Be familiar with the general trends of the major property crime types.

- Appreciate that an "absolute" explanation of property crime causation is currently unavailable.

- Appreciate the importance of using crime data to understand property crime trends and patterns, explaining crime, and recommending social policy.

- Appreciate the importance of applying an integrated and interdisciplinary approach when using crime data.

- Appreciate the benefit of using comparative criminology to lend further insight into the study and control of property crimes.

As we saw in the previous chapter, violent crime captures most of the public's attention but compared to crimes against property, it occurs infrequently. Property crimes account for approximately 60 per cent of all crimes known to the police each year and as indicated in the quotation above are costly to Canadians. And although, nationally, there has been a slight decline (c. 1 per cent per year

between 1991–1997), in the overall rate of property crimes in the latter half of the 1990s, the rate is still 50 per cent higher than it was in the late 1970s and early 80s. Regionally however, cities such as Vancouver experienced a 16 per cent increase in property crime between 1991 and 1995 (Vancouver Board…, 1997) while Ottawa experienced a 15 per cent decline (IBC, 1998).

FYI BOX 10.1

Not All Break and Enters Are the Same

Between 1993 to 1995, residential break and enters increased 20.6% and theft of automobiles increased 35.3% while only commercial break and enters declined (1.1%) (Vancouver Board…, 1997).

We live in a society that values material goods. News stories abound about people fighting, and even killing, to illegally obtain certain goods (e.g., running shoes, sport jackets, bicycles, motorized vehicles, etc.). A 1998 report, for example, cited that car theft is Canada's fastest growing crime (IBC, 1998). And although they may serve the same function, we seem to place greater value on certain items and labels than others. Even little children can sometimes rebel at attempts to remove an item they seem engrossed in. Possessing something can be a source of joy but it can also be the object of a property crime. In addition, while property crimes are legally considered less serious than violent crimes, victims may feel a sense of personal violation as well as significant emotional distress after a property crime occurs.

Crimes against property take various forms and, in this chapter, we will focus on five major **conventional** forms of property crime. They will include break and enter, fraud, theft, arson, and motor-vehicle crime. Property crimes have an economic element to them since they involve either the theft and/or destruction of property. As with the section on violent crime, we will examine offender and victim characteristics as well as their overall impact and policy/prevention strategies and implications.

Break and Enter

Break and enter (ss. 348–353) is usually done with the intent of stealing something from a residence, business, of some other fixed setting. Unlike robbery, a break and enter (B & E) does not involve face-to-face contact or the threat of force. Break and enter could be described as a more passive, non-violent crime. As depicted in movies, the "burglar" usually goes about his or her activities in a clandestine manner. However, that does not mean that victims of property crime take their victimization lightly. After the Prime Minister and his wife had their official residence broken into in 1995, there was an investigation into providing property security for them. In 1998, the residence underwent a $417,629 "security boost" to ensure such incidents would not happen again (Naumetz, 1998).

Is there a difference between break and enter and *burglary* (see Box 10.2)? These terms are sometimes used interchangeably. The United States and England still use the common law term "burglary" while in Canada we use the modern term "break and enter." Legally, they are comparable except that in the United States a burglar might use force if he or she encounters someone in the course of committing the crime. Technically in Canada the act would then become a robbery (see Chapter 9).

FYI BOX 10.2

Redefining Burglary

Under old English common law, burglary was an offence only if it was "breaking and entering of a dwelling during the night with the intent to commit a felony." Canada used this classification and description until the law was amended. It was no longer specified that burglary had to be in a dwelling and omitted the specific time frame of "night time" (Carrigan, 1991).

Patterns and Characteristics in Break and Enters

In 1997, there were 373,355 break and enter incidents reported to police. And the number of incidents has fluctuated since the early 1990s, with the rate of B & Es declining from 1,546 in 1991 to 1,233 in 1997 (see Table 10-1). The rate means that the home of at least 1 in every 50 residents was broken into in 1997. B & E represented approximately 25 per cent of all reported property crimes (*CCJS*, 1998:18(12)) and accounts for about $2.6 billion in stolen household goods each year.[1]

Between 1985 and 1997, residential B & E rates have fluctuated with an overall increase of 2.7 per cent. However, between 1996 and 1997, business-related B & Es declined nearly 10 per cent and other types of B & E declined 13.1 per cent. In absolute terms, residential B & Es account for 60 per cent of all B & Es while business premises make up 28 per cent and "other" premises the balance at 12 per cent.

TABLE 10–1

BREAK AND ENTERS: 1990–1997

YEAR	RATE PER 100,000	NUMBER
1990	1, 365	379, 364
1991	1, 546	434, 602
1992	1, 497	427, 153
1993	1, 404	406, 421
1994	1, 326	387, 867
1995	1, 319	390, 784
1996	1, 322	397, 057
1997	1, 233	373, 355

Source: *CCJS*, 1998:18(5) Assorted Canadian crime statistics. (Annual Reports)

Data from the 1993 GSS indicate that urban dwellings are more likely to be targeted than rural dwellings, and "that semi-detached homes, row houses and duplexes were more likely targets than single, detached dwellings. Rented dwellings were a more likely target than owner-occupied dwellings" (*CCJS*, 1996:16(11):9). Geographically, the western provinces report the highest rates.

The GSS victimization survey also reveals that victims of B & Es were more likely to report their victimization to the police than other types of crime. Only about one-third choose not to report their victimization. People are likely to report their B & Es in order to file an insurance claim. For 1994, the Insurance Bureau of Canada reported claims totalling $267 million for homeowner insurance claims from B & E related thefts. The most frequently stolen items are audio/video equipment (32 per cent) and jewellery (13 per cent). Another $63 million came from tenant insurance claims and $110 million for commercial claims. Money, cheques, or bonds are the most common items stolen (22 per cent) followed by office equipment (20 per cent) (*CCJS*, 1998:18(5)).

Because they are easy to carry away and to sell, audio-visual and electronic equipment has been the most common type of property stolen from residential B & Es. Burglars are opportunists and they are not interested in holding onto "hot" items. As for commercial premises, money and office equipment are the main targets and in other types of B & E (e.g., (open) garages and sheds), machinery and tools are the most common targets.[2] In a unique study conducted by Wright and Decker (1994) the authors interviewed active burglars, rather than those who were incarcerated, and reported that efforts to reduce B & E through *target hardening* (better locks and home security devices) were not overly effective. The primary reason was that most homeowners become careless about maintaining effective use of their security devices. In addition, even if the alarm is armed most burglars spend less than five minutes in a house—much less time than it takes an alarm company to respond. Rengert and Wasilchick (1985) also found that the more experienced burglars engage in systematic selection of a home. They take time to "case the joint." They look for subtle clues (closed windows, no lights, mail in the mailbox, etc.). They also take into account the location of the target, ease of escape, and general familiarity with the area. However, the general consensus in the literature is that most break and enter offenders are opportunistic young offenders. A Vancouver study found, for example, that there is perhaps only a core group of 40–50 property criminals who are responsible for a significant proportion of property crimes in their city (Vancouver Board …, 1997).

Given that B & Es are seen as crimes of *opportunity* and *rational choice*, burglars do not want to spend a lot of time planning, do not want to make noise, and prefer not to be seen. Therefore, it is not surprising that houses on the edge of an unoccupied area are at greater risk than those in the interior of a residential setting (Brantingham and Brantingham, 1981). Meanwhile, Rhodes and Conly (1981) found that residential burglars usually live within 1.6 miles (approximately 2 km) of their target, compared to 2.1 miles for robbers, and 1.2 miles for rapists. Wright and Decker (1994) found that the summer months (June, July and August) account for about 30 per cent of seasonal trends in B & Es. This is the time when school is out and people take their holidays, leaving their homes less secure. In keeping with the *rational choice theory* (Chapter 8), the majority of B & Es take place between the hours of 6 p.m. and 6 a.m. when people are either out or asleep.[3] The majority of those charged (nearly 45 per cent) are people aged 12–17 years with the median age being 19 for residential B & Es compared to 21 for business B & Es (see Box 10.3 and Box 10.4).

REALITY CHECK BOX 10.3
- -
HOME INVASION … B & E OR ROBBERY —"YOUR WORST NIGHTMARE COMES TRUE!"

Home invasions or intrusions are quickly becoming one of Canada's scariest forms of property crime. Not only does it involve being robbed but the victim is being robbed and terrorized in his or her own home. The robbery can turn violent, resulting in physical injury. Media reports show that home invasions have included sexual assaults, beatings, gunfire, and even murder. The motives range from wanting money, valuables, drugs, and crime-related revenge.

While there are some perceptions that Asians are prime targets, police officials note that no particular culture is directly involved. However, Asians are hit because many choose not to put their money in banks. In many incidents, this is the result of a mistrust of banks in their homeland.

The first official account of a home invasion in Calgary occurred in 1991. It involved a Chinese family who was robbed during the daytime (Mofina, 1991). By 1993, Vancouver was reporting that home invasions were becoming a serious concern in their city (Hall, 1993). Smaller cities also began to observe the emergence of home invasions. In 1994, Winnipeg began to experience a growth in home invasions. In early 1999, British Columbia became the first province to call for harsher punishment for home invaders. The request came in the aftermath of a series of home invasions. For convicted offenders, Premier Clark wants no parole and automatic election to adult court for young offenders. (Sutherland, 1999) What do you think of such measures? Would they act as deterrents? As with the experienced burglar, home invasion perpetrators usually know their victims and carefully plan their crimes.

A Criminologist's "Dilemma"

Crime clearance rates often tell us something about the nature of a crime and how effective crime prevention or intervention strategies are. In both Canada and the United Sates, B & E clearance rates are around 15 per cent! Fortunately for police, when offenders are ultimately caught, they usually confess to a string of B & Es. This strategy is usually done as part of a plea-bargain arrangement (Wright and Decker, 1994). The low clearance rates may also lend credence to some of the explanations for B & Es.

One of the major explanations employed for B & E is *rational choice theory* in which the offender weights the potential costs and rewards of the act (Cromwell, Olson, and Avary, 1991). In some centres, it could be argued there is an informal symbiotic support network that serves to perpetuate B & Es. The Vancouver Board report (1997:13), for example, noted that pawnshops often serve as "primary distribution centres for stolen goods ... public fencing outlets."

Along similar lines, Bursik (1995) suggests that burglars rely on environmental cues. Being a crime of opportunity, burglars tend to select homes they're familiar with, that are less visible to their neighbours, with ease of access, a general appearance of affluence, and that appear unoccupied. The police regularly provide crime prevention tips that focus on many of these issues. If you're going to be away, have someone collect your mail and cut your lawn and don't leave "gone on vacation" messages on your answering machine. Also, mark your belongings (e.g., Operation Identification) and post the decals in a visible place. This cannot guarantee you will never be a victim of a B & E, but will reduce your risk. However, as Repetto (1974) observed, these measures are likely to produce a *crime displacement* effect (i.e., move the target location, setting, time, etc.) rather than prevent it.

In **summary,** while B & Es do not involve direct confrontation they are often traumatic for the victim. They also pose a serious problem for the criminal justice system and insurance companies. They are one of the most prevalent crimes and their clearance rates are extremely low. In addition, research shows that in most B & Es, there is no prior relationship between the thieves and the victim. While some theories provide sound explanations for burglaries, they have done little to develop programs or strategies to abate them. As Greenberg (1996:165) observes, "fears about public safety among the general public appear to be on the rise. Clearly, restoring public faith in the justice system should be at or near the top of the Canadian agenda." How are the police going to do this? Given the police's general lack of success in clearing B & Es many police departments now regard B & Es as a low priority. Encouraging people to fortify their homes or not trust anyone: Is this the answer?

Fraud

FYI BOX 10.5

Fraud[4]

A 1996 public opinion survey showed that 43 per cent of Canadians agreed that it was easy to defraud an insurance company (*CCJS*, 1998:18(4), p. 7).

There are 16 sections (ss. 380–396) in the *Criminal Code* dealing with various aspects of fraud. Fraud is the taking of another's property (i.e., possessions) through deception, falsehood, or cheating. For example, imagine someone sold you a used car claiming it had never been in an accident. You bought it in good faith, only to find out later that it had been in a serious accident. This transaction would be fraudulent.

In this section we will deal only with property-related fraud. Many fraud cases could easily fall under the general heading of *white-collar crime* or *organized crime* (see Chapter 11), since they are committed by businesses and professionals.[5] Typically, property-related fraud includes cheque fraud, credit card fraud, and "other" fraud (e.g., breach of trust, false pretences, forgery, mail fraud, telemarketing fraud, and fraudulent manipulation of the stock exchange—see Box 10.6).

THE LURE OF MONEY

- On May 29, 1997 a Downsview mother and daughter were charged with fraud after a joint investigation by Peel Regional Police and Metro Toronto Police into the use of a rented vehicle in a staged accident. The mother-daughter duo was charged with Fraud Under $5,000 and Conspiracy to Commit Fraud. The charges arose after the car had become involved in an accident and three people filed claims, when only the driver had been in the car at the time of the collision. This represents a false (fraudulent) insurance claim and is a serious problem for insurance companies (Canada News Wire, 1997, May 29).
- In April of 1999, a former administrative secretary at a community college was charged with fraudulently depositing more than $12,000 in student tuitions into her bank account (Ex-college ..., 1999).
- On March 21, 1997 a Calgary man was charged with three counts of fraud over $5,000 in an employment insurance fraud. Between 1988 and 1993, the accused had used three variations of his name to claim UIC benefits of $93,523 (approx. $18,600 per year). Officials said that most cases are in the $5,000 to $6,000 range before they get caught. A spokesperson for a regional Human Resources Canada office said that while exact figures are not available, "more than $70 million—$30 million in Calgary—is recovered annually in the province in employment insurance fraud" (Slade, 1997).
- In February 1998, the Alberta Securities Commission discovered an elaborate scheme in which nearly 3,000 Albertans were swindled out of nearly $22 million! Two Calgary brokerage houses offered bogus securities in "prime bank instruments" with the promise that investors could double or even quadruple their money in a year. How can this happen? The article points out that "financial institutions around the world often do not thoroughly check on the authenticity of documents deposited in an account" (Mofina, 1998).

Patterns and Characteristics of Fraud

According to crime statistics the rate of fraud has steadily declined since 1991 from a high of 487 per 100,000 population to a rate of 319 in 1997. Fraud accounts for approximately 7 per cent of all property crime. McPhie (1996) notes, however, that in spite of media reports that the dollar value of losses through fraudulent activities rival those of dollar values normally associated with organized crimes, Statistics Canada reports neglect to present a breakdown of the crimes.[6] In terms of fraudulent activities, the Canadian Bankers' Association reported $50 million in losses from credit card fraud during the 1991 fiscal year. The Insurance Bureau of Canada reported that annual losses from bank robberies average about

$3.3 million (Morrison and Ogrodnik, 1994). Nevertheless, McPhie (1996:167) observes, most frauds are still "practiced by individuals or small groups who pass bad cheques, use found, stolen, or altered credit or bank cards, or who misrepresent themselves in some manner during financial transactions." In addition, persons charged with fraud are generally older than those accused of other property crimes. In February of 1999, 57-year-old Tory Senator Eric Berntson was found guilty of fraud "for devising illicit schemes to obtain $41,735.50 of taxpayers' money while he was deputy premier of Saskatchewan" (Aubry, 1999).

The Uniform Crime Report survey does however provide a breakdown by type of fraud. Between 1979 and 1993, cheque fraud (writing a "bad" cheque, referred to as *forgery* in the United States)[7] has remained the highest category, accounting for 68 per cent of all fraud in 1979 but declining to 50 per cent by 1993. The ratio of credit card fraud over the same period has doubled from 7 per cent to 14 per cent in 1983 and remained fairly stable since then. This is an interesting observation: while its ratio has not changed significantly since 1983, interest rates on credit cards have gone up dramatically. Why? The increase in part is due to the increase in dollar value lost through credit card fraud transactions, but also more and more credit cards are being used, and it is quite easy to commit fraud with a credit card. For example, have you ever used your parents' or significant other's credit card and signed your name, but done so knowingly and paid them for its use? The category "other fraud" covers a wide range of fraudulent behaviours, so its relative proportion should be seen in this light. It has gone from 25 per cent of all frauds in 1979 to 38 per cent in 1993. There are insufficient data to explain which types of fraud might account for the increase.

As with all crimes, there are geographical variations in fraud across the country. Saskatchewan has reported the highest rate (540 per 100,000 population) while Newfoundland and Quebec had the lowest rates (291 and 250 respectively). It is interesting to observe that "other fraud" accounts for the majority of fraud cases in the above four provinces. Cheque fraud was highest in Nova Scotia (66 per cent), and credit card fraud was highest in British Columbia (20 per cent) (see Box 10.7). No studies have been conducted to examine or explain the variations. However, we can assume they relate to an interaction of social, cultural, and personal situations.

A CLOSER LOOK BOX 10.7

The Price of Owning a Credit Card

In 1995, the Canadian issuers of MasterCard and Visa lost $73 million to payment card fraud. Nearly one-third of those loses were due to counterfeiting. Worldwide, bank card fraud losses to VISA and MasterCard alone increased from $100 million in 1980 to an estimated $1.63 billion in 1995. (Counterfeiting of currency and payment cards, 1996).

In 1994, approximately 124 million of the 193 million adults in the United States owned at least one credit card. The gap is expected to narrow at a rate of 2.4 million new cardholders per year until the new millenium. Credit card fraud is keeping pace with this growth.

While there are a variety of fraudulent schemes used, counterfeiting is the fastest-growing type of bankcard fraud. Asian gangs are the primary makers of counterfeit credit cards. Between 1991 and 1993, there has been a 370 per cent increase in credit card counterfeits in California alone.

Efforts to counter credit card fraud (e.g., holograms, photographs, fingerprints, personal histories) have all had only limited success because these measures could be readily altered. Companies continue to explore new technological deterrents as the world becomes ever more dependent on "plastic." By the year 2000, for example, gross bank card volume is expected to total $9.9 trillion and given current trends this would convert to $14 billion in fraud! In addition to increased police resources being directed to countering this crime, the so-called Smart-Card (it has computer chip technology that will make counterfeiting more difficult) is being touted as the latest deterrent strategy (Slotter, 1997).

Fraud is one type of crime in which youth is not well represented. In 1993, only 7 per cent of the total number of charges laid by police were against youth. In terms of adults, men account for the largest proportion of frauds (63 per cent) and women made up 30 per cent of all cases of fraud. Given that fraud is a non-violent act and requires no physical force, it may not be too surprising to find women more likely to be involved in fraud as compared to other types of property crime (23 per cent). Official data show that women are most likely to engage in cheque fraud (33 per cent)—or at least get caught at it. For example, Vito and Holmes (1994) report that women who had been arrested have a high rate of recidivism. However, why do people write "bad" cheques or use credit cards illegally?

Explaining Fraud

In his classic study of cheque forgers, Edwin Lemert (1953) observed that most forgers are *naive* and tend to commit the offence out of economic need. He also found that they tend not to be involved in other forms of property crime and to be older than most property offenders. But has forgery evolved as a crime? Trembley (1986) notes, for example, that in recent years there has been an increase in professional forgers who have developed sophisticated schemes and sometimes work in teams. "The elderly are among the preferred targets of such groups" (McPhie, 1996:173). They are easily accessible, some are looking for a little extra income on their fixed pensions, and because of possible embarrassment they are often reluctant to report their victimization.

Other explanations include techniques of *neutralization* (Chapter 7) in which people rationalize their actions by claiming that businesses make so much money they won't be hurt by a "little" loss. As for fraudulent transactions with people, the offender might rationalize that if someone is naive enough to fall for the false pretence they deserve to be taken advantage of. Some modern-day examples include direct-mail marketing, "900" telephone numbers that charge callers a nominal fee per minute for a service (e.g., sex lines and psychic lines), and scam ads in local newspapers. These and other techniques are all part of the ever growing schemes people have devised to fraudulently prompt people to give something of value to the wrongdoer. Fraud often capitalizes on people's greed and the ability of the perpetrator to win the victim's trust or confidence.

In **summary**, fraud is a commonly occurring form of property crime that can also take the form of organized criminal activity and white-collar crime (Chapter 11). The total value of financial losses incurred through fraud is not known because of the high rate of unreported incidents (McPhie, 1996). However, based on available data, fraud costs individuals, organizations, and government billions of dollars every year. And while the overall official rate for fraud may have declined in recent years, the variety of new forms of fraud may simply be one step ahead of police detection. For example, one of the fastest growing forms of fraud involves telemarketing scams aimed at seniors. One recent report observes that over 85 per cent of the victims are over the age of 60 (Brennan, 1999).

As long as most Canadians (and Americans) value economic success it will be difficult to develop social policies that will significantly reduce crimes of fraud. Meanwhile, although certain "target hardening" programs have been devised, criminals simply seem to find new twists to the old "snake bit" formula.

Theft—"Thou Shalt Not Steal"

There are 14 sections in the *Criminal Code* dealing with theft, ranging from theft of cattle (s. 338), to theft by spouse (s. 329), to theft with intent to deposit/deprive (s. 322). Needless to say, so many sections imply that theft is considered a serious form of property crime. Even before Confederation, theft was one of the more common crimes reported to police (Carrigan, 1991). In general terms, theft refers to the unlawful taking of property from the possession of another. However, unlike robbery, theft does not involve the use or the threat of force or overt deception.

In this section, we will deal only with "theft over" and "theft under." These two classifications represent the more conventional description of theft.

Patterns and Characteristics of Theft

The Changing Limits of Theft

In February 1995, the *Criminal Code* was amended to change the dollar cut-off for "theft under" and "theft over" to $5,000 from $1,000.

The crime of theft can serve as an excellent example of crimes being *evolving* and *relative* (Chapter 1). When the *Canadian Criminal Code* was first enacted, theft was known as *larceny*. Later, it was defined as theft and eventually subdivided into "theft under $200" and "theft over 200." In 1986, the cut-off for "under/over" was raised to $1000. Most recently, in 1995, it was again altered to "theft under $5000" and "theft over $5000." These changes reflect our social economy and the relative value of goods. And while general comparisons can be made over time, they should be viewed with some caution, since not all property has increased equally in value. Therefore, while describing the trends in theft, we will refer to them simply as "theft over" and "theft under."

Between 1990 and 1993, there was a steady increase in the rate of "theft over" incidents reported to police. However, since 1993, there has been a dramatic decline in the rate of "theft over" (see Table 10-2). The rate for cases involving "theft under," meanwhile, has fluctuated somewhat, but has remained relatively stable with steady declines since 1995. Combined incidents of theft accounted for approximately 55 per cent of all property crime in Canada.

TABLE 10-2

THEFT OVER AND UNDER*: 1990–1997

YEAR	UNDER	OVER	UNDER	OVER
	RATE PER 100,000		NUMBER	
1990	366	411	101,639	114,082
1991	418	496	117,540	139,345
1992	421	514	120,063	146,801
1993	2,680	408	774,293	117.765
1994	2,486	398	727,414	116,396
1995	2,772	142	820,908	42,080
1996	2,749	90	823,732	27,075
1997	2,503	79	758,025	24,026

Sources: Assorted *CCJS*. Canadian crime statistics. (Vol. 18(11):18 and Vol. 17(8):15).
* Note that the definition of theft over and theft under changed in 1995—see above.

In 1993, the most common types of "theft under" offences reported to the police were household articles (39 per cent), personal articles (17 per cent), and currency and stocks (13 per cent). Less than one per cent of household items stolen were firearms. The rate of young persons charged with "theft under" incidents is more than four times that for adults and more than twice the rate of "theft over" incidents (Hendrick, 1996).

Based on her survey findings, Ray (1987) reports that men and women are equally likely to shoplift. The "five finger discount," while often involving items considerably less than $5,000 in value (e.g., clothes, CD's, jewellery, etc.), costs some major retailers millions of dollars every year. Shoplifting has also increased in recent years and some studies estimate that about one in every nine shoppers steals from department stores. Buckle and Farrington (1984) suggest that shoplifting is so prevalent because of its low-risk detection: less than one per cent. However, accurate counts of shoplifting are difficult to establish because many businesses blend shoplifting losses into their *inventory shrinkage* —a figure that includes merchandise bookkeeping errors, breakage, employee theft, damages, as well as shoplifting losses. Although shoplifting occurs every day, the Christmas season is prime time for shoplifting and fraud. And given the cut-backs in staffing of some retail outlets, the problem may only become worse, although most major department stores now have hidden security cameras and have hired their own in-house security staff (see Box 10.9).

A CLOSER LOOK BOX 10.9

The Amateur vs. Professional Shoplifter

In a pioneering study on shoplifting, Mary Owen Cameron (1964) developed a typology of shoplifters.

The *snitch* is an amateur pilferer. This is the most common type and is usually a respectable person. Cameron believes that snitches are not driven by impulsive urges but usually respond to an opportunity that has been preceded by a stressful experience. When caught, older persons usually change their behaviour, while youths are less likely to be deterred (Klemke, 1978). Cameron estimates that snitches make up nearly 90 per cent of all shoplifters.

The *booster* or *heel* is the professional shoplifter who may steal for personal interest, like the snitch, but more often intends to resell the stolen merchandise to fences or pawnshops. Boosters usually sell the stolen goods at half to one-third the original retail cost. However, some boosters will steal to order. Based on a customer's request for certain goods the shoplifter will target these items.

A third type identified by Ronald Holmes (1983) is the *kleptomaniac*. These types of offenders are usually women, although not exclusively. Kleptomaniacs are not driven to steal for the material gain, but for the thrill and arousal they get from the experi-

Section III: Contemporary Issues in Canadian Criminology

As for "theft over"-related offences, theft from motor vehicles accounted for 49 per cent, in 1993. This was comprised mostly of car stereos and car CD's. It would be interesting to see whether the target has shifted with the new anti-theft stereos now available in most cars (Hendrick, 1996).

Geographically there is considerable variation in the rate of thefts across the country. In 1997, Regina reported the highest rate of auto thefts (1,479 per 100,000) followed by Winnipeg (1,352). The lowest rates of reported auto theft were in the east with St. John's (Nfld), 134 and Saint John (NB), 149. Meanwhile, the western provinces also had the highest median rate of "theft over" and "theft under" incidents.

According to the GSS, young persons aged 15–24 were the most likely to commit theft. Their rate is 93 per 100,000 population as compared to adults ages 45–64 whose rate is 29 per 100,000. Although male and female rates of victimization were nearly equal, younger women were more likely to be victimized than their male counterparts. Not surprisingly, living in an urban setting places a person (regardless of age) at greater risk than living in rural settings.[8] This general trend, however, does not explain why theft rates are so high in the Yukon, which is mostly rural.

The GSS also indicates that the clearance rates for theft are not very promising. In 1993, only 13 per cent of "theft under" incidents and 7 per cent of "theft over" incidents were cleared by charge. An additional 7 per cent of "theft under" incidents and 3% of "theft over" were cleared otherwise.

In 1993–94, "theft under" accounted for 78 per cent of cases heard in court and another 15 per cent involved "theft over" incidents. The most common disposition was probation (43 per cent), followed by community service orders (17 per cent), then open-custody (14 per cent) and secure-custody (8 per cent), while fines made up seven per cent. The median length of custody disposition for "theft over" was approximately 90 days, 30 days for "theft under" in secure facilities and 42 days for open custody placements. Probation order medians ran from 360 days for "theft over" to 270 days for "theft under." The median fines for "theft over" incidents were $200 and $100 for "theft under" (Hendrick, 1996).

Overall, it might be speculated that given the prevalence of theft, the current sentencing dispositions are not having a deterrent effect on offenders—especially among young offenders. Are the dispositions too lenient or are we simply using an ineffective approach? Criminologists need to examine such issues. However, it might also be the case that public apathy undermines crime prevention efforts. Most people view theft as a nuisance rather than a real threat (unless they are the victims) and with limited resources, criminal justice agencies may simply be mimicking public apathy.

Why is Theft so Prevalent?

In his study of college students, Klemke (1992) found that nearly 60 per cent of those surveyed had been involved in at least one shoplifting offence. Katz (1988) suggests that students participate in shoplifting as a release against boredom rather than out of financial need. However, any explanation must consider both individual and cultural factors. For example, after the wall came down in Berlin and Eastern Europeans were allowed to travel freely to the west, there was a sharp rise in shoplifting (along with other forms of criminal activity). Klemke (1992) offers the anomie and strain theories as plausible explanations. One of the North American dreams is economic success. Not being able to afford certain items may cause some (especially young people) to break the law quite readily for economic gain.

Other explanations of theft (and property theft in general) include the routine activities theory and crime for thrills—acts that are "sensually compelling" (see Katz, 1988). In a 1995 study involving almost 2,000 respondents, Bill McCarthy found that males and adolescents were more likely than females and adults to report getting a "high" from an object they considered stealing. Could this "high," however, be explained from an interdisciplinary perspective?

In **summary**, theft is one of the oldest crimes and one of the first common-law crimes created by English judges. Throughout our history, the criteria of theft have undergone a number of up-dates reflecting social and financial change. Other than theft from motor vehicles, shoplifting is the most common type of theft in Canada. Explanations have ranged from stealing for the thrill to *neutralization*—the justification that the store already makes enough profit. Those at risk tend to be the young, the single, the urbanite, the well-educated, the high-income earners, and the homeowners (Hendrick, 1996).

Attempts to control theft have focused on target hardening strategies such as using hidden cameras, hiring undercover staff, placing tags with electronic devices, to even securing some items to racks. But overall, these and other criminal justice measures have had little impact.

Arson

Sections 433–436.1 in the *Criminal Code* pertain to the legal definition and parameters of arson. While not classified as a property-type crime, arson is defined as the (willful) destruction of property through the use of fire or an explosion to property, either against another for fraudulent purposes, or by negligence. It is an extremely destructive act. In addition, while arson is far less common than theft or other types of property- or economically-related crimes, its motivation tends to be more diverse (see Box 10.10).

The Many Faces of Arson

The following incidents represent a cross-section of recent stories that reflect the diversity of reasons why people commit an act of arson.

- Feb. 24, 1997: About 500 tradesmen, many unemployed, descended upon a construction site in Sydney, N.S., to protest against the use of non-unionized workers. The new apartment construction site was set ablaze in protest by the tradesmen while the RCMP recorded the event (Protest by Arson?).
- April 1, 1997: IRA terrorists were involved in three arson attacks against the residences of three Protestants as well as setting fire to a Protestant church (Newsworld, Online).
- June 24, 1997: A 74-year-old man with a history of mental illness was charged with setting fire to the veterans' wing of Sunnybrook Medical Centre in Toronto. The incident occurred on June 14 and resulted in the deaths of three residents of the hospital. (Newsworld, Online). In January 1999, the man finally admitted to torching the rooms, but the court ruled that, given his age and mental condition, he could stay at the hospital (Freed, 1999).

Patterns and Characteristics of Arson

Between 1990 and 1997 the rate of arson incidents reported to police have remained stable (Table 10-3). It is interesting to observe that while the *Juristat* report for 1997 Canadian Crime Statistics provides a numerical account of the number and rate of arson incidents, the publication does not offer any discussion or description of the crime (see Box 10.11).

TABLE 10-3

ARSON: 1990–1997

YEAR	RATE 100,000	NUMBER
1990	32	8,778
1991	44	12,389
1992	46	13,146
1993	43	12,470
1994	46	13,509
1995	44	13,156
1996	43	12,830
1997	42	12,799

Sources: *CCJS*. Assorted Canadian crime statistics. (Vol. 18911):18 and Vol. 17(8):15).

ARSON: IS IT MISCHIEF, VANDALISM, OR AGGRAVATED VANDALISM?

Arson can be a very emotional subject depending on the motivation behind the offence. Under common law, the offence of arson was broad in scope. It was defined as "the malicious and willful burning of the house or outhouse of another man" and was generally classified as a form of *vandalism* (*Working Paper 36—Arson*, 1984:5). However, as societies evolved, so did the meaning of property and a desire arose to legally enunciate the gravity of the act (*actus reus*) and its underlying intent *(mens rea)*.

In response to the increase in arson attacks, The Law Reform Report (#36) attempted to clarify why arson should be treated differently than an act of vandalism.[9]

The Working Paper offered five recommendations in "an attempt to eradicate the complexities and redundancies of an area of law, which despite some unique problems, may be clearly and simply enunciated in our new *Code*" (p. 29).

The recommendations set out to treat arson as an aggravated form of vandalism that should carry a higher maximum penalty. In 1985, the recommendations were incorporated in the *Criminal Code* amendments. Today, arson is treated more seriously than mischief or vandalism, because the law reflects the emotional and personal value we place on our property.

Do you agree with these changes? Socially, what might arson represent?

Males are far more likely to be charged with arson than women (86 per cent vs. 14 per cent). In addition, while the median age of male fire setters is 19, it is almost double that for women—33 years. Why is there such an age difference? Part of the explanation might lie in understanding the different types of arson and the motivations underlying such acts.

In his study of young arsonists, Wayne Wooden (1991) identified four categories of juvenile arsonists:

1. The "playing with matches" fire setters are children, usually between the ages of four and nine, who start a fire accidentally while playing with matches carelessly left around.

2. The "crying for help" fire setter tends to be a little older (ages 7–13) and sets fires to reduce anxiety or stress. The source of such feelings is usually related to family-based issues such as divorce, abuse, death, or family strife. These youths have difficulty expressing their pain so they act it out. Gaynor and Stern (1993) suggest that they usually feel remorse for their actions.

3. The "delinquent" fire setter is the youth (ages 14–18) who sets fire to property in retaliation for some criticism he might have received (see Box 10.11 above). Gaynor and Stern (1993) found that delinquent fire setters are

mostly males (10:1) characterized by anger, antisocial personalities, and a lack of regard for social rules and norms.

4. The "severely disturbed" fire setter is a youth who has some personality disturbance and is likely to set numerous fires. The term *pyromaniac* is sometimes used to describe these individuals.

Even more recently, Swaffer and Hollin (1995) studied a group of female and male adolescent fire setters and came up with some slightly different categories. Although their sample size was small (N=17), it was interesting to observe that most of the youths said they set fires out of "revenge" (N=5). In two categories, three youths said they set fires either to conceal a crime or because of peer pressure. What is interesting to note is that all three females reported "self-injury" as the motivation for their fire setting.

Finally, the Alberta Juvenile Firesetter Handbook (Wijayasinghe, 1994) uses a combination of these categories and provides some interesting data comparing reasons for the act and the damage in dollar value (see Table 10-4).

TABLE 10-4

JUVENILE ARSONIST IN ALBERTA BY REASON 1987–1991

REASONS	FIRES	ARSONISTS	DEATHS	INJURIES	$ LOSS
Mischief	93	163	0	8	2,576,683
Pyromania	12	12	0	0	33,654
Cover Other Crime	11	14	0	0	609,186
Revenge	9	12	0	0	238,428
Spite	8	9	0	5	5,677,189
Mental	2	2	0	0	45,100
Unknown	46	68	0	2	296,194
Total	186	280	0	15	9,476,434

Not unlike juveniles, adults commit arson for a variety of reasons. The most common form is *arson for profit*. For example, the owner of a failing business might torch his or her building in order to claim insurance money. In an effort to reduce the risk of being caught, the owner might hire a professional lawyer (Bennett and Hess, 1984). Today, many insurance companies require a fire inspection before insuring buildings in an effort to make it more difficult to reduce fraudulent claims.

Other motives include *revenge* (Somers, 1984). In addition, some psychologists state that adult fire setters commonly suffer from personality disorders. Webb and her colleagues (1990) argue that most adult arson should be viewed as a mental health problem—not a criminal act. The emotionally disturbed *pyro-*

maniac usually attempts to cover or destroy evidence of another crime. Vito and Holmes (1994:315) cite an example in which a husband set fire to his house after killing his wife—hoping to incinerate the evidence. However, the fire department was able to put the fire out and find his wife's remains.

Finally, organized crime groups and political terrorists are also known to use arson. Between 1976 and 1980, Cecil Kirby, a Satan's Choice motorcycle club member, carried out over 100 contracts for the Mafia in Canada. Among the crimes he committed included arson, assault, bombing, and attempted murder (Carrigan, 1991). The Provisional Irish Republican Army (PIRA) is probably the best-known terrorist group to frequently resort to arson. Over the years, their activities are believed to be responsible for over 1,000 deaths and many more injuries.

According to research by Pettiway (1988), high arson patterns could be explained by *environmental/ecological theories* (Chapter 7). He found that the rate of arson was significantly related to the age of the housing—the older the house, the greater the likelihood of arson. Using the *routine activities theory* (Chapter 8) Stahura and Hollinger (1988) were also able to explain arson. They found that criminal motivation (e.g., percentage of poor, unemployed and youth) and criminal opportunities (e.g., percentage of old and multiple housing, number of commercial/industrial buildings) and guardianship (e.g., police resources, female labour force participation) were directly and/or indirectly related to arson rates.

In **summary**, arson, although not legally defined as a property offence, involves the willful destruction of private or public property. The motivation of arsonists is varied, and while the rate of arson has not changed significantly in recent years the dollar loss due to arson is extremely high.

It is sometimes difficult for investigators to determine whether a fire was accidental or deliberate. However, today virtually every major fire department has trained specialists who try to determine the cause of a fire. Because arson is so destructive and relatively easy to commit, criminologists need to better understand the motives underlying arsonist attacks so that they can be prevented.

Motor-Vehicle Crimes

REALITY CHECK BOX 10.12

MOTOR-VEHICLE CRIMES

In September 1996, the Ontario Provincial Police (OPP), in cooperation with several regional police forces and Canada Customs, successfully smashed a sophisticated ring of car thieves. The ring involved at least six members. The police had recovered

95 luxury vehicles valued at $2.5 million, destined mostly for Vietnam. The gang hired youths and adults and paid them from $300 to $500 to steal cars for a Mississauga import-export business.

The head of the OPP theft team pointed out that Ontario has the highest rate of stolen vehicles in Canada and observed that since 1990, auto theft had increased by 100 per cent.

Most of the cars recovered were Toyota Camrys and Honda Accords although the police know that the ring has also stolen higher-end models such as Lexuses, Mercedeses, and BMW's.

Police believe that stolen vehicles likely fetch a price in Vietnam at least three times higher than their Canadian market value.

Source: B. Mitchell (1996).

North Americans seem to have a "love-affair" with their automobiles. In 1994, there were nearly 18 million motor vehicles registered across Canada, of which approximately 13.7 million were passenger automobiles (*Canadian dimensions* ..., 1997). The fact that the auto industry in one of the biggest in North America is no coincidence. We spend billions every year maintaining and nurturing these vehicles. Therefore, it should come as no surprise that motor-vehicle crimes (i.e., carjacking, joyriding, theft, and vandalism) have been increasing in recent years.

Under the subheading "Offences Resembling Theft," section 335 pertains to motor-vehicle theft or "*vessel* without consent." Now, if you do not believe that Canadians take our means of transport seriously, reflect on the legal definition of a *vessel*. Section 214 defines a vessel as "a machine designed to derive support in the atmosphere primarily from reactions against the earth's surface of air expelled from the machine." Yet the punishment for taking a motor vehicle without consent is only punishable on a summary conviction.

In this section, we will look at some of the general patterns and characteristics of motor-vehicle crimes (MVC), in particular motor-vehicle theft. We will examine some of the strategies that have been introduced to combat the problem.

Patterns and Characteristics of MVC[10]

FYI BOX 10.13

Is Your Car Secure?

Car theft in North America occurs on average every 20 seconds (Shaw, 1997).

After a relatively stable rate between 1981 and 1987, the motor-vehicle theft (MVT) rate increased 62.7 per cent from 1988 to 1993. Starting in 1994 the rate began to nudge up (see Table 10-5). In 1995, MCV represented one in ten property crimes and, according to the 1993 GSS, losses from MVT, property theft from motor vehicles, and vandalism amounted to $1.6 billion (Trembley, Clermont, and Cusson, 1996).

TABLE 10-5

MOTOR VEHICLE THEFT: 1990–1997

YEAR	RATE	NUMBER
1990	411	114,082
1991	496	139,345
1992	514	146,801
1993	541	156,685
1994	545	159,469
1995	546	161,696
1996	601	178,123
1997	585	177,286

Sources: *CCJS*. Assorted Canadian crime statistics. (Annual Reports).

By now, you have probably surmised that MVC, like other property-related crimes, varies geographically as well. Throughout the 1990s, Quebec has had the highest motor theft rate (12.9 per 1,000 registration in 1993) with several of the western provinces taking turns at having the second highest rate. Newfoundland has consistently had the lowest reported rates (1.8 per 1,000 registrations in 1993) of motor-vehicle theft. Roy (1988 cited in Trembley et al., 1996:264) offers an explanation as to why Quebec may have a higher rate than other provinces. He points that "junked vehicles are allowed to go back on the street in Quebec and not in Ontario … as a result, wrecked vehicles are purchased by Quebec-based "retag operators"… and their vehicle identification numbers subsequently used to provide a legitimate number for a locally stolen vehicle."

Similar variations can be found internationally. Victimization data for 1988 reveal that France had the highest rate of car thefts while Spain had the highest rate of thefts from cars, and Canada the highest rate of car vandalism (Morrison and Ogrodnick, 1994). Overall, if you cherish your vehicle, Australia represents the country with the greatest risk of something happening to your car. Of the fourteen countries involved in the victimization survey, Switzerland had the lowest rates in all three categories (Ibid).

So which kind of car should you not own if you are worried about car theft? A few years ago (1992–93), the two-door Ford Mustang Cobra GT and two-door

Volkswagen Golf were the most common targets while the Mercury Sable and Oldsmobile Ninety-Eight had the best claim experience (least likely to be targeted) (Morrison, 1996). However, as can be seen in Table 10-6, more recently the trends have changed.

TABLE 10-6

RELATIVE FREQUENCY OF AUTO THEFT CLAIMS: 1995–96

WORST RESULTS		BEST RESULTS	
Honda Prelude	456	Ford Crown Victoria	12
Jeep YJ	455	Oldsmobile Eighty Eight	12
Suzuki Sidekick	328	Buick Regal 4-door	16
Acura Integra	313	Lincoln Town Car	16
Jeep Grand Cherokee	217	Hyundai Sonata	17

Source: Adapted from Bronskill, 1998, January 28. Calgary Herald, A2

Throughout the mid-1990s, youths aged 12–17 years accounted for almost half of the persons charged with MVT, one-third of those charged with theft from motor vehicles, and nearly one-quarter of those charged with automotive vandalism (Morrison, 1996). When youths steal a vehicle, most (approximately 76 per cent) of their acts amount to *joyriding*—taking vehicles for a short period for purposes of pleasure or transportation. Youths are more likely to steal vehicles during July and August—the summer holidays. However, research shows they rarely are suspected or apprehended. In 1994, only 10 per cent of MVTs were solved by the police. For example, the GSS shows that in 1993, 40 per cent of all motor-vehicle vandalisms "cleared otherwise" involved youths 12–17 years of age. Another 16 per cent were youths under the age of 12. The data indicated that most young offenders "are dealt with through avenues other than the formal criminal justice system" (Ibid, 197).[11]

Explaining Motor-Vehicle Crimes

Why are motor-vehicle crimes so prevalent and why do (mostly young) people become involved in motor-vehicle crimes? Morrison (1996) cites a number of studies whose explanations range from: (1) The symbolism we attach to motor vehicles. Cars are a status symbol and whether they are stolen for a joy ride or so decals can be removed, the action provides the offender with a sense of power, and (2) Initial MVC may be centred on peer influence, boredom, the desire to drive something with status, commission of another crime and money reward. The risk of auto theft is further enhanced by the fact that potential victims leave their valuables insecure and often in plain view.

In terms of theft for profit, Light, Nee, and Ingham (1993) found that these types of offenders developed a dependency on this type of income. However, they found that most youths simply grow out of the activity. It is not the legal sanction that deters them but simply "growing-up."

Finally, Tremblay et al. (1996) borrow from Felson's *routine activities theory* and suggest that one approach that might be used to understand the motivation of joyriders is to undertake a cross-sectional analysis of their responsiveness to structural features or urban environments. However, they point out that the process of developing a fruitful explanatory model requires "a much more detailed investigation of the routine activities and concerns of" all the factors that could be involved.

A number of years ago Karmen (1979) raised a number of interesting questions about the motivation of motor-vehicle crimes. Karmen pointed out that it is not only important to understand the relationship between motor-vehicle thieves/vandals and their victims but also the role the automotive industry plays in the design and security of cars. For example, why are cars easy to damage but expensive to repair? Why are cars still relatively easy to steal? Does the automotive industry have a personal stake? Surveys indicate that most people are willing to pay higher purchase prices for effective security features.

Recently, several of the automakers have taken steps to target harden their vehicles. In 1997, Ford Taurus introduced an electronic key that eliminates the ability to "hot wire" a car. Several leading automakers have equipped cars with GIS devices that enable the vehicle to be tracked via a satellite and pinpoint its location. Some American states such as Michigan have introduced an information hot line, *Operation HEAT* (Help Eliminate Auto Theft) which has helped to successfully recover over 900 vehicles, resulting in the arrest of 647 people (Siegel, 1995). Another novel program introduced in the States is the national *Watch Your Car Program*. Owners of vehicles "voluntarily display a decal or device, such as a state-issued, customized licence plate on their vehicles to alert police that their vehicles are not normally driven between the hours of 1 a.m. and 5 a.m." (The Watch Your Car program, 1996). The decals are tamper-resistant. Some states also use decals that indicate that the car is not normally operated near international borders or ports. For a nominal fee, all participants are registered with law enforcement officials.

Perhaps the most common device, which is relatively inexpensive and has received endorsements from the police and given considerable media attention, is "The Club"—the steering-column locking device.

When one takes into account all the target hardening measures that have been introduced and tried over the years, perhaps it is time to consider an alternative strategy. For example, crime prevention strategies should consider both the types of vehicles being targeted and the motivation of the perpetrator.

In **summary**, motor-vehicle crimes have increased in recent years. The patterns vary geographically as do the characteristics of offenders. The problem of motor-vehicle crimes is not unique to Canada, or North America. Sophisticated professional car stealing rings serve as reminders that in spite of all the security devices and safety programs that have been introduced these measures have done little to curb the problem.

As long as we continue to value automobiles and as long as the average cost of vehicles remains high, the opportunity for motor-vehicle crimes will not go away.[12] We need to focus not only on security measures but also to better understand the motivation behind these crimes. This will require an integrated and interdisciplinary approach. In the meantime, we might want to look to see what countries with low theft rates are doing.

Summary

Property crimes, also referred to as **economic crimes**, are generally committed with the intent of providing financial reward to the offender. The majority of property crimes are committed by youths or young male adults, and amateurs who are responding to opportunities. However, each property crime discussed also attracts professional criminals.

Several of the categories could readily cross over into violent crime (theft), organized crime (fraud), or white-collar crime (arson) classifications. This reflects the *relative* and *evolutive* nature of crime, in general. Furthermore, it was observed that most property crime and in particular theft have been legally revised throughout Canadian history to reflect social and economic changes.

Most crime prevention strategies have focused on **target hardening** strategies (e.g., automobiles, credit card industry, and home security). As Easton and Brantingham (1998) recently reported, Canadians spend nearly $200 million every year to protect themselves and their property with marginal or no success.

Most of the theories used to explain property crimes tend to be sociologically-based with a preponderance of such perspectives as routine activities theory, ecological theory, neutralization, economic deprivation, and social process. Although they offer conceptually sound explanations, the policies derived from them have had a questionable impact on reducing (reported) property crime incidents. Crime needs to take a new approach, an approach that is *integrated* and *interdisciplinary* and focuses on social, environmental, political, and individual factors. We need to develop models that can better explain the interaction between the individual and his or her environment, and whose recommendations have a measurable impact on crime. Given the recent inroads made in comparative studies, this line of inquiry may also hold promise.

Comparative criminology, it can be argued, has become a necessity as the world has become a "global village." Consider, for example, in 1996, Canada exported $2.8 billion worth of goods and imported $2.4 billion worth of goods (Imports and exports ..., 1998). Furthermore, many of the products we use and wear are manufactured somewhere else. Other signs of globalization are the forming of the European Common Market, the collapse of Communism in 1990, and in North America the North American Free Trade agreement. We are surrounded by examples of globalization.

Along with all the benefits of globalization have come new forms of transnational crime (e.g., drug, automobile, and property trafficking, computer crime, fraud, money laundering, organized crime, terrorism, etc.). Criminologists, therefore, must not only focus on regional trends but also engage in international cooperation to study violent and property crime and control it. We will return to the issue of comparative criminology in Chapter 14.

Finally, regardless of how the official sources try to play up the fact that conventional crime rates have declined throughout the mid-1990s, the rates are still alarmingly high compared with those from the 1960s through the 1980s. Now more than ever, criminologists must strive to understand the realities of conventional crime. Crime is the product of an interaction between human behaviour (more specifically, behaviour as the product of biological rather than psychological factors) and environmental factors (i.e., genetic, physical, and social factors). This will require an interdisciplinary approach. Social policies should endeavour to incorporate such approaches in their efforts to remedy these crimes. Among the most fundamental issues that criminologists need to resolve in forging their theoretical paradigms are the practical issues of social implications. Should we respond to (conventional) crimes legalistically (e.g., revise provincial Pawnshop Acts, devise alternative sentencing practices, improve monitoring systems, etc.), should we respond preventively (e.g., address substance addiction, educational programs, etc.) or find some balanced approach? We will explore some of these issues in Chapter 14. However, it is now time to move on to less *conventional* crimes—organized crime and white-collar crime.

Discussion Questions

1. What can the property crime statistics tell us about crime trends and patterns in Canada? Has the picture changed in recent years? Why?

2. Who is primarily responsible for committing property crimes? Are there common denominators? What are some of the major explanatory models for the different types of crimes covered?

3. Are there any common causal factors that can be used to explain both violent and property crimes?

4. Why are the crimes covered in the chapter referred to as *conventional* crimes? How do they differ from *non-conventional* crimes?

5. Throughout the semester collect at least a dozen media articles related to the "new" forms of crimes against property. What do they tell us about the nature and extent of the

problem? What kinds of solutions, if any, are offered? Do they pose a more serious threat to society?

6. Based on the highlights of the major federal parties (Appendix 5), which party do you think has the best approaches to control crimes against property? Why?

Key Concepts

Conventional crime	property crime	break and enter
Crime rate	home invasion	fraud
Theft	shoplifting	arson
Vandalism	motor-vehicle crime	clearance rate
Economic crimes	target hardening	

Weblinks

www.statcan.ca/english/pgdb/state/justice.html The homepage for Statistics Canada. A great way to keep up with the latest crime data.

www.undcp.or.at/unlinks.html The United Nations homepage on crime and crime statistics. Also has numerous international links.

www.fire.ottawa.ca/juvenile.html The Ottawa Fire Department established a "Juvenile Fire Setters" program in 1990. Their site offers tips to identifying juvenile fire setters and related information.

www.tap.net/~hyslo/ Homepage of the Fraud Information Centre. It has many useful links ranging from ethical issues to helpful hints and related Web sites.

With a little effort you can locate property crime data/information for virtually any country around the world and/or specific reports on any type of property crime. For example, by using the search engine "altavistacanada.com" and entering any of the property crimes, you will find many sites.

Footnotes

1. In 1994, insurance companies paid out $48M on B & E claims alone (Vancouver Board..., 1998).

2. In 1995, there were approximately 2 000 incidents of B & E involving the theft of firearms. Rifles accounted for 39 per cent, shotguns for 29 per cent, restricted weapons for 9 per cent and other types 23 per cent (*CCJS. Canadian crime statistics—1995*, 1997). Since 1991 people are more likely to be killed by a handgun then they are by a rifle or shotgun (*CCJS*, 1996:16(11)).

3. Statistics Canada only classifies the time of offences into four clusters of six hours each. While this may be practical since burglars are not interested in confrontation, studies might want to ask burglars more specific questions that help to explain and understand the decision-making process employed by B & E artists.

4. Fraud used to be called *false pretence*. It was introduced by the English Parliament in 1757 to cover an area of law not addressed by *larceny* (theft) statutes. As with many of England's classifications of criminal law, our original *Criminal Code* used the term "false pretence and fraud" until it was later changed to simply fraud (Carrigan, 1991).

5. Statistics Canada does not differentiate between property and white-collar related fraud. All fraud incidents are reported under property crime.

6. See *CCJS*, 1998, 18(11), and "A graphic overview of crime…," 1996.

7. An area that is a growing concern in academia has been cases of data fabrication, document fabrication, and even degree fabrication. Over the years several academics have been charged with "manipulating" their data to complement their theories, used other people's work and claimed it as their own, and claimed to have degrees that they did not earn. Students plagiarizing material is another form of document fabrication that can result in dismissal from the institution.

8. See Hendrick, 1996 for further details.

9. Prior to 1985, arson came under s. 392 (now s. 436).

10. This section will not differentiate between automobiles, trucks and minivans, motorcycles, or other motorized vehicles. While data are available, it is beyond the scope of this section to provide such a detailed breakdown. For further discussion see Trembley et al. (1996).

11. Youths under the age of 12 cannot be charged with a criminal offence and young offenders are either asked to pay restitution, given a warning, and/or their parents may be informed (Morrison, 1996). Pending legislation of the proposed *Youth Criminal Justice Act*, exceptions may be made.

12. For nearly 20 years, Japan's *Magazine X* has relied on sophisticated spying techniques to produce pictures and details on Japan's big automakers' concept designs and innovations. The magazine sells over 300,000 copies per month (Spies…, 1999).

Organized and Corporate Crime:
Economic Crimes of the Powerful

*"Reason why crime doesn't pay is that when
it does it is called by a more respectable name."*

(Justice) Tom Clark

Learning Outcomes

After you have completed this chapter, you should be able to:

- Describe the nature and significance of organized crime.

- Discuss the various types of organized crime groups in Canada.

- Assess the extent of corporate crime and the difficulty in regulating it.

- Discuss the causes of corporate crime.

- Evaluate what can be done to regulate corporate crime.

Introduction

In the previous two chapters we dealt with conventional crimes or "crimes of the street"—violent crimes and property crimes. Conventional crimes, typically, but not always, are committed by the middle and lower socio-economic classes. For the most part, conventional crimes can be committed by individuals or small

groups. Information on violent crimes and property crimes is readily available through official police records (Uniform Crime Reports—see Chapter 3). There are, however, other forms of crime whose impact can be more devastating and present unique challenges to criminologists.

Organized crimes and **corporate crimes** are typically committed by powerful and/or influential groups or individuals. As illustrated in Box 11.1, because of the powerful status they hold, the impact of their crimes can be costly in both human and financial terms. They can, and often do, have an international impact thereby making it difficult for criminal justice agencies to combat these types of crime. In this chapter, we will examine a variety of organized crimes and corporate crimes. We will examine their characteristics, methods, motives, trends, and review some of the major theoretical perspectives used to explain them. In addition, we will also examine what strategies criminologists have recommended and what the state has done to deal with these powerful groups and their illegal activities (see Box 11.2).

REALITY CHECK BOX 11.1

THE MANY FACES OF ORGANIZED CRIME

- Dec. 1996: Two Iranian nationals, living in Toronto, were charged with conspiracy to smuggle illegal immigrants (mostly Iranians) into Canada by using false travel documents. The smuggling ring originated in the Netherlands. The smugglers charged between $5,000 to $6,000 US to smuggle illegal immigrants into Canada. It is estimated that over a three year period, as many as 5,000 people have been smuggled into Canada (Refugee smuggling ring smashed).

- Dec. 1996: Two Nova Scotia men were sentenced to 20 years for conspiracy to import narcotics. They had been part of a $1 billion cocaine smuggling operation between Canada and Colombia. When arrested in 1991 they had approximately 1,500 kilograms of cocaine on their boat. They had been hired by a Colombian drug cartel to bring the cargo ashore (Massive smuggling ...).

- July 1997: A gang made up mostly of Romanian citizens has been involved in more than a dozen train robberies in Eastern Canada. The gang members break into container cars that are stopped. Then, once the train is moving they throw the items off to other gang members travelling in vehicles. CP and CN started loading their own cars but the bandits then began to cut access holes in the containers (Gang robbing ...).

- Oct. 1997: An organized group of poachers in northern Alberta were arrested and charged with 185 counts of illegally selling fish and wild game. Several local restaurants were also charged with trafficking in the illegal fish and wild game. Authorities said understaffing prevents them from better monitoring this lucrative activity (Arnold).

Organized Crime

History of Organized Crime

Probably since the dawn of time, human beings have been interested in gathering "goods and services" of one sort or another. Then, as we moved from being a hunting and gathering society to a mercantile and feudal system and from rural settings into urban settings, our methods of acquiring "profit" illegally began to flourish (Wright and Fox, 1978).

Piracy is among the earliest examples of organized crime. Some of the ancient Phoenicians (c. 1200 BC to 146 BC) roamed the Mediterranean Sea and plundered ships. From the close of the eighth century, the Vikings of Scandinavia were also known to practice acts of piracy and plunder throughout France, Scotland, England and Ireland. However, the most famous examples of piracy, made popular today through movie images, occurred during the 1600s. Flamboyant, swashbuckling pirates, wearing eye patches and bandannas, roamed the seas to plunder and pillage ships carrying goods to and from colonies in the New World.

Today, if you travel up the Thames River in London, England, you can still see the pubs along the water's edge named after some of the more notorious pirates. And even Canada had its pirates (see Box 11.3).

Piracy on the Canadian High Seas

Although old-style piracy had all but disappeared by the early nineteenth century, there were occasional incidents of piracy. In October of 1809, the schooner *Three Sisters* was en route to Halifax from Gaspé with a cargo of fish. One of the schooner's passengers, Edward Jordan, convinced the ship's mate to join him in a scheme to seize the schooner from its captain, John Stairs. Along with his ship's mate, Jordan went on a shooting spree, killing several of the crewmen, but Captain Stairs was able to jump overboard after being wounded. He was left to drown until a passing boat rescued him and informed the authorities in Halifax. Jordan and the schooner were soon found and captured. Jordan was tried and found guilty of piracy. He was then hanged, and his body gibbeted and put on public display. Carrigan (1991) provides an interesting account of similar incidents involving piracy during Canada's frontier days.

A quota has been placed on both Canadian and American fishers. BC fishermen were facing the seizure of their boats as well as charges for taking salmon illegally in Alaskan waters. In a similar case at the other end of the country, the captain of a Spanish trawler lied about taking halibut from Canadian waters. In 1997, he was charged by the European Union court with piracy (Spanish trawler..., 1997).

Starting in the late 1720s, honest officials began to clamp down on piracy. Several high profile pirates were executed and the state began to take back some control (Kenney and Finkenauer, 1995). However, Kenney and Finkenauer (1995:70) note that the age of piracy had flourished "only because the colonists wanted it to." In fact, Sir Robert Peel's London Metropolitan Police in 1850 was formed partly in response to a growing crime problem—many of the early police officers were involved in gang-type or criminal activities (Emerging Gangs, 1997).

During the Industrial Revolution and the rapid urbanization of the New World, there was a swelling of the poor and unemployed. Life for many was very difficult. Amid such conditions, crime began to flourish (see generally Carrigan, 1991). Youths turned to stealing, women to prostitution, and politicians to bribes as a means of economic gain. In some cases young men formed gangs in order to maximize their profits and protect themselves from the police (Kenney and Finkenauer, 1995). In many cases these gangs had ethnic lineage (e.g., Italian, Jewish, and Irish), and, more recently, Hispanic and Caribbean roots. These groups are typical of the new immigrant groups in the United States and Canada.

As Abadinsky (1994) observes, the city gangs were the forerunners of organized crime. With time they evolved into powerful and sophisticated groups who relied on careful planning and co-ordination of effort to acquire illegal profits. Today organized crime has become an international concern. Italy has La Cosa Nostra, Southeast Asia has the Triads, China, Hong Kong and Taiwan the Tong, Japan the Yakuza, Russia has its own Mafia, and Canada has various illegal motorcycle gangs such as the Hell's Angels, Rock Machine, Crim Reapers, and the Rebels, among 30 other bike gangs (CISC, 1998) (see p. 378).

Defining Organized Crime

Howard Abadinsky (1994), one of the leading North American authorities on organized crime observes that organized crime has been poorly defined. He suggests this may be because the *Organized Crime Control Act* of 1970 (revised in 1984 and 1986) does not offer a clear definition either.

A 1976 American Task Force defined organized crime as: Two or more persons who, with continuity of purpose engage in one or more of the following activities: (1) the supplying of illegal goods and services (e.g., loansharking and vice trade), and (2) predatory crime (e.g., fence rings, gangs, and terrorist activities).

Various criminologists (e.g., Maltz, 1990; Stamler, 1996) have all proposed their own definitions. However, they all share similar descriptors as offered by the 1976 Task Force definition. One of the challenges confronting a clear definition is the ability to "capture the essential aspects of the 'process' that certain criminals use in carrying out criminal activity" (Beare, 1996:266).

As stated earlier, the term "organized crime" does not appear in the Canadian *Criminal Code,* but legislation has provided provisions to combat organized crime. In 1989, the Proceeds of Crime legislation used the term "**enterprise crime**" and designated 24 offences to be enterprise/organized crimes (Baere, 1996) (see Box 11.4). Subsequently, several legislative amendments have been passed to strengthen the powers of criminal justice agents so they can more aggressively combat organized crime. The most recent legislative measure was Bill C-123 in 1993. Known as the *Seized Property Management Act* (S.C. 1993, Chapter 37), it provides the latest legal mechanism to combat organized crime.[2]

A CLOSER LOOK BOX 11.4

"Enterprise Crime Offences"—Proceeds of Crime

Under section 462.3 of the 1997 Canadian *Criminal Code*, "enterprise crime offence" means an offence against any of the following provisions, namely:
• Bribery of judicial officers;
• Weapons trafficking;

- Possession for purpose of weapons trafficking;
- Making automatic firearms;
- Importing or exporting knowing it is unauthorized;
- Bribery of officers;
- Frauds upon the government;
- Breach of trust by public officer;
- Corrupting morals;
- Child pornography;
- Keeping gaming or betting house;
- Betting, common bawdy-house;
- Betting, pool-selling, book-making, etc.;
- Keeping common bawdy-house;
- Criminal interest rate;
- Procuring;
- Extortion;
- Punishment for forgery;
- Uttering forged document;
- Fraud;
- Fraudulent manipulation of stock exchange transaction;
- Secret commissions;
- Arson;
- Making counterfeit money;
- Uttering, etc. counterfeit money;
- Laundering proceeds of crime; and
- An offence against possession of property obtained by crime (s. 354).

Note: As of 1998 several of the provisions had replaced 1995 classifications and the text had not yet been brought into force by the Governor in Council.

Appreciating the difficulty in defining organized crime, Abadinsky (1994), along with several other scholars, has focused on identifying a set of attributes that are commonly found among organized crime groups. They include, but are not limited to the following:

- *Nonideological*: Most organized crime groups have no political affiliation. Their goals are not directly motivated by political concerns.

- *Hierarchial*: There is a chain of command. Three or more permanent positions of authority usually exist within the group.

- *Limited or exclusive in membership*: Organized crime groups are sometimes formed along ethnic, racial, kinship, and prior criminal records lines. The powerful Bronfman family of Montreal, now seen as a leader in the entertainment industry, founded its fortune on alcohol smuggling to the United

States during prohibition (*Committee for a Safe Society,* 1997). Most members are male. Although women may be found within organized crime groups, their role is usually one of "service" to the male members.

- *Perpetuous*: Constitutes an ongoing criminal conspiracy designed to persist over time.
- *Organized through specialization or division of labour:* Members have certain areas of responsibility such as enforcers, soldiers, money movers, etc.
- *Monopolistic:* Organized crime groups strive for hegemony (dominance) over a geographic area, thereby restraining competition and increasing their own profit.
- *Governed by rules and regulations:* Virtually all organized crime groups require their members to take an oath of secrecy. Members of the Japanese Yakuza used to have to submit to having a joint of their little finger removed. Other gangs require new members to undergo a hazing, or beatings by fellow members, while others require a criminal act as part of their initiation.

Organized Crime Groups in Canada

REALITY CHECK BOX 11.5

RCMP NOT AS WELL ORGANIZED AS ORGANIZED CRIME FAMILIES!

Between 1990 and 1994, an undercover RCMP operation inadvertently helped Colombian drug traffickers and their associates import and sell almost 5,000 kilograms of cocaine. The drugs had an estimated street value of $2 billion. A report revealed that the sting operation failed as a result of insufficient police manpower, a reluctance of senior RCMP officials to respond to requests for assistance, and internal security breaches by at least two corrupt officers. The money was laundered through the RCMP company known as the Montreal International Currency Centre Inc. The RCMP fiasco is even suspected of helping "the clandestine drug pipeline between Colombia's cocaine cartels and Canadian biker gangs and Italian mafia gangs that import, distribute and sell cocaine to users and addicts in Canada" (McIntosh, 1998:A2). Koningsfeld (1998) points out that the art of money laundering has become very sophisticated through the use of "foreign legal persons" (e.g., companies, legal entities, or foreign legal persons) and the Internet. His Dutch-based organization specializes in tracking such enterprises. He calls for international cooperation and the establishment of databanks of all companies and their beneficial owners. As he states, "the weakest link is the problem of identification of the beneficial owner."

Several Canadian studies (Stamler, 1996; CACP, 1993) have identified a range of organized crime groups operating in Canada today. Moreover, although Canadian history is dotted with incidents of "gang" related crimes (see Carrigan, 1991), the government has never kept crime statistics on gangs, mobs, or organized crime groups. Most accounts come from media stories or special reports and, as discussed in Chapter 2, their coverage does not always provide a comprehensive picture of how extensive and pervasive organized crime is in Canada.

In this section, we will review several of the more prominent forms of organized crime groups that exist in Canada today. Although some forms differ in their orientation, they share many of the characteristics defined by Abadinsky (1994).

Aboriginal Crime Groups

During the early 1990s, three Indian reserves in eastern Canada, Akwesasne, Kahnawake, and St. Regis, were involved in cigarette smuggling operations. In addition, a few reserves have been known to be involved in smuggling alcohol and in illegal gaming operations. Beare (1996:272) describes the Aboriginal organized crime activities as "a perfect example of a 'manufactured' organized crime problem."

In February 1994, Canadian cigarettes were sold "duty and tax exempt" for export to the United States and to Europe as well as to special categories of customers such as duty-free stores, embassies, and the Aboriginals' reserves. In their campaign to deter smoking, the government began to dramatically increase the amount of tax on cigarettes to the point where the temptation to exploit this tax-exempt privilege became quite compelling for some groups. By 1993, a legally sold carton of cigarettes cost almost $50 compared to $22 for an untaxed carton available on the black market (Linden cited in Stamler, 1996:429). As Baere (1996) observed, cigarette smuggling took on the same aura as bootlegging (smuggling alcohol) in the 1920s when the public tended to sympathize with these entrepreneurs. Although legally a crime, smuggling is analogous to the Robin Hood scenario—turning a "bad" tax situation into a "good" profit. Between 1990 and 1993, over $1 billion of tax revenue was lost to smuggling activities (Linden cited in Stamler, 1996).

Aboriginal organized crime groups could make a profit of over a million dollars with a single tractor trailer loaded with 1,200 cases of cigarettes (Ibid, 272). Such crimes of "opportunity" combined with the ability to make easy profits have made intervention difficult. The problem of controlling or regulating smuggling activities among First Nations people is further compounded by their efforts to seek self-government rights over their reserves.

SMUGGLING RING GOES UP IN SMOKE

In December 1996, police arrested 14 individuals from Quebec and New Brunswick who had been involved in a smuggling ring worth $2 million in alcohol, cigarettes, and tobacco products. During the arrest, police seized $403,634 worth of contraband. The smugglers had bought their products from a supplier in the Akwesasne Reserve. The smugglers averaged $900 a day and their products ended up as far away as Vancouver (Smuggling ring..., 1996).

What can be done? As a crime of opportunity, it is difficult for law enforcement agencies to counter such activities. In 1994, the situation had become so critical that the government dramatically reduced cigarette taxes. Other measures involved closer cooperation among law enforcement agencies, and better prosecution and cooperation between Customs and Revenue Canada (CACP, 1994). However, perhaps the most effective strategy would be to inform the public and clarify its role and responsibility in not supporting organizations engaging "black market" activities. In criminology, this strategy is generally referred to as *crime prevention through social development* (see Chapter 14 for further discussion). However, what is the likelihood of not buying something at a reduced price if you know you are not likely to be prosecuted for it? Do you think it is right to levy such high taxes on alcohol and tobacco? Is the government being responsible in its actions? Are there alternative strategies that could/should be considered?

Cartels

The definition of a cartel is "a combination of independent commercial enterprises designed to limit competition." A special report in *Criminal Justice International* (1994) described cartels as a new breed of international organized crime that transcends nations. They are seen as threats to democracy, national security and development. The report estimates that in the early 1990s there were over 2,600 organized cartels around the world.

The Colombian cartels, for example, specialize in importing and trafficking in cocaine. Before Pablo Escobar, one of the Cali Cartel (in Colombia) leaders was caught, it is estimated that he had made $4 billion (U.S.) from trafficking in cocaine. It is estimated that in Colombia alone there are twenty organized crime families, four of which have major international operations (Stamler, 1996). It is estimated that they provide a least 75 per cent of the cocaine that is used in Canada and the United States (Ibid).

Cocaine—A Medicinal Drug?

Cocaine is derived from the leaves of the coca shrub where it has grown naturally in the Andean highlands since 1500 BC. It has been used for medicinal and tonic purposes. "Abuse" of the product began after 1862 when a German chemist was able to extract an alkaloid that he labelled "cocain." Its potent properties were soon being touted as a "magical substance" by Sigmund Freud in 1886. *Coca Cola,* in the late 1800s, placed the inscription "the tonic properties of the wonderful COCA Plant and the famous Cola Nut" on their bottles while several drug companies offered an energizing cocaine wine. Today, cocaine is used in a variety of pharmaceutical products. However, in 1961 a treaty ratified by 125 nations agreed to a ban on producing or processing cocaine,— except for medicinal purposes. It was shortly thereafter that cocaine became the drug of choice, and a marketable item for organized crime groups (White, 1989).

Although the Colombian government, helped by financial aid from the United States, has made efforts to curtail the drug cartels, the cartels' multi-billion dollar operation is not likely to be easily eradicated. Their sophisticated infrastructure, ability to corrupt officials, and preparedness to defend their illicit market will not readily succumb to government raids and the odd arrest.

Other known forms of drug cartels operating in Canada, and elsewhere in the world, include Nigerian operations, Japanese Yakuza or Boryokudan groups, and Jamaican groups known as "posses." One of the newest cartel groups in Canada and the United States is the Russian-based organized crime group (see Box 11.8). It is also established in other countries and is known for its excessive violence and wide range of organized criminal activity.

The Russian "Mafiya"

"The law cannot keep up with crime which is no doubt the biggest industry in Russia" (quote from the *Moscow Times,* cited in Goodwin, 1995:3).

With the collapse of the former Soviet Union in 1991, Eastern European organized crime began to flourish. However, its modern-day roots began in the 1970s and 1980s when it became increasingly involved in the "Black Market." This period coincided with the weakening of the Russian economy.

In 1991, the Russian Ministry of the Interior reported there were at least 785 organized crime groups operating throughout Russia. By 1995, their numbers had swelled to 5,700—a 1300 per cent growth. Today their influence plagues both economic and institutional reform in Russia. Murder rates have risen 25 per cent each year since 1991. The CIA estimates that more than "half of Russia's 25 largest banks have illegal ties to Russian organized crime" and there were accusations that at least 100 people with criminal records were running for the 1995 parliamentary elections (Goodwin, 1995:3). Coinciding with the 1991 collapse, the Russia Mafiya began to move beyond national borders. Between 1992 and 1994, the number of Russians applying for immigration status in Canada mushroomed from 151 to 1204. And while not all immigrants are members of Russian organized crime groups, a number of incidents indicate that a number of new immigrants have organized crime affiliations. By 1994, the Canadian Association of Chiefs of Police (CACP) described their activities as "potentially one of the most significant sources of corruption and discord operating in the world today." In fact, as recently as 1997, sophisticated Russian mobsters were allegedly active in at least 50 countries and had established alliances with Colombian and Nigerian drug cartels. Their presence has grown so fast that even Russian President Boris Yeltsin admitted his country has not been able to effectively counter the power of organized crime (Handelman, 1997).

Unlike conventional organized crime groups, they involve themselves in anything that will gain them a profit, rather than specializing in a specific market. They have been known to be involved in several drug "rip-offs" against the Hell's Angels and various Asian gangs. Their growing sophistication and ruthlessness has caused Canadian law enforcement agencies to establish a special task force to deal with the growing problem (CACP, 1994). In fact, one recent report noted that "nowhere has the influence of the mob been more evident than Russia itself" and that its "tentacles" are rapidly spreading around the world (Ward and Kinney, 1999:5).

At the tenth Annual Conference on Criminal Justice Futures: International Organized Crime: Internal and External Threats a major session was allocated to discuss Russian organized crime in North America.

Cartels are a prime example of the changing face of organized crime. Once little more than glorified regionalized gangs they have evolved to become international threats to nations' economies and political stability. Changes in the global economy, and political instability in various parts of the world, have created a rich environment for criminal organizations to flourish and spread their influence. This poses a major problem in trying to counter that influence. Most efforts have called for cooperation between law enforcement agencies that cross jurisdictions and international borders (OICJ, 1997). Laws could also be revised so that they are easier to enforce and can transcend international boundaries for certain organized crime groups. Criminologists should also explore proactive and interdisciplinary approaches in their efforts to understand and address opportunities. It also behooves criminology to adopt an international comparative perspective as in the work of the United Nations and Amnesty International.

Ethnic Groups

Canada is a country made up of many cultural and ethnic groups. Some of these groups, due to cultural and ethnic differences, do not assimilate as readily as others. Some groups (e.g., Vietnamese, Cambodians, Iranians, Nigerians, Somalis, etc.) come from war torn areas where violence, corruption, and extortion have become a way of life, while other minority groups, because of the image they project, may go largely unnoticed (see Box 11.9). On arriving in Canada they occasionally bring their conflicts with them. Among the more serious ethnic organized crime groups in Canada are Asian-based crime groups whose roots can be traced back to the first wave of Chinese immigrants, predominantly goldfield or railroad workers in the mid 1800s (Emerging Gangs, 1997).

REALITY CHECK BOX 11.9

THE MENNONITE DRUG PIPELINE

For the most part, the Mennonites are law-abiding people. However, no ethnic, religious, or social group is immune from the temptation of criminal opportunities. In May 1997, three Mennonites from southern Ontario were charged with operating a very sophisticated "drug pipeline" between Mexico and Canada. Starting in the late 1980s, they formed a lucrative marijuana smuggling pipeline that since 1991 has involved over $8 million in seizures. The three men were born in Mexico but also had Canadian citizenship, making it easier for them to move back and forth to establish the pipeline. Representatives from their community were quick to point out that such incidents are extremely rare among the Mennonite communities but that the men were victims of "socio-economic marginalization"—they came from impoverished environments. The three men each received 7 years for conspiracy to import narcotics and 5 years for possession of narcotics. The sentences were to run concurrently (Mennonite drug pipeline expanding, 1997).

Pace (1991) observes that ethnicity may affect a group's tendency to violence, its market of specialization, and accessibility to legitimate markets. Different groups are involved in different types of activities and use different strategies when engaging in their criminal behaviours.

Asian Triads and Vietnamese gangs can be found in every province. The greatest amount of activity, however, takes place in British Columbia, Ontario, and Quebec (Beare, 1996). Influenced by social and political circumstances in their native countries, these groups are known for their violence (e.g., drive-by shootings, home invasions, and extortion). The CACP (1993) has expressed concern over the influx of Asian criminals after the Chinese take-over of Hong Kong in July 1997. The wealth of many new Hong Kong immigrants may make them prime targets for extortion, drug trafficking, and other activities of Chinese crime groups. The leader of the Wo On Lok, also known as the Shui Fong (Water Rats), one of the most powerful Triads operating in Hong Kong, Tong Sang Lai, is living a posh life in east Vancouver while his gang (reported to be 3,000 strong) continues their turf war in Hong Kong. Investigation shows that corruption was involved in helping Mr. Tong to gain access into Canada (Criminal lands …, 1997). In December 1996, a search of a plane from Seoul, Korea in Vancouver found thirteen Iranians with false passports from Italy, Israel, Greece, and Spain. Although the Federal Immigration Department has introduced a new program to try and curb the entry of illegal immigrants, it appears that a fine of $3,200 per illegal immigrant is not a sufficient deterrent for some foreign carriers (Plane checked …, 1997).

Vietnamese gangs are known for their violence and general disregard for law enforcement. They often prey on members from their own communities through extortion and robbery, taking advantage of immigrants who are unfamiliar with Canadian ways and who, because of their cultural background, are afraid to go to the police (Carrigan, 1991). For many gang members, going to jail is seen as better than being in a refugee camp. The extent of their involvement in organized crime is not known because it is suspected that a significant number of their activities go unreported. One Vietnam-born police officer estimated that as much as "75 per cent of the crime committed by the Asian community is not reported" (Ibid, 194).

In her study of Vietnamese criminal organization in Canada, Prowse (1994:2) makes the comment that "the most powerful gang is the most violent gang; with violence, you get power, and with power, you get money." Relying on informant interviews, field notes, and a variety of media sources, Prowse (1994) further notes that the Vietnamese represent the second-largest Asian population in North America. Criminal activities among this group first came to the attention of Canadian authorities in the early 1980s but they were often mistaken for Chinese triads. Starting in the 1990s their level of violence escalated and they have since "undergone a transformation from loosely-structured crime groups … to well armed and semi-structured criminal organizations" (Ibid, 5). Involvement in Vietnamese gangs, according to Prowse, is grounded in their "conflicting demands of culturally-rooted financial obligation to family and the lack of a legitimate means of fulfilling their obligations" (Ibid, 8).

At the fourteenth Annual International Conference on Organized Crime, held in Calgary in 1995, a wide range of Asian Triad operations was identified. Among some of the more prominent Asian crime groups operating in Canada are the 14K, Sun Yee On, Wo Hop To, Wo On Lok, United Bamboo, and Big Circle Boys. These and other groups are involved in illegal activities ranging from running prostitution rings, making counterfeit credit cards, trafficking in drugs, operating nightclubs to launder their illegally-gotten monies, home invasions, organized break and enters, forgery, and selling contraband (see Box 11.10).

In 1996, Canada deported 5,838 people, of whom 1,838 (31 per cent) were known criminals. In 1995, Canada deported 4,798 people, of whom 1,756 (36.5 per cent) were known criminals (Tanner, A., 1997).

FYI BOX 11.10

Credit Card Fraud and Organized Crime

A 1998 RCMP report indicates that credit card fraud is either committed by, or can be traced back to, organized crime. In 1995, credit card fraud accounted for approximately $34 million in fraudulent credit card transactions and $1 billion (US) globally. It has become one of the world's most lucrative crimes (Counterfeit credit cards, 1998). Also see Chapter 10.

As with other forms of organized crime, efforts to combat Asian-based crime groups have posed major problems for law enforcement agencies. Today, there are annual international conferences whose primary focus is to find ways to fight organized crime as well as to try to understand the motivation of the various forms these crimes take. For example, a number of countries are not only forming their own special task forces to deal with these forms of organized crime groups but are also working collaboratively. In 1996, the Netherlands gave organized crime top priority and has joined forces with a number of other nations (e.g., Turkey, Latin America, the Caribbean, several Eastern European countries, and Russia). These countries have gone online to access and send out more information to more effectively combat organized crime.

Outlaw Motorcycle Gangs

Quebec has historically been a "hotbed" for motorcycle gangs in Canada, but, as with Asian gangs, they can be found in every province. Although it became the fashion in the 1980s for baby boomers to join motorbike clubs, some clubs have been involved in organized crime. For example, in 1994, there were 329,809 registered motorcycles and mopeds in Canada and most of them are law-abiding citizens who own Harley Davidson motorcycles and attend Harley Davidson motorbike conventions. The Hell's Angels are an outlaw gang who also own Harleys and may attend some of the conventions.[3]

In July 1997, the Hell's Angels began to make arrangements to set up a chapter of its organization in Red Deer, Alberta. It was met with considerable opposition from law enforcement representatives and drew widespread media attention. In Quebec the Rock Machine[4] and Hell's Angels compete for control of all the exotic dancer clubs, are involved in extortion, and intimidation of many other bars, as well as drug trafficking, prostitution and even contract killing.

One of the more perceptive accounts of an outlaw motorcycle gang in Canada is Daniel Wolf's (1991) book, *The Rebels: A Brotherhood of Outlaw Bikers*. The book is his doctoral thesis, based on Wolf's three years riding with the Alberta-based Rebels.

FYI BOX 11.11

Hell's Angels

Formed in the late 1940s, in Hollister, California, the Hell's Angels was made up of mostly ordinary individuals who were looking for a little recreation and excitement after the war. They called themselves the *Pissed Off Bastards of Bloomington* and formed the first American Motorcycle Association. It was only after a member of the group was arrested and not released that the group became more violent and renamed itself the Hell's Angels (Stamler, 1996).

Wolf applies a sociological perspective to interpreting the life of a biker and his subculture. He notes that most of the members come from the lower and working classes where they experience a sense of anomie—lack of purpose and identity. Being a member of the bike gang allows them to superficially romanticize their mundane life. With the backing of other members, they are able to lead a wild and carefree existence—a form of "rebellion" (see Chapter 7 for the modes of anomie theory).

A sense of "ritualism" is found in the colours they wear and the bikes they ride (i.e., riding only Harley-Davidsons, wearing the Rebels' logo on their jackets). These traditions are not only characteristic of bike gangs—the practices are also used to express their commitment and even serve as a form of intimidation. They also have their own jargon (see Box 11.12) to lend a sense of "retreatism."

FYI BOX 11.12

Glossary of Terms used by Outlaw Motorcycle Gangs

AFFL: Angels Forever, Forever Loaded.
Back Pack: Full colours tattooed on member's back.
Chopper: Chopped or cut-down motorcycle with all unnecessary equipment stripped off such as front brake and fender.
Crash Truck: A van, panel truck or converted school bus that follows or precedes the bike gang run and picks up broken down bikes.

Hawg or HOG: Law enforcement officers also known as "the man."

Mama: Any woman sexually available to all club members.

Old Lady: Wife (common-law or legal) or steady girlfriend of a club member.

Patch Over: Stronger of major clubs takes over defeated or probationary clubs. Can be accomplished peacefully or through war.

Striker: Canadian term for an applicant who wants to join an OMG (Outlaw Motorcycle Gang).

13: Patch worn by some outlaw bikers. The letter "M" is the 13th letter in the alphabet. It signifies methamphetamine and/or marijuana.

81: Hells Angels. "H" is eighth letter of alphabet, "A" is first.

666: Satan's sign, replaces the "Filthy few" but signifies the same message.

*: An asterisk tattooed between the thumb and forefinger indicates how many times the wearer has been in prison.

Note: This is only a sample of the terms/vocabulary used among outlaw bikers.

Source: Adapted from RCMP Gazette. (1994: (56)3 and (56)4: 39), as well as courtesy of N. Tusikov - Assistant Editor of the *RCMP Gazette.*

Wolf suggests one of the reasons why motorcycle gangs persist is because they represent an outgrowth of a capitalist system in which certain members of the working class feel alienated. In the gang subculture, they are able to share a common set of social norms that are usually in contrast to society at large. This draws social rejection and further reinforces their rebellious attitudes and behaviours. However, the characteristics of an organized crime group as identified above epitomize the gangs.

What Wolf does not explain is why more working-class people don't join motorcycle gangs or other sub-cultural groups. Why don't women become involved more in sub-cultural groups? Are violent sub-cultural groups a product of social conditions or is it possible that a number of individual, biological factors are also involved in the explanatory model? After all, we have seen that very few societies have ever been crime-free and that gangs, mobs, and organized crime groups have existed almost since the beginning of recorded history.

Motorcycle gangs have become very sophisticated in their activities. They are no longer the tattoo-laden, social misfits once portrayed in movies. They have become an international organization. Scaramella, Brenzinger, and Miller (1997) offer an overview of biker gangs in Europe. As in North America, the Hell's Angels have a very strong presence and are involved in many of the same activities (e.g., prostitution, illegal drugs, trafficking in weapons, etc.). For example, it is believed that the Italian Mafia hires bikers as muscle men and hit men. The

Mafia has also allegedly employed bikers to move drugs and carry out violent tactics such as bombings and arson.

Police efforts to control them, as evidenced in Montreal during the mid-1990s and the take-over of the Grim Reapers by the Hell's Angels in Alberta, in the late 1990s (see Sillars, 1996) have been limited. Other than harassing the bikers with various traffic violations as they rode into town, the police are unable to prevent the bike groups from going where they please and doing what they want. Yves Lavigna, a former crime reporter and author of *Hell's Angels: Taking Care of Business* (1986) and *Hell's Angels: Into the Abyss* (1996), describes the Angels and similar motorcycle gangs as North America's equivalent of the ethnic gangs commonly found in the underworld. Similar to the ethnic groups discussed above, bikers have their own roots in what Lavigna calls "white trash"—the social outcasts and rebellious youths. Yet, just as most of the ethnic groups have evolved and become more sophisticated, so have the Hell's Angels. Sillars (1996) points out that Vietnamese gangs and the bikers have carved out their separate territories, respecting each other's boundaries. Meanwhile, just as biker groups like the Hell's Angels are spreading their power and influence into new territory, law enforcement agencies in provinces like Alberta are facing financial cutbacks. This makes it increasingly difficult for them to counter the spread of organized crime alone. The situation is further compounded by police forces having to deal with legal constraints and court rulings that are undermining some of their efforts (see Palango, 1997).

Efforts to combat outlaw motorcycle gangs are hampered by their level of organization. The gangs consist of a vertical chain of command with at least three tiers. In addition, they are able to continue operating despite a loss of key members because of their organizational structure. And, as is common among most organized crime groups, they are prepared to use violence and bribery as a means of creating and maintaining their existence and monopoly over certain criminal activities (Scaramella, Brenzingen, and Miller, 1997). Finally, organized motorcycle groups have a clearly defined set of rules and regulations that govern membership (Abadinsky, 1994).

The only way to fight sophisticated crime is with sophisticated methods. This will require an integrated approach involving cooperation between all the elements of the criminal justice system and the input of support from society. Neither the police nor the law on their own will ever be able to arrest the growth of organized criminal activities. As the headline of one recent article read: "Force is 'rusting out,' says Alberta top Mountie." The official described the ability of the RCMP to combat any form of crime as "very near a critical situation" (Mofina and Ketcham, 1999).

"TRADITIONAL"[5] ITALIAN ORGANIZED CRIME FAMILIES

In July 1997, the powerful mob figure Carmen Barillaro, in the Niagara Region, was shot to death execution-style when he answered his door. Barillaro had been convicted of cocaine trafficking and had hired a woman to murder an ex-biker of the Outlaw biker gang over an outstanding drug debt. However, the woman turned informer and got Barillaro sentenced to three years. He had also been the former right-hand man to former mob-boss Johnny "Pops" Papalia. Papalia had been assassinated two months earlier.

While the killings appeared to be characteristic of a mob war, police were not able (or willing) to confirm such an association. They simply said, "our goal and intention is to solve the homicide" although there had been a series of other bombings and killings in the preceding months (Wilkes and Edwards, 1997).

Past and Present Status of the Mafia

Mafia-related organized crime has been reported in every province. Although their primary specialization has been drug trafficking, they have also been known to engage in illegal gambling, loan-sharking, union racketeering, counterfeiting, extortion, and the food supply industry, distribution of illicitly-operated video poker machines, and money laundering (Baere, 1996). Of particular concern to law enforcement agencies is their "extensive investment in legitimate businesses. These operations are used to invest their profits, to serve in a money laundering capacity, and as a cover or front for criminal operations" (Baere, 1996:271). Mafia-related movies often depict this stereotypical modus operandi of Italian organized crime families.[6]

The history of the Mafia shows an evolving process. It is believed that the "Mafia" originated during the ninth century on the island of Sicily when Arab invaders tried to oppress the original inhabitants. To survive, the inhabitants sought refuge in the hills of the island. The word "Mafia" means "refuge" in Arabic (*Mafia History*, 1997).

Subsequent attempts to force out the native inhabitants of the island led the families to form a secret society with its own infrastructure. Members were required to take an oath on initiation whose intention was to help create a sense of family based on ancestry and Sicilian heritage. The oath includes five fundamental principles:

- **Omerta:** A code of silence. A vow never to reveal any Mafia secrets or members under the threat of torture or death.

- Total obedience to the boss, or "don."
- Assist any befriended Mafia faction, no questions asked.
- Avenge any attack on members of the family, because an attack on one is an attack on all.
- Avoid any contact with the authorities (*Mafia History*, 1997).

The Mafia grew into a strong organization that relied on extortion and other forms of crime to gain what it needed. When Mafia members did not get their way they resorted to violence to force compliance. Soon families began to compete for power and territory. With this came competition between families that subsequently led to the emergence of organized crime families so often depicted in the movies. Names like Al Capone, Charles "Lucky" Luciano, Bugsy Siegel, and Meyer Lanksy have all been the subjects of various gangster movies.

Today[7] in Italy the Mafia poses a serious problem for the government. Moreover, while their *modus operandi* has evolved in recent years, they continue to be a major concern. In recent years, the Mafia has formed alliances with the Colombian cartels, as have outlaw motorcycle gangs (see above), as a means of facilitating international drug (primarily cocaine) trafficking. Recently, the FBI reported that the Mafia has infiltrated Wall Street. Although their influence is described as marginal, charges were laid against five mobsters suspected of stock manipulation (FBI expands ..., 1997). The article described how the mobsters used their usual tactics, such as threats of violence, to force brokers to manipulate certain stocks.

In spite of a few sensationalized cases in which "big-time" mobsters are arrested and prosecuted, efforts to weaken the influence of the Mafia in Canada have not been very successful. When arrested, they usually get relatively light sentences by plea-bargaining since they have access to the best legal talent available. While in prison they tend to be model prisoners and are usually paroled as soon as they become legally eligible. Furthermore, because they are not placed in isolation, they are still able to continue their entrepreneurial activities. Better policing, the use of informants, and successful prosecution bring occasional success but, the impact has been minimal.

Explaining Organized Crime

We have described a variety of organized crime groups in Canada. We have seen that organized crime is pervasive and has a dramatic impact on the social economy of the country. We have also seen that organized crime groups have become more sophisticated over the years as law enforcement and criminal justice efforts to counter organized crime have been introduced. Most recently, in 1997, the Nathanson Centre for the Study of Organized Crime and Corruption was established at Osgoode Hall, the law school at York University, to study the growing problem in Canada. Margaret Baere, a recognized expert in the field, is the Centre's new director (Galloway, 1997).

Hackler (1994:308) points out that explanations of "the Mafia, organized crime, and political crime differ." He observes that one approach is to describe and explain such criminal activities as "cancers that invade and destroy healthy societies" (Ibid.). Because of the economic consequences of most organized crime on governments, the cancer analogy is a popular interpretation. It enables governments to justify taking extreme measures (e.g., *War Measures Act*, passing special legislation to control outlaw motorcycle gangs, exercising special provisions for screening new immigrants, confiscating property, etc.). The assertion is that through aggressive crime control and intervention efforts, organized crime can be rooted out—or at least controlled.

Criminologists have also used a functionalist approach that sees organized crime as representing deficiencies in society—around the world. This approach emphasises such factors as *strain, blocked opportunity,* and *anomie* (see Chapter 7). In this sociological tradition, organized crime is seen as a normal adaptive response to the structural organization of society. Of particular importance is: "(1) the division of labour, (2) the nature and distribution of occupational roles, and (3) the opportunities available to obtain them" (Einstadter and Henry, 1995:145).

For groups such as the Mafia, Colombia cartels, and Aboriginal crime groups, —often relegated to the lower working class, without the same opportunities for upward mobility—the functionalist approach offers a plausible, albeit tenuous, explanation. However, the functionalist perspective is less adept at explaining crime groups such as the Yakuza in Japan, the criminal tribes of India, or the roving pickpocket gangs of Paris (Hackler, 1994). Furthermore, social disorganization, anomie, and sub-cultural theories cannot readily explain gender differences within organized crime.

As a *macro* approach, the functionalist theories are good at focusing on the criminogenic conditions of societies, but they are less adept at explaining the more *micro* social processes by which individuals choose to become involved in organized crime. In addition, the functional perspective, in accordance with its principles, assumes that organized crime (as with all existing things) performs some function. However, this is a tautological argument and not necessarily true. For example, if organized crime is *dysfunctional* to the stability of society and the state, then it could be reasoned that it would eventually cease to exist rather than evolve and expand.

In terms of the criminogenic conditions, organized crime is fluid. Its existence is more dependent on public and official readiness to cooperate with its illegal activities than on simply passing legislation that makes it easier to prosecute or harass organized crime groups. As Potter (1994:147) observes, organized crime does not produce the desire for vice (e.g., taking drugs, viewing pornography, prostitution)[8] rather "it merely fills an already existing social gap."

Should criminologists then study which vices might/should be legalized as a means of crime control? It is possible that organized crime does serve a functional symbiotic service as governments are still able to operate with varying degrees of corruption. If we legalized drugs, pornography, prostitution, and other vices (other countries have experimented with such measures) would this serve to lessen organized crime's power and its related problems? Whether such solutions would help or generate new problems is not clear and the subject of considerable debate. However, criminologists could engage in comparative studies where Canadian vices do not exist to see whether such measures might work. Kappeler, Blumberg, and Potter (1993) explore such issues in their book. They point out that the very existence of laws against consensual crimes simple serve to create the opportunity for organized crime. Furthermore, it would also be prudent for researchers to engage in an integrated and interdisciplinary approach. Organized crime is an evolving phenomenon that takes many forms today. Hence, criminologists need to view organized crime in terms of how society has structured its economic, political, and social resources to create an environment in which organized crime can both thrive and evolve.

Organized Crime versus Governments: Is There a Difference?

As was noted above, the definition of organized crime is not, and has not always been, clear. In many respects, the definition of organized crime is socially and politically relative. For example, it could be argued the Crusades of the eleventh–thirteenth century were a form of organized crime. Although sanctioned by the church, they amounted to little more than groups of armed Christians who invaded Moslem lands to kill, steal and rape.

In recent years, the terrorist activities of Islamic bombers have been interpreted as a type of organized crime. One person's fight for freedom may be seen as another's terrorist activities. Perhaps one of the most famous of all "terrorists," who the Cuban government described as being involved in organized crime, was the notorious guerrilla leader Ernesto "Che" Guevara. After he fled Cuba, he attempted to spread communism in Bolivia before being killed in 1967. In 1997, when his remains were returned to Cuba, he was treated as a national hero and thousands lined up to pay their respects for his return.

Other examples that blur the line between governments and crime include:

- Various governments have used criminal elements for their own ends (e.g., CIA and Mafia versus Castro in the 1960s, Japan's use of Yakuza (see above) as construction workers, General Chiang Kai-shek's rise from the Green Gang of Shanghai (*Committee for a Safe Society,* 1997).

- Is the use of lotteries by governments simply a "legalized" version of organized crime and number rackets?

- Numerous examples can be found in the literature in which government officials in many parts of the world are routinely bribed or receive campaign funding from organized crime groups (e.g., Colombia, United States, Italy, and Philippines).

- Governments in Nigeria, Cambodia, and Burma/Myanmar have been completely taken over by organized crime groups (*Committee for a Safe Society,* 1997).

- The American government sanctioning of the December 14, 1969 My Lai massacre in Vietnam.

- The Los Angeles police department's tolerance of the beating of Rodney King on May 19, 1991.

- The RCMP paying Clifford Olson $100,000 for disclosing information about the murders he committed during the 1980s.

- In 1998, Toronto City Council and the Toronto police finally gave "Jane Doe" an apology and awarded her $220,000. "Jane Doe" had been used as "bait" (without her awareness) by the city police to catch a serial rapist—12 years earlier (Gombu, 1998).

- The attempt by the Canadian military to cover up the shootings of citizens in Somalia.

- Only in 1998, after Dorothy Mill Proctor went public with her story, did the government admit that it had illegally subjected young women being held at the prison for women in Kingston to illegal experiments. An unconfirmed number of women had been the subject of LSD, sensory deprivation, and other "mind raping" experiments. What gives the state the right to conduct such experiments without the consent of the victim? (CBC Radio News, 1998).

The line between what, and how, organized crime groups operate may not be so dissimilar from some of the activities the government has been found guilty of engaging in. The differences may be more subjective than factually-based. The differences are *relative* as both parties can be accused of sharing many of the characteristics described under "Defining Organized Crime" (above).

Summary

Organized crime is widespread in society today. It is no longer confined to neighbourhoods, or even national boundaries. Its economic impact is far greater than that of conventional crimes. A few years ago, for example, an article in *Time* magazine estimated the illegal earning of the Mafia, or Cosa Nostra, to be around $52 billion (US) per year (Angelo, 1992).

The providing of **illicit markets** has a long history and attempts to control it (usually legal) have done little to eradicate its growth. Part of the problem is due to the nebulous definitions used to define organized crime. One of the consequences is that today some forms of organized crime are not only spreading but have also become international in scope and impact.

It was noted that not only is organized crime widespread, it is difficult to define and we have no official data on these activities. Most of the information available comes to us through the media and special reports. This may pose a problem in fully understanding the extent of organized crime. However, organizations such as the Office of Organized Crime Research at the Office of International Criminal Justice, in Chicago, is spearheading research and collaborative efforts to combat organized crime. The office recently dedicated an entire issue of their journal *Crime and Justice International* (1997, November) to the subject of organized crime. And in 1998, the Alberta government allocated $8 million to fight organized crime in the province. Part of the monies will go to establishing a new bureau that can better co-ordinate law enforcement agencies in tackling organized crime (Toneguzzi, 1998).

While organized crime continues to evolve its scope of operation, organized crime groups continue to share common characteristics (e.g., hierarchy, market monopoly, use of violence, etc.). And while organized families may share common traits such as ethnicity, race, and gender, their formation has less to do with ethnic succession or cultural transmission than with opportunities for entrepreneurial activity. Hence, it is prudent to study organized crime from an interdisciplinary and integrated perspective.

Corporate Crime[9]

Although substance abuse can be described as a "crime against public order" (see Chapter 12), consider the following facts in relation to corporate responsibility:

- According to the *Multinational Monitor* (1991), approximately 10 per cent of Americans are alcoholics. In Canada, about 5 per cent of Canadians drink every day and in 1991 the total per capita absolute alcohol consumption was 7.1 litres compared with 11.9 litres in France (*Canadian Year Book 1997*).

- In Canada, health studies report that automobiles mixed with alcohol are one of the leading causes of death. This is especially true among young adults. In 1970 the death rate among young adults was 25.6 per 100,000 and by 1992 the rate was 45.7 per 100,000 (*Canadian Year Book, 1997*).

- Burns (1988) reported that a teenager sees 100,000 alcoholic ads before reaching the legal drinking age.

In spite of these statistics, alcohol can now be easily obtained at wine special-ty stores across the country. With the exception of Quebec, this was not always the case. Liquor sales used to be completely controlled by the Liquor Control Board stores across the provinces. However in the 1970s and 1980s (varies by province), wine speciality stores began to get licencing privileges and then in the 1990s provincial governments began to decentralize the operations of liquor stores. They saw an opportunity for free enterprise to take over, offer more employment opportunities and generate even more revenue for provincial coffers.

Is this flagrant availability of a potentially dangerous drug an example of state corruption? Is it still possible for the government to ensure that underage youth are not now gaining easier access to alcoholic beverages? Should the provinces be allowed to place (high) taxes on a product that is the source of many social ills?

As with organized crime, corporate crimes are committed by another power-ful group in society. Both groups are interested in maximizing the profits of their organization and share several of the characteristics identified by Abadinsky (1994) (mentioned above). The difference is that these corporations are legiti-mate and are run by "high-status" members of society.

Corporate crime involves illegal acts by "big business" officials that benefit the corporation. For example, in early 1999, several members of the Salt Lake City Olympic organizing committee resigned in light of mounting evidence indi-cating that committee members and, allegedly, some Board members had engaged in bribes, fraud, and other illegal activities in order to win the Olympic bid (Mountlon, 1999). As Kramer (1984:31) points out, "they are the result of deliberate decision making by persons who occupy structural positions within the organization. The organization makes decisions intentionally to benefit itself." Many of these officials hold prestigious social positions and their individ-ual incomes are well above the national per capita income. Yet, as Snider (1993:1) observes "corporate crime ... actually does more harm, costs more money, and ruins more lives" than conventional crimes. Snider goes on to point out that more deaths result from corporate crimes in a month than all the deaths committed by mass murderers in a decade (see Box 11.14).

A CLOSER LOOK BOX 11.14

The "Not So Good" Corporate/Occupational Citizens

At the end of each year, the *Multinational Monitor*, founded by the renowned corpo-rate watchdog **Ralph Nader**, publishes a list of the 10 worst corporations in the United States.[10] The following is a sample from his 1996 list. This will be followed by a cross-section of Canadian-specific white-collar crimes during the 1980s.

- Archer Daniels Midland is considered a cutting edge corporation. The corporation was charged with *price fixing* to eliminate competition and cost shareholders nearly $500 million. Their fine was $100 million. The corporation has also been known to contribute millions of dollars to both American political parties.
- Top executives at Daiwa Bank Ltd. were found guilty of investing over $1 billion of investors' money in risky and reckless ventures. The executives tried to cover up the transactions by falsifying records and receiving regulators. Their punishment was to pay $340 million.
- The "family" corporation Disney was found guilty of using cheap child labour in Third World countries. For example, Disney paid Haitian workers 7 cents for making a pair of Pocohontas pyjamas that cost $11.97 at Wal-Mart.
- The mining giant Freeport McMoran had obtained a 30-year virtually *carte blanche* contract to mine copper and gold in Indonesia. In the process they have been charged with violating health violations and intimidating workers and were alleged to have been involved in the deaths of three civilians.
- The baby food company Gerber won a four-year battle to be able to sell its baby food products in Guatemala. In 1983, Guatemala became one of the first countries to sign an international agreement that promotes breast-feeding over breast-substitute products. The law forbids pictures of babies on baby food under 2 years of age.
- The mega-multinational company Mitsubushi continues to destroy tropical forests around the world.

Carrigan (1991) compiled a list of Canadian companies who have committed an assortment of white-collar crimes. The following represents a cross-section of the cases and their penalties during a seven-year period in the 1980s.

- Stone Consolidated Inc. charged with spilling PCB-laced transformer oil: fined $35,000.
- Shell Canada charged with price fixing: fined $100,000.
- Amway Canada charged with tax evasion: settled lawsuit for $45 million.
- BBM Lakeview Wholesale Lumber Ltd. of Vancouver found guilty of falsely labelling lumber: fined $100,000.
- Hoffman, LaRoche Ltd., a Toronto based drug company found guilty of breaking Competition Law: fined $50,000.
- Zellers Inc. found guilty in Nova Scotia of listing sales prices above advertised levels: fined $35,000.

Yet, as one study recently found, Canada still remains relatively free of corruption. In a survey of 85 countries, Mclearn (1998) reports that Canadian businesses ranked as the sixth least corrupt country. Denmark was the most honest while Cameroon was the most corrupt.

How do occupational crimes differ from conventional crimes? How would you explain the differences? Do you think there is a difference? Are the penalties fair?

Should there be separate penalties for corporate offenders? In spite of an increasing number of companies being prosecuted, why is white-collar crime increasing?

In 1977, Dowie accused the Ford Motor Company of intentionally covering up a life-threatening defect in their Pinto cars. The Pinto was a profitable subcompact so, rather than make the inexpensive modification (approximately $11 U.S. per car) the company chose not to disclose its findings. On impact at 25 miles per hour or more, the fuel tank could rupture and potentially explode. Recall would have cost Ford approximately $137 million while compensation to the 180 burn deaths eventually resulted in a copy loss of only $49.5 million (Carrigan, 1991)—a saving of $87.5 million.

Because of the deaths of three Indiana teenagers, resulting from a rear-end collision of their Pinto, Ford Motor Company was charged under the provision of reckless homicide in state law. Interestingly, the jury did not find the company guilty. Nevertheless, the case did set a precedent for being able to hold corporations criminally accountable (see Cullen, Maakestad, and Cavender, 1987). Unfortunately, as seen throughout this section, the impact is usually negligible and corporations continue to thrive. Although the impact of corporate crime is much greater than that of conventional street crime, the police cannot combat corporate crime as aggressively as they do street crime. Hence, the deterrent effect is minimal and the opportunity to exploit a market-driven economy remains inviting to those who are so motivated and have those skills.

Corporate crime is a modern-day crime. Only after the emergence of the Industrial Era and the market economy was it possible for corporate crime to manifest itself. And it was not until **Edwin Sutherland's** (Chapter 7) groundbreaking work in 1949 that corporate crime became a subject of interest to criminologists. Sutherland's work, *White Collar Crime*[11] was based on an analysis of the "life careers of the 70 largest U.S. manufacturing, mining, and mercantile corporations, examining the following legal violations: restraint of trade; misrepresentation in advertising; infringements of patents, trademarks, and copyrights; labour law violations; illegal rebates; financial fraud and violation of trust; violations of war regulations, and finally some miscellaneous offences" (Keane, 1996:282). The corporations studied averaged 19 judgements against them with the maximum number being 50! The most common (N=60) violation involved restraint of trade. Sutherland suggested that 90 per cent of the corporations were habitual criminals and 97 per cent were recidivists.

Although Sutherland's methodology and definition of white-collar crime have been criticized (see Geis and Goff, 1982) his general findings have been replicated in more recent studies. For example, Clinard and Yeager (1980) studied 1,553 federal files by government agencies. In addition, while virtually every kind of corporation was represented in their sample, the motor vehicle industry accounted for half of the hazardous product violations.

There has been a dearth of Canadian studies on corporate crime. Yet our economic history is rich with examples of corporate crime activities ranging from counterfeiting, embezzlement, forgery, and fraud, to regulatory offences (see Snider, 1988). Pioneering research in Canada was first undertaken by Collin Goff and Chuck Reasons (1978). Until their work, Canadian criminologists virtually ignored this area of inquiry because it was not seen as "real" crime and conventional criminological theory was not oriented towards the study of white-collar crime.

In examining the evolution of legislation aimed at preserving a competitive and free-enterprise system, researchers were able to describe how inept the government has been at enforcing the legislation. Similar views have been reiterated by Ralph Nader's Center for the Study of Responsive Law. For example, the Center points out that about one per cent of the public owns forty per cent of the wealth, whereas the bottom 95 per cent of the public own as much as the top 1 per cent!

Since their landmark study, there have been a number of other noteworthy studies conducted in an attempt to shed light on, and explain, Canadian corporate criminality (McMullan, 1992, Keane, 1996). The range of topics includes examination between:

- Corporate violence against women (DeKeseredy and Hinch, 1991);
- A review of how well various jurisdictional laws are enforced to protect consumers and the labour force (Snider, 1988);
- The nature and impact of crimes against consumers and employees through such activities as price fixing, illegal mergers, industrial espionage, and environmental pollution (Goff and Reasons, 1986); and
- An insightful account of the origins of *anticombines* legislation (Smandych, 1985) (see Box 11.15).

FYI BOX 11.15

Regulating Business Crime

Most forms of white-collar crime are dealt with not as corporate crimes per se but simply as fraud and embezzelement as defined under the *Criminal Code*. For the most part, regulatory agencies ranging from municipal government to the federal government define corporate offences and monitor their violation. The primary jurisdictional body concerned with overseeing corporate transgressions lies with the Ministry of Consumer and Corporate Affairs.

Until 1986, the most important regulatory statute was the *Combines Investigation Act* (CIA). Introduced in 1889, the act was intended to enable the state to protect consumers from unethical business practices such as price fixing, establishing a market monopoly, pollution, and safety and health violations, among other business practices. However, it only managed two convictions until it was replaced.

With the introduction of the *Competition Act* in 1986, cases now appear before a Competition Tribunal consisting of two Federal Court judges and a layperson who decide whether a company/corporation has violated their monopoly powers. Under the new Act, cases are tried under civil law, which does not require the same stringent burden of proof as criminal law.

In the spring of 1996, the Competition Bureau received complaints charging several petroleum companies with conspiring to fix gasoline prices. An independent review was unable to substantiate the charges. The report claimed there were too many possible intervening variables that might account for the fact that "in virtually all cities, short spike in gasoline retail prices" occurred!

Canada is one of the 11 nations that comprise the G10, which in 1997 attempted to establish international regulations for several international business operations (e.g., electronic banking). No consensus could be reached because they recognized "the different approaches that various countries have taken to regulations in the field" (Pressman, 1997).

Gordon and Coneybeer (1995:400) observe that, "the findings of this research and analysis are generally consistent with those presented in the international literature." They offer a number of general conclusions "... about corporate crime":

- Corporate crime is widespread and covers areas ranging from crimes against the economy, crimes against humanity and crimes against employees. In 1966, the chemical company Union Carbide was found to be violating health and safety standards at its plant in Bhopal, India. Over thirty years later the death toll in the aftermath of their gross negligence is over 10,000. Their out-of-court settlement was $470 million (*Multinational Monitor*, 1997, March).

- The losses in material, property damage, and physical injury are considerable. For example, Reasons, Ross, and Paterson (1981) noted that occupational deaths ranked third after heart disease and cancer. While not all occupational deaths could be directly associated with corporate wrongdoing or carelessness, they argue that it does account for a proportion of the deaths. An American study by Bohm (1986:195) estimated that "each year at least 10,000 lives are lost due to unnecessary surgeries, 20,000 to errors in prescribing drugs, 20,000 to doctors spreading diseases in hospital, 100,000 to industrial disease, 14,000 to industrial accidents, 200,000 to environmentally caused cancer, and an unknown number to lethal industrial products."

- Criminal law regulating corporate crime is poorly defined and violators are usually dealt with outside the criminal justice system in the form of compensations and victim appeasement. Perhaps the clearest example is the attempts on behalf of the American and Canadian governments to take legal action against the tobacco industry. After considerable legal posturing, tobacco companies have made a number of concessions to settle liability lawsuits. In the settlement, Joe Camel and the Marlboro ads will be permanently removed, all cigarette packages will carry clear warnings about their health hazards, and the industry will pay out $360 million U.S. over 25 years (most of which will go to anti-smoking campaigns), among a few other concessions. In return, tobacco companies will never face class-action lawsuits (*Newsworld,* June 20, 1997). Yet tobacco is recognized as the number one cause of premature death and illness in the United States and costs $52 billion (U.S.) in healthcare. Meanwhile, in Canada, British Columbia became the first province to pursue legal action against the tobacco industry in an effort to recoup health care costs linked to treating illnesses caused by smoking.

- Laws designed to prohibit forms of corporate behaviour are not only poorly enforced but are not effective deterrents.

- Because of their symbiotic relationship, governments usually work with corporations in constructing "appropriate" legislation and in determining appropriate measures to handle violators.

- The causes of corporate crime involve the complex interactions between individual, organizational, and social structural factors.

- Quality investigations into corporate crimes by criminologists are stymied by a variety of methodological problems (e.g., limited access to funding and data, and the complexities of corporate businesses).

In **summary**, corporate transgressions are pervasive throughout society. The economic, social, and political implications are often far reaching and yet the public is usually not well informed about these crimes. However, as an area of study, it poses a number of practical methodological problems.

Computer and High Technology Crime

As we have observed, white-collar crime is both highly profitable and relatively risk-free, and it appears to be growing. One of the more recent examples involved computer crime or cybercrime. And although a variety of computer crimes involve some form of theft (Chapter 10) it is addressed in this chapter because the victims and/or offenders often involve businesses.

Computer crime is any crime that uses computer-based technology to commit the offence. Some of the more commonly known forms of cybercrime include:

Unauthorized access to networks and their data: "Knowledge is power." Whether an individual or a corporation, gaining access to protected information can be used to gain an illegal advantage. For corporations this is referred to as *industrial espionage*. Corporations may be able to gain a competitive edge by "eavesdropping" on a competitor's new patent. Companies have been known to hire "cyberspies" or "cyberpirates" to illegally access information from a competitor's system without leaving any trace of intrusion. Relying on powerful and sophisticated technology, "cyberspies" can operate from virtually anywhere, making detection extremely difficult.

Another version of unauthorized access and use is *software piracy*. Have you ever obtained a copy of software from a friend and put it onto your computer? The duplication process is relatively simple. More sophisticated ventures might involve individuals or businesses copying software and then selling it as the original product—usually at a lower price.

FYI BOX 11.16

Counterfeiting Computer Software

On March 5 1998, Newmarket RCMP laid 11 charges against KCE Microcomputers Inc. They seized over 2500 disks and CD ROMs that were copies of Microsoft software and counterfeit-packaged. It is estimated the illegal products were worth at least $90,000 (Canada NewsWire, 1998, May 7).

Some of the techniques used to try and prevent access to sensitive data include *physical security,* such as key-operated hard disks and removable storage media. *Password or other forms of identification.* Most of us use a secret password for which we can set a limit to the number of wrong entries before the system shuts down. More advanced systems use optical imaging ("eyeball scanner") to recognize the owner's network of blood vessels on the retina.

Data encryption methods. This method involves using either hardware or software to convert information into gibberish until it is encoded by authorized users. Did you ever learn to write backwards or use pig Latin? Same sort of thing, just more sophisticated. The least sophisticated preventive method is *screen blanking.* In such situations, when a data entry station is left unattended for a fixed period of time it will go blank (Carter, 1995). As for software piracy, software companies are increasingly using compact discs and digital video disks which are more difficult (but not impossible) to duplicate.

Willful destruction of data: If you use a computer, you have most likely heard of those dreaded viruses (a computer program code).[12] "Hackers" may be laypersons or professionals with advanced computer programming skills. Remember the 'Melissa' virus planted by David Smith, 30, in March 1999? He disguised the virus as an e-mail message marked "important message from a friend" (Parello, 1999) (see Box 11.17).[13] Some of these individuals might use their skills to access networks and plant a set of hidden instructions that cause the computer to destroy its data or alter information. I have had more than one student tell me about "the" virus that ate their term paper—drat those computer gremlins. Is it possible? Viruses can be spread from one computer to another through disk swapping, using pirated or counterfeit software, or over access lines that link computers to another source.

"HACKERS": THE GOOD, THE BAD, ALL THOSE IN-BETWEEN

"The bad"
- In 1998, a 22-year-old Sudbury man was charged with hacking into NASA's computer system and in one case causing more than $70,000 in damage (Police make arrest..., 1998) There was also the high profile case of Kevin Mitnick who in 1995 was arrested and charged with breaking into the system of an Internet provider and stealing more than 20,000 credit card numbers.

"The not so bad"
An Australian-based survey, posted on the Internet, revealed some interesting findings about computer "hackers." Based on a sample of 101 respondents from around the world, Bavinton (1998) found that:
- Less than 4 per cent of hackers were women.
- Respondents were between 12–54 years of age. The average age was 22.
- The majority of respondents indicated that they hacked for the challenge, curiosity, fun, and the thrill. They were not the demented cybernerds typically depicted in the media.
- 82 per cent said stricter criminal laws would not serve as an effective deterrent.
- 78 per cent said more prosecutions would also not serve as an effective deterrent.
- 33 per cent had accessed a government network; 52 per cent had accessed a large corporation; 65 per cent a small company, and 81 per cent accessed school, college, or university networks.
- The majority did not see their hacking activity as criminal as long as they were not doing "any harm."

Every year there are new viruses to be aware of. Some Internet providers will warn their customers, assuming they find out. In addition, there are software programs that have "anti-virus" detection devices. The more sophisticated programs provide free downloads for virus updates. Since part of the act of hacking involves challenge, some hackers will always try to keep ahead of the technology. Therefore, it is always a case of computer users beware. Another option for users is always to make regular backups of their data.

"The good"
Doing business is a competitive enterprise and corporations and governments believe it is necessary to protect their interests for obvious reasons. Many companies spend considerable sums of money trying to ensure their networks are secure.

In 1992, a Calgary company was set up to test the security of networks. What is unique about M-Tech (short for Mercury Information Technology Services) is that it employs "professional hackers" who are paid by companies to try to break their security systems. The company prefers to use the term "penetration testing" and "ethical hacking" (Knapp, 1998).

Data manipulation: Data manipulation may be one of the most serious forms of high technology crime. It involves the ability to enter unauthorized into computer files and subsequently modify their data. The late 1980s movie *The Net* depicts a scenario in which a computer user accesses the Internet, accidentally discovers confidential information and uses it to create havoc. Shortly after the release of the movie, an article in *Maclean's Magazine* reported on the real-life risk of international terrorism being conducted with computers. The article notes that banks already transfer several trillion dollars around the world each day—money that is potential prey for technologically sophisticated computer criminals ("Crime in the Computer Age," 1988).

Data manipulation can range from students accessing their school grades and modifying them to accessing big companies and stealing files and/or money. An area of data manipulation that has posed a major challenge for law enforcement agencies has been Internet child pornography (see Chapter 12). Those who post such information on the Internet can use sophisticated technology to strategically hide and alter images (a technique referred to as *morphing*), making detection and apprehension difficult.

Combating Computer and High Technology Crime

Legally, ss. 342.1 and 430 of the Canadian *Criminal Code* define computer crime as involving destruction, altering data, rendering data meaningless and/or interfering with someone using legitimate data. However, as noted above, the likelihood of apprehending and prosecuting offenders is very difficult. Aside from the sophistication of technology used by computer criminals, offenders tend to be well-educated, highly skilled, and, generally, young.

Law enforcement resources are also limited. There are approximately 168 RCMP members who are trained in computer-related crime techniques. Only about one-half are assigned to commercial crime units across Canada. Considering the force has more than 50,000 members, it is a token number that performs a largely reactive role. Members are trained to provide technical guidance and expertise for information that is already known to the offenders. Unfortunately, once an offence has been recognized it is usually too late.

Although the intentions of computer criminals are in many cases similar to property offenders (financial gain), the impact of their crimes tends to be far more costly and more difficult to detect. Law enforcement agencies don't have the resources to effectively combat computer-based crimes and criminal law does not appear to be an effective deterrent—taking a "byte" out of crime, so to speak.

Computer crimes are an excellent example of the argument that traditional intervention and prevention strategies are both outmoded and ineffective. What is needed in an integrated and interdisciplinary approach that embraces redefining our cultural structure by drawing on the ideas presented throughout Chapter 8. As Barak (1997) argues, we are all capable of adapting, changing, and growing or "reintegrating" in a manner that will help to redefine our social contract so that we will all want to work towards eliminating crime. For example, many businesses are reluctant to report being victims of computer crime. Likely, they fear bad publicity. However, in the process they further isolate themselves from community support and involvement.

"Cut" From the Same Cloth?

We have examined two different forms of crimes by the powerful in society. We noted that they share common operational goals and motivations. The primary difference between the two was that most organized crime groups involve participants from the middle and lower classes, while corporate crime participants comprise the upper-class, esteemed members of society.

Criminologists, in their efforts to explain the crimes of the powerful, have found a number of other characteristics that suggest that, other than using the terms organized and corporate to distinguish the arena of operation, the participants share one important characteristic—both have criminal propensities.

Although no direct comparison has been made, research shows that participants in organized crime began their criminal careers early in life while white-collar criminals began their careers a little later (Weisburd, Chayet, and Waring, 1990). Similar to Sutherland's observations, Weisburd et al. also found that white-collar criminals are often repeat offenders. They found that recidivism rates varied from 10 per cent for bank embezzlers to 46 per cent for credit card offenders. Why do businesses do it?

Explaining Corporate Crime

Most of us might wonder why a big successful company would risk engaging in criminal activity when it appears to have so much going for it?

In his landmark work, **Edwin Sutherland** (1949) used his theory of **differential association** to explain white-collar crime. The theory, however, emphasizes the individual rather than the organization. Given the general definition of corporate crime, this posed a conceptual problem for explaining such activities. Therefore, as Clinard and Quinney (1973) suggested, Sutherland's theory is more applicable for explaining *occupational crime* (e.g., fraud, embezzlement, theft, and other "business crimes"). Nevertheless, is there any real difference between occupational crimes and white-collar crime? Do criminologists need to make a distinction? Without the individual to initiate the crime, it could not take place. Hirschi and Goffredson (1989) appear to recognize these points as they suggest that criminologists do not need a separate theory of crime to explain white-collar crime.

One possible solution is for criminologists to use a narrower definition of white-collar crime by limiting the definition to corporate crime and to regard crimes committed by individuals as common-law property offences. Accepting this line of reasoning would require an organizational theory that considers the factors that make up the environmental setting of the corporation (e.g., market competition, organizational stratification, and profit motivation).

In the context of a *conflict perspective,* or "external factors of influence" (Keane, 1996:283)[14] as part of the market economy and capitalism, businesses are motivated by maximizing profit, perpetual growth, a desire to monopolize their market, and to have free rein over their operations. Government regulations only serve to restrict natural growth. From a conflict perspective, capitalism contains the seeds of its own destruction. The price of "success" for corporations is to "run a tight ship" if they want to compete on the open market. So, while companies may not intentionally set out to cause harm, there will always be trade-offs.

In her book on corporate crime, Snider (1993) argues that the interests of corporations and the state are not always compatible and this can, and does, lead to the creation of distorted public images of "big business." For example, governments are sensitive to public pressure for job creation and keeping unemployment rates down. These are usually major issues during election campaigns. In 1997, BC Premier Glen Clark offered the lumber industry financial incentives to create more jobs. However, as the lumber industry has become more mechanized in an effort to compete on the international market, it has not needed to employ more people to support itself. Similarly, within the automotive industry, computers and robots are increasingly being used to produce vehicles more efficiently, with less human error, that ultimately increase profits (robots don't strike, they do not need to be paid wages, they can work 24 hours a day without faltering, etc.). Yet, the automotive unions have lobbied the government hard to preserve their jobs and high wages.

On the other hand, government regulatory bodies have served as watchdogs to minimize the risk of corporations destroying the environment in their zeal to make profits. For example, these bodies have been instrumental in regulations restricting clearcut logging, setting limits on how close loggers can cut near rivers and streams, setting catch limits for the fishing industry, requiring pollution devices to be placed on emission devices, etc. The balancing act between meeting social and environmental obligations and conducting business has evolved considerably in recent years (see Box 11.18).

FYI BOX 11.18

The Delicate Balancing Act
—The "Good" Corporate Citizen

- Lake Erie was almost totally void of life because of pollution in the 1960s and 1970s. Today, because of regulatory bodies, the lake has returned to life.
- Acid rain from pollutants emitted from factories in the 1970s was destroying lakes across Canada. New regulations have helped to curb the trend.
- In Newfoundland, the Grand Banks and other rich fishing holes were being depleted until the Fisheries ministry stepped in and placed a moratorium on the fishing industry (Carrigan, 1991).
- There are a variety of other companies which appear to reflect sound ethical business practices. For example, The Body Shop returns a percentage of its profit to support environmental causes as do a number of financial institutions.
- Do corporations become involved because they are concerned corporate citizens or because they want to present an image behind which they can deflect their preoccupation with making more money? A true exception may be Ted Turner, vice chairman of Time Warner Inc., and founder of CNN, who, in September 1997, pledged to donate one billion dollars to the United Nations over the next 10 years. The money will go to United Nations humanitarian programs (Newsworld, 1997, Sept. 19).

Another theory that has a certain level of appeal in explaining corporate crime is Sykes and Matza's (1957) theory of **neutralization**. In his chapter on corporate crime, Carl Keane (1996:228–229) offers a concise account of how the techniques of neutralization can be applied to the way corporations can justify illegal behaviour. We will use the tobacco industry as an example of how it might neutralize any responsibility:

- *Denial of responsibility:* The tobacco industry does not force people to smoke its cigarettes. It is an individual choice. The industry is simply providing a market demand. It places warnings on its packages.

- *Denial of injury:* There has never been conclusive evidence proving that tobacco causes cancer. Millions of smokers have lived long and healthy lives and died of natural causes. Deaths may be attributed to other related factors. By placing warning ads on their packaging the industry is fulfilling its legal obligation to warn people of the possible hazards.

- *Denial of victim:* Not all smokers die of lung cancer. If they are smokers and die, it is probably because they were predisposed.

- *Condemnation of the condemners:* Why does the government focus on cigarettes when alcohol, sugar, fast cars, and many other products are far more potential risks? This is the "Everyone is corrupt" defence.

- *Appeal to higher loyalties:* When the tobacco industry was under attack, a number of people pointed out that the government had been quite happy for years to collect the revenue generated from the high taxes levied on cigarettes. Hence, the tobacco industry did it to support the economy. Is it not hypocritical to sanction someone and yet continue to profit from the tobacco industries profits? Who is the (real) offender?

Criminologist Stanley Cohen (1993) used the term "culture of denial" to describe the fact that there is virtually no information (official and/or unofficial) on corporate crime. Moreover, when someone is caught and charged the penalty is nominal. For example, after the *Exxon Valdez* oil spill in Alaska, Exxon was not forced out of business. And, in spite of the overwhelming evidence linking tobacco to cancer, tobacco companies are allowed to continue business. And the list goes on.

FYI BOX 11.19

Exxon Valdez Update

In 1999, former *Exxon Valdez* skipper, Joseph Henderson, was given 1,000 hours of community service for his 1990 conviction of negligently discharging oil into Prince William Sound, an incident that drew international attention. Beginning in the summer of 1999, Henderson will spend each summer for the next five years picking up trash along Anchorage highways (*Exxon Valdez*...1999). Do you think this is a fair sentence?

The above explanations have reflected either micro- or macro-level external, internal, and individual factors impinging on how organizations conduct their business. Each approach has its strengths but also have its limitations. For example, although neutralization techniques have appeal, the techniques do not in themselves explain crime. Therefore, as a number of investigators have suggested, a more prudent approach might be to synthesize these findings in an integrated format.

Keane (1996) suggests that one of the underlying themes of most explanations is the concept of *stress.* It could be used, for example, to link the three elements (i.e., micro-macro external, internal, and individual). Strain is an external factor as corporations strive to compete in an open market. Internal stress is expressed by the owners and employees as they try to conduct business within the confines of existing regulations, and individual stress can result from the potential risk of failure or shut-down. In other words, the causes of corporate crime are as involved and as complex, as operating a successful corporation.

A more realistic attempt to integrate macro and micro elements is to apply an interdisciplinary approach. As much as we might want to view corporate crime at an organizational level that consists of external, internal, and individual factors, the white-collar offender is still a biological and psychological individual. Without *mens rea* and *actus reus* (i.e., an individual) there can be no crime. The only difference is that the offender commits the crime within the organizational structure of the corporation. Therefore, when studying corporate crime, criminologists must integrate biological, psychological, social, and legal levels of analysis.

Historically, the criminal justice system has replied on criminal law to control corporate crime as well as organized crime. Perhaps it is time for criminologists to adopt a new theoretical framework that is integrated and interdisciplinary and better addresses the complexity of human behaviour. Then criminologists can begin to recommend effective social policies for the control of corporate crimes. To date, this line of inquiry has not received much attention. The following section will illustrate how the state has attempted, more typically, to regulate corporations.

Regulating Corporate Crime

There is little doubt that corporate crime has a major social and economic impact. What is somewhat more difficult to agree on is how the state should respond to the crime. While the state follows traditional punishment rationales of retribution and just deserts, it is less clear whether the state should prosecute the offender or the corporation. Alternatively, should prosecution involve the individual(s) and the corporation?[15] The decision process is further complicated by the interests of the state. For example, as noted above, penalizing the tobacco industry would lose the state considerable revenue. Similarly, video lottery terminals or lottery tickets generate millions of dollars every year for the state. Yet in sanctioning such activities, the state opens the way for a number of people to become addicted to these vices and many end up ruining their lives to support their habit (see Box 11.20).

A CLOSER LOOK BOX 11.20

Shame On You!

In 1989, **John Braithwaite** introduced his theory of reintegrative shaming in *Crime, Shame, and Reintegration*. It has been described as both a general theory of crime as well as offering an integrative explanation of crime. The theory combines elements of "labeling, subcultural, control, opportunity, and learning—the positive and negative aspects of lawbreakers" (Barak, 1997:203).

According to Braithwaite, not all forms of social disapproval are the same. Braithwaite distinguishes between *disintegrative shaming* and *reintegrative shaming*. The former is negative in orientation and does not provide the offender with any opportunity to make amends for his or her behaviour. This type of shaming usually results in driving the offender into further acts of deviance or crime.

Reintegrative shaming involves efforts to bring offenders back into the community. While the offender is expected to experience some shame around his or her behaviour, it is through the efforts of community involvement that the offender is given an opportunity to reintegrate. The general concept works well in homogeneous societies such as Japanese, Aboriginal communities, and other "communitarian" societies that are characterized by a high degree of concern for the welfare of others.

Since its introduction into criminology, the concept has been applied in many settings, including corporate crime. One of the earliest studies involved interviews with seventy white-collar offenders who had been convicted of a white-collar crime. Benson (1990) found that most of the offenders experienced disintegrative shaming, usually at the hands of the media. However, while reintegrative shaming has been adapted into restorative justice-based programs for conventional crimes and youth, there is little evidence that it has been applied to white-collar offenders. The criminal justice system has, and continues to be, largely reactive in its approach to economic crimes. Economic crimes happen because such criminals are proactive and are able to take advantage of opportunities. In order to regulate corporate crime, criminologists and criminal justice agencies must learn to be sensitive to international issues, differences in law, differences in law enforcement, changing technology, as well as market and social trends. The ideological issues of how countries respond to corporate offenders vary by country. For example, according to Hackler (1994), government tolerance is less common in Australia, Britain, Japan, and Sweden, while in the United States and Canada corporations have a tendency to resist regulation.[16]

In summary, criminology and policy makers have a tall order in front of them. We are ill-equipped at present to address economically-motivated crime (Kappler, Blumberg, and Potter, 1993). Financially, individual countries cannot afford to combat the spread of crime, and criminal justice systems, by themselves, have been slow to change their traditional, and failed, approaches. It is time to look beyond our parochial and provincial ideas. Criminologists and criminal justice agencies have to collaborate in their efforts and ideas on how best to combat these crimes. In addition, an integrated and interdisciplinary approach will be required, one that recognizes that "home-grown" theories and single explanations and strategies will never work.

Summary

Organized crime and corporate crime, or, simply, economic crimes, are pervasive. We live in a materialistic world where demands for goods and services make it expedient to foster illegal markets in a symbiotic manner. While they may differ on a number of descriptive characteristics, their *modus operandi* are very similar. They both share the motive of economic gain through illegal means. They both strive to monopolize the economy and both resort to varying forms of threats, intimidation, and deceptions to succeed. In other words, the line between organized crime and corporate crime hardly exists and is really more practical for criminologists interested in researching the topics than in reality. However, organized crime has been subject to more study than has corporate crime.

Neither American or Canadian leaders (see Appendix 5) have addressed the generic problem of corporate crime and violence. They have both, however, directed considerable energies and resources to combatting organized crime. Why? Could it be because organized crime does not provide direct support to the political parties while big business does? It is not wise to bite the hand that feeds you! Such situations make it very difficult for criminologists to study corporate crime. Governments and corporations have no vested interest in funding such research unless there is a direct benefit for them. Furthermore, organized crime and corporate crime have been fraught with definition difficulties. They are subject to change with the passage of time and are often culturally relative.

The temptation to make money and/or acquire power has always been the poisonous fruit of the capitalist system. While we might respect the notion that businesses deserve to make a profit, we are sometimes torn by how much profit is acceptable (e.g., the profit margins of Canada's banks or the notion that amalgamating two or more banks would be in the best interests of their clients). The likelihood of attaining such goals (see anomie theory—Chapter 7) often outweighs the risk of apprehension or the penalties associatedwith such transactions. We saw that the rapid expansion of governments and corporations has given rise to an increasing number of organized crime and corporate crime. We also saw that no one, not even judges, lawyers, prison guards, or police officers are immune to the vices of money and power.

Traditionally, we have relied on sociologically-based theories to explain organized crime and corporate crime. However, such approaches have had limited success in explaining such crime or in offering sound policy recommendations. It was suggested that criminology must extend its approach beyond conventional lines and embrace an integrated and interdisciplinary perspective as well as adopt an international/comparative approach. Both organized crime and corporate crime have crossed national boundaries to become transnational crimes. Criminology and criminal justice agencies need to share information and work towards a common goal. Until then, individual efforts will continue to produce marginal results.

The research on organized crime is more established than the literature on white-collar crime, but no official records are kept on their activities, and at best, we have only rough estimates as to their extensiveness. Why is this? Do our political institutions and our criminal justice systems in some way help to perpetuate the growth of economic crimes? As Clinard and Yeager (1980:21) observed, "corporate crime provides an indicator of the degree of hypocrisy in society." Recently, six Canadian law professors filed a complaint with the Competition Bureau of Canada charging that seal processors conspired to fix prices in 1996. They argue it points to the fact that this sanctioned government enterprise is conducted illegally and with the government's blessing (Law professors…, 1998).

The general lack of control, lenient sentences, and lack of public awareness have all contributed to the problem of trying to understand and address this form of non-conventional crime. And while such crimes reflect generally the "role of greed and a lack of ethics and values" in society (Carrigan, 1991:165), criminologists have been less adept at explaining the other causes of criminal activity.

Throughout the chapter, it was suggested that criminologists need to view these forms of crime as a product of human behaviour. Until we can understand the workings of the human brain and its interaction with the environment, our efforts to simply use the law to maintain social control will have a minimal impact. For example, our ancestors were hunters and gatherers. Are economic crimes simply an evolving representation of an innate trait? Just as bears need to hibernate, will people take the risk to accumulate wealth and power when presented with the opportunity? Does the solution lie in better control, better detection, stiffer penalties, or in better understanding human behaviour, or none of these?

Discussion Questions

1. What are the similarities and differences between organized crime and corporate crime?

2. Should organized crime and corporate crime be treated differently than conventional crimes (robbery, murder, theft, etc.)?

3. Why is it difficult to detect and prosecute organized crime and/or corporate crime offenders?

4. To what extent might corporations be prime targets for organized or corporate crime?

5. Why is it better to apply an interdisciplinary approach to the study of organized and corporate crime?

6. Do outlaw motorcycle gangs serve a useful function in society? Other than their level of organization, why else can authorities not stop the expansion of these organized groups? What should criminologists focus on when studying such groups so that they might be able to offer sound advice?

7. Collect several articles on organized crime and corporate crime. Using the material covered in this chapter, analyze your selected articles.

8. Using Salt Lake City's 2002 Olympic scandal as an example, explain why members of the committee would take such a risk. Describe why it is difficult to regulate corporations.

9. In recent years there has been increasing public demand to stop environmental pollution and destruction (e.g., logging the rainforests of British Columbia, toxic spills in the North West Territories, various oil spills, etc.). Can laws effectively prevent such crimes from happening? Are there alternatives that might be more effective?

Key Concepts

Organized crime	corporate crime	enterprise crime
Mafia	illicit market	cartels
Aboriginal crime groups	ethnic crime groups	motorcycle gangs
Omerta	virus	high technology crime
Ministry of Consumer and	hacker	reintegrative shaming
Corporate Affairs	neutralization	differential association
Computer crime		

Key Names

H. Abadinsky	R. Nader	J. Braithwaite
E. Sutherland		

Weblinks

www.yorku.ca/nathanason/search.htm The homepage for the Nathanson Research Institute on organized crime and corruption at York University. Offers a comprehensive bibliographical database search engine and many informative links.

www.mts.net/dcaskey/index.htm The homepage for the RCMP Analytical Division. Excellent links for organized crime and white-collar crime.

www.mafia.spb.ru/ An at times offensive information link but worth the educational visit.

www.rcmp.grc.ca The RCMP homepage. They have numerous fact sheets on a wide variety of corporate crime and organized crime. Also worth trying are regional RCMP sites such as the Regina RCMP Web site—very useful links.

www.essential.org/monitor/monitor/html The homepage of the *Multinational Monitor*. The watchdog Internet magazine of corporate crimes, which every year publishes the ten worst companies around the world.

Footnotes

1. For **corporate crime**-based movies, see *Wall Street* and *Other People's Money.* Both offer insightful depictions of crimes of "the suit."

2. This is not unlike the famous RICO (Racketeer-Influenced and Corrupt Organization Act) and CCE (Continuing Criminal Enterprise Act) in the United States. These acts gave the government power to seize the personal assets of drug traffickers and sell them to the public to help recover costs and hit the criminals (Inciardi, 1991).

3. Perhaps one of the ironies is that Harleys are also prized by many police officers for recreational riding and many police departments use Harley Davidson motorbikes.

4. In May 1997, the Quebec provincial police undertook a major raid of the Rock Machine and seized millions of dollars in assets. The police believe the raids seriously weakened the Rock Machine and their deadly activities against the Hell's Angels over the province's illegal-drug trade. The raid resulted in the arrest of twenty people and in the seizure or freezing of nearly $5 million in property, land, weapons and explosives. Over the years, the war between the Rock Machine and Hell's Angels has claimed almost 50 victims (Noel, 1997).

5. Defining organized crime has presented criminologists with challenges. Some definitions limit the definition of "traditional" mobs to *La Cosa Nostra* (Italian for "our affair"). Scaramella et. al. (1997) notes that *La Cosa Nostra* "refers to traditional Italian organized crime in the United States." Yet it shares many similar characteristics to the Mafia. In this section, we will focus only on the activities of the Mafia.

6. For an interesting, true life account of an Italian mobster read Peter Mass's *Underboss Sammy the Bull Gravano's story of life in the Mafia* (1997) by NY: Harper Collins. The book is written in a narrative fashion and provides a thorough overview of life as one of the top Mafia underbosses in New York City.

7. It is not known exactly when the Mafia, or "Black Hand" as they were also referred to, began operations in Canada. However, during the 1920s and 1930s they became actively involved in drug operations in Montreal and in bootlegging alcohol to the United States during Prohibition (Carrigan, 1991). Since then their enterprises have expanded and they have become a major force in the criminal underworld.

8. The notion that organized crime exists because immigrants (e.g., Italian, Vietnamese, Jamaican, etc.) corrupt the law-abiding and prey on our weaknesses is based on the mythical *alien conspiracy model* first put forth in the 1950s (see Potter, 1994, Cressey, 1969—for a classic depiction of this view).

9. In this section, we will focus on corporate crime rather than *occupational crime*. While there is debate in the literature as to whether they are separate, or should be treated as such, for the purpose of this section we will limit the definition by the characteristic nature of each. Corporate crimes are crimes done for the benefit for the corporation while occupational crimes are committed by individuals within a business setting for their own advantage. For example, a bank might commit fraud by trying to "hide" its assets from the gov-

ernment. However, the bank teller who embezzles money from bank through manipulating transactions, is committing the crime for his or her own personal benefit (Daly, 1989a). This is generally referred to by criminologists as *occupational crime*. Former RCMP commissioner Norman Inkster estimates annual losses from all types of white-collar crime and fraud at $20 billion per year in Canada. He points out that law agencies simply do not have the resources to effectively combat their rapid growth (White collar …, 1997).

10. No comparable publications/data are available for Canada.

11. Since most crimes of this nature are committed by big businesses, Sutherland coined the term "white-collar crime" to describe the general characteristic of the type of individuals (i.e., upper-class) involved in business crimes. However, due to definitional issues and changing format of some businesses, the term corporate crime is more commonly found, or is used interchangeably. Another term that has been used to describe business and corporate crime is "suite crime" (Ermann and Lundman, 1982). As with the term white-collar crime, suite crime reflects the nature of origin of most corporate crime—in the offices of the corporation.

12. Viruses can damage data by way of *data diddling* (software manipulation); *Trojan Horses* (implanting instructions designed to destroy, or alter, a program); *logic time bombs* (instructions that are executed at a pre-set time to cause damage); or *macroviruses* (newest variety of virus. They target documents and spreadsheets from popular programs like Excel and MS Word).

13. Smith was tracked down and arrested within 10 days. At the time of preparing this chapter, he faced a maximum of 40 years in prison and a $480,000 U.S. fine. However, his lawyer argued the virus did not corrupt, erase, or delete any files. All it did was forward an innocuous message to 50 other people.

14. Keane (1996) describes six external factors that can be used to explain corporate crime. They include capitalism, competition, strain theory, environmental uncertainty, market structure, and opportunity theory. Because companies are goal-oriented, these external factors can individually or collectively cause some businesses to resort to criminal activities in order to meet their goals.

15. In a study of corporate prosecutions in California, Benson, Maakestad, Cullen, and Geis (1988) found that individuals were more likely to be prosecuted than their organization. They also observed that prosecutions were less likely to occur if there was a major impact on the local economy.

16. The *Multinational Monitor* (MM) (1992) cited a report by the Environmental Crimes Project in which then President Ronald Reagan discouraged and often prevented federal investigators from prosecuting environmental crimes. The *Monitor* also noted that the rates for other forms of corporate crime began to increase dramatically after Reagan assumed the Presidency. In the April 1996 issue of MM an article pointed out that a House seat in the American Congress cost approximately $520,000 (U.S.) while a seat in the Senate cost $4.5 (U.S.) million. The article suggests that very few give money out of "love for democracy." Rather, it is for power and vested interests.

CHAPTER 12

Crimes Against
Public Order

*"The greatest happiness of the greatest number is the
foundation of morals and legislation."*

Jeremy Bentham (1742–1832)

Learning Outcomes

After you have completed this chapter, you should be able to:

- Recognize the relationship between law and morality.

- Appreciate the characteristics and nature of public order offences such as gambling, prostitution, pornography, and substance abuse.

- Have an awareness of the theories and implications of public order offences on society.

In earlier chapters, we discussed several of the important elements of crime. It was observed that the criminalization of certain behaviours is *relative* and *evolving*. It was also noted that our perception of what constitutes "wrongful" behaviour varies widely throughout society. That is, there is little consensus as to what behaviours should be classified as criminal as opposed to being *deviant* or simply *social diversions*. Within criminology, there are a number of acts that are often referred to as public order crimes or victimless crimes.

The term **victimless crime** is somewhat confusing in that it implies there is no "complaining victim." Because there is no victim, some criminologists question whether the acts should be considered criminal. **Public order crimes** include gambling, prostitution, pornography, vandalism and graffiti, substance abuse and hate crimes. And while a number of these crimes are covered in this chapter, they could also have been allocated to a variety of other chapters. For

example, prostitution and pornography could have been covered in Chapter 11 and gambling in Chapter 10. However, given that many of these acts are victimless events, we have grouped them together as public order crimes.

In this chapter, we will examine some of the current forms of public order offences. In the process, we will discuss the characteristics and patterns of such acts. We will also review some of the explanations and policy implications of these "victimless" acts. First, however, given the controversy surrounding public order offences, we will look at the relationship between law and morality.

Law and Morality

"People committing acts in obedience of law or habit are not being moral"
W.H. Auden.

Consider the following questions:

- Legally you can buy lottery tickets. Why are you not allowed to gamble?
- Legally you are allowed to have intimate relations with your partner. Why are you not allowed to pay someone for such services?
- People fly the Canadian flag in various states of disrepair but why is it illegal to burn a flag in protest?
- If you are of legal age, you are allowed to drink alcohol. Why are you not allowed to smoke marijuana or snort cocaine?
- Part I of the *Canadian Charter of Rights and Freedoms* (1982) guarantees every Canadian the "freedom of speech" and "freedom of the press," yet why is some gangsta rap groups' music sanctioned?
- Legally you are allowed to watch certain forms of adult dancers in strip bars but lap dancing, a form of stripping, was declared illegal by the Supreme Court of Canada in March of 1997 (Makin, 1997). Is there a discernable difference between suggestive behaviour as opposed to overt sexual expression?
- Why are women allowed to sell their eggs for profit and enable other women to have children, when the public at large is not allowed to sell its organs? Is there a moral difference between donating and selling?
- Although abortions are permitted during the first trimester of pregnancy, fierce dispute continues over whether the aborted fetus qualifies as a true victim (e.g., a form of murder). How can the law, let alone science, determine when life begins?
- The Bible implies that God destroyed the ancient cities of Sodom and Gomorrah because their residents engaged in deviant behaviour and supposed homosexual practices (see Box 12.1). Why is the practice of homosexual behaviour legal today when public support is mixed? (see Box 12.2).

FYI BOX 12.1

Homosexuality

Prior to 1968, homosexuality was a punishable crime in Canada. Because of social and cultural changes in the 1950s and 1960s, the passage of Bill C-150 legalized the practice of homosexuality (149 to 55 voted in favour of the Bill). For some years after it was viewed as a disease rather than a crime (Duhaime, 1996).

REALITY CHECK BOX 12.2

TRYING TO RULE ON MORALITY

In 1991, Delwin Vriend was dismissed from a Christian college in Edmonton when he admitted to being a practicing homosexual. Until his dismissal, Vriend had been working at the college for seven years without incident. His only "wrongdoing," according to the college, was his involvement in gay rights. It was not until April of 1998 that the Supreme Court of Canada ruled that Vriend's dismissal was a violation of human rights law (Chase, 1998).

Shortly after the ruling the *Calgary Herald* presented a debate on the pros and cons of the decision. The debate included opinions from the court, private citizens, and politicians. Of those who supported the ruling, comments focused on such issues as these: protecting the interests of a minority who have historically been the target of prejudice and discrimination, serving to raise everyone's consciousness of the importance of human rights issues and suggesting that the ruling simply reflected what Albertans had been saying for years.

The comments of those who opposed the ruling focused on such issues as these: morality should not be the domain of the courts, the ruling represents another example of how special interest groups are circumventing democratic processes and the ruling will open the doors to the legitimization of other controversial behaviours (e.g., pedophilia) (The Vriend decision, 1998).

These and related questions raise a serious dilemma for criminologists and policy makers. How does society decide which acts should be sanctioned and which ones should be criminalized?

The primary purpose of the law is to protect society by legislating behaviours that society at large considers immoral and socially harmful. However, what is the foundation of morality? Surely, as the German philosopher Immanuel Kant (1724–1804) argued, morality cannot rely on religious doctrines. Rather, according to more recent philosophers such as Wolf (1989), morality must be established on grounds that can withstand skeptical challenges and enrich the lives of all.

These philosophical points have been the subject of many debates. How does one determine whether an act presents a clear and immediate harm to all those who partake? For example, how should criminology respond to certain acts that take place between consenting individuals (e.g., gambling, prostitution, euthanasia, etc.)? What proportion of the population needs to share those views before such acts can be defined as immoral/moral and declared illegal/legal? Where does one draw the line between the victimless participants who are being coerced into their acts? If, for example, a prostitute prefers not to take part in certain sexual acts and yet the customer makes such a request (and is willing to pay extra), is this coercion? If the client applies force, does the act then become a crime?

Answers to the above questions are complicated by an assortment of related variables. How old are the participants? How much force was used? Is there a greater social and moral issue at stake? For example, does allowing prostitutes to walk the streets send an inappropriate message to young impressionable people? Does it promote the entry of the homeless and runaways into such acts as a means of survival? Does it result in their unnecessary exploitation?

There are no clear-cut answers to these types of questions. They are questions of morality and, as will be discussed throughout the chapter, it is uncertain whether criminal law can be effectively used to regulate these subjective behaviours.

Since antiquity, social conventions and rules of etiquette have been the guiding principles for maintaining social harmony. As societies evolved it became necessary to codify their norms and values in order to maintain a sense of social harmony. This codification resulted in the creation of formal criminal law. The formation of law is seen as subscribing to one of two general theoretical orientations—either the consensus model or the conflict perspective—which are not necessarily mutually exclusive.

Among criminologists who subscribe to the **consensus model** (see Figure 1–1), laws are seen as representing the interests (i.e., needs and values) of a given society. Conversely, those criminologists who adopt a **conflict perspective** interpret the legislation of laws as representing the interests of the vocal majority and those who are in a position of power (see Box 12.3). For example, most Canadians probably agree that murder should be a crime. Since murder is a criminal offence we can say that the law reflects a consensus perspective. On the other hand, Canadians appear to support a reinstatement of capital punishment. For example, a Nova Scotia public school student conducted a survey of his grade 8 classmates and discovered that 59 per cent supported a reinstatement of the death penalty (Brett, 1996). Similarly, Honeyman and Ogloff (1996) reported that 59 per cent of the university and college students they surveyed supported a reinstatement of the death penalty. Their study revealed that 66 per cent of males versus 54 per cent of females were in favour of a return of capital punishment. Criminologists might argue that this reflects a conflict perspective in the law.

For Whose Benefit? The Long Arm of the Law and Exotic Dancers

The following sections of the Canadian *Criminal Code* can and have been applied against women, at various times, working as exotic dancers at clubs:

- Indecent act in a public place, s. 173
- Immoral theatrical performance, s. 167
- Common "bawdy-house," s. 210
- Nudity, s. 174
- Obscenity, s. 163
- Causing a disturbance, s. 175
- Communicating for the purpose of prostitution, s. 213.

Going Topless: Tolerance vs. Rights

Under section 174 of the *Criminal Code,* anyone "who, without lawful excuse, (a) is nude in a public place, or (b) is nude and exposed to public view while on private property ... is guilty of an offence ... For the purpose of this section, a person is nude who is clad as to offend against public decency or order." And depending on the jurisdiction, law enforcement officials could also enforce section 175 of the *C.C.* as it pertains to "causing disturbance and indecent exhibition." However, on a hot summer day in 1991, Gwen Jacobs strolled the streets of Guelph, Ontario without wearing a top. She was charged with committing an indecent act. Claiming it was discriminatory, Jacobs went to court, and in 1996 won her case. The decision declared that going topless was now legal for women. Ontario Premier Mike Harris expressed concern about the decision and feared the impact it could have on the province's impressionable young people (Baring breasts..., 1996). In addition, in 1997 a province-wide poll of 928 adult Ontario residents revealed that sixty-five per cent disapproved of the law. Forty-five per cent of males surveyed thought it was OK while only twenty-one per cent of women surveyed expressed similar views (Ontario cool..., 1997).

Since the landmark case, women across the country have begun to test the limits of the law. Yet, as much as many women advocate their rights in this matter, not all provinces are prepared to tolerate such actions.

As a result of two topless incidents in Regina during the summer of 1997, the Saskatchewan Attorney General's office made it clear that unless there is an amendment to the *Criminal Code*, going topless is still illegal and "offenders" may risk facing charges. One of the cases involved a Caucasian women and the other a Native woman. The former was not charged, the latter was. In addition to outraging special interest groups, there were cries of possible discrimination (Hall, 1997).

The architects of the Canadian Constitution recognized this inherent dilemma in the law. In formulating the Constitution they attempted to strike a balance between respecting natural law (i.e., utilitarian principles) and the relative and evolving nature of social norms and values. From a criminological (primarily sociological perspective) standpoint, criminal prohibitions have their roots in the social forces of society. In courses such as the "sociology of law," students explore the forces and elements that contribute to the formation of criminal law. Among the aspects studied are the "moral entrepreneurs"[1] who campaign to have their values legitimized and embodied in law. Canadian examples include the prohibition period, environmental groups such as Greenpeace and the Sierra Club, abortion activists, gay and lesbian groups, hemp growers and users, and more recently the right of women to go topless in public. Although these groups do not represent a majority or necessarily hold high social positions, many of the groups have gained a voice by using various laws along with pleas to public sympathy to have their rights protected.

In general, the above issues are part of *legal jurisprudence*. A number of criminology programs, most law schools, and some political science programs offer courses on the history of criminological thought which usually address some of the above issues.[2] But the tension between the balance of social order and individual freedoms is one that will not, nor is likely to be, resolved in our multi-ethnic, multi-cultural, pluralistic society. To illustrate the point, let us now turn to several specific examples.

Gambling

"Gambling is not a healthy commercial activity. It is an activity that shows a society is morally bankrupt." Marie Lucie Spoke (1998, Ottawa—Citizens Against Gambling Expansion).

Have you ever bought a lottery, raffle, or pull-ticket? Have you ever been to a casino, played bingo, or participated in **nambling** (net gambling)? Have you ever made a bet with a friend, at the track or with yourself? If you are like most people, you have probably participated in one or more of these activities "just for fun" (see Box 12.4). However, why are some forms of gambling considered socially acceptable and quite innocent while other forms have been legally sanctioned? What is the point of the dress code in casinos? Why do bingo halls not have a dress code? How are such decisions made and what is the impact of gambling on individuals and society? Of what interest is gambling to criminologists? What does the law say about gambling?

Is it Just for Fun or Something More Serious?

AADAC Gambling Screen

1. In the past 12 months have you:
   - ☐ played bingo
   - ☐ bet on sporting events
   - ☐ purchased lottery tickets
   - ☐ played games of skill for money (e.g. cards)
   - ☐ played slot machines, video lottery machines (poker machines)
   - ☐ gambled in a casino
   - ☐ gambled at the track (include off-track betting as well)
   - ☐ participated in any other form of gambling?

2. In the past 12 months have you spent more money than you intended on any of these activities?
   - ☐ Yes   ☐ No

3. In the past 12 months has your involvement in the above activities created financial difficulties for you or your family?
   - ☐ Yes   ☐ No

4. In the past 12 months has anyone expressed concern about your involvement in these activities?
   - ☐ Yes   ☐ No

5. In the past 12 months have you been concerned about your involvement in these activities?
   - ☐ Yes   ☐ No

If you answer "yes" to any one of questions 2–5, or if you show significant gambling activity in question 1 but answer "no" to questions 2–5, further assessment is recommended. Contact your local AADAC office or call the Gambling Help Line at 1-800-665-9676 for confidential referral.

To contact your local AADAC office: _____ .

Source: Adapted from AADAC Gambling Screen quiz.

Let us first begin by defining the meaning of gambling as described in the *Criminal Code*. Then we will examine some of the characteristics and trends of gambling before focusing on some of the social problems associated with it. The section will conclude with an examination of several theoretical explanations of gambling.

Gambling and the Law

The first thing you will notice when you look up gambling in the Canadian *Criminal Code* is that gambling is referred to **gaming and betting**. It covers sections 197 through 210 in the Code. One of the key legal terms is the concept of "betting," generally defined as "a bet that is placed on any contingency or event that is to take place in or out of Canada, ... includes a bet that is placed on any contingency relating to a horse-race, fight, match or sporting event that is to take place in or out of Canada." The term "gaming" refers to "a game of chance or mixed chance of skill."

Under section 207 of the Code, the law describes the terms and conditions under which the government of a province may legally conduct and manage a lottery scheme. Such schemes must be "fair" in their structure, they must be associated with a charitable or religious organization, and they must receive licencing by the Lieutenant Governor in Council of a province. Therefore, when you buy a lottery ticket, a percentage of the money you spend is funneled back to the public in the form of winnings and a percentage goes to charitable organizations. The rules and regulations are defined under each province's Gaming and Liquor Commission.

Blickstead (1990) observes that in 1985 Canadians spent $2.7 billion on lottery tickets. Perhaps you have been involved in a fund raising activity in school or with a local club. You sell a select number of tickets. Then, based on the prize structure, your charitable organization gets to put the profits towards a school trip, purchasing new equipment, or some other benefit. In 1986, on average, every Canadian spent about $146 on lottery tickets—up from $102 in 1982. Blickstead further notes that those making between $50,000 and $60,000, in 1986, spent the most (approximately $238 per capita) while those making over $60,000 per year spent slightly less—$207. Playing the lotteries became more commonplace in 1969 when they were legalized in Canada. Every province now sponsors local lotteries and the federal government is also involved in sponsoring several national lotteries (see Box 12.5). As Walker (1994 cited in Barkan, 1996:449) notes, "the old moralist objections have collapsed" as the line between legalized gambling and illegal gambling, in many respects, has been reduced to mere legal discourse.

In 1997, Jim Gray, Chairman of Canadian Hunter Explorations and chair of the conservative Canada West Foundation think tank stated that Alberta was addicted to VLT revenue. He pointed out that the province netted about $500 million annually from VLTs alone and that "somewhere between two and five per cent of your population becomes pathologically addicted. That's between 50,000 and 200,000 Albertans" (Chase, 1997). Other reports estimate that compulsive or pathological gamblers spend more than $380 a month on VLTs alone (see Table 12–1).

VLTS EXPANDING

In 1998, several Alberta MLAs suggested that one solution to the numerous VLT outlets throughout the province would be to limit them to casinos. In June of 1998,
Ontario announced that it was opening four giant casinos. Three of the casinos border
the United States—hoping to lure American gamblers the way Niagara Falls and
Windsor already do (Welsh and Donavan, 1998). What do you think about these ideas?

TABLE 12—1

GAMBLING IN ALBERTA*

	TOTAL GROSS			PER CENT OF WINNING OF GROSS		
	'91–'92	'93–'94 (000)	'95–'96	'91–'92	'93–'94	'95–'96
Bingo	297,258	337,718	301,334	70.2	70.7	69.6
Casino	224,311	297,634	294,631	80.9	82.4	82.7
Pull-ticket	103,644	86,480	38,986	74.0	74.3	74.5
Raffles	24,022	45,022	58,585**	41.6	40.3	44.5

- * In 1998, it was reported that six thousand VLTs were in operation in Alberta pubs and lounges.
  An Alberta Web site reports that VLTs generate nearly a billion dollars in extra revenue for the
  Provincial Government" (VLT..., 1998). However, a spokesperson from the Alberta Gaming and
  Liquor Commission noted that VLTs generate approximately $500 million per year for the
  Provincial Government.
- ** Not including raffles under $10,000
- Source: *Gaming in Alberta 1991–92, 1993–94, 1995–96* and personal communication with the
  Alberta Gaming Commission.
- An April 1998 survey conducted by the Angus Reid Poll for the *Calgary Herald* revealed that 52
  per cent of Calgarians were in favour of removing VLTs from bars and lounges. Women were more
  opposed (49 per cent) to VLTs than males (41 per cent) (Cunningham, 1998).

Whether you are betting on the "horses," or buying tickets for a car raffle, you
are involved in a game of chance. Should any form of risk-taking be legally sanctioned? Does it matter whether illegal gambling usually involves lower odds of
winning than legalized forms of gambling?[3] The law seems to think so.

Gambling and Legalization

The line between what is defined as acceptable chance taking and what is defined as illegal has become less clear. Increasingly, many forms of gambling are being legalized. Why?

In the previous section, it was observed that legalizing gambling activities undermines the ability of organized crime groups to exploit that opportunity. Other explanations include the observation that the public has become more tolerant about a variety of vice crimes (e.g., gambling, prostitution, substance abuse, and pornography). Since the legalization of many forms of gambling, we have seen public attitudes shift and the shift is being reflected socially. Today, it is possible to buy lottery tickets in every province and territory. Most provinces operate their own lotteries and run video lottery machines. Several are even legally operating casinos.

Another rationale for legalization is the opportunity for municipal, provincial and federal levels of government to use gambling venues to generate much-needed revenue. For example, First Nations people have been granted the right to run casinos as a means of supporting their desire for self-government. A news release from the Government of Saskatchewan stated that granting a company owned by the Star Blanket Cree Nation the right to set up a gift shop at Casino Regina, would "employ up to six people, part of the 352 jobs created by the operation of the casino. An additional 150 jobs were created by the casino construction and renovation project" (Casino Regina ..., 1996).

Are the legislative bodies preying on human weakness? Moral entrepreneurial groups such as Gamblers Anonymous, the Canadian Foundation on Compulsive Gambling, along with many religious groups, warn against the temptation and vice of gambling. While their reasoning may differ they all agree that the harm done to families, individuals, and the impact on crime is a very real issue.

Characteristics and Trends

A recent story observed that cash-starved Atlantic provinces were looking for ways to capitalize on legalized gambling. In the article, the Auditor-General of the Atlantic Lottery Corporation noted that the lottery industry was a "cash cow" for the eastern provinces. For example, New Brunswick, with its 3,588 gambling machines, generated $82 million in 1996, Nova Scotia, with its 2,573 machines, generated $105 million, Newfoundland generated $74 million from its 2,084 machines, and Prince Edward Island managed a profit of $14 million from 621 machines. The article went on to point out that, although New Brunswick has the most machines it does not generate the most money. Suggestions were made about how to improve these odds.

Interestingly, nothing was said about the social impact on society or on individuals who might be problem gamblers, or about the potential criminal spin-offs of such activity.[4] The focus of the report was on how to maximize the provinces' jackpot "winnings" (Morris, 1997). However, in an article that appeared a few weeks later it was observed that 525,000 of 760,000 people (approximately 70 per cent) had gambled at some point in their life, but "only 9,400" (approximately 2 per cent) were considered to be problem gamblers (Video gambling ..., 1997).

Because gambling can take many forms, it is difficult to estimate how many people gamble legally and illegally. One recent American study revealed that boys gamble more often than girls and ninth and twelfth grade students gambled more than sixth grade students. Mexican/Latin American students gamble more than Asian American and white students. Comparing rates of gambling between 1992 and 1995, Stinchfield (1997) found that gambling among youths frequently included antisocial behaviour and frequent use of alcohol. This area remains mostly unexplored but one Canadian article reported that nearly 70 per cent of youths 9–14 years of age had gambled at least once. Only 5 per cent claimed to gamble at least once per week. But adolescents are more inclined to play video arcade games, which are mostly games of skill and chance where gambling habits may get rooted (Moore, 1994).

In a related study, Stinchfield and Winters (1997) found that 61 per cent of adult gamblers were males, the average age was 39, only 16 per cent were college graduates, and nearly 66 per cent were employed full-time. In addition, almost half (49 per cent) had previously sought assistance for their gambling problem, 33 per cent had received chemical dependency services, and most had started their gambling addiction before adulthood.

While it is possible to obtain figures on how much Canadians spend on lottery tickets, it is difficult to estimate how much money the average person spends each year on other, gambling-related activities. As we saw in Chapter 11, many organized crime groups are heavily involved in gambling-related activities (sometimes referred to as the "numbers racket"). Any attempt to estimate the amount of profit organized crimes groups make from illegal gambling activities is sheer speculation. Criminal justice agencies are aware of the extent of it and prefer instead to direct their attention to understanding it and curbing its activity.[5]

Along with the recent liberalization of gambling laws in Canada (and North America), most provinces now have lottery operations ranging from simple ticket operations to video lottery machines. A growing number of provinces now have legalized casinos. As noted above, the lotteries provide a significant proportion of provincial and federal revenue. In addition, as noted in the example above, it could be suggested that some provinces are overly dependent on these "cash cows." This point is further illustrated in a study by Blickstead (1990). Examining Canadian lottery revenue, Blickstead observed that 48 per cent of revenue goes to prizes, 33 per cent is returned to the provinces, 3 per cent goes to the government, 10 per cent is used for operating expenses, and 6 per cent goes to the thousands of retailers who sell the tickets.

What is sometimes overlooked when presenting raw data on gambling are the moral consequences of gambling? What is the social impact? What kind of spin-off consequences might result? What is the impact on organized crime?

The "Catch-22"

As stated above, and in Chapter 11, gambling represents a major source of revenue for organized crime groups. However, the recent liberalization of gambling laws throughout North America has reduced organized crime's income from gambling.[6] In response, organized crime has turned its efforts to other illegal venues such as extortion, illicit drugs, immigration fraud, money laundering, and pornography. The catch, as indicated above and as expressed by the Canadian Foundation on Compulsive Gambling, is that now that many forms of gambling have been legalized, more people have become problem gamblers and the ensuing negative social effects have escalated accordingly.

Although there is no hard data on the numbers of people who have become problem gamblers, there is sufficient research to demonstrate that gambling is a social vice that threatens public order, increases health care costs, and increases criminal activity.

Those individuals who experience serious gambling problems are sometimes referred to as compulsive gamblers. The problem is generally seen as symptomatic of an emotional disorder—low self-esteem, inability and/or unwillingness to accept reality, immaturity, or obsessive behavioural patterns. In 1995, it was reported that in Alberta there were an estimated 100,000 people who are "slaves" to gambling. Of those who sought help, many said the VLTs (video lottery terminals) provided them with an escape from reality that became addictive. The article recounts an incident in which an individual spent nearly five hours in his van with a gun and a ski mask trying to get up enough courage to rob a local pub to recover all the rent and food money he had gambled away on VLTs (When it's no ..., 1995). Fortunately, he finally turned himself in. Such stories are not isolated examples. Compulsive gambling is a serious problem (see theoretical explanations below). Yet, in spite of the fact that two-thirds of Albertans oppose VLTs, they have not been removed or declared illegal.[7]

A study conducted by the Harvard School of Medicine in 1997 concluded that 3.9 per cent of the adult population is likely to have experienced mild to severe gambling-related problems during the past 12 months. The researchers examined the findings of more than 150 studies done throughout North America since 1977 and concluded that problem gamblers are on the rise even though they admit that "medical science still isn't sure how to define problem gambling and positively identify those suffering its financially and emotionally destructive symptoms" (Alm, 1997).

Criminologists, among other social scientists, have attempted to identify the warning signs of a compulsive gambler. Moreover, while the indicators are dependent on varying environmental, psychological, and social factors, it is possible to identify "warning signs" (see Box 12.4).

By definition, gambling is seen as a social problem and problem gamblers require attention. In January 1957, Gamblers Anonymous was formed to help people deal with their compulsion to gamble. GA operates on the premise that gambling is an illness, that it is progressive in nature and cannot be cured—only arrested. Gamblers Anonymous does not believe will power will work. Only adherence to spiritual principles can help to control the moral vice.

Today, this organization has chapters all around the world. In 1997, the Calgary Addiction Centre of Alberta set up the very first residential program, in Canada, exclusively for women who are gambling addicts. The executive director of the centre believes that the problem will only get worse as the provinces further relax laws on gambling. She notes that women are less likely to disclose their addiction problems to men than they are to women. She also suggests that women are turning to gambling as a way to escape boredom, marital problems, and depression (Treatment planned ..., 1997). Since then, other provinces are looking into setting up similar programs. But why do people gamble?

Explaining Gambling

Berman and Siegel (1992) provide three explanations commonly found throughout the literature. The *psychological theories* focus on such individualized factors as "too much" or "too little" parenting: the child's basic emotional needs were not met. In addition, a disproportionate number of gamblers have (had) parents who were unable to provide proper role modelling for their children due to their own problems—either alcohol, drugs, gambling, or emotional. Such conditions typically lead to prolonged frustration and undermine the child's self-esteem. Later, as an adult, the "victim" might turn to gambling as a way of trying to be a "big shot."

Other psychological perspectives view gambling as an unconscious desire to take risks and lose, as a response to their feelings of guilt, emotional isolation, and pain. The later is analogous to Freud's "death instinct" (Chapter 6)—a desire to be punished.

Although not widely embraced in North America because of underlying perceptions of gambling, *biological theories* interpret gambling as an impulse disorder with a biochemical link. For example, Berman and Siegel (1992) cite studies that have found compulsive gamblers have low levels of *serotonin* and increased responsiveness of the *noradrenergic system* (associated with poor control of impulses). Studies have also found an association between low levels of *norepinephrine* (which regulates arousal, thrill, and excitement).

These conditions, left medically untreated, only make it more difficult for problem gamblers to stop their addiction. Any attempts to stop are likely to lead to depression and other emotional difficulties. That will eventually lead the individual back to his or her gambling habits that in turn will temporarily alleviate the depression.

The final explanation Berman and Siegel (1992) review is the *learning/perception theories*. These sociologically-based theories view gambling as a learned behaviour. It is dependent on random reinforcement that prompts the gambler to believe that he or she will win again. After winning, a gambler might rationalize that winning was due to skill alone. Furthermore, the media tend to reinforce a superficial perception of gambling by focusing on the "positive" aspects of winning—the holiday, the new car, paying off debts, and quitting your boring job.

In **summary**, criminologists will likely have to accept the fact that for better or worse, gambling is here to stay. As has been said in many different ways "life itself is a gamble."

In addition to defining the characteristics of gamblers and which forms of gambling pose a greater risk to criminal activity than others, criminologists should focus on articulating the extent to which gambling is or is not a victimless crime. In terms of social policy, criminologists should study whether offering help lines, establishing support groups/programs, and having trained staff at gambling facilities, can minimize the damage gambling causes.

One small irony of possible gambling venues is the fact that organized crime has not infiltrated the greatest gambling enterprise in North America—the stock market! Why is it that criminologists typically direct their attention to "ordinary" forms of gambling and pay minimal attention to people who play the stock market? As the Bre-X scandal of 1997 showed, the cost of playing the stock market can be more financially devastating than ordinary gambling.

Where and how can, or should, criminal law distinguish between acceptable forms of gambling and illegal forms of gambling? Is there really any difference between betting on the horses and betting on stocks? It could be argued that the idea of democracy itself (as a form of government) represents a type of gambling. Based on a majority vote we hope that politicians will reflect the will of the people who voted them in. Yet most Canadians are in favour of reinstating capital punishment, toughening the *Young Offenders Act* (i.e., *Youth Criminal Justice Act*) and eliminating section 745.2 (the "faint hope" clause) of the *Criminal Code*, among other major reforms.

Prostitution

We have probably all heard the phrase that prostitution is the "oldest profession in the world." Yet, as a social institution, it has run the gamut from being tolerated and even condoned to being defined as a serious moral interdiction.

In ancient Greece, prostitution was openly accepted while in pre-twentieth-century Japan, geisha girls were considered desirable for marriage because "they knew how to please a man"[8] (Vito and Holmes, 1994). Also during ancient times, there existed a class of sacred prostitutes in the Middle East known as *qedesha* or *kedesha* (*Britannica*, 1997). During the 1700s and 1800s, many European cities permitted licenced brothels and required the women to submit to regular medical examinations (Bullough and Bullough, 1987). Closer to home, during the Yukon gold rush in the late 1800s, prostitution operated openly. Most of the prostitutes during this period were Aboriginal women, "many of whom were lured into the business through alcohol addiction, or were forced into it by fathers, husbands, and others who bought and sold Native women for prostitution" (Carrigan, 1991:263).

Although there is a considerable volume of Canadian literature on prostitutes or "sex workers" (McIntyre, 1994) today, most of this literature did not begin to emerge until the early 1980s. Prostitution became a politically relevant issue when special interest groups such as POWER (Prostitutes and Other Women for Equal Rights), CORP (Canadian Organization for the Rights of Prostitutes), SWAV (Sex Workers Alliance of Vancouver),[9] and Dans La Rue attracted considerable attention to the needs and rights of prostitutes.[10]

The deluge of research was further accelerated after the publication of two major federally commissioned studies. In 1981, the Committee on Sexual Offences Against Children and Youth (commonly referred to as the **Badgley Report**, after its primary author) examined child abuse and youth prostitution. Among its numerous findings the report revealed that young prostitutes were more likely to be sexually precocious than youth not involved in prostitution. It also reported that a significant number of young prostitutes were the victims of unwanted sexual acts committed against them as children and/or in adolescence. However, Lowman (1995) and Brannigan (1996), among several other subsequent studies, point out that the Badgley Report did not specify the nature of abuse, its prevalence, or describe how often abuse occurred (see Brannigan, 1996, for an overview).

Notwithstanding the methodological shortfalls, the report, along with subsequent studies (see Lowman, 1995 for a general review) indicates that many young prostitutes come from dysfunctional family backgrounds. The growing body of evidence prompted a review of laws pertaining to youth prostitution.

Although no amount of adolescent prostitution should be tolerated, the increase in official counts needs to be placed in perspective. For example, the new legislation against prostitution (specifically Bill C-15—"The Child Exploitation

Law"—see Brannigan, 1996 for an overview) resulted in significant changes in law enforcement practices.[11] Similar trends, after the introduction of new legislation to protect child exploitation, have been experienced in the United Kingdom and Australia (Ibid).

Adult prostitution was subsequently addressed by the Special Committee on Pornography and Prostitution (SCPP—also referred to as the **Fraser Report**) in 1983. Its mandate was to review the status of prostitution and pornography and their related regulatory laws. In order to fulfill its objectives, the committee sponsored several other related studies.

One of the recommendations of the Fraser Report was to amend the outdated *Bawdy House Act*. The authors of the report argued that the Act represented an outmoded morality law that makes criminals of people who may simply be living an alternative lifestyle.[12] Under the law, it is not only illegal to operate a bawdy house, it is also a crime to simply be found in a bawdy house. The problem of the act revolves around the concept of "acts of indecency," which is not defined in the *Criminal Code* (see Lowman, 1995).

In this section we will limit our coverage to a more general overview. We will begin by looking at the legal definition of prostitution. Then we will look at some of the characteristics and trends of prostitution before examining the notion of prostitution representing the "oldest profession." The section will conclude with the criminological (and social) dilemma of whether prostitution should continue to be criminalized, regulated or abolished. Davis and Shaffer (1994:3) point out that the three regimes share two common policy considerations:

1. "The protection of prostitution from exploitation by third parties, and
2. The protection of the public from adverse affects of exposure to prostitution."

However, before we get ahead of ourselves, let's begin by reviewing the definition of prostitution.

Defining Prostitution

Technically speaking, prostitution is legal in Canada. What is illegal is practising prostitution. In fact, it is almost impossible for a prostitute to work without violating laws. And while other western countries have moved away from criminalizing prostitution, Canada appears to have moved in the opposite direction. In 1990, for example, the Standing Committee on Justice recommended that on arrest, prostitutes should be fingerprinted and photographed and those charged with communication have their drivers' licences removed. Subsequent studies have placed an emphasis on better enforcement of existing laws (Davis and Shaffer, 1994).

In the 1999 *Criminal Code,* sections 210–213 pertain to "keeping common bawdy-house"—indoor prostitution, "procuring" or living off the avails of prostitution, and "offences in relation to prostitution" (e.g., any person in a "public place" who attempts to stop any person for the purpose of engaging in prostitution). These sections make up the legal meaning of prostitution. Lowman (1995) argues that sections 210 through 212 are intended to protect prostitutes from third parties while section 213 is designed to protect the public from the "nuisance" effects of prostitution.

Do these laws work? Davis and Shaffer (1994) and McIntyre (1994), among others, argue no. They point out that the law has only prompted prostitutes to devise better means of avoiding detection rather than focusing on health and safety issues.

Historically, however, prostitution was more narrowly defined. As with much of our legal heritage, Canada's first prostitution-oriented laws were based on British law. Prostitution was initially prohibited by vagrancy laws (Lowman, 1995). The first vagrancy act was the *Nova Scotia Act* of 1759.

The laws were not directed at the act per se but at the "nuisance that was created by streetwalkers and 'bawdy-house' (brothel) activities" (Ibid, 333).[13] In spite of existing laws, enforcement of the laws in Britain, and the United States was only superficially enforced. This was especially evident in the frontier areas of Canada and the United States where "red-light" areas of town were openly tolerated by the police (see Brannigan, Knafla, and Levy, 1989).

FYI BOX 12.6

Red-Light Districts

The term "red-light district" became popular in North America during the railroad-building era in the 1800s. When visiting a prostitute, a railroad worker would hang his red signal light outside the woman's tent so that if he was suddenly needed for work he could be quickly found (Bullough, 1980).

Finally, in 1957, a commissioned study on laws governing sexual behaviour in Great Britain eventually brought about new standards, with the *Sexual Offences Act* in 1967. The commission produced a report known as the *Wolfenden Report*. Among its recommendations, the report argued that any legislation pertaining to sexual behaviour should focus on the sexual acts that offend public decency or disrupt order and not concern themselves with trying to legislate morality.

While the law grapples with the definition of prostitution and public decency (see Box 12.7), the public also has varying perceptions as to the meaning of prostitution. The SCPP (1985) reports that 90 per cent believe prostitution is the exchange of sexual services for money. Fifty-three per cent believe that prostitution involves sex in return for material goals (e.g., a place to sleep, drugs, a free trip or ride). Moreover, only 62 per cent of Canadians surveyed feel that exchanging sex for money is indecent and worthy of disapproval. A 1994 poll by *Maclean's* showed that 49 per cent of Canadians believe that prostitution should be legalized (*Maclean's,* 1994, Jan., 1).

A CLOSER LOOK BOX 12.7
- -

Prostitution in Foreign Countries

The following examples illustrate variations in foreign attitudes towards prostitution, age of consent, and related issues:

- Japan: although the Prostitution Prevention Law of 1956 made prostitution a punishable criminal offence, Yokoyama (1995) has observed that there has been an increased demand for prostitution that appears to coincide with the rapid socio-economic changes in Japan with the result that the law is seldom enforced.
- Australia: prostitution is not illegal but street prostitution is in some regions. In Victoria, for example, street prostitution is legal but it cannot happen near schools, churches, or hospitals. Age of consent is generally 16.
- Brazil: prostitution is legal. The age of consent is 14.
- Costa Rica: prostitution is legal and workers are required to be licenced and carry ID cards. Age of consent is 18.
- Denmark: prostitution is legal, but it is illegal to make a living off it. In other words, a prostitute must have another source of income. Age of consent is 15.
- Greece: prostitution is legal. Recent provisions have been proposed to require prostitutes to retire at 55 with the state providing social and medical benefits. Workers are required to undergo health checks every two weeks.
- Netherlands: prostitution has never been outlawed in the Netherlands. Since 1988 prostitutes have joined the Service Sector Union as a legal profession and workers have been required to pay income taxes since 1996. No health checks are required. Age of consent is 16.
- New Zealand: although prostitution is not officially legal, prostitutes advertise their services in the yellow pages, magazines, and even on the radio. Age of consent is 16.
- Vietnam: In the mid-1970s after North and South Vietnam united, the communist-oriented government began a major campaign to rid the country of prostitution. Today, giant billboards warn against illicit sex, gambling, and other vices, but prostitution is thriving. Authorities attribute the resurgence of prostitution to the emergence of the market economy.

Other than the general one of providing a sexual service, the survey reveals that among Canadians there is no consensus on a definition of prostitution. Such being the case, how can we expect the law to adequately address and control prostitution? Both American and Canadian studies have found that regardless of how strict the laws and how well-enforced, they do not serve as effective deterrents (Davis and Shaffer, 1994; Cao, 1987).

Characteristics and Trends

A recent Statistics Canada report reveals a number of characteristics of prostitutes. They include:

- The average age of female prostitutes is 28 while male prostitutes' average age is 35.
- In 1995, only 3 per cent of those charged were under 18 years of age.
- Police are more likely to charge female prostitutes than male prostitutes.
- Regina averages the highest rate of charges per capita. Vancouver and Edmonton ranked second and third.
- One in every five charges laid for procuring the services of a prostitute involves an assault, sexual or otherwise.
- One in 20 (N=63) of those people murdered between 1991–95 were known prostitutes.
- It is believed that 50 of 63 prostitutes were killed by their customers while the balance (N=13) were killed either by their pimps or partners.
- Thirty-four (54 per cent) of the cases remained unsolved as compared to 20 per cent for all other murders.[14]
- The report concludes by noting that prostitutes are a common target for victimization (Durkan, 1997).

As reflected in the points above, the data seem to support earlier findings which found that most people view prostitutes stereotypically, as social misfits suffering from low self-image, who use prostitution to support their drug habits, work for "pimps" (anyone who lives off the avails of a prostitute),[15] and do not like men or enjoy sex (SCPP, 1985). Most of these perceptions, while not completely absent, have not been empirically supported. For example, Carman and Moody (1985) found that most male and female prostitutes are heterosexual and have satisfying sex with their partners. The SCPP (1985) found that only one per cent of male and ten per cent of female prostitutes worked for a pimp. The SCPP survey also found that approximately 60 per cent of Canadians surveyed believe prostitution is controlled by organized crime. While there is some evidence that organized crime is involved in prostitution (see Chapter 11), that influence is not as pervasive as imagined. Another inconclusive finding (Carman and Moody, 1985) is that prostitutes are drug users—they prostitute themselves to support their drug habits. However, a number of North American studies found that this is not the case (see, Committee on Sexual Offences …, (1984)(Canadian); James (1977) (United States)).

Another interesting possible misconception is the extent of prostitution. If one can believe what one obtains through the media, prostitutes are well-represented in society. Relying on an ethnomethodological approach, Lowman (1984) estimated the number of prostitutes in Vancouver to be between 60 and 70, increasing to 100 during peak periods. The Vancouver City police meanwhile set the estimates at 600. A few years later, Lowman estimated that the "murder rate of British Columbia women involved in street prostitution was roughly 60 to 120 times the rate of other adult women" (Bindman, 1996). Solving murders involving prostitutes is very difficult given the number of strangers they come into contact with and because of their low social status.

One of the earlier Canadian studies on prostitution found that prostitutes usually enter the profession in one of three ways. Lautt (1984) found that the younger prostitutes (ages 12–16) are more often recruited through *exploitation*. Street pimps will patrol bus stops, airports, train stations, and other entry points in a city looking for prospective young girls and boys who can be enticed into prostitution with the promise of food and shelter. MacLauren (1996:184) reports that "a percentage of runaway and homeless youth become involved in prostitution while living on the streets." Yet he goes on to note that these youth do not leave home "with the goal of taking up prostitution, but rather, that entering into prostitution occurs as a result of the street situation" (Ibid, 184).

A second means by which females can end up prostituting is through the influence of a *"big sister."* In this situation an older prostitute will recruit a naive 15- to 19-year-old girl. While participation may initially be for "fun" because of the sexually active lifestyle, Lautt (1984) points out that the girls get hooked once they prostitute for financial gain.

The third type identified by Lautt (1984) are those prostitutes who enter the trade for the *independent pragmatic decision*. These women tend to be more mature individuals aged 18 to 24. They choose prostitution on pragmatic grounds—usually out of economic necessity. Women, and occasionally men, come from all walks of life, including students and employed women seeking extra money (SCPP, 1985).

Silbert and Pines (1982 cited in McIntyre, 1994:54) found that approximately 32 per cent of young persons acquire their knowledge of prostitution through movies, books, and/or magazines. Similarly, Brannigan et al. (1989) found that 39 per cent of those they interviewed knew someone working in the sex trade business. This average was later reaffirmed by McIntyre (1994) who found that 36 per cent of those involved in prostitution became involved because of someone they knew in the business. Needing money, being products of dysfunctional families, and suffering from personal problems, the opportunity to *drift* (as defined by Matza (1964)) into the sex trade business for "easy money" becomes compelling for some.

In her "tell all" story, Norma Jean Almodovar (1993) recounts how as a traffic enforcement officer with the Los Angeles Police Department (LAPD) she became so disgusted with the rampant theft, corruption, and the sexual exploitation of women in the force that she left the police force to become a prostitute. As she describes it, working her own hours, selecting her clients, leading "the good life" and making good money seemed like a logical choice. Today, she is an advocate for the rights of prostitutes.

Types of Prostitution

Like other forms of crime, deviance, and occupations in general, there are several different types of prostitution. And just as with most professions, there is a status hierarchy among prostitutes.

1. **Streetwalkers.** Streetwalkers are the most visible and most common form of all prostitutes as they ply their trade in public view on the streets of most urban centres. When movies portray prostitutes, it is the streetwalker who is most commonly featured. Yet they generally represent the lower rung of the prostitution hierarchy. Given all the attention they receive, it is not surprising that they tend to be the type most commonly researched by criminologists and subject to the most intervention strategies.

A common misconception of streetwalkers is that they are all "ladies of the night" and that they all work for "pimps." While female prostitutes do constitute the largest proportion of streetwalkers, men also work the streets as prostitutes. While women are more likely to have pimps that are male prostitutes, most women work independently (SCPP, 1985). As a result of their street presence and lack of security (other than relying on their "street smarts," streetwalkers run the greatest risk of arrest and injury. They are among the few groups in society who regularly get into vehicles with strangers. In addition, they are at greater risk than most other types of prostitution for being raped by customers, not being paid for services (even though most prostitutes demand their money up front), robbery, and being exploited by their pimps (see Box 12.8).

Streetwalkers solicit their clientele through public solicitation. Most prostitutes have a "stroll," a geographic area that they use to work in to solicit potential "johns" (a generic name denoting the preference of most clients to remain anonymous). Although streetwalkers patrol the streets awaiting a client, they wait for the "john" to initiate discussion and interest. In this way they avoid the risk of entrapment by plainclothes police officers. While working, prostitutes dress in tight clothing and provocative attire in an effort to solicit a "trick." According to the SCPP (1985) study, most prostitutes conduct their business from Wednesday through Saturday, and mostly in the evenings. In larger urban centres, however, they may also cater to the "lunch-time quickie crowd."

Most major Canadian cities have well-known areas where streetwalkers can be found. Within larger communities, there may be more than one geographic area. If so, streetwalkers can usually be discerned by the kind of clientele they cater to. At the bottom of the ladder are the "tough broads," "drunks," and "druggies" who are less refined, less discriminating in who they service, and at greater risk of victimization. If you live in, or near a major urban centre, you might want to follow the news for a period of time to see whether you can identify these areas. If solicitation is illegal, why do the police allow streetwalkers at all?

FYI BOX 12.8

Youth at Risk

The first piece of legislation introduced to protect young children from being exploited in Canada in Upper Canada came into effect with the *Seduction Act* of March 1837. The Act enabled the "domestic servant's father to sue the daughter's employer for seduction of the daughter" (Bailey, 1991:159). The Act also amended the common law by making a father liable for the support of his illegitimate child (Ibid). Until the *Family Law Act* was introduced in 1986, laws protecting the exploitation of children underwent a number of revisions. However, in spite of the laws intended to protect the exploitation of children, Bailey (1991) notes the number of girls exploited and abused was substantially greater than that for boys.

In 1997, the United Nations Rights Commission estimated that there are 10 million prostitutes in the world. The report notes that this figure is growing by about 1 million per year. The most problematic areas are southeast Asia and Latin America (Social Implications of Child Prostitution, 1998). In 1999, Alberta became the first province to put into effect the *Protection of Children Involved in Prostitution Act*. Under section 2 of the Act, a police officer or director under the *Child Welfare Act* may "apprehend and convey the child to a protective safe house ... to confine the child for up to 72 hours to ensure the safety of the child" and assess their risk (*Protection of Children ...* 1999). It remains to be seen how effective this Act will be, but it reflects a growing awareness and concern about the welfare of young people who might end up in prostitution."

2. **Bar prostitutes.** Also known as B-girls, bar prostitutes operate out of public drinking establishments such as bars and taverns. Contrary to public opinion, these establishments range from seedy taverns to luxurious hotel lounges. B-girls usually work such establishments with the cooperation of the management. For example, management will water down drinks served to the bar prostitutes, charge full fare for each drink, and then pass the B-girl's customer the bill. In this manner the bar makes money off the drinks and the B-girl remains sober to perform her services, the payment for which she usually splits with management.

This is especially true in cases where the establishment may provide rooms for services rendered.

Transactions usually begin with the B-girl approaching a prospective client and asking him if he would like to buy her a drink. Then the B-girl engages in general flirtatious conversation, providing the client with an opening to negotiate a sexual service. In this manner the B-girl cannot be caught for soliciting.

If successful the parties will discreetly retreat to the room where the transactions take place.

Police do not interfere with B-girls as much as with streetwalkers. B-girls have a higher social status than streetwalkers, especially if they work in expensive hotel lounges.

3. **Massage-parlour prostitutes.** Next to streetwalkers, prostitutes are often associated with massage parlours. Historically this has created a negative image for legitimate massage practitioners. However, while this image has changed somewhat in recent years, it is still possible to find massage parlours operated for purposes of prostitution. Parlours tend to use suggestive language to indicate the type of service available—e.g., "all muscles massages," or "seven seas parlour."

To avoid entrapment, a client will enter and pay a fee comparable to that of legitimate parlours. While the masseuse may provide suggestive contact, it remains the responsibility of the client to request "extra services" and to negotiate a fee. Sansfacon (1985) reports that fellatio (performing oral sex) and sexual intercourse are usually not part of the fee structure but other sexual services can be negotiated.

Because of the way such parlours operate it is sometimes difficult for the police to lay charges of solicitation and keeping a common bawdy house (Sansfacon, 1985). For example, it is up to the client to request "extra" services. This provides the parlours with a ready defence against criminal charges, although such defences have not always been successful (Ibid). In 1997, an international Asian smuggling ring was caught bringing young Asian women into Canada to work in brothels and parlours (see Box 12.9). The smugglers charged the girls considerable sums of money that most could not afford. In return the girls had to promise to work off their passage to North America (Asian women…, 1997).

A CLOSER LOOK BOX 12.9

Organized Crime and Sex Slave Markets

In many parts of the world, organized crime has been involved in prostitution. In the 1990s, one of the fastest growing crime groups to become involved in sexual slavery has been organized Russian crime groups. Stone (1998:7) reports it has "become one of the fastest growing criminal enterprises on the international black market," and since the fall of the USSR, "Slavic women have become the most valuable commodities on this market." For example, Stone observes:

- Slavic sexual slaves outnumber all other nationalities today.
- In Milan, Italy, 80 per cent of the prostitutes are foreigners.
- Gangs lure women with the promise of good jobs, better wages, and in some cases use front companies such as modelling agencies and mail order ads to recruit innocent victims.
- Each prostitute can average about $215,000 U.S. per month for the gang.

4. **House prostitutes.** In the 1970s Xaviera Hollander, the madam who titled her book *The Happy Hooker,* described in graphic detail the exploits of her life. The book opened the floodgates for similar material and led to a number of such books being written by women who were living off the avails of prostitution.

If you have seen your share of western movies you have likely seen scenes involving a madam operating a brothel, a house of ill-repute, or whorehouse, as they are also called. The madam, usually a retired prostitute, manages the brothel and the prostitutes she has working for her. And while there are no legal brothels in Canada, American states such as Nevada have special provisions in which brothels may operate, if a county so elects.[16] In Canada, brothels can still be found and are easily located with access to the Internet.

House prostitutes are generally considered higher on the social ladder than massage and street prostitutes. Again, their status depends on the nature of the brothels.

5. **Rap session booth.** In cities like Amsterdam and in London's red-light districts it is possible to visit adult bookstores or shops that provide little "rap session booths" for clients to converse with a prostitute. The prostitute sits behind a glass booth while the client passes money through an opening in the booth. Based on an informal fee structure the prostitute will remove her clothing. There is no direct sexual contact between the prostitute and the john.

Rap session booths are not legal in Canada but today, with 900 lines and pay per use Internet sites, it is possible to receive comparable services (see Box 12.10). Again, while not legal, it is extremely difficult to censor these types of services.

REALITY CHECK BOX 12.10

POLICING THE INTERNET: OLD FANTASIES IN A NEW PACKAGE

In 1998, it was estimated that there are 50 million Internet users worldwide and the numbers are growing (CSIS, 1998).

In February 1997, the first European conference on combatting violence and pornography on the Internet was held in England. The following points are a summary of conference proceedings.

- Monika Gerstendforfer, a British psychologist, defined "pornography" as the torture of women and children as well as acts of bestiality. She believes real and computer-generated images can have damaging effects on children that are both physical and psychological.
- Damien Eames, a consultant, pointed out that regulatory standards are too vague to effectively police pornography on the Internet, although the Internet Watch Foundation is making strides to facilitate such efforts.
- Liz Kelly and Dianne Butterworth, of the University of North London, expressed the opinion that while certain forms of pornography may represent a violation of human dignity, any attempt to develop a rating system is futile.
- Elizabeth Massonnet, of the French Ministry for Telecommunications and Postal Affairs, raised the question as to whether self-regulation is the same as self-censorship (Akdeniz, 1997).
- Jeffrey Shallit (1997), of the University of Waterloo, an expert on Internet censorship, argues that the Internet is no more at fault for breaking the law than traditional media sources. He also suggests that we may be overreacting, given the fact that, compared to the number of users, "there have been so few incidents of this type" (i.e., breaking the law).[17]

6. **Call girls.** Call girls represent the aristocrats of all prostitutes and they charge the most. Because call girls keep an exclusive and comparatively small and select group of clients, they keep the names of their clients in a "black book" that sometimes falls into the hands of the media, police, or blackmailers. When the names involve prominent people the media often get considerable mileage out of the story, while the call girls are suddenly seen as guardians of morality.

7. **Escort services.** If you look in the classified ads of any major city paper, or look in the yellow pages, you will find numerous ads with names like "A Geisha's Touch," "A Fantasy Mistress," and "Endless Possibilities."[18] Most call girls use, or have their own, escort agency that is used to screen for vice squads and clients not considered suitable. All agencies offer total discretion and confidentiality.

On contacting an escort service, the client may be shown photos, watch a video clip, and/or listen to an audio tape of prospective escorts whose services he might like to seek. This "privilege" costs the client a fee. Because the service is recognized as a legal operation, it is possible for clients to pay with a credit card, cheque, or cash. As Sansfacon (1985) observes, escort services are seldom targeted by the police because of the privacy of the transactions and because of the relatively high social standing of many of the clients.

Male Prostitution

Until recently, the subject of male prostitutes was largely overlooked. One of the first of such studies was conducted by the sociologist Albert Reiss (1961). While studying young offenders, he found that a number of them had been involved in homosexual contact with older men as a means of making money. Yet Reiss observed that, when questioned, the boys denied they were prostitutes. It has been studies such as Reiss's that have created the myth that male prostitutes are gay

A more recent study by Cates and Markley (1992) lends support to Reiss's general finding that the major reason males engage in prostitution with older males is to find a "sugar-daddy" who will support them. This financial motivation is similarly found among many female prostitutes.

Canadian studies of male prostitutes are limited. One recent study was conducted in Vancouver. Relying on interview data, Wright (1997) found that 84 per cent of the male prostitutes interviewed were survivors of sexual abuse. Wright also observed that like female prostitutes, male prostitutes felt a lack of belonging and intimacy and felt more like a commodity. Furthermore, he found that most of the male prostitutes cope with their pain and sex-trade work through disassociating from it.

Other characteristics that the "male hustlers" share with female prostitutes are being harassed by police, raped and/or assaulted by johns, and being the subject of gay bashing even though many are not gay. Wright (1997) concludes his observations of male prostitutes by noting that there is a serious service gap for these men as well as an information gap that criminologists should be looking at.

Explanations of Prostitution

Why do they do it? Explanations as to why women and men enter prostitution are quite varied. Based on his review of the literature, Lowman (1995) suggests there are at least six types of theoretical perspectives on prostitution. They range from biological positivism (Chapter 5) to the feminist approach (Chapter 8). He also suggests none is particularly Canadian, but given that prostitution is a universal phenomenon, not an isolated practice, why should they be? Nevertheless, there are a number of perspectives that have been favoured in Canadian-based research.

The Badgley Committee offers a social-psychological perspective on prostitution. The committee focused on such characteristics as family stability, social background, and unwanted sexual acts and/or physical violence. While much acclaimed for its ground-breaking efforts, Lowman (1995) identifies a number of limitations of the study and its theoretical approach. For example, "very little is said about the effect of unemployment structures and the marginal position of youth," "it negates any kind of structural analysis of the family as a social unit," and pays limited attention to "gender relations generally" (Ibid, 349). These are elements that are usually examined when using a social-psychological perspective. In a follow-up to a series of studies on prostitution over the years, Van Brunschot and Brannigan (1997) adopted a social-psychological approach with an emphasis on social control theory (Chapter 7). Consistent with other social-psychologically-based studies, they found a significant relationship between involvement in prostitution and a history of physical abuse, non-traditional familial structure, expulsion from school, and a history of running away. Similarly, McIntyre (1994) found that almost 75 per cent of male and female prostitutes began sex work prior to their sixteenth birthdays. Over three-quarters of those interviewed had been sexually and/or physically abused prior to their involvement in sex work. Furthermore, and consistent with other studies, running away, school difficulties, and having a low self-image "were not uncommon features" among the study group (Ibid).

By contrast, the Fraser Committee, a conservative think tank, presents a political economy interpretation of prostitution that is influenced by the feminist approach (Lowman, 1995). Its approach stresses inequalities in job opportunities, earning power, and "sexual socialization as the structural factors responsible for making prostitution appear to be a choice at all" (Ibid, 349). Hence, prostitution is described as being motivated out of economic necessity, with women being the victims of a patriarchal power structure. Brannigan (1989) found that 77 per cent of women and 84 per cent of men stated that money was their primary motivation for entering the sex trade. By contrast, McIntyre (1994) found that the need for money only accounted for 30 per cent of those who entered the sex trade business.[19] Some feminists view prostitution as men exploiting women and using them as expendable commodities to be bought and sold.

Liberal feminists have argued that some women become involved because they don't have access to legitimate opportunities. By contrast, Marxist/socialist feminists view prostitution as a product of women being subjugated into the trade, while radical feminists "believe that prostitution is the result of the role women are trained into in the serving of men" (McIntyre, 1994:144). All feminists, regardless of their theoretical orientation, support the decriminalization of prostitution.

A third perspective that has received varied support is the *functionalist* approach. Drawing on the work of sociologist Kingsley Davis in the late 1930s, functionalism views prostitution as part of our social institution. And while it condemns the practice of prostitution on the one hand, functionalism also thinks that it contributes to stability in society by providing men with a sexual outlet—a supposed innate drive (see Freud—Chapter 6). This view reflects a double standard, while reinforcing the status quo. For example, in 1982 Portugal legalized prostitution in partial response to the number of upper-class men who frequented prostitutes while their wives stayed at home (Geis, 1989). Feminist groups applauded the liberalization of laws but still oppose the exploitation of women. From this perspective, it can be argued that only if the needs of society are equated with the needs of men, could prostitution be considered functional.

Finally, John Lowman, winner of the 1997 Sterling Prize for Controversy at Simon Fraser University, argues that Canadians need to "cut the hypocrisy and work out what we want prostitution law and social policy to accomplish" (Sterling Prize …, 1997). In order to do this, Lowman identifies four goals in a decriminalization process: "prevent sexual procurement of children and youth; protect prostitutes from pimp coercion and customer violence; encourage prostitute self-employment; and protect bystanders from nuisance" (Ibid). While evocative, Lowman's goals neglect a fundamental aspect of criminology that has repeatedly been noted throughout this book: Laws and policy cannot prevent crime. Criminology needs to examine the causes and meaning of prostitution from an interdisciplinary perspective. There is a reason why prostitution is the "oldest profession."

In summary, prostitution is one of the oldest vices, one of the more dangerous ones for the worker, and one that has never been successfully eradicated.[20] And in spite of its long history, there are many misconceptions as to who prostitutes are and why they enter this profession. While most prostitutes come from abusive backgrounds or are coerced to enter prostitution, Carman and Moody (1985) report that a small percentage of prostitutes come from respectable backgrounds. They enter the profession for economic gain, understand the risks and are not disturbed, or hooked on drugs.

The issue of whether prostitution should be legalized remains controversial. There are competing groups and organizations in society that offer compelling arguments for both camps. One area on which there is strong consensus is the exploitation of youth in prostitution. Being largely based on social and cultural values, it is also argued that young prostitutes are not capable of making an informed decision about such a life-style. However, as long as child abuse continues to be prevalent in our society, it is not likely that we will be able to prevent men from seeking the services of a young prostitute. Finally, because other crimes are considered more serious than prostitution, it is not likely that sufficient resources will be directed to addressing the issue.

Pornography

"There is evidence that pornography is sometimes associated with crime and depravity, but there is little evidence that this association is a casual relationship. When books are blamed for evil consequences and anti-social conduct the fault is generally with the reader rather than the book" Alec Craig.

Have you read any of the following books: *The Stone Angel* by Margaret Lawrence, *Ulysses* by James Joyce, *Lady Chatterley's Lover* by D.H. Lawrence,

Fanny Hill by John Cleland, or *Moll Flanders* by Daniel Defoe? These books were all considered to be obscene at some time or another. In 1999, Calgary Reform MP, Art Hanger, called for the removal of *Lolita*, a book first published in 1958 (McGoogan, 1999), from Canada's Parliamentary Library because the book is about an older man's infatuation with a 12-year-old girl. Have you ever looked at a copy of *Chic, Forum, Hustler, Penthouse, Playboy,* or *Playgirl*? These are legitimate magazines, as long as you are eighteen years or older. Yet there are other pornographic magazines that are illegal in Canada (e.g., child pornography magazines). Have you every listened to the rap group "2 Live Crew"? In 1990, they were charged in the United States for producing obscene material. Several of their songs (e.g., Me so horny) contain sexually explicit lyrics (Lacayo, 1990). Yet in the 1970s the former wife of Beatle great John Lennon, Yoko Ono, produced an album in which it sounds very much like she is having an orgasm. Why did her album not receive the same bad press as Marilyn Manson, or "2 Live Crew"? When does art become obscene or pornographic?

FYI BOX 12.11

Violent Images in Adult Magazines

In conducting a content analysis of 373 issues of *Playboy, Penthouse,* and *Hustler* magazine between 1953 and 1984, Reisman (1997) found 6,004 child images as well as over 14,000 images of crime and violence. Reisman further observed that since 1975, *Penthouse* and *Hustler* have increased their coverage of depictions of children, crime and violence.

Like prostitution, pornography has been around a very long time. Plato, over 2,300 years ago, is sometimes credited with beginning the debate over the role of the arts in a good society (Salomon, 1988). His simple question as to what is the proper role or function for art continues to be debated. Pornography was common in ancient Greece and Italy and was especially popular in ancient India and Japan. For example, the Indian manual *Kama Sutra* provides readers with ways to use their bodies for love. The term pornography is derived from the Greek *porno*, meaning "prostitute" and *graphen* meaning "to write." Therefore, the term pornography literally means writing about the activities of prostitutes. Today, pornographic material is available from a wide range of sources, including books, magazines, videos, and, in recent years, on the Internet. Most major cities have specialty stores that specialize in providing "adult" entertainment. Although I would not want to guess how many such specialty stores there are now in Toronto alone, in the early 1970s I was a research assistant for an instructor in the only "sex shop" in the city. My responsibilities were to simply act as a salesperson and observe the interactions of people visiting the shop. Then, as today, everything was very professional and discreet. Having attended school in Europe several years earlier, I was somewhat used to this Canadian novelty.

A term that is sometimes used interchangeably and considered by some "moral entrepreneur" groups to be synonymous with pornography is obscenity, derived from the Latin *caenum* for "filth." The *Concise Oxford Dictionary* defines obscenity as "indecent, especially grossly or repulsively so; lewd, ... morally repulsive." The difficulty in controlling pornography revolves around the legal definition of obscenity. Law enforcement officials can only seize material that is defined as obscene. In 1987 the U.S. Supreme Court modified its 1973 ruling by stating pornographic material could be judged obscene, and thus banned, if a "reasonable person" could conclude that the work lacked any social value. However, as Albanese (1996) points out, the term "reasonable person" lacks any objective standards. And despite two presidential commissions the Supreme Court is no closer to successfully defining the term.

In the next section we will begin by looking at the laws as they relate to freedom of speech or censorship of pornography. Then we will examine the controversial issue of whether pornography causes violence.

Pornography and the Law

Crimes pertaining to pornography, or more precisely obscenity, are listed under the section *Offences tending to corrupt morals* in the Canadian *Criminal Code*. They include sections 163–169. One deals specifically with "child pornography." Introduced in 1993, the law specifically prohibits the exploitation of children (i.e., anyone under the age of 18) in any manner that involves explicit sexual activity. The maximum penalty is five years imprisonment. The law also prohibits the importation, selling, or any other distribution of child pornography (see Box 12.12).

The British legal system has adopted a different approach to defining pornography. Unlike the Canadian or American definitions, their definition does not refer to any inherent danger in pornography. In fact, pornography may be prescribed by a sex therapist for patients experiencing sexual difficulties. Using a *functional theory* approach, Ellis (1987:31) suggests that "prostitution and pornography are functional for society, because by permitting the expression of anti-social sex, they act as a safety valve and so help keep families together." (The British legal definition focuses on the negative effect on public morals, especially those of children. For example, the British Home Office (1979:103) defines pornography as:

A *pornographic* representation combines two features: it has a certain function or intention, to arouse its audience sexually, and also a certain content, explicit representation of sexual materials (organs, postures, activity, etc.)).

Finally, Ellis (1984 cited in Scott and Schwalm, 1988:40) simply defines pornography as "anti-culture, anti-conscience, anti-God, anti-family, anti-child, and anti-women. Pornography brutalizes and insults society." All these definitions share a common theme. They all view pornography as a violation of social values and norms. What is also evident is that none of the definitions provide a clear and concise explanation. There is an inference that the definitions reflect a consensus, but we live in a heterogeneous society and it may not be possible to reach a consensus.

REALITY CHECK BOX 12.12

CHILD PORNOGRAPHY ON THE NET

In the mid-1990s there was a rash of cases involving individuals being charged with downloading child pornography from the Internet and distributing the material for a fee. One case of note involved a former scientist with the Department of National Defence—Dr. Blair Evans. In 1996, Evans was charged with four counts of distributing child pornography and one charge of possession of child pornography material. Before being arrested, the father of two had downloaded more than 20,000 child pornography images from the Internet using a National Defence computer (Ex-DND..., 1997).

In another unusual case, a 41-year-old Ontario man was given a 12-month conditional sentence for possessing child pornography. After his house security system malfunctioned, the police responded to the alarm. On checking the house for evidence of a break-in they came across the man's computer where a child pornographic scene was depicted on the screen-saver (Man sentenced..., 1997).

Finally, McMaster University professor, David Jones suggests that the Internet porn danger is overblown. He argues that eighty per cent of Canadians have "no meaningful interaction with the Internet" and that the media focus too much on the few incidents that do involve pedophiles on the Internet. He further points out that the introduction of telephones, radio and television brought similar sorts of hysteria. For example, Jones notes that "less than one per cent of 11,000 discussion forums or newsgroups contain sexually explicit material" (Internet porn ..., 1998).

These and other cases present new challenges for criminal justice officials.

Does Pornography Cause Violence?

Aside from the moral issue, criminologists have shifted their focus more recently to the question of whether pornographic material contributes in any way to violence, victimization of women and children, and possibly against men. As University of Calgary Professor Chelsea Daeger (1997) notes, there is ample literature indicating that many women are being forced to participate in pornography and in some cases are being harmed while participating.

Public surveys conducted in the United States in the '80s showed that most Americans believe there is a relationship between pornography and violence/

crime (*The Report of the Commission ...*, 1970). However, after reviewing the academic literature, the Commission concluded that exposure to erotic materials is *not* a causal factor in sex crimes or sex delinquency, even though the report neglected to differentiate between the kinds and the extent of erotic materials. Many thought the issue would quickly die but spurred, in part, by the women's movement and various fundamentalists, literally hundreds of studies were conducted on this question in the following years. After reviewing many of these studies in 1984, the Attorney General's Commission, in the United States, concluded that while erotic material may not cause sex crimes, viewing such material can lead to a greater acceptance of sex crimes through an habituation to pornography (Adler, Mueller, and Laufer, 1991). These findings provided feminists with the evidence to argue that pornographic material should be censored and that it does undermine the status of women in general.

Today, the literature generally concurs on the point that regular exposure to erotic material can facilitate expressions of anger and violence (Conklin, 1997). Radical feminists, for example, argue that exposure to pornography often leads to violence against women by linking coercion and violence with sexual stimulation (Berger et al., 1991). However, it does not appear to be the sexual acts per se, but the degree of violence depicted in the acts that triggers violence. For some, these images may weaken condemnation of sex crimes by men and women. For example, Scott and Schwalm (1988) point out that after Denmark repealed all bans of sexually-oriented material in the late 1960s, sex crimes actually declined in the country. Similarly, Japan has a flourishing pornography trade and yet their rape rates are less than one-quarter the rate for Germany or Great Britain, and one-fourteenth the rate for the United States (cited in Livingston, 1992). As pointed out in Chapter 9, sexual assault in Canada has increased since new legislation was enacted in the 1980s. Although a percentage of the increase may be due to reporting patterns and greater public awareness, and changes in the legal definition of rape, surely such factors cannot account for the dramatic increase. Furthermore, since some pornography involves depictions of men, what standards, if any, should be applied in their case?

These comparative rates lend credence to the idea that sex crimes are related to certain cultural climates. If so, criminologists need to explore what the possible critical cultural factors are that differentiate high rape rates from countries with low rape rates. Knowing such factors may enable countries to better regulate pornography. Already, we have seen dramatic changes in our level of tolerance of those desiring alternative lifestyles (e.g., gay marriages, graphic depiction of sex and violence on the screen and through the Internet, music videos, etc.). Our notion of pornography is really a relative concept that poses a major challenge to criminologists interested in studying any criminogenic relationship. Finally, the issue that remains unanswered is the matter of morality and our constitutional right to freedom of speech and the press. Pornography is therefore both a criminological issue and a civil issue (see Box 12.13).

WHAT DO YOU THINK? BOX 12.13

IS IT PORNOGRAPHIC, IS IT OBSCENE, OR IS IT "UNUSUAL"?

- For women to walk around in public topless?
- To practise homosexuality?
- For women to read magazines such as *Playgirl?*
- For women to wear "suggestive" clothing?
- For men to wear "suggestive" clothing?
- To take personal pictures of your partner?
- To display art work that is revealing and/or suggestive in content?
- To have lewd fantasies?
- To kiss in public?

All these questions have, and in some cases are still, considered sanctionable in different parts of the world on the grounds they are pornographic, indecent, and/or obscene.

The two primary opponents of pornography, fundamentalists and feminists, continue to be vigilant about how society embraces pornography. If the influx of pornographic material is any indication, these "moral entrepreneurs" are fighting a losing battle. The fundamentalists adopt the argument that pornography erodes public morality and respect for human life. In the early 1980s the "Squamish Five," in addition to bombing the Litton Systems plant in Toronto, also bombed several pornographic video stores in British Columbia. The group was protesting against businesses that degraded women by selling such videos (see Salomon, 1988).

Meanwhile, feminists view pornographic material as being antiwoman, representing hate literature against women (e.g., bondage, submissive positions, etc.). They also argue that the material violates women's civil rights on the grounds of equality and free speech (Scott and Schwalm, 1988). The "rape shield" law in the mid-1980s received considerable impetus from feminist groups across the country. Women's groups have also been instrumental in limiting access to child pornography, by getting magazine distributors to put shrink wrap on their material and having businesses display the magazines above normal eye level.

In **summary**, pornography is a controversial issue and to date there is no conclusive evidence that either completely refutes any link between pornography or sex crimes or supports possible links. While sex surveys show that most adults engage in acts that are found in pornographic literature, when it occurs between "consenting" adults we think little of it. Do people have an innate desire for sexual adventure? Exactly when does sexual contact or sexual interaction constitute a moral wrong that deserves to be sanctioned?

Since many "non-consenting" acts are precipitated by drugs or alcohol, is there a possible biological or biochemical cause for obscene behaviour, or is the behaviour learned through association? To date, there is no conclusive empirical evidence to support one theoretical perspective over another. Therefore, until we can understand the roots of pornography and clearly define it, we will have to join Plato and simply continue to engage in rhetoric. In the meantime, pornography will continue to fuel the underground economy (e.g., through organized crime groups and other means). Criminologists need to adopt an interdisciplinary approach that enables them to recognize the unique elements of the environment and individual characteristics and/or traits associated with pornography and violence. It may also be time to deal with the issue as a civil matter, not a criminal one.

The final public order offence we will cover in this chapter is substance abuse. It is regarded by many Canadians as one of the country's most serious social problems. A review of several recent (late 1990s) *Juristat* and *Forum on Corrections Research* reports clearly indicate that drugs and/or alcohol are present in many criminal events.

Substance Abuse

"She threw into the wine which they were drinking a drug which takes away grief and passion and brings forgetfulness of all ills" Homer (700 BC).

In Chapter 5 we looked at the relationship between the biochemical effects of alcohol and criminal behaviour. It was also noted that an inordinate number (as high as 65 per cent according to Single, Robson, Relm, and Xie, 1996) of violent crimes involved the use of alcohol and/or drugs. For example, between 1992 and 1996, the number of official drug-related offences increased from 55,881 to 65,106. This represents a rate per 100,000 increase from 206 to 217 (Kong, 1997).

Abuse of alcohol and legal and illicit drugs can affect the sense of public order through the altered behaviour expressed by the substance abuser. And if we can believe half of what we read and see in the media, North Americans have been part of a drug epidemic since the 1960s. Millions of dollars are spent every year to curb the abuse of alcohol and drugs.[21] As we will see below, the social, financial, and personal costs are staggering.

In this section, we will examine the research evidence concerning criminal behaviour and substance abuse. We will also review several of the key policy issues as they relate to treatment and legalization. First, however, we will take a brief historical look at the issue of drugs and its definition.

A Brief History of
Substance Use and Abuse

According to Schlaadt (1992) there is virtually no society in which people cannot be found using mind- and mood-altering substances. Throughout the ages, we can find numerous examples of how alcohol was used in everything from religious rites to social celebration to simply complementing a meal. For example, in countries such as France and Italy, it is common for many families to share a bottle of wine over lunch and dinner on a daily basis.

While *alcohol* was not the only psychoactive (i.e., the potential to alter mood or behaviour) substance used in ancient times, it was the most prevalent (Ibid). In fact, both the Greeks and Romans had gods of wine many years before the birth of Christianity. For the Greeks it was *Dionysus*, also the god of vegetation, while for the Romans it was *Bacchus*. As the Roman Empire spread throughout Europe, the Romans brought their love of wine and copious consumption with them. The French, Spanish, Germans, and even the British were quick to embrace the practice and began to cultivate their own wines. Schlaadt (1992:3) observes that some historians believe that the eventual downfall of the Roman Empire was due in part to alcoholism, along with greed, corruption, and self-indulgence.

The church even got into the act, using wine in such rituals as the sacrament of Communion. And today, there are a number of monasteries throughout Europe that are known for the alcoholic beverages they produce. For example, *Benedictine* was made by the Benedictine Brothers of France.

In areas where grapes could not be grown, other spirits were invented. The Scots were the first to manufacture whisky around 1500, the Dutch introduced gin in 1672, and the Portuguese produced port around 1670. By the nineteenth century, alcohol was both plentiful and frequently abused throughout Europe.

Not surprisingly, given that Europeans colonized the "New World," they brought their drinking habits with them. In fact, research shows that between 1720 and 1820, alcohol consumption was twice that between 1830 through the 1970s (Schlaadt, 1992).

The use of *drugs* has an equal, if not longer history than alcohol. Egyptian records show that from 1500 BC opium was already being used for medicinal purposes. The Indians in ancient Peru chewed coca leaves containing cocaine, and Native Americans discovered the use of mescaline as a mood-altering substance (Fishbein and Pease, 1996). It appears that most cultures have chosen some drug that can be readily found in their area as a socially-accepted way of altering their state of consciousness.

It was not until the late 1800s and early 1900s that drug regulation became an issue in North America. Fishbein and Pease (1996) suggest there were two important factors that contributed to this awareness and the subsequent move to regulate drugs. The first was an alarming increase in the "rates of narcotic addiction" and the second factor was "the association of drug use with minority groups" (Ibid, 11).

Drugs and the Law

What exactly is meant by "drug abuse"? Who has ever gone on a weekend binge? Who enjoys a regular glass of beer or wine with an evening meal? Who has ever experimented with an illegal drug? How many of you smoke cigarettes? If so, how much do you smoke? How many of you drink coffee every day or at least several times a week?

Generally, we think of drug abuse as overuse or physical and/or psychological dependency. But, as Blackwell (1988) notes, the meaning is ambiguous. For example, how much, or how many drinks, joints, or pills does one need to take before they qualify as harmful? Drug abuse is not a readily definable construct.

The *Controlled Drugs and Substance Act* replaced the former *Narcotic Control Act* in 1996. The new Act covers everything from "possession of substance" to "punishment," forfeiture of proceeds of crime," and "determination of amount." Schedules I through VIII, which are located at the back of the Act, provide a list of all the controlled substances. With respect to the extensive list of controlled substances, what is interesting to note is s. 60 of the Act. It pertains to "amendments to schedules" and reads:

> The Governor in Council may, by order, amend any of Schedules I to VIII by adding to them or deleting from them any item or portion of an item, where the Governor in Council deems the amendments to be necessary in the public interest.

The wording of the section reflects recognition of how new drugs can be manufactured and used in harmful ways (e.g., steroids). What is less clear is what constitutes "necessary in the public interest." For example, cannabis is a banned substance and yet it has been used for medicinal purposes.[22] In 1999, the Mayor of Grand Forks in British Columbia suggested that the city obtain federal licencing to become Canada's primary supplier of medical marijuana. The mayor points out that the region is well-suited for growing marijuana and that the crop would be a boost for the economically-depressed community (Ketcham, 1999).

The recent legal controversy over the right to grow hemp (a member of the cannabis family) attracted national attention when Chris Clay was arrested in London, Ontario in 1995 for selling small cannabis-cutting plants. The arrest was somewhat ironic as Clay had been operating the first Canadian hemp store for nearly two years before the police decided it was time to punish him for breaking the law. Then, in December 1996, the police raided a hemp farm in Ontario and seized over $40,000 worth of inventory (Hempnation, 1997). These and other related incidents have prompted a constitutional backlash since a number of Canadian farmers feel that industrial hemp is both safe and a highly beneficial product. It does not have the potency of marijuana and it can be used to make very durable clothes as well as be used as a health food product. Today, hemp is commercially grown in such countries as France, England, Spain, Romania, and on several experimental farms in Canada.

In 1997, the first Canadian cannabis café opened in the heart of Vancouver's historic Gastown. In addition to offering a vapourizer that provides marijuana steam, the café displays dozens of artifacts and merchandise that are made with hemp (Ibid). To further promote the hemp cause, Chris Clay, along with other hemp supporters, launched a Web site to promote awareness and the benefits of hemp. As we enter the twenty-first century, hemp stores are springing up across the country.

From a criminological perspective, it will prove interesting to see how the courts handle the growing support for hemp. It will also draw further attention to the controversy of how one defines "social harm," and how we should respond to such crimes.

Characteristics and Trends

Alcohol and Controlled Substances

According to the Canadian Centre on Substance Abuse, alcohol consumption declined between 1990 and 1994 from 79 per cent to 72.3 per cent. For 1992/93 the average adult consumed the equivalent of 7.58 litres of absolute alcohol. The report also shows that young adults, males, and those with higher incomes drink more than other Canadians (McKenzie and Single, 1997).

Based on findings from the 1993 GSS, approximately ten per cent (9.2 per cent) said they had problems with their drinking. Of those, 5.1 per cent reported they experienced physical health problems and 4.7 per cent had financial problems.[23] In 1992 there were 6,701 alcohol related deaths and over 86,000 hospitalizations attributed to alcohol.

One of the more dramatic statistics on the "evils" of alcohol is the number of automobile accidents that is attributed to alcohol. This was perhaps epitomized on August 30, 1997 when the driver of Diana, Princess of Wales, Dodi Fayed, and his bodyguard, was found to have a blood alcohol level three times above the French legal limit. While the paparazzi got most of the blame for Diana's and Fayed's deaths, in all likelihood the driver's judgment and motor skills were sufficiently compromised by his alcohol levels to cause the car to crash.

At some level Canadians are aware of the risks associated with alcohol consumption. Based on 1994 data, nearly 75 per cent of Canadians supported increases in prevention programs while 75.5 per cent supported severe intervention programs. Furthermore, 66.7 per cent were opposed to selling alcohol in convenience stores and 69.5 per cent were in favour of placing warning labels on bottles containing alcoholic beverages. A question that was not asked was: Do Canadians favour the government privatizing liquor store operations in certain provinces? In Alberta, for example, there has been an explosion of liquor outlets since the government relaxed its licencing laws.

With the exception of those countries where religion forbids the consumption of alcohol (e.g., Islamic[24]) it continues to be consumed in great quantities. Knowledge about the harmful effects of alcohol and tobacco has had no significant impact on consumption. As a vice, should we view alcohol as a disease rather than a crime? How should criminologists deal with the latest scientific evidence that states people who use modest amounts of alcohol are less likely to experience health problems like arteriosclerosis, heart attacks and strokes? John Bland from the University of Vermont College of Medicine points out that there are "cleansing and neurophysiological benefits to alcohol" (cited in Pela, 1997:74).

FYI BOX 12.14

Controlled Substances

"In 1982, the abuse of narcotic drugs, LSD and marijuana cost 505 Canadians their lives. Compare this figure with those for the most costly and deadly drugs in Canada that year—alcohol and tobacco. Almost 900 Canadians died in traffic accidents in which alcohol figured prominently as a cause" (Gomme, 1998:316).

Research evidence shows a strong link between controlled substance abuse and criminal behaviour. Several studies have found that offenders with a substance abuse problem commit a high percentage of violent crimes (Gropper, 1985; Zawitz, 1992); that drug addicts commit more crimes while under the influence than when sober (Nurco, Cisin, and Ball, 1985); and Speckart and Anglin (1985) observed that substance abuse was highly related to high levels of property crime.

In many respects the public may seem hypocritical in its condemnation of the illicit drug problem in Canadian society. As noted in the quote from Gomme above, more Canadians die every year from legal drugs than from illicit drugs. Similarly, our focus seems to shift from decade to decade. In the 1960s we were preoccupied with the evils of marijuana,[25] in the 1970s the focus shifted to hallucinogens (e.g., LSD, PCP, MDA, etc.), while in the 1980s cocaine and crack (a synthetic form of cocaine) became the drugs of concern. All the while little attention or concern seems to have been directed at the number one drug killers—alcohol and tobacco.

It is true that the government has set limits on how alcohol and tobacco can be advertised, but out of fear of losing millions of dollars in revenue from the high taxes levied on these products, the government is not prepared (or able) to ban them. Boyd (1991) is quite critical about the hypocrisy that sees Canadians viewing legal drugs as less harmful than illegal drugs. As he states "we are a country of drug takers. About 80 per cent drink alcohol, 70 per cent drink coffee, and about 30 per cent smoke tobacco" (Ibid, 1).

As reflected in the settlement between the American tobacco industry and the lawsuits levied at them in 1997, the tobacco industry is a multi-billion dollar enterprise. Even after paying nearly 10 billion dollars in damages, it continues to survive and even thrive. All this in spite of the fact that in Canada alone approximately 35,000 people die directly and indirectly as a result of cigarettes. Cigarettes have been linked to lung cancer, heart disease, emphysema, and chronic bronchitis (Canada Year Book, 1997). In fact, lung cancer is the leading cause of death among men in Canada while breast cancer is the leading cause of death among women (Ibid). According to the Lung Association, a person's chances of surviving lung cancer are only about 5 per cent. Yet the association claims that 85 per cent of lung cancers can be avoided if a person refrains from smoking.

Perhaps one of the reasons the public is less inclined to think of smoking as a drug is that, other than the physiological addiction to the nicotine, there is no psychomotor or cognitive impairment involved. In other words, smoking does not alter your ability to drive, talk, or perform delicate tasks. It is a silent killer and a relatively inexpensive one. In 1998 a package of cigarettes cost approximately $5.50 while a hit of cocaine cost approximately $50, a marijuana cigarette about $2, and a bottle of spirits around $10. Withdrawal effects from smoking have been reported to be more difficult than withdrawal from heroin. The relapse rate is nearly 70 per cent. How many of you have ever tried to stop smoking?

Our concern about the dangers of controlled substance abuse, according to a number of Canadian experts, is based on misconceptions. Blackwell (1988) found that illegal drug use changed little throughout the 1980s while Blackwell and Erickson (1988) report that the addictive properties of most illicit drugs is not as extreme as often portrayed. They also argue that the notions that soft drug use naturally leads to hard drug use are also not supported in the literature. Finally, Blackwell and Erickson further point out that the image of drug pushers lurking around schoolyards is grossly overstated. These observations are not meant to undermine the potential dangers of illicit drugs but rather to draw attention to some of the misconceptions.

Growing up in the 1960s and 1970s, I found I and many of my friends were more interested in seeking out older kids to buy us a bottle of cheap wine than in buying illicit drugs. Many of us were simply modelling what we saw among the adult population. While frequently reminding us about the dangers of smoking and drinking, most of our parents would hypocritically engage in the very practice from which they were trying to deter us. Well, if it was good enough for them, why not us? Even though such reasoning was not very astute, in psychological terms it is referred to as learned behaviour.

In 1985, United Way published a study stating that 39 per cent of American High School seniors are problem drinkers (Burns, 1989). Even though these numbers have declined a few percentiles in recent years, the numbers are still alarming—88 per cent, in 1992, reported having tried alcohol at some time in their lives (Fishbein and Pease, 1996). Among college students there is a tendency to be weekend drinkers: over 70 per cent of those surveyed reported drinking a great deal on the weekend while their weekday drinking habits were more limited.

Alcohol the Drug

If you have ever set a match to alcohol you know how rapidly it evaporates. When put into the body alcohol is absorbed quickly and completely. In fact, there are few other drugs that can be as quickly absorbed into the bloodstream. However, absorption and rate of impact are also moderated by the concentration of alcohol in the drink, which can range from 5 per cent in regular beer to 40 and 50 per cent in distilled liquor (Fishbein and Pease, 1996).

The psychological and psychoactive effects of alcohol are well-documented. For example, one of the serious consequences of drinking is that over time drinkers develop a tolerance for alcohol, meaning they require more in order to get the same effect. As they drink more, there is an increased tendency to develop a dependency on the alcohol to sustain the false sense of well-being. Then, because of the biochemical changes that occur with sustained heavy drinking, drinkers develop withdrawal symptoms when they try to go without. The addiction begins to take hold and the symptoms escalate. Another damaging consequence of alcohol addiction is the transference of biochemical changes into newborns. Babies born to mothers who are chronic drinkers are highly susceptible to fetal alcohol syndrome (see Chapter 5). So alcohol not only puts drinkers at risk, but their children also.

Illicit Drugs

There are three broad classes of psychoactive drugs that affect the central nervous system: *stimulants, depressants,* and *hallucinogens*. Although not always mutually exclusive they describe the general effects related drug types create. For example, marijuana is known as a "cross-over" drug, as it initially acts as a stimulant and then a depressant as the effects wear off. Depending on the potency and amount smoked it can also create sensory distortions similar to those of hallucinogens.

Stimulants tend to elevate the user's sense of well-being. Sometimes referred to as "uppers," these drugs keep the user alert and able to resist fatigue. The most common examples are nicotine and caffeine—that morning pick-me-up cup of coffee. Other examples include cocaine, crack, and the sythesized drugs called amphetamines. Stimulants, as with all drugs, vary in potency and addictive properties. According to a study cited by Fishbein and Pease (1996:85) nicotine is the most addictive (nearly 100 per cent) of the stimulants, with crack being a close second. Caffeine is the least addictive of the stimulants (approximately 85 per cent).

Depressants, as the term suggests, slow down the central nervous system. They are also referred to as "downers." They can induce sleep, alleviate pain, relax muscles, reduce anxiety, and create a false sense of euphoria—a "nothing bothers me" effect. The most common depressant is alcohol. The opiate drugs (heroin, morphine) and barbiturates, antihistamines, PCP (phencyclidine), and a variety of aerosol sprays act as depressants. Alcohol is the most addictive of the depressants (approximately 87 per cent) followed closely by heroin.

Hallucinogens are designed to create an altered state of awareness, a distortion of reality. Popular in the 1960s with the hippie generation, they were glorified by Carlos Castaneda in his books as well as by Timothy Leary, both of whom became major spokespersons for the benefits of hallucinogenic drugs such as LSD and "magic mushrooms." Users of hallucinogens report "out-of-body" experiences such as hearing sounds, seeing images, hearing colours, and distortion of time and place. The most popular hallucinogen is marijuana, although in the 1960s peyote (a mushroom) was very popular. It also contains mescaline that can be made synthetically. Other synthetic hallucinogens include LSD (lysergic acid diethylamide) and PCP. LSD is derived from a natural fungus known as ergot and it grows on such grains as rye. Before its discovery it was possible to feel some of the minor effects of LSD if one ate rye infected with the fungus (Fishbein and Pease, 1996). PCP became vary popular in the 1980s and is the most addictive of the hallucinogens. Also known as angel dust, hog, or green, PCP is easily made and comparatively inexpensive.

However, stories of drugs causing violent and uncontrollable behaviour seemed to cause it to become less desirable. But, just as the preference for other social vices goes in cycles, is it possible that hallucinogens might regain status among groups who want to be violent?

Finally, in Table 12-2 we see a breakdown of the various drugs used by Canadians, and their impacts. As has been stated throughout this section, and as illustrated in the table, Canadians are more likely to use/abuse legal drugs and the associated health risks are much higher. Why do so many people continue to use/abuse drugs?

TABLE 12-2

CANADA'S DRUG USERS, COSTS, AND ATTRIBUTABLE DEATHS

DRUG	ANNUAL NUMBER OF USERS	COST PER WEEK FOR THE AVERAGE USERS	POSSIBILITY OF OVERDOSE DEATHS	DRUG RELATED DEATHS PER YEAR
Alcohol*	16,000,000	$10 $100	YES	3000–15,000
Amphetamines	<100,000	$100–$500	YES	<100
Cocaine	300,000–500,000	$10–$5000	YES	<100
Heroin	<100,000	$50–$5000	YES	<100
LSD	<100,000	<$20	NO	<10
Marijuana	1,500,000–2,500,000	$10–$100	NO	<10
Tobacco*	6,000,000–8,000,000	$30–$100	NO	35,000
Tranquillizers*	1,500,000–2,500,000	$0–$20	NO	<10

* Denotes drugs that are legal.

Source: Used with permission from *High Society* by Neil Boyd, Key Porter Books.

Explanations of Addiction

Fishbein and Pease (1996:82) point out that while there are many theoretical explanations of drug use and addiction, "many theories do not distinguish between those factors that contribute to the reasons to first use a drug, reasons to maintain drug use, and reasons for relapse." After reviewing biological, psychological, and a variety of sociological theories of addiction, they note that none of the perspectives is able to address all the factors. Instead, they suggest that a *multidisciplinary* approach is necessary. Specifically they refer to the diathesis-stress model that recognizes elements of the social environment, perceived environment, personality, biological/genetic factors, and behaviourial factors. Each element has risk factors as well as protective factors. An individual's risk of developing alcohol problems is dependent on the extent of the stressors within each of the major elements.

While this is a comprehensive model, Fishbein and Pease (1996) point out that the conditions necessary for predicting alcoholic tendencies are still too non-specific. However, they believe that only through this line of inquiry will we be able to predict and prevent alcohol abuse.

Drug Use: Is it a Moral Issue?

We have seen throughout this section that there is a wide range of psychotropic drugs available. While many of these drugs are illegal, a number of them are legal. And some of these legal drugs have stronger addictive properties than illicit drugs. We have also seen that throughout history some of the drugs that are illicit today were once legal and even used for medical purposes. Similarly, we saw that legal drugs like alcohol were not always legal in Canadian history.

A conflict and/or Marxist interpretation of the relative legal status of drugs focuses on drugs being viewed as a social problem by various social classes who feel a certain drug threatens their social stability (i.e., power). In other words, they would sanction a drug only if they could monopolize the making and selling of the drug. From this point of view, the best way to combat an "evil" drug would be through thought reform and education.

Drugs, whether you use them or not, present a moral dilemma for society. Whether one subscribes to the psychological position of Erich Fromm, that we learn to desire those things that go along with our economic and social system, or the sociological position put forth by Max Weber, who stated that society rewards those who are industrious, both positions leave the door open for cultural values to dictate what "pleasure-seeking" outlets are acceptable or unacceptable. If our desire to use drugs can be traced back to earliest recorded history, perhaps the drug controversies are a reflection of a cultural lag between existing laws and people's changing feelings and values.

How many of you take vitamins, herbs, or some other alternative to traditional medicine? In Canada and the United States, allopathic medicine has dominated the medical arena for nearly two hundred years. However, in recent years alternative medicine (e.g., herbalism, homeopathy, and naturopathy) has begun to gather a significant following. Even though most provinces do not provide medical coverage for some of the alternative forms, there has been a significant shift in the number of people turning to these practitioners. The result has been a desperate backlash by pharmaceutical companies, the Canadian medical community, and even the Canadian Health Protection Branch (Ludde, 1997). They have combined their interests and are attempting to suppress the growth of the alternative health movement. The backlash has largely taken the form of trying to legally restrict the scope of practice of alternative practitioners in order to neutralize their effectiveness. As Ludde (1997:52) observes "the drug lords pull all the strings." In addition, pressure has been applied by the mega-pharmaceutical companies to ban over the counter sales of products found to be highly beneficial. "Drugs" such as DHEA, yohimba, tryptophan, melatonin, and ma-huang, among many others, now require prescriptions (Jensen, 1997). Quebec physician, Guylaine Lanctot (1994) believes so strongly that the large pharmaceutical companies are corrupt that he has sacrificed his career and personal assets to defend the rights of individuals to choose their own health care options. Is it not morally wrong when medical drugs destroy health and growth and inhibit basic life functions? For example, with respect to conventional cancer research, Ludde

(1997) points out that in spite of "40 years of research they don't have a cure and the rate of mortality is steadily rising."

This example reflects how people's values and beliefs have changed regarding certain drugs. Yet the law and the power brokers have attempted to maintain the status quo. Fortunately for the alternative field, the groundswell of support for legal reform to protect people's right to have their voices heard seems to be taking hold.

Society is forever evolving and some of these changes are accompanied by social consequences that pose challenges to criminologists. Only by adopting an interdisciplinary perspective can we try to understand the role of crime versus morality.

Summary

Public order crimes being age-old "problems," I will draw on age-old wisdom in summarizing this chapter. Both Aristotle and Plato believed that once a bad moral state exists it is not easily amended. Yet they both believed that human behaviour is a matter of choice because we have free will. However, they also argued that no one intentionally falls prey to a social vice. As Plato (1980:196) observed, "no one will ever voluntarily accept the supreme evil into the most vulnerable part of himself and live with it throughout his life."

In this chapter, we covered a range of vices, or public order offences or victimless crimes, as they are also called. It was observed that an attempt to legislate issues of morality in a heterogeneous society is complex and controversial. Criminologists have never successfully resolved the question of whether public order offences should be treated as criminal or civil matters. Yet public order offences represent the "most widespread organization of lawlessness" (Sutherland and Cressey, 1959:230). Not only do most people engage in varying forms of vices but criminal organizations (and in some cases non-criminal organizations) feed society's demands.

After discussing the issue of morality, we shifted our attention to examining four primary forms of public order offences. First we looked at gambling. It was noted that while the law sanctions certain forms of gambling it condones other forms. It was also noted that problem gambling represents a breakdown in the will and self-control of the offender/victim. In pointing out that life itself is a gamble, the question was raised as to how best criminologists can explain (illegal) gambling practices and how best they can control a behaviour that almost appears innate.

Next we looked at the "oldest" profession in the world—prostitution. Again, we are confronted with a behaviour that has run the gamut—from being held in the highest esteem to being described in derogatory terms. It was further noted that prostitution has endured the full criminological spectrum of theoretical explanations. None of the theories, however, has been able to provide a clear understanding of why mostly females enter prostitution, let alone provide a solid basis for controlling prostitution.

The dilemma of trying to legislate morality in the context of understanding human behaviour will continue to pose a major challenge for criminology. Perhaps the Athenian, in Plato's *The Laws* (1980:337), put it best when he said "suppose some impatient young man were standing here, bursting with seed, and heard us passing this law" (on sexual conduct). "He'd probably raise the echoes and his bellows of abuse and say our rules were stupid and unrealistic." Rather than criminologists trying to balance concerns of morality that serve the greater common good, the solution (as the Athenian reasoned) might lie in teaching morality and self-control. How realistic is this solution? Again, the Athenian offers a solution. He suggested that any man (or woman) "must do so without any man or woman getting to know about it" (Ibid, 340). Failure to do so warrants punishment.

This chapter does not condone prostitution. The above comments simply highlight an issue for which there is no clear solution. Laws will never prevent men, or women, from seeking the services of a prostitute. Therefore, instead of focusing on reforming the law, criminologists should direct their attention to understanding this expression of human behaviour from an integrated and inter-disciplinary perspective.

The third public order offence we examined was pornography. Like gambling and prostitution, the history of pornography runs deep in society. It was suggested there is no clear answer to the problem, when even today criminologists struggle with the definition, the boundaries, the effects and possible consequences of pornography. To paraphrase an old saying, "one man's food is another man's poison."

As criminologists, do we focus on the aftermath of the effect or do we attempt to understand the role of pornography in an integrated and interdisciplinary manner? Perhaps Plato and Aristotle are both correct. Using pornography can be both evil and good but the law cannot decide these matters. Only a person's conscience can decide. Or as the Roman philosopher, Seneca (3 BC–65 AD) stated, "shame may restrain what law does not prohibit" or cannot control. It will be interesting to see how criminologists and the criminal justice system respond to the recently criminalized public order acts on stalking or criminal harassment (see Chapter 9) and the growing problem of illegal organ transplants (see Box 12.15).

ORGAN TRANSPLANTS: DO WE REGULATE?

We value life because it is precious. Since we were first able to transplant human (and even animal) organs there has been an ongoing debate about the moral and ethical implications. Today, we must also contend with a growing crime problem around the trade of human body parts. Thousands of transplants are performed every year and yet the number of people awaiting transplants grows every year. Hence, the demand outstrips the supply. A transnational industry, and in some cases an illegal one, has emerged. In July 1998, a CBC Radio special reported that Chinese prisoners were used for their organs, some even murdered for them. Other stories involve poor parents selling their children's body parts for a little extra money. Perhaps an even more fundamental dilemma concerns donating a needed organ to a loved one. If the donor is doing so out of a sense of guilt, a sense of obligation, and/or giving the organ to someone who abused their bodies, is this morally right, and should it somehow be regulated?

The final vice we examined was substance abuse. Once again, we saw the history and meaning of substance abuse parallel the trends and patterns of the other vices we covered. Whether legal or not, all drugs have psychoactive properties. The differentiation in legal status is a man-made construction. Often the definition of what is deemed legal as opposed to illegal is defined only by the power brokers. But self-serving laws cannot and do not deter users. It is simply not possible to legislate morality or what is outmoded or puritanical in attitude.

As with the other public order offences covered in this chapter, criminologists need to bridge the gap between man-made laws and social science. They need to focus on the acts as they relate to human behaviour from an integrated and interdisciplinary perspective. Only by recognizing the complexity of human behaviour and by approaching any criminological issue in this manner will criminologists begin to understand what such behaviours mean. But it does not necessarily follow that we will be able to control them, or that we should endeavour to do so.

Having presented an overview of the oldest and most widespread forms of "lawlessness," let us now look at one of the newest areas of criminological interest—the female offender. Ironically, gender issues are as old as Adam and Eve but within criminology, we have only begun to pay attention to women and crime.

Discussion Questions

1. Should criminologists try to legislate issues of morality? What issues need to be taken into consideration when making such a decision?

2. To what extent does involvement in any public order offence involve voluntary participation?

3. To what extent might trying to control public order offences contribute to the criminal population? To what extent does it promote the involvement of organized crime groups?

4. How do criminal justice agencies attempt to monitor child pornography? Where does one draw the line in defining obscenity? How do these laws affect our rights to freedom of speech and expression? From a criminological perspective it raises such questions as: What motivates people to take such risks and how do we explain their behaviour? Should such behaviours be sanctioned? Is the problem "overblown"? Where should we draw the line in terms of human rights?

5. Should people suffering from serious illnesses be allowed to use soft drugs like marijuana for medicinal purposes? What moral and/or ethical issues might be involved?

6. Why have conventional theories (e.g., psychological and sociological ones) been relatively ineffective in explaining public order offences and in helping to formulate effective social policy?

7. Discuss anti-drug campaigns presented in the media. What is their orientation? How do they try to convince us not to use the drug? Contrast these ads with ads for drugs that are legal. What is their orientation? How do they try to convince us that it is safe to use the drug?

8. How could an interdisciplinary and integrated approach be applied to address public order crimes?

Key Concepts

Public order crimes	victimless crimes	gambling
Consensus model	conflict perspective	gaming and betting
Nambling	prostitution	Badgley Report
Bill C-15	streetwalkers	Fraser Report
Massage-parlour prostitution	house prostitution	bar prostitution
Call girls	political economy perspective	rap session booths
Pornography	substance abuse	psychoactive
Controlled substances	diathesis-stress model	stalking
Criminal harassment	obscenity	

Weblinks

www.ccsa.ca/ The Canadian Centre of Substance Abuse.

www.acjnet.org/docs/prosjhs.html An excellent link for information on a wide variety of public order issues such as prostitution, gambling, and substance abuse.

www.hempnation.com The homepage for the legalization of hemp. Offers a number of interesting links and addresses a variety of ethical, legal, and moral issues.

www.walnut.org/csis/groups.swav/ The homepage for the Vancouver- based Sex Workers Alliance of Vancouver. Also includes numerous other useful links on prostitution and related issues.

www.gov.ns.ca/heal/gambling/ The Nova Scotia government Gamblers Anonymous homepage. Has lots of interesting links.

www.culture/crime/crimes/sex-crimes/child-pornography/ Offers additional information on the child pornography controversy.

Other related crimes against public order links can be found through Cecil Greek and Malaspina University College Web sites identified in earlier chapters.

Footnotes

1. The American sociologist, Howard Becker first coined this term in his classic *Outsiders* (1963). He used the term in reference to those people, who usually hold high social positions, giving them the power to enforce their values, who wish to control the definition of morality as a means of eliminating evil in society. He points out that such crusaders tend to only see their way as representing the right way—they can be described as being "self-righteous."

2. In Chapter 4 and Appendix 5, several of the important pioneers in criminological thought are presented. The fact remains that while criminologists debate the merits of morality in law and whether or not the two can, or should, be treated separately, there are a variety of public order acts that have been defined as sanctionable under criminal law.

3. The statement is perhaps somewhat trite as your odds of winning the "649 lottery," depending on the volume of tickets old across Canada, are usually one in several million. A number of charitable lotteries list the number of tickets sold and will identify your chances of winning something. However, the reality of winning the *big* prize still remains extremely low.

4. See organized crime in Chapter 11.

5. The problem of gambling is considered serious enough to warrant its own academic venue for publications—the *Journal of Gambling Studies*.

6. In the mid-1990s, Alberta relaxed their laws pertaining to gambling even more by allowing casinos to extend their hours and serve liquor at tables (Treatment planned…, 1997).

7. The small Alberta community of Rocky Mountain House voted on February 24, 1997 to remove VLTs from their hotels and lounges. While the local businesses felt the financial impact of the ban, a follow-up survey showed that "gamblers drive to other nearby towns to get their video fix." For example, the nearby community of Caroline noticed a significant increase in customers after the ban in Rocky Mountain House. Even so, a number

of communities have come forward requesting a plebiscite on the machines in their community. Under the initial legislation, towns and cities could hold a plebiscite within 90 days of filing a petition. However, in the spring of 1997, Ralph Klein's Conservative government changed the rules delaying votes until the next civic election in October 1998 (Cunningham, 1997). In Alberta, as in most provinces, the government does not appear interested in losing the revenue it collects from the machines.

8. Japanese prostitutes do not enjoy the same status today.

9. SWAV has a weblink that can be reached at www.walnut.org/csis/groups/swav/. They have a wide range of information on the sex-trade, John Schools, etc.

10. The American counterpart is COYOTE (Call Off Your Old Tired Ethics).

11. In spite of such legislation, child prostitution remains a serious problem. A CBC news special (aired June 17, 1998) noted that Saskatoon has the highest per capita rate of child prostitution in Canada. Of the 259 known child prostitutes in 1997, 88 (34 per cent) were under the age of 14. A member of the local outreach program observed that there are no treatment programs available for these youths.

12. Alternative lifestyle groups can include the National Leather Association, Fetish Night Hostess Madam X, Boudoir Noir Magazine, among other groups. In 1997 New York city opened the first restaurant, La Nouvelle Justine, in which customers can "order" a spanking from the maitre d' for $20 US. An assortment of other "mild" sadomasochism is also available (Restaurant serves..., 1997).

13. For a historical overview of prostitution in Canada see Lowman (1989).

14. Between 1988–1995, 48 sex-trade workers were murdered in BC. The solution rate is 25 per cent lower for them than for those murdered in the general population (Smith, 1997).

15. According to Prus and Irini (1988) a "pimp" offer a sense of comfort and support, as in most conventional marriages. However, unlike most conventional relationships pimps receive financial remuneration for their "support." Occasionally pimps may be boyfriends, lovers, or husbands. And contrary to public image, pimps do not regularly abuse the women working for them (SCPP, 1985).

16. Nevada law requires working women to be fingerprinted and carry identity cards. County laws also usually require prostitutes to submit to regular medical examinations. Local laws also dictate where brothels can be located and usually confine prostitutes to plying their trade within the brothel. They may not go onto the street and solicit business (Brown, Esbensen, and Geis, 1991).

17. For further reading on the implications of pornography on the Internet, Jo Bindman and Jo Doezma have published *Redefining Prostitution as Sex Work on the International Agenda*, in 1998. Their book examines over 10,000 pornographic images between 1995–96 on case-law examples from Canada and several other countries.

18. A survey of the Calgary yellow pages revealed nearly 20 pages of advertisements for female and male escort services. It is likely that a number of escort services represent fronts for prostitution.

19. Negative family history accounted for 16 per cent, survival another 12 per cent, and wanting to live in the fast lane and/or being naive accounted for 12 per cent as well. Other explanations were negligible.

20. In 1998, Winnipeg gained national media attention when their chief of police touted the benefits of "John Schools." The idea was to have those caught seeking the avails of street prostitutes attend a class for a day where they would be educated on the risk of transmittable diseases, the havoc prostitution causes neighbourhoods, and other social "ills." SVAT, and similar groups (see footnote 9) have argued that such schools simply encourage prostitutes to move into escort services and that the police are enforcing morality, not the law.

21. According to Single et al. (1997), there has been no attempt, in Canada, to estimate the total cost associated with the use and abuse of psychoactive substances. Based on available information, they estimate it at around $18.5 billion, or 27 per cent GDP, or $649 per capita.

22. According to an American judge, marijuana in its natural form, is one of the safest therapeutically-active substances known to man (Hempnation, 1997). In 1997, California became the first American state to allow patients with certain serious illnesses (e.g., AIDS, epilepsy, and various forms of cancer) to possess marijuana for medical use. However, in 1998, several of the cannabis clubs were charged with alleged illegal sales of the drug. To date no insurance companies will provide coverage for the "treatment" (Gilionna, 1998). The right of Canadians to use marijuana for medical purposes received a blow in June of 1998 when Calgarian Grant Krieger, suffering from multiple sclerosis, was charged with possessing and cultivating a narcotic. Krieger has been campaigning to allow those suffering from painful illnesses to use marijuana for medicinal purposes (Engman, 1998).

23. The numbers do not add up to 9.2 per cent because of a rounding error.

24. In most Islamic countries coffee, tobacco, and variations of mind-altering herbs along with opium are very popular psychoactive drugs (Boyd, 1991).

25. For an amusing account of how marijuana was portrayed in the 1930s and 1940s see the video *Reefer Madness*.

CHAPTER 13

Women and Crime

*"There can be no doubt about
women's violent potential."*
F. Heidensohn (1992)

*"Women commit the majority
of child homicides."*
P. Pearson (1998)

Learning Outcomes

After you have completed this chapter, you should be able to:

- Appreciate the heritage of the subject of women and crime in criminology.
- Identify the important elements regarding gender issues in criminology.
- Appreciate the need to see female crime not only as a social construct but also as a bio-social disorder.
- Appreciate the importance of female offenders as an area of interest within criminology.
- Recognize the nature and characteristics of female offenders, as well as explanations of female offenders.

As discussed in Chapter 8, crime is ever present in our world and it is not age-, gender-, or social class-specific. Hardly a day goes by when we do not hear or read about a criminal incident in the news. If you have listened carefully you will have noticed that while women are typically portrayed as victims (e.g., rape and assault),[1] you might also have noticed that they also commit crimes (see Box 13.1). Boritch (1997) has observed that until recently criminologists have also tended to focus on female victimization and spent less time studying women and crime.

Two rationales for this lack of attention include the facts that "women represent a minority of all offenders, across time and culture," and most crimes com-

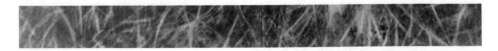

mitted by women are petty property offences (Ibid). In addition, the patriarchal aspects of the criminal justice system and criminology have typically viewed female offending as "sick" or "pathological" and not a serious social problem. Swigert and Farrell (1976) observed that being female seemed to serve as a mitigating factor when women's criminality was assessed. They used the term **pedestal effect** to describe a social and definitional orientation that they feel contributes "to the less severe treatment accorded women accused of homicide" (p. 80). The view of women, as needing protection, means they have traditionally been less likely to be arrested and incarcerated and more likely to receive lighter sentences. This benevolent attitude towards women has also been referred to as the **chivalry hypothesis**.

In spite of an apparent lack of interest in female offenders, the number of women being charged with criminal offences in North America is increasing (Boe, 1992). Furthermore, earlier attitudes have since been mostly discredited. Therefore, it is important for criminology to pay attention to criminal behaviour trends and patterns among women.

BY THE NUMBERS BOX 13.1

WOMEN AND CRIME

- In 1991, 12 per cent (N=13,000) of all Canadians charged with violent crime were women. Between 1970 and 1991, the number of all charges against women for violent offences rose from 8.1 per cent to 13.6 per cent. Yet the majority of these offences involved minor assaults.
- Between 1974 and 1984 the number of female offenders in American prisons increased from 8,091 to 20,853. This represents an increase of 158 per cent. Over the same period the increase for men was "only" 100 per cent (Nesbitt, 1985). More recently, Dowling (1997) reports the number of women in United States prisons has increased five fold between 1980 and 1997. Again, their rate of increase is greater than that among male offenders. Yet, as in Canada, women offenders only account for 11 per cent of all violent crime in the United States.
- Between 1960 and 1990 in Canada, aggravated assault and robbery among women increased more than twice the rate for men (Pearson, 1998).
- Between 1986 and 1996, the rate of violent crime among young females increased 179 per cent compared to 85 per cent among young males (see Chapter 9)

This chapter will begin with a historical overview of the role of women and the female offender. As Boritch (1996:5) points out, a historical perspective is important to understand "the legacy of the past in understanding the contemporary context of women's criminality and the criminal justice system response to women."

She claims many of the issues surrounding our misconceptions about female offenders and their treatment are the product of misplaced stereotypical images perpetuated by men (and women) through the ages. Women were seen to be innately more moral then men and hence less likely to fall prey to social vices. If, and when, such incidents occurred women were seen to have "fallen" from grace.

Next, we will examine a number of specific crimes that are perpetrated by women. In addition to discussing the extent and nature of female offending, we will focus on how female offenders differ from male offenders on such variables as motivation, age, race and social class. Where possible, Canadian information will be used. But, as many researchers have observed, most "sources available for literature searches in Canada are primarily American or North American" (Shaw and Dubois, 1995:2).

The third major section will provide an overview of some of the early, as well as more recent, theoretical explanations of why women commit crimes. We will begin by looking at the early biological explanations that stigmatized the female offender and progress to the feminist perspectives that attempt to provide an integrated and interdisciplinary approach to understanding the female offender.

Before we get into these issues, let us begin with a historical overview of women and crime.

The History of Female Offenders

One of the first works on female offenders was written by one of the pioneers of criminology, **Cesare Lombroso** (Chapter 4). Lombroso, in collaboration with his son-in-law, G. Ferrero, wrote *La Donna Delinqente, La Prostituta e La Donna Normale*. First published in 1893, it appeared in English and several other languages in 1895 and was titled *The Female Offender.*

Many of the stereotypes that preceded Lombroso's work can be found in his book. For example, Lombroso described women as being very child-like in their emotions and level of sensibility. Relying on historical and some ethnological (i.e., the science of human races and their relationship to one another) material Lombroso suggested that "prostitutes and prostitution represent reversionary or *atavistic*[2] phenomena" (Wolfgang, 1973:254). Relying on the examination of their physical traits he argued that genuine female offenders "are endowed with the same fundamental peculiarities found in male criminals, and that prostitutes and other genuine criminal feminine types are characterized by a lack of 'mother-sense' " (Ibid, 255).

While popular in the nineteenth century, such views have since been largely discredited. However, consistent with today's crime statistics, Lombroso did point out that while females commit fewer crimes than males, they commit far more crimes than official statistics show.

In spite of Lombroso's contribution to understanding the female offender, between 1983 and the 1960s, very little else was written on the female offender. Among the more noteworthy studies to have an impact was the 1930s research project undertaken by Sheldon and Eleanor Glueck in which they attempted to discover the biological and environmental causes of crime. They included women in their study project. And although their findings were decidedly sociological, their work inspired others to examine the causes of female crime. In the 1950s, **Otto Pollak** was among the first to attempt to break the stereotype that women offenders are biological aberrations. Instead, he emphasized the importance of family structure in determining a women's activities. He suggested that women tend to commit crimes that are deceitful in nature, supposedly using deceit to compensate for their physical weaknesses. Pollak described crimes committed by women as "masked crimes." As Pollak did not use empirical data to support any of his assertions, when the feminist movement emerged it were quick to condemn Pollak's work for perpetuating stereotypes and for being unable to provide evidence (see Gavigan, 1987:52—also see below for further discussion).

It was, however, the prefeminist writings of **Freda Adler** (1975) and **Rita Simons** (1975) that renewed interest in the relationship between gender and crime. Both Adler and Simon argued that the women's liberation movement (see Box 13.2) helped women's access to legitimate and illegitimate opportunities. While their claims about future trends in female criminality have been overstated (Barak, 1998), their efforts were instrumental in compelling criminology to study female criminality. Additional impetus for the feminist perspective on criminology came from the first anti-rape group in the early 1970s. Known as the *Bay Area Women Against Crime*, the group included criminology students expressing feminist ideas in action, ideas that were instrumental in bringing about criminal justice reforms (Schwendinger and Schwendinger, 1991). These and other efforts helped make women a central subject in criminology.

A CLOSER LOOK BOX 13.2

Women's Liberation Movement

The term "women's liberation" was first used by the French feminist writer Simone De Beauvoir in her 1953 book *The Second Sex* (Feminist Chronicles, 1997). The term was used to refer to women as deserving of equal status to men, in every way, whether educational, political, social, and/or economic. Or, as Canadian author and feminist Donna Laframboise (1996:1) phrased it: "when little girls grow up they should be able to be anything they want to be—doctors, lawyers, political leaders or fighter pilots." However, the history of the women's movement has been a path met with (male) resistance.

In her book, *Her Story II: Women from Canada's Past,* Merritt (1995) chronicles the lives of 16 Canadian Aboriginal and black women who have had a significant impact on women's issues and rights. Her account includes Eunice Williams, an Iroquois, though Mohawk by choice, who challenged the taking of children from their Aboriginal setting, and Piseolak (1904–1983), an Inuit who, after being moved from the Northwest Territories to the permanent settlement at Cape Dorset, escaped her impoverished life by becoming the most famous of the Cape Dorset artists.

Federally, women have only been able to vote since May 24, 1918. They did not acquire legal status as "persons" until 1929. Since then many Canadian women have reached prestigious positions. Jeanne Sauvé became the first female Governor General, first female Speaker of the House of Commons, and the first female Member of Parliament from Quebec to be a Cabinet Minister. Kim Campbell was the first female Prime Minister and Audrey McLaughlin the first woman to serve as head of a federal political party in Canada and North America (Then and Now, 1997).

Did you know?

- It was illegal to distribute information about birth control as late as 1969.
- Canada didn't get its first female Supreme Court judge until 1982.
- As recently as the early 1970s, many females weren't permitted to wear trousers to school or work because it was considered "unfeminine" (Laframboise, 1996).

In terms of a "movement," most literature points to the 1960s when the women's movement began to truly gather momentum at a societal level. However, it was not until the 1970s that feminists began to make inroads into the male-dominated arena of criminology.

Many early studies not only lacked empirical support but they were at times also demeaning of women. For example, in the 1938 *Report of the Royal Commission to Investigate the Penal System of Canada* (Archabault Report), when referring to the 32 women at Kingston Penitentiary for Women (P4W), the authors concluded:

> The number of trainable women is very small, and the women prisoners apart from young prisoners who are capable of deriving benefit from continued education would constitute a small class (cited in Gavigan, 1987:79).

One of the first Canadian studies on women offenders appeared in the *Canadian Journal of Corrections* (now the *Canadian Journal of Criminology*) in 1969. Then in 1976, Phyllis Haslem, Executive Director of the Elizabeth Fry Society (Toronto Branch) wrote a chapter on female offenders for McGrath's (1976) criminal justice textbook. In her chapter Haslem expressed the belief that, contrary to popular opinion, female offenders are not any more difficult to work with than men. Nevertheless, she says that women need to be treated differently to men in order for them to "gain or regain a sense of her own worth" (p. 475). Haslem offered eight general recommendations for change. They ranged from eliminating the mandatory physical search on entry into prisons to providing "suitable, colourful, well-fitted clothing."

While the early literature and research was sporadic, it was not until the emergence of the feminist movement in the 1970s that a more concerted effort was directed to understanding both the female offender and the female victim.

The Emergence of Feminist Interests

Throughout most of the twentieth century, the Elizabeth Fry Society (see Box 13.3) championed the cause of female offenders and female victims. However, one of the most significant reports that helped bring the issue of female crime into the limelight in Canada was the 1986 government commission entitled *A Feminist Review of Criminal Law* (cited in Adelberg and Currie, 1987). It was the first report to approach Canadian criminal law from a woman's perspective. Ellen Adelburg and Claudia Currie (1987) were among the first Canadians to write about the Canadian female offender. As they said "we feel compelled to break the historical silence surrounding women offenders" (Ibid, 11).

A CLOSER LOOK BOX 13.3

Elizabeth Fry Society

Elizabeth Fry (Gurey) (1780–1845) was born into a family of Quakers in England. Quakers were among the first denominations to believe in the equality of women. Being brought up in such a setting had a profound impact on Elizabeth Fry in her work at London's Newgate Prison. She became a strong proponent of the humane treatment of women prisoners and was instrumental in promoting prison reform (Canadian Association of Elizabeth Fry Society (CAEFS), 1997).

The first Elizabeth Fry Society was established in Vancouver, BC., in 1939 and the CAEFS was incorporated as voluntary non-profit organizations in 1978.[3] Today there are 21 member societies across Canada (Ibid).

CAEFS is a federation that works with, and on behalf of, women involved with the justice system. The member societies emphasize community-based services and programs for "marginalized women, advocating for legislation and administrative reform" (Ibid).

On May 5, 1995, Herb Gray then Solicitor-General of Canada and Marie Cadieux, director of the National Film Board productions *A Double Tour* and *Twice Condemned*, helped to launch National Elizabeth Fry Society Week, held the week before Mother's Day. Member societies organize public information events to promote awareness and support. Volunteerism is an essential part of the society (Ibid).

In **summary**, although feminism is more than a century old, it has only been since the 1960s that its influence has been felt in criminology. However, many of the early patriarchal stereotypes as to the causes of female crime still prevail. Until recently, criminology has tended to focus on female victimization rather than on female offenders. Much of the credit for the exponential growth in literature on the plight of female victims and female offenders can be attributed to the feminist movement of the 1960s and 1970s. In addition, there has been a smattering of non-feminists, primarily from the critical criminology perspective, who have also championed interests in women's crime and criminal justice issues. Some of the notable Canadians include: Walter DeKeseredy and Ronald Hinch (1991) who have written extensively on the abuse of women, Holly Johnson (1996) and her work on violence against women and Vince Sacco who has researched the general victimization of women. But while there is a growing body of information on female victims, there is little on female offenders. Yet, based on the titles of some recent books (e.g., *Too Few to Count* by Adelberg and Currie (1987), *The Invisible Woman* by Belknap (1996), *When She was Bad* by Pearson (1997), and *Casualties of Community Disorder* by Baskin and Sommers (1998)), it appears that the female offender is gaining a platform of interest. However, when compared to the extent of material available on the male offender, there is much room for research here. This chapter may inspire others to study the female offender, not just as a gender issue but as part of an integrated and interdisciplinary approach to the study of crime and criminality.

We will now turn our attention to the female offender.

The Female Offender

"Part of reclaiming women's history is documenting our oppression in all facets of life" Adelberg and Currie, 1987:21.

As noted above, the 1960s and '70s in North America marked a dramatic increase in the attention given to women's equality and rights. It has been argued that women received differential treatment at all levels of the criminal justice system. However, it has only been recently that the movement for the rights of female offenders and prisoners made any inroads. In this section we will begin by examining the notion of women as morally "bad." We will then examine the characteristics and the extent of female crime.

Gender Differences

Observable and measurable differences between males and females have been known for some time. Maccoby and Jacklin (1974) identified four major differences between the genders:

- Females are more verbal (left hemisphere);
- Females are less visual, aural, and spatial (right hemisphere);
- Females are less adept in science and mathematics; and
- Females are less physically aggressive, dominant, and curious.

While some of these traits can, and have been, explained in terms of the socialization process, such perspectives cannot account for all the differences. Nor should we assume that an *either/or* relationship exists when making female-male comparisons. For example, both "males and females vary between being highly aggressive and very unaggressive" (McKie, 1987:19). Hence, as we will see later, it is important to adopt an interdisciplinary perspective in trying to understand gender differences.

One example in which the importance of social and biological differences illustrate the need for an integrated and interdisciplinary approach is the famous study of Kalat in the late 1980s (cited in Blum, 1997). Kalat studied the impact of socialization on sexual behaviour among young males in the Dominican Republic. Because of a genetic defect, the boys do not have a fully developed penis until adolescence. Until then, they are raised as females. Once their gender identity becomes clear they are treated as males (which they were all along). Although they were raised as girls, the boys readily adapt to their "new" identity. Similar studies have been done of males who lost their penises shortly after birth due to an accident or during circumcision. Most of the documented cases indicated that the male preferred to behave in a "male way."

Therefore, in spite of the social reinforcement of being raised as females, the effects of biology (e.g., testosterone and hypothalamus differences) also play a determining role in any behaviour. Other classic examples where "nature" appears to play a significant role in gender identity (in spite of social stigmas) involve those individuals who undergo physical sex changes and/or those who experience same-sex orientations. Unfortunately, because of the social sensitivity involved concerning whether or not sexual orientation involves a biological component, politics can not only interfere with such research, but it can "blind us to the results" (Blum, 1997:157).

Women as Morally "Bad"

Karlene Faith (1987), from Simon Fraser University, argues that the media tend to portray female offenders as violent individuals (e.g., and/or predator lesbians). She claims that female offenders "are mocked by B-grade movies about women's prisons which feature male-oriented sex-and-violence plots complete with predatory characters who prey on young, innocent types" (Ibid, 183). These movies also stereotypically portray female wardens and/or female staff as cold, "masculine" females. Faith describes these B-grade movies as insulting to both female staff and those who are in prison.

While Faith makes a number of poignant points, much of what she describes —sexual violence, "masculinity" among women offenders, exploitation of women by other women, etc.—are also regularly found in male-oriented B-grade prison theme-based movies. In not drawing gender comparisons on such important issues, it is difficult to gauge the extent to which such problems are unique only to female offenders and female prisons. Faith does, however, make the occasional reference to male and female prisoners. For example, in one incident, Faith notes how a male inmate told her how he felt humiliated after being "treated like a women" while a female prisoner told her how degrading it was to be treated like a child (Ibid, 199). Unfortunately, anecdotal incidents a case do not make! There is, however, considerable evidence showing that female victimization and fear of victimization is often associated with women being portrayed as objects who can be controlled by men (see Belknap, 1996).

At another point, Faith suggests that there is "no basis for believing that the violence that does occur in P4W" (Kingston's Prison for Women) is comparable to such Canadian movies as *Turning to Stone* in 1986. She considers the movie to be a realistic depiction of female offenders and life in women's prisons. Yet, in April 1994, P4W was the subject of one of the worst scandals in Canadian prison history. Female inmates were brutally assaulted by male prison staff while the female warden allegedly turned a (knowing) blind eye to the whole incident. While the warden may not have been fully aware of what had happened during the "shakedown," the incident shows how women can be, and are, the subject of male exploitation.

Notwithstanding a number of methodological shortfalls in her article, Faith makes a poignant observation in suggesting the media could be used to educate the public about the realities of social and cultural issues surrounding female offenders and female prisons. Unfortunately, her general observation that distorted stereotypes continue to prevail in society has done little to help the plight of female offenders in general.

Until the widely-publicized case of Paul Bernardo and his now ex-wife, Karla Homolka in 1995, few Canadians probably gave much thought to female offenders. Their gruesome story, however, captured media attention as few other criminal cases ever have in Canadian history. Until then, if asked about female crime, most of us would probably point to such crimes as prostitution, shoplifting, and fraud as the primary types of crime committed by women. Homolka assisted her husband in the sexual slaying of two teenage girls (Leslie Mahaffy, 14, from Burlington and Kristin French, 15, from St. Catherines) (Boritch, 1996). She also contributed to the death of her own sister, Tammy, a murder she was never convicted of. Pearson (1998) suggests that this may have been the result of Homolka's defence lawyer trying to use the "battered wife syndrome" to deflect direct responsibility to Paul Bernardo. Needless to say, the public was repelled. (Boritch, 1996).

Is Homolka an anomaly among women (see Box 13.5)? Do women commit crimes for the same reasons men do? What kinds of crimes do they commit? We suddenly wanted to know more—or at least the media were giving us the opportunity to learn more. Female offenders had a public platform.

A Growing Concern

Referring to official UCR data, there has been a significant increase in the absolute number of women being officially charged with criminal offences. Between 1962 and 1992, the number of women charged for all offences rose from 27,530 to 115,770. This represents more than a 400 per cent increase (Boritch, 1997). Yet, among the adult offender population, women only represent 8 per cent of all those sentenced (Lipinski, 1991). The number of women admitted under sentence to provincial/territorial facilities has increased by 13 per cent since 1986–87. Yet as reflected in the comment from Hedlin above, this figure does not account for those crimes that go undetected and/or unreported.[4] Therefore, it can be assumed that the actual growth in female crime is even greater than reported.

Violent offences among women rose from 843 in 1962 to 9912 in 1989. This represents an increase of approximately 1100 per cent (Lipinski, 1991)! In fact, the number of women charged with property offences and other federal charges has also increased dramatically.

Boritch (1997:19) argues that since these numbers are absolute numbers over an extended period, "it is not immediately clear whether the growth in female criminality has kept pace with the growth in Canada's female population." However, in referring to Campbell's 1990 special *CCJS* report, Boritch observes that even when the numbers are converted into charges per 100,000, female crime rates increased from 476 in 1962 to 1092 in 1989. Still, the majority of violent offences committed by women in Canada involve minor assaults (Kong, 1997).

Similar trends have been observed in the United States. For example, the number of women sentenced for violent offences rose from 22,777 to 39,917 between 1986 and 1991 (Snell, 1994). This represents a 75.2 per cent increase, compared with a 52.9 per cent increase in the number of men who entered U.S. prisons over the same period. The report also shows that the most common violent offence among women is murder. However, similar to Canadian trends, nearly half of all women in American prisons, in 1991, were serving sentences for nonviolent offences such as drugs and fraud. Women convicted of violent offences are more than twice as likely as violent men (36 per cent vs. 16 per cent) to commit violence against someone close to them. For example, in 1991 the victims of women in prison for homicide included: relatives—17 per cent, intimate (i.e., husband, ex-husband, or boyfriend) 31.9 per cent, well-known—14.3 per cent, acquaintance—12.8 per cent, stranger—21.3 per cent, and known by sight only—2.7 per cent (Profile of female …, 1996). Female offenders are less likely than male offenders to have a previous criminal history (see below) but are more likely than male offenders to have a partner with a criminal history than vice versa. Meanwhile, Allen and Simenson (1997:302) report that "the female prisoners' population growth outpaced that of males." Between 1986 and 1991, the number of adult women arrested increased 23.5 per cent vs. 16.7 per cent among adult male offenders (Snell, 1994). They also note that nearly one-third of female inmates reported they were under the influence of a drug at the time of their offence. Nearly 40 per cent claimed they had been physically or sexually abused at some time in their lives. Allen and Simenson conclude by suggesting that the profile of the average imprisoned (American) female inmate "hardly reflects a dangerous offender for whom incarceration in prison is required" (p. 304). Similarly, Edmonton lawyer Laura Stevens (1997) points out that women appear in criminal courts far more often as victims than as accused.

Although the number of incidents of female offenders has been increasing since the 1960s, *Juristat* has not released a report on female offenders since 1990. Is this observation a continued reflection of the criminal justice system's lack of interest in the female offender? Does it reflect the ideological bias that still dominates Canadian criminology and criminological thought?

FYI BOX 13.6

Women and Violent Crime[5]

- Between 1985 and 1994, 234 men were killed by their spouse while 761 women were killed by their partner. This represents a 300 per cent difference! (Leesti, 1997).
- In 1996, a male judge in Quebec received considerable criticism when he suggested that a women "gone bad" is capable of more harm than any man (Steven, 1997).

Kelly Blanchette (1997:14) recently pointed out: "violent crime has traditionally been viewed as a uniquely male phenomenon." In fact, Shaw and Dubois (1995) observe that not only do men outnumber women by a large margin but the difference holds true "across countries, over time, at all ages, and in relation to different types of violence." We have been conditioned to believe that women are only the victims of crime and when they do commit crimes it is a result of mitigating circumstances—"acts of necessity." However, as noted above, since 1989, there has been a steady increase in the rate of females committing violent crime. Between 1992 and 1993, violent crime among Canadian women increased by 18.7 per cent. Yet Canadian female offenders represent less than 10 per cent of admissions to prisons for 1995–1996 (Reed and Morrison, 1997).

Relying on the Offender Intake Assessment process used in Canadian Corrections, Blanchette examined available demographic data on 182 federal female offenders since 1994. Among other findings, she reports:

- 106 (58 per cent) were designated as violent.
- 76 (42 per cent) were designated as non-violent.

- Average age of entire population was 33.8. Violent offenders' average age was 32.4, non-violent offenders' 34.5.
- 40 (22 per cent) of the federal female offenders were Aboriginal, of which 68 per cent were classified as violent vs. 56 per cent of the non-Aboriginal women.

Men still commit more violent crimes than women, but women are more likely to be charged with minor assaults than men are. Very few Canadian women are charged with robbery or sexual assault (Shaw and Dubois, 1995). In 1997, 581 individuals were charged with murder or manslaughter. Less than 10 per cent of the accused were women. However, a key difference between male and female killers is that women are more likely (64 per cent in 1997) to kill a family member. Only 32 per cent of the men killed a family member the same year (*CCJS*, 1998: 18(12)). As illustrated in Table 13–1, violent female offenders more often lack family ties during childhood. Female offenders were more likely to have a poor employment record, more frequently use drugs, and were more likely to have weak interpersonal skills combined with a poor attitude towards the different elements of the criminal justice system.

Of particular interest in trying to better understand offending behaviour by women, the criminal history profile of the violent and non-violent group revealed that adult female offenders were statistically more likely to become violent adult offenders than those who those who did not experience major difficulties (Blanchette, 1997). The female offenders expressed difficulty under the youth court system and in their personal lives. However, since the association between negative criminal justice experiences was not very strong, the indicator should not be seen as a major predictor. Blanchette did, however, observe other significant differences. Using multiple indicators, she identified five areas in which violent female offenders expressed statistically significant greater difficulties than the non-violent group (see Table 13–1).

TABLE 13–1

AREAS OF EXPRESSED NEEDS OF VIOLENT AND NON-VIOLENT FEMALE OFFENDERS AT ADMISSION

TYPE OF NEED	VIOLENT (N=106) %	NON-VIOLENT (N=127) %
Employment	80.2	70.1
Marital/Family	87.8	68.5
Substance Abuse	73.6	45.7
Personal/Emotional	97.2	82.7
Attitude	35.8	20.5

Source: Adapted from Blanchette (1997:15).

In addition to violent and non-violent expressive differences, Blanchette also found that 55 per cent of the violent women's group have *attempted* suicide in the past. This is more than double the figure for the non-violent group. Some have used this type of data to lend support to the notion that violent female offenders are somehow psychologically (if not biologically) unstable or different than non-violent female offenders. Yet Farrell (1993), among others, argues that violent women do not experience any more psychological disorders than non-violent females or males, they simply report it more. For example, Asher (1996) reports that male suicide rates in Canada are 376 per cent higher than among females. In fact, male suicide rates are currently double the rates they were during the 1930s, the Depression years. On the other hand, federal female inmates are more likely to have a history of suicide attempts (48 per cent) than men (13 per cent).

These and other related issues pose interesting and challenging questions for gender-based violence. Much more research needs to be conducted in relation to the female offender.

Although considered exploratory in nature, Blanchette's study does reveal that violent female offenders "present higher need levels than their non-violent counterparts" (Blanchette, 1997:18). Consistent with other literature of female and male offenders (see Chapter 9) the violent female offender typically has a history of substance abuse.

The increasing number of incidents involving women appears to further support the assertion that there is an interaction of social and biological factors. As Blum (1997), among others, notes, there is a growing body of knowledge that suggests that genetics might also play a role.

While most criminologists/researchers call for intensive treatment programs to provide assistance for these individuals, very few researchers point to the fact that substance abuse is part of a multi-level problem that involves environmental factors and biochemical elements. In Chapter 8, we discussed the *bio-environmental theory* and *bio-social theories* and that, as interdisciplinary approaches, they represent a more fruitful way by which to both understand and treat women and men who abuse alcohol and/or drugs (see below). Espousing the general philosophy of Corrections Canada, Blanchette only recommends support "for the ongoing, intensive substance abuse programming ... especially for those women convicted of violent offences" (Ibid, 18).

FYI BOX 13.7

Female Violence

In November 1997, a 14-year-old Saanich, BC, girl was found dead near a riverbank. Seven of her assailants were female. Only one boy was involved (Teen tormented...

Women kill far less frequently than men. In 1997, 61 women were killed by their spouse or ex-partner as compared with 14 men killed by their female partner or ex-partner (*CCJS*, 1998:18(12)). Historically, the sex ratio of partner homicide victimization has remained fairly stable. Yet there is a growing body of research that shows that when women do kill, their methods and reasons for killing are usually different from those of their male counterparts.

Dougherty (1993:94) asserts that not only have female perpetrators of child abuse and infanticide (i.e., killing of children, see Box 13.7 above) been virtually ignored in the literature, but researchers have relied on "gender neutral psychiatric factors and defects in character structure" to explain their behaviour. Official data indicate, however, that "there was a large increase in the number of mothers accused of killing their children." Between 1996 and 1997, the number of children killed by their mother rose from 13 to 15—half of all children killed (*CCJS*, 199:18(12)). Two-thirds of the children were under the age of one when killed. And while it is generally true that women spend more time with children than men, the fact remains that women do commit such crimes. And while a majority of women who kill their partners have been victims of abuse, it is less clear why a women would kill a child. In 1998, Sherry Perrault, of Regina, was sentenced to three years in prison for stomping on her adopted daughter's belly. A week after the incident, the five-year-old died from the injuries (O'Hanlon, 1998).

Female Serial Killers

Another area of female violence that has received minimal attention has been the subject of female serial killers. Several years ago, Keeney and Heide (1994) estimated that 10 to 15 per cent of serial killers are women. They found that females use different *modus operandi* than do males. For example, while males are more likely to use violence and torture, and have more direct physical contact with their victims, females are more likely to poison or smother their victims. Women are more likely to lure and seduce their victims to their deaths while men typically track and stalk their victims. For example, in 1992, Aileen Carol Wuornos of Florida was found guilty of killing seven men. She would pose as a hitchhiker and wait for men to pick her up. She would then rob and kill them and leave their naked bodies on the roadside. In her account of nine female serial killers, Manner (1995) notes that female serial killers average 9.2 years of killing before being caught. Female serial killers average 8 to 14 victims before being caught. Men average 8 to 11 victims before being caught (Hickey, 1997). In addition, he reports that female serial killers tend to be slightly older (32 years of age) than male serial killers. Nearly one-third are housewives.

Finally, Hickey (1997) comments on how the media stereotypically portray female serial killers as having more psychopathic tendencies than their male counterparts. This gender-bias is also reflected in the criminal justice system as women serial killers are less likely to end up on death row (in the United States), more likely to be placed in a psychiatric facility and generally receive shorter sentences.

Additional research needs to be conducted in order to better understand why some women kill. If women are by nature nurturing, how is it that they can kill? It also remains to be answered: Why do women continue to account for fewer violent crimes than males?

Aboriginal Women and Violent Crime

In terms of homicide, Lavigne, Hoffman, and Dickie (1997) report that Aboriginal women are overrepresented in the female offender population (see Box 13.8). Although they represent less than five per cent of the population, Aboriginal women represented 29 per cent of total sentenced admissions among women in 1989–90 (Lipinski, 1991). However, by 1995–96, their representation among the female offender population had dropped to 16 per cent (Reed and Morrison, 1997).

Lavigne et al. (1997) also found that Aboriginal women are more likely to be convicted of second degree murder (approximately 50 per cent) as opposed to manslaughter (34 per cent), or first degree murder (11 per cent). As in Blanchette's study, Lavigne et al. found many of the same demographic factors that related to violent female offenders also related to women convicted of homicide. Women who killed usually only killed one person. Most offenders did not live with their victim, although in 18 per cent of the cases the victim was an acquaintance and in 14 per cent the victim was their husband. Strangers only accounted for 7 per cent of their victims, while 15 per cent of the homicides "involved the death of a child in the care of the offender (biological and non-biological)." Perhaps because this study was also exploratory in nature, the authors fail to offer any theoretical explanation or propose any intervention/prevention strategies.

FYI BOX 13.8

Are Aboriginal Women More Likely to Kill Out of Protection?

Although Aboriginal women commit more violent crimes than non-Aboriginal women, Silverman and Kennedy (1988) found that they are more likely than Caucasian women to defend themselves against violent men and are better at protecting themselves than Caucasian women.

Finally, LaPrairie (1993) reports that not only are Aboriginal women over- represented in the female prison population, but they are more likely to commit violent crimes than non-Aboriginal women. LaPrairie, among others, attributes the increase in Aboriginal women's violent crime to increasing marginalization and a breakdown of traditional cultural norms and values (see Box 13.9). As LaPrairie states, "Aboriginal women offenders are a product of historical socio-economic forces and background factors" (p. 243). However, as important as these social factors are, it is important to understand the extent to which long-term substance abuse, dietary history, and genetic predisposition exacerbate the plight of Aboriginal people. This is a politically sensitive issue that has not yet been explored.

A CLOSER LOOK BOX 13.9

Violence Against Inuit Women

As partial fulfillment of her doctoral thesis, Evelyn Zellerer (1996) examined violence against Inuit women in the Canadian Eastern Arctic (i.e., Baffin Island). She notes that while there is a growing body of literature that examines violence against women, there is a dearth of information on violence against indigenous women or rural women abuse. Adopting an interdisciplinary perspective, Zellerer examined a variety of information between 1992 and 1994. In addition to official statistics, she relied on in-depth interviews and personal observations.

Overall, Zellerer found that Inuit women were the subject of a "startling" amount of violence. She further noted that there are few resources available to such victims, and raises a number of concerns about community-based justice initiatives.

In their review of the literature, Shaw and Dubois (1995) note that in the United States, violent crime is higher among black women and they are more likely to be charged with violent offences than other women. Both American black women and Aboriginal women have been described as being products of "historical socio-economic forces and background factors" that marginalize their opportunities. Hence, both groups must struggle against racial/cultural bias and gender prejudice and often represent the lower social class. Interestingly, Stevens (1997) makes the same observation of the female offender. She notes that such women typically come from impoverished backgrounds, have a history of abuse, and often feel powerless.

Women and Property Crime

"In Canada the first person to be officially condemned to death in 1640, was a French girl, sixteen years old. She was convicted of theft" Carrigan, 1991.

Section III: Contemporary Issues in Canadian Criminology

Property Crime among Women

In 1965, 45.1 per cent of all Canadian women convicted were charged with property-related offences without violence. By 1975 the proportion had risen to 55.5 per cent, and 58.1 per cent by 1985 (Johnson, 1987). However, by 1992 the percentage of total female charges for property-related offences declined to 40.7 per cent (Boritch, 1997).

More specifically, the most common property offence among women is theft. In 1992, women accounted for 66.8 per cent of property-related charges. Most (over 90 per cent) of the charges were for theft under $1,000 and 83 per cent of these were for shoplifting (Ibid). Of this number, 62.7 per cent were convicted of theft (Shaw and Dubois, 1995).

Based on their practical experience while working in the criminal justice system, Adelberg and Currie (1987) note that most of the women were young and poor. Few had finished high school and still fewer had any training for the job market. In addition, the institutions that housed them offered very limited opportunities for upgrading social, educational, and practical skills. Overall, they observe that "women offenders' lives did not seem to improve after coming into contact with the criminal justice system" (Ibid, 13). Furthermore, they noted that the vast majority of Canadians are quite naive about the actual workings of the justice and corrections system.

The general increase in female criminality, and property crime in particular, can be partly explained by the changing patterns of criminal opportunity for women. As noted earlier, Freda Adler (1975) argued that the women's liberation movement would not only help break down barriers to equality between men and women but would also result in increased aggressive criminal behaviour in women. Although a number of subsequent studies supported this view, other studies pointed out that the largest increase in women's offending has been in property crime (see, generally, Shaw and Dubois, 1995).

The increase in property crime has been explained in terms of increased poverty among women. Even though the percentage of women in the labour force has increased steadily since the late 1960s (38 per cent in 1969 to 58 per cent in 1989) women are still disproportionately employed in lower-paid service industry jobs (e.g., clerical and services) (O'Neill, 1994). However, the overall impression in the literature is that no one (conventional) explanation can satisfactorily account for the increase in violent crime. Chunn and Gavigan (1991) suggest changing social attitudes towards prosecuting women may be a viable explanation. On the other hand, Thomas (1993) argues that the changing role of women (e.g., single parents, women working in order to support the family, increased divorce rates, etc.) have added extra stress and subsequently predisposed both men and women to lead more aggressive lives.

Women and White Collar Crime

As more and more women enter the professional work force, it should come as no surprise that women have also been charged with white-collar crimes. Data on women who commit these crimes are very limited. Although there are no specific data on women in the professional workforce, several years ago an American study found that women represented approximately 26 per cent of those charged with white-collar offences. The most common charges against women in this area were embezzlement (41 per cent) and forgery (30 per cent) (U.S. Justice Department, 1987).

Women and white-collar crime is an area that deserves further investigation in criminology. Ogle, Maier-Katin, and Bernard (1995) offer a number of propositions about women that suggest that women's violence and/or crime may be motivated differently from men. Among their propositions, they suggest:

1. Women experience higher stress than men.
2. Women have more blockages on anger-coping mechanisms than men.
3. Women are more likely than men to develop overcontrolling personalities.
4. Women are more likely than men to explode in an episode of extreme uncontrolled violence when experiencing high stress.

Although Southerland, Collins, and Scarborough (1997) argue that these propositions do not appear to apply directly to the workplace they did find that women are more likely to leave the workplace and were more effective in their attempts to commit suicide. They also observed that female offenders were younger than their male counterparts (median age 30 vs. 36 years) and they were more likely to receive shorter prison sentences than men for similar crimes. Overall, however, Daly (1979) reports that in spite of entering into professional positions in increasing numbers, women do not appear to be responding to the opportunities as men do.

In **summary**, as criminology pays increasing attention to the female offender, research indicates that, while not equally represented, more and more women are coming into conflict with the law. Over time they have become more involved in a variety of crimes, including those traditionally thought of as "male crimes" (e.g., crimes of violence and white-collar crimes). Hence, rather than simply focusing on gender-related issues, criminology needs to embrace an integrated and interdisciplinary perspective when trying to understand how and why women become more involved in "non-conventional" crimes. But why are they underrepresented and less criminal than men?

Competing Explanations

Thanks in large part to the feminist movement in the 1970s, researchers have begun to study female crime separately from male crime. It has become politically and socially correct to recognize these differences. Over the years, a number of perspectives have evolved to explain female crime. We will look at four divergent explanatory models, summarized in Figure 13–1.

FIGURE 13–1

PERSPECTIVES ON FEMALE CRIME

THEORIST	BIOLOGICAL/ PHYSICAL CHARACTERISTICS	PSYCHOLOGICAL/ PERSONALITY FLAWS	GENDER ROLE SOCIALIZATION	WOMEN'S LIBERATION	FEMINIST THEORY
Adler 1975			X		
Chesney-Lind '73				X	
Cowie et al. '68	X	X			
Hagen et al. '79			X		
Heidensohn '85					X
Hoffman-Bustamonte '73			X		
Konopka '66		X			
Lombroso 1889	X				
Pollak et al. '61		X			
Schafer '46	X				
Simon '75				X	
Smart '76					X
Steffensmeier '78				X	
Thomas '23		X			

Source: Adapted from S.E. Brown, F-A Esbensen, and G. Geis, (1991:525). *Criminology: Explaining Crime and its Context.* Cincinnati, OH. Anderson Publishing Company.

Biological Positivism

The biological perspective is perhaps the oldest and most controversial perspective. As discussed above, Lombroso was among the first to offer some scientific verification of the biological determinism of female offenders. And while his ideas of being able to differentiate criminal from non-criminals on their physical traits have since been debunked, other researchers have focused on other observable traits. For example, Susan Edwards (cited in Gavigan, 1987) cites literature that supposedly linked female crime to menstruation, menopause, and even to pregnancy and childbirth. Even the Canadian media got mileage out of publishing articles in the 1980s linking pregnancy to crime (Ibid).

Such images reinforced the stereotype that female offenders are not "true" criminals but women who are "sick" at a given point in their life, a condition that predisposes them to commit a crime. Unfortunately, as has been the case with much of the biological research until recently (see Chapters 5 and 8), the research has often been methodologically weak. It is interesting to note that most discussions of any biological link are often limited to Lombroso and many of the earlier studies.

Another commonly cited work is that of **William Thomas** (1923). Although a sociologist, he was influenced by the works of Lombroso and Ferraro. For his research, Thomas relied on case studies of delinquent girls. From these observations, he reasoned that human behaviour was dominated by four key wishes: new experiences, security, response, and recognition. He further contended that the four wishes had a biological basis and are expressed in the form of anger, fear, love, and the desire to gain power or status. Then, based on these assertions, Thomas inferred that women need to give and receive love. Failure to do so often led to immoral acts such as prostitution.

Although it looked like a double standard, Thomas's work had an enduring impact—especially on a male-dominated discipline. And in many respects his efforts to use social and biological factors to explain female delinquency reflect an integrated and interdisciplinary perspective.

Even citing the research of John and Valerie Cowie and Eliot Slater, in 1968, does little to give credibility to the biological perspective. For example, in the classic tradition of Lombroso and Ferraro, the authors claimed that "delinquent girls more often than boys have other forms of impaired health; they are noticed to be oversize, lumpish, uncouth and graceless, with a raised incidence of minor physical defects" (Ibid, 166–167). But as Rosenbaum (1991) notes, they only studied female delinquents who were more than likely to come from troubled homes. They also failed to distinguish between biological variables and cultural variables such as gender, i.e., Cowie et al. neglected to acknowledge any environmental influences.

While such chauvinistic attitudes might still prevail in some circles today, it is obvious that female crime is not restricted to the lower socio-economic class, that female crime is not just restricted to prostitution, or that all female offenders look like men.

Although there is a growing body of literature that links biological traits and/or characteristics to environmental situations that can trigger criminal and deviant behaviour, until researchers and authors begin to pay full attention to such information, biological factors will remain a politically sensitive line of inquiry when it comes to gender-based issues. Fortunately, however, research is being conducted in different disciplines that are slowly finding their way into criminological literature and opening the doors for an integrated and interdisciplinary approach. For example, Kolata (1995) reports that there are measurable brain differences between women and men, which affect behavioural, cognitive, and emotional functioning. Although still in its infancy, a number of researchers have begun to explore the possible interaction of biological and environmental factors and gender differences (see, for example, Raine, Brennan, Farrington, and Mednick (1997)).

Psychological "Flaws"

In 1966, Gisealla Konopka interviewed several hundred delinquent girls who had been sentenced to a Minnesota institution. Relying on the traditional psychological perspective, she sought to identify some pathological traits in the girls. In adopting this approach, Konopka focused on stereotypical traits that might distinguish deviant behaviour from non-deviant behaviour among young girls.

Similar to Thomas's (1923) work, she believed that women have a greater need for love and affection than men. Women who fail to make themselves loveable to men were more likely to experience distrust, fear, loneliness, poor self-image, and come from poor and/or broken homes. She further noted that these traits are less expressive in males, though males also seek them. Konopka concluded that female delinquency is the result of gender instability and an inability to adjust to basic female needs.

Again, although her research was methodologically flawed and her model lacked clear operationalization of fundamental constructs, such as what loneliness is and what constitutes poor homes, her work still attracted considerable attention. Rosenbaum (1991) observed that the double standard of morality and the perpetuation of delinquency among females supposedly being related to individual maladjustment, justified social workers and clinicians treating female delinquents as promiscuous and unloved.

One of the more frequently-cited studies from the sixties that used a psychological approach is Otto Pollak's (1961). He believed that female criminality was more prevalent than was officially recognized because women are better able to deceive men through sexual play-acting and manipulating situations. This assertion is not dissimilar from Farrell's (1993) discussion of why women get treatment for their psychological problems while men commit suicide. For example, nearly two-thirds of female offenders seek psychological help as opposed to one-third of male offenders. But Farrell argues that women may not experience more psychological or emotional disorders because various self-report studies have shown that an "equal number of men and women experience depression"—men just don't seek help for it. It may be that it is simply more socially acceptable for women to appear to suffer more from psychological disorders (Gray, 1992).

Pollak also asserted that the nature of women's social roles (in the sixties, primarily one of housekeeper and caretaker of children) provided them with ample opportunities both to commit crimes and to readily disguise them. As Carol Smart (cited in Rosenbaum, 1991:511) observed, this is hardly an original notion as "it has its origins in the biblical story of Adam and Eve." Pollak also suggested that women do occasionally abuse and neglect their children but that it goes largely unreported—it gets "masked."

Both Konopka and Pollak's work focused on trying to identify female delinquent traits based in individual factors. And in spite of their questionable methodologies and weak theoretical foundation, their findings were embraced by practitioners eager to address the growing concern with female criminality. The merits of their ideas appeared to be reflected in crime data. Female delinquency and female criminality *appeared* to be increasing throughout the twentieth century. And even though some of the increase can be explained as a result of increased awareness, the fact remains that such perceptions contributed little to the understanding or control of female crime. This eventually set the stage for the next wave of theoretical inquiry and explanation—gender-role socialization and women's liberation.

Socialization and Women's Liberation

As noted earlier, the 1970s marked a significant change within criminology and the study of female crime. It was a period in which more women entered the field and a period in which women's liberation became a "tour de force."

Hoffman-Bustamonte (1973) for example, asserted that women and men were socialized differently. Boys were socialized to be tough, to not cry, and fight back when confronted, while girls were socialized to be caring, non-violent, and passive.[6] Hoffman-Bustamonte suggested that since socialization processes are different, girls have less illegitimate opportunities than males, hence the lower female crime rate. But does this mean women have any less propensity for committing crimes?

While Hoffman-Bustamonte's work was instrumental in shifting the focus away from individual traits and *role theory*, it has been described as a starting point for feminist criminology (Rosenbaum, 1991).

A less controversial sociological perspective that has been frequently used is the middle-class value approach. It is premised on the observation that girls have traditionally been brought up to be quiet and well-behaved. They are expected to stay home until old enough to look after themselves. Haslem (1976) points out that such images are entwined with double standards. Boys who date numerous girls, engage in sex, and go out a lot with their friends are considered to be normal while girls engaging in similar behaviour are considered to have "morally fallen." Hence, criminal behaviour among women is seen as a form of rebellion against traditional standards. Or is it that as values and norms change, society has been reluctant to accept role convergence?

In her influential book, Adler (1975) argued that the old stereotypical image of being "pregnant and barefoot in the kitchen" was no longer the dominant way in the 1970s. She suggested that the rise in female crime was related to the emancipation of women. With their newfound freedom, there were more opportunities available to women to commit crimes. Her argument became known as the *liberation hypothesis.* Furthermore, she speculated that with the convergence of gender role expectations, female crime would increasingly resemble male crime.

Official crime statistics seemed to lend support to Adler's assertions, as property crime among women increased significantly in the 1970s. But how much of the increase could be accounted for as a result of increased attention to female crime and how much the manner in which the criminal justice system was responding to female offenders? And has "liberation" created a catch-22? American data show, for example, that between 1970 and 1994, arrests among women for drug abuse grew by 217 per cent (compared to 104 per cent for men), and liquor violations by 22 per cent (FBI, 1994).

Not surprisingly, the work of Adler and others during this period came under fire. Using data from before 1970 and into the 1970s, Steffensmeir (1978) argues that the empirical links between women's liberation and female crime were weak at best. Nevertheless, momentum was gathering and the volume of research directed at women and crime was growing. The movement gained a strong ally in the feminist criminology that blossomed in the 1980s.

Feminist Criminology

In Chapter 8 we noted that the feminist perspective is not a single perspective but can be divided into several different fundamentally different orientations.

The **power-control theory**, developed by Hagan, Simpson, and Gillis (1979) and elaborated on in subsequent studies, gained attention as they suggested that female delinquency was linked to the patriarchal family. They asserted that both mothers and fathers control girls more—both a type of repression and sheltering. Again, this perspective reflects the double standard orientation. As the control is dissipated it creates opportunity in which greater female delinquency can occur.

Although a gender-based theory, it was also one of the first integrated theories of female crime. It combined a Marxist, conflict, and control theory with classicist assumptions about human behaviour. While a commendable effort to combine structural (macro) constructs with individual level (micro) constructs, research evidence has not been favourable. For example, Caspi and his colleagues (1994, 1995) have been conducting a longitudinal study in New Zealand of more than 1,000 children born in 1972 and 1973, and have found no significant difference in the personality and structural indicators suggested by Hagan and his associates. Instead, they found that delinquency among male and female youth corresponded to neuropsychological problems. Such problems could be traced to poor nutrition during pregnancy, birth complications, exposure to lead and other toxic substances—all of which, they suggest, result from issues in the social and family environment of the youths that can be prevented. As promising as their research might appear, Caspi and his associates have not addressed the critical issue of causal order nor have they been able to account for possible spurious relationships. However, they do draw attention to a possible interaction between biological, social, psychological, and environmental elements. Their research, in many respects, can be described as interdisciplinary.

In recent years, feminist criminology has gained considerable influence amongst criminologists. As noted in Chapter 8, the *British Realists* and *post-critical criminologists*, among others, have begun to embrace ideas put forth by feminist criminology. The volume of literature has been prodigious. And as we saw earlier, female offenders, characteristically, are not all that dissimilar from male offenders. For example, as noted earlier, they both tend to come from minority groups, have been brought up in lower socio-economic conditions, are often under-educated, are under-unemployed, have a history of substance abuse themselves and/or in the family, and both predominately commit property-related crimes. However, based on *reported* incidents, female offenders tend more often to be the victims of physical and/or sexual abuse, and/or neglect. Rosenbaum (1991:523) suggests that, for women, the picture of the female offender is one "with survival as her goal."

In **summary**, criminology needs to not only remain sensitive to female crime (and the female victim) but it also needs to explore the differences between male and female crime in the context of an integrated and interdisciplinary perspective, in a balanced manner. Not only must there be a convergence of feminist ideas and criminology but there must be a convergence of interdisciplinary perspectives if we are going to truly understand the differences between female offenders and male offenders. After all, men are still more likely to be victims of violent crime (see Box 13.11) than women and they are still more likely to commit violent crimes.

A CLOSER LOOK BOX 13.11

Fostering a Better Understanding of Gender (In)equality

Few would dispute the fact that the (violent) female offender is still a relative anomaly in criminology. Yet the female offender, and more particularly the female victim, has become the centre of intense research since the 1970s. Nevertheless, in our socially and politically-charged climate, we sometimes neglect to see things in balance. Consider for example:

- Men are sent to fight in wars and women aren't.
- Women live longer then men.
- Women tend to get shorter sentences than men when committing similar crimes and sharing comparable backgrounds (Cose, 1995).
- Women have used PMS as a legal defence while no male offender has ever been able to use elevated testosterone as a defence (Pearson, 1998). Recent discoveries show that women suffering from premenstrual syndrome have neurotransmitters similar to men's (Moir and Jessel, 1997).
- Other than rape, men are the victims of violent crime far more than women (Brott, 1995)
- In 1993–94, over $11 million was allocated to the Canadian Violence Against Women's Commission after the commission released its report. No mention was made of violence perpetrated against men (Asher, 1996).
- In some countries such as England, under the *Infants Act*, a mother cannot be found guilty of murdering her child within the first twelve months of its life. She can only be charged with manslaughter. The rationale underlying the act is that it allows the court to consider a biological basis for possible postnatal depression (Moir and Jessel, 1997).
- Men are more likely to die via suicide, being killed, or assaulted while in prison than are incarcerated female offenders (Leibling, 1998). According to Corrections Canada data for 1997, the profile of the incarcerated female and male offender is similar on such variables as age (20–34) and marital status. Significantly more women (62.9 per cent vs. 53.4 per cent for men) are serving sentences of less than six years. Yet proportionately more women (15.5 per cent) commit murder than men (13.7 per cent).
- In 1997, we spent approximately $78,000 looking after incarcerated women as compared to spending an average of $45,000 to incarcerate an adult male offender.

The above points are not intended to undermine the gravity of violence directed at women today. Rather, it is a plea for a gender transition movement that will foster a better, and objective, understanding between women and men. For as Farrell (1993) and others have observed: "when one gender loses, they both lose."

Summary

This chapter focused on the study of the female offender. We began the chapter by tracing the historical roots of female criminality. It was noted that until the feminist movement little attention had been paid to the female offender. What little research had been done of female offenders tended to view their criminal behaviour as "sick" or morally "bad." However, feminists such as Adler (1975) began to enlighten criminologists and to compel them to take the subject of female crime seriously. We slowly moved away from making sweeping statements about female offenders based on case studies and/or questionable methodologies.

The chapter then described female crime and the female offender. We looked at some of the trends and patterns of female crime, noting that for many types of offences the characteristics of female crime differ from those of men across such variables as age, race, motivation and social class. It was also observed that an increasing number of women are being charged with white-collar offences.

The third section of the chapter explored four of the major theoretical explanations of female crime. It was noted that while they each offer insight into the female offender, criminology must embrace an integrated and interdisciplinary approach in order to understand crime as it relates to gender differences. Collectively, the explanations reflect the relative and evolving nature of female crime and criminologists' efforts to explain it.

In reading this chapter, I hope it has become clear that there have been a number of important changes since the 1970s in the rate at which women commit crimes. There have also been some major shifts in criminology concerning female offenders and how criminologists explain their behaviour. Rosenbaum (1991) observed, for example, that in the 1960s there were less then a dozen studies on female offenders.

Today, hundreds of studies exist and more recently there have been a number of conferences focusing on women and crime. For example, the *First International Conference of Women, Law and Social Control* was held in Mont Gabriel, Quebec in July 1991. There are even journals that deal specifically with female issues and with women in the criminal justice system. For example:[7]

- *Women and Criminal Justice*
- *Canadian Journal of Women and Law*
- *Journal of Women in Culture and Society*
- *International Journal of Women's Studies*
- *Women's Studies*
- *Canadian Woman Studies*
- *Women's Studies: An Interdisciplinary Journal*

The differences between female and male crime rates have important implications for criminology. We have seen that those traditional explanations (e.g., physiology, sociology, psychology, the environment, and the feminist perspective) are unable to adequately account for gender crime rate differences. While there has been an increase in property-related crimes, embezzlement, forgery, and fraud among women, the rate of violent crime has not increased as sharply—although it does get considerably more press.

Future research needs to pay more attention to the plight not only of the female victim but also the female offender. Any such attention, however, should be done in an integrated and interdisciplinary fashion.

Discussion Questions

1. Why is it important to appreciate the history of the female offender?

2. Are female offenders different from male offenders? What are the important differences that need to be considered? How can an interdisciplinary and integrated approach facilitate understanding female crime?

3. Why is female crime increasing? Is it becoming more serious?

4. What areas of female crime deserve further research?

5. Collect at least a dozen articles on women-related crime issues. What is their general focus? What types of crimes are portrayed? What kinds of explanations are offered?

6. Are female offenders "invisible"?

7. Is there a social and cultural bias between the genders? If so, to what extent does it mask our understanding of how criminology and the criminal justice system view female criminality?

Key Concepts

Pedestal effect	chivalry hypothesis
Elizabeth Fry Society	feminist movement
Psychological "flaws"	middle-class value approach
Feminist criminology	power-control theory
Women's movement	

Key Names

C. Lombroso	O. Pollak	F. Adler
R. Simon	L. Neve	W. Thomas
M. Moore	E. Fry (Gurey)	P. Haslem

Weblinks

A scan of such classic links as *Cecil Greek's Criminology* will provide a host of links. Entering any of the key concepts in a search engine will also provide an array of links. Given the social and political sensitivity of gender issues, you may have to exercise some judgement as to the reliability of Internet information. The journals listed above may represent an excellent starting point for further research.

Footnotes

1. A 1999 U.S. Department of Justice report found that nearly 32 per cent of female inmates claimed to have been either physically or sexually abused as compared to 12 to 17 per cent in the general population (Marcoux, 1999).

2. The term refers to certain individuals resembling earlier, less evolved, ancestors.

3. For an overview of the John Howard Society, the male advocacy counterpart to the Elizabeth Fry Society, see Chapter 4.

4. Rosenbaum (1991) offers figures for the United States that suggest that the increase in female crime is a North American phenomenon. Between 1971 and 1985, crime among males arrested increased 6 per cent while for females it increased 37 per cent.

5. For an interesting historical overview of other Canadian women who have killed in ways that could rival Karla Homolka read Frank Anderson's (1997) book *A Dance with Death: Canadian Women on the Gallows 1754–1954*. Aside from covering 49 different cases, he also discusses the various reactions of society and the criminal justice system towards these women.

6. This notion was not new. Lloyd DeMause (1988) observes that these patterns existed thousands of years earlier. In his discussion of childrearing modes, DeMause asserts that even in ancient times, gender-role socialization was not dissimilar from what it is today.

7. For a comprehensive list of references on female offenders see Snell (1997).

CHAPTER 14

Future Directions in Criminology

"It was only gradually, ... that I realized that what is interesting is not necessarily useful."

J.Q. Wilson (1985:56)

Learning Outcomes

After you have completed this chapter, you should be able to:

- Discuss the importance of developing an interdisciplinary and integrated approach to the study of criminology.

- Be cognizant of the dynamic nature of crime and criminality.

- Recognize some of the likely trends in crime and criminological research.

- Appreciate the need to merge criminology and criminal justice issues.

- Discuss the importance of comparative criminology in bridging criminological issues.

Criminologists have a personal stake in the issues they study, publish, and bring to the public's attention. Whether they focus on criminological theory, sociology of law, victimology, or any of the other elements that make up the criminological enterprise, all areas continue to evolve with the ebb and flow of cultural, political, and social trends as well as with the growing body of scientific evidence. However, we must always be careful about what we believe to be true (see Box 14.1).

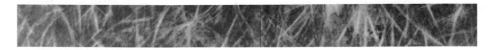

The Fleeting Image of Reality[1]

- "Computers in the future may weigh no more than 1.5 tons." *Popular Mechanics*, 1949.
- "There is no reason anyone would want a computer in their home." Ken Olson, Pres., Chairman and founder of Digital Equipment Corp., 1977.
- "We don't like their sound, and guitar music is on the way out." Decca Recording Co. rejecting the *Beatles*, 1962.
- "I'm glad it'll be Clark Gable who's falling on his face and not Gary Cooper." Gary Cooper on his decision not to take the leading role in *Gone with the Wind*.
- "Stocks have reached what looks like a permanently high plateau." Irving Fisher, Professor of Economics, Yale University, 1929.
- "Louis Pasteur's theory of germs is ridiculous fiction." Pierre Pachet, Professor of Physiology at Toulouse, 1872.

In the chapter-opening quote, Wilson is referring to the gap between what criminologists do and what criminal justice practitioners do. Although they are interested in the subject of crime control they have not always worked in concert. The recommendations each has offered have been as diverse as human nature itself. Criminology lacks the stability of the natural sciences and its research often follows fads that often have short life spans. For example, under the current wave (i.e., late 1990s) of post-positivism and post-modernism (Chapter 8), many of the conventional concepts of the discipline are being challenged. Dragan Milovanovic (1997:5) recently suggested that the modernist conventional views of criminology (e.g., determinism, Newtonian ideas, and adherence to a structural functionalist approach to knowledge) lead him to conclude that the "search for overencompassing theories of society and social development" is fundamentally flawed. He claims the new postmodern paradigm "is neither fatalistic or nihilistic" but is an approach that claims to view knowledge differently and in a way that may hold more promise than the ways we have traditionally studied crime (Ibid, 23).

Throughout this textbook we have examined the subject of criminology and its major elements. We have seen that it is evolving into an interdisciplinary and integrated science. As John Short noted in his 1997 Presidential address to the American Society of Criminology, criminology "cuts across professions as well as disciplines." Similarly, in his 1998 presidential address to the Academy of Criminal Justice Science, Gennaro Vito also called for a merging of the disciplines and for criminal justice and criminology scholars to work towards bridging and integrating their differences.[2]

Throughout the book, it has been suggested that criminology must move beyond its traditional disciplinary biases and "cross boundaries and build new bridges" in order to overcome the challenges that face criminologists. Although the concept of crime has always been dynamic, the challenges that lie ahead are perhaps more exciting than ever. As crime continues to draw wide attention, and as issues of accountability escalate, so will competing philosophies of crime control. Policy-makers will need to work more closely with criminologists. Criminologists, in turn, will have to move beyond their cherished ideologies or favourite policies that have no scientific foundation.

Although I lay no claim to being able to predict the future, in this final chapter, we will examine some of the issues that criminologists will have to contend with. Predicting anything is a risky business. This is especially true in criminology. Crime, being a *relative* and *evolving* construct, presents unique challenges. Notwithstanding these challenges, we will rely on criminology's relatively brief academic history, and its present history, to formulate a number of observations. If we are going to improve our sense of social justice, reduce crime, and improve inequalities, criminology must find a balance between responding to complex human behaviour issues while dealing with the more pragmatic policy-based criminal justice decisions.

Criminology: A Frame of Reference

Repeatedly throughout this textbook we have seen that the ultimate objective of criminology is crime control or the science of controlology—a term coined by Ditton (1979). The objective and rationale is to maximize the quality of life for the greatest number in society—the *utilitarian* principle. However, as has been noted, this textbook and others that espouse an integrated and interdisciplinary approach struggle with how best to address the issue of crime control and/or social order. Until recently, there have been three basic approaches to crime control: conservative, liberal, and radical (Conklin, 1998). More recently, the integrated and interdisciplinary approach has been drawing attention. Therefore, we will briefly summarize its key principles as well.

The **conservative approach**, as discussed in more general terms in Chapter 4, emphasizes:

- Preserving the status quo from criminals;
- Focusing on conventional crimes;
- Attributing crime to the lower and middle classes;
- Focusing on improving family values;
- The legitimacy of the legal order;
- Placing an emphasis on incarceration and just deserts;

- Larger and less restrained police force; and
- Compromising individual freedoms in the name of social control.

One of the critical questions that the conservatives must grapple with is laws that are not "humanistic" in their intent (bridging cultural and scientific knowledge) but are political and power-based. With the conceptualization of law being increasingly driven by the latter, it is "becoming an instrument of utility, removed from its proximity to the cultural institutions" (Christie, 1996:182). For example, Christie (1996), among others, argues that as an instrument of social control, the law is becoming more political than scientific. In the process it is losing its roots in the "core area of human experience" (Ibid,182). However, as evidenced throughout this textbook, relying on the law to control the crime problem has not been very effective.

The **liberal approach**, as discussed in more general terms in Chapter 4, emphasizes:

- Crime control is possible by addressing the underlying causes;
- Criminal activity is the result of social and economic circumstances;
- A labelling and/or interactionist approach;
- Lack of opportunity for certain groups increases the probability of crime occurring;
- Placing an emphasis on social reform through vocational training, social assistance, job creation, and community involvement. Liberals tend to focus on conventional crimes; and
- Placing an emphasis on treatment and rehabilitation as the means to crime control.

Although the liberal approach has received considerable attention and support in the past thirty years, its struggle to account for anti-crime policies has been only marginally successful and its search for crime causation has been wanting.

The radical approach, also generally discussed in Chapter 8, emphasizes:

- Focusing on crime by both the lower classes and the upper-class/white-collar groups;
- Relying on unofficial sources (e.g., self-report and victimization surveys) to indicate that crime can be found across all social classes;
- An anti-establishment view of social order;
- That crime problems are ultimately a reflection of media hype, competing interest groups, and recording patterns;
- Viewing competition (i.e., capitalism) as an underlying motivator of crime, and focusing on non-conventional crime (e.g., political crime, white-collar crime, and corruption);

- Shifting the focus from the offender to the system; and
- Conklin (1998:530) notes that radicals offer few specific solutions to the crime problem, other than calling for the construction of a new and fundamentally different social system. Other critics have been less conciliatory. For example, Klockar (1980 cited in Fattah, 1997:296) described radical criminology as "poor scholarship, embarrassing empirical failures, for their strident moral and political imperialism."

Finally, the integrated and **interdisciplinary approach** views crime as:

- A product of human behaviour;
- An interaction between the individual and the environment (i.e., nature vs. nurture);
- An individual is characterized by his or her genetic and biological traits and attributes (i.e., determinism vs. free will); and
- An interdisciplinary approach adapts a "soft-deterministic"[3] approach to the study of human behaviour (i.e., objective vs. subjective).

The integrated and interdisciplinary attempt to reconcile differences between the previous three approaches is a tall order—to say the least! However, as stated in previous chapters, we can only overcome the fragmentation in criminology by embracing this relatively new approach. This will require the bridging of the varieties of the *criminological enterprises* (Chapter 1) and being interdisciplinary in how we view crime. Yet, admittedly, this approach will undergo its share of growing pains as reflected in Chapter 8 and the range of emerging integrated and interdisciplinary theories.

Although the divisions of the above perspectives risk being too simplistic, each view emphasizes a different way to interpret crime and offer different strategies of crime control. It is no small challenge for criminologists to choose which camp to align themselves with. It is perhaps an even bigger challenge for those who administer justice and legislate criminal policy.

Inevitably, choosing one perspective over another will carry a price. While social control is an inherent element of criminology and a facet of political life, criminology must build a model of social control that respects people's sense of freedom and dignity. The interdisciplinary approach represents one such approach. However, it still requires refinement. It remains to be seen whether criminology becomes interdisciplinary and whether the agents of the criminal justice system will be able to move from a legalistic/classical approach to a more scientific and humanistically-based discipline. There are signs, however, that criminology has started to evolve in this direction. One such example occurred at the forty-ninth Annual American Society of Criminology meetings in 1997. John King (1997), in discussing the new Caribbean Criminology Association, suggests that greater cooperation among criminologists and criminal justice practitioners is needed if we are to address the growing international nature of crime, not just in the Caribbean but worldwide.

Criminology and Prediction

As noted at various points throughout this book, the need to integrate science and law is gaining an increasing following. However, is this necessarily the "right" path to follow?

It is easy to be critical of existing events, theory, and social policy. However, it is an unenviable task to try to offer constructive insights. For example, many criminologists have espoused great policy recommendations only to find they have met with limited success. Perhaps the most infamous of these ideas came from the work of Robert Martinson (1974) and his colleagues, who suggested in the 1970s that "nothing works" in the correctional arena. While there was general sentiment to support his conclusions, we know today that his conclusion was not just an overstatement but one which had an enduring impact on how criminologists viewed crime and crime control. In many respects, it marked the end of an era of conservatism and a return to a model of retribution and theories that focused on social structures as representing the underlying causes of criminality. It was also marked by the growth of *critical criminology, radical criminology, feminist criminology,* and *structural criminology* (see, generally, Chapter 8). Criminologists became agents for social change—a mantle that some may be carrying with reservations.

Criminology is a dynamic discipline and human behaviour perhaps the most complex of the phenomena it must understand. However, if Charles H. Cooley (the father of sociology in the United States) was correct when he said that all human beings have a common ground (in that we all share the same basic human experiences), why then has it been so difficult to explain and control criminal behaviour? Do we not all share a common "gut" feeling of right and wrong, "and some common basis for sensing when impossible conflicts arise" (Christie, 1996:179)?

As elusive at it appears to be, crime control will likely continue to occupy a prominent place in academia and in society at large. Universally, we value freedom and life. As long as we continue to do so, deviance and crime will remain focal concerns. The challenge for criminologists is how to best approach a concern that is enveloped in cultural, political, and social concerns. As in the past, in the future the theoretical and practical direction criminology takes will follow the prevailing intellectual climate. However, as already mentioned, with increasing public and political awareness, criminology will need to undergo fundamental paradigm and theoretical shifts. In addition to adopting an interdisciplinary perspective, criminology will also need to embrace an integrated approach that pays increasing attention to comparative criminological research.

Comparative Criminology

Until recently, the idea of engaging in comparative criminological research was met with varying support at best. It was suggested that language barriers, definition barriers, reporting and recording practices, and administrative variations interfere with the ability to do comparative research (see Winterdyk, 1997). It was thought that these, along with other barriers, simply resulted in fragmented knowledge. However, with advances in technology and methodology, international and comparative research of criminological issues has become a major area of study (see Box 14.2). Nevertheless, Reichel (1994:19) cautions that even though comparative criminal justice is a "synthetic scheme,"[4] it serves an essential role in classifying and presenting information in a way that allows for constructive comparisons. This can be evidenced by the growing number of textbook and academic journals that adopt such an approach (generally, see Bernie and Hill, 1991).

A CLOSER LOOK BOX 14.2

Helping To Make a Positive Change

The Canadian Foundation for the Americas is part of *The International Centre for Criminal Law Reform and Criminal Justice Policy*. In response to the problems of civil war and social and political unrest in Latin America and the Caribbean, the Foundation has provided assistance by providing expertise in crime prevention and criminal justice programs. The Foundation promotes cooperation between governments, and through such agencies as *Canadian International Development Agency* (CIDA), funds have been directed to building bridges that encourage international participation in decision-making. As Dandurand and Paris-Steffens (1997:27) have noted, our support has been described as "lepid," yet at least it represents a constructive effort.

The criminology program at the University of Montreal has also been involved in international (especially with Europe) and comparative research projects for many years. However, because of language barriers (most of the work is produced in French) their work is not generally known to English-speaking Canadian scholars. In addition, the Canadian International Centre for the Prevention of Crime is located in Montreal.

In spite of its historical antecedents, North American criminologists have been slow to embrace a comparative approach. Fattah (1997:303), for example, notes that the words comparative research or comparative criminology "hardly appear in any of the subject indexes of American textbooks in criminology." The vacuum in criminology is largely due to the "provincial attitudes" among North American criminologists and criminal justice officials. In a 1996 chapter contribution, Hackler asserts that "many anglophones still complacently assume that their legal systems are superior to others," when in fact they are "now inferior to those in most of the developed world" (p. 258). In examining the juvenile justice systems in Australia, France, and Fiji, Hackler (1996) suggests that some of their practices deserve to be examined by such countries as Canada. He notes that our young offender system is fraught with political inefficiency that is not in the best interests of young offenders. For example, in France, youths cannot be detained for more than one night, judges must undergo special training to work with young offenders, and a greater emphasis is placed on re-education than on punishment. French judges prefer a less scientific approach to assess the guilt or innocence of a youth. In addition, French judges are well informed about their cases and effectively apply their *inquisitorial* model to assess the circumstances surrounding a youth's behaviour. In many respects, the French juvenile justice system is similar to the principles of *restorative* justice, rather than the *retributive* justice that characterizes the Canadian system.

Not only is the demographic composition of Canada changing, so is the nature of crime. As Canada becomes more multi-cultural and multi-ethnic, it becomes increasingly important to understand how these cultural differences influence crime and criminal trends. For example, home invasions and drive-by shootings were virtually unknown to Canadians until the 1980s. Along with the influx of new immigrants, we are experiencing new forms of **transnational crimes** (see Chapter 10). The price of globalization has brought many benefits to Canada but it has also introduced many new forms of crime that are best dealt with from an international and comparative perspective.

Canadians are not the only ones who can benefit from a comparative approach. Kuhn (1997) reports that even though the number of inmates in the United States more than tripled between 1978 and 1994, the rates of incarceration in some European countries (e.g., Austria, Finland, and Germany) have decreased since the mid-1970s. This has been accomplished largely through the use of alternative programs, with no significant increases in the official crime rates. Such findings should excite criminologists and criminal justice officials and encourage them to examine how these countries are able to create such trends. Only through cross-national and cross-cultural research that attempt to marry theory and practice will it be possible to learn about such programs.

In his informative account of the mystical international police association *Interpol*, Fooner (1989) points out that criminal justice and public safety policy need to focus on an international approach. Global crime is already a reality and criminologists and criminal justice agencies have been slow to respond. Fooner (1989) suggests that the professional community and institutions of higher learning have ignored international issues. He states "there is a large gap in our understanding of the nature of crime in our society ... and a deficiency in our capacity for coping with the hazards" (p. 179).

Today, 150 nations belong to Interpol. Canada joined in 1949. The RCMP serves as a link to the collection of documents and information pertaining to international law enforcement, and forwards the information to Interpol (McKeena, 1998). Interpol Canada played a key role in the 1996 capture of Albert Walker. Before fleeing to England, Walker had defrauded his Canadian clients of millions of dollars while posing as a financial advisor in Paris, Ontario. Interpol also helped to nab Blair Down, whose real estate scams and lottery tele-marketing operations in the late 1990s rival the notorious crimes in our land.

Until criminologists begin to work towards an international or "global" perspective in explaining, describing and predicting crime and criminality, and understanding foreign criminal justice and legal systems, transnational and international crime activity will continue to expand.

In recent years, there has been a groundswell of researchers venturing into the arena of comparative criminology. And while it is gaining acceptance as part of the criminological enterprise, scholars such as Nowak (1989 cited in Oyen, 1992:8) point out that in addition to providing descriptive comparisons of criminological concepts and criminal justice issues, such studies need to ground themselves in some type of theoretical framework. Until criminology can bridge this gap, comparative and/or cross-cultural studies will likely be limited to titillating ideas and academic rhetoric.

At the Commonwealth Finance Ministers' annual meeting in 1996, a number of legal strategies were proposed to counter the expanding international problem of money laundering. It was noted that current estimates place money laundering practices at $500 billion. In an effort to curb such trends, Switzerland has proposed reporting suspicious transactions to authorities while Australia, Canada, and United States already have such practices in place. Germany has extended police powers, including phone tapping, while Great Britain has set up a separate police unit for money laundering (*CJ Europe*, 1996: Nov./Dec., 6).

Although these are commendable steps that forge international cooperation, it is unlikely that such measures will deter at the level of sophistication being employed by many organized crime groups.[5] Laws alone cannot ensure compliance with social values and norms. Instead, criminology needs to understand the root causes of these behaviours rather than focusing on the acts per se. An interdisciplinary and comparative approach can provide the venue for such inquiries.

In the mid-1980s, the United Nations tried to develop guidelines for the administration of juvenile justice. The "Standard Minimum Rules for the Administration of Juvenile Justice," more commonly referred to as "the Beijing Rules" (see Box 14.3) reflect the *welfare* model advocated by the UN. However, as several researchers have noted, few countries have tried to incorporate the model or the guidelines. In fact, in 1998, Justice Minister Anne McLellan reported that the government was planning to toughen the *Young Offenders Act* by introducing a new act which would be called the *Youth Criminal Justice Act*. This represents a break from the United Nations Convention on the Rights of the Child, of which Canada was a signatory member. (Bronskill and Bryden, 1998).

A CLOSER LOOK BOX 14.3

Highlights of "the Beijing Rules" (1984)

- *Fundamental perspectives:* 1.1 To further the well-being of the juvenile and her or his family; 1.2 To develop conditions that will ensure a meaningful life in the community for the juvenile; 1.4 Administration of juvenile justice should represent an integral part of the natural development process of each country.
- *Age of responsibility:* 4.1 The beginning age shall not be fixed at too low an age level, bearing in mind the facts of emotional, mental, and intellectual maturity.
- *Aim of juvenile justice:* 5.1 Emphasize the well-being of the juvenile and shall ensure that any reaction to juvenile offenders shall always be in proportion to the circumstances of both the offender and the offence.
- *Scope of discretion:* 6.2 Efforts made to ensure sufficient accountability at all stages and levels in the exercise of any such direction.
- *Protection of privacy:* 8.1 Right to privacy shall be protected at all stages in order to avoid harm being caused by undue publicity or by the process of labeling. 8.2 No information that may lead to the identification of a juvenile offender shall be published.

Source: Adapted from J. Winterdyk (1997: viii).

Nevertheless, we can identify three reasons why criminology should engage in cross-national and cross-cultural studies.

- "To benefit from the experience of others;
- To broaden our understanding of different cultures and approaches to problems; and
- To help us deal with international crime problems such as terrorism and drug smuggling" (Fairchild, 1993:3).

Comparative criminology is driven by substantive problems of crime, social control, and crime control. Borrowing from Robert K. Merton's notion that we should abandon the quest for an all-encompassing theory, comparative criminology may force criminology to deal with "theories of the middle range." As Merton notes "our task today is to develop *special* theories, applicable to limited ranges of data—theories, for example of deviant behavior, or the flow of power from generation to generation, or the unseen ways in which personal influence is exercised" (cited in Wallace and Wolf, 1995:56).

Finally, at the 1995 United Nations Crime Prevention and Criminal Justice meetings, Coldren (1995:10) emphasized the need "to rely on the best thinkers in the world and to share our ideas and experience with our colleagues because we can all benefit from such efforts." It is perhaps realistic to speculate that comparative criminology will play a primary role in leading criminology out of the ideological approach that has dominated it and into the interdisciplinary model.

The Knowledge Explosion in Criminology

"This is the bitterest pain among men, to have much knowledge but no power."
Herodotus (c. 485-425 BC).

As with many areas of interest today, criminology is an expansive discipline. In Chapter 1, we discussed the six important elements that make up the criminological enterprise. Its expansiveness is also evidenced by the growing number of journals (see Appendix 2) that criminology has available to it nationally, internationally, and in other disciplines. The number of criminology textbooks on the market, and even the number of true crime novels, lend credence to the perception that crime is a serious topic. At the 1997 American Society of Criminology Conference there were over 400 different sessions over the four-day meetings. It was impossible to attend them all. Criminology has not always been this way.

In the early part of this century, criminology was dominated largely by sociologists and in particular a small group who were based out of the University of Chicago—known more generally as the **Chicago School** (Chapter 7). After WW II, the study of criminology expanded into the disciplines of psychology, geography, and biology, and even economics and political science. Slowly, criminology became a growth industry with many competing perspectives. Today, it is nearly impossible to master criminological knowledge. Although there is no shortage of criminological theories (see Chapters 5-8), and although these theories have been dominated by sociological and psychological perspectives, no one theoretical orientation has prevailed. They seem to compete for a small part in explaining criminological phenomena. In fact, in recent years a growing number of criminologists has commented on the growing diversity of criminological thought and its general lack of soundness. For example, as Henry (1990 cited in Einstadter and Henry, 1995:297) said in their evaluation of the "new" postmodernist movement within criminology, it "is merely a provisional metaphor, insufficiently developed to merit the grand description 'theory'." Martin Schwartz (cited in Eintadter and Henry, 1995:298), commenting on reading postmodernism, is even more forceful in saying, "I really do not know what the hell they are talking about."

The debate as to the soundness of criminological theory appears to have reached new heights in the 1990s. Yet a number of criminologists have suggested that a number of "scientific" theories in criminology are often based on untested assumptions and therefore these "theories" are reduced to the status of myths. Similarly, Matthews and Young (1986:1) noted that criminological theory is in a state of "theoretical bankruptcy." Such dilemmas pose a major hurdle for criminology because evaluation and policy-making must often rely on "informed" opinion. However, our vast resources, high-technology communication and information dissemination seem to have complicated the process of criminological study rather than expedited it (see below). There always seems to be something else to consider.

In the 1960s and 1970s, there were but a handful of introductory criminology textbooks, usually written by sociologists. Today, their numbers have increased and individuals from a variety of disciplinary backgrounds have written them. It has become increasingly difficult to convey the "essential" information to students in a rapidly changing world. While the general concept of crime remains constant, its meaning continues to shift. Criminologists must grapple with these issues when deciding what topics need to be studied, how they should be studied, from what perspective they should be examined, and what objective they hope to attain. As discussed in Chapter 1, "doing" criminology can involve aggregate data research, experimental research, longitudinal research, and/or survey research. The intent of the varied techniques is to measure the nature and extent of criminal behaviour. Each technique has its strengths and weaknesses, not to mention its methodological (e.g., evaluation designs and appropriate control or comparison groups) and ethical issues. Hence, we return to the plea for criminology to become an interdisciplinary science. As such, it must move beyond its dependency on law, psychology, sociology, and other "soft" sciences and integrate the hard sciences (e.g., biology, genetics, mathematics and physics).

A review of international criminology journals reveals that while there may be a plea among some criminologists for an integrated, interdisciplinary and comparative approach, a survey of citations in major international criminology journals suggests otherwise (Cohn and Farrington, 1998). Each country tends to reflect a provincial bias for "homegrown" criminologists. And while this is to be expected, students should be sensitive to the trend and encouraged to review other major criminological journals (see Appendix 2) if they wish to obtain an international perspective and draw comparative analyses.

The exception to the publication trend was the *Canadian Journal of Criminology*. As suggested in Chapter 1 and reflected in Appendix 4, Canadian criminologists have been slow in forging their own identity. Of the four journals, the Canadian journal was the only international journal in which the two most frequently-cited authors (Murray Strauss and Anthony Doob) do *not* live in Canada.

It is interesting to observe that the list of names in the *Canadian Journal of Criminology* conduct research primarily in the area of young offenders and/or family violence issues. In the United States the focus is more on social control theory and the general theory of crime (see Chapter 7). In England, there is a split between crime prevention and British realism theory (Chapter 8) and the focus in Australia has evolved around restorative-based issues and reintegrative practices.

Overall, Cohn and Farrington (1998) observe that the five most frequently-cited scholars[6] across the four major journals tended to focus on criminological theories, while the most frequently-cited scholars between 1986-90 were more concerned with criminal career research and measuring crime. Their findings point to the relative and evolving nature of criminology.

Charles Tittle (1997:101) has cautioned that while theoretical integration is the most useful approach for criminologists interested in improving their theories, there are a number of limitations that still need to be resolved: "(1) the necessity for compatible dependent variables, (2) agreement on the purpose and nature of theory, (3) difficulty in articulating interconnections of parts, and (4) inadequacy of data for checking out problematic elements." Even though his points have considerable merit, the overriding benefit of adopting an integrated and interdisciplinary approach is that it is more likely to enable a more realistic examination of crime. And as the explanatory models evolve it is hoped they will become more robust as we develop theoretical and methodological strategies that bridge the current gaps.

As noted scholars such as Don Gibbons (1992) and James Q. Wilson (1975) have observed, thinking about crime is hard work and serious business. Not only must we deal with a complex world in which crime is prevalent, but we must realize that crime is only one part of the complexity of human behaviour. In his preface, Gibbons (1992) boldly asserts that after six tries (i.e., his sixth edition), he believes that he "is finally getting it right"—writing an introductory criminology textbook! Well, perhaps I can find consolation in such a statement and excuse any less-than-perfect coverage in this first edition. As souls, we are all here to learn and it is a never-ending process. Once we have attained absolute knowledge then perhaps the need for the vices that plague humanity will cease to exist. Until then, perhaps it is more prudent to agree with Milovanic (1997:207) that criminology "is a perpetually unfinished project." Only when we are free of crime and the fear of crime will I feel that we have gotten it right.

The knowledge explosion in criminology has been both a blessing and a curse for criminologists. While it has helped to create an identity and an image of importance, the knowledge explosion also reinforces the old adage "the more we know the more we realize how little we know." This is a sobering thought—or at least should be for anyone interested in the study of crime and/or deviance, let alone human behaviour.

Criminologists must realize and accept the limits of their knowledge. They must learn to accept slow and perhaps painful growth in their understanding of criminal behaviour. They must also explore, with great care, the interdisciplinary nature of people's behaviour in relation to themselves and the world around them. A simple challenge, but one we have not yet come close to mastering. As Einstadter and Henry (1995:318), among many others, have noted: "there are no simple explanations; there are no simple solutions. Complexity is the nature of social science." Yet Akers (1994:194) reminds us that "opinion in criminology favors the search for parsimonious, empirically valid integrated explanations of crime and criminal justice." Even so, what direction an integrated approach will take (or should take) has not been resolved. Furthermore, how we might consolidate all the criminological information also remains a puzzle.

Criminology, as a discipline, has evolved considerably from the time Toppinard first coined the term *criminology* in the late 1800s. The ensuing years have seen criminology progress through a wide range of perspectives, much of them based on "faulty" assumptions about the causes of crime. Consequently, the recommendations for crime control were also misguided. For example, in Chapter 9, we saw that with the exception of a few short periods in Canadian history, the crime rate has steadily increased among both adults and youth. While some of the increases can be explained (e.g., shifting demographics), the explanations cannot account for all the increases or all types of crime.

Today, criminologists not only have a vast array of academic journals devoted to criminological topics available, but the Internet and its powerful search engines to provide access to information on many levels. For example, it has been an interesting exercise for students to follow such high profile cases as those of Guy Paul Morin, Paul Bernardo, Lisa Neve, Stan Faulder, Albert Walker, the Truth and Reconciliation Commission in South Africa, the devastation of the Amazon rainforest (environmental crime), the Clinton impeachment proceedings, and the genocide in Kosovo. On the other hand, it is not always possible to evaluate the accuracy of the information. Furthermore, these sources cannot answer the pertinent question, "what does it mean?"

As you have gathered from reading earlier chapters, whether it is break and enter, corporate crime, or public order crime, criminologists have accomplished little more than being able to describe the nature of many of these crimes. The number of competing interpretations and explanations can appear overwhelming. The challenge will be for criminology to uniformly recognize that the causes of crime and criminality are linked to a number of interrelated variables— *multicausality,* which, in addition to requiring an integrated and interdisciplinary approach, also requires the use of sophisticated statistical and research techniques to figure out their meaning.

This textbook has attempted, where possible, to draw these parallels. However, given the relative infancy of this perspective, there is still considerable room for refinement.

The Future and Crime

While all crimes can be classified into either property-related or personal-type offences, they have taken many different forms. We are truly a creative, innovative and adapting species. As the saying goes, "where there is a will there is a way." Nevertheless, many traditional crimes (e.g., break and enter, fraud, murder, and theft) persist today and will likely continue to do so for centuries to come. The new emerging forms will pose additional challenges to criminology.

Fattah (1997:286) expresses the belief that the invention of the automobile is "the most important single factor responsible for the fundamental changes in the nature of crime in the 20th century." Yet he points out that very few criminologists study the role the "car has played in transforming many types of crime and in producing new forms of criminality" (Ibid). While Fattah's observation deserves consideration, similar arguments could be made for the introduction/invention of the monetary system, airplanes, computers, credit cards, radios, telephones, and a wide variety of other technologies introduced that have improved the quality of life. With each new technological advance someone has found a way to illegally capitalize on it. A story that garnered national attention in 1998 was the sudden increase in debit card fraud. Daw (1998) reports that between 1996 and 1997 debit card fraud increased between 60 and 80 per cent. Daw points out that most Canadian banks "still lack the necessary computer systems to monitor unusual account activity with debit cards." Daw also observed that this new crime wave has been made possible by the increasing number of people using debit cards and not properly protecting their access codes.[7] The new inventions have changed the nature of criminal enterprises, influenced how we deliver criminal justice services, and how we respond to crime.

As we enter the twenty-first century, few would dispute the suggestion that crime and criminality will continue to evolve. Among the areas that *may* pose increasing challenges for criminology and crime control are (also see Box 14.4):

- Computer and other high-tech based crimes;
- International sex trade;
- International trade in human organs;
- Transnationally-based organized crime groups;
- Transnational corporate crime;

- Bio-social factors and crime;
- International terrorism and new forms of terrorist violence—from businesses and government organizations to religious leaders and cyberterrorism; and
- International money laundering, gemstone scams, land sale scams, etc.

FYI BOX 14.4

The Evolving Nature of Crime

The following highlights have been taken from a variety of sources and reflect some of the emerging forms of crime.

- In Bulgaria, one of Europe's least scientifically advanced countries, criminal gangs were writing computer software and selling it abroad with the specific aim of helping hackers break into computers (Moseley, 1995: July/August: 1).
- Organized crime is using its vast financial resources and sophisticated command of technology to launder money, move huge sums around the world in seconds and infiltrate legitimate businesses (Ibid).
- Police are ill-equipped to deal with computer crime which can "occur in 3 milliseconds with a programming code instructing the software to 'erase itself' after the action is executed by the computer" (Ibid, 4).
- In Africa, where many banks are ill-equipped to handle electronic money transfers, organized crime cartels use legitimate "front" companies to launder illicit crime earnings (Ibid).
- Eastern Europe battles a transnational auto theft problem. In 1987, 5,500 stolen cars were reported to police while by 1992 the number had risen to 16,500—an increase of 300 per cent (*CJ Europe,* 1996: Nov./Dec.).
- Militant groups are spreading internationally. For example, unofficial counts of Neo-Nazi skinheads range from 5,000 in Germany, to 4,000 each in Hungary and Czechoslovakia, 3,500 in the United States, 2,500 in Poland, 1,500 each in United Kingdom, and Brazil, 1,000 in Sweden, and 500 each in France, Switzerland, and Canada (*CJ Europe,* 1996: Nov./Dec.).

What forms these crimes will take, assuming they emerge as major concerns, poses an even bigger challenge for criminologists. It will become even more important for criminologists to develop theoretical understandings that transcend cultural, gender, and political boundaries. Although it has been argued that only an integrated and interdisciplinary perspective will be able to shed light on these new trends, that perspective also continues to evolve.

In addition, it is interesting to speculate whether the new forms of crime will cease to exist if we can identify the underlying causes of the "traditional" forms of crime. Our current practice of theory development often reflects the social and political trends within society. Furthermore, as Williams and McShane

(1994) have noted, the number of theories in criminology can be overwhelming for students. The number of theories is in part a reflection of the complex nature of crime and criminality. As they conclude, "contemporary criminology is now fermenting nicely" (Ibid, 266).

The conventional trend of theory development seems little more than criminologists trying to develop a "better mousetrap" as each successive paradigm (especially from the traditional theoretical perspectives) is found wanting or is little more than a variation on an old theme. While the exact direction criminological theory takes may be in doubt, it does appear that we are on the verge of a paradigm revolution. One thing seems certain. The twenty-first century will be an exciting time for criminology as it continues to determine whether prevention or punishment is the most effective means of crime and social control.

Social Control: Prevention or Punishment?

Consider the following facts from the Canadian International Centre for Crime Prevention in Montreal, in 1997:

- In Canada, Australia, the Netherlands, and the United States, the cost of crime accounts for more than 5 per cent of the Gross Domestic Product.[8]

- An international survey of seven countries, including Canada, shows that the average citizen pays $200 for police, courts, and prisons, $400 for the shattered lives of victims, $100 for private security, and $25 for lost property per year.

- The number of persons incarcerated has risen approximately 10 per cent since 1970.

These and other statistics presented throughout this textbook emphasize the need for governments to find cost-effective ways to control crime.

In Chapter 1, one of the definitions of crime is an offence against individuals and/or society. It was also noted that crime carries a negative connotation. Our primary mode of response has been *retribution* or *revenge* (Chapter 2). Even the notion of treatment implies that criminal behaviour is bad and in need of correction.

In the mid to late 1990s the American government spent $3 billion in state and local crime prevention programs. A team of distinguished criminologists, led by Lawrence W. Sherman, was commissioned to evaluate the effectiveness of these programs in terms of the prevention of crime and the increased protection of society (Chin, 1997).

The authors of the report suggest that effectiveness depends on whether money and resources are being directed at urban areas with concentrated poverty. Sherman and his associates examined five different institutions involved in crime prevention efforts. They included: communities, family-based programs, school programs, policing, and criminal justice system programs. Within each major area they looked at programs that fell within the domain of these areas (Chin, 1997).

Unfortunately, no comparable study has been undertaken in Canada.[9] However, since we share many of the same concerns, a summary of Sherman's findings are presented in Figure 14-1.

FIGURE 14—1

CRIME PREVENTION: WHAT WORKS AND WHAT DOESN'T*

COMMUNITIES

Most programs suffer weak evaluations.

What's promising:

- Gang violence prevention.
- Community-based mentoring.
- After school recreation.

What doen't work:

- Gun buy-back programs.
- Community mobilization (e.g., lobbying against renewal of tavern liquor licenses).

FAMILY-BASED CRIME PREVENTION

What works:

- Early infancy and pre-school visitations.
- Parent training or family therapy for high-risk adolescents and early childhood.

What's promising:

- Battered women's shelters.
- Orders of protection for battered women.

What doesn't work:

- Home visits by police after domestic violence incidents fail to reduce repeat violence.

SCHOOL-BASED PROGRAMS

What works:

- For youth, programs aimed at building capacity to initiate and sustain innovation.
- Clarifying norms of behaviour and ensuring they are consistently enforced in schools.
- For substance abusers, using behaviour modification programs and programs on "thinking skills."

What's promising:

- Use of small groups within a school setting that provide the opportunity for supportive interaction and greater flexibility to students' needs.
- Behaviour modification programs.

What doesn't work:

- Counselling and peer counselling.
- Alternative activities such as recreation and community services for substance abusers.
- Instructional programs focusing on information dissemination, fear arousal, and moral appeal.

POLICING

What works:

- Increased police presence at "hot spots" of crime.
- Proactive arrest, drug testing, drunk driving programs.

What's promising:

- Community policing with community participation.
- Zero tolerance of disorder, if circumstances are justified.
- Problem-oriented policing generally.

What doesn't work:

- Neighbourhood Block Watch.
- Arrest of unemployed suspect for domestic assault.
- Community policing with no clear crime-risk factor focus.

CRIMINAL JUSTICE SYSTEM

What works:

- Rehabilitation programs with particular characteristics.
- Incapacitation of repeat offenders.

What's promising:

- Day fines.
- Juvenile aftercare.
- Drug courts combining both rehabilitation and criminal justice control.

What doesn't work:

- Rehab programs that: use vague, non-directive, unstructured counselling, and/or programs that rely on shock intervention strategies.
- Programs directed at low risk offenders with vague behavioural targets.
- When not combined with rehabilitation programs such as intensive supervision, home confinement, community residential programs, and urine testing.

*Note: For an interesting overview of "special" treatment and rehabilitation programs for young offenders that have varying degrees of success see Romig, Cleland, and Romig (1989: Chapter 5). At the 1997 American Society of Criminology meetings, Canadian criminologist Richard Trembley reported on some preliminary findings in which he suggests that it may be possible to detect future delinquent tendencies by simply watching the overt interactions of babies between the ages of 14–25 months. The more aggressive, the greater the likelihood they will offend.

In a comprehensive study conducted for the American Office of Juvenile Justice and Delinquency and Prevention, it was reported that the "only way to substantially reduce serious and violent offending is through prevention and early intervention with youth who are on paths toward becoming serious violent chronic offenders" (Howell, 1995:6). The report points out that in order to control the growth of violent youth crime it is necessary to recognize that such behaviours are characterized by *multiple risk factors* (e.g., background indicators such as family, school, peers, and neighborhood characteristics). The report also notes that these factors have an interaction effect and are not necessarily linear in their relation to one another. However, the authors of the report further point out that it is possible to have *protective factors*. And while they may only have a minimal impact on a singular basis, collectively they can serve as deterrents to prevent high risk youth from becoming chronic offenders. Protective elements can include family, school, and peer groups, among other factors.

Finally, the study identified three *developmental pathways* young offenders "take to problem behavior and serious, violent, and chronic offending" (Howell, 1995:5). The pathways include the *authority conflict pathway*. At this level delinquency amplifies when stubborn behaviour eventually gives way to authority avoidance (e.g., staying out late, running away from home). The *covert pathway* begins with youths engaging in secretive behaviours and then progressing to overt behaviour such as property damage that may in turn escalate to more serious acts (e.g., break and enter, fraud, and theft). The third model is the *overt pathway.* In this phase, behaviour begins with minor aggression and can progress into more serious violence (e.g., assault and sexual assault).

Howell (1995) notes that approximately 75 per cent of high-risk offenders fit into one or more of these pathways. Along with his colleagues, Howell further observes that their findings lend support to the evidence that only a small proportion (between 6–14 per cent—depending on source cited) of young offenders commit the majority (excess of 70 per cent—varies by age) of serious and violent crimes.

One of their prevention strategies involves the social development model. This strategy is designed to address "target risks in a way that enhances protection" and lead to healthy beliefs and healthy behaviours. An example Howell (1995) refers to is teaching children in the 1980s to "Just Say No" to drugs. A similar initiative in the 1990s is the "Stop the Violence" campaign. Critical to the success of any such program is the ability of youths to "bond" with the message (Howell, 1995). This involves youths being able to experience a sense of involvement, being able to contribute and/or participate in the campaign, and receiving recognition for their involvement.

Although an impressive study, it reflects the traditional limitations found in explanatory models: limited to integrated sociological and/or psychological factors. For example, the report neglects to examine the role of victims in the implementation of crime prevention initiatives (see Tonry and Farrington, 1995).

A general approach that is capturing the attention of some Canadian scholars is the crime prevention concepts of **opportunity reduction** and **social development** (see Box 14.5).

Opportunity reduction (Chapter 8) is not a new concept but one that has emerged in response to escalating difficulties in the administration of justice and the cry among criminologists for proactive intervention. Opportunity reduction involves such strategies as target hardening (e.g., use of alarm systems, deadbolts, gated communities, increased street lighting, and surveillance equipment). This approach is also referred to as **primary prevention**. The risk of embracing a physical security mentality is the threat it poses to placing humanity into isolated pockets, fearful of all but our immediate friends and family. As Fattah (1997:294) observes, such a move could simply serve to "undermine the social democracy it wishes to protect."

FYI BOX 14.5

- -

Opportunity Reduction as a Means of Crime Control— Crime Prevention

The following points reflect the varied findings about the effectiveness of crime control through opportunity reduction.

- Research from both sides of the Atlantic suggests conventional attempts (i.e., more policing, more laws, longer sentences, etc.) to control and/or reduce crime are not very fruitful (Pease and Litton, 1984).
- In the 1970s, the United Kingdom introduced steering column locks and official statistics showed a noticeable drop in the number of new cars stolen (Ibid).
- After the French introduced closed-circuit television cameras in their supermarkets, they observed a 33 per cent drop in losses (Ibid).
- When the Dutch introduced a law requiring drivers of motorized bicycles to wear helmets, theft of such cycles dropped by one-third (Ibid).
- Cheque frauds dropped significantly after Sweden introduced stricter cheque guarantee regulations.
- Since the 1960s, much of the effort on preventing crime in Canada has focused on crime reduction through law enforcement, corrections, and opportunity reduction (Federation of Canadian..., 1997).
- The Federation promotes opportunity reduction through *social development* (see below).

Secondary prevention, on the other hand, focuses on trying to predict who should be targeted. For example, knowing the relationship between the use of drugs and crime, programs have been developed to educate youth about the hazards of drugs. While these ideas are appealing, Lab (1997) observes that in the future criminologists will need to focus more clearly on which strategies are the most promising. However, will/can such programs work for individuals who demonstrate a propensity for criminal activity? What is the risk of over-predicting?

The final form of opportunity reduction is **tertiary prevention**. This strategy is reserved for individuals who have already violated the law. Although the bulk of criminological and criminal justice efforts have been directed at punishment, rehabilitation, or some other intervention strategy, they have had a dismal track record. It will be interesting to see whether criminology can change its focus to one that is interdisciplinary in its theoretical perspective, and proactive in its objective to reduce crime and fear of crime.

Opportunity reduction means using devices to limit the likelihood of potential victimization. While such strategies may reduce the risk of criminal victimization they provide minimal insight into why someone chooses to commit a crime in the first place. For example, why are some individuals more prone to commit crimes than others, given the same situation, and why are they more prone than others to place themselves in situations that favour criminal activity?

On the other hand, Sacco and Kennedy (1994:317) note that "crime prevention through social development is focused on the serious repeat offender." The literature concurs in observing that approximately six per cent of offenders account for a disproportionately large number of crimes. Yet, in spite of attempts to predict and correct the criminogenic social conditions, traditional approaches have had limited success. Nevertheless, Sacco and Kennedy (1994:317) suggest future success may lie in such strategies as policing "shifting their attention from crime fighting ... to compliance policing, which is more directly integrated into the community." They assert that by involving community participation in defining and solving problems, the social development concept can work (see Box 14.6).

A CLOSER LOOK BOX 14.6

Part of the Solution—Community Policing

Christine Silverberg, chief of the Calgary Police Service, in a two-part series on youth crime in the *Calgary Herald*, publicly offered her assessment of how to solve the youth crime problem in Canadian society. Among the points she made were:

- There is no panacea to the maintenance of order or the problems of crime and disorder.
- There must be an integrated and comprehensive approach to crime control.
- The police must work in concert with governments, institutions, and the community to counter (youth) crime.
- Responding to crime necessitates both traditional and advanced investigative techniques (Silverberg, 1997).

While our ability to control crime may depend on our ability to understand where crime comes from, it appears less realistic that applying the principles of structural functionalism would prove very effective. Such an approach assumes a social system based on linear progression rather than being "composed of inter-locking, intersecting, and interpenetrating relational sets which are in dynamic change" (Milovanic, 1997:196).[10] What prevention efforts have been put in place have had modest success. In fact, a number of years ago, a major survey of 589 prison inmates serving sentences for property crime rated crime prevention policies as poor to no good (Crime prevention ..., 1988). In the future, any social development programs will have to be subject to more rigorous evaluation, larger sample sizes, and clearer operationalization of key terms (Tonry and Farrington, 1995). In addition, as former federal Justice Minister Allan Rock argued, the government needs to free up more money to support efforts by the national Crime Prevention Council. Yet it also was noted in the article that Rock allocated less than one per cent of his department's budget to crime prevention (Alden, 1996). For example, in 1995-96, the direct cost of crime is about $17 billion, of which $9.1 billion (over 50 per cent) went to policing—crime control (Easton and Brantingham, 1998).

In 1994, the newly elected government of the Netherlands decided to take a proactive stance on their growing crime problem by directing $100 million into crime prevention. As part of the initiative, the Dutch Ministry of Justice tested four hypothetical models of crime control. They included: (1) doing nothing, (2) increasing the number of police officers, (3) increasing situational prevention measures and (4) increasing social prevention. While situational prevention had some success, the most effective model involved social prevention. The program has been introduced in four major cities and involves four levels of intervention. They include: providing employment, particularly in the socially disadvantaged groups; improving education and reducing school drop-out rates; improving target hardening for property-related offences; and facilitating the quality of life through promoting inter-racial harmony (Preventing crime within ..., 1997).

Does it work? As of 1998, an evaluation of its impact has not yet been completed. However, similar programs have been initiated in Edmonton where a 41 per cent drop was observed in the number of criminal offences between 1991 and 1995. Meanwhile, in 1989, Toronto introduced a target hardening and social development program that appears to have had some success. Official results have not yet been calculated but the program is being replicated in Brisbane, Australia (International Centre ..., 1997).

Regardless of which crime control strategy one might prefer to follow, criminologists will always have to contend with politics. Whether we choose to follow the punishment model or the crime prevention model in the future, we need to come to terms with the "true" extent of the crime problem. Although a variety of techniques can be used by which to gauge the level of crime, political agendas are often driven by public attitudes. Research has clearly shown that fear of crime levels among the public is disproportionate to the true magnitude of crime. Hence, future techniques must be cognizant of both the real and perceived levels of crime and must be prepared to attack crime in all its aspects. Ekstedt (1995:307) suggests that "policy-making is concerned with competing values and the achievement of social purpose." Criminal policy seeks to effect compromises between basic social values that are in tension (i.e., liberty and security). In other words, crime policy seeks to balance utilitarian principles with those that aim to protect society at large. This is no small task and until recently, criminologists have largely ignored it.

Finally, as our world becomes "smaller," societies will no longer remain homogeneous or mono-cultural. Canada's rate of growth is due primarily to immigration. These cultural changes combined with growing urbanization, ease of travel and communication will add to the "global village" scenario so often talked about in the media.

Criminologists will have to think globally and criminal policy will have to evolve with these trends. These changes will require criminologists to redefine their approach. Currently, criminologists and criminal justice officials continue to be treated, and treat each other, as separate entities. We continue to have separate conferences for each group. Theory and practice (i.e., policy) are often also treated as separate entities and the gap widens between them. Finding the balance between principles of restorative justice, reintegrative **shaming**, and other moral and value-laden programs will require diligent theoretical and methodological attention by criminologists. Such change has been slow in coming.

A recent article on "innovative" incarceration practices in the state of Wisconsin and Maryland noted that inmates will be required to "wear stun belts which fire 50,000 volts through their bodies if they try to escape" (Gordon, 1997:A3). These states are continuing with the program in spite of urging from Amnesty International that such practices represent "cruel and unusual punishment." Gordon (1997) concludes by observing that "shame, hard work and harsh conditions are increasingly seen as part of crime and punishment." Yet, there is no criminological theory to support such notions.

Criminology and Criminal Law

Criminal law plays an important role in maintaining social order and in the study of crime. Yet, historically, the study of crime and the role of criminal law have been treated as an *interdependent* relationship. Since the definition of crime is dependent on its legal definition, any changes in the *Criminal Code* influence what criminologists focus on. What is less clear is how criminal law will evolve in the future.

Norval Morris (1973) suggested that the criminal law of the future would be predominantly administrative as it responds to our increasing "obsession with the right of property." If this is the case, we will also see a shift in social control, from the law focusing on imprisonment to one of compensation and restitution.

Should criminal law make such a shift then the radical view of criminal law being an instrument of the elite would no longer hold true. Instead, criminal law would be designed to protect the values and norms of a higher order of a more universal nature.

Wollan (1980 cited in Fattah, 1997:289) observed that criminology will "become somewhat more concerned for values and, hence, to shift slightly from the empirical, scientific end of the spectrum toward the normative, philosophical end." Given that approximately twenty years have passed since Wollan's observations, it may be optimistic to think that criminology will/can make such a dramatic shift. At best, such views may become a part of the criminal justice network.

It has been noted that criminal law has had a minimal effect in curbing crime trends. In Canada, we now have more than 90,000 laws covering substantive offences while the United States had more than 250,000 such laws. Yet neither system has been able to demonstrate a positive relationship between criminal behaviour and crime control. If anything, it could be argued that criminal law only serves to (artificially) inflate crime statistics (generally, see Goff, 1998).

Criminologists need to recognize this inherent contradiction. Furthermore, with the constant changing nature of crime, current parochial attitudes are no match for the changing forms of crime. Today crime knows no boundaries, but our legal system does.

It is likely that we will see criminal law shift increasingly from a reactive response to law violation to a model wherein criminal law and criminologists focus on promoting observation of the law and crime prevention. This will require criminologists to rethink how they view crime and how they respond to it.

Expanding the Scope of Criminology

The assertion that criminal law will move towards the normative and philosophical end suggested by Wollan is likely to be further hampered by the growth of science and technology as they become a major part of criminology. Criminalistics or forensic science, in particular, is a rapidly growing area.

In a general sense, forensic science is "the application of science to law" (Saferstein, 1998:1). Forensic science offers "the knowledge and technology of science for the definition and enforcement of such laws" (Ibid, 1).

For many the term forensic probably conjures up images of *Quincy, Millennium, Profiler,* or perhaps Sherlock Holmes. In all cases the key actor worked either in crime laboratories or specialized in trying to get into the minds of heinous criminals and was a master at finding clues that linked the criminal to the crime scene.

First launched in January 1995, VICLAS (Violent Crime Linkage Analysis System) represents an attempt by the RCMP to update its computer system for tracking the nation's most serious crimes. In 1997, it was estimated that "roughly 20 serial killers and 200 serial rapists are walking the streets of Canada" (Upgrades to computer ..., 1997).

The system currently holds information on over 17,000 major crimes committed across Canada. VICLAS allows police to cross-reference details of crimes committed across the country. And in an effort to facilitate the process, in 1997, 30 new employees were added to the team. This brings the total number of staff to about 100. That is a lot of resources for a category of crime that accounts for a small percentage of all conventional crimes—let alone non-conventional crimes.

Aside from the practical issues, VICLAS is a classic example of how criminology and the criminal justice system remain more preoccupied with apprehending high profile criminals rather than focusing on petty crime offenders, white-collar, political, and other forms of criminality.

Crime: The Elusive Enigma

In Chapter 9, we learned that crime is very much present in society. Official statistics show us that crime rates have increased since the UCR were introduced in the early 1960s. Furthermore, self-report studies and victimization surveys generally reinforce these observations. However, we also learned that public interest as well as that of the criminal justice system, is as predictable as the weather. Our focus shifts as the media grapple to find news stories to pique our interest. How often now do we hear anything more about Clifford Olson, Paul Bernardo, Karla Homolka, Brian Mulroney, Alan Eagleson, O.J. Simpson, or any other individuals who captured considerable media coverage at one point or another (other than the tabloids perhaps)?

The point is, new social issues appear regularly. And while many of them carry a similar theme (e.g., young offenders, corporate crime, biker gangs, drug abuse, etc.), these stories only reinforce our awareness and remind us of the strong presence of crime in society. As Kappler, Blumberg, and Potter (1990:331) observe, crime waves "become mental filters through which social issues are filtered." They refer to crime problems as *crime myths* since they carry no concrete significance in and of themselves. Rather, they simply feed misconceptions of crime and criminal justice.

For example, we continue to believe that if crime is so serious, then more police officers with high-tech equipment are needed to combat crime. Yet classic studies such as the Kansas City Patrol Study in the 1970s dispelled these myths. All the same, the police continue to argue they need more officers and better technology to fight criminals. Similarly, the evidence strongly indicates that imprisonment of violent offenders is not an effective deterrent. All it does is temporarily remove individuals from society, and recidivism data hardly argue for a continued use of imprisonment. Yet we continue to build new institutions. As for our judicial system, one need only look at the plight of our young people to know that the punishments meted out by the courts are laughable. Furthermore, the most likely losers are minority groups and the lower and middle classes. The winners are white-collar offenders who seldom receive criminal sentences but whose crimes are often more costly to society. The racial issue was recently seen in Nova Scotia. In 1997, the Supreme Court heard a case involving a black Nova Scotia judge who allegedly engaged in "reasonable apprehension of bias" because of race-related comments (Bindman, 1997). In the same article, a Nova Scotia government lawyer conceded that racism is found in both society and the legal system.

The implications of the misconceptions not only help to create and perpetuate myths about crime and criminals but also serve to stymie the introduction of new ideas. So while criminologists struggle try to determine which philosophical orientations best explain and predict criminal behaviour, the criminal justice system continues to rely on antiquated ideas of punishment and treatment.

Perhaps one of the more innovative alternatives to gain momentum in the 1990s is the concept of restorative justice or *communitarianism* as it is sometimes referred to in Sweden (Lindstrom, 1997).

Restorative Justice: A Flickering Candle of Hope[11]

Throughout the textbook, we have seen that criminology and the criminal justice system in general, is in a state of crisis. Despite a decline in the crime rates in the late 1990s, they are still alarmingly high. The criminal justice system is struggling to maintain some sense of social control, public support is waning, and criminological theory is in a state of disrepair. Should we feel a sense of despair? Being an optimist by nature, my answer would be no!

One area of criminological inquiry that is drawing considerable attention in the 1990s is the concept of restorative justice. Throughout most of history, we have adopted a negative approach to crime and applied principles of retribution and revenge to crime control. Our preoccupation with the Hammurabi Code's principle of *lex talionis*, the law of retaliation, "an eye for an eye and a tooth for a tooth," has accomplished little in our efforts to control crime. I was recently told by a retired lawyer friend that in 3,400 years of recorded history we have had only about 265 war-free years. Perhaps it is time to break from the traditional modes of criminological thinking.

One of the champions of an alternative form of justice is Ezzat Fattah. Fattah (1995) presents a list of reasons as to why punishment does not, and never will work (see Box 14.7).

WHAT DO YOU THINK? BOX 14.7

PUNISHMENT—IS THERE EVER A TIME FOR IT?

- *Punishment is ineffective:* The United States sends more people per capita to prison than any other Western country, yet their crime problem shows no serious signs of reversing. China has been executing offenders liberally in an attempt to stem the tide of crime. Singapore's zero tolerance for many crimes is beginning to show signs of faltering. Do we want to embrace such concepts?

- *Punishment is costly:* As noted elsewhere in this book, the financial costs of administering criminal justice have been escalating as a result of inflation, increased number of legal cases to process, and growing prison populations. What social and financial good has ever come of placing an offender in prison? Recidivism rates are a reality in our system. What good does locking up the offender do?

- *Punishment treats human beings as a means to an end:* While punishing someone can have a cathartic effect on the victim and the public, it does little or nothing for the individual being punished. Those who repent and reform are few compared to those who feel degraded, humiliated, and stigmatized in ways that can never be corrected. Is there no better solution? Has our system truly evolved or simply become clouded in "civilized" protocols?

- *Punitive penal sanctions amount to punishing the victim:* Regardless of the etiology one uses to explain criminality there is no logical justification for punishment. When someone falls from grace, we want to punish them. The outcome is that the offender loses and the victim has no real recourse to heal. Is this true justice?

The common link as to why punishment does not work is that the legal system has ignored the victim's rights to heal. Virtually every religion has long since recognized this oversight in the legal system. As Christian moralists have always advocated, an evil deed can always be put right by doing good.

The major principles and philosophy of restorative justice include:

- When a wrong (crime) is committed the offender is obliged to restore the victim, and by extension the community. This involves a shift from moral responsibility to social responsibility.

- The process has strong psychological and sociological underpinnings for the offender. Research has shown that publicly shaming an offender can serve as a powerful tool to re-integrate the individual.

- Retribution focuses on the crime as being a violation of the state while restoration focuses on the crime as being a violation of people. This involves a shift from a guilt orientation to a consequence orientation. Existing programs include VORP (Victim Offender Reconciliation Program), VOM (Victim Offender Mediation), CJJ (Community Justice Circles), RPP (Reparative Probation Program) and in New South Wales, Australia, reintegrative shaming and transformative justice.

- Crime is not an abstraction but an injury and violation to a person and a community that should be repaired. This involves a shift from revenge and retribution to emotional, physical, social, and spiritual restitution.

- The process should respect all parties—victim, offender, and justice colleagues.

Although thought to be a "new" idea, the Mennonites were among the first in North America to formally put restorative principles into practice. However, University of Calgary law professor Chris Levy (1997) has observed that evidence of these principles can also be found in the late 1800s and early 1900s in England, when the government practised a minimalist approach to justice. The community was encouraged to resolve its own disputes before bringing them to court.

Informally, the Aboriginal people of Canada had practised elements of restorative justice for hundreds of years. However, as the Europeans settled and conquered the "new world" they forced the Aboriginal people to give up the ways of their culture, subjecting them to cultural genocide. Today, our criminal justice system bears the scars of our ill-conceived notions. It is now well-documented that Aboriginal people are over-represented in our criminal justice system, the child welfare system, juvenile justice system, unemployment, and drug and alcohol treatment systems (Sinclair, 1994).

Before Aboriginal people were subjected to colonialism, they embraced principles that relied on the community to resolve disputes and emphasized informal social process, reintegrating the offender into the family and community through a gradual restoration of trust and forgiveness. The process is commonly referred to as a *circle sentencing* conference. As Hazelhurst (1996:1-2) noted, "many of these fundamental mechanisms, institutions, social processes and inter-personal skills need to be relearned or regenerated" within the Aboriginal community.

Again, whether or not restorative justice becomes the flavour of the new millennium for criminology will likely be dependent on the nature of social order and the political-economic system. Given the political-economic changes in Canada in the 1990s, not to mention internationally (e.g., the European Community), it does not require a leap of faith to suggest that we are in for some major changes.

Whether we become an advanced capitalist society or whether an economic collapse occurs (e.g., the collapse of Asian economic markets in the late 1990s, the unstable dollar, and instability of precious metals), is still unclear. If we can continue to embrace the evolving character of crime and criminality in this post-modern era, then we may be in for a pleasant surprise, perhaps allowing peace-making and other interdisciplinary paradigms to emerge. However, from a prag-matic perspective, Nicholl (1997) points out that a balance needs to be struck in the gap between the criminal justice system's focus on crime control and the terms of reconciling through conferencing. It also remains to be seen whether there is enough community support to effectively engage in a meaningful process. Nevertheless, the Canadian Criminal Justice Association along with var-ious provincial associations are trying to bridge the gap between theory and prac-tice. In many respects, through the restorative initiatives, we are witnessing an integration of ideas with practice, a break from the history of public policy and theory seldom complementing one another.

Summary

I would like to conclude this chapter with a quote from the philosopher Bertrand Russell (1872-1970). "Three passions, simple but overwhelmingly strong, have governed my life; the longing for love, the search for knowledge, and the unbear-able pity for the suffering of mankind." I would add the search for spiritual growth.

Throughout this textbook, it has been implied that criminology must embrace a systems approach and an interdisciplinary approach to the study of human behaviour and criminological issues. Without a human action (*actus reas*) there can be no crime. While the focus of the textbook has been on the study of crime from a criminological perspective, criminal justice elements and issues have also been interwoven. In an effort to embrace an integrated and interdisciplinary approach it has been argued that much of what criminologists do has, or can have, direct (or indirect) applications to how policy-makers respond to criminals and crime.

In this chapter we addressed some of the issues criminologists will likely have to deal with in the coming years. As a dynamic discipline, criminology has always had its share of challenges. However, it has become more evident than ever in our heterogeneous society that criminologists, while still needing to focus on crime (social) control, need to resolve some long-standing barriers. Criminology must bridge the competing classical school (legalistic) ideas and positivist school (scientific) perspectives of crime causation. Criminology must move toward an integrated and interdisciplinary model of criminology. We must also move beyond our provincial boundaries and embrace cross-cultural and cross-national approaches to studying crime and criminality. Any constructive social policy can only be attained within the context of global social reform.

Crime control is the cornerstone to criminology. In this chapter, it was suggested that criminology must build models that universally respect human freedom and dignity. As Beccaria noted over 300 years ago, it is better to prevent crime than to punish it through means that have consistently been proven not to work. For example, it was suggested that restorative justice might represent one such approach. Criminologists should feel morally and ethically bound to develop a new approach to understand and control criminal behaviour. As the **postmodernists** have said—we need different knowledge and we need knowledge differently.

It is with these objectives in mind that I share the ideas presented in this book. I place the gauntlet before you. As students interested in criminology, you have the opportunity to forge new ideas and new approaches. I hope you will see this book as a stepping stone in our quest to answer the theoretical and practical issues facing criminology. I encourage you to bring criminology into the new millennium, to find the path that will unify criminology in an interdisciplinary fashion and enable it to unravel the challenges facing it.

Discussion Questions

1. Which of the four frames of references do you think is "best" suited to address criminological concerns? Why?

2. Why is it so difficult for criminologists to predict crime and criminal behaviour accurately? How can an integrated and interdisciplinary perspective help improve prediction?

3. What are the barriers to conducting comparative research? What are the advantages for criminology in trying to overcome them?

4. Why has the knowledge explosion been a "blessing and a curse" in our pursuit of finding solutions to crime and in formulating policy? How can we begin to synthesize all this knowledge?

5. What challenges will the crimes of tomorrow present for criminologists? How do they reflect the *relative* and *evolving* nature of crime?

6. Based on your readings, and regardless of what may be in vogue, what do *you* think is the most effective strategy for crime control? With which perspective does it align?

7. Using the concept of restorative justice, what could we do at a local and national level to implement new policies and of social/crime control?

Key Concepts

Frame of reference	conservative approach	liberal approach
Radical approach	interdisciplinary approach	comparative research
Beijing Rules	knowledge explosion	transnational crime
Restorative justice	social development	opportunity reduction
Secondary prevention	primary prevention	tertiary prevention
Postmodernism	shaming	

Weblinks

www.realjustice.org The homepage for the 1998 conference proceedings on "restorative" justice.

www.opc.on.ca/ohcc/communit.htm Ontario's St. Leonard Society homepage. Interesting links and perspectives on restorative justice.

www.crime-prevention.intl.org The Canadian International Centre for the Prevention of Crime based in Montreal.

www.law.ubc.ca/centres/icclr/index.html The International Centre for Criminal Law Reform and Criminal Justice Policy, based in Vancouver.

www.copnet.com A rich site for information on crime trends and issues of the future as well as what is currently being done from a law enforcement perspective.

www.cjprimer.com/circles.htm. Offers an extensive article on restorative justice. It is co-authored by a Canadian and an American criminologist.

www.acsp.uic.edu The homepage for the Office of International Criminal Justice at the University of Illinois at Chicago. An excellent site for seeing what is happening internationally in crime and justice.

Again, there are numerous other informative and interesting links. By simply using some of the key concepts identified above, you will likely find lots of sites.

Footnotes

1. Most of the following points were sent to me by Ron Tuck, a colleague from Australia.

2. A reading of the School of Criminology description on the Internet (www.sfu.ca/criminology/) shows that they describe their objective as the attempt to "study of all aspects of crime through an *integrated* and *interdisciplinary* approach."

3. Arguments for soft-determinism can be found in David Matza's *drift theory* (Chapter 7), Travis Hirschi's *control theory* (Chapter 7), among a variety of other sociological theories. In essence, soft determinism acknowledges that factors in our life serve as predisposing factors that under the "right" conditions may or may not result in criminal or deviant acts.

4. Understanding is based more on observation and description than on analysis of the nature of the subject.

5. For an interesting and insightful read see Howard Marks' autobiography *Mr. Nice* (1997) by Random House.

6. They include Travis Hirschi (US), David Farrington (UK), Michael R. Gottfredson (US), Alfred Blumstein (US), and John Braithwaite (Aus).

7. In one incident, criminals had placed a very small camera in the area of a debit machine that simply recorded people as they entered their pin numbers!

8. Note, in Chapter 1, a 1996 *Fraser Forum* publication noted that the cost of crime as a per-

centage of the GDP for 1994 was 2.3 per cent. Although they admit it was a conservative estimate, the difference reflects the argument that the administration of criminal justice is becoming increasingly expensive.

9. Students might want to check such publications as *Forum* (a publication by Corrections Canada that examines a wide range of programs in the Canadian correctional arena). Back issues of the *Canadian Police College Journal* (it is no longer being published), the *RCMP Gazette*, among others, for police-based programs. The John Howard Society and Elizabeth Fry Society have reports on an array of offender programs. Various religious organizations (e.g., Mennonites and Presbyterian Church) produce publications on the rights of offenders and treatment of offenders. Finally, most criminology departments within Canadian university and some college settings have Web sites where research findings and projects are often posted.

10. This view has spawned a new critical criminological theory that borrows its analogy from physics. It is referred to as the *chaos theory*. In essence, the theory is based on the premise that no two events are ever repeated in exactly the same way (e.g., the two snowflakes analogy). Yet it is supposedly possible to calculate a finite (deterministic) boundary to behaviour.

11. Many of the ideas in this section are drawn from Winterdyk (1998).

References

Abadinsky, H. (1994). *Organized crime* (4th ed.). Chicago: Nelson Hall.

Adams, J. (1976). *Learning and memory: An introduction*. NY: Dorsey Press.

Adams, R. (1973). Differential association and learning principles revisited. *Social Problems*, 20:458–470.

Adams, S. (1998a, January 28). Diet found to play role in attention deficit disorder. *Calgary Herald*, B4.

Adams, S. (1998b, June 17). Taming the demons. *Calgary Herald*, B6.

Adelberg, E., & Currie, C. (1987). *Too few to count*. Vancouver: The Press Gang.

Adler, F. (1975). *Sisters in crime: The rise of the new female criminal*. NY: McGraw-Hill.

Adler, F., Mueller, G.O.W., & Laufer, W.S. (1991). *Criminology*. NY: McGraw-Hill.

Agnew, R., & White, H.R. (1992). An empirical test of general strain theory. *Criminology*, 30:475–499.

Aichorn, A. *Wayward youth*. (1935). NY: Viking Press.

Akdeniz, Y. (1997). *Policing the Internet*. (Online).

Akers, R. (1977). *Deviant behavior: A social learning approach* (2nd ed.). Belmont, CA: Wadsworth.

Akers, R. (1992, September). Linking sociology and its specialties:The case of criminology. *Social Forces*, 1–16.

Akers, R.L. (1994). *Criminological theories: Introduction and evaluation*. Los Angeles, CA: Roxbury.

Akers. R.L, & Brugess, R. (1966). A differential association – Reinforcement theory of criminal behavior. *Social Problems*, 14:128–147.

Akman, D.D., & Normandeau, A. (1967). The measurement of crime and delinquency in Canada. *Criminal Law Quarterly*, 9:323–238.

Albanese, J. (1996). Looking for a new approach to an old problem: The future of obscenity and pornography. In R. Muraskin and A.R. Roberts (Eds.), *Visions for change: crime and justice in the twenty-first century*. Upper Saddle River, NJ: Prentice-Hall, (pp. 60–72).

Albert, S. (1996, March 16). Hanger's cliffhanger. *Calgary Herald*, A3.

Alden, E. (1996, August 26). Rock wants more money to battle crime. *Calgary Herald*, A3.

Alm, R. (1997, December 6). Problem gamblers are on the rise. *Calgary Herald*, A3.

Almodovar, N.J. (1993). *Cop to call girl*. NY: Avon Books.

American Friends Service Committee. (1971). *Struggle for justice*. NY: Hill and Wane.

American Society of Criminology: 49th Annual Meeting. (1997, November 19–22) *Crossing boundaries and building bridges: The discipline and the profession of criminology*. San Diego, CA.

Ancel, M. (1994). Social defence. In J.E. Jacoby (Ed.). *Classics of criminology*. Prospect Height, Ill: Waveland, (Chapter 41).

Anderson, F.W. (1973). *Hanging in Canada: A concise history for a controversial topic*. Calgary: Frontier Books.

Anderson, F.W. (1982). *Bill Miner: Stagecoach and train robberies*. Vancouver: Frontier Books.

Anderson, F.W. (1997). *A dance with death: Canadian women on the gallows 1754–1954*. Fifth House Publishing.

Andrew, D.A., & Bonta, J. (1994). *The psychology of criminal conduct* (2nd ed). Cincinnati, OH: Anderson.

Andrews, D.A., & Bonta, J. (1991). *The psychology of criminal conduct*. Cincinnati, OH: Anderson.

Angelo, B. (1992, April 13). Wanted: A new godfather. *Time*, p. 30.

Arnold, S. (1997, October 17). 36 arrests as major poaching ring busted. *Edmonton Journal*. (Online).

Asian women were forced into prostitution. (1997, September 11). *Calgary Herald*. (Online).

Atkinson, L. (19970. Juvenile justice in Australia. In J. Winterdyk (Ed.), *Comparative juvenile justice*. Toronto: Canadian Scholars Press.

Average hours per week of television viewing, by age and sex, Canada and the provinces, fall 1004. (1004). Statistics Canada. Cat. No. 87–211.

Bachusy, J. (1998, October 24). Stiffer fines sought for workplace deaths. *Calgary Herald*, B1–2.

Badgley Report. (Chair). (1984). *Committee on sexual offences against children and youths*. Ottawa: Supply and Services Canada.

Baldwin, J., & Bottoms, A.E. (1976). *The urban criminal*. London: Tavistock.

Ballard, J.D. (1998, March 10–14). *The Oklahoma City bombing case, the media and public policy on domestic terrorism*. Paper presented at the Academy of Criminal Justice Science 35th Annual Meeting. Albuquerque, NM.

Bandura, A. (1965). Vicarious processes: A case of no-trial learning. In L. Berkowitz (Ed.), *Advances in experimental social psychology*. Vol. 2, NY: Academic Press. (Chapter 1).

Bandura, A. (1979). The social learning perspective mechanisms of aggression. In H. Toch (Ed.), *Psychology of crime and criminal justice*. NY: Holt, Rinehart, & Winston.

Bandura, A., & Walters, R.H. (1959). *Adolescent aggression*. NY: Ronald Press.

Bank Robbery. (1997). (Online general search).

Barak, G. (1998). *Integrating criminologies*. Boston, Mass: Allyn & Bacon.

Barbara, J.S. (1995). *Media violence and real life aggression and militarism*. (Online).

Baring breasts in public not right: Premier. (1996, December 11). *Calgary Herald*. (Online).

Barkan, S.E. (1997). *Criminology: A sociological understanding*. Englewood Cliffs, NJ: Prentice-Hall.

Barkan, S.E., & Cohn, S.F. (1994). "Racial prejudice and support for the death penalty" by whites. *Journal of Research in Crime and Delinquency*, 31: 202–209.

Barnes, A.R., Fisher, D.G., & Dellinger, A.B. (1993). *The value of hair and blood analysis in the identification of manganese*. Annual meeting of the Academy of Criminal Justice Science, Kansas City, Missouri.

Barry, J.V. (1973). Alexander Maconochie. In H. Mannheim (Ed.). *Pioneers in criminology* (2nd ed.). Montclair, NJ: Patterson Smith.

Baskin, D.R., & Sommers, I.B. (1998). *Casualties of community disorder: Women's careers in violent crime*. Boulder, CO: Westview.

Bartol, C.R. (1995). *Criminal behaviour: A psychological approach* (4th ed.). Englewood Cliffs, NJ: Prentice-Hall.

Bavinton, F. (1998). *Hacking: a questionnaire*. (Online: www.arts.unimelb.edu.au/dept/crim/hack/quest.htm).

Beare, M. (1996). Organized crime and money laundering. In R.D. Silverman, J.T. Teevan., & V.F. Sacco (Eds.), *Crime in Canadian society* (5th ed.). Toronto: Harcourt Brace.

Beardsley, T. (1999). For whom did the bell curve toll? *Scientific American*. Vol. 9(4): 30–31.

Beasely, J.D., & Swift, J.J. (1989). *The Kellogg Report*. Annandale-on-Hudson, NY: The Institute of Health Policy and Practice, The Bard College Center.

Beccaria, C. (1963). *On crimes and punishment*. (Trans. Henry Paolucci). Indianapolis, IN: Bobbs-Merrill.

Becker, H.S. (1963). *Outsiders*. NY: The Free Press.

Becker, R.O., & Selden, G. (1985). *The body electric: Electromagnetism and foundation of life*. NY: Quill.

Bedau, H.A. (1996). *Capital punishment*. Microsoft (R) Encarta (R) 96 Encyclopedia.

Belknap, J. (1996). *The invisible woman: Gender, crime, and justice*. Belmont, CA: Wadsworth.

Beneteau, R. (1990). Trends in suicide. In C. McKie & K. Thompson, *Canadian Social Trends*. Toronto: Thompson Educational Pub., pp. 93–97.

Bennett, W.W., and Hess, K.M. (1984). *Investigating arson*. Springfield, Ill: Charles C. Thomas.

Benson, M.L. (1990). Emotions and adjudication: Status degradation ceremonies among white collar criminals. *Justice Quarterly*, 7:515–528.

Benson, M.L., Maakested, W.J., Cullen, F.T., & Geis, G. (1988). District attorneys and corporate crime: Surveying the prosecutorial gatekeepers. *Criminology*, 26:505–518.

Bentham, J. (1789). *An introduction to the principles of morals and legislation*. NY: Kegan Paul. (Reprinted 1948).

Berger, T.R. (1982). *Fragile freedom*. Toronto: Irwin.

Berkowitz, L. (1962). *Aggression: A social-psychological analysis*. NY: McGraw-Hill.

Berman, J., & Siegel, M-H. (1992). *Behind the 8–ball: A guide for families of gamblers*. NY: Simon and Schuster.

Bernard, T. (1987). Control criticisms of strain theories: An assessment of theoretical and empirical adequacy. *Journal of Research in Crime and Delinquency*, 21: 353–372.

Bernie, P. (1991). Inventing criminology: The "science of man" in Cesare Beccaria's Dei Delitti E Delle Pene (1764). *Criminology*, 29(4):777–820.

Bernie, P., & Hill, J. (1991). *Comparative criminology: An annotated bibliography*. NY: Greenwood Press.

Bernie, P., & Messerschmidt, J. (1991). *Criminology*. San Diego: Harcourt Brace Jovanovich.

Bernier, L., Mailloux, M., David, G., & Cote, H. (1996, May). An innovative treatment approach to incestuous fathers. *Forum*, pp. 28–30.

Bieler, H.G. (1965). *Food is your best medicine*. NY: Ballantine Books.

Bindman, J., & Doezma, J. (1998). *Redefining prostitution as sex work on international agenda*. Vancouver, B.C.: Commercial Sex Information Service.

Bindman, S. (1996, March 11). The world's most dangerous profession. *Calgary Herald*, A3.

Birckbeck, E., & LaFree, G. (1993). The theoretical analysis of crime and deviance. *American Review of Sociology*, 19:113–137.

Bischof, L. (1964). *Interpreting personality theories*. NY: Harper and Row.

Blackwell, J.E. (1988). Sin, sickness, or social problem?: The concept of drug dependence. In J. Blackwell and P. Erickson (Eds.). *Illicit drugs in Canada*. Scarborough: Nelson.

Blackwell, J.E., & Erickson, P.G. (Eds.). (1988). *Illicit drugs in Canada: A risky business*. Scarborough: Nelson.

Blanchette, K. (1997, May). Comparing Violent and Non-violent Female Offenders on Risk and Need. *Forum on Corrections Research*. pp. 14–18.

Blickstead, M. (1990). Lotteries. In C. McKie and K. Thompson (Eds.), *Canadian Social Trends*. Toronto: Thompson.

Blum, D. (1997). *Sex on the brain: The biological differences between men and women*. NY: Viking.

Blumer, H. (1969). *Symbolic interactionism: Perspectives and method*. Englewood Cliffs, NJ: Prentice-Hall.

Boe, R. (1992). *Correction Service of Canada offender population forecast for 1993 to 2002*. Ottawa: Corrections Service Canada.

Boers, K., & Sessar, K. (1966). Do people Really want Punishment. In K. Sessar & H-J. Kerner (Eds.), *Developments in crime and crime control research*. NY: Springer-Verlag, 1991.

Boggs, S. (1986). Urban Crime Patterns. *American Sociological Review*, 30:899–908.

Bohm, R.M. "Crime, Criminal, and Crime Control Policy Myth." *Justice Quarterly*, 3: 193–214.

Bohman, M., Cloninger, R., Sigvardsson, S., & von Knoring, A.L. (1982). Predisposition to Petty Criminality in Swedish Adoptees. I.

Genetic and Environmental Heterogeneity. *Archives of General Psychiatry*, 39:1233–1241.

Bonta, J., LaPrairie, C., & Wallace-Capretta, S. (1997). Risk prediction and re-offending: Aboriginal and non-aboriginal offenders. *Canadian Journal of Criminology*, 32(2): 127–144.

Borgaonkar, D.S., & Shah, S.A. (1974). The XYY chromosome male or syndrome? *Progress in Medical Genetics*, 10:135–142.

Boritch, H. (1997). *Fallen women: Female crime and criminal justice in Canada.* Scarborough: Nelson

Boulding, K. (1978). Sociobiology or biosociology? In M.S. Gregory, A. Silvers, & D. Sutch (Eds.), *Sociobiology and Human Nature.* San Francisco: Jossey-Bass.

Bourque, B.B., Cronin, R.C., Felker, D.B., Pearson, F.R., Han, M., & Hill, S.M. (1996, May). *Boot camps for juvenile offenders: An implementation evaluation of three demonstration programs.* Rockville, MD: National Institute of Justice.

Box, S. (1983). *Power, crime, and mystification.* London: Tavistock.

Boy charged with murder prompts debate on crime. (1997, November 7). *Calgary Herald*, A7.

Boyd, N. (1988). *The Last Dance: Murder in Canada.* Scarborough, ON: Prentice-Hall.

Boyd, N. (1991). *High Society: Legal and Illegal Drugs in Canada.* Toronto: Key Porter Books.

Boyd, N. (1993). *High Society.* Toronto: Seal Books.

Boyle, J. (June, 1998). Corruption prevails in many former Soviet States. *Crime and Justice International*, 8.

Bracken, D.C., & Leowen, R.J.L. (1992). *Confronting individual and structural barriers to employment: The employment and skill enhancement (EASE) program for prisons.* In K.R.E.

Brady, T.V. (1996,December) *Measuring What Matters.* National Institute of Justice. Washington, DC: U.S. Dept. of Justice.

Braithewaite, J. (1989). *Crime, Shame and Reintegration.* Cambridge: Cambridge University Press.

Braithewaite, J. (1989). The State of Criminology: Theoretical Decay or Renaissance? *Australian and New Zealand Journal of Criminology*, 22(3): 129–135.

Braithwaite, J. (1981). The Myth of Social Class and Criminality Reconsidered. *American Sociological Review*, 46:41

Brannigan, A. (1989) *Social and Legal Differences in the Conduct and Control of Prostitution: Street Soliciting v. Escort Services in Calgary.* Prepared for presentation to the Annual Meetings of Canadian Law Society Association, Laval University, June, 1989.

Brannigan, A. (1996). The Adolescent Prostitute: Policing Delinquency or Treating Pathology? In J. Winterdyk (Ed.), *Issues and Perspectives on Young Offenders in Canada.* Toroto: Harcourt Brace (Chapter 9).

Brannigan, A. (1998). Criminology and the Holocaust: Xenophobia, Evolution, and Genocide. *Crime and Delinquency*, 44(2): 257–276.

Brannigan, A., Knafla, L., & Levy, C. (1989). *Street Prostitution: Assessing the Impact of the Law,* Calgary, Regina, and Winnipeg. Ottawa: Department of Justice.

Brantingham, P.J., & Brantingham, P. (1981). (Eds.), *Environmental criminology.* Beverly Hills, CA: Sage.

Brantingham, P.J., & Brantingham, P.L. (1984). *Patterns in crime.* NY: Macmillan.

Brantingham, P. J., Mu, S., & Verma, A. (1995). Patterns in Canadian Criminology. In M.A. Jackson and C.T. Griffiths (Eds.), *Canadian Criminology* (2nd ed.). Toronto: Harcourt-Brace.

Braswell, M.C., McCarthy, B.R., & McCarthy, B.J. (1996). *Justice, crime and ethics.* Cincinnati, OH: Anderson.

Brennan, B. (1999, March 22). "Fraud squad: Calgary seniors tell their peers how to protect themselves against scams, cons." *Calgary Herald*, B6.

Brennan, P., & Raine, A. (1996). *Biosocial bases of antisocial behavior: Psychophysiological, neurological, and cognitive factors.* (Paper sent to author while in review).

Brenzinger, M.A. (1998, May) Serial Rapists and Their Use of Clandestine Chemicals. *Crime and Justice International.* (pp: 6, 28–29).

Brillon, Y. (1987). *Victimization and fear of crime among the elderly.* Toronto: Butterworths.

Britannica. (1997). *Wolfenden Report.* (Online).

Bronskill, J. (1998, January 28). Vehicle thefts hit Record Level in '97. *Calgary Herald,* A2.

Bronskill, J. (1998, June 29). Gulf War Vets' Kids suffer more Birth Defects: Study. *Calgary Herald,* p. A1–2.

Bronskill, J., & Bryden, J. (1998, April 21). Grits fear Tough Laws could break UN Treaty. *Calgary Herald,* p. A9.

Brown, S., Esbensen, F-A., & Geis, G. (1991). *Criminology: Explaining Crime and its Context. Cincinnati,* OH: Anderson.

Brown, S.E., Esbensen, F-A., & Geis, G. (1996). *Criminology: Explaining Crime and its Content* (2nd ed.). Cincinnati, OH: Anderson

Brundt, R. (1997, January 27). "Antichrist in a Black G-string." *Alberta Report,* pp. 42–43.

Buckle, A., & Farrington, D.P. (1984). An Observational Study of Shoplifting. *British Journal of Criminology,* 24:63–73.

Bullough, V.L., & Bullough, B. (1987). *Women and Prostitution: A Social History.* Buffalo, NY: Prometheus.

Burns, E.T. (1989). *Anatomy of a Crisis.* Needham Heights, MA: Ginn Press.

Bursick, R.J. (1995). The Distribution and Dynamics of Property Crime. In J.F. Sheley (Ed.), *Criminology: A Contemporary Handbook.* Philadelphia: Temple University Press. pp. 211–257.

Bursick, R.J., & Grasmick, H.G. (1993). *Neighbourhoods and Crime.* Toronto: Maxwell Macmillan.

Business Week. (1993, December, 13). pp. 72–75, 78–80, 85.

Calgary Herald. (1995, February 27). *When It is no longer a Game.* B3.

— (1996, May 24). *Special Report – public perception of crime.* (Online).

— (1996, December 11). *The world's most dangerous profession.* (Online).

Cambell, D.T., & Fiske, D. W. (1959). Convergent and Discriminant Validity by the Multitrait-Multimethod Matrix. *Psychological Bulletin,* 56:81–105.

Cameron, M. O. (1964). *The Booster and the Snitch.* NY: Free Press.

Canada NewsWire.

(1998, May 7) 90,000.00 Worth of counterfeit software seized in Markham.

(1997, April 4). Police officers sentenced in Mississauga home invasion.

(1997, June 12). Major incidents.

(1997, June 16). The British Columbia College of teachers announces final decisions in disciplinary cases.

(1997, May 29). Peel Regional Police – This was no accident.

Canada Year Book 1997. (1996). Ottawa: Ministry of Industry.

CACP – Canadian Association of Chiefs of Police (1993). Ottawa: Strategic Planning Committee, Canadian Association of Chiefs of Police.

—— (1994). Ottawa: Strategic Planning Committee, Canadian Association of Chiefs of Police.

Canadian Association of the Elizabeth Fry Society (CAEFS). (1997). (Online).

Canadian Centre for Justice Statistics. (1996). *A graphic overview of crime and the administration of criminal justice in Canada.*

CCJS – Canadian Centre for Justice Statistics.

Robbery in Canada. (1992). Vol. 12(10).

Trends in Justice Spending, 1988–89 to 1992–93. (1994). Vol. 14(16).

Criminal Justice Processing of Sexual Assault Cases. (1994). Vol. 14(7).

Motor Vehicle Crimes. (1996). Vol. 16(2).

Canadian Crime Statistics, 1995. (1996). Vol. 16(10).

Homicide in Canada – 1995. (1996). Vol. 16(11).

Justice Spending in Canada. (1997). Vol., 17(3).

Canadian Crime Statistics, 1996. (1997). Vol. 17(8).

Homicide in Canada – 1996. (1997). Vol. 17(9).

Justice Fact finder. (1997). Vol. 17(13).

Sentence Admissions: 1996–97. (1998). Vol. 18(3).

The Changing Nature of Fraud in Canada. (1998). Vol. 18(4).

Breaking and Entering in Canada, 1996. (1998). Vol. 18(5).

Victim Survey. (1998). Vol. 18(6).

Adult Criminal Courts Statistics, 1996–97. (1998). Vol. 18(7).

Canadian Crime Statistics, 1997. (1998). Vol. 18(11).

Homicide in Canada, 1997. (1998). Vol. 18(12).

Adult Criminal Court Statistics, 1997–98. Vol. 18(14).

Canadian *Criminal Code*. (1999). Toronto: Carswell.

Statistics Canada (1997). Canadian Dimensions – Motor vehicle registration, the provinces and territories, 1994. (Online).

Canadian Year Book 1997. (1997). Ottawa: Ministry of Industry.

Cao, L. (1987). Illegal traffic in women: A civil RICO proposal. *The Yale Law Journal*, 96: 1297–1306.

Carman, A., & Moody, H. (1985). *Working women: The subterranean world of street prostitutes*. NY: Harper and Row.

Carrigan, D.O. (1991). *Crime and Punishment in Canada: A History*. Toronto: McClelland and Stewart.

Carter, J.G. (1997). The Social Construction of the Serial Killer. *RCMP Gazette*, 59(2): 2–21.

Carter, P. (1995, September). Violence: From the Grave to the Cradle. *Financial Post Magazine*, pp. 23–48.

Casino Regina Gift Shop Contract Awarded. (1996, January 23). Government of Saskatchewan. (Online).

Cates, J.A., & Markley, J. (1992). Demographic, Clinical, and Personality Variables Associated with Male Prostitution by Choice. *Adolescence*, 27:695–714.

CBC Radio News. (1998, July 9). Calgary, AB.

Chambers, A. (1997, December 6). Alberta Pledges Curb on Violence. *Calgary Herald*, A18.

Chambliss, W. (1975). *The box man: A professional thief's journal, by Harry King*. NY: Harper Row.

Chambliss, W. (1988). *On the Take* (2nd ed.). Bloomington, ID: Indiana Un. Press.

Chambliss, W.J., & Yassa, A. (1995). Law School Admission Criteria and Criminal Justice Undergraduate Majors. *ACS Today*, XIV(2): 1,3.

Charges against RCMP officer dropped. (1998, February 11). *Calgary Herald*, A10.

Chase, S. (1997, October 26). Oilman backs VLT plebiscites. *Calgary Herald*, A1–A2.

Chase, S. (1998, April 3). Klein won't fight ruling on gays. *Calgary Herald*, A1–A2.

Chase, S. (1998, January 16). Young offenders on hit list. *Calgary Herald*, A1,2.

CJ Europe, (1996, November/December). *Chemical castration considered for sex offenders*. p. 11.

Chermak, S.M. (1995). *Victims in the News: Crime and the American News Media*. Boulder, CO: Westview Press.

Chesney-Lind, M., & Sheldon, R.G. (1992). *Girls, Delinquency and Juvenile Delinquency*. Pacific Grove, CA: Brooks/Col.

Chin, E. (1997, October). Crime Prevention: Is It Working? *Crime and Justice International*, pp. 21–22.

Chopra, D. (1990). *Quantum healing*. NY: Bantam Books

Christiansen, K. A. (1977). Preliminary Study of Criminality among Twins. In S.A. Mednick & K. Chrisitiansen (Eds.), *Biosocial bases of criminal behavior*, (89–108). NY: Gardner Press.

Christie, N. (1996). *Crime control as industry* (2nd ed.). London: Routledge.

Christie, N. (1997). Four blocks against Insight: Notes on the Oversocialization of Criminologists. *Theoretical criminology*, 1(1): 11–23.

Chunn, D., & Menzies, R. (1997). The Getting of Wisdom, The ideology and experience of graduate education among students enrolled in anglophone Canadian criminology programs. *Canadian Journal of Criminology*, 39(1): 1–26.

Chunn, D.E., & Gavigan, S.A.N. (1991). Women and Crime in Canada. In M. Jackson & C.T. Griffiths (Eds.), *Canadian Criminology*. Toronto: Harcourt Brace, Jovanovitch.

CISC Annual Report. (1998). (Available: www.cisc.gc.ca/)

Cisneros, H.G. (1995). *Defensible Space: Deterring Crime and Building Community*. Washington, D.C.: Secretary of Housing and Urban Development.

CJ Europe. (1996, November/December).

CJ International. (1996, September/October). p. 7.

Clark, L., & Tifft, L. (1966). Polygraph and interview validation of self-reported deviant behaviour. *American Sociological Review*, 31: 516–523.

Clarke, J. J.W. (1982). *American assassins: the darker side of politics*. Princeton, NJ: Princton University Press.

Clarke, R.V., & Felson, M. (1993). Introduction: Criminology, routine activity, and rational choice. In R.V. Clarke and M. Felson (Eds.), *Routine activity and rational choice*. New Brunswick, NJ: Transaction, (pp. 1–14).

Clarkson, M. (1990, December 8). One in 10 victims haunted by disorder which biologically alters brain. *Calgary Herald*, B6.

Clermont, Y. (1996). Robbery. In L.W. Kennedy and V.F. Sacco (Eds.), *Crime Counts: A Criminal Event Analysis*. Scarborough: Nelson.

Clinard, R., & Quinney, R. (1973). *Criminal behavior systems: A typology*. NY: Holt, Rinehart and Winston.

CNN Interactive. (1998, April 16) *Study finds more violence in prime-time TV shows*. (Online).

Cohen, A. (1955). *Delinquent Boys: The Culture of the Gang*. NY: Free Press.

Cohn, E.G., & Farrington, D.P. (1998). Changes in the most cited scholars in major international journals between 1986–90 and 1991–95. *British Journal of Criminology*, 38(1):156–170.

Cohen, L.E., & Felson, M. (1979). Social Change and Crime Rate Trends: A routine activities approach. *American Sociological Review*, 44:588–607.

Cohen, L.E., & Machalek, R. (1988). A general theory of expropriate crime: An evolutionary ecological approach. *American Journal of Sociology*, 94: 465–501.

Cohen, L.E., & Vila, B. (1996). Self-control and social control: An exposition of Gottfredson-Hirschi/Sampson-Laub debate. *Studies on Crime and Crime Prevention*, 5(2): 125–150.

Cohen, S. (1985). *Visions of social control*. Cambridge: U.K.: Polity.

Cohen, S. (1994). Social control and the politics of reconstruction. In D. Nelken (Ed.), *The future of criminology*. London, U.K.: Sage.

Coldren, J.D. (1995, July/August). Change at the speed of light: Doing justice in the information age. *CJ International*, 8–12.

Colgan, M. (1996). *Hormonal health*. Vancouver, BC: Apple Pub.

Committee for a Safe Society '97. (1997). The Office of International Criminal Justice. (Online).

Committee on Sexual Offences Against Children and Youth. (1984). Sexual offences against children. Ottawa: Department of Supply and Services.

Conklin, J. (1975). *The impact of crime*. NY: Macmillan.

Conklin, J. (1998). *Criminology* (6th ed.). Boston: Allyn and Bacon.

Corcoran, K., & Fischer, J. (1987). *Measures for clinical practice*. NY: Free Press.

Cornish, D.B., & Clarke, R.V. (Eds.). (1986). *The reasoning criminal: Rational choice perspectives on offending.* NY: Springer-Verlag.

Correctional Research and Development Correctional Services of Canada. (1995).No. B-10: Ottawa. *A profile of robbery offenders in Canada.* Research Brief.

Corrections in Canada – 1994 edition. Ottawa: Ministry of Supply and Service Canada.

Corrections in Canada – 1997 edition. Ottawa: Ministry of Supply and Service Canada.

Corrections population growth: First report on progress. (1997, February). (Online – Solicitor General of Canada).

Counterfeit credit cards. (1998). (Online: http://heads-up.oanet.com/pub009.htm).

Counterfeiting of currency and payment cards. (1996). (Online – www.rcmp-grc.ca/html/ccandpc.htm).

Cousineau, F.D., & Verdun-Jones, S. (1979). Evaluating research into plea bargaining in Canada and the United States: Pitfalls facing the policy makers. *Canadian Journal of Criminology,* 21: 293–309.

Cowie, J., Cowie, V., & Slater, E. (1968). *Delinquency in girls.* London: Heinemann.

Cowles, E.L., & Castellano, T.C. (1995). "Boot camps," drug treatment and aftercare intervention: An evaluation review. Rockville, MD: National Institute of Justice.

Cox, D.N., Roesch, R., & Zapf, P.A. (1996). *Psychological perspectives on criminality.* In R. Linden (Ed.), *Criminology: A Canadian perspective* (3rd ed.). Toronto, ON: Harcourt Brace. (Ch. 8).

Coyle, J. (1998, May 9). Road rage is driving us around the bend. *Toronto Star.* Online: www.thestar.co).

Cressey, D.R. (1969). *Theft of the nation: The structure and operations of organized crime in America.* NY: Harper & Row.

Crime in the computer age. (1988, January 25). Maclean's Magazine. pp. 28–30.

Crime prevention efforts get poor rating by criminals. (1988, December). *Law and Order,* p. 66–67.

Crime rate drops: we're just too old? (1995, October 23). *Calgary Herald,* A3.

Crime Times. (1997). Alcohol's legacy: High crime rates seen in FAS/FAE. 3(1):5–6.

Criminal Justice International. (1994). Vol. 10 (1):4–5.

—— (1997). Vol. 13(10).

Criminal lands in Canada. (1997, July 13). *Calgary Herald.* (Online).

Cromwell, P.F., Olson, J.N., & Avary, D.W. (1991). *Breaking and entering: An ethnographic analysis of burglary.* Newbury Park, CA: Sage.

Crowe, R. (1974). An adoption study of antisocial personality. *Archives of General Psychiatry,* 31:785–791.

CSC. Corrections Service Canada. (Online).

CSI Statistics. (1997). *Crime Stoppers International.* (Online).

CSIS. (1998, March 20). *Commercial sex information service: Today's special.* (Online: www.walnut.org/csis/specials.html).

CSOACY. (1984). Committee on Sexual Offences Against Children and Youth. Ottawa: Ministry of Supply and Service.

Cullen, F.T., Maakestad, W.J., & Cavender, G. (1987). *Corporate crime under attack: The Ford Pinto case and beyond.* Cincinnati, OH: Anderson.

Cunningham, J. (1997, October, 2). Convicted killer can apply for parole in 1999. *Calgary Herald,* B4.

Cunningham, J. (1998, April 5). Majority of Calgarians favor limiting access to VLTs. *Calgary Herald,* A4.

Dalton, K. (1961). Menstruation and crime. *British Medical Journal,* 2:1752–1753.

Daly, K. (1989a). Gender and varieties of white-collar crime. *Criminology,* 27(4):763–793.

Daly, K. (1989b). Neither conflict nor labeling nor paternalism will suffice. *Crime and Delinquency,* 35:136–168.

Daly, K., & Chesney-Lind, M. (1988). Feminism and criminology. *Justice Quarterly,* 5: 497–533.

Dandurand, Y., & Paris-Steffens, R. (1997). *Beyond wishful thinking.* Vancouver, BC: Canadian/Latin American Cooperation in Criminal Law Reform and Criminal Justice.

Darling, J. (1998, July 18). Kidnapping is big business. *Calgary Herald*, H1.

Data on hate-motivated violence. (August, 1995). http://canada.justice.gc.ca/orientations/reforme/naine/hate_en_7.html

Date rape. (1997). (Online search).

Date rape: Drug smuggled from Mexico. (1998, February 5). *Calgary Herald,* B1–B2.

'Date rape drug' an 'epidemic'. (1998, January 31). *Calgary Herald*, A17.

Davis, S., & Shaffer, M. (1994). *Prostitution in Canada: The invisible menace or the menace of invisibility?* (Online).

Daw, J. (1998, January 20). Huge jump in debit card fraud. *Toronto Star.* (Online: www.thestar.com).

Death on the Internet. (1996). (Online).

Decision '97. (May 15, 1997). Bulletin, Ottawa: Canadian Criminal Justice Association.

DeKeseredy, W., & Hinch, R. (1991). *Woman abuse: Sociological perspectives.* Toronto: Thompson.

DeKeseredy, W., & Schwartz, M.D. (1996). *Contemporary criminology.* Belmont, CA: Wadsworth.

DeMause, L. (Ed.). (1988). *The history of childhood.* New York: Peter Bedrick Books.

Denisoff, R.S., Callahan, O., & Levine, M. (1974). *Theories and paradigms in contemporary sociology.* Itasca, Il: Peacock.

Denno, D. (1988). Human biology and criminal responsibility: Free will or free ride? *University of Pennsylvania Law Review*, 137:615–671.

Denter, R.A., & Monroe, L.J. (1961). Social correlates of early adolescent theft. *American Sociological Review*, 26: 733–743.

Derber, C. (1996). *The wilding of America: How greed and violence are eroding our nation's character.* NY: St. Martin's Press.

Desroches, F. (1995). *Forces and fear: Robbery in Canada.* Scarborough: Nelson.

Desroches, F. (1996). *Behind the bars.* Toronto: Canadian Scholars' Press.

Deutschmann, L.B. (1994). *Deviance and social control.* Scarborough: Nelson.

Deutschmann, L.B. (1998). *Deviance and social control* (2nd ed.). Scarborough: Nelson.

Dialogue with Richard Quinney. (1971). *Issues in Criminology*, 6:41–54.

Ditton, J. (1979) *Controlology: Beyond criminology.* London: MacMillan.

Dobbie, J., & Bill, P. (1978). *Fetal alcohol syndrome.* Toronto: Alcohol and Drug Addiction Research Foundation.

Dollard, J., Doob, L.W., Miller, N.E., Mowrer, O.H., & Sears, R.R.(1939). *Frustration and aggression.* New Haven, Conn: Yale University Press.

Doob, A.N., & Roberts, J.V. (1982). *Crime and the official response to crime: The views of the public.* Ottawa: Department of Justice.

Douillard, J. (1991). *Invincible athlete.* Lancaster, MA: Sports Organization of Maharishi Ayur-Veda.

Dubro, J. (1985). *Mob rule: Inside the Canadian Mafia.* Toronto: Totem Books.

Duffy, A. (1997, May 18). Bre-X an epic hoax. *Calgary Herald*, A8–9.

Duiguid, S. (1979). History and moral education in correctional education. *Canadian Journal of Education*, 4:81–92.

Dunn, C.S. (1976). *Patterns of robbery characteristics and their occurrence among social areas.* Washington, DC: U.S. Dept. of Justice.

Durkan, S. (1997, February 14). Most hooker killers go free. *Toronto Star.* (Online).

Durkheim, E. (1895). *Rules of sociological method.* Trans. S.A. Soloway and J. H. Mueller. NY: Free Press (Reprinted 1965).

Eastern Spectrum 1997. Toronto: Guidance Centre OISE.

Easton, S., & Brantingham, P. (1998, June), *The cost of crime.* Vancouver, BC: Fraser Institute.

Eggertson, L. (1998, July 21). Liberals lift ban on controversial gas additive. *Toronto Star.* (Online).

Einstadter, W., & Henry, S. (1995). *Criminological theory: An analysis of its underlying assumptions.* NY: Harcourt Brace.

Ekstedt, J. (1995). Canadian justice policy. In M.A. Jackson & C.T. Griffiths (Eds.). *Canadian criminology: Perspectives on crime and criminality* (2nd ed.). Toronto: Harcourt Brace.

Ekstedt, J., & Jackson, M. (1997). *Keepers and the kept.* Scarborough, ON: Nelson.

Ekstedt, J.W., & Griffiths, G.C. (1988). *Corrections in Canada: policy and practice* (2nd ed.). Toronto: Butterworths.

Elderly Crime Victims 1994. (1994). Washington, DC: Bureau of Justice Statistics: Bulletin.

Eliany, M. (1994). Alcohol and drug consumption among Canadian youth. In E.T. Pryor (Ed.), *Canadian social trends* (vol. 2). Toronto: Thompson Education Pub.

Elias, R. (1986). *The politics of victimization: Victims, victimology and human rights.* NY: Oxford University Press.

Elias, R. (1993). *Victim still: The political manipulation of crime victims.* Newbury Park, CA: Sage.

Elliot, D.S., Ageton, S.S., & Canter, R.J. (1979). An integrated theoretical perspective on delinquent behavior. *Journal of Research in Crime and Delinquency,* 16(1):3–27.

Elliot, D.S., Huizinga, D., & Ageton, S.S. (1985). *Explaining delinquency and drug use.* Beverly Hills, CA: SAGE.

Ellis, D. (1989). *The wrong stuff.* Toronto: Collier Macmillan.

Ellis, D., & DeKeseredy, W. (1996). *The wrong stuff* (2nd ed.). Scarborough: Allyn & Bacon.

Ellis, L. (1982). Genetics and criminal behavior. *Criminology,* 20(1): 43–66.

Ellis, L. (1987). *Theories of rape: Inquiries into the causes of sexual aggression.* NY: Hemisphere.

Ellis, L. (1988). Genetic influences and crime. In F.H. Marsh & J. Katz (Eds.), *Biology, crime and ethics: A study of biological explanations for criminal behavior.* Cincinnati, OH: Anderson. pp. 65–92.

Ellis, R. (1986). *The politics of victimization: Victims, victimology and crime victims.* NY: Oxford Un. Press.

Elmer, M.C. (1982). Century-old ecological studies in France. In G.A. Theodorson (Ed.), *Urban patterns: Studies in human ecology.* Philadelphia, PA: Pennsylvania State University Press.

Emerging gangs: An International trend? (1997, October). *Crime and Justice International,* pp. 4–5.

Encarta (R). (1996). *Encyclopedia.* 1993–1995 Microsoft Corporation.

Endell, R.V. (1983). Bioenvironmental criminology: Political and policy implications for crime prevention strategies. *Journal of Juvenile and Family Court,* 34(1):43–62.

Engman, K. (1998, June 17). Marijuana advocate convicted. *Calgary Herald,* p. B6.

Ennis, B.J., & Litwack, T.R. (1974). Psychiatry and the presumption of expertise: Flipping coins in the courtroom. *California Law Review,* 62: 693–752.

Ericson, R., & Carriere, K. (1994). The fragmentation of criminology. In D. Nelken (Ed.), *The futures of criminology.* Thousand Oaks, CA: Sage. (Chapter 4).

Ericson, R.V., Baranek, P.M., & Chan, J.B.L. (1987). *Visualizing deviance: A study of new organizations.* Toronto: Un. of Toronto Press.

Ericson, R.V., Baranek, P.M., & Chan, J.B.L. (1991). *Representing order: Crime, law, and justice in the news media.* Toronto: Un. of Toronto Press.

Ermann, M.D., & Lundman, R.J. (1982). *Corporate deviance.* NY: Holt Rinehart and Winston.

Evans, J., & Himelfarb, A. (1992). Counting crime. In R. Linden (Ed.), *Criminology: A Canadian perspective* (2nd ed.). Toronto: Harcourt Brace.

Evans, J., & Legar, P. (1979). Canadian victimization surveys. *Canadian Journal of Criminology,* 21(2): 166–183.

Ex-college secretary charged with fraud for putting students' tuition in her account. (1999, April 9). *Calgary Herald*, B9.

Ex-DND worker faces more charges. (1997, May 29). *Calgary Herald*. (Online).

Eysenck, H.J. (1977). *Crime and personality*. Frogmore, England: Paladin.

Eysenck, H.J. (1998). Intelligence. NY: Transaction.

Fairchild, E. (1993). *Comparative criminal justice*. Belmont, CA: Wadsworth.

Faith, K. (1987). Media, myths and masculinization: Images of women in prison. In E. Adelberg and C. Currie (Eds.), *Too few to count*. Vancouver: The Press Gang.

Farrell, W. (1993). *The myth of male power*. NY: Simon and Schuster.

Farrington, D.P. (Ed.). (1994). *Psychological explanations of crime*. Aldershot, UK: Dartmouth.

Fattah, E.A. (1991). *Understanding criminal victimization*. Scarborough: Prentice-Hall.

Fattah, E.A. (1995). Restorative and retributive justice models, A comparison. In H-H. Kuhne (Ed.), *Festschrift fur Koichi Miyazawa*. Baden-Baden, Germany: Nomos Verlagsgesllschaft.

Fattah, E. A. (1997). *Criminology: Past, Present and Future*. NY: St. Martin.

Fattah, E.A., & Sacco, V.F. (1989). *Crime and victimization of the elderly*. NY: Springer-Verlag.

FBI expands investigation into Mafia stock scams. (1997, November 27). *Calgary Herald*, p. A24.

FBI. Uniform Crime Report, 1970–1994. Washington, DC: Government Printing Office.

Federation of Canadian municipalities: Policy statements on community safety and crime prevention. (1997). (Online: http://www.fcm.ca/newsite/newsite/pp/97crime-eng-polstat.htm).

Felson, M. (1997). A "Routine Activity" analysis of recent crime reductions. *The Criminologists*, 22(6):1,3.

Fernandez, K., & Neiman, M. (1997). *The geography of fear of crime*. Paper presented at the 49th American Society of Criminology Annual Meetings. San Diego. (November 19–22).

Feyerabend, P.K. (1986). *Against method*. London: New Left Books.

Finckenauer, J.Q. (1984). *Juvenile delinquency and corrections: The gap between theory and practice*. Orlando, Fl: Academic Press.

Fishbein, D.H. (1992). *Biological perspectives in criminology*. Criminology, 28(1): 27–72.

Fishbein, D.H., & Pease, S.E. (1996). *The dynamics of drug abuse*. Needham Heights, Mass: Allyn and Bacon.

Fisher, A. (1991). A new synthesis II: How different are humans? *Mosaic*, 22(1):2–15.

Fleming, T. (1985). Prospects for a working-class criminology in Canada. In T. Fleming (Ed.), *The new criminologies in Canada: State, crime, and control*. Toronto: Oxford Un. Press.

Fooner, M. (1989). *Interpol: Issues in world crime and international criminal justice*. NY: Plenum.

Foot, D. (1996). *Boom, bust, and echo*. Toronto: Macfarlane, Walter and Ross.

Forde, D.R., & Kennedy, L.W. (1997). Risky lifestyles, routine activities, and the general theory of crime. *Justice Quarterly*, 14(2): 265–294.

Fortune, E.P., Vega, M., & Silverman, I. (1980). A study of female robbers in southern correctional institutions. *Journal of Criminal Justice*, 8: 317–325.

Foucault, M. (1977). *Discipline and punish: The birth of prison*. NY: Vintage.

Fox, R.G. (1969). XYY chromosome and crime. *Australian and New Zealand J. of Criminology*. 2(1): 5–19.

Franklin, J.L., & Thrasher, J.H. (1976). *An introduction to program evaluation*. NY: John Wiley and Sons.

Fraser Forum. (1995, May). *Capital punishment no deterrent?* (Document - Folio Infobase).

Fraser Forum (1996, September). Critical Issues Bulletins — 1996. *The crime bill: Who pays and how much?* Vancouver, B.C. (Online).

Friedrichs, D.O. (1991). Introduction: Peacemaking criminology in a world filled with conflict. In B.D. MacLean & D. Milovanovic (Eds.), *New directions in critical criminology*. Vancouver: Collective Press.

Galloway, G. (1997, March 7). Centre eyes organized crime. *Calgary Herald*. (Online).

Gamblers Anonymous International (1997). (Online).

Gambling. (1997). Mayo Health Oasis. (Online).

Gang robbing cargo trains. *Calgary Herald*. (Online).

Garfinkel, H. (Ed.). (1967). *Studies in ethnomethodology*. Englewood Cliffs, NJ: Prentice-Hall.

Gavigan, S. (1987). Women's crime: New perspectives and old theories. In E. Adelberg and C. Currie (Eds.), *Too few to count*. Vancouver: The Press Gang.

Gaynor, J., & Stern, D. (1993). *Child and juvenile firesetters: Examining their psychological profiles*. Firehouse, 18: 24–26.

Gebotys, R.J., Roberts, J.V., & DasGupta, B. (1988). News media use and public perceptions of crime seriousness. *Canadian Journal of Criminology*, 30(1), 3–16.

Geis, G. (1973). Jeremy Bentham. In H. Mannheim (Ed.), *Pioneers in criminology* (2nd ed.). Montclair, NJ: Patterson Smith.

Geis, G. (1989). Prostitution in Portugal. In N. Davis (Ed.), *International handbook of prostitution*. Westport, CT: Greenwood.

Geis, G., & Goff, C. (1982). Edwin H. Sutherland: A biological and analytical commentary. In P. Wickman and T. Daily (Eds.), *White-collar crime and economic crime*. Lexington, Mass: Lexington Books.

Gendreau, P., & Gossin, C. (1996, September). Principles of effective correctional programming. *Forum*, 8(3): 38–41.

Gendreau, P., & Ross, R.R. (1987). Revivification of rehabilitation: Evidence from the 1980s. *Justice Quarterly*, 4: 349–407.

Georges-Abeyie, D.E. (1981). Studying black crime: A realistic approach. In P.J. Brantingham & P.L. Brantingham (Eds.), *Environmental criminology*. Beverly Hills, CA: Sage. (pp. 97–109).

Gibbens, T.C.N. (1961). *Trends in juvenile delinquency*. Geneva: World Health Organization.

Gibbons, D. (1979). *The criminological enterprise: Theories and perspectives*. Englewood Cliffs, CA: Prentice-Hall.

Gibbons, D. (1992). *Society, crime, and criminal behavior* (6th ed.). Englewood Cliffs, NJ: Prentice-Hall.

Gibbons, D. (1994). *Talking about crime and criminals: Problems and issues in theory development in criminology*. Englewood Cliffs, NJ: Prentice-Hall.

Gibbs, J. (1972). *Sociological theory construction*. Hinsdale, Ill: Dryden.

Gibbs, J. (1975). Crime, punishment, and deterrence. *Southwestern Social Science Quarterly*, 48: 515–530.

Gibbs, J. (1987). The state of criminological theory. *Criminology*, 25: 821–840.

Gibbs, W.W. (1995, March). Seeking the criminal element. *Scientific American*, p. 100–107.

Gilligan, C. (1982). *In a different voice: Psychological theory and women's development*. Cambridge, MA: Harvard University Press.

Glaser, B.G., & Strauss, A.L. (1973). *The discovery of grounded theory: Strategies for qualitative research*. Chicago: Aldine.

Glenn, H.S. (1988). *Raising self-reliant children in a self-indulgent world*. Fair Oaks, CA: Sunrise Press.

Glionna, J. (1998, June 13). 'It makes the pain easier to bear': Last-ditch supply centre for Californians with incurable diseases now in jeopardy. *Calgary Herald*, H2.

Globe and Mail. (1996, August 2). (Online).

Goff, C. (1997). *Criminal justice in Canada*. Toronto: Nelson.

Goff, C., & Reasons, C.E. (1978). *Corporate crime in Canada: A critical analysis of Anti-Combines legislation*. Scarborough, ON: Prentice-Hall.

Gollin, A.E. (1988). The media's influence is limited. In B.L. Bender & B. Leone (Eds.), *The mass media*. San Diego, CA: Greenhaven Press. (pp. 116–120).

Gombu, P. (1998, July 10). Jane Doe gets apology. *Toronto Star*. (Online).

Gomme, I.M., Morton, M.E., & West, W.G. (1984). Rates, types, and patterns of male and female delinquency in an Ontario community. *Canadian Journal of Criminology*, 26(3): 313–323.

Goodwin, T. (1995, Winter Solstice). Crime in Russia: Bitter fruit of capitalism and democracy. *Synapse*. (Online).

Gordon, H. (1997, March, 12). State has stunning plan for jailbreakers. *Calgary Herald*, p. A3.

Gordon, R., & Coneybeer, I. (1995). Corporate crime. In M. A. Jackson and C.T. Griffiths (Eds.), *Canadian criminology: Perspectives on crime and criminality* (2nd ed.). Toronto: Harcourt Brace.

Gordon, R.A. (1987). SES versus IQ in the race-IQ delinquency model. *International Journal of Sociology and Social Policy*, 7: 29–56.

Goring, C.B. (1913). *The English convict: A statistical study*. London, HMSO.

Gosgnash, T. (1998). *Promise Keepers anticipate better year*. (Online: http://www.christian-week.org/stories/vol11/no23/story3.htm).

Gottfredson, M.R., & Hirschi, T. (1990). *A general theory of crime*. Stanford, CA: Stanford University Press.

Gottschalk, L.A., Rebello, T., Buchsbaum, M.S., Tucker, H.G., & Hodges, E.L. (1991). Abnormalities in hair trace elements as indicators of aberrant behavior. *Comprehensive Psychiatry*, 32(3): 229–237.

Graci, S. (1997). *The power of superfoods*. Scarborough: Prentice-Hall.

Graham, P. (1998, June 26). Ex-hockey czar gets out of penalty box July 7. *Calgary Herald*, A18.

Grasmick, H.G., Tittle, C.R., Bursik Jr., R.J., & Arneklev, B.J. (1993). Testing the core empirical implications of Gottfredson and Hirschi's general theory of crime. *Journal of Research in Crime and Delinquency*, 30:5–29.

Grassberger, R. (1973). Hans Gross. In H. Mannheim (Ed.), *Pioneers in criminology* (2nd ed.). Montclair, NJ: Patterson Smith.

Great Victoria Crime Stoppers. (1996). (Online).

Greenberg, P. (1996). Break and enter. In L.W. Kennedy and V.F. Sacco (Eds.), *Crime counts: A criminal event analysis*. Scarborough: Nelson. (Ch. 9.)

Greenfeld, L.A. (1994, March). Criminal victimization in the United States, 1992. Bureau of Justice Statistics. U.S. Department of Justice.

Grescoe, T. (1996, September). Murder he mapped. *Canadian Geographic*, pp. 49–52.

Griffin, J. H. (1961). *Black like me*. Boston: Hougton Miffin.

Griffiths, C.T., & Verdun-Jones, S. (1994). *Canadian criminal justice* (2nd ed.). Toronto: Harcourt Brace.

Griffiths, C.T., & Verdun-Jones, S.N. (1989). *Canadian criminal justice*. Toronto: Butterworths.

Gropper, B.A. (1985). Probing the link between drugs and crime. Washington, DC: National Institute of Justice.

Groth, N. (1979). *Men who rape: The psychology of the offender*. NY: Plenum.

Grygier, T. (1988). A Canadian approach or an American band-wagon? *Canadian Journal of Criminology*, 30(2): 165–172.

Guilford, J.P. (1954). *A factor-analytic study across domains of reasoning, creativity, and evaluation. Report from the psychology lab*. Los Angeles, CA: Un. of Southern California.

Hackler, J. (1994). *Crime and Canadian public policy*. Scarborough: Prentice-Hall.

Hackler, J. (1996). Anglophone juvenile justice. In J. Winterdyk (Ed.). *Issues and perspectives on young offenders in Canada*. Toronto: Harcourt Brace.

Hagan, F.E. (1997). *Research methods in criminal justice and criminology* (4th ed.). NY: Macmillan.

Hagan, J. (1970). *The disreputable pleasures: Crime and deviance in Canada*. Toronto: McGraw-Hill.

Hagan, J. (1985). *Modern criminology: Crime, criminal behaviour and its control*. New York: McGraw-Hill.

Hagan, J. (1987). *The disreputable pleasures: Crime and deviance in Canada* (2nd ed.). Toronto: McGraw Hill.

Hagan, J. (1989). *Structural criminology*. New Brunswick, NJ: Rutgers University Press.

Hagan, J. (1991). *The disreputable pleasures: Crime and deviance in Canada* (3rd ed.). Toronto: McGraw-Hill.

Hagan, J. (Ed.). (1989). *Structural criminology*. New Brunswick, NJ: Rugters Un. Press.

Hak, J. (1996). The Young Offenders Act. In J. Winterdyk (Ed.), *Issues and perspectives on young offenders in Canada*. Toronto: Harcourt Brace. (Ch. 3).

Hakim, S., & Buck, A.J. (1989). Do casinos enhance crime? *Journal of Criminal Justice*, 17:409–416.

Hall, C.S., & Lindzey, G. (1970). *Theories in personality* (2nd ed.). NY: John Wiley & Sons.

Hall, N. (1993, April). Big-city crime wave hits the "burbs": Home invasion, prostitution on the rise. *The Vancouver Sun*, B4.

Hall, V. (1997, August 9). Topless still illegal. *The Leader-Post* (Regina). (Online).

Halleck, S.L. (1967). *Psychiatry and the dilemmas of crime*. NY: Harper and Row.

Hamm, M.S. (1994). *The American neo-Nazi skinheads: Hyperactive conformists or rebels without a clue?* Paper presented at the 46th American Society of Criminology Annual Meetings. Miami, Fl. (November 9–12).

Hamm, M.S. (1998). *Ethnography at the edge: Crime, deviance, and field research*. Paper presented at the Academy of Criminal Justice 35th Annual Meeting. Albuquerque, NM. March 10–14.

Handelman, S. (1997, September 30). Russia exports "criminal state." *Toronto Star.* (Online).

Hare, R. (1996). Psychopathy: a clinical construct whose time has come. *Criminal Justice and Behavior*, 23(1):25–54.

Harris, J. R. (1998). *The nature assumption*. NY: Free Press.

Hartnagel, J. (1995). Correlates of criminal behaviour. In R. Linden (Ed.), *Criminology: A Canadian perspective* (3rd ed.). Toronto: Harcourt-Brace.

Hasenpusch, B. (1979). Future trends in crime in Canada. *Canadian Police College Journal*, 3(2): 89–114.

Haslem, P.G. (1976). The women offender. In W.T. McGrath (Ed.), *Crime and its treatment in Canada* (2nd ed.). Toronto: Macmillan.

Hatch, A. (1995). Historical legacies of crime and criminal justice in Canada. In M.A. Jackson & C.T. Griffiths (Eds.), *Canadian criminology* (3rd ed.). Toronto: Harcourt-Brace. (Ch. 7).

Hazelhurst, K. (1996, August). *Community healing and restorative justice: Two models of recovery in aboriginal Australia*. CBA Commonwealth Law Conference. Canberra.

Heidensohn, F. (1992, February). Sociological perspectives on violence in women. Paper given at the University of Montreal.

Heimer, K., & Matsueda, R. (1994). Role-taking, role-commitment and delinquency: A theory of differential social control. *American Sociological Review*, 59:400–437.

Hempnation (1997). (Online) www.hempnation.com

Hendrick, D. (1996). Theft. In L.W. Kennedy and V.F. Sacco (Eds.), *Crime counts: A criminal event analysis*. Scarborough: Nelson. (Ch. 11).

Hentig, H. von. (1948). *The criminal and his victim: Studies in the sociobiology of crime*. New Haven, Conn: Yale University Press.

Herrnstein, R.J. (1989). *Biology and crime*. National Institute of Justice. Rockville, MD: U.S. Department of Justice.

Herrnstein, R.J. (1989b). IQ and falling birthrates. *The Atlantic*, 263(5): 72–84.

Hickey, E.W. (1991). *Serial murderers and their victims*. Pacific Grove, CA: Brooks/Cole.

Hiller, H.H. (1982). *Society and change: S.D. Clark and the development of Canadian sociology*. Toronto: Univ. of Toronto Press.

Hillman, J. (1996).*The soul's code*. NY: Random House.

Hinch, R. (1994). *Introduction: Theoretical diversity. In R. Hinch (Ed.), Readings in critical criminology*. Scarborough: Prentice-Hall.

Hindelang, M., Hirschi, T., & Weis, J. (1981). *Measuring delinquency*. Beverly Hills, CA: Sage.

Hippchen, L.J. (Ed.). (1978). *Ecological-biochemical approaches to the treatment of delinquents and criminals*. NY: Van Nostrand Reinhold.

Hirschi, T. (1969). *Causes of delinquency*. Berkeley, CA: University of California.

Hirschi, T. (1979). Separate and unequal is better. *Journal of Research in Crime and Delinquency*, 16:34–38.

Hirschi, T., & Gottfredson, M. (1987). Causes of white-collar crime. *Criminology*, 25(4): 949–974.

Hirschi, T., & Gottfredson, M.R. (1989). The significance of white-collar crime and a general theory of crime. *Criminology*, 27(2):359–372.

Hirschi, T., & Hindelang, M.J. (1977). Intelligence and delinquency: A revisionist view. *American Sociological Review*, 42: 571–582.

Hoffman-Bustamonte, D. (1973). The nature of female delinquency. *Issues in Criminology*, 8:117–136.

Holmes, R.M. (1983). *The sex offender and the criminal justice system*. Springfield, IL: Charles C. Thomas.

Holmes, R.M. (1991). *Sex crimes*. Newbury Park, CA: Sage.

Holmes, R.M. (1993). *Serial murder*. Beverly Hills, CA: Sage.

Holmes, R.M., & Homes, S.T. (1993). *Murder in America*. Thousand Oaks, CA: Sage.

Home Office (1979). *Report of the Committee on Obscenity and Film Censorship*. London: Her Majesty's Stationery Office.

Home Office. (1997). (Online).

Honeyman, J.C., & Ogloff, J.R.P. (1996). Capital punishment: Arguments for life and death. *Canadian Journal of Behavioural Science*, 21(1).

Hood, R., & Sparks, R. (1970). *Key issues in criminology*. London: Weidenfeld and Nicolson.

Hooton, E.A. (1931). *Crime and the man*. Reprinted by Greenwood Press, Westport, CT. 1968.

Horowitz, I.L., & Rainwater, L. (1970). Journalistic moralizer. *TransAction*, 7(7):5–7.

Howe, C. (1995). Universities gearing for change. *The Globe and Mail*, A6.

Howell, J.C. (Ed.). (1995). *Guide to implementing the comprehensive strategy for serious, violent, and chronic juvenile offenders*. Washington: U.S. Dept. of Justice. Office of Juvenile Justice and Delinquency Prevention.

Hucker, S.J., Webster, C.D., & Ben-Aron, M-H. (Eds.). (1981). *Mental disorder and criminal responsibility*. Toronto: Butterworths.

Huff, D. (1954). *How to lie with statistics*. NY: W.W. Norton.

Humphrey, L. (1970). *Tearoom trade: Impersonal sex in public places*. Chicago: Aldine.

Hyder, K. (1998, May 27). Muggers defy hi-tech spies to send crime rate soaring. *Evening Standard*, 5.

IBC (1998). Insurance Board Canada: facts book. (Online: www.stratgem.on.ca/ibc/facts/10fact.htm).

Imports and exports of goods on a balance-of-payments basis. (1998). *Canadian Statistics*. (Online).

Inciardi, J.A. (1991). *The drug legislation debate*. Newbury Park, CA: Sage.

International Centre for the Prevention of Crime. (1997). (Online: http://www.crime-preven.../chap2.htm#anchor805002).

Internet porn dangers overblown, says professor. (1998, March 21). *Calgary Herald*, A14.

Jackson, M., & Griffiths, C.T. (1995). *Canadian criminology: Perspectives on crime and criminality* (2nd ed.). Toronto: Harcourt Brace.

Jackson, W. (1995). *Doing social research methods*. Scarborough, ON: Prentice-Hall.

Jacobs, J.B., & Henry, J.S. (1996). The social construction of a hate crime epidemic. *Journal of Criminal Law and Criminology*, 86:366–391.

Jacoby, J.E. (1979). *Classics of criminology*. Prospect Heights, Ill: Waveland.

Jacoby, J.E. (1994). *Classics of criminology* (2nd ed.). Prospect Heights, Ill: Waveland.

Jahrig, G. (1996, June 22). "IQ exam isn't smart testing, says Harvard researcher." *Missoulian*. Missoula, MT. B1.

James, J. (1977). Prostitute and prostitution. In E. Sagarin and F. Montanino (Eds.), *Deviants: Voluntary action in a hostile world*. Glenview, Il: Scott, Freeman.

Jeffery, C.R. (1965, September). Criminal behavior and learning theory. *Journal of Criminal Law, Criminology, and Police Science*, 56: 294–300.

Jeffery, C.R. (1973). The historical development of criminology. In H. Mannheim (Ed.), *Pioneers in criminology* (2nd ed.). Montclair, NJ: Patterson Smith. (Ch. 25).

Jeffery, C.R. (1978). Criminology as an interdisciplinary science. *Criminology*, 16(2): 149–170.

Jeffery, C.R. (1990). *Criminology: An interdisciplinary approach*. Englewood Cliffs, NJ: Prentice-Hall.

Jeffery, C.R. (1993). Biological perspectives. *Journal of Criminal Justice Education*, 4(2): 292–293.

Jeffery, C.R. (1996). The genetics and crime conference revisted. *The Criminologist*, 21(2):1,3.

Jensen, K. (1997, September 15). Personal communication. (President of the Alberta Naturopathic Association).

Johnson, H. (1996). Sexual assault. In L. Kennedy & V. F. Sacco (Eds.), *Crime counts*. Scarborough: Nelson. (Ch. 8).

Johnson, H. (1996b). Violence against women: A special topic survey. In R.A. Silverman, J.J. Teevan, and V.F. Sacco (Eds.), *Crime in Canadian society* (5th ed.). Toronto: Harcourt Brace. (pp. 210–221).

Johnson, H. A. (1988). *History of criminal justice*. Cincinnati, OH: Anderson.

Johnson, J.A., & Fennell, E.B. (1983). Aggressive and delinquent behaviour in childhood and adolescence. In C.E. Walker & M.C. Roberts (Eds.), *Handbook of clinical child psychology*. NY: John Wiley.

Junger-Tas, J., Terlouw, G-T., & Klein, M.W. (Eds.). (1996). *Delinquent behaviour among young people in the western world*. NY: Kugler.

Justice Association (1989). Cited in *"What causes youth crime?" Tough on crime*, Calgary John Howard Society, 1993:3.

Kaczynski plea bargain rejected. (1997, December 30). *Calgary Herald*, A13.

Kantrowitz, B., & Wingert, P. (1993, April 12). No longer a sacred cow: Head Start has become a free-fire zone. *Newsweek*, 51.

Kappler, V.E., Blumberg, M., & Potter, G.W. (1993). *The mythology of crime and justice*. Prospect Heights, Il: Waveland Press.

Karman, A. (1996). *Crime victim* (2nd ed.). Pacific Grove, CA: Brooks/Cole.

Karman, A. (1990). *Crime victim* (2nd ed.). Pacific Grove, CA: Brooks/Cole.

Karmen, A. (1979). Victim facilitation: The case of automobile theft. *Victimology*, 4(4): 361–370.

Katz, J. (1988). *Seduction of crime: Moral and sensual attraction of doing evil*. NY: Basic Books.

Katz, J., & Chambliss, W.J. (1995). Biology and crime. In J.F. Shelly (Ed.), *Criminology: A contemporary handbook*. Belmont, CA: Wadsworth.

Keane, C. (1996). Corporate crime. In R.A. Silverman, J.J. Teevan, and V.F. Sacco (Eds.), *Crime in Canadian society* (5th ed.). Toronto: Harcourt Brace.

Keane, C., Maxim, P., & Teevan, J. (1993). Drinking and driving, self control, and gender: Testing a general theory of crime.

Journal of Research in Crime and Delinquency, 29:30–49.

Kelling, G.L., & Coles, C.M. (1996). *Fixing broken windows*. NY: Touchstone.

Kempf, K. (1993). The empirical status of Hirschi's control theory. In F. Adler and W.S. Laufer (Eds.), *New directions in criminological theory* (Col. 4, pp. 143–185). New Brunswick, NJ: Transaction.

Kenison, F.R. (1973). Charles Doe. In H. Mannheim (Ed.), *Pioneers in criminology*. Montclaire, NJ: Patterson Smith.

Kennedy, L. W., & Forde, D.R., (1990). Routine activities and crime: An analysis of victimization in Canada. *Criminology*, 28:137–152.

Kennedy, L., & Baron, S. (1993). Routine activities and a subculture of violence: A study of violence on the street. *Journal of Research in Crime and Delinquency*, 30:88–112.

Kennedy, L.W., & Forde, D.R. (1995). *Pathways to aggression: Towards a theory of 'Routine Conflict'*. Conflict Series Paper No. 1, Centre for Criminological Research, University of Alberta, Edmonton.

Kennedy, L.W., & Sacco, V.L. (1996). *Crime count: A criminal event analysis*. Scarborough, ON: Nelson.

Kenney, D.J., & Finkenauer, J.O. (1995). *Organized crime in America*. Belmont, CA: Wadsworth.

Kerans, R.P. (1993). Two nations under law. In D. Thomas (Ed.). *Canada and the United States: Differences that count*. Peterborough, ON: Broadview.

Kerlinger, F.N. (1979). *Foundation of behavioral research* (2nd ed.). NY: Holt, Rinehart, & Winston.

Ketcham, B. (1999, January 10). Mayor wants Grand Forks to go to pot. *Calgary Herald*, A6.

Kidder, L.H. & Judd, C.M. (1986). *Research methods in social relations* (5th ed.). NY: Holt, Rinehart & Winston.

Kiedrowski, J., & Jayewardene, C.H.S. (1994). *Parental abduction of children: An overview and profile of the abductor.* Report prepared for the Missing Children's Registry, RCMP. (Also available Online: www.childcybersearch.org/rcmp/recmp6.htm).

Kinberg, O. (1960). *Basic problems of criminology*. Copenhagen.

King, J. (1997, November 19–22). Crime, geography and migration: The need for criminological collaboration in the Americas. *American Society of Criminology*. San Diego, CA.

Kingsbury, A.A. (1973). *Introduction to security and crime prevention surveys*. Charles C. Thomas.

Kinsella, W. (1994). *The web of hate*. Toronto: Harper Collins.

Kittrie, N. (1971). *The right to be different*. Baltimore, MD: John Hopkins University Press.

Klemke, L W. (1978). Does apprehension for shoplifting amplify or terminate shoplifting activity. *Law and Society Review*, 12: 390–403.

Knapp, S. (1998, June 28). Hackers find the cracks in systems. *Calgary Herald*, TL16.

Knobler, P., & Bratton, W.W. (1998). *Turnaround: How America's top cop reversed the crime epidemic*. (Available online: amazon.com).

Koenig, D.J. (1992). Conventional crime. In R. Linden (Ed.), *Criminology: A Canadian perspective* (2nd ed.). Toronto: Harcourt Brace. (Chapter 13).

Kohlberg, L. (1969). Stage and sequence: The cognitive developmental approach of socialization. In D.A. Goslin (Ed.), *Handbook of socialization theory and research*. Chicago: Rand McNally.

Kohlberg, L. (1986). The just community approach to corrections. *Journal of Correctional Education*, 37(2):54–58.

Kohlberg, L., Kauffman, K., Scharf, P., & Hickey, J. (1973). *The just community approach in corrections: A manual*. Niantic, Conn: Department of Corrections.

Kolata, G. (1995, February 28). Man's world, woman's world? Brain studies point to differences. *New York Times*, C6–C7.

Koningsvelf, J. (1998, December 3). *"Money laundering and FIOD."* Summary of paper presented at the FATF meeting in London, U.K. (November 1998).

Konopka, G. (1966). *The adolescent girls in conflict.* Englewood Cliffs, NJ: Prentice-Hall.

Kotulak, R. (1997). *Inside the brain: Revolutionary discoveries of how the mind works.* Kansas City: Andrews McMeel.

Kozak, P. (1998, April 15). Talk smarter, not louder. *Calgary Herald*, E8–9.

Kramer, R.C. (1984). Corporate criminality: The development of an idea. In E. Hochstedler (Ed.), *Corporations as criminals.* Beverly Hills, CA: Sage.

Krisberg, B., & Austin, J. (1978). *Children of Ishmael.* Palo Alto, CA: Mayfield.

Kuhn, A. (1997, November 19–22). *Prison populations: What can be learned from the Austrian, Finnish and German decreases?* Paper presented at the American Society of Criminology 49th annual meeting. San Diego, CA.

Kuhn, T. (1970). *The structure of scientific revolution* (2nd ed.). Chicago: Un. of Chicago Press.

L'Opinion:Independante. (1996, May). Media clip sent by A. Normandeau to the author.

Lab, S.P. (1997). *Crime prevention: Approaches, practices and evaluations* (3rd ed.). Cincinnati, OH: Anderson.

Lacayo, R. (1990, June 25). Rap against a rap group. *Time*. p. 18.

Lad, V. (1985). Ayurveda: *The science of self-healing.* Wilmot, WI: Lotus Press.

Laframboise, D. (1996). *Am I a feminist?* (Online). http://www.razberry.com/raz/laframboise/feminist.htm.

LaHaye, T. (1988). The media's influence undermines America's morality. In D.L. Bender & B. Leone (Eds.), *The mass media.* San Diego, CA: Greenhaven Press. (pp. 111–115).

Lanctot, G. (1994). *The medical Mafia.* Miami: Guyarian Press.

Langan, P.A., & Harlow, C. W. (1994). *Child rape victims, 1992.* Washington, DC: Bureau of Justice Statistics, 1994.

Lanier, M.M., & Henry, S. (1998). *Essential criminology.* Boulder, CO: Westview.

LaPrairie, C. (1990). The role of sentencing in the over-representation of Aboriginal offenders in correctional institutions. *Canadian Journal of Criminology*, 32:429–440.

LaPrairie, C. (1993). Aboriginal women and crime in Canada: Identifying the issues. In E. Adelberg & C. Currie (Eds.), *In conflict with the law: Women and the Canadian justice system.* Vancouver, BC: Press Gang.

Laub, J.H., & Sampson, R.J. (1993). Turning points in the life cycle course: Why change matters to the study of crime. *Criminology*, 31:301–326.

Lauritsen, J.L. (1993). Sibling resemblance in juvenile delinquency: Findings from the National Youth Survey. *Criminology*, 31:387–409.

Lautt, M. (1984). *A report on prostitution in the prairie provinces.* Working Papers on Pornography and Prostitution Report No. 9. Ottawa: Department of Justice.

Lavigna, Y. (1986). *Hell's Angels: Taking care of business.* Toronto: Harper Collins.

Lavigna, Y. (1996). *Into the Abyss.* Toronto: Harper Collins.

Lavigne, B., Hoffman, L., & Dickie, I. (1997, May). Women who have committed suicide. *Forum on Corrections Research*. pp. 25–28.

Law professors accuse seal processors of price-fixing. (1998, May 5). (Online: interactive.cfra.com/1998/05/05/32600.html).

Lawton, V. (1994, January). Home-invasion crime on the rise. *Winnipeg Free Press*, A3.

Lazerfeld, P. F. (1959). Problems in methodology. In R.K. Merton, L. Brown and L.S. Cottrell Jr. (Eds.), *Sociology today: Problems and prospects.* NY: Basic Books.

Lea, J., & Young, J. (1984). *What is to be done about law and order?* NY: Penguin.

Leard, F. (1980, March). Case management and the juvenile offender. *Corrections Newsletter*. Victoria, BC: Attorney General.

LeBlanc, M., & Ferchette, M. (1989). *Male criminal activity from childhood through* youth: Multilevel and developmental perspectives. NY: Springer-Verlag.

Lejins, P. (1983). Educational programs in criminal justice. In S.H. Kadiosh (Ed.), *Encyclopedia of crime and justice*. New York, Free Press.

Lemert, E. (1953). An isolation and closure theory of naïve check forgery. *Journal of Criminal Law and Police Science*, 44: 297–298.

Lenneberg, E.H. (1967). *Biological foundations of language*. NY: John Wiley.

Leonard, E.B. (1982). *Women, crime and society: A critique of criminological theory*. NY: Longman.

Letkemann, P. (1973). *Crime as work*. Englewood Cliffs, NJ: Prentice-Hall.

Levy, C. (1997, May 22–24). Presentation given at the annual Alberta Criminal Justice Association meetings. Red Deer, Alberta.

Lewin, T. (1993, February 8). New laws address old problems: The terror of a stalking threat. *New York Times*, A1.

Leyton, E. (1986). *Hunting humans*. Toronto: Seal Books.

Liebling, A. (Ed.). (1998). *Death of offenders: The hidden side of justice*. Winchester, UK: Waterside Press.

Light, R.C., Nee, C., & Ingham, H. (1993). *Car theft: The offender's perspective*. Home Office Research Study No.130. London Home Office.

Lilles, H. (1997, May 24). *Conditional sentencing: One judge's perspective*. Alberta Criminal Justice Association Conference. Red Deer, Alberta.

Linden, R. (1978). Myths of middle-class delinquency: A test of the generalizability of the social control theory. *Youth and Society*, 9:407–431.

Linden, R. (Ed.). (1996). *Criminology: A Canadian perspective* (3rd ed.). Toronto: Harcourt-Brace.

Linden, R. (Ed.). (2000). *Criminology: A Canadian perspective* (4th ed.). Toronto: Harcourt Brace.

Lindstrom, P. (1997, November 19–22). *Communitarianism and restorative justice in Sweden: Potentials and pitfalls*. Paper presented at the American Society of Criminology 49th annual meetings. San Diego, CA.

Lines, R. (1996). Dare to struggle... Political prisoners and the criminalization of dissent in the U.S.: Insidious implications for Canadians. In K.R.E. McCormick & L.A. Visano (Eds.). *Canadian penology*. Toronto: Canadian Scholars' Press. (Ch. 15).

Lipinski, S. (1991). Adult female offenders in the Provincial/Territorial corrections systems, 1989–90. *Juristat*, 11(6).

Lippert, R. (1990). The construction of Satanism as a social problem in Canada. *The Canadian Journal of Sociology*, XV(4): 417–440.

Livingston, J. (1992). *Crime and criminology*. Englewood Cliffs, NJ: Prentice-Hall.

Locke, D. (1993). Court services in Canada. *Juristat*, 13(2). Canadian Centre for Justice Statistics. Ottawa: Publication Division, Statistics Canada.

Lofland, J. (1984). *Analyzing social settings*. Belmont, CA: Wadsworth.

Loftus, E.F. (1979). *Eyewitness testimony* (2nd ed.). Cambridge, MA: Harvard University Press.

Longmire, D.R. (1983). Ethical dilemmas in the research setting. *Criminology*, 21: 333–348.

Lonsdale, D., & Shamberger, R. (1980). Red cell transketolase as an indicator of nutritional deficiency. *American Journal of Clinical Nutrition*, 33: 205–212.

Lorenz, K. (1966). *On aggression*. NY: Harcourt Brace Jovanovich.

Lowey, M. (March 22, 1997). Diagnosis: We're healthy, but there's room for improvement. *Calgary Herald*, A14–15.

Lowman, J. (1984). *Vancouver field study of prostitution*. Ottawa: Department of Justice.

Lowman, J. (1989). Prostitution in Canada. In N. Davis (Ed)., *International handbook of prostitution*. Westport, CT: Greenwood.

Lowman, J. (1995). Prostitution in Canada. In M.A. Jackson & C.T. Griffiths (Eds.), *Canadian criminology* (3rd ed.). Toronto: Harcourt Brace. (Ch. 10).

Lowman, J., & MacLean, B.D. (Eds.). (1992). *Realist criminology: Crime control and policing in the 1990s*. Toronto: University of Toronto Press.

Ludde, F. (1997). The case for democratic health care. *Alive*, (#180)· 52–53

Lunden, W.A. (1972). Emile Durkheim. In H. Mannheim (Ed.), *Pioneers in criminology*. Montclair, NJ: Patterson Smith.

Lynch, J.P., & Cantor, D. (1992). Ecological and behavioral influences on property victimization at home: Implications for opportunity theory. *Journal of Research in Crime and Delinquency*, 29:335–362.

Lynch, M.J. (1988). The extraction of surplus value, crime and punishment: A preliminary examination. *Contemporary Crises*, 12:329–344.

Lynch, M.J., & Groves, W.B. (1989). *A primer in radical criminology* (2nd ed.). Albany, NY: Harrow & Heston.

Maccoby, E.E., & Jacklin, C.N. (1974). *The psychology of sex differences*. Stanford, CA: Stanford University Press.

MacDonald, V. (1997, January 27). Psychoanalyst links dreams with impending illness. *Calgary Herald*, D2.

Maclean, B.D. (1986). *The political economy of crime*. Scarborough, ON: Prentice-Hall. (Chapter 7).

MacLean, B.D. (1996). State expenditures on Canadian criminal justice. In B.D. MacLean (Ed.), *Crime and society: Readings in critical criminology*. Toronto: Copp Clarke Ltd.

Maclean, B.D., & Milovanovic, D. (Eds.). (1991). *New directions in critical criminology*. Vancouver: Collective Press.

Maclean's. (1994, January, 1).

Macleans, (1991, January 7). High anxieties. pp. 30–31.

Mafia History. (1997). (Online).

Makin, K. (1997, March 13). Lap dancing an indecent act, top court rules. *Globe and Mail*, A1.

Maletzky, B.M. (1991). *Treating the sexual offender*. Newbury, CA: Sage.

Maltz, M. (1990). *Measuring the effectiveness of organized crime control efforts*. University of Illinois at Chicago. Office of International Criminal Justice.

Man sentenced after cops find porn on screen. (1997, July 19). *Calgary Herald*. (Online).

Mannheim, H. (Ed.). (1973). *Pioneers in criminology* (2nd ed.). Montclair, NJ: Patterson Smith.

Manning, P. (1973). On deviance. *Contemporary Sociology*, 2:697–699.

Marlowe, M. (1993, April 27). Personal correspondence. Appalachian State University, Boone, North Carolina.

Marlowe, M., Bliss, L., & Schneider, H.G. (1994). Hair trace element content of violence prone male children. *Journal of Advancement in Medicine*, 7(1): 5–18.

Marotte, B. (1997). V-chip man is a big believer in curbing explicit television. *Calgary Herald*, C10.

Marron, K. (1983, November, 7). TV dubbed a "violent teacher." *Globe and Mail*, p. 1.

Martin, R., Mutchnick, R.J., & Austin, W.T. (1990). *Criminological thought: Pioneers past and present*. NY: Macmillan.

Martinson, R. (1974). What works? Questions and answers about prison reform. *Public Interest*, 35:22–54.

Marx, K., & Engels, F. (1848). *The communist manifesto*. (NY: International Pub., 1979).

Mass, P. (1997). *Underboss Sunny the Bull Gravani's story of life in the Mafia*. NY: Harper Collins.

Massive drug smuggling trial wrapped up. (1996, December 24). *Calgary Herald*. (Online).

Matsueda, R. (1992). Reflected appraisals: Parental labelling, and delinquency: Specifying a symbolic interactionist theory. *American Sociological Review*, 97: 1577–1611.

Matthews, R. (1987). Taking realist criminology seriously. *Contemporary Crisis*, 11:371–401.

Matthews, R., & Young, J. (1986). *Confronting crime*. London: Sage.

Matthews, R., & Young, J. (1992). *Issues in realist criminology*. London: Sage.

Matza, D. (1964). *Delinquency and drift*. NY: Wiley.

Maxfield, M.G., & Babbie, E. (1995). *Research methods for criminal justice and criminology*. Belmont, CA: Wadsworth.

May, R. (1969). *Love and will*. NY: Norton.

Maybury, R. (1993). *Whatever happened to justice?* Placerville, CA: Bluestocking.

Mayhew, P., Clarke, R.V., Sturman, R., & Hough, J.M. (1976). *Crime as opportunity*. Home Office Research Study No. 34. London: HMSO.

McLearn, M. (1998, October 29). Corruption sours foreign business dream. *Calgary Herald*, E1–2.

McCord, W., & McCord, J. (1959). *Origins of crime*. NY: Columbia University.

McCormick & L.A. Visano (Eds.), *Canadian penology: Advanced perspectives and research*. Toronto: Canadian Scholars Press.

McDevitt, J., & Levin, J. (1993). *Hate crimes – The rising tide of bigotry and bloodshed*. NY: Plenum.

McGraham, P. (1986). Brantingham and Brantingham: Patterns in crime. *Canadian Journal of Criminology*, 28(1): 89–91.

McGrath, W.T. (Ed.). (1976). *Crime and its treatment in Canada* (2nd ed.). Toronto: Macmillan.

McIntosh, A. (1998, June 11). RCMP's sting aided drug lords. *Calgary Herald*, A1–2.

McIntyre, S. (1994). *The youngest profession: The oldest oppression*. Unpublished Ph.D. thesis. Department of Law, University of Sheffield, Sheffield, England.

McKenzie, D., & Single, E. (1997). *Alcohol*. Canadian Centre on Substance Abuse. (Online).

McKie, C. (1989). Life style risks: Smoking and drinking. In C. McKie & K. Thompson (Eds.), *Canadian social trends*. Toronto: Thompson. (pp. 86–92)

McKie, C. (1994). Population ageing: Baby boomers into the 21st Century. In C. McKie (Ed.), *Canadian social trends*. Toronto: Thompson Educational Publication.

McMullan, J.L. (1992). *Beyond the limits of the law: Corporate crime and law and order*. Halifax: Fernwood.

McPhie, P. (1996). Fraud. In L. W. Kennedy and V.F. Sacco (Eds.), *Crime counts: A criminal event analysis*. Scarborough: Nelson.

Mednick, S., & Christiansen, K.O. (1977). *Biosocial bases of criminal behavior*. New York: Gardner Press.

Mednick, S., Moffit, T., & Stack, S.A. (1987). *The causes of crime: New biological approaches*. Cambridge, U.K.: Cambridge Un. Press.

Mednick, S., & Volavka, J. (1980). Biology and crime. In N. Morris and M. Tonry (Eds.), *Crime and justice*. Chicago: Univ. of Chicago Press. (pp. 85–159).

Mendelson, B. (1963). The origin of the doctrine of victimology. *Excerpta Criminologica*, 3: 235–244.

Menninger, K. (1968). *The crime of punishment*. NY: Viking.

Mennonite drug pipeline expanding. (1997). *Toronto Star*. (Online).

Menzies, R. (1992). Beyond realist criminology. In J. Lowman & B. D. MacLean (Eds.), *Realist criminology*. Toronto: University of Toronto.

Messner, S.F., & Rosenfeld, R. (1994). Racial inequality and racially disaggregated homicide rates: An assessment of alternative theoretical explanations. *Criminology*, 30: 421–445.

Messner, S.F., & Tardiff, K. (1985) The social ecology of urban homicide: an application of the "routine activities" approach. *Criminology*, 23:241–268.

Metcalfe, R. (1999, January, 15). Kidnapping has become an industry in Columbia. *Calgary Herald*, A15.

Millar, R.W. (1973). John Henry Wigmore. In H. Mannheim (Ed.), *Pioneers in criminology* (2nd ed.). Montclair, NJ: Patterson Smith.

References

Mills, C.W. (1959). *The sociological imagination*. London: Oxford University Press.

Milovanovic, D. (Ed.). (1997). *Chaos, criminology, and social justice: The new orderly (dis)order*. Westport, Conn: Praeger.

Missoulian, (1996, July 18). *DNA test gives back freedom*. A2.

Mitchell, B. (1996, September 26). Police smash ring sending stolen cars to Vietnam. *Toronto Star*. (Online).

Moir, A., & Jessel, D. (1997). *A mind to crime*. Toronto: Signet.

Moffit, T., Lynam, D.R., & Silva, P.A. (1994). Neuropsychological tests predicting persistent male delinquency. *Criminology*, 32: 277–300.

Moffit, T.E. (1993). Adolescence-limited and life-course-persistent antisocial behavior: A developmental taxonomy. *Psychological Review*, 100(4):674–701.

Mofina, R. (1991, August 6). City Asians prey to home invasions. *Calgary Herald*, B1.

Mofina, R. (1996). Young offenders and the press. In J. Winterdyk (Ed.), *Issues and perspectives on young offenders in Canada*. Toronto: Harcourt Brace.

Mofina, R. (1998, February 1). 3,000 Calgarians may be fraud victims. *Calgary Herald*, A1–2.

Mofina, R. & Ketcham, B. (1999, February 7). Force is "rusting out," says Alberta's top Mountie. *Calgary Herald*, A1, 14–15.

Monachesi, E. (1973). Cesare Beccaria. In H. Mannheim (Ed.), *Pioneers in criminology* (2nd ed.). Montclair, NJ: Patterson Smith.

Monahan, J. (1981). *Predicting violent behaviour*. Beverly Hills, CA: Sage.

Montagu, A. (1997). *Man's most dangerous myth: The fallacy of race* (6th ed.). Walnut Creek, CA: Altamira Press.

Moore, L. (1994, October 6). Playing video games leads adolescents to gamble more. *Montreal Gazette*. A5.

Moore, M. (1997, June 18). Argument over man's sexuality turns violent. *Missoulian*, B1.

Morris, C. (1997, January 2). Auditor general questions lottery earnings. *Calgary Herald*. (Online).

Morris, N. (1973). *The law is a busy body*. Copyright by the New York Times Co. (Reprinted by World Correctional Service Centre).

Morrison, P. (1996). Motor-vehicle crimes. In L.W. Kennedy & V.F. Sacco (Eds.), *Crime counts*. Toronto: Nelson.

Morrison, P., & Ogrodnick, L. (1994). Motor vehicle crimes. *Canadian social trends*, 34: 21–26.

Moseley, R. (1995, July/August). Conference: High-tech crime looms as major global concern. *CJ Europe*, 1, 4.

Motiuk, L.L., & Belcourt, R. (1995). *Statistical profiles of homicide, sex, robbery and drug offenders in federal corrections*. Research Brief, B-11. Research Division. Correctional Service of Canada.

Motiuk, L.L., & Porporine, F. (1992). *The prevalence, nature and severity of mental health problems among federal male inmates in Canadian penitentiaries*. Research Report R-24. Correctional Service of Canada: Ottawa.

Moulton, K. (1999, January 10). Two execs took blame, but where was the board? *Calgary Herald*, D1.

Mueller, G.O.W. (1969). *Crime, law, and the scholars*. Seattle: Un. of Washington Press.

Multinational Monitor. (1991, December). (Online).

Multinational Monitor. (1992, December). (Online).

Multinational Monitor. (1996, April).(Online).

Multinational Monitor. (1997, March). (Online).

Murder down for fourth year in a row – CTV coverage up. (1996, September). *Fraser Forum*, 1–2.

Murphy, C. (1995). Traditional sociological approaches. In M.A. Jackson & C.T. Griffiths (Eds.), *Canadian criminology* (3rd ed.). Toronto: Harcourt Brace. (Ch. 6).

Murray, J.P. (1990). Status offenders: Roles, rules, and reactions. In R.A. Weisheit & R.G. Culbertson (Eds.), *Juvenile delinquency: A justice perspective*. Prospect Heights, IL: Waveland. (pp. 17–26).

Nagel, W.H. (1963). The notion of victimology in criminology. *Excerpta Criminologica*, 3: 245–247.

Nagin, D.S., Farrington, D.P., & Moffitt, T.E. (1995). Life-course trajectories of different types of offenders. *Criminology*, 33:111–139.

Nash, J.M. (1997, March 10). The age of cloning. *Time*. pp: 34–41.

Naumetz, T. (1999, January, 14). Control of death penalty could shift to regions. *Calgary Herald*, A6.

Nelken, D. (Ed.). (1994). *The future of criminology*. Thousand Oaks, CA: Sage.

Nettler, G. (1982). *Killing one another*. Cincinnati, OH: Anderson.

Nettler, G. (1984). *Explaining crime*. NY: McGraw-Hill.

Nettler, G. (1987). *Explaining crime* (2nd ed.). Toronto: McGraw-Hill.

Newman, G., & Marongiu, P. (1990). Penological reform and the myth of Becarria. *Criminology*, 28: 325–346.

Newman, G.R. (1977). Problems of method in comparative criminology. *International Journal of Comparative and Applied Criminal Justice*, 1(1): 17–31.

Newman, O. (1972). *Defensible space*. NY: Macmillan.

Newman, O. (1996). *Creating defensible space*. Washington, D.C.: U.S. Dept. of Housing and Urban Development.

Newsworld.

(1997, April 1). *IRA terrorists*. (Online).

(1997, June 20). *Tobacco*. (Online).

(1997, September 19). *Turner donates $1 billion to UN*. (Online).

Nicholl, C. (1997, November 19–22). *Implementation issues in restorative conferencing*. Paper presented at the American Society of Criminology 49 annual meeting. San Diego, CA.

Noel, A. (1997, May 23) Rock machine crippled: Police. *Montreal Gazette*. (Online).

Normandeau, A. (1968). *Trends and patterns in crimes of robbery*. Ph.D. Dissertation. Philadelphia: University of Pennsylvania.

Normandeau, A. (1973). Charles Lucas. In H. Mannheim (Ed.), *Pioneers in criminology* (2nd ed.). Montclair, NJ: Patterson Smith.

Normandeau, A., & Hasenpush, B. (1980, July). Prevention programs and their evaluation. *Canadian Journal of Criminology*, pp. 307–319.

Normandeau, A., & Leighton, B. (1990). *A vision of the future of policing in Canada – Challenge 2000*. Ottawa: Police Security Branch: Solicitor General Canada.

Nurco, D.N., Cisin, I.H., & Ball, J.C. (1985). Crime as a source of income for narcotic addicts. *Journal of Substance Abuse Treatment*, 2, 113–115.

O'Neil, J.A., Wish, E., & Visher, C. (1990). *Drugs and crime – 1989*. Washington, DC: National Institute of Justice.

O'Reilly-Fleming, T. (Ed.). (1996). *Post-critical criminology*. Scarborough: Prentice-Hall.

O'Reilly-Fleming, T. (Ed.). (1996). *Serial and mass murder: Theory, Research and Policy*. Toronto: Canadian Scholars' Press.

Officer's 'lost' lighter a ruse: Morin probe told. (1997, August 6). *Globe and Mail*, A5.

Ogle, R.S., Maier-Katin, D., & Bernard, T.J. (1995). A theory of homicidal behavior among women. *Criminology*, 33(2):173–193.

O'Hanlon, M. (1998, November 7). Woman jailed for girl's death. *Calgary Herald*, A15.

OICJ. (1997, November). The evolution of organized crime. *Crime and Justice International*. 13(10).

Ontario cool to topless women: Poll. (1997, June 23). *Calgary Herald*. (Online).

Ontario Spectrum 1997. Toronto: Guidance Centre OISE.

"Orion: Geographic profiling software". (1996). Vancouver, BC: Environmental Criminology Research Inc.

Overholser, W. (1973). Issac Ray. In H. Mannheim (Ed.), *Pioneers in criminology*

(2nd ed.). Montclair, NJ: Patterson Smith. (Chapter 11).

Oyen, E. (1992). *Comparative methodology: Theory and practice in international social research*. London: Sage.

Pace, D.F. (1991). *Concepts of vice, narcotics, and organized crime* (3rd ed.). Engelwood Cliffs, NJ: Prentice-Hall.

Palango, P. (1994). *Above the law*. Toronto: McClelland and Stweart.

Palys, T. (1998). *Research decisions: Quantitative and qualitative perspectives* (2nd ed.). Toronto: Harcourt Brace Jovanovich.

Parello, N. (1999, April 3). Melissa suspect charged in New Jersey. *Calgary Herald*, E1.

Paternoster, R., Saltzman, L.E., Waldo, G.P., & Chiricos, T.G. (1983). Perceived risk and social control: Do sanctions really deter? *Law and Society Review*, 17: 457–480.

Pavarini, M. (1994). Is criminology worth saving? In D. Nelken (Ed.), *The future of criminology*. Thousand Oaks, CA: Sage.

Pearson, P. (1998). *When she was bad: Violent women and the myth of innocence*. Toronto: Random House.

Pease, K., & Litton, R. (1984). Crime prevention: Practice and motivation. In D.J. Muller, D.E. Blackman, & A.J. Chapman (Eds.), *Psychology and law*. NY: John Wiley & Sons.

Pela, R.L. (1997, Winter). High hopes: A spirited guide to aging and alcohol. *Prime Health and Fitness*. pp. 72–76.

Pepinsky, H. (1991). Peacemaking in criminology. In B.D. MacLean & D. Milovanovic (Eds.), *New directions in critical criminology*. Vancouver: Collective Press.

Pepinsky, H., & Jesilow, P. (1984). *Myths that cause crime* (2nd ed.). Cabin John, MY: Seven Locks.

Perry, P. (1996). Adolescent substance abuse and delinquency. In J.A. Winterdyk (Ed.), *Issues and perspectives on young offenders in Canada*. Toronto: Harcourt Brace. (Ch. 7).

Peters, M. (1995). Does brain size matter? A reply to Rushton and Ankney. *Canadian Journal of Experimental Psychology*, 49(4). (Online – ww.cpa.ca).

Pettiway, L.E. (1988). Urban spatial structure and arson incidence: Differences between ghetto and nonghetto environments. *Justice Quarterly*, 5: 113–130.

Pfohl, S., & Gordon, A. (1986). Criminological displacements: A sociological deconstruction. *Social Problems*, 33:S94–11.

Pfuhl, E.H., & Henry, S. (1993). *The deviance process* (3rd ed.). NY: Aldine.

Philip, D. (1996, July 29). The bikers are coming! Stop the cut backs! *Alberta Report*, pp. 26–27.

Philpott, W.H. (1978). Ecological aspects of antisocial behavior. In L.J. Hippchen (Ed.), *Ecological-biochemical approaches to treatment of delinquents and criminals*. NY: Van Nostrand Reinhold.

Planes checked for illegal immigrants. (1997, February 17). *Calgary Herald*. (Online).

Plato. (1980). The laws. London: Penguin Classics.

Platt, A.M. (1969). *The child savers*. Chicago: The University of Chicago.

Police make arrest in NASA computer hacking case. (1998, April 6). *Sudbury Star*. (Online).

Polk, K. (1991). Book review of Michael R. Gottfredson and Travis Hirschi, A general theory of crime (Stanford, CA: Stanford University Press). *Crime and Delinquency*, 37:575–581.

Pollak, O. (1961). *The criminality of women*. NY: Barnes.

Poterfield, A.L. (1943). Delinquency and its outcome in court and college. *American Journal of Sociology*, 49: 199–208.

Potter, G. (1994). *Criminal organizations: Vice, racketeering, and politics in an American city*. Prospect Heights, Ill: Waveland.

Potter, G., & Kappeler, V. (1998). *Snowblind: The major media, the Contras and crack*. Paper presented at the Academy of Criminal Justice Sciences 35th Annual Meeting. Albuquerque, NM. March, 10–14.

Powell, K. (1998, January 9). What makes Lisa Neve so dangerous, court asks. *Edmonton Journal*. (Online: http://www.southham. com/edmontonjournal.html).

Pressman, A. (1997, May 8). *USA: Big countries differ on regulating electronic money*. (Online: Reuters – www.bizinfo.reuters.com).

Preventing crime within a framework of urban social development (The Netherlands). (1997). (Online: http://www.crime-prevention-intl.org/english/how to/city action/048.htm).

Preventing crime: Current issues and debates. (1990). *Canadian Journal of Criminology*. 32(1).

Prison News Service. (1995, April). (Online search).

Prosecution calls for life term for Carlos. (1997, December 23). *Calgary Herald*, A9.

Protest by arson? (1997, February 24). *Calgary Herald*. (Online).

Prowse, C. (1994). Vietnamese criminal organizations: Reconceptualizing Vietnam "gangs." *RCMP Gazette*, 56(7): 2–8.

Prus, R., & Irini, S. (1988). *Hookers, rounders and desk clerks: The social organization of the hotel community*. Salem: Sheffield.

Quay, H.C. (Ed.). (1987). *Handbook of juvenile delinquency*. NY: John Wiley.

Question: How do you feel about stupid quizzes? (1998, March 25). *Edmonton Journal*. (Online: www.southam.com/edmontonjournal).

Quick facts – Media violence. (1998). (Online: http:www.screen.commnet/eng/iss...olence/quikfct/vioquik.htm#canprev).

Quinney, R. (1970). *The social reality of crime*. Boston: Little, Brown.

Quinney, R. (1977). *Class state and crime*. New York, David McKay.

Quinney, R. (1991). Oneness of all: The mystical nature of humanism. In B.D. MacLean & D. Milovanovic (Eds.), *New directions in critical criminology*. Vancouver: Collective Press.

Quinney, R., & Wildeman, J. (1991). *The problem of crime: A peace and social justice perspective* (3rd ed.). London: Mayfield.

Quiros, C.B. de (1911). *Modern theories of criminality*. Translated by A. deSalvio. Boston: Little, Brown. (1969).

Radzinowicz, L. (1965). *The need for criminology*. London: Heinemann.

Raine, A. (Ed.). (1993). *The psychopathology of crime: Criminal behavior as a clinical disorder*. NY: Acaemic Press.

Raine, A., Brennan, P., & Farrington, D. (1997a). Biosocial bases of violence: Conceptual and theoretical issues. In A. Raine, P. Brennan, & D. Farrington (Eds.), *Biosocial bases of violence*. NY: Plenum.

Raine, A., Buschshaum, M., & LaCasse, L. (1997b). Brain abnormalities in murderers indicated by position emission tomography. *Biological Psychiatry*, 42:508.

Raine, L.P., & Cillufo, F.J. (Eds.). (1994). *Global organized crime: The new empire of evil*. Chicago: Centre for Strategic and International Studies.

Random drug testing to be introduced for officers. (1996, November/December). *CJ International*, p. 8.

Ratner, R.S. (1985). Inside the liberal boot: The criminological enterprise in Canada. In T. Fleming (Ed.), *The new criminologies in Canada*. Toronto: Oxford University Press.

Ray, J-A. (1987). Every twelfth shopper: Who shoplifts and why? *Social Casework*, 68:234–239.

RCMP Gazette. (1994, November). Hells Angels forever!

RCMP violated suspect's rights on body samples, top court rules. (1997, March 21). *Calgary Heral*. '7.

Reasons, C.E. (1986). Workplace terrorism. *The Facts*, 9(3):6–11.

Reasons, C.E., Ross, L., & Paterson, C. (1981). *Assault on the worker: Occupational Health and Safety in Canada*. Toronto: Butterworths.

Reckless, W.C. (1970). American criminology. *Criminology*, 8(1):4–20.

Redl, F., & Wineman, D. (1951). *Children who hate*. Glencoe, Ill: Free Press.

Reed, M., & Morrison, P. (1997). Adult Correctional Services in Canada: 1995–1996. *Juristat Service Bulletin*, 17(4).

Refugee smuggling ring smashed. (1996, December 6). *Calgary Herald*. (Online).

Reich, C.J. (1994, March). (Personal communicate).

Reichel, P.L. (1994). *Comparative criminal justice systems: A topical approach*. Englewood Cliffs, NJ: Prentice-Hall.

Reid, S.T. (1982). *Crime and criminology* (3rd ed.). NY: Holt Reinholt Winston.

Reisman, J.A. (1997). *Images of children crime and violence in Playboy, Penthouse, and Hustler*. Washington, DC: Department of Justice.

Reiss, A.J. (1961). The social integration of peers and queers. *Social Problems*, 9:102–120.

Rengert, G., & Wasilchick, J. (1985). *Suburban burglary: A time and place for everything*. Springfield, Il: Thomas.

Rengert, G.F. (1989). Spatial justice and criminal victimization. *Justice Quarterly*, 6:543–564.

Reoffence risk high – study. (1998, June 5). *Calgary Herald*, B13.

Repetto, T. (1974). *Residential crime*. Cambridge, MA: Ballinger.

Restaurant serves up spankings. (1997, August 13). *Missoulian*. A2.

Retson, D. (1998, February 14). After 6 years, Hedlin calls it quits as director of Sexual Assault Centre. *Edmonton Journal*. (Online: http://www.southam.com/edmontonjournal/news/html).

Rhodes, W.M., & Conly, C. (1981). Crime and mobility: An empirical study. In P.J. Brantingham and P. Brantingham (Eds.), *Environmental criminology*. Beverly Hills, CA: Sage. pp. 161–178.

Ritual Abuse. (1966, Jan 21). http://limestone.–kosone.com/people/ocrt/ra.htm

Ritzer, G. (1992). *Sociological theory* (3rd ed.). NY: McGraw-Hill.

Roberts, J., & Geboyts, R. (1992). Reforming rape laws. *Law and Human Behavior*, 16(5): 555–573.

Roberts, J., & Grossman, M. (1994). Changing definitions of sexual assault: An analysis of police statistics. In J. Roberts and R. Mohr (Eds.), *Confronting sexual assault: A decade of legal and social change*. Toronto: University of Toronto Press.

Roberts, J.V. & Gabor, T. (1990). Lombrosian wine in a new bottle: Research on crime and race. *Canadian Journal of Criminology*, 3292): 291–313.

Roberts, J.V. (1988). Public opinion about sentencing: Some popular myths. *Justice Report*, 5: 7–9.

Roberts, L. (1990). Nettler: Criminology lessons. *Canadian Journal of Criminology*, 32(2): 353 357.

Roesch, R., & Winterdyk, J.A. (1985). *The Vancouver convenience store robbery prevention program*: Final Report. Ottawa: Ministry of the Solicitor General of Canada. No. 1985–42.

Ronald Arthur Biggs. (1996). (Online).

Roneck, D.W., & Maier, P.A. (1991). Bars, blocks, and crimes revisited: Linking the theory of routine activities to the empiricism of "hot spots." *Criminology*, 29:725–753.

Rosenbaum, J. J.L. (1991). Female crime and delinquency. In S.E. Brown, F-A. Esbensen, & G. Geis (Eds.), Criminology: *Explaining crime and its context*. Cincinnati, OH: Anderson.

Ross, J.I. (Ed.). (1995). *Violence in Canada: Sociological perspectives*. Don Mills, ON: Oxford.

Ross, R. (1993). Evaluating the Canadian Centre for Justice Statistics. In J. Hudson and J. Roberts (Eds.), *Evaluating justice*. Toronto: Thompson Educational Pub.

Ross, R.R., Fabiano, E.A., & Eweles, C.D. (1988). Reasoning and rehabilitation. *International Journal of Offender Therapy and Comparative Criminology*, 32: 29–35.

Rossmo, D.K. (1995). Place, space, and police investigations: Hunting serial violent criminals. In J.E. Eck & D. Weisburd (Eds.), *Crime and place*. Washington, DC: Criminal Justice Press.

Rowe, D.C., & Farrington, D.P. (1997). The familial transmission of criminal convictions. *Criminology*, 35(1):177–201.

Rubin, S. (1998, June 3). Bre-X's Walsh suffers stroke. *Federal Post*. (Online: www.sunmeadia.ca).

Rush, F. (1980). *The best kept secrets: Sexual abuse of children*. NY: McGraw-Hill.

Rushton, J.P. (1995). *Race evolution, and behaviour: A life history perspective*. New Brunswick, NJ: Transactional Pub.

Rushton, J.P., & Ankney, D. (1995). Brain size matters: A reply to Peters. *Canadian Journal of Experimental Psychology*, 49(4). (Online – www.cpa.ca).

Rushton, J.P., & Harris, J.A. (1994). *Genetic and environmental components to self-report violence in male and female twins*. Paper presented at the American Society of Criminology annual meetings. Miami. (November).

Rutter, M., & Giller, H. (1984). Juvenile delinquency: Trends and perspectives. NY: The Guilford Press. *Criminology*, 223–240.

Sacciol, P. (1998, March 09). Personal communicatation. (Director of Security for the Canadian Banking Association.

Sacco, V. F. (1982). The effects of mass media on perceptions of crime. *Pacific Sociological Review*, 25(4): 475–493.

Sacco, V.F., & Kennedy, L. (1994). *The criminal event*. Scarborough: Nelson.

Sacco, V.F., & Kennedy, L.W. (1998). *The criminal event* (2nd ed.). Scarborough: Nelson.

Saferstein, R. (1998). *Criminalistics: An introduction to forensic science* (6th ed.). Upper Saddle River, NJ: Prentice-Hall.

Salomon, E.D. (1988). Homosexuality: Sexual stigma. In V.F. Sacco (Ed.), *Deviance: Conformity and control in Canadian society*. Scarborough: Prentice-Hall.

Samenow, S.E. (1984). *Inside the criminal mind*. NY: Random House.

Sampson, R.J., & Laub, J. (1988). Unraveling families and delinquency: A reanalysis of the Glueck's data. *Criminology*, 26: 355–380.

Sampson, R.J., & Laub, J. (1993). *Crime in the making: Pathways and turning points through life*. Cambridge, Mass: Harvard Un. Press.

Sansfacon, D. (1985). *Prostitution in Canada: A research review report*. Ottawa: Department of Justice.

Sapstead, D. (1999, January 4). Terrorist chief renews call for holy war. *Calgary Herald*, A1.

Scaramella, G., Brensinger, M., & Miller, P. (1997, October). Outlaw motorcycle gangs: Tattoo-laden misfits or sophisticated criminals? *Crime and Justice International*, pp. 10–13.

Schafer, S. (1976). *Introduction to criminology*. Reston, VA: Reston.

Schlaadt, R.G. (1992). *Alcohol use and abuse*. Guilford, CT: Duskin.

Schmalleger, F. (1996). *Criminology today*. Englewood Cliffs, NJ: Prentice-Hall.

Schoentahler, S., & Doraz, W. (1983). Diet and crime. *International Journal of Biosocial Research*, 4: 29–39.

Schoenthaler, S., Amos, S., Eysenck, H., Hudes, M., & Korda, D. (1995). *A controlled trial of the effect of vitamin-mineral supplementation on the incidence of serious institutional rule violations*. Unpublished manuscript - courtesy of H. Eysenck.

Schroeder, D.P. (1994). Fetal alcohol syndrome and effects. (Online search).

Schuessler, K.F., & Cressey, D.R. (1950). Personality characteristics and criminals. *American Journal of Sociology*, 55: 476–484.

Schur, E. (1972). *Labelling deviant behavior*. NY: Harper & Row.

Schur, E. (1973). *Radical non-intervention*. Englewood Cliffs, NJ: Prentice-Hall.

Schwendinger, H., & Schwendinger, J. (1970). Defenders of order or guardians of human rights. *Issues in Criminology*, 5:123–157.

Schwendinger, H., & Schwendinger, J. (1983). *Rape and inequality*. Beverly Hills, CA: Sage.

Schwendinger, H., & Schwendinger, J. (1991). Feminism, criminology and complex variations. In B.D. MacLean, B, & D. Milovanovic (Eds.), *New directions in critical criminology*. Vancouver, BC: The Collective Press. (Chapter 7).

Scott, J.E., & Schwalm, L.A. (1987). Pornography and rape: An examination of adult theater rates and rape rates by State. In J.E. Scott and T. Hirschi (Eds.),

Controversial issues in crime and justice. Newbury Park, CA: Sage.

Scott, P. (1973). Henry Maudsley. In H. Mannheim (Ed.), *Pioneers in criminology* (2nd ed.). Montclair, NJ: Patterson Smith. (Chapter 12.)

Seagrave, J. (1997). *Introduction to policing in Canada.* Scarborough: Prentice-Hall.

Selected trends in Canadian criminal justice. (1984). Ottawa: Solicitor General of Canada, Program Branch.

Sellin, T. (1931). The basis of a crime index. *Journal of Criminal law and Criminology,* 22: 335–336.

Sellin, T. (1938). *Culture conflict and crime.* Bulletin 41; New York: Social Science Research Council.

Sellin, T. (1973). Enrico Ferri 1856–1929. In H. Mannheim (Ed.), *Pioneers in criminology* (2nd ed.). Montclair, NJ: Patterson Smith.

Sexual assaults not seen as serious: Professor. (1997, June 8). *Calgary Herald.* (Online).

Shah, S., & Roth, L.H. (1974). Biological and psychophysiological factors in criminality. In D. Glaser (Ed.), *Handbook of criminology.* Chicago, Il.: Rand McNally. (pp. 101–73).

Shallit, J. (1997). *Ten fallacies of Internet censorship.* (Online search).

Shaw, C., & McKay, H. (1969). Juvenile delinquency and urban areas: A study of rates of delinquency in relation to differential characteristics of local communities in American cities. Chicago: Un. of Chicago Press.

Shaw, G. (1997, September 5). Car theft in North America, it occurs on average every 20 seconds. *Calgary Herald,* G12.

Shaw, M., & Dubois, S. (1995). *Understanding violence by women: A review of the literature.* Ottawa: Corrections Service Canada. (Online: http://198.103.98.138/crd/fsw/fsw23/fsw23e02.htm).

Shearing, C. (1989). Decriminalizing criminology: Reflections on the liberal and topological meaning of the term. *Canadian Journal of Criminology,* 31(2):169–178.

Sherman, L.W., Patrick, R.G., & Michael, E.B. (1989). Hot spot of predatory crime: Routines activities and the criminology of place. *Criminology,* 27:27–55.

Sherman, L.W., Smith, D.A., Schmidt, J.D., & Rogan, D.P. (1992). Crime, punishment, and stake in conformity: Legal and informal control of domestic violence. *American Sociological Review,* 49: 261–272.

Sherman, R. (1994, April 18). Crime's toll on the U.S.: Fear, despair and guns. *National Laws.* (1994–95 Greenview)

Short, J. (1997, September/October). President's message: On communicating, cross boundaries and building bridges. *The Criminologist.* pg. 1.

Siegel, L.J. (1992). *Criminology, theories, patterns, and typologies* (4th ed.). St. Paul, MN: West.

Siegel, L.J. (1995). *Criminology: Theories, patterns, and typologies* (5th ed.). Minneapolis/St. Paul, MN: West.

Sillars, L. (1996, July 26). Where Angels do not fear to tread. *Alberta Report,* pp. 24–29.

Silverman, R.A. (1988). Interpersonal criminal violence. In V.F. Sacco (Ed.). *Deviance: Conformity and control in Canadian society.* Scarborough: Prentice-Hall.

Silverman, R.A., & Kennedy, L. (1992). *Deadly deeds: Murder in Canada.* Scarborough: Nelson.

Silverman, R.A., & Teevan, J.J., Jr. (1986). *Crime in Canadian society* (3rd ed.). Toronto: Butterworths.

Silverman, R.A., Teevan, J.J., Jr., & Sacco, V.F. (1991). *Crime in Canadian society* (4th ed.). Toronto: Butterworths.

Simon, R. (1975). *Women and crime.* Lexington, MA: D.C. Heath.

Simonds, M. (1996, March/April). Code of arms. *Canadian Geographic,* pp. 45–56.

Simpson, S. (1989). Feminist theory, crime and justice. *Criminology,* 27: 497–538.

Sinclair, M. (1994). Aboriginal peoples and Euro-Canadians: Two world views, aboriginal self-government in Canada. In J.H.

Hylton (Ed.,) *Current trends and issues*. Saskatoon, Sask.: Purich.

Single, E., Robson, L., Relm, J., & Xie, X. (1996). *The cost of substance abuse in Canada*. Toronto: Candian Centre for Substance Abuse.

Skinner, B.F. (1971). *Beyond freedom and dignity*. NY: Knopf.

Skinner, B.F. (1979). *The shaping of a behaviourist*. NY: Knopf.

Slade, D. (1997, January 15). Man bilked pogey fund of $93,500. *Calgary Herald*, B1.

Slade, D. (1999, January 16). Unusual circumstances cited in lenient sentence. *Calgary Herald*, B1.

Slade, D. (1999, February 26). Mountie slammed by judge over cash seizure. *Calgary Herald*, B1.

Slotter, K. (1997, June). *Plastic payments: trends in credit card fraud*. FBI Law Enforcement Bulletin. (On-line).

Smandych, R. (1985). Re-examining the origins of Canadian anticombines legislation, 1890–1910. In T. Fleming (Ed.), *The new criminologies in Canada*. Toronto: Oxford University Press.

Smith, C. (1997, July 2). Critics say school for Johns doesn't make the grade. *The Georgia Strait*. (Online: ww.walnut.org/csis/news/vancouver_96/straight.html).

Smith, M. (1983). *Violence and sports*. Toronto: Butterworths.

Smuggling ring goes up in smoke. (1996, December 4). *Calgary Herald*. (Online).

Smythe, P. (1996). Terrorism in Canada: Recent trends and future prospects. *RCMP Gazette*, 58(10): 18–22.

Snell, T.L. (1994). *Women in prison*. Washington, DC: Bureau of Justice Statistics Bulletin. (Online).

Snider, L. (1993). *Bad business: Corporate crime in Canada*. Scarborough, ON: Nelson.

Snodgrass, J. (1982). *The jack-roller at seventy: A fifty year follow-up*. Lexington, Mass: D.C. Health.

Social implications of child prostitution. (1998).

(Online: http://www.taasa.org/childprostit.htm).

Sociology, 49: 199–208.

Soderman, H., & O'Connell, J. (1945). *Modern criminal investigation*. NY: Funk and Wagnell.

Solicitor General of Canada. (1998). (Online).

Somers, L.E. (1984). *Economic crimes*. NY: Clark Boardman.

Southland, M.D., Collins, P.A., & Scarborough, K.E. (1997). *Workplace violence*. Cincinnati, OH: Anderson.

Spanish trawlers given hook. (1997, March 10). *Calgary Herald*. (Online).

Special Committee on Pornography and Prostitution. (1985). *Pornography and prostitution in Canada*. Ottawa: Department of Supply and Services.

Spies get the scoop on Japan auto industry. (1999, April 13). *Calgary Herald*. F6.

Spoke, M.L. (1998, June 27). Quoted in M. Welsh and K. Donovan. Four giant casinos on the way. *Toronto Star*. (Online).

Sprott, J. (1996). Understanding public views of youth crime and the youth justice system. *Canadian Journal of Criminology*, 38: 271–288.

Stahura, J.N., & Hollinger, R.C. (1988). A routine activities approach to suburban arson rates. *Sociological Spectrum*, 8:349–369.

Stalking and domestic violence in America. (Online: www.ojd.usdoj.gov/vawgo/stalk98/chapter1.htm) [January 15, 1999].

Stamler, R.T. (1996). Organized crime. In R. Linden (Ed.), *Criminology: A Canadian perspective* (3rd ed.). Toronto: Harcourt Brace.

Stansfield, R.T. (1996). *Issues in policing: A Canadian perspective*. Toronto: Thompson Educational Pub.

Stark, R. (1992). *Sociology* (4th ed.). Belmont, CA: Wadsworth.

Statistics Canada. (1997). *Justice spending, by sector*. (Online: http://www.statcan.ca/english/pgdb/state/justice/legal13.htm).

Statistics for 95. (1997). *Crime and justice statistics for Western Australia* (1995). Perth, WA: Faculties of Economic and Commerce,

Education and Law. The University of Western Australia.

Steffensmeier, D.J. (1978). Crime and the contemporary women. *Social Forces*, 57: 566–584.

Steinert, H. (1997). Fin de siècle criminology. *Theoretical Criminology*, 1(1):111–129.

Sterling prize winner challenges prostitution law. (1997, Fall). *Simon Fraser University Alumni Journal*, p. 8.

Stevens, L. (1997). Gender bars: Sentencing the female offender. *Law Now*. (Online: www.extension.ualberta.ca/lawnow/female/htm).

Stinchfield, R. (1997). *Youth gambling*. (Online).

Stinchfield, R., & Winters, K. (1997). *Gambling treatment outcome study*. (Online).

Stitt, B.G., & Giacopassi, D.J. (1992). Trends in the connectivity of theory and research in criminology. *The Criminologist*, 17(1): 3–6.

Stoff, D.M., & Cairns, R.B. (Eds.). (1996). *Aggression and violence: Genetic, neurobiological, and biosocial perspectives*. Mahwah, NJ: Lawrence Erlbaum Assoc.

Stoff, D.M., & Cairns, R.B. (Eds.). (1996). *Aggression and violence*. Mahwah, NJ: Lawrence Erlbaum Assoc.

Stoff, D.M., & Vitieloo, D. (1996). Role of serotonin in aggression of children and adolescents: biochemical and pharmacological studies. In D.M. Stoff and R.B. Cairns (Eds.), *Aggression and violence: Genetic, neurobiological, and biosocial perspectives*. Mahwah, NJ: Lawrence Erlbaum Assoc.

Stone, T. (1998, May). Slavic women in demand in sex slave markets throughout world. *Crime and Justice International*, pp. 7–8.

Straten, M. van. (1994). *Gurana*. Saffron Walden, U.K.: C.W. Daniel Co.

Streissguth, (1997). *Crime Times*. (Online).

Sulloway, F.J. (1979). *Freud: Biologist of the mind*. NY: Basic Books.

Surette, R. (1992). *Media, crime and criminal justice*. Pacific Grove, CA: Brooks/Cole.

Sutherland, E. (1937). *The professional thief*. Chicago: University of Chicago Press.

Sutherland, E. (1947). *Principles of Criminology* (4th ed.). Philadelphia, PA: J.B. Lippincott.

Sutherland, E. (1949). *White collar crime*. NY: Holt, Rinehart and Hart.

Sutherland, E., & Cressey, D. (1955). *Principles of criminology* (5th ed.). Philadelphia, PA: Lippincott.

Sutherland, E., & Cressey, D. (1960). *Principles of criminology* (6th ed.). Philadelphia, PA: J.B. Lippincott.

Swaffer, T., & Hollin, C.R. (1995). Adolescent firesetting: why do they say they do it? *Journal of Adolescence*, 18: 619–623.

Swigert, V.L., & Farrell, R.A. (1976). *Murder, inequality, and the law*. Lexington, MA: Lexington Books.

Sykes, G., & Matza, D. (1957). Techniques of neutralization: A theory of delinquency. *American Sociological Review*, 22:664–670.

Synnott, A. (1996). *Shadows: Issues and social patterns in Canada*. Scarborough: Prentice-Hall.

Tabakoff, B., Whelan, J.P., & Hoffman, P.L. (1990). Two biological markers of alcoholism. In C.R. Cloninger & H. Begleiter (Eds.), *Genetics and biology of alcoholism*. Cold Spring Harbor, NY: Cold Spring Harbor Laboratory Press.

Tannenbaum, D.J. (1977). Personality and criminality: A summary and implication of the literature. *Journal of Criminal Justice*, 5: 225–235.

Tanner, A. (1997, October 17). Asian crime ring fail deportation order. *Calgary Herald*, A6.

Tanner, J. (1997). *Teenage trouble: Youth and deviance in Canada*. Scarborough: Nelson.

Taylor, I., Walton, P., & Young, J. (1973). *The new criminology: For a social theory of deviance*. London: Routledge and Kegan Paul.

Taylor, R.B., & Harrell, A.V. (1996). *Physical environment and crime*. Washington, D.C.: National Institute of Justice.

Teevan, J.J. (Ed.). (1986). *Introduction to sociology: A Canadian perspective*. Scarborough: Prentice-Hall.

Teevan, J.J., & Blute, M. (1986). What is sociology? In J.J. Teevan (Ed.), *Introduction to sociology: A Canadian perspective*. Scarborough: Prentice-Hall. (Chapter 1).

Texas executes Karla Faye Tucker for 1983 pickaxe slaying. (1998, February 4). *Edmonton Journal*. (Online).

The book of vital world statistics: *The Economist*. (1990). NY: Random House.

The complete history of cannabis in Canada. (1997, January 3). (Online).

The Metro Toronto research group on drug use. (1996, August). *Facts on Rohypnol*. (Online: http://sano.org/geninfo/rohypnol.htm).

The Report of the Commission on Obscenity and Pornography. (1970). Washington, DC: U.S. Government Printing Office.

The Ultimate price. (1997, June 8). *Calgary Herald*. A9.

The Vriend decision: What it means for Albertans. (1998, April 3). *Calgary Herald*, A7–A8.

The watch your car program. (1996, November). Washington, D.C.: Bureau of Justice Assistance fact Sheet.

Theodorson, G.A. (Ed.). (1982). *Urban patterns: Studies in human ecology*. Philadelphia: The Pennsylvania State University Press.

Thomas, J., & O'Maolchatha, A. (1989). Reassessing the critical metaphor: An optimistic revisionist view. *Criminology*, 6(6): 143–172.

Thomas, S.P. (Ed.). (1993). *Women and anger*. NY: Aldine de Gruyter.

Thomas, W.I. (1923). *The unadjusted girl: With cases and standpoint for behavior analysis*. NY: Harper and Row.

Thompson, M. (1996). Zeroing in on the serial killer. *RCMP Gazette*, 58(3):14–15.

Thornberry, T.P., & Farnsworth, M. (1982). Social correlates of criminal involvement: Further evidence on the relationship between social status and criminal behavior. *American Sociological Review*, 47:505–518.

Tifft, L. Forward to D. Sullivan (1980). *The mask of love*. Port Washington, NY: Kennikat Press.

Tjaden, P. (1997, November). *The crime of stalking: How big is the problem?* Washington: National Institute of Justice.

Toneguzzi, M. (1997, April 1). Calgary researchers win funding. *Calgary Herald*, B3.

Toneguzzi, M. (1998, November 4). Province declares $8M war on crime. *Calgary Herald*, A1–2.

Tonry, M., & Farrington, D.P. (Eds.). *Building a safer society: Strategic approaches to crime prevention*. Chicago: The University of Chicago.

Treatment planned for women gambling addicts. (1997, August 11). *Calgary Herald*. (Online).

Trembley, P. (1986). Designing crime: The short life expectancy and the workings of a recent wave of credit card bank frauds. *British Journal of Criminology*, 26: 673–690.

Trembley, P., Clermont, Y., & Cusson, M. (1996). Jockeys and joyriders. In R.A. Silverman, J.J. Teevan, and V.F. Sacco (Eds.), *Crime in Canadian society* (5th ed.). Toronto: Harcourt Brace. (Ch. 20).

Tunnell, K. (1993). Inside the drug trade: Trafficking from the dealer's perspective. *Qualitative Sociology*, 16:361–381.

Turk, A. (1964). Toward construction of a theory of delinquency. In H.L. Voss (Ed.). (1970). *Society, delinquency, and delinquent behavior*. Boston, Mass: Little, Brown and Co.

Turk, A. (1995). Transformation versus revolutionism and reformism: Policy implications of conflict theory. In H.D. Barlow (Ed.), *Crime and public policy:Putting theory to work*. Boulder, CO: Westview Press. (pp. 15–28).

UCR. (1994). Uniform Crime Reporting Program Press Release. U.S. Department of Justice. (Online).

Underwood, N. (1991, January 7). High anxiety. *Maclean's*, pp. 30–36.

Unis, A.S., Cook, E.H., Vincent, J.G., Gjerge, D.K., Perry, B.D., Magon, C., & Mitchell, J. (1997). Platelet serotonin measures in adolescents with conduct disorder. *Biological Psychiatry*, 42:553–559.

United Nations. (1995). *Ninth United Nations*

Congress on the Prevention of Crime and the Treatment of Offenders. Cairo, Egypt, 29 April - 8 May. Vienna, Austria: United Nations.

University Medical Research Publishers. (1993). *Amazing medicines the drug companies don't want you to discover*. Tempe, AZ.

Upgrades to computer system will make it easier to track felons. (1997, November 9). *Calgary Herald*, A4.

Van Brunschot, E.G., and Brannigan, A. (1997). Youthful prostitution and child sexual trauma. *International Journal of Law and Psychiatry*, 20(3): 337–354.

Vancouver Board of Trade Information. (1997, June). *Report on property crime in Vancouver- June 1997*. (Online: www.vancouver.boardoftrade.com/crime_report.html).

Van Dijk, J.J.M., Mayhew, P., & Killias, M. (1990). *Experiences of crime across the world*. Boston: Kluwer.

Vest, J., Cohen, W., & Tharp, M. (1997, June). Road rage. *U.S. News and World Report*. (Online).

Video gambling under attack. (1997, February 7). *Calgary Herald*. (Online).

Vikkunen, M., & Linnoila, M. (1996). Serotonin and glucose metabolism in impulsively violent alcoholic offenders. In D.M. Staff & R.B. Cairns (Eds.), *Aggression and violence*. Mahwah, NJ: Lawrence Erlbaum Assoc.

Violence Research Foundation. (VRF). (1994). Material forwarded by R. Hodges, President of the VRF, Tustin, CA.

Violent crime among youth shows increase. (1992, October 17). *Globe and Mail*, A9.

Violent crime in Canada 1996 (Vol. 16(6)). *Juristat Service Bulletin*. Canadian Centre for Justice Statistics.

Vito, G.F., & Holmes, R.M. (1994). *Criminology: Theory, research, and policy*. Belmont, CA: Wadsworth.

VLT, Video Lottery Terminals, slot machine, on... (1998). (Online: www.telusplanet.net/public/gibson/intro.htm).

Vold, G. (1958). *Theoretical criminology*. New York: Oxford University Press.

Vold, G.B., & Bernard, T.J. (1981). *Theoretical criminology* (2nd ed.). NY: Oxford.

Von Hentig, H. (1948). *The criminal and his victim: Studies in the sociobiology of crime*. New Haven, Conn: Yale Univ. Press..

Von Hentig, H. (1973). Gustuv Aschaffenburg. In H. Mannheim (Ed.), *Pioneers in criminology* (2nd ed.). Montclair, NJ: Patterson Smith. (Ch. 22).

Walker, M. (December 1994). Excessive tissue manganese as a cause of antisocial behaviour. *Townsend Letter for Doctors*, 1328–1334.

Walker, N. (1987). *Crime and criminality: A critical introduction*. NY: Oxford University Press.

Wallace, R.A., & Wolf, A. (1995). *Contemporary sociological theory: Continuing the classical tradition* (4th ed). Englewood Cliffs, NJ: Prentice-Hall.

Waller, I., & Okihiro, N. (1978). *Burglary: The victim and the public*. Toronto: University of Toronto Press.

Walters, G.D. (1992). A meta-analysis of the gene-crime relationship. *Criminology*, 30(4): 595–613.

Wannell, T. (1990). Losing ground: Wages of young people, 1981–1986. In C. McKie & K. Thompson (Eds.), *Canadian social trends*. Toronto: Thompson Educational Pub. (pp. 221–223).

Warr, M. (1993). Age, peers, and delinquency. *Criminology*, 31: 17–40.

Warren, M.Q., & Hindelang, M.J. (1986). Current explanations of offender behaviour. In H. Toch (Ed.), *Psychology of crime and criminal justice*. Prospect Heights, Ill: Waveland Press. (pp. 166–182).

Webb, N., Sakheim, G., Towns-Miranda, L., & Wagner, C. (1990). Collaborative treatment of juvenile firestarters: Assessment and outreach. *American Journal of Orthopsychiatry*, 60:305–310.

Weichman, D. (1994). Caning and corporal punishment: Viewpoint. *CJ International*, 10(5): 13–20.

Weisburd, D., Chayet, E.F., & Waring, E.J. (1990). White-collar crime and criminal careers: Some preliminary findings. *Crime and Delinquency*, 36: 342–355.

Weiss, D.S. (1988). Personality assessment. In H.H. Goldman (Ed.), *Review of general psychology*. Norwalk, CT: Appleton & Longe. (pp. 221–232).

Wellford, C.C. (1997, December). Two goals of criminal justice. *Crime and Justice International*, p. 4.

Wellford, C.C. (1975). Labelling theory and criminology. *Social Problems*, 22:313–332.

Wellford, C.F. (1997). 1996 Presidential Address: Controlling crime and achieving justice. *Criminology*, 35(1):1–12.

Wells, L.E. (1995). Explaining crime in the year 2010. In J. Klofas & S. Stojkovic (Eds.), *Crime and justice in the year 2010*. Belmont, CA: Wadsworth. (Ch. 3).

Welsh, M., & Donovan, K. (1998, June 27). Four giant casinos on the way. *Toronto Star* (Online – www2.thestar.com).

Wertheim, A.H. (July 1995). What's wrong with sugar? *Townsend Letter for Doctors*, 85–86.

West, G.W. (1984). *Young offenders and the state*. Toronto: Butterworths.

Western Spectrum 1997. Toronto, ON: Guidance Centre OISE.

When it's no longer a game. (1995, February 27). *Calgary Herald*, B3.

White collar crooks steal billions – ex-Mountie. (1997, October 2). *Calgary Herald*, B10.

White, J. (1991). *Terrorism: An introduction*. Pacific Grove, CA: Brooks/Cole.

White, P.T. (1989, January). An ancient Indian herb turns deadly: Coca. *National Geographic*. (pp. 2–47).

Wijayasinghe, M.S. (1994). *The Alberta Juvenile Firesetter Handbook and Resource Directory*. Edmonton, AB: Fire Commissioner's Office of Alberta Labour.

Wijsman, M. (1990). Linkage analysis of alcoholism: Problems and solutions. In C.R. Cloninger & H. Begleiter (Eds.), *Genetics and biology of alcoholism*. Cold Spring Harbor, NY: Cold Spring Harbor Laboratory Press. (pp. 317–326).

Wilkes, J., & Edwards, P. (1997, July 25). Mobster murdered answering his door. *Toronto Star*. (Online).

Williams, K.R. & Hawkins, R. (1986). The meaning of arrest for wife assault. *Criminology*, 27: 163–181.

William, F.P. III., & McShane, M.D. (1994). *Criminological theory* (2nd ed.). Englewood Cliffs, NJ: Prentice-Hall.

Williams, F.P., & McShane, M.D. (1988). *Criminological theory*. Englewood Cliffs, NJ: Prentice-Hall.

Williams, R.J., & Kalita, D.K. (1977). *A physician's handbook on orthomolecular medicine*. NY: Pergamon Press.

Wilson, E.O. (1975). *Sociobiology: The new synthesis*. Cambridge, MA: The Belknap Press of Harvard University Press.

Wilson, E.O. (1978). Introduction: What is sociobiology. In M.S. Gregory, A. Silvers, & D. Sutch (Eds.), *Sociobiology and human nature*. San Francisco: Jossey-Bass.

Wilson, J.Q. (1975). *Thinking about crime*. New York: Vantage (Reprinted in 1983).

Wilson, J.Q. (1994, September). What to do about crime? *Commentary*, 25–34.

Wilson, J.Q. (1995). Crime and public policy. In J. Wilson & J. Petersilia (Eds.), *Crime*. San Francisco, CA: ICS Press. pp. 489–507.

Wilson, J.Q., & Herrnstein, R. (1985). *Crime and human nature*. NY: Simon & Schuster.

Winfree, L.T., Jr., Griffiths, C.T., & Sellers, C.S. (1989). Social learning theory, drug use, and American Indian youths: A cross-cultural test. *Justice Quarterly*, 6:395–417.

Winterdyk, J. (1993, February). "Respectable" crime. *Law Now*, pp. 20–21.

Winterdyk, J. (1996). The looking glass: Canadian Centre for Justice Statistics. *Law Now*, 20(5): 14–17.

Winterdyk, J. (1997a, February/March). Law school admission: Is there anything you can do? *Law Now*, pp. 31–34.

Winterdyk, J. (Ed.). (1997b). *Juvenile justice systems: International perspectives*. Toronto: Canadian Scholar's Press.

Winterdyk, J. (1998, April/May). It's time, it's time, is it time for restorative justice? *Law Now*, 20–22.

Winterdyk, J. (Ed.). (2000a). *Issues and perspectives on young offenders in Canada* (2nd ed.). Toronto: Harcourt Brace.

Winterdyk, J. (Ed.). (2000b—forthcoming). *Corrections in Canada: Social Reactions to Crime.* Scarborough, ON: Prentice Hall.

Winterdyk, J., & Roesch, R. (1982). A wilderness experiential program as an alternative to probation: An evaluation. *Canadian Journal of Criminology*, 24(1): 39–50.

Wolf, D. (1991). *The Rebels: A brotherhood of outlaw bikers*. Toronto: University of Toronto Press.

Wolff, R.P. (1971). *Philosophy: A modern encounter*. Englewood Cliffs, NJ: Prentice-Hall.

Wolfgang, M.E. (1963). Uniform Crime Reports: A critical appraisal. *University of Pennsylvania Law Review*, 111: 708–738.

Wolfgang, M. E. (1973). Cesare Lombroso. In H. Mannheim (Ed.), *Pioneers in criminology* (2nd ed.). Montclair, NJ: Patterson Smith.

Wolfgang, M.E. (1996, May). *Delinquents in China: Study of birth cohort*. National Institute of Justice. Rockville, MD: U.S. Dept. of Justice.

Wolfgang, M.E., & Ferracuti, F. (1967). *The subculture of violence*. London: Tavistock.

Woman complains over RCMP inaction. (1997, August 19). *Calgary Herald*. (Online).

Wooden, W. (1991). Juvenile firesetters in cross-cultural perspective: How should society respond? In J. Hackler (Ed). Official responses to juvenile problems: Some international reflections. *Fire Journal*. Onita, Spain: Onita Pub.

Woodward, J. (1997, January 27). The university turns New Age. *Alberta Report*, p. 38.

Working Paper 36 – *Damage to property: Arson*. (1984). Ottawa: Law Reform Commission of Canada.

Wright, B., & Fox, V. (1978). *Criminal justice and the social sciences*. Philadelphia, PA: W.B. Saunders.

Wright, D. (1997). *Acknowledging the continuum from childhood abuse to male prostitution*. (Online: http://www.netizen.org/narc/bcifv/backiss2/spring95/nf_continuum.html).

Wright, R. (1998). *The most-cited scholars and works in criminological theory*. Paper presented at the Academy of Criminal Justice Sciences 35th Annual Meeting. Albuquerque, NM. March 10–14.

Wright, R., & Decker, S. (1994). *Burglars on the job: Streetlife and residential break-ins*. Boston, MA: Northeastern University Press.

Yochelson, S., & Samenow, S.E. (1976). *The criminal personality*. (Vol. 1: A profile for change). NY: Jason Aronson.

Yokoyama, M. (1995). Analysis of prostitution in Japan. *International Journal of Comparative and Applied Criminal Justice*, 19(1):48–60.

Young, A. (1990). Television viewing. In C. McKie & K. Thompson (Eds.), *Canadian social trends*. Ottawa: Thompson Educational Publications.

Young, J. (1986). The failure of criminology: The need for a radical realism. In R. Matthews & J. Young (Eds.), *Confronting crime*. London: Sage.

Youth Court Statistics 1995–96: Highlights. (1997). *Juristat Service Bulletin*, 17(10).

Zawitz, M. W. (1993). *Highlights from twenty years of surveying crime victims*. Washington, D.C.: Bureau of Justice Statistics.

Zawitz, M.W. (Ed.). (1992). *Drugs, crime, and the justice system: A national report from the Bureau of Justice Statistics*. Washington, D.C.: Department of Justice, Bureau of Justice Statistics.

Zehr, H. (1995). A restorative lens. In N. Larsen (Ed.), *The Canadian criminal justice system: An issues approach to the administration of justice*. Toronto: Canadian Scholar's Press. (Ch. 25).

Zellerer, E. (1996). *Violence against Inuit women in the Canadian Eastern Arctic*. Doctoral Thesis, School of Criminology, Simon Fraser University, Burnaby, BC.

Zimring, F.E., & Hawkins, G. (1975). *Deterrence: The legal threat to crime control*. Chicago: University of Chicago Press.

Glossary

Abduction is the illegal apprehension of another person for the purpose of financial gain, retribution, or trying to achieve personal or political gain. Also referred to as kidnapping, abductions are an indictable offence.

Aboriginal crime group refers to a form of organized crime that involves Aboriginal groups in Canada. They have been involved in crimes ranging from smuggling of cigarettes to running illegal gambling establishments.

ADD or **Attention Deficit Disorder** is a psychological and/or biologically-rooted disorder that is characterized by the individual being unable to concentrate for periods of time. Many inmates are thought to suffer from some degree of ADD.

Anomie is a sociological term that refers to a state of normlessness in society. It is usually attributed to decreased homogeneity, which provides a social environment conducive to crimes and criminality.

Archambault Report, published in 1938, amongst other aspects is perhaps best noted for its recommendation that the reformation of the offender should be the primary objective of the correctional system.

Arson involves the willful burning of property. Legally, it used to be considered a form of vandalism but its increase has now caused it to be defined as its own defence.

Assault is a type of violent crime that has several sub-classifications under the *Criminal Code*. In general, it refers to the unlawful, intentional attempt to inflict injury on another person.

Atavism is a term first used by Cesare Lombroso and other early supporters of the positivist school of criminology. It refers to a biological condition that allegedly renders the recipient incapable of living within the social norms of a society.

Avoidance learning is a form of behavioural learning in which the individual learns to avoid an undesirable behaviour (being punished) by performing a desirable behaviour.

Badgley Report, released in 1984, was the first major Canadian study on the abuse of children and young people.

Behaviour modification is a psychological theory and treatment that emphasizes changing behaviour, rather than personality. The process relies on a series of either rewards or undesirable punishments.

Behavioural learning is the psychological theory that asserts that all behaviour is learned through some type of stimulus (negative or positive). It assumes behaviour consists of determinable relationships.

Beijing Rules were created in 1984 at a United Nations meeting in Beijing. The rules established a set of guidelines which all member countries should use when dealing with young offenders. The primary emphasis was a welfare approach in which young people should be given special consideration and support.

Bias crimes is a term sometimes used to describe certain forms of hate crime in which the act is perpetrated on the grounds of ethnic origin, race, religion, or sexual orientation.

Break and enter is a form of property crime that involves the illegal entry into a building or dwelling without permission and with the intent of committing a theft or an act of violence.

Burden of proof is a legal term referring to the duty or necessity of proving a fact in question as a case progresses.

Canadian Centre for Justice Statistics (*CCJS*) is an agency introduced in 1980, responsible for collecting and compiling crime data on a wide range of criminological and criminal justice topics. Its findings are published in the *Juristat Bulletin*. These are readily available in most libraries.

Canadian *Criminal Code* is the legal source where one can find a listing of all criminal offences, their penalties, and guidelines pertaining to the administration of justice. Most criminal codes also include all major federal statutes.

Canadian Urban Victimization Survey was conducted during the 1980s and was the first major attempt to survey Canadians who had been victims of crime. The data generally shows that certain crimes are far less reported than others.

Cartels refer to major organized crime groups who have an international network of criminal activity. Such groups can include the Colombian drug cartels who traffic drugs from Colombia to around the world.

Case law is a concept handed down from the early English tradition of trying cases. It is based on the notion that preceding judicial decisions, court interpretations or rules made by courts can be made in the absence of written statutes or other sources of written decisions.

Cause implies that the outcome of one event is due to the influence of another. Criminologists strive to identify causal relationships. The assumption is that if causal relationships can be found then prevention measures can be more accurately defined.

Chivalry hypothesis refers to the benevolent attitude the criminal justice system is sometimes accused of using when processing female offenders. The hypothesis asserts women need special protection.

Chromosomes is the term used to describe the amino acid chain upon which all our genes are located. We have 46 pairs of chromosomes. Each chromosome is responsible for a different physical, emotional, and behavioural trait.

Civil law traces its roots to early Roman law. It pertains to those laws concerned with the rules and enforcement of private or civil rights. Unlike criminal law, civil law actions tend to seek personal compensation for the wrong done rather than seeking criminal punishment.

Classical conditioning, sometimes referred to as Pavlovian conditioning, involves the process of using an *unconditioned stimulus*

to obtain a desired response—a *conditioned response.*

Classical school of criminology can trace its origins to the work of Cesare Beccaria in 1764. Its main assumptions were that criminals (we) are rational, being capable of free will, and that the severity, swiftness, and certainty of punishment should serve as an effective deterrent to crime.

Clearance rate refers to the rate at which crimes are solved over a fixed period of time. The rate varies considerably between types of offences and is generally considered a reasonable indicator as to how effective crime prevention strategies are.

Cognition is a term used in social psychology that refers to the processes by which we come to "know" something. Association, frustration, reward or punishment are possible ways by which we might come to learn and/or know something.

Common law originated in England and was adopted in early Canadian law. It refers to those laws that are based on customs and traditions, as opposed to court-derived decisions or written statutes.

Comparative research (criminology) is the cross-cultural and cross-national study of crime and its control. Researchers then attempt to develop theories and strategies that cut across social, economic, and political boundaries.

Computer crime is a form of high-technology crime that involves the use of computer equipment and technology to commit a range of crimes (e.g., data theft to data destruction and illegal transfer of money, etc.). It can be described as a high-tech form of theft crime.

Concentric-circle theory is one of the early forms of ecological theory. It is based on the premise that crime radiates out in a predictable fashion from inner cities to the suburbs. The circles relate to observable social and environmental characteristics.

Conflict theory asserts that crime is the product of social and/or economic disparity in society. People are seen as social creatures who, when subjected to division and competition, may resort to criminal activity.

Conflict view of crime is a sociological and criminological term that refers to the theory that people disagree on norms and act out of self-interest to further their own needs.

Consensus view (model) of crime is a sociological and criminological term that refers to the theory that people agree on norms and work towards a common good and that crimes should be sanctioned.

Conservative approach is an ideology that relies on the criminal justice system to deter and incapacitate criminals as a means of controlling crime.

Conventional crime refers to those crimes that most commonly come to mind when we think of crime. They typically include violent crimes such as murder, robbery, and assault. They also include property crimes such as break and enter, motor-vehicle theft, and arson. They also tend to be the crimes most commonly dealt with by the criminal justice system. Conventional crimes are usually divided into crimes of violence (crimes against the person) and property crimes. They represent those crimes most commonly known to the public and for which official crime statistics are readily available.

Corporate crime is a form of white-collar and/or economic crime involving a legal violation by a corporate entity. Crimes can vary from price-fixing to the dumping of hazardous waste and violence in the workplace.

Correctional statistics are an official source of crime data. The data are based on federal and provincial offenders and include an array of information ranging from offenders' age, gender, and offence, to prior convictions.

Correlation is a term used to refer to the observed association between two or more variables. The higher a correlation between the variables the greater the likelihood that they are associated in some way (many prostitutes have a history of sexual abuse). Criminology seeks to find correlations between a crime and possible related factors or characteristics.

CPTED (Crime Prevention Through Environmental Design) represents a proactive means of preventing crime. The model emphasizes and targets the physical environment to minimize target suitability.

Crime control involves the use of the criminal justice system and community resources to prevent and punish crime. The "crime control model."

Crime data refers to information that people and/or criminal justice agencies collect on criminal events. Depending on the source of the collection, they may or may not be substantiated cases.

Crime is a socially-constructed concept used to categorize certain behaviours as requiring formal control and warranting some form of social intervention.

Crime rate refers to the number of offences in a category recorded in a fixed ratio such as per 1,000, per 10,000, or per 100,000 population. The *Uniform Crime Report* provides crime rates for most crimes. It is thought to be a more reliable indicator of crime trends as it standardizes the actual occurrence.

Criminal defence is the case put forth by the defendant's defence attorney in a criminal trial from the point of arrest to final appeal.

Criminal harassment is also known as *stalking*. It represents a criminal offence that evolved from domestic violence. It pertains to unlawful following and willful harassing of another person. It usually involves people known to each other.

Criminal justice is the term generally used when referring to the three formal elements involved in the detection, apprehension, processing, and handling of offenders. It is made up of the police, the courts, corrections and all their supporting agencies.

Criminal law pertains to those laws dealing with crimes, their punishment, and defences.

Criminal personality is a theoretical perspective that asserts that criminals differ from non-criminals based on identifiable personality differences. The perspective also assumes that in most cases these personalities can be corrected.

Criminalistics had its origins in Europe. It is the science of crime detection and investigation that relies on scientific methodology.

Today there are many sub-areas ranging from weapons specialists to DNA analysts.

Criminological enterprise refers to what criminologists do. Criminologists engage in everything from the examination of crime data to the study of criminal behaviour and victimology.

Criminologists are behavioural scientists who are interested in the identification, classification, and description of types of criminal behaviour.

Criminology is the integrated and interdisciplinary approach to the study of crime and criminality and its accompanying enterprise of criminal justice services.

Critical criminology calls for a "self-critical" approach to understanding crime and criminality. It emphasizes the importance of critically examining the social, economic, political, and ideological traditions within criminology.

Cultural transmission is a sociological theory that views crime as a socially-learned behaviour that is transmitted through successive generations. It is more likely to occur in disorganized urban settings.

Dark figure is a term coined in the 1970s that refers to that element, or portion, of crime that goes undetected or unreported by official sources.

Date rape is a form of sexual assault involving unlawfully coercing sexual interactions with someone (usually females) against their will within the context of a dating relationship.

Dependent variable is a research methodology term that refers to an element/event that is the subject of a study and for which criminologists attempt to discover relationships with other variables or factors.

Determinism is a doctrine that maintains that our decisions are decided by predictable and/or inherited causes that act on our character. For example, the reason you committed theft is because your father took you along when he used to commit theft.

Deterrence is one of the forms of social response to a potential offender. It is based on the premise that the risk or fear of punishment may be enough to prevent/deter someone from committing (a) further crime(s).

Deviance is a sociological term that refers to a behaviour that violates a social norm but which is not necessarily sanctioned under law. For example, it is impolite to stick your tongue out at someone but it is not a crime to do so.

Diathesis-stress model refers to a mutidisciplinary approach for treating substance abusers. The model focuses on both risk and protective factors.

Differential association is a sociological construct that suggests criminal acts are the result of exposure to negative influences either directly or vicariously. Crime is seen as a form of socially-learned behaviour.

Differential identification refers to the sociological explanation that views crime as the product of identifying with a real or imaginary person and interpreting that person's behaviour as acceptable.

Discretion is a criminal justice system term denoting the process by which an authority exercises his or her judgment rather than follow specific rules and facts.

Ecological school of criminology involves the study of how elements of the physical environment (from buildings to climate and social settings) interact to create a criminal environment. Also the basis of *CPTED*.

Economic crime refers to those crimes designed to bring financial gain to the offender(s). They typically involve organized crime and white-collar crimes.

Elizabeth Fry Society was created by a Quaker woman, Elizabeth Fry (Gurey), in the mid-1800s in response to the perceived need to promote prison reform for women prisoners. Elizabeth Fry Society agencies can be found across the country.

Empiricist refers to researchers who rely on an experimental approach to the study of crime and criminality.

Ethnomethodology is an investigative technique that was developed by sociologists. It involves observing how people come to construct their own sense of reality.

Etiology refers to the variety of explanatory models of crime and criminality.

Evolutive is a term coined by Maurice

Parmalee in 1918 to describe the process by which the nature and characteristics of crime can change over time. For example, computer crime is a modern day version of theft.

False positive is a research methodology concept that refers to the risk of making a prediction about an event/individual that may not be true.

Feminist perspective draws attention to the female offender and female victim. While there are several different strands of feminism, they emphasize the patriarchal bias in society and call for greater equality between the genders within the criminal justice system, and theory construction.

Functionalism is a sociological perspective that views all parts of society as being interrelated and contributes to the maintenance of society.

General theory of crime is a sociological perspective that asserts criminal behaviour is a product of defective socialization processes that make it difficult for a potential offender to exercise self-control. The theory represents a modification of the social control theory.

Hate crimes involve acts of intimidation or violence directed at groups or individuals considered undesirable because of their race, sexual orientation, religion, or ethnicity.

Illicit market encompasses economic-based crimes such as organized crime groups that provide services, often illegal, for their own economic gain.

Indictable offence is an offence that is considered more serious than a summary offence and usually carries a more serious penalty. It includes such crimes as murder, robbery, and assault. Sentences are usually served in a federal institution.

Integrating criminologies involves the general and specific attempt to construct an interpretive model of crime and crime control.

Interdisciplinary approach to criminology to integrate the various sub-areas of knowledge (e.g., biology, economics, law, psychology, and sociology, and other fields) to formulate an interdisciplinary theory of behaviour and form the basis for intervention and prevention strategies.

Just deserts is a type of punishment that asserts an individual who commits an offence deserves to suffer for it. Also referred to as "retribution."

Labelling is a sociological construct used to explain why someone might commit a crime. It asserts that a direct or indirect negative characterization can predispose the individual to feel "tagged" and like an outcast.

Liberal approach proposes to control crime by focusing on alleviating social inequalities and by providing legitimate opportunities for everyone.

Life-course theory is an integrated theory that involves the study of changing in the offending pattern of an individual over the course of their life. Researchers attempt to identify differentiating factors (early in life) that predispose individuals to criminal activity.

Middle-class value approach, also referred to as the "middle-class measuring rod" is a sociological theory that asserts that people from the lower class strive to attain middle-class standards. When they fail to do so, it gives rise to anger and frustration with the conventional values. These feelings may then trigger criminal behaviour.

Moral development is a psychological theory that asserts that morality is a development process that is dependent on how we are able to meet certain needs at different development stages of life. Criminals are thought to exhibit a lower level of moral development.

Moral entrepreneurs is a term used to describe those individuals who use their power and/or influence to shape the legal process to their advantage.

Moral insanity is a concept devised by the legal profession that provided physicians with an opportunity to offer a medical diagnosis and treat the condition as a form of mental illness.

Moral panic is a sociological term that refers to people's concern over crimes of morality (e.g., prostitution, pornography, gambling, etc.).

Neoclassical theorists subscribe to the assertion that different situations or circumstances can make it impossible to exercise free will. If identifiable they can be used to exempt the accused from conviction (e.g., insanity, compulsion, self-defence, etc.).

Neo-positivism is the perspective that evolved after the positivist school and has been characterized as part of the school of *social defence*.

Net widening refers to the process by which social control mechanisms (e.g., laws, administrative decisions) are used to expand its control over behaviour.

Norms refer to the informal standards of behaviour that are shared by members of a given society. As a sociological term they represent the common expectations of appropriate and inappropriate behaviour.

Operationalization involves defining criminological concepts or events so that they can be observed and measured in a scientific manner.

Paradigm shift is a sociological term that refers to the process when a prevailing model or theoretical orientation undergoes a conceptual shift.

Peacemaking theory is a sociological perspective that is based on a humanistic approach to crime control. Rather than use punishment and retribution as a means of social control, advocates of the peacemaking perspective emphasize reconciliation through mediation and dispute settlement.

Pedestal effect is a term occasionally used to describe the differential treatment and processing of female offenders. It is also sometimes interchangeably used with the "chivalry hypothesis." The terms reflect the assertion that women offenders have been treated more kindly than male offenders.

Political economy perspective has its roots in feminist theory. Used to explain prostitution, the perspective emphasizes social inequalities that force some women to turn to prostitution out of economic necessity.

Pornography is the portrayal of sexually-offensive material prohibited by law (e.g., child pornography). It is a type of public order offence.

Positivist theories believe the study of crime should emphasize the individual. They focus on the treatment over punishment as a means of correcting behaviour. They rely on the scientific method to quantify and measure behaviour.

Postmodernism is a theoretical framework derived from *critical* criminology that essentially rejects the self-evident reality of distinctions made by conventional scientific knowledge and/or common-sense.

Power-control theory is a sociological perspective that emphasizes the importance of class structure within the family setting in explaining delinquency and crime. Key concepts involve the nature of power and control within a family setting and how they relate to patriarchy and gender role socialization.

Prevention is a proactive concept that focuses on strategies that will prevent crimes before they occur. There are three major types of prevention. *Primary prevention*, or situational crime prevention, refers to the use of targeting known risks by increasing natural guardianship (e.g., locks, high intensity street lighting, etc). *Secondary prevention* involves trying to predict who should be targeted and developing programs to target the potential risk. *Tertiary prevention* is intended for those who have already violated the law. Prevention can range from detention to various intervention strategies (e.g., shaming).

Primary deviance is a sociological concept that refers to a criminal act that not been socially labelled as deviant.

Psychoactive refers to a substance that has the potential to alter an individual's mood or behaviour.

Psychoanalysis was developed by Sigmund Freud and views crime as the expression of conflict and tension within the individual. The source of conflict is believed to stem from unresolved and often unconscious experiences during one's childhood. Treatment involves trying to resolve these conflicts.

Psychopath is considered by some to be a psychological and/or biological condition in which an individual's behaviour is characterized by a lack of empathy, low arousal levels, and an inability to learn from experience. There is a growing body of literature suggesting that many chronic offenders suffer from some degree of psychopathy.

Radical approach attempts to address both conventional and non-conventional crimes by attempting to eliminate structural inequalities brought on through capitalism.

Random error pertains to observations that are not predictable because of some unforeseen intervening variable.

Rationalism refers to the "common-sense" process by which individuals attempt to determine the reality of a situation.

Reintegrative shaming is a method of correction that encourages offenders to confront their wrongdoing by performing some gesture that earns reacceptance.

Relative is a term that refers to the notion that the meaning and nature of crime can vary across time and location.

Reliability in research methodology refers to the likelihood that an observed relationship between two or more variables can or will be observed in a consistent manner.

Restitution is a theory of punishment that asserts the offender must reimburse the victim either financially or with services.

Restorative justice is a sentencing model which emphasizes restitution and community participation with the intent of restoring a sense of community and reintegrating individuals back into their communities.

Retribution is a theory of punishment that asserts offenders should be punished for crimes committed because they deserve it.

Routine activities theory is a sociological explanation that views crime as a predictable function of normal activities of daily living. Target suitability is identifiable based on their lack of guardianship.

Schizophrenia is a form of psychosis that is characterized by thought disorders that may be accompanied by delusion, fantasy, and incoherence.

Secondary deviance is a sociological term that refers to deviant behaviour as the result of being labelled. (See primary deviance).

Self-help justice was one of the earliest forms of crime control. A victimized person would seek revenge against the offender and/or if possible their significant others. It was an early form of vengeance.

Self-report data are types of unofficial crime data that involve asking individuals to disclose whether they have ever committed an offence. Given that a great deal of youth crime goes undetected, self-report studies are popular among this group.

Social conflict theory is a sociological approach that is based on the premise that people are more different than they are alike. The conflict over differences can evolve around issues of power and control.

Social contract is a philosophical doctrine premised on the belief that people are bound to society only by consent. Therefore, we are responsible for society and society is responsible for the individual. Furthermore, the doctrine maintains that society should have the fewest laws possible while still ensuring the rights and protection of its citizens.

Social control refers to the ability of society and its institutions to control, manage or direct human behaviour.

Social disorganization is a sociological theory that defines deviance and crime in terms of a breakdown of social control bonds, areas characterized by social decay, and/or associations involving other deviant groups.

Social structure is a sociological concept used to describe consistent and stable patterns of social interactions.

Somatotyping is a technique used for catagorizing the behaviours or temperaments of individuals based on specific body types or physique.

Stalking is a form of harassment in which the offender intentionally and repeatedly follows another person with the intention of causing emotional and/or physical discomfort.

Strain is a sociological concept that interprets emotional turmoil and conflict as the result of being unable to achieve desired goals through legitimate means.

Summary offences, unlike indictable offences, are considered less serious. Penalties are restricted to six months imprisonment and/or a $5,000 fine. Sentences are usually served in a provincial institution.

Symbolic interaction is a sociological perspective that focuses on the ways in which people communicate through symbols and how they use symbols to express behaviour.

Systematic error is the predictable error in observation. When collecting data, the observer is aware of the approximate error in the reliability of the observation.

Terrorism involves the use of propaganda, violence, or dangerous acts against some organization or agency for the purpose of obtaining concessions or rewards for their cause for personal and/or political reasons.

Token economy is a term used by behavioural therapists to describe a reinforcement strategy.

Transnational crime involves a criminal act(s) or transaction that violates the laws of more than one country, for example, international drug smuggling rings, money laundering, and various organized crime activities.

Triangulation is a research methods technique that involves using more than one source of criminological data to access the validity of what is being observed.

Uniform Crime Report (UCR) is the official crime data collected by Statistics Canada and which is published under various areas by the Centre for Justice Statistics of Canada. Most reports are available through the *Juristat* publication.

Unofficial (crime) data pertains to crime data that is not collected by official criminal justice agencies. It can include self-report data, victimization data, field observations, among other sources. It is usually used to elucidate existing official data and verify the validity of official data sources.

Utilitarianism is an ethical and classical school concept that states that any laws should respect the greatest good for the greatest number.

Validity in research methodology pertains to the likelihood that relationships being observed and measured are in fact real.

Victimization data involves collecting data from individuals who have been victims of crimes, or in some cases know of someone who has been a victim, and asking a range of questions regarding the incidents.

Victimless crimes are a type of public order offence. These crimes interfere with the normative order in society. Examples include prostitution, gambling, sexual practices, substance abuse, and disorderly conduct.

Violent crime is a general category of crime classification that includes such crimes as murder, robbery and assault. They are considered serious crimes and are mostly indictable offences, incurring sentences of two years.

Wallace Wheel illustrates the process by which researchers engage in scientific study. The wheel consists of four major elements—theory, hypothesis, observation, and empirical generalization.

White-collar crime is a sociological concept encompassing crimes committed by individuals or a group of persons, who capitalize on their legitimate occupations or pursuits. Such crimes can involve theft, fraud, embezzlement, insider-trading, and false advertizing.

Women's (liberation) movement emerged in the late 1950s and drew attention to the rights of women and their equal status to men in all economic, political, and social settings.

XYY chromosome theory is a constitutional theory that asserts there is a relationship between the extra Y chromosome, found in some males, and a propensity toward criminal/anti-social behaviour.

Appendices

Appendix 1

Where to Study Criminology in Canada

A 1995 Statistics Canada Report revealed that not only are employment prospects bleak and getting bleaker for high school graduates but, as the author of the report said, "times are tough, and if you want to make headway you had better study hard and get a university degree" (Howe, 1995). Although a generic statement, it can hardly be disputed today that seeking post-secondary education for almost any line of work is prudent.

As can be seen in this appendix, colleges in eastern Canada tend to focus on more practical applications of criminal justice employment while the western provinces tend to have a cross-section of applied and two-year university transfer-based programs. Nevertheless, given the number of programs available across the country it can safely be said that criminology has emerged as an academic and professional discipline. Students interested in gaining employment in this field are astute if they obtain specific training in the area that most interests them.

An area of study not covered in this appendix, but which attracts a great number of students, is criminal law. It might appear to be a logical assertion that a degree in criminology/criminal justice would place you at an advantage when applying to law school. Chambliss and Yassa (1995) failed to confirm this in their survey of American universities. In fact, they found that American law schools ranked students with undergraduate degrees in English, philosophy, and economics as preferred. Criminology/criminal justice programs ranked among the lower three! A similar survey conducted of Canadian law schools by Winterdyk (1997a) revealed that no preference was given to any undergraduate background. Rather, academic performance, LSAT scores, and letters of reference were used in the selection process.

The following list has been drawn from National Guide 1996: College and Universities Programs and then cross-referenced with the 1997 Eastern, Ontario, and Western Spectrum. For reasons of consistency and practicality, the list of programs is by region.

Note: *Many of the programs listed below may be accessed through the Internet. It is also possible that the references are incomplete. While I have endeavoured to identify all university and college programs across the country, a few may have been omitted (If so, I apologize. Please forward any corrections and/or omissions and I will be happy to update the list).*

EASTERN REGION— Atlantic Provinces and Quebec

Criminology
Memorial University of Newfoundland (St. John's)
• Division of Continuing Studies
• Certificate with 9 courses
Saint Mary's University

- Certificate with 4 credits
- Must be enrolled in a degree program (or completed)

Université de Montreal
- Baccalauréate: 6 semesters
- Certificate: 2 semesters

CEGEPs

John Abbott College
- Professional Police Program: 6 semesters
- Correctional Intervention: 6 semesters

Marianopolis College
- Law and Social Justice: 5 credits taken in conjunction with another program

Dawson College
- Law and Society: 4 semesters

Ontario

Criminology

Université d'Ottawa
- Baccalauréate
- Masters (Applied)

University of Toronto
- Baccalauréate
- Masters
- Certificate (2-3 years)

York University
- Baccalauréate in Law and Justice

University of Windsor
- Baccalauréate
- Certificate

Criminology and Criminal Justice

Carleton University (Ottawa)
- Baccalauréate

Police Learning Foundations

Algonquin (Ottawa)
- Diplomas in security and alarm systems technician; security management; and Police learning foundations
- Four semester programs

Cambrian (Sudbury)
- Diploma in police education, Native justice education
- Four semester programs

Canadore (North Bay)
- Police learning foundations: 4 semesters

Conestoga (Kitchener)
- Police learning foundations: 4 semesters

Confederation (London)
- Police learning foundations: 4 semesters

Durham (Oshawa)
- Police learning foundations: 4 semesters

Fanshawe College (London)
- Police learning foundations: 4 semesters

Georgian College (Barrie)
- Police learning foundations: 4 semesters

Correctional Worker/ Community Worker

Algonquin (Ottawa)
- Diploma: 4 semesters

Cambrian (Sudbury)
- Diploma: 4 semesters

Canadore (North Bay)
- Diploma: 4 semesters

Centennial (Scarborough)
- Diploma: 4 semesters

George Brown (Toronto)
- Diploma: 4 semesters

Lambton (Sarnia)
- Diploma: 4 semesters

St. Lawrence (Kingston)
- Diploma: 4 semesters

Sheridan (Oakville)
- Diploma: 4 semesters

Sir Sandford Fleming (Peterborough)
- Diploma: 4 semesters

WESTERN PROVINCES

Criminal Justice/Criminology
University of Alberta (Edmonton)
- Baccalauréate (Special)—1 + 3 years in Dept. of Sociology

Camosun (Victoria, BC)
- Diploma or associate degree: 2 years

Douglas (New Westminister, BC)
- Certificate—1 year and diploma—2 years
- Areas: corrections, criminology, law enforcement, and a transferable agreement to third year at Simon Fraser University (SFU)

University College of Fraser College (Abbotsford, BC)
- B.A. in criminal justice: 45 credits
- Two-year diplomas in corrections, criminology, law enforcement (all transferable to SFU third year criminology)

Kwantlen (Surrey, BC)
- Same as Douglas College

Langara (South Vancouver, BC)
- Same as Douglas College

Lethbridge (Lethbridge, AB)
- Two-year diplomas in corrections, law enforcement, and security
- One-year certificate available to Aboriginal persons only

Malaspina (Nanaimo, BC)
- Same as Douglas College

Mount Royal (Calgary, AB)
- Two-year diplomas in corrections, law enforcement and two-year university transfer to SFU, Carlton, Ottawa, Regina, Great Falls, and several other American universities

New Caledonia (Prince George, BC)
- See Douglas College

Red Deer (Red Deer, AB)
- Two-year university transfer

University of Regina
- The program is called Human Justice Service
- Three-year program with a strong practicum

Simon Fraser University (Burnaby, BC)
- Three-year B.A.
- Masters and Doctoral programs

Yukon (Whitehorse, YT)
- One-year certificate in criminal justice, northern justice/criminology

Note: For a comprehensive overview and link to some colleges and all universities across Canada visit: ***www.fes.uwaterloo.ca/cdnuvic.html***. You can also access all Ontario colleges by visiting: **http//ctoc.ocas.on.ca/tab2.htm**.

Appendix 2

Sampling of Criminology Journals

The following list, although not exhaustive, illustrates the diverse range of journals that are commonly used and in which criminologists tend to get their work published in North America. A growing number of these journals can now be accessed directly through the Internet. It should be noted that over the years some journals have changed their titles to reflect the evolutive changes within criminology. For example, the *Canadian Journal of Criminology*, in the 1970s, used to be titled *The Canadian Journal of Criminology and Corrections*—not unlike the title of Gillin's introductory textbook in 1926.

The list does not include the vast volume of specialized magazines or international journal publications (virtually every country has a criminology program or criminological institute that produces a criminology journal in their country). While some of these may be available they may not be as readily accessible at smaller criminology programs and many may pose reading difficulties because of their language.

American Journal of Criminal Justice
Canadian Journal of Criminology
Canadian Journal of Women and the Law
Crime and Delinquency
Federal Probation
International Journal of Comparative and Applied Criminal Justice
Journal of Criminal Law and Criminology
Journal of Personality and Social Psychology
Journal of Interpersonal Violence
Journal of Human Justice
Journal of Criminal Justice Education
Journal of Quantitative Criminology
Justice Quarterly
Law and Society Review
RCMP Gazette
Social Problems
The Criminologist
The Prison Journal
Violence and Victims
Youth and Society

American Sociological Review
Canadian Journal of Law and Society
Corrections Today
Criminology
International Journal of Adolescence and Youth
International Journal of Offender Therapy and Comparative Criminology
Journal of Police Science and Administration
Journal of Research in Crime and Delinquency
Journal of Criminal Law
Juvenile and Family Court Journal
Law and Psychology
Law Now
Police Chief
Social Forces
Sociology of Criminal Law
Theoretical Criminology
Victimology

Appendix 3

What Can You Do With a Degree/Diploma in Criminology/Criminal Justice/Human Justice?

A quick scan of the diploma program titles listed in Appendix 1 will provide the reader with a primary list of possible employment areas. The primary areas include law enforcement, the judiciary, and corrections. There are a number of related fields where students can gain employment. As you can see in Box A, criminology is a rich and diverse field. It offers graduates a wide range of areas in which to seek employment. Can you think of any employment opportunities that might have been omitted?

BOX A

EMPLOYMENT OPPORTUNITIES FOR CRIMINOLOGY-RELATED DEGREES/DIPLOMAS

- Fish and Wildlife Officer
- Customs Officer
- Probation Officer
- Parole Officer
- Correctional Officer—adult and juvenile system
- Youth Care Worker
- Private security: The Bay, Eatons, Zellers, Gas companies, private residential areas, etc.
- Private Investigators
- Law enforcement: municipal, provincial, federal
- Legal services/courts
- Legal Aid Workers
- Family and social services
- Criminal investigator—forensics
- Human Rights Commission
- Office of the Ombudsman
- Criminal Injury Section—Workers' Compensation Board
- Criminal Justice Training Institutions
- Community Residential Workers
- Related programs at community colleges and universities
- Provincial and Federal Department of Justice, Solicitor General, Corrections
- Voluntary community services (e.g., Victim Assistance Programs)

Appendix 4

"Canadian" Pioneers of Criminology

The word Canadian appears in quotation marks because most of the Canadian pioneers are first-generation Canadians. Their varied international experience has had a noticeable impact on Canadian criminological thought. It is perhaps also because of this diversity that Canadian criminology has been slow in forging its own unique identity. Instead, there appear to be pockets of criminological perspectives. Furthermore, given its youth, it was not easy to identify a handful of pioneers who reflect what has been happening in Canadian criminology.

The overview attempts to follow a chronological order. In preparing this section, a bio-profile was compiled and sent to a number of "obvious" pioneers. These individuals were then asked to identify other notable Canadian pioneers in criminology. Based on their feedback and a review of the literature I selected the six criminologists presented below. When I received the profiles, I composed a biographical sketch of each contributor before returning it to them for accuracy and possible clarification.

Denis Szabo—The "Father" of Canadian Criminology

Professor Szabo was born into a military family in Budapest, Hungary, on June 4, 1929. His post-secondary education began at the University of Budapest in 1947 where he completed his matriculation in sociology, philosophy and history. Szabo then went to the Christian University in Louvain (Belgium) where he completed his Masters degree in Political Science and Sociology. Thereafter, he obtained his doctorate degree in 1956. He then taught sociology for several years in France before going on to complete post-graduate work at the Sorbonne in Paris.

In 1958 Szabo joined the department of sociology at the Université de Montreal. Shortly thereafter, in 1960, Szabo became the founding director of the first criminology program in Canada. He perhaps deserves to be referred to as the "founding father of Canadian criminology." He established a Master of Science program in 1960 that was followed by a B.Sc. and a doctoral program in Criminology in 1962 and 1964.

In 1969, he founded a research centre in cooperation with the International Society of Criminology at the University of Montreal. It is named *The International Centre for Comparative Criminology*. And over the years, it has been the source of many fine research projects. He served as its director until 1984 and is today the chairman of its board of directors.

In 1969, he also founded the journal *Criminologie* for which he was the editor until 1987. The journal, published twice a year, is a thematic periodical. Over the years, the majority of its issues focused on crime, delinquency, and criminal justice research and their application to policy issues.

Over the years Szabo has held teaching or research positions at various universities throughout France. He has also taught in Brussels, Budapest, Tokyo, and held a fellowship at the renowned Max Planck Institute in Freiburg, Germany.

Among his numerous awards, he received the distinguished Sutherland award from the American Society of Criminology in 1968 and the Beccaria Gold Medal in 1970 from the German Society of Criminology. In 1973 Szabo became a fellow of the Royal Society of Canada and has received a number of honorary doctorate degrees from European universities.

Szabo's professional career has been punctuated with numerous international and national accolades. It is unfortunate for English-speaking Canadian criminology students that most of his work has been published in French. For example, very few anglophone criminology textbooks acknowledge any of his fine work, let alone that of any of his Quebec criminology counterparts. Fortunately, the bilingual publication, the *Canadian Journal of Criminology*, has published many of his articles and several of his books have been reviewed in English. For example, in a recently edited book with Marc LeBlanc, *Traite de Criminologie Empirique, deux-ième edition*, Rick Linden notes how "Quebec criminology reflects a willingness to deal with problems and issues rather than getting mired in sterile debates about procedural issues" (1996:335). Linden suggests a translation of the book would be a significant contribution to English-speaking criminologists.

The works of Leo Strauss and Emile Durkheim have played an important role in Szabo's thinking and theoretical orien-tation. Strauss's influence also prevented him from being swayed by the radical relativism which often characterizes much of the work done in the field of crime and justice today. Durkheim's influence, meanwhile, oriented Szabo's research to a strong empirical foundation in sociological theorization. From Durkheim, he learnt the importance of viewing social facts in their psychological and historical context. Consequently, Szabo has retained, as he described it, "a mild positivism in my empirical research."

Szabo's primary areas of interest include sociological and legal issues as they pertain to criminal justice and criminology as well as the importance of historical trends. He has a keen interest in the prevention of youth crime, most notably on sexual conduct in youth and family. Over the years, he has produced a number of major monographs on the subject.

His vast international experience has added significantly to his knowledge base and helped to forge recognition of criminology in Canada. Szabo, along with his fellow Quebec criminologists, has also been instrumental in bridging European traditions of law and medicine with the social science traditions of North America. Among his more notable students who have gone on to work in the criminal justice system or teach in the area, include Ezzat Fattah, André Normandeau, Pierre Landerville, Maurice Cusson, Guy Lemire and Jean Trepanier.

When asked to comment on his impression of the state of criminology in Canada, Szabo feels we are at a crossroads in North American and European criminology. A focus on public order has taken on a significant orientation. Nowadays, traditional correctional research is not as popular as it was in the 1960s. More interest is devoted to the functioning of the criminal justice system, sentencing and the maintenance of public order. Criminology, he suggests, is very much involved in the area of policing and it has to balance its interests between a scrupulous respect for human rights and the efficient carrying out of duties that serve the security of the citizenry.

Finally, Szabo points out that criminology is inseparable from criminal policy. Being a social science discipline, there are always two faces to the same reality. It is a value-laden discipline, not free of conflicts between the requirements of simultaneous aspirations for freedom and security, order and change. While Szabo's influence may be felt through his students' ideas and writings in English, it is hoped that more of his works and ideas will be translated into English. In this way, all Canadian criminology students can appreciate the significance of his work.

Ezzat A. Fattah—The pioneer of (Canadian) Victimology and Champion of Restorative Justice

Ezzat A. Fattah was born on January 1, 1929 in Assiant, Egypt. During his formative years he developed a strong interest in law, human rights, and political science. Combined with the influence of an uncle, who was a judge of the Supreme Court of Egypt, Ezzat's destiny seemed to take form early in life.

Fattah's academic career has been long and varied. He earned his first degree in law from the University of Cairo in 1948. After several years as a state attorney he left feeling disillusioned with the practice of law and the criminal law's inability to solve social problems. After a visit by Professor Roland Grassberger, then Director of the Institute of Criminology at the University of Vienna, Fattah moved to Austria to study criminology and social science.

At the University of Vienna (1961–1964) Fattah became interested in victimology, while studying under and working closely with Roland Grassberger. After completing his studies at the University of Vienna, Fattah moved to the Université de Montreal to further his studies. There he studied under Henri Ellenberger in the School of Criminology. On completing his Ph.D., Fattah became the first person in Canada to hold such a degree from a Canadian institution. He then spent several years teaching at the university before being invited, in 1974, to set up a criminology program at Simon Fraser University in Burnaby (British Columbia)—the first in western Canada. Today, the School of Criminology is the largest in English-speaking Canada and has a faculty of 25 full-time members.

Fattah's interest in victimology may have been a natural choice in many respects, given his experiences while living under a totalitarian regime in Egypt. These experiences led him to become a staunch defender of human rights and a champion of citizens against the abuses of state power. Fattah was one of the early scholars who led the fight against the death penalty that was still in effect at the time. His 1972 study, *A Study of the Deterrent Effect of Capital Punishment with Particular Reference to the Canadian Situation* was frequently cited in the parliamentary debates that ended the abolition of capital punishment in 1976.

Fattah's views and dedication to preserving human rights have earned him international recognition. In 1977, he was invited to be a rapporteur for the death penalty conference convened by Amnesty International (AI) in Stockholm. One of the landmark proclamations of the conference was the Stockholm declaration that stated that the death penalty was the ultimate cruel, inhuman and degrading punishment and violated the right to life. Subsequently, Fattah was sent on several AI missions around the world.

Ezzat Fattah's criminological thinking was influenced by various European and North American scholars. Several of these scholars include Roland Grassberger from Austria and German scholar Hans von Hentig and his work on victimology. Other European scholars whom he acknowledges include Nils Christie in Norway, Inkeri Anttda in Finland, Louk Hulsman in the Netherlands, and Leslie Wilkins in the United Kingdom, whose collective work is very critical of clinical and dispositional criminology and of punitive criminal policy. In particular, Christie and Hulsman belong to the *abolitionist school* which, among other perspectives, calls for the abolition of prisons and dealing with crimes as conflicts.

Among North America influence, Fattah credits Denis Szabo who integrated European and American theories (see above) and Henri Ellenberger who inspired him to follow his interest in victimology.

Ezzat Fattah's work on victimology dates back to 1966 and his seminal article *La Victimologie—Qu'est-elle et Quel est Son Avenir* was published in 1967 in *Revue Internationale de Criminologie et de Police Technique*. In addition to his books and interest in victimology he has authored or co-authored numerous books, chapters, and scholarly papers published in learned journals in ten languages. Throughout the 1990s, Fattah has been actively involved in various restorative justice projects (see Chapter 14).

The current reputation of the School of Criminology at SFU is in large part due to his commitment to excellence. Fattah is a genuine pioneer in his area and his international experience and focus have been instrumental in promoting criminology as an interdisciplinary subject area. And even though Professor Fattah retired in 1997, he continues to write, research, and contribute his knowledge and expertise to an area of criminology that until recently had largely gone unrecognized.

Gwynne Nettler—"A scholar with broad interests and serious beliefs" (L. Roberts, 1990).

Gwynne Nettler was born on Manhattan Island, New York City on July 7th, 1913. When he was three, his family moved to

Los Angeles, California, where he spent his youth and eventually earned his bachelor's degree in history from the University of California (LA) in 1934. He then went on to earn a master's degree in psychology from Claremont College, 1936, and then at the relatively young age of 33, his Ph.D. in psychology and sociology from Stanford University in 1946. His dissertation, *The Relationship between Attitude and Information Concerning the Japanese in America* is the study in which Nettler invented and applied "know-group" validations. This procedure was first reported in *American Journal of Sociology*, 1946: v.52 and the entire dissertation has since been reprinted in a series edited by R. Merton and H. Zuckerman in 1980.

Before moving to Canada, Nettler taught at several schools throughout the United States. Then in 1963, interested in returning to teaching, and reading and writing, he accepted a joint appointment with the Departments of Psychology and Sociology at the University of Alberta. Shortly after arriving at the university, he moved to Sociology because two "halves" proved to be more than one whole and because criminology was being taught largely in the sociological sector. He remained there until he retired in 1989.

Nettler's long and distinguished career has not been limited to criminology. In fact, his primary area of academic interest and research lies more directly in the examination of the boundaries of social scientists' competence. That is, what and how can social scientists contribute to the understanding of social issues? Nettler credits a broad range of scholars with influencing his thinking and work. Among the list, he sites A. Leonard, an astronomer, W.F. Ogburn, a sociologist, S.I. Franz, a psychologist, and several philosophers, including A.J. Ayer, John Mackie and George Santayana.

Nettler's list of publications dates back to the 1940s. Although many of his works primarily bridge the psychological and sociological literature, his books on crime have been repeatedly cited and referenced by academics in criminology and by criminology students across Canada (and North America). Perhaps the most notable of his criminological writings was his book *Explaining Crime* (McGraw-Hill), first published in 1974. It became a standard textbook in most criminology and deviance courses across the country. Roberts (1990) describes Nettler's work as "an intellectual challenge, and recommend that any intelligent person interested in criminological topics can profit from exposure to the issues presented in this book ... this volume is both instructive and a delight to read ... (and) deserves our serious attention" (p. 357).

Nettler currently lives in San Diego, having in some respects returned to his roots. And while he no longer actively teaches, he offers occasional lectures and continues to produce scholarly works.

Among his more notable graduate students, Nettler cites John Hagan and Ron Gillis (both at the University of Toronto), William Avison (University of Western Ontario), and Marlene MacKie (University of Calgary). Other students include John Evans who directs statistical research in the Department of Justice and Carol Ross, a prominent attorney in Vancouver.

When asked to comment on the state of Canadian criminology, Dr. Nettler notes that as a discipline, it is weak. He finds criminology and sociology to be heavily ideological—that is, to confuse political preference with science. He claims that political commitment is hostile to truth-seeking and truth-telling. While criminology presents itself as a policy science, its impact on criminal activity and governmental response to crime is minimal. Criminologists' most useful talent, he claims, lies in assessing the results of programs others develop as, for example, in evaluating the efficacy of offender-rehabilitation and the utility of the death penalty.

Tadeusz Grygier—Social Protection Code

Professor Grygier was born on October 2, 1915 in Warsaw, Poland. His attraction to criminology may be described as having followed a sequence of events in his life.

At the age of twenty (1935) he obtained the equivalent of a B.Sc. Hons. in political science and economics at the Jaqiellonian University (in Cracow). The next year he completed and received his Master of Law (canonical and civil) from Warsaw University.

In 1939, Hitler began his campaign of terror across Europe and after his pact with Stalin, Poland became a victim of both tyrants. Grygier became a Soviet prisoner and was sent to the Gulag Archipelago (1940-1942). He was released on parole in 1941 only to be kid-

napped by the Russian secret police and subjected to Pavlovian-style conditioning. He survived by redefining himself not as a victim but as a lucky scientist who could observe and analyze the effects of oppression.

Released in 1943 he spent some time working for Polish, British and American intelligence (1943-1945) in Iran. From there, he eventually ended up in London and decided to continue his studies at the London School of Economics (LSE). It was there he met several of his mentors. Among the list Grygier includes Herman Mannheim (law and criminology), Sir Frederic Bartlett (experimental psychology), Sir Karl Popper (philosophy and science), Sir Claus Moser (his statistical advisor), Sir Raymond Firth (anthropology), and Edward Shils (a visiting professor of sociology from Chicago). None of the above was knighted at the time. Except for Bartlett and Shils, they were mere lecturers at the LSE.

Grygier's Ph.D. thesis was published as *Oppression: A Study in Social and Criminal Psychology*, twice in 1954 and then again in 1973. Shortly thereafter, Mannheim recommended him to the University of Toronto where he taught and conducted research in criminology, psychology and social work, as well as working part-time as director of research and policy advisor for the government of Ontario.

In 1967, Gyrgier moved to the University of Ottawa where he was invited to set up a research centre in criminology. Two years later he established two interdisciplinary, bilingual programs, one leading to a Master of Arts

(M.A.) degree in criminological research and the other to a professional degree of Master of Correctional Administration (M.C.A.). These programs reflect Grygier's passion for research and the importance of the proper application of criminological knowledge. Later, in 1980, the University established an undergraduate program in criminology.

Grygier's interests are as varied as his life has been. This appears to reflect his vast international experience and zest for research. He has engaged in research covering a wide range of topics such as the use of mathematical models for social problems and Arctic Studies. While he has done considerable work in the area of criminology, his early publications (1945-1983) were mainly in psychology and personality assessment.

Grygier has enjoyed supervising graduate students to reach their potential. Several of his students include Maurice Cusson, R.R. Ross, Bill Outerbridge, and Ezzat Fattah. He describes his orientation as empirical and eclectic, and like several other Canadian pioneers, he is directed more by the quest to seek practical solutions rather than testing theories. One common theme of his work is his interest in rehabilitation and a humanitarian approach to justice. He asks (in McGrath, 1965:40): "Could we be safer if we were less ruthless?" He continued to argue that Canada's retributive philosophy be replaced by the concept of the *protection of society*—a concept that was adopted by the Canadian Committee on Corrections in 1969.

When asked to comment on the state of criminology in Canada, Grygier expressed his disappointment with the general lack of influence of criminological studies on legislation. He recently referred to this resistance as "tunnel vision." In Grygier's opinion this was the state of the law in the sixteenth century and it is still the situation in Canada and elsewhere. He believes we need facts, not presumptions based on legal precedents. As he observed, "a criminal law oriented to the past" cannot help us to build "a just, peaceful and safe society."

James C. Hackler— "When I was young I admired clever people; now that I am older I admire kind people." (Excerpt from his autobiography)

In talking to former students of Hackler, the above quote appears to exemplify this highly intelligent and charming man.

Hackler was born on June 15, 1930 to a family of modest means in Stockton, California. After graduating from junior college, he entered the University of California at Berkeley. His first degree was in Business Administration. After graduating he joined the Medical Service Corps and spent several years working as a doctor's aide and lectured on malaria and "other things." After moving on he spent the next five years teaching in a junior high school before deciding to enter the sociology program at the University of Washington in Seattle. Even though Hackler describes the unfolding of his life as "being in the right place at the right time," this last choice would have a major impact on his future academic path.

Herbert Costner and Clarence Schrag were the most important scholars in his Ph.D. program as well as his mentors. From Costner he learned the importance of applying the scientific approach to knowledge. This influence can be found in one of his recent textbooks, *Crime and Canadian Public Policy* (1994). In the book, he discusses the importance of applying a scientific approach to knowledge and points out how this area is neglected by many teachers of criminology. Costner's early influence also carried over into Hackler's dissertation research. Working with the Opportunities for Youth Project (based on Cloward and Albert Ohlin's opportunity theory—see Chapter 7) he eventually discovered that the project did not work. Subsequently, Hackler has come to adopt a framework about crime prevention that can be summarized in four points: (1) most things don't work very well, (2) some things work a little, sometimes, (3) we're not sure what works better than anything else, and (4) doing less is probably better than doing more.

In 1965, he joined the sociology department at the University of Alberta (Edmonton). There he spent the first seven years trying to establish the MA program in criminal justice and then the BA program in criminology. Although meeting with some resistance, both programs came on line in the early 1980s.

In addition to being a prolific researcher and writer, he gives a considerable amount of his time and energy to community level concerns around crimi-

nal justice issues. While the later "pastimes" may not be considered scholarly, being in a field where research can have real consequences, his community work represents an approach and attitude often found failing among academic criminologists today.

His primary area of interest, within criminology, is juvenile justice and comparative juvenile justice issues. His list of scholarly publications is numerous—dating back to before his graduate school days. In a 1996 chapter contribution Hackler discusses some of his concerns about the damage we are doing to juveniles in Canada as a result of our preoccupation with an adversarial model of youth justice. He poignantly argues that in Canada we "need to widen our horizons and counter some of the ethnocentrism that characterizes" much of our thinking about juvenile justice (p. 272).

Another area that Professor Hackler has written extensively on is the nature and quality of applied research in criminology. He suggests that some Canadian criminologists' use of rigorous scientific procedures have been lacking and that "if they understood and utilized scientific procedures more" they would be more productive (Hackler, 1994:63).

In 1996, Dr. Hackler moved to the University of Victoria to study Aboriginal juvenile justice in the many small communities there. He hopes to be able to play a role in the implementation of the Gove Report. The report led to the creation of a Ministry of Children and Youth which brings together a variety of agencies and services which had been scattered among different areas of government.

Hackler describes his theoretical orientation as left-realism (see Chapter 8). As for the current state of criminology in Canada, he is not impressed with the situation, arguing that we suffer from provincial ideas and a general lack of concern for humanity.

It is perhaps unfortunate that at a time we can benefit from his wisdom and compassion he is nearing retirement. But then again several of his students, including John Hagan and Rick Linden, appear to be carrying on his tradition of academic excellence as can be evidenced by their fine work.

André Normandeau— A passion for the study of crime

André Normandeau is a bilingual French Canadian born (May 4, 1942) and raised in Montreal.

After graduating from high school, Normandeau went on to complete a bachelor's degree in sociology at the Université de Montreal in 1964. Thereafter, he moved south to the University of Pennsylvania (U of P) in 1964 to pursue his Master's in criminology. U of P was something of a criminology hotbed at the time with such notables as Thorsten Sellin and Marvin Wolfgang teaching there. These years were marked by a close intellectual relationship between the graduate students and their mentors.

Having a thirst to further his knowledge, Normandeau then entered a doctoral program in sociology at the University of Pennsylvania. His dissertation was on *Patterns and Trends in Robbery* in the so-called tradition of Wolfgang, on homicide. After completing his Ph.D. in 1968, still not feeling finished with his quest, Normandeau completed a post-doctoral degree in criminology at the University of California in Berkeley.

Normandeau especially enjoyed working with Sellin (1896–1994), a criminologist, historian, and penologist whose work and ideas have impacted numerous criminologists over the years. Sellin was accomplished in eight languages. From Sellin, Normandeau developed a strong interest in historical knowledge as well as the value of being multilingual and multicultural.

In addition to Sellin, Normandeau credits Marvin Wolfgang as also having significantly influenced his academic career. Wolfgang's interest in violence prompted Normandeau to eventually engage in considerable research in such areas as violence (subculture), robbery, and crime statistics. Normandeau eventually replicated in Canada (in 1970) the famous Sellin–Wolfgang index of crime.

Normandeau strongly believes in empirical criminology. Facts and statistics are a religion, he asserts, but they are the bottom line of criminology as a full-fledged social science.

While he has published over 500 articles in twelve countries and authored or co-authored over a dozen books, his primary areas of interest include the sociology of the police, community policing, sociology of prison and alternatives and justice policies. His theoretical orientation could be described as a "classical functionalist" in a Mertonian style, who thinks crime can be partly controlled by an efficient criminal justice system, a functional system.

In addition to his illustrious academic career, Normandeau stood as a Parti Quebecois candidate in four elections (1973, 1976, 1981, and 1985). This is not unusual, as a number of Quebec criminology scholars have become very involved in community activities and government initiatives—more so than any other criminology centre in Canada (Hackler, 1994). For example, in an article that appeared in the 1996 May issue of *L'Opinion: Independante,* Normandeau pointed out that "(I)n closing five prisons (recently) Quebec has made a courageous choice preferring to invest in alternative measures, that's to say community measures." Furthermore, with respect to the use of electronic surveillance, Normandeau expressed the view that "it is more a punitive addition than a true alternative means ... In Quebec, as in France, one remains prudent with this measure."

Finally, when asked to comment on his impressions on the state of Canadian criminology, Normandeau is perhaps a bit more complimentary than some of the other Canadian pioneers covered in this appendix. He notes that Canadian criminology is now at par with American criminology. More specifically he feels that English Canadian criminology is a bit more theoretical while Quebec criminology tends to be a bit more applied in its orientation.

He affirms that the major criminological teaching and research centres in Canada are doing a "great job." In fact, he says, "we are doing an even greater job

because Canadian criminologists often integrate knowledge from Europe and America, which is not usually the case for the typical American criminologist."

Paul and Patricia Brantingham—the Environmental Criminologists

Space permitting, I could justify covering these two pioneers separately. However, given the parameters of this book/chapter, such will not be the case. Instead, the review will focus on their major contributions as Canadian pioneers in criminology.

Both were born in the United States, Paul in Long Beach, California and Patricia in St. Louis, Missouri. Patricia is the older by one day—born June 28, 1943.

Paul and Patricia met while both were completing their Bachelors' degrees at Columbia University. And while their subsequent education followed different paths, they eventually came to a common ground. Patricia (Matthews) Brantingham obtained a Masters degree in mathematics first and then her Master of Science and eventually her doctorate in urban and regional planning at Florida State University. Paul Brantingham obtained a JD at Columbia and then went on to receive a diploma in criminology at Cambridge University in England.

Pat acknowledges that it was Paul who drew her away from traditional urban planning and showed her that urban crime was an essential issue in urban planning. Paul meanwhile credits C.R. Jeffery with showing him the importance of looking at the *criminal event*, not just the criminal or criminal law. This involves three key elements: 1) the precursors of the event, 2) how the interactions among events define the outcome, and 3) the aftermath of the event, ranging from reporting the event to the public reaction to the event (Sacco and Kennedy, 1994:137). And from his wife, Paul learnt the importance of the environment and how its structure shapes crime.

Together they co-developed the field of environmental criminology (i.e., micro-spatial criminology) and the pattern theory of crime. Many of their ideas are extensively covered in their books, *Patterns in Crime* (1984) and *Environmental Criminology* (1991), among other publications. Their work on patterns of crime and environmental criminology has drawn both Canadian and international respect and acclaim. And while they have different theoretical orientations (Paul describes himself as a conflict theorist and Patricia describes herself as an "intuitionist"— which, although not a criminological term, involves a phenomenological approach) the significance and impact of their work speaks for itself. Since moving to Canada, in 1977, they have become the leaders and authorities on environmental criminology.

As with all good scholars, their work is not limited to one area of expertise. They have been conducting pioneering research on legal aid in Canada since the early 1980s and have been involved in numerous projects for the Department of Justice and the Fraser Institute, based in Vancouver.

When asked to comment on Canadian criminology, Pat Brantingham notes that Canadian criminology is at an important juncture. She suggests "there are different theoretical approaches, a range of diverse issues, and varied methodologies." Current and prospective Canadian criminology students can benefit from this by being prepared to see variety and similarity in our future concerns. She feels it is an exciting time for Canadian criminology as we choose our path.

Paul noted that one of the developments in Canadian criminology is the adoption of the principles of environmental criminology at the operational level in police departments and criminology detachments. In particular, he points to the CPTED (Crime Prevention Through Environmental Design) and community policing movements in western cities such as Calgary, Edmonton, and Vancouver. In fact, Leslie Kennedy and several of his associates in the sociology department, at the University of Alberta as well as Kim Rossmo with the Vancouver City Police (see Chapters 4 and 7) have successfully adopted mapping strategies to the study of crime. And students interested in studying this general subject area are drawn to the School of Criminology at Simon Fraser University where the Brantinghams both work and teach.

Appendix 5

Highlights of the Major Federal Parties' '97 Election Platform in the Areas of Criminal Justice: Who Would/Did You Vote For?

Liberal Party:

- New sentencing alternatives to incarceration for low-risk, non-violent offenders (e.g., community diversion programs and greater use of assessment techniques).

- Continued support of the gun control legislation that is among the toughest in the western world.

- Strengthening the *Young Offenders Act* such as longer sentences for younger offenders and improved mechanisms for transferring serious violent young offenders to adult court. They also proposed establishing special programs to help youth gangs members to exit these groups.

- Just prior to election campaign, the Liberal government launched a national "flagging" system to assist the Crown in identifying high-risk offenders at the time of prosecution. In addition, new legislation was introduced to enable high-risk offenders to be placed on supervision of up to 10 years following their release from prison.

- New legislation was introduced to protect women and children from violent crime. For example, they eliminated self-intoxication as a defence for violent crimes.

- Following up on their anti-smuggling strategy, the Liberals propose to continue to take an aggressive stand against organized crime.

- The Liberals propose to improve the mechanisms for sharing information across the justice system.

- At the focal point of the Liberal campaign against crime is their focus on crime prevention through the initiation of crime prevention programs through social development initiatives (e.g., Canada Child Tax Benefit, Centres of Excellence for Children's Well-Being, the Aboriginal Head Start program, etc.).

Bloc Quebecois:

- As noted in the *Bulletin* issue (May 15, 1997:6), "the text is not available in English and a communications official of the Bloc Quebecois has requested it not be translated." Not being sufficiently fluent in French to provide a translation and given the request of the Bloc representative, no effort will be made to translate. For the curious reader, please refer to pages 6–8 of the *Bulletin*.

Reform Party:

- Recognizing the importance of crime prevention the Reform party believes the key to crime prevention is by strengthening families and communities rather than relying on the criminal justice agencies.

- While respecting the rights of the accused, Reform advocates a shifting of balance towards the rights of the victim and law-abiding citizens. They offer eight specific criteria for protecting the rights of the victim. They range from "the right to be informed at every stage of the process" (p. 8) to "the right to be informed, in timely fashion, of the details of the Crown's intention to offer a plea bargain before it is presented to the defence." (p. 9).

- They propose redefining the age of responsibility by lowering it to 10. In addition, they feel that any offender over 15 should be tried as an adult. Furthermore, they would publish the name of any convicted violent young offender.
- Unlike the Liberals, they would repeal Bill C-68, the universal firearms registry legislation. Instead they would implement a "zero tolerance" policy for criminal offences involving firearms.
- They would repeal s. 745 of the *Criminal Code* (the so-called "faint hope clause"), introduce a "two strikes" legislation, and revise the criminal justice system to better represent the interests of Canadians generally.

New Democratic Party:

- They propose to be tough on crime, and more specifically to be tough on the causes of crime. They point to such problem areas as unemployment, child poverty.
- The New Democrats propose holding criminals accountable for their crimes but they did not specify how this would differ from current processes.
- Age would not be the only factor when determining the consequences of a young offender.
- They would introduce special treatment programs for victims of sexual and physical abuse.

- The NDP would introduce literacy programs and provide social assistance programs to help children with behavioural and learning disorders.
- Along with the Liberals, the NDP proposes introducing tougher sanctions to combat white-collar crime.

Progressive Conservative (PC) Party:

- Their essential solution to crime problems "is a strong, growing economy that provides more jobs and opportunity" (p. 12).
- The PCs advocate a tough but balanced and realistic approach to responding to criminals and respecting the interests of victims.
- They propose introducing a "Safer Street" initiative that would balance both prevention and punishment of offenders. For example, they would abolish the provision in s. 745 that enables first degree murderers to seek parole.
- Like the Reform party the PCs propose to lower the age of responsibility from 12 to 10. In addition, they want to see judges given "more power to impose mandatory treatment or therapy on troubled youths" (p. 14). Like most of the parties, they would also propose to make it easier to transfer serious violent youth crime cases to adult court.
- The PCs would see the *Firearms Act* repealed and replaced with stiffer penalties for those convicted of using a firearm in the commission of a crime.

Source: Abbreviated from "Decision '97." *Bulletin,* May 15, 1997:1–14.

Index